WOMEN OF IDEAS

By the same author

Man Made Language

DALE SPENDER

WOMEN OF IDEAS

AND WHAT MEN HAVE DONE TO THEM
From Aphra Behn to Adrienne Rich

Routledge & Kegan Paul
London, Boston, Melbourne and Henley

First published in 1982
by Routledge & Kegan Paul Ltd
39 Store Street, London WC1E 7DD,
9 Park Street, Boston, Mass. 02108, USA,
296 Beaconsfield Parade, Middle Park,
Melbourne, 3206, Australia, and
Broadway House, Newtown Road,
Henley-on-Thames, Oxon RG9 1EN
Set in 10/12pt Sabon by
Input Typesetting Ltd., London SW19 8DR
and printed in Great Britain by
T. J. Press (Padstow) Ltd.,
Padstow, Cornwall

Library of Congress Cataloging in Publication Data

Spender, Dale.
Women of ideas and what men have done to them.
Bibliography: p.
Includes index.
1. Women intellectuals. 2. Women intellectuals—
Case studies. 3. Sex discrimination against women.
I. Title.
HQ1206.S68   1982   305.4   82-12208

ISBN 0–7100–9353–5

For
my mother,
my sister,
my friend, and
my self

The number is larger than appears on the
surface, for the fear of public ridicule,
and the loss of private favors from those
who shelter, feed and clothe them, withholds
many from declaring their opinions and
demanding their rights.

Elizabeth Cady Stanton,
Susan B. Anthony,
Matilda Joslyn Gage,
History of Woman Suffrage, vol. I, 1881

CONTENTS

ACKNOWLEDGMENTS

I have many debts and cannot begin to acknowledge them all. To the women of the past who have now so shaped my life I have debts I can never begin to repay. To the Fawcett Library, where so many of their words are housed and for which so many women have worked so arduously to preserve them I give my greatest thanks. To David Doughan and Catherine Ireland, the librarians, who have treated the words of women past with so much care and concern, who have given me so much assistance, and who have ensured a warm and welcome reception to all who seek to 'dig', I want to express my gratitude and my deep admiration.

To many of my friends who have sent snippets of information, provided references and answered queries, many thanks. I am grateful to Liz Stanley and Sue Wise, Angeline Goreau, Leslie Wheeler and Pat Staton, and to Angela Miles, Mary O'Brien, Gaby Weiner and Ivy Spender for the information they provided me with, but which I was unable to include.

But I also want to acknowledge that this book has been time consuming to write and that I have not given to my family and friends what they have all so generously given me over the last year. Without criticising my decision to devote myself exclusively to this task, they have done everything to make it possible for me to do little but read and write, and have supported me in so many ways. The only way I know to repay what has been so willingly given is to say – my mother, I shall come and see you and reciprocate for those many replenishing letters, we will sit in the sun together and talk of Elizabeth Cady Stanton at leisure. My sister. . . . where do I begin? For the days you have spent reading and writing, for the support and availability, which I know is work; I thank you for every ounce of care and assure you that it is your turn for the next year – we will drink our (Australian) red wine and worry not about whether I will be able to write afterwards. Renate, I will answer your difficult post, look after my own pot plants as well as yours, make your soup when you get the flu, read your writing with pleasure, and help keep the days warm.

And Ted, who stands in contradiction to my entire thesis on men, I swear to be emotionally available some of the time and to help replenish the resources which you have so freely given over the last year and without which I would have lost my way.

Lizzie, we will divide the work in half instead of you doing 90 per cent;

Glynis, you can get some sleep instead of staying up until all hours magically transforming the scrawl into clear, clean type, and wondering what will happen in the next instalment; Anne and Kerry you need never look up references again – I'll do them for you. Pippa, you can call anytime without writing understanding notes to see if it will be all right.

My brother, I promise that for a while we will talk of your problems for a change; my father, we can have a discussion on any topic you elect. And all my friends who know about interruptions and who have in their show of support kept the world away, I thank you enormously and now suggest we practise what we have learnt – that feminism is fun too.

HISTORY
OF
WOMAN SUFFRAGE
VOL. I
1881

THESE VOLUMES
ARE
AFFECTIONATELY INSCRIBED
TO THE
Memory of

MARY WOLLSTONECRAFT,
FRANCES WRIGHT, LUCRETIA MOTT, HARRIET MARTINEAU,
LYDIA MARIA CHILD, MARGARET FULLER, SARAH AND ANGELINA GRIMKÉ,
JOSEPHINE S. GRIFFING, MARTHA C. WRIGHT, HARRIOT K. HUNT, M.D.,
MARIANA W. JOHNSON, ALICE AND PHEBE CAREY, ANN PRESTON, M.D.,
LYDIA MOTT, ELIZA W. FARNHAM, LYDIA F. FOWLER, M.D.,
PAULINA WRIGHT DAVIES,

Whose Earnest Lives and Fearless Words, in Demanding
Political Rights for Women, have been,
in the Preparation of these Pages,
a Constant Inspiration
TO
THE EDITORS

INTRODUCTION

1 Why didn't I know?

This book has its origins in my personal experience: in the late 1960s an over-riding issue in my life was to find out whether other women felt and thought as I did in a male-dominated society. It soon became apparent that I was not alone. As many of us began to talk to each other – sometimes for the first time – we found we had a wealth of common experience which had been 'submerged'. Books such as *The Feminine Mystique* (1963) by Betty Friedan, *Sexual Politics* (1969) by Kate Millett and *The Female Eunuch* (1970) by Germaine Greer both confirmed and stimulated our ideas, and as we talked more our isolated fears and questions gave way to more collective and visible understandings. We realised that the problems we faced, and the discrepancies we encountered between what we were supposed to be and feel and what we were and felt in our own terms, were not idiosyncratic in origin, nor a product of individual deficiency as many of us had believed. Looking back, I know that we thought when we found that there was nothing 'wrong' with ourselves that we had discovered something 'new' (which in a sense, we had) and we experienced a feeling of elation that goes with finding a more meaningful and positive way of viewing the world and ourselves.

But then many of us began to ask whether we were the first generation of women to have felt this way. Some of us were vaguely aware that we did have a past, but even when we had an idea that something like this had happened before, it was usually based on a shadowy impression – from a discussion with one's grandmother, a reference or a quotation in an old book, a comment from one's father about silly and unsexed suffragettes. There was little coherence in the fragments which many of us had found by random means and which we brought with us to our new understandings. For many reasons, however, vague suppositions gave way to more systematic and persistent questions: were there women who had felt like this in the past, how many of them were there, what had they said?

Some of these questions began to be answered comparatively quickly by women who obviously shared similar concerns: in 1970, Leslie Tanner edited *Voices from Women's Liberation* and the section entitled 'Voices from the Past' included excerpts from Abigail Adams to Florence Kelley

with Mary Wollstonecraft, Harriet Taylor and Harriet Martineau in between; in 1971, came Elaine Showalter's *Women's Liberation and Literature* (from Mary Wollstonecraft to Mary Ellmann); in 1972, Wendy
Martin's *The American Sisterhood: Writings of the Feminist Movement
from Colonial Times to the Present*, and Miriam Schneir's *Feminism: The
Essential Historical Writings*, which again began with Abigail Adams and
Mary Wollstonecraft, ended with Virginia Woolf, and included Sarah
Grimké, Sojourner Truth, Lucretia Mott, Lucy Stone, Elizabeth Cady Stanton, Charlotte Perkins Gilman, Emmeline Pankhurst and Emma Goldman;
in 1973, there was Alice Rossi's *The Feminist Papers: from Adams to de
Beauvoir*. With the advent of these publications (and others) the question
of whether women had thought and felt this way before was put to rest —
they had! Another question arose in its place: why didn't I know, why
didn't *we* know?

This was not just simply a superficial or intellectually interesting question, but one which was central to our understanding of patriarchy. Why
were women of the present cut off from women of the past and how was
this achieved? While we had been ready to believe the lessons of our own
education and to accept that there was but a handful of women in the past
who had protested against male power, that they were 'eccentric' at best,
and more usually 'neurotic', 'embittered' and quite unrepresentative, then
the absence of women's voices from history seemed understandable. But
when it began to appear that there had been many women who had been
saying in centuries past what we were saying in the 1970s, that they had
been representative of their sex, and that they had disappeared, the problem
assumed very different proportions.

For years I had not thought to challenge the received wisdom of my
own history tutors who had — in the only fragment of knowledge about
angry women I was ever endowed with — informed me that early in the
twentieth century, a few unbalanced and foolish women had chained themselves to railings in the attempt to obtain the vote. When I learnt, however,
that in 1911 there had been twenty-one regular feminist periodicals in
Britain (see Elizabeth Sarah, 1982b), that there was a feminist book shop,
a woman's press, and a women's bank run by and for women, I could no
longer accept that the reason I knew almost nothing about women of the
past was because there were so few of them, and they had done so little.
I began to acknowledge not only that the women's movement of the early
twentieth century was bigger, stronger and more influential than I had ever
suspected, but that it might not have been the *only* such movement. It was
in this context that I began to wonder whether the disappearance of the
women of the past was an accident.

Why didn't we know about these women? Was it possible that we
were not meant to? And if women who raised their voices against male
power became but a transitory entry in the historical records, what was to
be the fate of the present women's movement?

For me, the comfort of finding so many women of the past began to
give way to the discomfort of wondering about the present. I began to ask
quite seriously how are women made to disappear? If such a huge move-

ment as that of 1911, with so many and various voices, could have so effectively disappeared within the space of fifty years, what were the implications for the apparently smaller movement of my own time? What was the process by which women were erased; and was it still in operation?

These questions are the substance of this book. I have come to accept that a patriarchal society depends in large measure on the experience and values of males being perceived as the *only* valid frame of reference for society, and that it is therefore in patriarchal interest to prevent women from sharing, establishing and asserting their equally real, valid and *different* frame of reference, which is the outcome of different experience.

It is men who have decreed that women occupy a different place from themselves in a patriarchal universe, but men do not know what it is to be in that different place. Yet without any direct experience of what it feels like to be half of humanity, men have proceeded to describe and explain the world from their own point of view, and have assumed that their *partial* experience of the world is all that exists. Women's experience is non-existent, invisible, unreal from the outset, and it is my contention that if patriarchy is to be preserved, women's invisibility must remain. Obviously, this is not, for me, a state to be desired.

Men are in charge in our society: not only do they hold the most influential positions and own and control most of the resources,[1] but their positions and resources enable them to be the 'experts' who make the pronouncements on what makes sense in society, on what is to be valued, indeed, even on what is to be considered real, and what is not. It should not be surprising therefore that these influential men should consider their own frame of reference – based on their own experience and values, which include seeing themselves as centrally important to society – as the basis for their judgements. They may put forward very 'good', 'sound' reasons as to why it is that they should be the experts and why it is that the male sex is justified in being 'superior', and these reasons may come to be accepted by the whole society; but what is frequently overlooked – particularly by the men who are responsible for decreeing the social values and social arrangements – is that the origin of this belief system lies with men, and not women. It is a belief system which may fit very comfortably with men's view of the world, and themselves, but one which may be very uncomfortable for women.

So while men are justified in feeling confident that (for them) there is no great mis-match between their own lived experience and the beliefs of society (for after all, they constructed the beliefs of society on the basis of their own experience) they are *not* justified in generalising that it is the

---

[1] The United Nations statistics will emerge throughout this book with monotonous regularity: given that these statistics are based on information supplied by member nations, and one assumes therefore that they are the most flattering interpretation available, the fact that women do two-thirds of the world's work, for less than 10 per cent of the world's salary, and own less than 1 per cent of the world's wealth, is probably a conservative estimate. These statistics do help to suggest that there is some discrepancy between the 'power' of the sexes.

same for women, that their male experience is the sum total of human experience.

When a woman confronts the existing value system of a society and finds that it is men who are valued she, unlike a man, does not find this particularly self-enhancing knowledge. When she finds that it is men who occupy the influential positions in society and who own and control the resources, she does not feel a strong surge of confidence and self-esteem. When she learns – as she quickly does in the education system (Dale Spender, 1982a) – that it is men who are authoritative, that it is male experience that counts, and that it is males who influence the environment, she does not experience a feeling of liberation and a sense of autonomy. Instead, she usually comes to accept in part that the world is made for men and that her place within it, is as a subordinate – for 'good' and 'sound' reasons.

But what if this view of the world does not match with a woman's own experience of herself and others? Surely these discrepancies and contradictions would be of such central concern to her that they would become a condition of her daily existence and would cause her persistently to question the social values and arrangements? To be confronted every day with the injunction to be subordinate when one does not feel subordinate, to manifest deference to males when one does not see them as superior, to be urged to give way to men in the name of reason when it feels most unfair, to be obliged to give consensus to male problems being the basis of society's problems when one believes that women's problems are equally, if not more, central and significant, could be to inhabit a chaotic, conflicting and confusing world. How to account for these discrepancies and contradictions could well become one of the most pervasive and perplexing questions of existence, under the circumstances. Any woman confronted with this problem could well make it a matter of priority to develop a philosophy which helps to explain what she has got *wrong*: is it herself and her own experience that is at fault, or is there something wrong with what society believes?

Such a philosophy, and the questions which give rise to it, would not ordinarily be developed by men, who often do not know what women are talking about when they try and explain and explore their state of being 'in the wrong', for it is not a permanent condition of man's existence. Yet while men rule, and therefore have the ruling ideas, while male experience serves as the frame of reference for explaining society, this common experience of women and the problems it creates are not deemed to exist. Simone de Beauvoir may have stated the case admirably, hundreds of women may have outlined the nature of the problem, but from the point of view of men who have not experienced it, and who have decreed that what is outside their experience is 'unreal', no such problem exists.

Even to put forward a radically different frame of reference for explaining the world (and seeing the world through the eyes of those who are oppressed rather than through the eyes of those who do the oppressing *does* make a radical difference) is to enter the realm of the unknown, the invisible, the neurotic, and invites not serious consideration, but ridicule and abuse. Am I, a woman of the limited, non-authoritative, emotional, deviant and wrong sex, unschooled in the art-and-science of philosophy, being so presumptuous as to fly in the face of centuries of established philosophical tradition and to suggest that there is a fundamental, philosophical question about the nature of human existence that my 'superiors' have not addressed? If no such question has arisen in the philosophical circles of the masters, can I not see that it must not be important — that is, if it is indeed a *real* question and not just a product of my sense of grievance and embitteredness, because I happen to be born of the wrong sex?

The suggestion that men have omitted fundamental questions about the nature of existence in their years and years of checking with each other, is a preposterous one in a patriarchal world. It casts aspersions on the accumulated wisdom of men, and their status as authority figures. It is therefore a suggestion which will be met with considerable resistance, and many are the mechanisms the ruling group has made available to discredit and devalue any member of the 'ruled' who dares to put it forward. This practice of penalising insubordination is not just a peculiarity of modern times, however. It is a practice which has been going on for centuries and which allows men to 'punish' women who challenge male authority.

As this book demonstrates, for centuries women have been challenging men, and men have used punitive measures against them; for centuries women have been claiming that the world and men look very different from the perspective of women. Far from being an unusual claim, it is a common assertion of women of the past and a familiar issue in contemporary feminism[2] that women's meanings and values have been excluded from what have been put forward as society's meanings and values.

For many women, for many years, a crucial consideration in daily life has been male power; it has been a problem in numerous ways: it has had implications for virtually every aspect of women's existence. That we have not inherited a tradition in which male power is perceived as a problem, in which it is described, analysed or criticised, is not because it has not been a fundamental issue to women, nor because they have not attempted to explain it, but because male power is not ordinarily a problem for men, and it is men who ordain what the real and significant issues of society are to be.

Patriarchy requires that any conceptualisation of the world in which men and their power are a central problem should become invisible and unreal. How could patriarchy afford to accept that men were a serious social problem, to gather together what women have said on the subject and make it the substance of the educational curriculum, to treat women's version of men with respect, and to discuss at length and with impartiality the origins of male power and the means by which it is maintained?

---

[2] While I would prefer not to define or restrict the meaning of feminism, I feel obliged to give some indication of my usage of the term. I suggest therefore that a feminist is a woman who does not accept man's socially sanctioned view of himself and that feminism refers to the alternative meanings put forward by feminists. That should leave enough room.

This is a nonsense in a patriarchal society. It is akin to asking christianity in the past to put favourably the case of heretics, or the scientific community in the present to devote an equal amount of time to address with equal good will such areas as alchemy, faith healing, astrology (or even the case against nuclear power) which it has outlawed, and against which it sets itself up as authoritative.

Groups in power validate themselves by reference to those out of power – which they dismiss as *wrong* – and justify their own power in the process. Those who would try to put forward an alternative to science in a society where the scientific method serves as a basis for our view of the world (and for many reasons they are often women) are also dealing with the invisible and incomprehensible and are likely to be dismissed as superstitious or silly. Those who try to put forward an alternative to patriarchy and male values, when male values are the basis of society and men's opinions the very standard of reasonableness and veracity, are being *extremist* and acting as *politicos*. They too can be dismissed as subversive – or stupid, or sick.

Openly questioning the way the world works and challenging the power of the powerful is not an activity customarily rewarded. Non-believers are not respected for their different frame of reference but are defined as wrong, and treated accordingly, sometimes even being institutionalised for their lack of belief. It can therefore be appreciated why women might have chosen to remain silent. But many women have spoken out, and have discussed the issue of finding themselves permanently in the wrong. Yet the generations after generations of women who have put forward this view have found no sanctioned place in the records of our society. If they were to be visible, of course, it would mean that we were members of a society which was prepared to admit that patriarchy was a problem.

Because men have power, says Dorothy Smith (1978), they have the power to keep it. All human beings are constantly engaged in the process of describing and explaining, and ordering the world, but only a few have been, or are, in a position to have their version treated as serious, and accepted. These few Dorothy Smith aptly terms the 'circle of men' – who are the philosophers, politicians, poets and policy-makers – who have for centuries been writing and talking to each other about issues which are of significance to them. The descriptions and explanations of this circle of men extend backwards in time as far as our records reach, claims Smith, and each new generation is instructed in this particular yet partial view of the world, from which women are absent.

This is part of the insidious nature of the problem, for we are born into a society in which we come to our human-ness by making sense of the world through this inherited patriarchal tradition, and having learnt this system, we find it difficult to escape its influence. We must be socialised in order to become members of society, we must learn the language and the meanings if we are to describe and explain the world; but the society, the language, the meanings we take on, are ones developed by males and in which male power is promoted and justified. Having been socialised into a patriarchal society, having learnt the words, the concepts, the *sense* of male power, our vision is circumscribed, our possibilities for envisaging and explaining an alternative are limited. We have entered a *system* and, dislike it as we may, it is the only one that is available, and within which we must work.

So before we begin we find the world weighted in favour of men. For centuries they have been consulting each other, developing their view of the world and encoding a language to embody and construct their meanings in which they are central, and in which all else (including women) is defined in relation to them. They have formulated a tradition in which their power is taken for granted and is perceived as unproblematic; they have preserved their own pronouncements from Aristotle to Freud and have dismissed and 'lost' those views which are not consistent with their own. In order to become members of the society in which they hold sway, we must learn *their* rules; we must learn that we are women, that we do not occupy the privileged position men do, that we do not count as much, that we do not have the same human needs; and yet we must also learn that these conditions of our existence are not open to discussion.

If we wish to protest that this is neither just, nor justifiable, then we must do so from a position of subordination – and defensiveness. It could be argued that our prospects do not look good.

For centuries, says Dorothy Smith, this process has been going on, where men have excluded women from the circles in which society's meanings are constructed, where they have deprived women of the possibility of defining or raising to social consciousness the problems which concern them. Women 'have never controlled the material or social means to the making of a tradition among themselves or to acting as equals in the ongoing discourse of intellectuals. . . . The universe of ideas, images and themes – the symbolic modes which are *the general currency* of thought – have been either produced by men or controlled by them. Insofar as women's work and experience has been entered into it, it has been on terms decided by men and because it has been approved by men' (pp. 281–2).

It is men, not women, who *control* knowledge, and I believe that this is an understanding we should never lose sight of. It is because men control knowledge that we do not know about our traditions as women; it is because men control knowledge that the knowledge we produce can be used against us in the same way that the knowledge of our foremothers was used against them, and is denied to us.

We *can* produce knowledge, we have been doing so for centuries, but the fact that it is not part of our traditions, that it is not visible in our culture, is because we have little or no influence over where it goes. We are not the judges of what is significant and helpful, we are not influential members in those institutions which legitimate and distribute knowledge. We are women producing knowledge which is often different from that produced by men, in a society controlled by men. If they like what we produce they will appropriate it, if they can use what we produce (even against us) they will take it, if they do not want to know, they will lose it. But rarely, if ever, will they treat it as they treat their own.

That these ideas are not even the common currency of our culture is not because women have not been expressing them, but because men control what is *believable* knowledge and what is not. When it is not their experience that women's knowledge is treated differently, why should they believe a woman who says it is?

Dorothy Smith's stand is currently supported by many women: the meanings that are missing from society, says Jean Baker Miller (1978), are 'precisely those perceptions that men because of their dominant position could *not* perceive' (p. 1) What we know about power, says Elizabeth Janeway (1980), makes it seem pretty acceptable, but then, it is the powerful who tells us this and who are giving us the benefit of their own experience of power (p. 3). For as long as we know, says Janeway, women have been on the other end of that power, making adjustments as the subordinate partners in power relationships, but we know little or nothing of their meanings and understandings, 'for the meaning of female experience has been fed only rarely into the larger reservoir of valued social knowledge' (p. 4). When we look for women's view of the world, from the position of 'the weak', or the oppressed, from the *underside* as Elise Boulding (1976) calls it, we encounter little but silence, for, says Janeway, 'what women know, learned and relearned in our long sojourn in the country of the weak, is the geography of the uncharted territory of human existence'(p. 5).

However, it is not just that we are initiated into a society in which women's experience of the world is absent and unreal, it is that we are also led to believe that the reason 'women have had no written history until very recently, no share in making religious thoughts, no political philosophy, no representation of society from their view, no poetic tradition, no tradition in art' (Smith, 1978, p. 282), is *because women have nothing worthwhile to contribute*. So argue those who control knowledge, the *gatekeepers* as Dorothy Smith calls them, who sanctimoniously declare that women are absent from the records because they are 'not up to standard' without adding that significant piece of information that the standard to which they refer is peculiarly and exclusively *male!*

Why should they disclose this information? In all likelihood it does not occur to them to do so, for are not male standards human standards; is not the male the norm, and the experience of the male, universal?

This is the area where men have their cake and get to eat it too, for while they decree themselves as representative of humanity, women who argue that men are not, are simply showing how little they know! And when men's standards are defined as human standards, then women who assert that women are different, demonstrate how 'inhuman' they are. It is a real 'Catch 22'.

As a woman I either accept that women are not up to standard, that they have made no cultural contribution, and resign myself to 'inferiority'; or else I assert that women have a different but autonomous view of the world, that we have different standards, different priorities, different problems (men among them) in which case I help to signal my 'maladjustment' to my society, my failure to accept the rules of society, my distance from the human standard, my deviancy – and must therefore resign myself to my 'inferiority'. Men win, women lose, while men control knowledge.

Does it have to be this way? I think not.

Fundamental to patriarchy is the invisibility of women, the unreal nature of women's experience, the absence of women as a force to be reckoned with. When women become visible, when they assert the validity of that experience and refuse to be intimidated, patriarchal values are under threat. When we know that for centuries women have been saying that men and their power are a problem, when we are able to share our knowledge of today and combine it with that of the past, when we construct our own alternative meanings and traditions, we are no longer invisible, unreal, non-existent. And when we assert that the reason for women's absence is not women, but men, that it is not that women have not contributed, but that men have 'doctored the records', reality undergoes a remarkable change.

Then we *do* feel that self-esteem, that confidence, that sense of liberation that men take for granted in encountering their own past and finding themselves central; but we do far more. We challenge male authority to describe and explain the world, to encode themselves as positively human and to define woman as other; we portray men in an unflattering light in which they rarely if ever portray themselves. We make male power a social issue: we make it problematic.

The simple answer to my question – why didn't I know about all the women of the past who have protested about male power – is that patriarchy doesn't like it. These women and their ideas constitute a political threat and they are censored. By this means women are 'kept in the dark', with the result that every generation must begin virtually at the beginning, and start again to forge the meanings of women's existence in a patriarchal world, so that in Catharine Stimpson's terms, every fifty years women have to reinvent the wheel.

All this is relatively easy to see: but the question is, how do they do it? For if we do not understand the process by which hundreds of women – often influential in their own time – have been made to disappear, how can we believe that what has happened to our foremothers, will not happen to us?

The arguments which I put forward in this book are not part of an abstract thesis of women's subordination and oppression, they reflect the daily realities of women's lives. Our existence as women in a patriarchal society is one of interruptions and silences, in the presence of men. Over and over again we find ourselves in situations where it is men who do the talking, men who define the terms and pass judgement, men who determine what the *real* issues are. Over and over again we find that if we are permitted to talk at all, our words can be appropriated, and few are the women unfamiliar with the occasion when a woman's words seemingly go unnoticed but are shortly afterwards repeated by a man and greeted with approval if not applause. Over and over again we find that our words can be distorted, misrepresented, 'turned round' to suit a man's needs and to deny our own. This aspect of women's existence, however, is not confined to conversation; what men do with our spoken words today, they have done to women's written words of the past.

As Adrienne Rich (1980) has pointed out, our existence, and our tradition, is one of interruption and silence: 'The entire history of women's struggle for self determination has been muffled in silence over and over. One serious cultural obstacle encountered by any feminist writer is that each feminist work has tended to be received as if it emerged from nowhere; as if each one of us had lived, thought, and worked without any historical past or contextual present. This is one of the ways in which women's work and thinking has been made to seem sporadic, errant, orphaned of any tradition of its own' (p. 11).

It is disturbing to recognise that what we today have in common with women of the past is our experience of being silenced and interrupted; our experience of becoming a member of society in which women have no visible past, no heritage; our experience of existing in a *void*.

Men take their past for granted: they look back to it for guidance, confirmation, inspiration. But even at the most elementary level, women usually encounter an absence when we seek to find ourselves reflected and resonated in past generations. 'Imagine', says Louise Bernikow (1980), 'a woman is wandering in the countryside; at the foot of a gnarled tree or at a crossroads she encounters another woman making a journey. . . .' This is the stuff of which men's myths are made, men's existence empowered with meaning; we have no equivalent. 'I want to leap, pretending to have a confidence none of us has,' adds Bernikow, 'into a place in our imaginations where our mothers stand on firm ground, along with our sisters, daughters, friends, lovers, grandmothers, aunts, nieces, to a place where we become the mythmakers, and these female connections are the stuff of our myths and we consider these to be the *primary* stories, the *Odyssey,* the *Iliad,* Greek drama, Shakespeare, Tolstoy. To work of this stature we bring all we know. . . . Imagine that we conjure up a world that is safe for mothers and daughters. A great celebration takes place at the birth of a daughter. The mother is honored; the girl child is honored. . . .' (ibid., p. 69) Just imagine! What different meanings life could have.

We are by no means the first generation of women who have faced the necessity and tasted the joy of reconstructing our own past, of piecing together our traditions in order to invest our present with symbolism and meaning. This was a task Mary Beard set herself in 1946 in *Woman as Force in History,* and before her, in 1928 Virginia Woolf had recreated women's traditions in order to explain herself in *A Room of One's Own.* In the nineteenth century, Matilda Joslyn Gage wrote about women's strength, women's power in the past, so that the present could be more meaningful and the future more promising, and before her Margaret Fuller had written *Woman in the Nineteenth Century* (1845) for the same reasons. All of these women had predecessors.

Women's past is at least as rich as men's; that we do not know about it, that we encounter only interruptions and silence when we seek it, is part of our oppression. Unless and until we can reconstruct our past, draw on it, and *transmit it* to *the next generation,* our oppression persists.

The reason I did not know that so many women had thought and talked and written on so many of the issues that concern us today is because to *know* this is a source of strength. In a male-dominated society where men are able to control knowledge, they are in a position to deprive us of this source of strength. They are able to assert that it is *they* and *their* experience which is to be valued, and to insist that it has always been this way. This is partly how patriarchy is perpetuated.

2 Objections: sustained and over-ruled

Like Louise Bernikow, my method for finding out about women of the past has been to become 'an archeologist, digging for relics . . . unearthing layers of evidence. The masculine vision was only the first layer. My life and the life around me was another' (1980, p. 8). In the absence of sanctioned methods and meanings for undertaking this task, I have tested the past against the criteria in my own feminist circles today. In many respects this is what men have done as they have consulted with each other within their own circles and tested their meanings against their own experience. But there is an essential difference: such activities of men are sanctioned by centuries of tradition, while the activities of women are not. And in a context where women do not control knowledge, untangling the threads of women's past, and finding their 'disappearance', is a process fraught with difficulty, for there are so many mechanisms that can be called upon to discredit those who undertake such a task.

I am not oblivious to some of the pitfalls that await me, and I have come to accept that some of them cannot be avoided, but because I think it important to try to be explicit about how it is I come to think and know as I do, I have decided to go through some of the objections that I raised to myself, and to indicate how I did, or did not, overcome them.

(i) Portraying men as the enemy

This caused me little loss of sleep. The more women of the past I encountered, the more I came to appreciate that for centuries many women have perceived men as the enemy, even when they have been told again and again it is neither a nice, nor a useful, thing to do. But this is to be expected in a patriarchal society where men can determine the values. They are not likely to encourage women to call them the enemy and to make male power a problem. In a heterosexual society it is more in men's interest to argue for the *interdependence* of the sexes, and in a society where women have been allocated a nurturing and passive role, it is more likely that men will argue that women should understand, mediate, conciliate, appease, and endure, rather than resist and confront.

As no equivalent 'good manners' are required in relation to race and class, as no similiar concern is shown in these contexts to refrain from calling the oppressor the enemy, I see no good reason for making sex an exception. Objection over-ruled.

(ii) Studying women 'out of context'

I have looked primarily at women's past and have treated the behaviour of men largely as irrelevant. This does not mean that I have overlooked the fact that women's ideas have been produced and received in a male-dominated society, but it does mean that the particular battles, economic crises, political intrigues that men were engaged in while an individual woman was writing about the problems of male power, have, in the main, gone unelaborated.

If, in a patriarchal society one response to my explanation for the disappearance of women is to claim that they have been studied 'out of context', I will feel some measure of gratification, for studying women 'in context' almost always means studying them in relation to men, locating them in terms of what men were doing or saying at the time.

I do not want to study women in relation to men, partly because most of the women who are quoted in these pages refused to see themselves in relation to men. That I choose to follow in their footsteps, rather than the socially sanctioned ones of my forefathers, appears to me good sense. Objection over-ruled.

(iii) Treating all women the same

This is a more difficult issue: I *know* that the experience of women today is not identical to the experience of women in the past; I *know* that time, colour, class, culture, sexual preference, age, disability, all make significant and undeniable differences to women's position in and perception of the world. But I suspect that those various positions and perceptions are bounded by a common framework. There is even a diversity of descriptions and explanations among us when we share a common basis of time, colour, class, sexual preference or age, but I believe that diversity can be valued and built upon, rather than used to divide us.

I know that I am a product of a particular group in a particular culture and that I am being critical of another group that has presumed to treat its particular and limited experience as the whole. I would not wish to make the same mistake as those of whom I am critical. I do not assume that my experience of the world is all that there is.

Given these limitations, I am still inclined to the view that as women we do have a common experience which can be described and explained: it is the experience of being women in a men's world. I live in a patriarchal society as do women now in the western world, and as did all the women of the past whom I have included for discussion. We share the experience of oppression by men; we share our exclusion from the male frame of reference, our lack of knowledge of a past, our invisibility, our deviancy, our wrongness. Now, as in the past, we have been on the receiving end of male power, we have been obliged to obtain access to the world's resources, through men, as owners, fathers, husbands, employers. This is the common frame of reference which we share.

But I have other more consciously political reasons for wanting to emphasise what we have in common, rather than what there is to divide. Because women have no control over the knowledge we produce, I think it unwise, if not plain destructive, to produce knowledge which can be used against us. There are differences among women, and some of them are the substance of this book, but I have deliberately tried to pre-empt the possibility that these differences may be used to divide us.

It is not my intention to make available to patriarchy knowledge which allows men to divide and rule. As women's resources are appropriated by men (the case put by many of the women in the following pages, see particularly Matilda Joslyn Gage) then all I am prepared to 'supply' is a positive portrayal of women — a commodity not much in 'demand' in a patriarchal society.

Because I do suspect that women share a common frame of reference, and because I think it subversive and empowering to emphasise our unity, and its positive nature, I have tended to treat women as a group, in contrast with, and often in conflict with, men.

Objection over-ruled.

(iv) The limitations of the sample

My research for women of the past has not been exhaustive and my coverage does not even begin to be comprehensive. I have only been able to 'dig' in certain places, and even then, just below the patriarchal surface. Already I am aware of glaring omissions (for in defiance of 'order', I am of course writing the introduction, *after* I have finished the book). But even if it were possible to provide a comprehensive coverage (and this book has just kept expanding and expanding until, under pressure, I arbitrarily called a halt) it would not necessarily mean that the case for women having a past was more convincing.

Had I decided to wait until I had pursued every clue (and double-checked every record) I would never have come to write the book, for every fragment uncovered points to many more. What I wanted to do was to make it clear that for centuries women have been saying many of the things we are saying today and which we have often thought of as new; what I wanted to do was to explore our silences and interruptions and to try and explain why and how they have occurred. I wanted to share my excitement and joy in the reclaiming of our foremothers, and my anger at their erasure from our heritage. To do this, it is not mandatory to find *all* the women who have ever contributed to our traditions, nor is it necessary to suggest that I have provided a definitive account of their lives and their ideas.

I can think of nothing better than future debates among women as to whether Matilda Joslyn Gage was arguing that *all* women's resources were stolen by men, whether Charlotte Perkins Gilman's explanations for women's behaviour are more accurate and useful than Freud's, whether Christabel Pankhurst was a product of a repressive Victorian morality or a courageous woman who chose to be independent of men, whether Mary Beard's thesis that a belief in women's oppression based on the past, is a primary condition for oppression in the present: after all, men take such debates about themselves and their forefathers for granted; there are industries built upon the discussion of men's ideas, and for women it would be a pleasant and productive change to be able to build upon, elaborate and modify the ideas of our foremothers.

But although I have over-ruled the objection in relation to my inability to be comprehensive, I cannot over-rule my own objection to the limitations of the printed word as a sample. It is in the nature of my task that in order to establish how women *disappear*, I am confined to those women who, in the first place, made their *presence* known, and this has invariably meant women who have been published.

Women who have been published are, generally speaking, a small and select group, and are unlikely to be representative of ordinary women. Making them *visible* once again also comes perilously close to constructing a tradition of 'heroines' simply to parallel the male histories of 'heroes', to which many of us have valid objections. But at this stage I feel there is really little choice, for if we are to reconstruct our past, to find out who has 'been and gone' in the records of our culture, then it is to published material we must initally go, despite its limitations. All we can do is to try and be aware of those limitations.

I have not, of course, been engaged in the traditional tasks of an historian. My goal has been to find some of the women who in the past have published their ideas about male power, and then I have tried to establish what has happened to them, to discover what men have done to them. This has meant locating some of the women below the patriarchal surface of their 'absence', and then following their entry into the records: how have they been reported, what have critics and commentators had to say about them, what sort of biographical details have been conveyed? Almost always, however, I have been dealing with published records, and the lives and experience of most women are not entered in those records in patriarchal society (see Lynne Spender, forthcoming, for a discussion of women's exclusion from the published word). And almost always the women who do make their way into the published records are literate.

However, it cannot be assumed that the women who were literate and who left the written records of their lives, and their ideas, were necessarily a privileged group well supplied by men's financial resources. Some were; some most definitely were not. Without access to the financial resources of men, many women past and present have found themselves in the same boat – destitute. When men today own 99 per cent of the resources – and I am assuming that the pattern was not dramatically different in the past and that it could have been even worse given that for much of the nineteenth century married women were not permitted to own property – there are not many independently wealthy women who can devote themselves to the business of writing, and the number who have been able to support themselves entirely by writing has been few. Some of the women whose works are included here supported themselves by alternating between the 'oldest' and the 'newest' professions for women, between prostitution and writing.

It was the personal experience of many of these women that survival was dependent on access to the resources controlled by men; some of them made this a major concern of their writing; some of them argued that this was the common experience of women.

Nevertheless, the fact remains that in some respects these women were not representative: some of them were wealthy when most of the population lived in poverty; they were literate at times when the majority of the population was not. And there is also the consideration of the extent to which access to education and literacy constructs its own world view.

But, as some of them have argued, it has been their education and their rare independence – their £500 and a room of their own, as Virginia Woolf (1928) called it – which has allowed them to register their protests in the name of their sex.
Objections: some sustained.

(v) The western world

The women included are from the English-speaking world.[3] I do not assume that this tradition which I have outlined is of relevance outside that world. In an ideal situation (and with an understanding publisher) perhaps it would be possible to take account of more than one – imperialistic – world view, but it is not possible here.

Patriarchy may know no cultural boundaries but its expressions vary from culture to culture and this explanation, restricted as it is to one frame of reference, may have no application in societies where patriarchy manifests itself in different forms. I make no claims for the universality of my explanation but regret that it takes no account of the women who do not share the English language. I would want to suggest, however, that it is not self-indulgence to assert that male power, in the English-speaking world, is one of the most pressing problems of our age.
Objection: partially sustained.

(vi) The realm of the intellectual

In a society where theorising has been the province of men, and where their theories have so often been used to mystify, to intimidate and to oppress, it is well that we as women should be wary of what we have come to see as theorising – and theorists. We have witnessed elites using their power to justify their position: from the rich we have heard that the poor are responsible for their own poverty, from the whites that blacks have only themselves to blame for their depressed position in society, and from men that women are content with their lot and choose their subordination.

---

[3] There are exceptions such as Frederika Bremer, Georges Sand, Colette, and Simone de Beauvoir who have been translated into English and who have been influential in the English-speaking world.

'Theory' has been used to construct a division between those who know and those who do not, and, like most divisions in our hierarchical society, it is not a division of equal parts. And this is one of the reasons that the women's movement, quite rightly, has often been suspicious of theories and theorists. But our impatience with theory is not just because most of the 'theories' we are introduced to have been produced by men, or even that they have used them in their own interest, but that in times of economic hardship, in times when violence against women appears to be becoming greater and violence among men is becoming increasingly threatening to us all, we are likely to sympathise with Christabel Pankhurst's stand and to argue that it is *Deeds Not Words* that are required.

We need to redefine theory and theorist; we need to see theory not as something which is frequently to be resisted, but something we can use in our own interest. And we need to see that men have no monopoly on theory: theorising is an activity engaged in by *all* human beings.

Frances Wright said that all human beings are equally knowledgeable, that we all theorise, and that we all have a responsibility to engage in free enquiry and to examine why it is we believe what we believe; Lady Mary Wortley Montagu claimed that it is vital that as women we ask who profits from what we believe; and Mary Ritter Beard argued that part of women's oppression has its origins in our acceptance of the belief that women are powerless. All of these ideas, these theories, are part of our heritage, they help explain our circumstances, they suggest the options for change – that is why we benefit from knowing them. They are theories we can use in a society where most theories have been used against us.

We need to know how patriarchy works. We need to know how women disappear, why we are initiated into a culture where women have no visible past, and what will happen if we make that past visible and real. If the process is not to be repeated again, if we are to transmit to the next generation of women what was denied transmission to us, we need to know how to break the closed circle of male power which permits men to go on producing knowledge about themselves, pretending that we do not exist.

And this is to enter the realm of theory – not to mystify, intimidate or oppress, but to describe and explain the experience of women in a male-dominated society which says that if such experience does exist, then it is of no account.

Into a context in which women have grave doubts about the potential of the intellectual, I am going to introduce the argument which contends that this is no accident; I am going to suggest that patriarchy has found it profitable to turn us away from the intellectual. We have been discouraged from formulating and building theories, for patriarchy finds this a dangerous activity on the part of women. This is why the theories we have constructed, again and again, and which show many similar features, have so effectively disappeared.

Problem partially resolved: I understand why we need to be suspicious of theory, but I believe that theory, and the discussion of the history of women's ideas, can be profitable, can help us to understand the present and to plan for the future.

3 Mocking our minds

That women have not been treated as serious intellectual beings is an understanding that is central to my explanation for women's disappearance. It is an understanding put forward – in varying forms – by almost all the women in this book, who have argued that men have taken away women's creativity and intelligence, that they have denied our ability to reason and think, and that they have supported a division of labour in which mental work is seen as the province of men, and service as the province of women.

From Aphra Behn to Matina Horner women have argued that men have claimed for themselves a monopoly of the mind, they have described and legitimated themselves as the 'authoritative' sex, the sex with the capacity to be 'objective', the sex who comprise the 'natural' intellectuals, philosophers, poets, politicians, policy-makers, etc. It seems that in the long struggle for equality women have achieved few if any gains in this area. 'Stupidity' is just as desirable today, in the female sex, as it was when Aphra Behn wrote her plays in the seventeenth century; it seems that intellectual competence in women then was just as threatening as it is now.

Women *are* intellectually competent, and even the repudiating devices of patriarchy cannot always conceal this. But even where women's intellectual competence is 'undeniable', men are still able to 'deny' it, and take it away. Women who reveal their intellectual resources are often described as having 'masculine minds', which is a clever device for acknowledging their contribution while at the same time it allows it to be dismissed, for a woman with a 'masculine mind' is unrepresentative of her sex, and the realm of the intellectual is still retained by men.

Even when we display our power to think in terms men have validated, to follow their arguments and reach their conclusions, we will rarely receive 'credit' for it. Once again our existence can be dismissed even at the point at which we display it. For the consensus will invariably be that it was not *reason* that we used to arrive at our conclusions, but a much inferior, capricious and lucky process – *intuition*. Again, men retain their ownership of the mental world by this classification, and women's intellectual competence is denied.

Most women know those subtle and insidious pressures which work upon us to produce what Florence Howe (1974) has called 'selective stupidity'; most women know those forces which are applied in a society where it is considered essential for men to be seen as 'superior' and where in Cicely Hamilton's (1909) terms we are coerced into 'not showing men up'. This may not be a topic frequently addressed in the traditions into which we have been initiated, but it is one which is raised again and again in the traditions that have been lost. No man is required to relate to a man as a woman is required to relate to a man, and this common practice among women of enhancing men's intellectual status at the expense of our own may be unknown to men, but it is not unknown to women.

Why do we do it? is one of the questions raised, and the answer seems to be relatively simple: it is not politic, says Cicely Hamilton, to bite the hand that feeds you, and the hand that feeds women has claimed the right to the realm of the intellectual. So for survival, we agree; we help to construct the image of men as our mental superiors. What is the effect?

The answer to this question is not so simple, but it can be readily recognised that when the reality – constructed by women and men – is that men are intellectually superior, that their arguments carry more weight, and are of a better 'standard', then there are many reasons for claiming that women's words, women's ideas, women's intellectual contributions, no matter what they are are not of the same quality as men's, and are therefore more likely to be 'rationally' excluded from the social reservoir of knowledge transmitted to the next generation.

There is also the effect upon women; the effect of having our intelligence denied, even of denying it ourselves. Berenice Carroll (1981)[4] has helped to show how men have denied women's intellectual existence, how they have constructed a whole set of beliefs which portray themselves in a flattering light and which we have too often come to accept, and to help 'come true'. At the heart of this belief system, she argues, are words like *originality, innovativeness, quality, excellence,* amorphous and subjective concepts (despite the fact that they originate with the 'objective' sex), which defy explicit classification and measurement, but which none the less have been unhesitatingly used to substantiate the thesis that the male is intellectually superior.

To illustrate her case, Carroll refers to the entries in James et al., *Notable American Women* (1971), a source which covers the contributions of women in many different fields, as they are assessed by a range of authors, and Carroll finds again and again that the entries contain disparaging – but unsupported – statements about women's intellectual ability. One woman's philosophy is superficial, her thinking constricted and largely derivative; another is not an innovator, but an expositor; another is not among the first rank; another has deficiencies in her critical and analytical faculties; another relied on her personality, not her ideas; another could absorb but not create, could systematise but not originate. . . .

Yet these assessments have little if any basis. Sometimes they stand out even as stark contradictions in a list of a particular woman's achievements, as in the case of Elizabeth Blackwell, for example. 'Of Elizabeth Blackwell, physician and medical sociologist', Carroll states, 'her biographer writes: "Not all her views were soundly based" (a reference to Blackwell's opposition to vaccination and animal experimentation). And she concludes: "But despite these negative strands, and although she made no contribution to medical science," her stress on preventive medicine, sanitation, sexual problems and public health were "in advance of her time".'

What Carroll reports here is not a phenomenon peculiar to the entries in *Notable American Women* but the manifestation of an intellectual 'double standard' (something of a euphemism) that operates within a patriarchal society, an intellectual double standard practised by women as well as men. Our attitudes towards intelligence in women have not advanced very far,

---

[4] I am very grateful for Berenice Carroll's generosity in sharing her ideas with me so readily.

says Matina Horner (1974) since Aristotle claimed 'that women never suffered from baldness because they never use the contents of their heads', for it is still a deeply entrenched conviction that intellectual competence cannot co-exist with 'femininity' (p. 44). This conviction finds expression again and again.

It is why Philip Goldberg (1974) found that women rated the same essay as 'impressive' when they thought the author a man, and 'mediocre' when they thought the author a woman; this is why women writers have often used male pseudonyms to get published (see Lynne Spender, forthcoming) and to obtain 'protection' from the critics; it is why teachers can mark the essays they believe to be written by boys as better than those they believe written by girls, and why 'messy' work when the writer is thought to be a boy can be called evidence of creativity and divergent thinking, and when the writer is thought to be a girl – carelessness (see Dale Spender, 1982a). This is why many teachers believe boys to be brighter – even when their test results are not as good as the girls (see Birgit Brock-Utne, 1981; Katherine Clarricoates, 1978; Michelle Stanworth, 1981; Dale Spender, 1982a).

While the belief persists that males are more intellectually competent, and while women subscribe to it in any way – from practising selective stupidity to abstaining from 'showing up men' – I think it fair to say that women will continue to disappear, and also that women are facilitating the process. While women are *not* perceived as intellectual and creative beings there is a ready-made rationale available for minimising and dismissing their contributions.

But as I have described this process so far, it appears to be one of unintended bias, and this is not the impression I seek to give. Generally speaking, when women of the past have been examined, it is often by someone who has specialised in the study of an individual woman, and often the finding that gross and wilful misrepresentation has occurred is assumed to be an 'isolated' case, the product of a particularly vicious critic, commentator, biographer, historian. But when these studies are brought together, when repeatedly one finds these ostensibly 'isolated' cases, one begins to suspect that they are not isolated at all, but the systematic pattern of the treatment of women's intellectual contribution in a male-dominated society.

We must begin to accept what Berenice Carroll points out, that the terms *original, innovative, creative, first rank, excellent*, are *political* terms, in that they are terms used by the gatekeepers to exclude women from entry in the 'worthwhile' records of our society. They are unsubstantiated terms used to maintain and justify a male monopoly on intelligence. They are based not on the contribution itself, but on the *sex* of the contributor, and they permit the 'superior' sex to be the producers of 'superior' work.

'There is something about women who try to engage in intellectual, scholarly and creative work', says Berenice Carroll, 'which elicits from many of their biographers a sense of obligation to comment negatively on the quality and originality of their contributions.' They are in the wrong place; they are usurping the rights of men who have defined themselves as the rightful thinkers and authorities.

Sometimes the emphasis shifts slightly from *what* is said, to *how* it is said, but the value judgements remain the same. Over and over again the women who are discussed in this book have their presentation, their 'style', called into question, and there is usually no more basis for this devaluation than there is for the devaluation of their ideas.

We find that Aphra Behn was too bawdy, Mary Wollstonecraft too rambling and too unsystematic, Catherine Macaulay too dense (she should be left on the library shelves where she belongs!). We are told that it is difficult to understand the appeal of Harriet Martineau's immensely popular writing, and that Margaret Fuller, while she was a good conversationalist, unfortunately could not write!

Reading these commentaries, one can begin to understand how it is that women are helped to disappear. Who would wish to go to the trouble of finding an obscure woman and to read her work, when informed that it is poorly presented, incoherent, badly planned and badly argued, rhetoric and polemic rather than reason, and utterly unconvincing? Only a rare and determined few would have persisted (and would thereby have had any chance of discovering any of the discrepancies), which is one of the reasons women have so often disappeared – without a fuss.

If women are to cease disappearing we must cease operating an intellectual double standard. In the interest of 'fair play' I have assumed that, in the absence of well-substantiated evidence to the contrary, women are intelligent, reasonable, logical human beings, who present their ideas in a competent manner. Treating women as positively intellectual and creative, however, in a society which regards them as negatively intellectual and creative, will no doubt be seen as distortion and bias. This gives me little cause for concern: it gives me considerable satisfaction to believe that patriarchy will not know how to use such knowledge biased in favour of women.

4 Harassment

In 1893, Matilda Joslyn Gage argued that women's resources were stolen by men; in 1909, Cicely Hamilton argued that women were required to trade their persons in return for bread; in 1946, Mary Ritter Beard argued that women's activity, force and will could even be denied at the moment they were demonstrating it: and in 1979 Catharine MacKinnon brought together many of these understandings in her description and explanation of sexual harassment.

It is part of the normal pattern of relationship of the sexes, argues MacKinnon, for men to see women as 'available' to them and for them to feel that it is in order for them to 'take' women's resources. At the workplace where women are still defined in terms of their sex and not their work, this pattern is likely to persist, and women, who find that men have more authority by virtue of their sex, and often by virtue of their position in the workforce, are often required to 'trade their person' in order to keep their job. If women resist or protest about this *normal* pattern of relations between the sexes, then where that resistance and protest is acknowledged to exist (and frequently it is not) the women are often perceived to be behaving in an unreasonable manner and can quickly become targets for abuse.

Sexual harassment works to keep women in their place, argues Mac-Kinnon, for it reinforces the power of men and denies women any other role than that of sexual availability. It constitutes a double-bind for women who do not *initiate* this behaviour in men (despite the fact that they are frequently held responsible for it). They are damned if they do 'trade' and damned if they do not.

This pattern also prevails in relation to women's intellectual work, where again, women are customarily defined in terms of their sex and not their work. One of the most striking features that emerges in a survey of women's ideas and men's evaluation of them, is the frequency with which *no* mention is made of a woman's ideas while the substance of discussion centres on her sexuality – or lack of it!

From Aphra Behn through Mary Wollstonecraft to Germaine Greer we witness the technique of bringing a woman's character into disrepute by means of her sexuality, so that her ideas need not be addressed at all. Almost all the women who are discussed here have been ridiculed or reviled in this way, for if a woman can be classified as 'promiscuous' then her ideas can be classified as unreliable and not worthy of serious consideration, and if she can be classified as embittered and twisted (almost an automatic assumption in the case of women who protest about male power, particularly if they live independently of men), then the same rule applies.

Women do not *initiate* these discussions of their sexuality, nor are they in a position to avoid them, for, as so many women have been pointing out for so long, the only definitions available to women in a patriarchal society are in terms of their sexuality and in relation to men. Women perform intellectual work, they produce their ideas and feed them into a male-dominated society, where their sex, and not their work, can become the immediate focus. One result is that their ideas can slip away unnoticed, unaddressed, and unrefuted. This is one way in which women's analysis of male power has persistently been ignored.

In the records which discuss women's contribution we are likely to come across entries which do not just suggest that a particular woman was a populariser and not a creative thinker, a purveyor and not an originator of ideas, we are also likely to encounter suggestions that the woman concerned was unbalanced in some way, abnormal, unrepresentative, and not to be trusted. So Harriet Martineau is portrayed as a crank, Christabel Pankhurst as a prude, Aphra Behn as a whore, Mary Wollstonecraft as promiscuous, and the list of distinguishing characteristics goes on, right up to the present day, where women who are associated with women's protest against men are likely to be the recipients of considerable ridicule and abuse.

Often the most offensive and repellent terms of the times have been used to describe a particular woman's character, and by implication to discredit her ideas. Such abuse has served to discourage other women from expressing their ideas, or else has indicated the good sense of expressing them anonymously and thereby trying to find a measure of protection. This also helps women to be invisible and promotes their disappearance.

What does one do with forty-six different anonymous women? At one stage this was the number contained in my own index, and the fact that there is no ready-made solution for including them in a reference system helps to indicate that those who designed the system did not find anonymous women a problem. But there are other difficulties presented as well: in many cases it is impossible to find out more about these anonymous women authors and, in a society where women have difficulty in establishing their human individuality, in constructing an identity, in distinguishing themselves from the over-riding definition of their sex, women's anonymity helps to serve patriarchal ends. There seems to be no easy way around this problem, for one can still appreciate why it is that women today might also seek to protect themselves from vilification in a male-dominated society.

The abuse that women received in the past has served to intimidate women in the past, but it can also function today to discourage us from seeking out our foremothers, if we take such abuse at its face value. If we do *not* accept it, if we persevere, and go from reports of women's lives and writing, to the women's *own* accounts of their lives and their work, we are often in for a considerable shock. Marie Mitchell Olesen Urbanski (1980), for example, was outraged when she found from Margaret Fuller's own account of her life the extent to which the editors of Fuller's *Memoirs* had distorted her character and ignored her ideas. Alice Rossi (1970) was upset by the discrepancies between the realities of Harriet Taylor's life and the way she had been reported, and suggested that it revealed much more about the fears of the reporters than about Harriet Taylor. I was so angry when I began to see how historians had dismissed Christabel Pankhurst's ideas and strategies by the simple technique of presenting her as a frustrated but none the less frigid woman who gave expression to her pent-up disappointments through a series of emotional outbursts against men.

I have to say that crude (and predictable) as these techniques are, they seem to work. They work by initially discrediting a woman and helping to remove her from the mainstream, they work by becoming the basis for any future discussion about her, and they work by keeping future generations of women away from her. This is a form of literary and historical harassment that keeps women in their (invisible) place.

5   Aphra Behn: a case study

When I first undertook the research for this book I began with the woman I thought had started it all: Mary Wollstonecraft. I immediately encountered the problem that Wollstonecraft did not always see herself this way:

she thought she had predecessors (Catherine Macaulay among them) and what is more, she was convinced that they had not been given the recognition she thought they deserved. Wollstonecraft was very concerned with the contempt in which women's intelligence was held, and with women's exclusion from the intellectual mainstream, and she linked both of these problems with women's exclusion from education. There would be no equality between the sexes, argued Wollstonecraft, until women were recognised as intellectually competent, and this was one of the reasons she demanded education for women, on the premise that when both sexes were educated, both sexes would demonstrate intellectual competence and would be intellectually responsible.

With education for women, so Wollstonecraft believed, the problem of women's inferior intellectual status and their consequent exclusion from the intellectual realm would be overcome. This would enable women to become part of the visible traditions of society, to take their full and proper place in the community and the culture.

My study of Wollstonecraft revealed that long before her time women had been generating ideas and men had been erasing them, and that, like patriarchy itself, there was no satisfactory way of pinpointing 'when it all started'. Virtually any woman chosen as a 'beginning' would have predecessors (which as Berenice Carroll, 1981, points out, makes a mockery of the concept of 'originality' as it is often used) and those predecessors would probably have disappeared, at least partially. The beginning, then, which I wanted to be *before* Wollstonecraft, was going to have to be arbitrary. (There are many 'anonymous' precedents – which I have deliberately retained in the bibliography – but because I do not know any of the details of these women, they could not be a satisfactory starting point.) However, there was one *name* that seemed to demand attention – that of Aphra Behn. She flitted in and out of some of the records, particularly those of women who had already attempted to reconstruct the past and to outline women's traditions, and she had an 'identity', as well as a number of publications. Virginia Woolf's comment on Aphra Behn suggested that she was a likely candidate for the role of demonstrating that it didn't all begin with Wollstonecraft, for in *A Room of One's Own* (1928), Woolf said 'All women together should let flowers fall on the tomb of Aphra Behn . . . for it was she who earned them the right to speak their minds' (p. 66).

As I knew almost nothing about Aphra Behn, I could presume that she had virtually disappeared, and so I began 'digging' and was helped immeasurably by Angeline Goreau's book, *Reconstructing Aphra* (1980). Nothing, however, could have prepared me for this 'classic case' of what happens to a woman who challenges male power. Because the treatment of Aphra Behn constitutes an example of almost every technique men have used to abuse, devalue, and erase women, because she is my starting point, and because the harassment she received helps to indicate that there have not been many changes over the last three hundred years in this area, I am using Aphra Behn here as a case study to illustrate what happens to women and their ideas in a patriarchal society.

From our perspective there can be no doubt about her achievement;

this is how Goreau summarises it: 'The life she led would have been extraordinary in any age, but for a woman of the seventeenth century not born to fortune or position, it was nearly unheard of. Aphra Behn was an adventuress who undertook the long and dangerous voyage to the West Indies, became involved in a slave rebellion there, and visited a tribe of Indians who had never before seen Europeans. She was a spy for Charles II against the Dutch. She was a debtor imprisoned for expenses incurred in the service of the King. She was a feminist who vociferously defended the right of women to an education, and the right to marry whom they pleased or not at all. She was a sexual pioneer who contended that men and women should love freely and as equals. She was a political activist who argued the Royalist point of view at Will's Coffee House and from the stage of the Drury Lane Theatre. She was an early abolitionist whose novel *Oroonoko* contained the first popular portrayal of the horrors of slavery. Finally, she was a writer who not only insisted on being heard but successfully forced the men who dominated the jealous literary world of Restoration England to recognize her as an equal. In a London that boasted only two theatres, she had seventeen plays produced in seventeen years. She wrote thirteen novels (thirty years before Daniel Defoe wrote *Robinson Crusoe*, generally termed the first novel) and published several collections of poems and translations.

'Along with her friend and colleague John Dryden, she is buried in Westminster Abbey – Dryden in poet's corner; Aphra outside, at the entrance to the cloisters, where her stone has almost been worn smooth by three centuries of indifferent feet' (Goreau, 1980, p. 3–4).

This woman was remarkable, and yet her 'disappearance' was so complete that in 1953/4, according to Goreau, a Mr A. Purvis was able to prove that Aphra Behn had died four days after she was born and that any claims made about her contribution were therefore based on nothing but myths. Mr Purvis, however, was just one of a long line of 'de-biographers (who) returned her to the silence thought proper for a woman of her time' (ibid., pp. 10–11).

But what has happened to Aphra Behn historically also had its parallels in her own lifetime. She was excluded from education, excluded from the circles of power in the literary world, and her achievement even then denied by the 'critics'. When her plays were so demonstrably successful, her force, her power, her effort, was still denied. It was frequently suggested, for example, that her work was not hers at all, but must have been written by a man (it was said to be her lover), or else, if it was hers, then it was of no value and her popular success could not be taken as a measure of her artistic or aesthetic ability.

This is how women's active existence in the world can be negated, and how the realms of creative and intellectual achievement are retained by and for men, even when a woman demonstrates her own competence in their terms. It was not just Aphra Behn's success, however, that made the male critics so vicious, it was also that they were rather distressed by what she had to say, for she often made them – and male power in general – the substance of her writings.

Her first play, *The Forced Marriage* or *The Jealous Bridegroom* was performed on Tuesday, 20 September 1670, at Lincoln's Inn Fields, and in it she presents in both implicit and explicit form the *different* experience of women in a male-dominated world. She speaks on behalf of her sex, and she looks at men through women's eyes (which was partly why so many men were enraged by her insolence) and acknowledges the significance of her entry, as a woman, to the male domain of literature.

As many women after her were to do (and perhaps as many before her had done) she raised the problem of trying to obtain a fair hearing from the men who held power and who certainly did not want to hear what she had to say. While most definitely seeking to put forward a woman's version of experience, Aphra Behn readily admitted that men would find it 'offensive' and were likely to take their revenge. So on occasions she tried to present her point of view without alienating the men who were in many respects responsible for her livelihood, and certainly for her reputation: 'Her fighting declaration of her entry into the sphere of wits is equivocated by her reluctance to risk being considered unfeminine', says Goreau. 'Her desire to be taken seriously is countered by her wish to charm' (ibid., p. 124). Aphra Behn assumes this is an experience that is common to women: it is something women have commented upon fre- quently from her own day to ours (see Matina Horner, 1974).

Often Behn makes this very dilemma the topic of her writing; she acknowledges that men want to listen to women who are modest, pleasing, agreeable and deferential. But while she recognises this, she also insists on the falseness and the injustice of the practice. Those women who will not talk to men in the terms men desire are dismissed as unfeminine, impolite, impertinent: 'Impertinence, my sex's shame', she writes, but then adds with her marvellous defiance, 'Your kind opinion was the unflattering glass in which my mind found how deformed it was' (from one of her poems, quoted in Goreau, 1980, p. 231).

Aphra Behn was acutely aware of the unjust way women were treated. She appreciated that their worth was measured in terms of their physical attractions, that they were sex-objects whose value – unlike the value of men – declined with age. She was conscious of the bartering and exchange of women which took place and she made this the dramatic issue in much of her work.

She also accepted the common human elements of the two sexes and argued that what was good for one sex must be good for both. Within this framework she accorded equal sexual desire to women and men and accepted that if it were permissible to portray physical passion and activity in men, on stage, then it was permissible to portray women giving expres- sion to their passion – even if it were not a form that men found comforting or flattering. One of the fundamental features of her work is that her woman characters frequently undermine the accepted patriarchal image of women – and of men – and that they expose the discrepancy between men's view of the world, and women's view of the world. For example, it was generally accepted that the period was one of sexual permissiveness in which greater freedom was allowed for both sexes, but Aphra Behn points out that this view is very one-sided and that, while there may have been greater sexual freedom for men, this resulted in increased difficulty, danger and penalties for women.

She also exposed some of the male myths. Her poem 'The Disappointment'[5] is about impotence, and most definitely not from a male perspective: it does not, therefore, offer the same explanations or portray the experience in the same way as a male might do.

But this was not all that Aphra Behn did. Not content simply to confine herself to presenting an alternative point of view, she often explicitly argued for its authenticity and attacked those critics who wished to dismiss her and her ideas. 'She gave her enemies ammunition', state Mary Mahl and Helene Koon (1977), 'by refusing to accept attacks with modesty, tears or admissions of inferiority: instead she fought back, and her prefaces are often sharp counterattacks . . .' (p. 166).

She became involved in the contemporary argument about the purpose of drama – partly because her own work was criticised on the grounds that it was written by an uneducated woman who could not appreciate the classical dimensions of drama because she knew neither Latin nor Greek. To the male literary establishment it was bad enough that she should write plays, successful plays that undermined their authority, but it was intolerable that she should put herself forward as an alternative authority. It was equally intolerable to Aphra Behn that they should persist in their own misguided apprehensions that 'the male way was the right way' and in 'An Epistle to the Reader' (reprinted in Goulianos, 1974, pp. 98–100) she produced a scathing attack on male supremacy.

Men, states Aphra Behn, deny women access to education so that Latin and Greek becomes a sort of secret code which lets them feel superior: by permitting only men to learn Latin and Greek, and by insisting that Latin and Greek are essential, they are able to 'reason' that women have no worthwhile contribution to make. Ridiculous, scoffs Behn, who proceeds to ridicule her critics.

First of all she denies the essential nature of Latin and Greek: Shakespeare did not know them, yet Jonson did: 'we all well know that the immortal Shakespeare's plays (who was not guilty of much more of this than often falls to women's share) have better pleased the world than Jonson's works' (ibid., p. 99). But secondly, and more bitingly, she makes it abundantly clear that, if her critics are to be taken as examples of the advantages conferred by a classical education, then women are not handicapped by not knowing Latin or Greek. 'Literature in the English language had rarely, if ever, seen such a diatribe in print with a woman's name signed at the bottom,' says Goreau (1980, p. 133).

While the purpose of the criticism against her was undoubtedly to make Aphra Behn 'withdraw' from the debate, it did not work. As Goreau

---

[5] I do not know of another poem in the English language that treats this topic from this perspective – yet I assume it is not a most uncommon experience for women. I appreciate that it is a subject on which the subordinate's view might not be welcome and presume this has been an influential factor in promoting the silence on the topic.

says 'Defiantly sarcastic, she is first of all refusing to be intimidated into a sense of inferiority because of her sex's ignorance' and she insists on 'dismissing the much vaunted "learning" that she has been denied as so much "academic frippery" ' (ibid.). Aphra's experience is not uncommon, even if her response is.

Her caricatures of the 'wits' and their pretentions is savage and recognisable and her understandings about 'academic frippery' and the way it is used to intimidate women no less applicable today. But in the course of our education few women have had access to this range of meanings because Aphra Behn like the women who went before and came after – has been silenced.

Always her work met with derision and dismissal on the grounds of her sex, and much of her energy – and wit – went into arguing that there was no reason that women could not write as well and authoritatively as men, except the 'reasons' (or prejudices) which men put forward from their limited or 'half-witted' position.

> I here and there o'erheard a coxcomb cry
> Ah, Rot it – 'tis a woman's comedy,
> One, who because she lately chanc'd to please us,
> With her damn'd stuff, will never cease to tease us.
> What had poor woman done, that she must be
> Debarred from sense, and sacred poetry? . . .
> As for you half wits, you unthinking tribe,
> We'll let you see, what e'er besides we do,
> How artfully we copy some of you:
> And if you're drawn to the life, pray tell me then,
> Why women should not write as well as men.

(Epilogue from *Sir Patient Fancy*, reprinted Goreau, 1980, p. 234)

The male-dominated literary establishment kept getting angrier, and Aphra Behn kept adding fuel to the fire. The more they harassed her, the more she mocked them in print, and so the process went on.

One of the most common techniques the critics used to discredit her was to accuse her of plagiarism and 'Though she often put up a front of saucy reply to her detractors', says Goreau, she 'was in truth far from indifferent to the siege of criticism and insult' (ibid., p. 231). The charges of plagiarism were so persistent and widespread in the case of *Abdelazer* that she felt obliged to defend her professional reputation in a postscript to *The Rover*. But even here she did not bow down submissively but instead pointed to the jealousy and envy of those who had made the accusations. If the play 'had succeeded ill', she states, 'I should have no need of imploring justice from the critics, who are naturally so kind to any that pretend to usurp their dominion' (ibid.).

Aphra Behn's popularity was a constant source of embarrassment to the male literary establishment who consistently accused her of being uneducated and creatively and intellectually inferior. But they also used her sexuality as a means of defining her work, and as a means of devaluing both herself and her work. William Wycherley was among those who sought to put her in her place. Although much less successful at the time than Aphra Behn (he had only four plays produced to her seventeen), he has managed to remain part of our tradition (I remember having to study his dreadful plays) while she has not, and part of the reason she has not is because of the efforts made by Wycherley and his ilk to disparage her as disreputable. He wrote a poem addressed 'To Sappho of the Age, Supposed to Lye-In' and makes full use of his wit to sustain the argument that a woman who earns a 'reputation' loses her good name. His poem is but another version of 'the only good woman is an invisible one' and any woman who becomes visible therefore has her modesty, femininity, desirability, called into question.

While Aphra Behn kept writing her plays (and people kept flocking to see them) then, even though she was outside the structured centres of power (the literary establishment), she was still *visible*. Once she ceased to produce her plays, however, it was unlikely that anyone within the literary or scholarly establishment would 'speak up' for them, and help maintain their and her visibility. With her death, she could effectively be removed. There are, however, some derogatory references to her among the men, after her death. In 'The Apotheosis of Milton' in the *Gentleman's Magazine* (1738), there is a fictional account of a meeting to admit Milton to the 'Club' of all the writers who were buried in Poets' Corner of Westminster Abbey. Aphra Behn tried to join in the meeting, but Chaucer tells her that no woman has a right to membership in the club. As none of the members present want her to stay, 'she flings out of the assembly' (p. 469). This is presumably a reference to her burial *outside* the mainstream of Poets' Corner, and unwittingly, a self-revealing male commentary on the position and treatment of women.

Over the last three centuries, Aphra Behn's name has occasionally made its way into debate, only to be dismissed, and usually on the grounds of her sex. One of the most common justifications for her exclusion has been that she wrote 'bawdy', unforgivable in a woman, despite the fact that it was the style of her age and that it has not ever been necessary to forgive her male contemporaries. Towards the end of the nineteenth century some of her work was republished, but, as only five hundred copies were printed, it was not intended that she reach a wide audience. Even so, the reviewer in the *Saturday Review* was not content to leave her demise to chance:

> Mrs. Behn is still to be found here and there in the dusty worm
> eaten libraries of old country houses, but as a rule we imagine she
> has been ejected from all *decent* society for more than a generation
> or two. If Mrs. Behn is read at all, it can only be from a love of
> impurity for its own sake, for rank indecency . . . even in her own
> day. Mrs. Behn's works had a scandalous reputation . . . it is true
> that this did not prevent her from attaining honourable burial in
> Westminster Abbey but it is a pity her books did not rot with her
> bones. That they should now be disinterred from obscurity into

which they have happily fallen is surely inexcusable. ('Literary
Garbage', *Saturday Review*, vol. 33, 27 January 1862, p. 109)

And of course there have been the 'scholarly' activities which have been
concerned with discrediting her existence as well as her work. Among those
who played their part in undermining her authenticity was one Ernest
Bernbaum who in 1913 wrote an article entitled 'Mrs. Behn's Biography:
a Fiction' in which he asserted that the biography of Aphra Behn, written
by 'One of the Fair Sex', and which had been used to establish her identity,
was not written by one of the fair sex at all but by a man; that she had
never been to the West Indies, that there had been no Mr Behn and that
her exploits as a spy were not to be believed.

'Why did Bernbaum want to discredit Aphra?' asks Goreau. 'Why
dismantle her history? The evidence he gave for doubting her word was
purely speculative – he had discovered no new "fact" that established an
alternative version of her story. "Mrs. Behn's Biography: a Fiction" it
seems, was based more on an unwillingness to believe that a woman of
Aphra's time could have lived the life she did than on any compelling
evidence to the contrary' (Goreau, 1980, p. 10).

That women *cannot* make a worthwhile creative or intellectual contribution to our culture is a deeply entrenched belief in our society, and if
this belief is to be maintained women who *do* make such a contribution
consistently have it – and themselves – negated and denied. Sometimes it
is their womanliness that can be found to be deficient – they may have too
little sense of modesty, and can therefore be labelled as 'bawdy', or too
little sense of emotion and sensitivity and can be labelled as having a
'masculine mind', or too little understanding of any depth or substance and
therefore be labelled as 'trivial', or too little concern for men and be labelled
as embittered. If it is not themselves then it is their contributions that are
found to be deficient – they may not be 'up to standard'. And if all this
fails and their intellectual capacity persists in being visible, then it is almost
mandatory to insist that their ideas must have originated with a man.

It is this treatment of a woman's contribution where the judgements
are made on the basis of her *sex*, and not her *work*, that I am describing
as harassment, and which I am suggesting is part of the normal pattern of
the relationship between the sexes. By such harassment, women are kept
in their place, and men's claim to ownership of the realm of ideas and
creativity is upheld.

Men have a *double* power, in that they have the power to decree how
a *woman* will be evaluated in a male-dominated society, and the power to
determine how her *work* will be received. This power they use to make
women who threaten the system *disappear*. This is why I suspect that it is
extremely subversive to insist on women's intellectual competence and to
assert the 'realness' of women's intellectual existence in a patriarchal
society.

PART ONE

MARY WOLLSTONECRAFT AND HER FOREMOTHERS

1 Alone or together?

When I first began to reconstruct the tradition of women's ideas, Mary Wollstonecraft seemed the obvious starting point – the provisional title for this book was 'From Mary Wollstonecraft to Adrienne Rich'. So frequently is the women's movement dated from Mary Wollstonecraft that initially I did not even ask myself whether indeed Mary Wollstonecraft was the *first* – or, whether this was significant.

But I did start with the particular image of Wollstonecraft that is usually presented, and I did wonder how accurate it was. She is usually perceived as a 'lone figure' who 'started it all', but more than this, as someone who – in times past and before the recent era of sexual permissiveness – has been presented as 'immoral' and 'unstable'. There is often the implication among women as well as men that she was a bad advertisement for women's cause, that her behaviour and her protest were sufficiently offensive to scare people away and that she retarded the development of a women's movement. It was because she frightened people away, because she stood as a 'warning' to those who might be tempted to follow in her footsteps, that there was nothing but silence after her, for fifty years – so I was led to believe.

What was clear to me was that whether this portrayal of Wollstonecraft was accurate or not, it wasn't very helpful. There is little in it that imbues us with a sense of confidence or inspires us with a desire to emulate her ways and yet there was a lot in it that led us to dissociate ourselves from her. And interestingly, although many many women I asked could tell me about Mary Wollstonecraft – that she was a founding mother and had an unfortunate life – few had ever read her work. To me, there were some 'odd' things about Wollstonecraft, but they weren't the 'oddities' presented by the conventional portrayal. Almost everywhere I read accounts of her she was presented as 'alone' and it was because this 'clashed' with my own experience that I began to question her standing as the solitary individual who started it all.

'Mary is an obvious pioneer,' says Margaret George (1970), 'there were other possible candidates before her – Aphra Behn, the talented playwright of the restoration and the first Englishwoman to support herself by writing, or Mary Astell who under the anonymity of "a Lover of her Sex" published in 1694 *A serious Proposal to the Ladies*, or a lady identifying herself only as "Sophia, a Person of Quality" whose pamphlet of 1739 was entitled *Woman not Inferior to Man*, and she had ambitious contemporaries including Catherine Macaulay, Olympe de Gouges, and Helen Maria Williams, but her position is unchallengeable' (p. 6).

As at this stage I knew nothing of Mary Astell, 'Sophia', Catherine Macaulay, Olympe de Gouges or Helen Maria Williams, I could have accepted this assessment and continued to date women's protest from the end of the eighteenth century – although I remember thinking that *Woman not Inferior to Man* looked rather promising.

Emily Sunstein (1975) accords Mary Wollstonecraft and her protest pride of place and quotes Ruth Benedict in support: 'It was in Ruth Benedict's words "a fight for which the world was not yet ready, which seemed worth fighting to only one soul then living, to Mary Wollstonecraft herself" ' (p. 207). This portrayal of Wollstonecraft as completely unrepresentative left me feeling distinctly uneasy. It was not just that she was unrepresentative in her own time, with no one else experiencing either the need or the capacity to protest, but that she is also unrepresentative in our own time when few (if any) women go off on their own to raise their consciousness about patriarchy.

I can well appreciate why it is that a capitalist society based on premises of individual competition and accumulation of wealth would seek to describe the realm of ideas in terms of individual competition and in terms of the *ownership* of ideas, and would find no inconsistency in portraying Mary Wollstonecraft as a solitary figure who produced her ideas on her own and who deserves full 'credit' for them; but this interpretation would not fit with what I have come to know about ideas in a context of women.

Among many women today, ideas and consciousness-raising are inextricably linked and I suspect it would be somewhat foolhardy to advocate that women should retreat into solitude if they wish to engage in consciousness-raising and develop their ideas about patriarchy. Rather than sticking to the rules which generally govern the academic community (presumed to have a monopoly on ideas), where ideas are frequently 'hoarded' until publication, and due recognition of ownership and credit can be granted, women have tried to organise more co-operative contexts in which ideas can be shared, pooled, and ordered – to the extent that even if it were considered desirable to identify the owner of a particular point, connection, concept, it would often be impossible to do so.

How could I reconcile this knowledge with that of Mary Wollstonecraft as someone who thought it up all by herself? Today we can conceptualise (albeit vaguely) the possibility of collective ideas as a product of consciousness-raising, and this helps to suggest the way we are establishing a viable (and very subversive) alternative. Mary O'Brien (1981) pointed out that the use of the footnote has paralleled the rise of capitalism and, she suggests, this is no coincidence. Apart from raising interesting questions about the role of footnotes, think what it would mean if we began to devise a referencing system that catered for collective ideas? Yet there would be no room for the prevailing portrayal of Wollstonecraft in such a framework.

While the spoken word has been given greater prominence in consciousness-raising, it is not the only means by which ideas are generated. Numerous women today testify to the importance of a particular book – 'it changed my life' – even though they generally want to talk (or write) about it. But even that would have to be ruled out if Wollstonecraft was the *first*, for there simply wouldn't have been any books for, by, about, women that she could have turned to.

Virtually everything I first found out about Wollstonecraft, then, contradicted what I knew from my own experience. I could, of course, have come to the conclusion that human processes had changed drastically over the last two centuries and that while today insights about male power were more likely to be forged in a collective context, two hundred years ago it was possible to do it alone. Somehow this didn't seem feasible. Besides, there were so many facets of Mary Wollstonecraft's life which, far from being unique, suggested that we shared much in common with her. Trying to account for Wollstonecraft's protest, Virginia Woolf said in 1932 that: 'If Jane Austen had lain as a child on the landing to prevent her father from thrashing her mother, her soul might have burnt with such a passion against tyranny that all her novels might have been consumed in one cry for justice.' Woolf adds: 'such had been Mary Wollstonecraft's first experiences of the joys of married life and then her sister Everina had been married miserably, and had bitten her wedding ring to pieces in the coach. Her brother had been a burden on her; her father's farm had failed and in order to start that disreputable man with the red face and violent temper and the dirty hair in life again, she had gone into bondage among the aristocracy as a governess' (1969, p. 194).

Nancy Hartsock (1981) sees so many similarities between Wollstonecraft's experience and our own that she has stated that Wollstonecraft's life reads like a feminist 'How–To' manual, which makes it more difficult to regard her as unrepresentative, and incidentally, helps to reveal the commonalities of women's experience, over time, in a male-dominated society. Reading about her sister's miserable marriage – and post-natal depression – raises the question of how far the notion of *progress* is confined to male experience, and the extent to which the restrictions placed on women in a patriarchal society are so encompassing that women's experience is structured in much the same limited way regardless of the century in which it occurs.[1]

If she shares some of the features of women's contemporary existence, she also seems to share some of the forms of resistance. Many of her

---

[1] I recognise that many historians – including Gerda Lerner, whose work (and life) I greatly admire – have warned against assuming that there are shared experiences with women of the past and that it is dangerous to treat women as an undifferentiated group, and I appreciate the inadequacies of my classification. But I also suspect that there is an area – of being subordinate to men, of being defined in relation to men, of being the nurturing sex in an exploitative society – where women do share a common experience and I would not want to lose sight of this.

biographers emphasise the way she vehemently asserted the validity of her personal experience – even when it defied existing beliefs – and made it the substance of her insights (see particularly Margaret Walters, 1976). This is why, says Miriam Kramnick (1978),[2] her argument has a freshness and immediacy 'as if the author herself had only now entered the contemporary debate on women's rights' (p. 7). She may not have had the benefit of the current slogan, but there is little doubt that to Wollstonecraft the personal was political.

There is yet another aspect of her life with which we can identify: she experienced a considerable amount of harassment. For her life, her work, her protest, she was rebuffed and ridiculed; she was called everything from a 'philosophic sloven' (a reference to her failure to dress in a feminine form) to a 'hyena in petticoats'. One could almost write a book on the abuse that has been levelled at her and which ranges from a denial of her intellectual and creative ability to a condemnation of her habit of serving tea in cracked cups!

Mary Wollstonecraft seems to be in many respects peculiarly modern. But the 'fact' that she is without precedents, and the 'fact' that she forged her ideas about patriarchy without benefit of a community of women, makes her distinctly different. But the question to be asked is whether this representation of Wollstonecraft, as first and alone, reflects the realities of her life, or the needs of patriarchy. If we could establish that she was neither the first, nor alone, if we could show that she was one of a long line of women who protested about male power and that she had many contemporaries who shared her views, how significant would this information be? If we could demonstrate that she was neither unrepresentative in her own time, or in ours, that she was one of a group of women who thought it reasonable and normal to object to male power, what meaning would it have for us today? And what then would we make of the official objective records, and the 'gatekeepers' who have controlled the knowledge (or absence of it) that we have inherited?

In retrospect I think that, had I not had my doubts born of my own personal experience about the likelihood of Mary Wollstonecraft bursting forth from nowhere as a solitary (and not very attractive) figure, I would probably have accepted the (patriarchal) portrayal of Mary Wollstonecraft as the *first*. I would probably have dated women's protest from the end of the eighteenth century and would not have come to believe – as I now do – that while ever there has been male power there has been female resistance. I might even have constructed an argument based on the concept of *progress*, from the first passionate stirrings of Mary Wollstonecraft, to the beginnings of a 'movement' fifty years later, to the demand for suffrage, the gaining of the vote – and somehow fitted in the current feminist revival. It was partly because I decided to find out who said what *before* Mary Wollstonecraft that I have reached my current conclusions – that as far back as we can go we find evidence of women's protest against male power, and evidence of male power being used to eradicate it from the record.

---

[2] Miriam Kramnick is now Miriam Brody.

When one begins to appreciate what Aphra Behn, Mary Astell, 'Sophia', Catherine Macaulay and Olympe de Gouges said (and I must apologise for the omission of Helen Maria Williams who proved to be a little too elusive), the notion of *progress* becomes meaningless. 'Coming and going', 'appearing and disappearing', beginning anew virtually every fifty years and sometimes not attaining comparable insights to those who have gone before but who remain unknown, does not resemble progress. It does, however, constitute women's tradition.

In suggesting that Mary Wollstonecraft was not alone, and that she had foremothers, I do not want to devalue her 'originality' or minimise her contribution – that has been done systematically and enthusiastically by the masters – but I do want to suggest that she is one of many (and there will be countless more that my 'diggings' have not unearthed) and that it has been in patriarchal interest to silence and conceal such women. I do want to suggest that we should be suspicious of the treatment of women as lone figures, for it is by such a process that they become isolated from their sex, that they are classified as an aberration and of little or no relevance to women, that they are made vulnerable while the contributions of women around them are made invisible. I do want to suggest that when we know that for centuries women have been saying many of the things we are saying today, and that men have been interrupting them, we do feel confident, we do feel inspired to emulate some of those women we have reclaimed. It is because such knowledge of women of the past – and there have been hundreds of them – is empowering for women that every effort has been made to make it disappear in a patriarchal society where power is perceived as the prerogative of men.

2 Mary, Mary, quite contrary

For at least one hundred years before Mary Wollstonecraft there were women who were turning their critical attention to the arrangements of society and the role that men had provided for themselves, and women, in the organisation that they established. It has been stated that Aphra Behn, through her pioneering efforts, ushered in a new age of thoughtful and articulate women who were prepared to assert the authenticity of their own personal and different experience. Of Aphra Behn, Vita Sackville-West stated in 1927 that she was 'the first woman in England to earn her living by the pen' and to open up new possibilities for women, for 'she entered the open pits. She was an inhabitant of Grub Street with the best of them ... a troop of women followed in the steps she had so painfully cut; Elizabeth Rowe, Mary Pix, Eliza Haywood, Jane Barker, Penelope Aubin, Mary de la Rivière Manley, to name but a few were her direct successors' (p. 13); and they were also Mary Wollstonecraft's direct predecessors.

It is fascinating to find that Vita Sackville-West was engaged in the same task earlier this century as we are today, of reconstructing women's past (as was Virginia Woolf, of course – this is the substance of *A Room*

of One's Own and *Three Guineas*). But it is difficult to trace some of the
women she names, for they are not entered in the catalogue of the British
Library or listed in the biographical dictionaries. However, where they can
be traced fairly readily, and where they did adopt a women's perspective,
it becomes immediately obvious that they received a comparable response
to their work as Aphra Behn who went before and Mary Wollstonecraft
who came after – they were ridiculed, belittled and abused, in short,
sexually harassed – condemned more often as women rather than responded to as writers or thinkers.

   The Grub Street women to whom Vita Sackville-West refers were not
the only women who preceded Mary Wollstonecraft and left written records
of their criticism and their social analysis. There were other women who
followed on more from 'Orinda' (Katherine Phillips) and the Duchess of
Newcastle, and while they may have been more privileged they were no
less critical of male power (see Goreau, 1980, and Mahl and Koon, 1977).
In fact, it could be argued that it was because they did not have to earn
their living by their pen and meet the demands of 'the public' (invariably
construed as 'male') that they were able to engage in more radical protest.
Among them were two 'Marys' who would most definitely have been
viewed as 'contrary': Mary Astell (1668–1731) and Lady Mary Wortley
Montagu (1689–1762). They were close friends (and they had other women
friends) and they both produced clear and caustic criticisms of male power.

   In many ways they generated the concept of *patriarchy* (although they
did not use the name) that we have come to use and accept as a reality
today, and their contribution must not be underestimated.[3] It is not an easy
task to describe the world in terms that have not been part of the culture
and not learned. Some linguists state that it is almost impossible, but
women's experience suggests otherwise (see D. Spender, 1980). Mary Astell
and Lady Mary Wortley Montagu did not accept the conventional cultural
view of the world (which they both acknowledged was encoded by men
and based exclusively on the limited experience of men) but reconceptualised it from the perspective of women who must daily deal with male
power and the consequent constraints it imposes on women. They described
the world in their terms and sexual inequality was one of its most fundamental features. They took the enormous step of rejecting this inequality
as divinely ordained, natural, or inevitable (the then current conventional
explanations). They re-evaluated the roles of women and men, they re-
evaluated work, and manners and morals and explanations, and the relationship and interaction of the sexes. They developed a new frame of
reference, which related to women. In the process they conceptualised
women as an independent category, an entity in themselves, and this necessitated breaking the mental set which defined women only in relation to
men; in classifying women as an autonomous category, they were also
required to conceptualise men as a different and opposing force.

---

   [3] I recognise the danger of assuming that they were the 'first' and that they had no
antecedents, but I have to stop somewhere or the process could be endless: the two
'Marys' constitute an arbitrary dividing line for their successor, the third Mary.

It is unfortunate that one of the consequences of knowing so little about our past, about what women have thought and how their ideas have been treated, is that we tend today to have a 'superior' notion about our own position and to rate what little we do know against our own current understandings. In a society where differences are readily ranked (which may be cause, or effect, but which is certainly not unconnected to sexual difference and inequality), it is sometimes tempting to interpret the differences between our own insights and those of the past in our own favour – to be critical of those women who did not adopt the same priorities as we do today. There *are* differences, but rather than rank them, rather than emphasise where I think our foremothers have been 'mistaken', I want to emphasise what we have in common, where we are the 'same'. With Mary Astell, the task is not at all difficult; there is much that we share.

To label *A Vindication of the Right of Woman* by Mary Wollstonecraft as the first major feminist treatise is to do Mary Astell a serious injustice, for, almost one hundred years before, in 1694, she put forward a very similar thesis. In a context in which women are judged according to manners and appearance – even today – Katharine Rogers (1979) has said of Mary Astell that she was 'forbidding in appearance, blunt in manners' (p. 26). Rogers, however, goes on to add that Astell was 'utterly contemptuous of masculine gallantry which she regarded "as insults in disguise, impertinently offered by men through a secret persuasion that all women were fools" ' (ibid.). Such biting criticisms of the 'superior' sex are typical of Astell and one of the reasons that her writing is so acceptable today and may have been so relevant to Mary Wollstonecraft. *A Serious Proposal to the Ladies* (1694) and *Some Reflections upon Marriage Occasioned by the Duke and Duchess of Mazarine's Case* (1700) are Astell's two major works which contain her astute analysis of 'patriarchal society', but, as Mary Hays (1803), a good friend of Mary Wollstonecraft's, points out, Astell also wrote *A Letter to a Lady, Written by a Lady* (1696), a humorous essay in defence of her sex. (This can be disputed, see Kinnaird, 1979.)

Reading some of Astell's work today is a joy; I was both amazed and amused by the satirical and entertaining way (from a female point of view) in which she attacked her targets. Reading some of the comments made about her – past and present – is not such a joy (not that there are many comments; as Rogers says, only one book has been written about Astell – and that in 1916 by Florence M. Smith. Ruth Perry (1981), however, is currently working on a biography of her and see also Joan K. Kinnaird, 1979, and forthcoming). Like other women who have described sexual inequality in the light of their experience as those who have less resources, Mary Astell was belittled and ridiculed. She herself said of her critics: 'They must either be very ignorant, or very malicious' (Stephen and Lee, 1973, p. 674). But detracting from her contribution is not an activity confined to past, unenlightened decades; it often continues today in the form of disallowing the value of her ideas. Katharine Rogers (1979), for example, is critical of Astell for her theoretical rather than practical stance (this, as the evaluation of a woman who helped to bring the concept of patriarchy into existence), and thereby reinforces the belief that it is inappropriate for

women to enter the realm of ideas. And Rogers makes only a mild concession to Astell's satire – another area that males appear to own. She also
chooses to portray Astell's life – which was quite courageous in many
respects – in a negative way, so that we are asked to see her as somewhat
strange and invited to distance ourselves from her, rather than identify with
her. For example, Rogers says that it was Astell's preference for celibacy
which 'accounts for the relative indifference to improving the lot of
wives. . . . While clearly recognizing their oppression, she does not suggest
that the laws of state or church be modified to alleviate it,' and, in the case
of *Some Reflections on Marriage*, 'Perhaps, however, the irony which per-
vades much of this tract was meant to extend to its apparently uncompromising insistence on the subjection of wives' (ibid., p. 27).

I have many objections to this treatment of Astell. In relation to the
ciriticism of her as *understanding* the oppression of women, but not
attempting to change the laws of church or state which reflected or reinforced this oppression, I wonder if in years to come Germaine Greer, Kate
Millett, Adrienne Rich and Mary Daly, for example, will be condemned
for their theoretical and analytical critiques of patriarchy. There are many
parallels, because in spite of the intervening centuries, these women were
beginning again to reformulate the concept of patriarchy for a new generation, without always appreciating how often and how well such a concept
had been generated before. Yet, are Greer, Millet,, Rich and Daly (to name
but a few), who have helped to map out the dimensions of patriarchy,
going to be criticised for their failure to argue for Anti-Sex Discrimination
Laws or the Equal Rights Amendment? Treating Astell in the way Rogers
has done is akin in many respects to judging Greer, Millett, Rich and Daly
as those who identified the oppression of women but who were indifferent
to improving women's position, because they made no recommendations
about changes in the law.

Looking for a legal solution to the problem is very much a
nineteenth-century strategy, and, I would argue, depends greatly on knowing what the problem is.[4] Mary Astell was a pioneer when it came to
formulating that problem, with all its complexities. And I think there are
many dangers in asserting that it is preferable for women to engage in
'practical' activities, rather than 'theoretical' ones. Even today, many
women would be prepared to argue that seeking to improve women's
position within a male-dominated society, via legal means which males
control, is only one way – and not necessarily the best way – of ending
women's oppression. Trying to understand the way in which male domination works is no less laudable or useful an activity – although it does
have more connotations of the 'intellectual'. It is probably correct to say
that Mary Astell, Lady Mary Wortley Montagu and Mary Wollstonecraft
(the same criticism has been levelled at her) did not address the iniquities
of the legal system in the same way as their nineteenth-century sisters did,
but it is entirely another matter to declare whether this is a strength or a
weakness. I think it fair to suggest that much of the reform of the nineteenth

---

[4] This is discussed in more detail in Part II, page 518.

century could not have been visualised, let alone enacted, if these women had not *named the problem* (a concept developed more recently for us by Mary Daly, 1973) and that in outlining the tradition of women it is even fairer to acknowledge that we are indebted to *both*, to the theoretical feminists and the practical feminists (and to those who combined both in their own lives, for is it not a political and practical activity to write the pamphlets and the books that have changed people's lives?), and that women's position is unlikely to be changed if we have one, but not the other.

In relation to the treatment of Mary Astell, I also have many objections to her celibacy being seen as problematic and used to explain her 'weaknesses' in other areas: why could it not have been said that 'Mary Astell was not impressed by marriage, which perhaps explains why she chose not to enter the ostensibly blissful state: that she is aware of all its many disadvantages for women is very obvious, and they are frequently the focus of her satire'? To perceive Astell's writing in this way, however, is to accept that she *is* a satirist and this introduces another aspect of the same problem: satire too has an 'intellectual' dimension and is therefore often judged as 'out of bounds' for women. (Men are satirical – it is clever; women are nasty or bitchy – which is a reflection of their temperament.)

Those who took Jonathan Swift seriously when he suggested that babies be boiled to solve the famine problem in Ireland were scoffed at themselves in turn for being unable to understand the biting criticism he was putting forward by advocating such a 'solution'. But when Mary Astell suggests that women should submit totally to the tyranny of men, she is criticised for her conservatism, and allowed only the slim possibility that she is mocking or condemning the existing arrangements. That we have no tradition of women satirists is not because women have not written powerful and persuasive satire since the time of Aphra Behn (and perhaps before), but because satire is seen as the prerogative of men, demanding the qualities appropriated by men – intelligence, wit, a sense of humour! Women should put Mary Astell to the test themselves: whether she harangues (as a celibate woman could be expected to do in a society where men determine the values) or whether she satirises can be judged from her writing.

In 1694, when Mary Astell wrote *A Serious Proposal to the Ladies*, she made no attempt to conceal or deny the differences between women and men (even if they did portray women in an unflattering light), but attempted to account for these differences *outside* the conventional interpretations of them as 'divinely ordained' and 'natural'. In seeking to explain the world in a different way she also came to generate a concept which is still fundamental today – that women are blamed for events over which they have little or no control. She saw that men appeared superior and too often women appeared silly, but she attributed this to the power which men had to arrange society in their own interest, and this included the power to provide explanations – such as that these differences were natural, and, in contradiction to this, that it was women's *fault* that they were inferior. Again, while not using the word, Mary Astell provided a substantial analysis of 'woman as scapegoat'.

It was male power, and socialisation, that were to Astell responsible for the differences between the sexes, and part of the oppression of women was that they were 'blamed' for the social arrangements that men devised. 'Women are from their very infancy debarred those advantages, with the want of which they are afterwards reproached, and nursed up in those vices which will hereafter be upbraided to them' (Astell, 1694, reprinted in Rogers (ed.), 1979, p. 28).

Mary Astell stated that the problem was one of education; men educated themselves, denied education to women, and then blamed women because they were not educated (precisely the same point as that made by Aphra Behn). But Astell went further: she stated categorically that men liked it that way, and that even while they castigated women for their foolishness, they continued to cajole and coerce them into being foolish, in order that men should appear more masterful: 'So partial are men to expect bricks where they afford no straw', stated Astell, 'and so abundantly civil as to take care we make good that obliging epithet of *ignorant*, which out of an excess of manners they are pleased to bestow on us' (ibid.). Satire?

Like Mary Wollstonecraft and many more women who came later, this is not a woman trying to win approval from a male audience. Some of the women who came later and who looked to a reform of the laws in order to improve the position of women needed male assistance in their efforts, and therefore were obliged to try and win men over to their arguments,[5] but Astell does not depend on the goodwill of men (although one would like to know more about her publisher), and makes no attempt to demonstrate her worth to men, in the terms laid down by men (in this pamphlet). On the contrary, she engages in a scathing attack on men and their silly ways. She outlines some of the artful tricks they employ in order to appear superior themselves and to have women appear inferior – and accept it.

Of course men will pay women compliments, and be chivalrous to helpless, hapless women, argues Astell, and of course men will be critical – even outraged – if women cease being foolish and ignorant, and begin to challenge the apparent superiority of males. But men who try to woo women by praising their incompetence and delighting in their ignorance are false lovers, declares Astell, for their words are but the 'deceitful flatteries of those who under pretence of loving and admiring you, really serve their *own* base ends' (ibid., p. 30).

Astell's analysis, written almost three hundred years ago, is not only relevant but is radical today – her argument is that women who are admired and valued for their figure and foolishness, and who accept this as a sign of genuine worth, are deceived, because they are simply serving the interests of male supremacy; this argument has its contemporary counterpart. Men who deal in such flattery are but feigned and cunning lovers, argues Astell,

---

[5] The suffragettes, of course, stopped trying to seek male approval as a means of getting men to change their laws so that they were less unfavourable to women.

for they would pretend that you are admirable, with the result that they will divert you and keep you from obtaining those very qualities that could make you admirable and strong.

In encountering these words of Mary Astell, I find strength and excitement, but I also feel frustration and rage – anger that they were not available to me twenty years ago, when they would have explained and enriched my life, when they would have made such a difference. But there is also the growing conviction that it is precisely because they would have made a very big difference to my own life, and the lives of many other women, that Mary Astell's words have disappeared. If I had known about her she would have been such a marvellous model for demonstrating how men's arguments could be turned back on men themselves. She is a source of so many 'quotable quotes', of humour, wit *and satire*. For example, taking the arguments that men have used to deny women the possibilities for intellectual development, she quickly and neatly turns them around when she says: 'If any object against a learned education that it will make women vain and assuming, and instead of correcting increase their pride, I grant that a smattering of learning may,' and she adds cryptically, *'for it has this effect on the men: none so dogmatical and so forward to show their parts as your little PRETENDERS to science'* (ibid., pp. 34–5, my italics). She then assures her readers (and it must be noted that she is addressing herself to women – in itself subversive in a male-dominated society, see D. Spender, 1980) that such a form of education is precisely what she does not want; she seeks the 'substance' not the 'show'.

Her response to the argument that it is undesirable for wives to be more intellectually competent than their husbands is superb, and could and should be used more often today: 'The only danger [of intellectual development for women] is that the wife be more knowing than the husband', she says, 'but if she be *'tis his own fault*,' and she demolishes the argument that even for this, women are held at fault. It is the man who is to blame for such a state of affairs, she says 'since he wants no opportunities for improvement; unless he be a natural BLOCKHEAD', she adds, 'and then such an one will need a wise woman to govern him, whose prudence will conceal it from public observation, and at once both cover and supply his defects' (in Rogers, 1979, pp. 35–6, my italics).

With alacrity, Astell strips men of their pretence and exposes their many weaknesses: she develops a concept of patriarchy and outlines some of the ways in which it works; she proposes to put an end to this ridiculous masquerade which bestows learning and authority on men and assists them to appear superior, by providing for women the facilities to become learned and authoritative – then, she believes, the 'apparent' supremacy of men will be ended. To this end she advocated establishing a college for women: 'You are therefore, Ladies, invited into a place, where you shall suffer no other confinement but to be kept out of the road of sin: you shall not be deprived of your grandeur, but only exchange the vain pomps and pageantry of the world, empty titles and forms of state, for the true and solid greatness of being able to despise *them*' (ibid., p. 29). There can be no doubt of what Astell thinks of the society designed by men – she wants women to despise the vain pomps and pageantry of the world, the empty titles and forms of state which men have devised and on which they place such value. And she wants them to acquire a new value system in a 'women-only' college.

That women should condemn the pageantry, pomp, and prestige of the male-ordered world was a point taken up by Virginia Woolf in 1938 in *Three Guineas* (and by other women in the interim). Woolf acknowledged her debt to Astell – but many generations of women have had no such debt to acknowledge; they did not know of her existence. Both Astell and Woolf are acutely aware of the deficiencies and inadequacies in the way males have organised the world, and neither of them seeks for women simply a greater share of power in male-defined institutions.

But what was the response to Astell's proposal? She herself knew it would be predictably varied, according to sex and vested interest: 'The Ladies, I am sure, have no reason to dislike this Proposal; but I know not how the men will resent it, to have their enclosure broken down, and women invited to taste of that Tree of Knowledge, they have so long unjustly monopolised. But they must excuse me, if I be as partial to my own sex as they are to theirs, and think women as capable of learning as men, and that it becomes them as well' (ibid., p. 33).

Astell was not frightened to assert the value of her sex and the validity of her personal experience: she signed the *Proposal* as 'a Lover of her Sex' and it was partly because she had gained so much satisfaction from her own studies that she was able to assert from her personal experience (which defied accepted beliefs) that it was possible, worthwhile, and *becoming* for women to undertake serious study and to be educated. But, unlike many women since who have believed that all that was necessary was to convince men of the justice of their cause, and 'rights' would be forthcoming, Astell knew that men would resist moves which threatened or undermined their power and consequent superiority.

Her project of a women's college did not come to fruition and both Mary Hays (1803) and Virginia Woolf (1938) explained why: 'A lady of fortune, impressed by these publications, proposed to contribute £10,000 towards erecting a seminary or college, for the education of young women, and also to serve as an asylum for those whom misfortune, studious habits, or other circumstances, should render desirous of retiring from the world. The execution of this laudable and rational project was prevented by Bishop Burnet, from a puerile apprehension, that its resemblance to conventual institutions would reflect scandal on the Reformation' (Hays, 1803, pp. 214–15).

Virginia Woolf seems to be of the same opinion. Of Astell she says: 'Little is known about her, but enough to show that almost 250 years ago this obstinate and perhaps irreligious desire was alive in her: she actually proposed to found a college for women. What is almost as remarkable, the Princess Ann was ready to give her £10,000 – a very considerable sum then, and, indeed, now, for any woman to have at her disposal – towards the expenses.' And then, says Woolf, we meet with Bishop Burnet, who was against it, on religious grounds. 'The money went elsewhere; the college was never founded' (Woolf, 1938, p. 47).

Establishing a college for women was a project quite dear to Mary Astell and not just because she had 'experienced in the study of letters a fruitful source of *independent* pleasure' and 'became solicitous to impart to her sex the satisfaction she enjoyed' (Hays, 1803, p. 214, my italics), nor because it was a systematic way of undermining the supremacy men had claimed for themselves, but because, also, it would have been for her a haven. Astell knew, as many women since have known, that it is enormously difficult for women to have time and space to themselves. Mary Hays says of Astell that, 'To preserve herself from the interruption of frivolous visits, from such persons as relieve themselves from the burthen of time unemployed by breaking in upon their more rational and industrious acquaintance, she was accustomed, from her window, jestingly to inform intruders, that "Mrs Astell was not at home" ' (ibid., p. 216). Many a similar ruse is employed today!

Mary Astell would have liked the *freedom* – and the legitimacy – that such a college could offer. To see her proposal as one of confining or restricting the growth and development of women is to see it from the perspective of men who, historically, have insisted that men are necessary for women's happiness, and that to remove oneself from their presence is 'self-denial'. For women, who see male power as problematic, who experience men as a source of restriction and limitation, to remove oneself from their presence has a connotation of 'freedom',[6] but this perspective, of course, rarely surfaces in records kept by men. So Astell was disappointed, but it was not only disappointment she had to deal with, but also calumny.

The project collapsed 'but not without drawing upon its well-intentioned proposer a still more unmerited and, unfortunately, a more widely circulated aspersion.' The 32nd, 59th and 63rd editions of the *Tatler* contained gross misrepresentations of Mary Astell and mounted a vicious personal attack on her. In the 63rd edition 'it is stated (no doubt with the intention of turning the whole affair into ridicule) that Mrs Manley, authoress of that vile work, the *New Atlantis*, was to be directress of the new institution. The whole story would be unworthy of mention, were it not that it appeared in so famous a paper as the *Tatler* and that the great names of Swift and Addison are supposed to be connected with the writing of it' (Stephen and Lee, 1973, p. 674).

Swift and Addison were, of course, very witty, clever men. It would be interesting to note how many things such men have written would be termed satire, which today we would label 'sexual harassment' (and conversely how many ostensibly 'vile' and nasty things written by women, which from our perspective we could rename as women's satire): the difference is that as males have the power to impose their values, it is no coincidence that when women engage in the same activities as men, less

---

[6] This is one of the bases for arguing for single-sex schools – *for girls*; see Dale Spender, 1982a.

value is attached to those of women. This is what patriarchy is in part about; it was what Mary Astell was documenting and explaining.

Astell was not cowed by her critics: in 1700 she produced another 'feminist tract' in which she argued that there is little prospect of happiness in marriage for women. Once more she identifies male power as her major target. She challenges men's ability to see reason rather than appeal to them on their own terms; she dismisses them if they cannot follow her arguments, but understands why their own lead them in a different direction where their own interests are protected. Of wives, Astell says that 'a reasonable man can't deny that she has by much the harder bargain' (In Rogers, 1979, p. 38) because a wife has no redress, and is completely at the mercy of her husband. But perhaps it is too much to ask men to see it from this perspective, says Astell, for it undermines their own, and they are masters of the double standard which allows them to argue, that it is not the same for a woman: 'Whatever may be said against passive obedience in another case', observes Astell, 'I suppose there's no man but likes it very well in his own' (ibid., p. 39).

If Astell's assessment of marriage were to be published today, it would be considered very radical (and would no doubt give rise to 'satirical' accounts of her as a *man-hater*) for she does not gloss over the harsh realities (for women) with a layer of sentiment or romantic love, but bluntly describes the arrangement; the privileges it bestows on one sex and the penalties it exacts from the other. In some ways it is even more of a radical critique than that given by Jessie Bernard (1972) in *The Future of Marriage*. Mary Astell calmly and concisely lists what it is that men want in a wife (and what wives lose in the process) and anticipates by almost three hundred years, Jessie Bernard's contention that in every marriage, there are two perceptions, two positions, *his* and *hers*, and *his* marriage is immeasurably better than *hers*.

'For under many sounding compliments, words that have nothing in them', says Astell, 'this is his true meaning: He wants one to manage his family, an housekeeper, one whose interest it will be not to wrong him, and in whom therefore he can put greater confidence than in any he can hire for money. One who may breed his children, taking all the care and trouble of their education, to preserve his name and family. One whose beauty, wit, or good humour and agreeable conversation will entertain him at home when he has been contradicted and disappointed abroad, who will do him the justice the ill-natured world denies him; that is, in anyone's language but his own, soothe his pride and flatter his vanity, by having always so much good sense as to be on his side, to conclude him in the right, when others are so ignorant or rude as to deny it. . . . In a word, one whom he can entirely govern, and consequently may form her to his will and liking, who must be his for life, and therefore cannot quit his service, let him treat her how he will' (Astell in Rogers, 1979, pp. 41–2).

Astell has described the difference in power between women and men in terms of the way it impinges on women in marriage. She states that the man will not experience it this way ('in anyone's language but his own'); her goal, and her achievement, is to dislodge the male version of marriage as it affects women, and to construct in its place a well-documented and substantiated female version of 'the facts'. That they may be given less credence is not because they are less 'real' or 'accurate' but because they *are* a woman's view in a male-dominated world (a point pursued by Jessie Bernard, 1972). Those who rule having the ruling ideas.

In many ways, the picture of marriage which Astell portrays could well be a picture that 'fits' for many a contemporary housewife: if we were to add to Astell's description that a man may also seek a wife who has an interesting job as well, which not only makes for a more interesting companion but contributes to the family coffers, reducing his responsibility, then it could well be a picture of a contemporary *superwoman*. There has been little 'progress' for women as a result of their centuries-old struggle if, despite all the 'practical' reforms, the underlying problem as perceived by Astell remains much the same.

Astell also tackles the argument – frequently put forward now as then – that women are happy to submit to men. Not only does she ask where this idea comes from, and whose interest it serves, she also shows how women are manoeuvred into this submissive position – and then obliged to support it. In highly satirical vein she begins by stating that it is understandable that women should come to recognise that they count for little in comparison to men for 'Have not all the great actions that have been performed in the world been done by men? Have they not founded empires and overturned them? Do they not make laws and continually repeal them?' She asks in a tone that reveals that she is not impressed by the male version of male achievement. She goes further and outlines the destructive 'other side' of their so-called achievement. 'Their vast minds lay kingdoms waste, no bounds or measures can be prescribed to their desires', and scathingly continues, 'What is it they cannot do? They make worlds and ruin them, form systems of universal nature and dispute eternally about them; their pen gives worth to the most trifling controversy', she says (in Rogers, 1979, p. 42).

But, in a style that is characteristic of her, Astell dismisses the notion that women are content to bow down to this brand of supremacy, and turns male arguments back upon men. In marriage, men are tyrants, states Astell, and women are required passively and unprotestingly to accept such tyranny, yet, 'If the great and wise Cato, *a man*, a man of no ordinary firmness and strength of mind, a man who was esteemed as an oracle, and by the philosophers and great men of his nation equated even to the gods themselves, if he with all his Stoical principles was not able to bear the sight of a triumphant conqueror . . . but out of a cowardly fear of insult, ran to death to secure him from it; can it be thought that an ignorant weak woman should have patience to bear a continual outrage and insolence all the days of her life?' (ibid., p. 144). Almost one hundred years later Mary Wollstonecraft was to use much the same argument.

Astell continues with a warning, a warning which contains a veiled threat, when she says to men that they would be foolish to believe that women are fulfilled by this arrangement. You could not seriously contend that a woman is happy, she says, in such circumstances, 'Unless you well suppose her a *very ass*, but then, remember what the Italians say, – since they being *very* husbands, they may be presumed to have some authority in the case, *an ass, though slow, if provoked, will kick*' (ibid., p. 54).

In moving from the explanation that the relationship between the sexes is divinely ordained and natural to the explanation of 'socialisation' accompanied by power, Astell carves out a new framework for the location of women's experience, and understands, and excuses, the way in which her sex behaves, instead of blaming them for a condition over which they have no control. She accepts that: 'Women are for the most part wise enough to love their chains, and to discern how becomingly they fit' for, without autonomy or power, what else can they do? 'They think as humbly of themselves', says Astell, indicating the role played by men, 'as their masters can wish' and can be 'so sensible of their own meanness as to conclude it impossible to attain to anything excellent' (ibid., p. 46). When women come to accept men's definitions of women, male supremacy goes unchallenged, but when women draw on their own personal experience to repudiate the male version of female, it is a very different matter.

Not that this happens often, admits Astell. Too frequently women collude with men to support a system which keeps women slaves. They deny their own experience and she finds this frustrating. On occasion she directs her anger against women who do not seem to recognise the destructive process they are engaged in. This is understandable. No doubt she felt betrayed by many members of her own sex. Passionately she states that women should authenticate their own personal experience, that women 'are, or ought to be best acquainted with their own strength and genius' and perhaps it is personal regret that leads her to say of women 'she's a fool who would attempt their deliverance or improvement' (ibid). What is certain is that Astell understood some of the links between the personal and the political, between women's personal, positive experience of the world unmediated by males, and the power of males to blanket and repress women's knowledge.

Astell is most definitely not arguing for the preservation of the status quo when she suggests that it is going to be difficult for women to break free of their bondage or when she expresses exasperation that women have become so convinced of their own aptitude for servitude. This is part of the picture of patriarchy that she is trying to portray, and which she perceives as a problem. There is no suggestion that she is serious when she states somewhat bitterly: 'No, let them enjoy the great honour and felicity of their tame, submissive and depending temper. Let them receive the flatteries and grimaces of the other sex, live unenvied by their own, and be as much beloved as one woman can afford to love another' (ibid., p. 46). Astell herself indicated how little she subscribed to the idea of 'competition' and divisiveness among women (a consequence of a male-dominated society where women are required to compete for men) when she signed her *Proposal* as 'a Lover of her Sex'; she indicated how abhorrent she found tame, submissive dependency in her writing and in her own life. It is a measure of the way she has been treated in the male-dominated society which she set out to describe that she could be construed as 'against' women, and for the status quo.

In so many ways Astell exposed the workings of patriarchy: she took up and developed the idea that it was man – not God, *or* woman – who was responsible for sexual inequality. In the seventeenth century she made the connections which today we would call the phenomenon of the double-bind, a product of a double-standard, where women were damned if they were foolish, and damned if they were responsible and serious. She knew that she could see things that men could not, she could see the inconsistencies in their arguments which were arranged to suit their own needs, and she knew of their need not to be threatened or contradicted by 'conflicting evidence' which had its origins in women's experience. She knew women were *blamed* for all manner of injustices (including sexual injustices) which men themselves created; women, she said, are 'blamed for that ill conduct they are not suffered to avoid', and, she added, 'reproached for those faults they are in a manner forced into' (ibid., p. 45). That men do not understand this, that they cannot grasp these reasons, is because they experience the world differently, from a position of power over women.

In *Some Reflections upon Marriage* (1700) Astell makes a final statement which I take as satirical: Let women, she says 'not by any means aspire at being women of understanding, because no man can endure a woman of superior sense, or would treat a reasonable woman civilly but that he thinks he stands on higher ground and that she is so wise as to make exceptions in his favour and to take her measures by his direction' (ibid., p. 47). She shows how fragile the whole structure is with its dependence on women, *not* to challenge men's version of themselves, the world, and women's place within it. But Astell herself clearly indicates that she does not take *her* measure by men's directions, she does not see male 'authority' as superior. She is not a woman who has been intimidated, who lacks confidence because she is 'different' and attempts to explain it in terms of her own inadequacy as countless of us are tempted to do. Hers are the arguments of an independent woman; they are statements which could well be made by feminists today, which we have believed to be radical and 'sophisticated' and which we have believed – too often – distinguish us from the women who have gone before. They are statements which stand outside the patriarchal value system and beyond patriarchal explanations, for they are located in the personal experience of a woman who trusts their authenticity and asserts their validity.

They are also statements that have been repeated, at intervals, over the last three hundred years.

Although not part of a widespread women's movement, it is clear that Mary Astell neither stood alone in her own time, nor was she completely lost to her successors. Lady Mary Wortley Montagu shared many of Mary Astell's understandings, and biographers mention the close association between Mary Astell, Lady Hastings,[7] and Lady Catherine Jones: if it was Princess Ann who offered £10,000 towards the establishment of a women's

---

[7] Lady Hastings was the student of Bathsua Makin (1608?–1675?), a female scholar, see J. R. Brink, 1980.

college (there is some suggestion that it was Lady Hastings) then perhaps Princess Ann was a member of that circle of privileged women who used their resources to develop critiques of patriarchy. Whether Mary Wollstonecraft knew of Mary Astell is open to some debate, but it is unlikely that Wollstonecraft had not read her work, partly because of the striking resemblances in some of their arguments, and partly because Mary Astell was most definitely known to Mary Hays, one of Wollstonecraft's close friends.

In her discussion of Mary Astell, Mary Hays (1803) says that: 'Her death was occasioned by a cancer in her breast; a painful and terrible disease, which, for some years, she carefully concealed even from the most intimate of her friends. It is not improbable that this disorder originated in a severe and sedentary life, by which the blood is impoverished, and the system debilitated' (p. 220). Not exactly a form of encouragement for other women to follow in Astell's steps; she died from the operation to remove the cancer.

There is little reason to believe today that we have witnessed a new era for women's liberation when so much of our analysis and so many of our arguments – which we consider 'new' and capable of leading us towards the elimination of patriarchy – are in many respects so 'old' and have not proved to be particularly productive. Perhaps the only knowledge we have that Mary Astell did not is that we are part of a long tradition. It could not be said that she did not know how men responded to women's ideas, nor that she did not appreciate the lengths to which they would go to protect their position. She even understood the limitations of male reason that posed as human reason. Three hundred years later one of the things we can add to the account she provided is that men facilitate the disappearance of ideas such as hers, and women are required to revive them, periodically.

3 Lady Mary Wortley Montagu (1689–1762)

Of Lady Mary Wortley Montagu it has been said that she was, 'One of the most glittering figures of the Augustan Age' (Halsband, 1947, p. ix); the list of her 'achievements' is great, with 'beauty' of course frequently being cited as one of her first claims to fame. She was a staunch advocate of feminism, a 'friend' of literary figures,[8] and a patron of young writers, a prolific letter-writer and the person who introduced smallpox inoculation in England. She was also a friend of Alexander Pope for a while; they quarrelled and he later referred to her vitriolically (as 'Sappho') in some of his verse and it is often for this 'notoriety', rather than her own resources, that she is known.

Like so many other women of her time she was deprived of provision for systematic education, but in her case she was fortunate enough to be 'left to educate herself, reading voluminously in her father's library and

[8] She was a 'literary figure' herself but, as is customary, is reported as *knowing*, rather than *being*, a genuine literary personage.

even teaching herself Latin' (Rogers, 1979, p. 48). She eloped with Edward Wortley Montagu in 1712, and when in 1716 he was appointed ambassador to Turkey, she accompanied him, 'sending home a series of fascinating letters' (ibid.). The letters were later published and, 'Mary Astell wrote a preface for the Collection in 1724, pointing out their superior originality to travel accounts written by men and urging women to lay aside envy and "be pleased that a *woman* triumphs" ' (ibid., pp. 48–9).

Apart from her *Letters*, she also produced a political periodical in support of Robert Walpole's government. Entitled *The Nonsense of Common Sense*, its aim was to combat the propaganda of the opposition journal, *Common Sense*. Feminist ideas are reflected in much of her writing in the periodical, particularly in Number VI. Lady Mary's entry into the 'political arena' is quite remarkable in many ways and not just because the area was the institutionalised prerogative of men. The periodical bridges the distance between the world of letters and Grub Street. Although she did not attach her name to the publication, and stated that she would never write for money or fame and that those who did so were obliged to produce libels and obscenities (Halsband, 1947, p. xxvi), Lady Mary found that producing a *public* political periodical is a considerably different activity from writing verse and letters to be circulated *privately* among one's friends. She was one of the first women political journalists – the honour of being the first has been variously attributed at different times to Mary de la Rivière Manley, Mary Wollstonecraft, Margaret Fuller and Harriet Martineau – among others. *Women not Inferior to Man* (1734) and *Woman's Superior Excellence over Man* (1743) have also been attributed to Lady Mary Wortley Montagu: again there are complications when the author uses a pseudonym, in this case 'Sophia, a Person of Quality'.

If Lady Mary was indeed the author of *Woman not Inferior to Man*, then not only does she share many of Mary Astell's ideas about the nature of society and the fundamental feature, and fallacy, of male superiority, she expands and develops some of these ideas. If not, and it is but her *Letters* and the periodical which reflect her analysis, then she did not go quite as far as Astell, though their ideas on learning and marriage show they have much in common. Lady Mary, like Astell, concluded that, in a society where males held power, there were for women many advantages to be gained from learning (but, of course, it had to be hidden from men) and very few from marriage. (She herself was separated from her husband later in life and appears to have been 'exiled'; she returned to England on his death.)

For many years Lady Mary's only contact with her daughter (and her granddaughter) was through letters and they are therefore quite illuminating. In them there is many a shrewd assessment of the way male-controlled societies work against women. Giving advice about her granddaughter's education, Lady Mary says that: 'The second caution to be given her (and which is most absolutely necessary) is to conceal whatever learning she attains with as much solicitude as she would hide crookedness or lameness' (Wortley Montagu in Rogers, 1979, p. 66). Learning in women *is* a deformity as far as men are concerned, and men make up the rules. Lady

Mary's advice has its parallels today when many women are counselled that, 'it doesn't pay to be too bright' (see Horner, 1974).

Lady Mary also counsels her granddaughter against marriage (perhaps not such prevalent advice today) and urges that the ultimate end of her education be 'to make her happy in her virgin state. I will not say it is happier but it is undoubtedly safer than any marriage. In a lottery where there are (at the lowest computation) ten thousand blanks to a prize, it is the most prudent choice not to venture' (in Rogers, 1979, p. 67). She has the experience of her own marriage to go upon, as well as the knowledge of Mary Astell's 'celibate state', and had no hesitation in recommending the latter to her dear granddaughter. Regardless of the reasons put forward for women's entry to marriage (economic necessity, and fulfilment), Lady Mary has more faith in her own personal experience (and presumably the economic motive was not so imperative).

Her satire, in her *Letters*, while less biting than that of Astell, is none the less humorous and frequently directed against men. For example, in a letter to her daughter, Lady Bute (6 March 1753), Lady Mary declared that she did not believe that nature had placed women in an inferior rank to men, 'no more than the females of other animals, where we see no distinction of capacity though I am persuaded', she adds ironically, that 'if there was a commonwealth of rational horses (as Doctor Swift has supposed) it would be an established maxim among them that a mare could not be taught to pace' (ibid., p. 69). Men make up the rules without reference to the evidence provided by women, states Lady Mary, but women must conform even though it necessitates repudiating their own capacity.

Another of her targets was the (male) medical profession that resisted her attempts to introduce smallpox vaccination into England. She had learnt the method in Turkey and had even used it on her own son, and, while she intended to publicise this life-saving method, she had no illusions as to what the medical response would be, when their control over knowledge – and their income – was threatened in any way: 'I am patriot enough to take pains to bring this useful invention into fashion in England', she stated in a letter to Sarah Chiswell in 1717, 'and I should not fail to write to some of our doctors about it if I knew any one of 'em that I thought had virtue enough to destroy such a considerable branch of their revenue for the good of mankind, but that distemper is too beneficial to them not to expose all their resentment the hardy wight that should undertake to put an end to it' (ibid., p. 56). Curiously contemporary words.

The Nonsense of Common Sense is a topical journal and perhaps many of its references are lost on us today and this may detract from its relevance and wit. But, if the passing of time were not sufficient to reduce some of its value, those who have commented on Lady Mary's contribution have added their own evaluations which help to 'minimise' it even further. In the first and only reprint of the periodical in 1947, Robert Halsband extols his praise of Lady Mary – for her beauty and wit, among other attributes – but then measures her 'success' in this venture primarily in terms of how far her efforts were helpful to Robert Walpole. (Male political journalists, even among her contemporaries, are rarely judged according to the extent to which their 'chosen' candidates were able to hold office.) That Halsband sees Lady Mary in relation to men is obvious, and, in persisting with this framework, he misses the point of much of her work, which, paradoxically, could have been directed at him and the values he held, which 'clouded his reasoning'.

Unable to accept the possible independence of a woman (and unable to state that she was under the influence of her husband, for, although he had a political career, he did *not* support Walpole), Halsband states that there is: 'Evidence that Walpole did control Lady Mary's pen' (1947, p. xix). He glosses over the significance of a woman in the eighteenth century producing a political periodical – which reflects a departure from her husband's political position despite the fact that he is in politics – with 'Lady Mary's marital obedience, perfunctory in other respects, certainly did not extend to politics' (ibid., p. xx).

In analysing the nine numbers of *The Nonsense of Common Sense*, Halsband devotes considerable space to an outline of the male political scene, and under the heading 'Social Satire' includes a paragraph on her 'feminism' which, in line with male definitions of the world, does not constitute 'politics'. Having relegated feminism to the periphery, it is hardly a compliment when he states: 'feminism is her most lively topic' (ibid., p. xxiv); nor does he conceptualise Lady Mary and her work as serious when he adds that she 'dabbled' in literature and therefore had some insights into 'the republic of letters' (ibid., p. xxvii), which he sees, predictably, as a male domain.

Despite the fact that he claims that Lady Mary's feminist writing was her most lively, he pays scant attention to it; he could not have made some of the comments he did if he had grasped the points she was making. It appears that her critique of men's ability to reason was lost on him. She stated that: 'Men that have not sense enough to shew any Superiority in their arguments hope to be yielded to by a Faith, that, as they are Men, all the reason that has been allotted to human kind has fallen to their Share – I am seriously of another opinion' (ibid., p. 27). Having made much of Lady Mary's beauty and her 'pair of fine piercing eyes', how could Halsband respond to her statement that: 'I have some thoughts of exhibiting a Set of Pictures of such meritorious Ladies, where I shall say nothing of the Fire of their Eyes, or the Pureness of their Complexions: but give them such Praises as benefits a rational sensible being' (ibid., p. 28)?

Lady Mary does not want women to be made insignificant, reduced to the status of sex-objects and perceived only in terms that men find pleasing. She asserts the rationality of women's experience and explanations and pours scorn on men's logic which leads them to believe that the only valid view of the world is their own. While her *Letters* and *The Nonsense of Common Sense* do not constitute a systematic conceptualisation and critique of patriarchy, they none the less indicate that Lady Mary is not fooled by the arguments and reasons men put forward for keeping women in their place, a place men are not required to occupy and which has been constructed by men to serve as a foil, and substantiate their own claims for their own supremacy.

Woman not Inferior to Man,[9] is, in contrast, a sustained, systematic and satirical thesis, a comprehensive overview of patriarchy. As Lady Mary did not 'claim' the pamphlet (which could be understood, given its challenging contents), I shall refer to the author as 'Sophia' despite the fact that there is consensus that it came from her pen (Sherry O'Donnell, 1981).

From start to finish this is a radical feminist analysis which introduces many of the areas that have become identified as 'priorities' among feminists today: it still has a contribution to make to the contemporary debate and could not be dismissed as of mere historical interest. The Introduction is concerned with how it is we come to know what we know, the origin of our beliefs, and the way they influence our behaviour, the role that men play in formulating and imposing their beliefs on those who would possibly otherwise not share them, and the conviction that all the pieces fit together to ensure that males emerge as superior in a structure they have created.

'Sophia's' analysis ranges from the construction of knowledge, to women as sex-objects and reproductive machines, from women's intellectual competence to their exclusion from public office. Elizabeth Janeway's (1980) statement that the most important power is the power to decide what is important finds expression throughout the course of the pamphlet as 'Sophia' repeatedly urges women to examine the advantages men gain when women accept the male version of the nature of the universe. She repeatedly exhorts women to put forward and to validate a women's version which is in the interest of women, and not to be intimidated by men's claims of reason and logic, claims which it suits men to make.

It is little short of a tragedy that her clear and passionate critique should have 'disappeared', for she enters at a point where many of us today have only recently, and sometimes tentatively, arrived, after a decade of discussion and analysis. So much time and energy has been wasted as we have laboured to catch up to her 250 years later – but, of course, that is, I believe, one of the major reasons that her work was unknown and has never formed part of our cultural heritage. We would have a very different culture today if she had been part of that heritage.

There are many similarities – in argument and style – between 'Sophia' and Mary Astell; like Mary Astell, 'Sophia' devotes the first part of her pamphlet to 'demystifying' male reason and logic. She does not seek to convince men in the terms which they have laid down, but challenges those terms. She does not expect men to be able to follow her arguments (so she states, provocatively) because they are beyond male experience. Throughout the book she is ruthless in her analysis of *Man*, scoffing at his petty pretentions, his vanity, his inability to reason, and at the same time she is uncompromising in her assertion that it is men who are to blame for sexual inequality and for their own limitations. Like Mary Astell, she also lays to rest the suggestion that women have no sense of humour (although, in accord with conventional male values, when men are the butt of the joke,

---

[9] The edition used throughout is the 1975 Facsimile Reprint of the Fawcett Society; references are therefore retained as 1739.

the author is generally classified as a 'man-hater' and no doubt such accusations could be laid at 'Sophia's' door); like Mary Astell she makes a
number of points that we have believed – erroneously – to be but recent
understandings; like Mary Astell she makes no bid for male approval and
like Mary Astell, her writing promotes excitement, and anger, that we were
not raised on her concept of reason.

'Sophia' begins by stating how *custom* has been confused with *nature*,
and, in order to illustrate the point she is making, uses analogies that
bear a striking resemblance to those of the women's movement in the
early 1970s as women – once again – undertook the difficult task of trying to reconceptualise the world, with themselves at the centre, and to
demonstrate that what were thought to be the inherent characteristics of
female and male (including the centrality of men and the marginality of
women) were nothing other than social constructs. The difference between
'Sophia's' arguments and those of today is that where she uses the word
custom we should use the term *socialisation:* that is the mark of 250 years
of progress.

It is the origin of these *customs* that concern 'Sophia' who states that
men, 'biased by custom, prejudice and interest, have presumed boldly to
pronounce sentence in their own favour, because possession empowered
them to make violence take place of justice. And the Men of our times,
without trial or examination, have taken the same liberty from the report
of other Men' (1739, pp. 7–8).

When in 1978 Dorothy Smith's thesis on the exclusion of women from
the production of cultural forms was published, in which she explained the
phenomenon in terms of men listening to and attending to only what other
men have said, I was among those who heralded it as a 'break-through',
yet 'Sophia', had introduced a similar thesis in 1739. Men check only with
other men, states 'Sophia', and what they decide about women (and men)
embodies their own interests. If they could only divest themselves of their
partiality for themselves, they would be able to understand that it is only
their prejudice, *for* themselves and *against* women, which makes them set
less value upon women and greater excellence and nobility upon men.
'But', she admits, philosophically, 'as there are extremely few among them
capable of such an abstracted way of thinking' they cannot be expected to
be objective and logical (ibid., p. 8).

She makes it perfectly plain that men can only see women in relation
to themselves and as creatures for their own use, and that they have no
conception of the way their arrangements impinge on women: 'was every
individual *Man* to divulge his thoughts of our sex, they would all be found
unanimous in thinking, that we are made only for their use, that we are fit
only to breed and nurse their children in their tender years, to mind
household affairs, and to obey, serve and please our masters, that is themselves forsooth' (ibid., p. 11). Boldly 'Sophia' asserts that even in the terms
which men set down, their argument is untenable and that, on the contrary,
reason leads elsewhere, for it is the other way round, and it is precisely
because men *depend* on women – to produce and nurse children – that

there is a logical case for stating 'that *Men* were made for our use rather than we for theirs' (ibid.).[10]

She also argues that men have been irrational – in their own terms – in denying women public office. 'Are not the *women*', she asks, who produce and nurse children, 'entitled to the greatest share in public esteem, who are incomparably the greatest contributors to the public good?' (ibid., p. 13). If we are going to use male logic, argues 'Sophia', then women should be valued more, not less, than men. But she is also very mindful of the trap that has been set, and in line with many modern feminists who assert the value and worth of motherhood, hastens to warn that in relation to reproduction, 'being so much more capable than the male kind to execute that office well, *no way proves us unqualified to execute any other*' (ibid., p. 15, my italics). She well appreciates how men have used women's reproductive capacity against women.

Predating by 250 years some of the current sociological understandings, 'Sophia' outlines the way men require women to accept male definitions of the world, which includes the definition of women as inferior and irrational. Again she turns the argument around and states unequivocally that the only proof of irrationality in women would be if they agreed to male definitions and denied their own knowledge of themselves: 'I hope, while *Women* have any spirit left', she says, 'they will exert it all, in showing how worthy they are of better usage, by not submitting tamely to such misplaced arrogance' on the part of men (ibid., p. 17). A 'good' woman in 'Sophia's' terms was one who was prepared to protest.

Men, she argues, have made up so many myths and it is 'always the opinion of the wisest among them, that *Women* are never to be indulged the sweets of liberty; but ought to pass their whole lives in a state of subordination to the *Men*, and in absolute dependence on them' and in what has become to me one of the most significant statements, declares '*It must be observed, that so bold a tenet ought to have better proofs to support it, than the bare word of persons who advance it*' (ibid., p. 20, my italics). This, argues 'Sophia', is a crucial test: when men profit, as they do, from all the definitions of what is right and proper for women, their definitions are more than suspect. When they assert that it is in a woman's interest to be subordinate, to do what she is told, remember, she warns, that these are the words of those who have not experienced this predicament but who gain immensely from the rationalisation that women enjoy a status that they as men could not endure.

Chapter III is entitled 'Whether *Women* are inferior to *Men* in their intellectual capacity or not', and, not content with the assertion that women *are* the intellectual equals of men (a comparison 'Sophia' finds insidious because of the centrality it accords men), 'Sophia' implies an even more radical suggestion that women are probably 'superior' because they can follow men's arguments, identify their limitations, and put forward more comprehensive explanations of their own, which account for women's

[10] Throughout 'Sophia' identified with women – referring to *we* and *us*, another mark of modernity.

experience, as well as men's. Sixty years before Mary Wollstonecraft (and Catherine Macaulay), 'Sophia' makes the categorical statement that women are intellectually competent and 'explains' the evidence which suggests the contrary, as the result of the definitions – and education, or lack of it – that are imposed on women in a male-dominated society.

'Sophia' lists the ways in which women and men *are* equal and, in a statement that parallels Ruth Hubbard's (1981), delcares that: 'All the researches of Anatomy, have not yet been able to show the least difference [apart from reproductive organs] between *Men* and *Women*' (ibid., p. 24). While during the nineteenth century it became even more common practice to build a whole system of beliefs (which helped to justify women's subordination) on the basis of this *one* difference, 'Sophia' demonstrates her affinity with many contemporary feminists when she concentrates on the physical and *biological* features which are *common* to both sexes and explains their supposed sex *differences* in terms of power.

Throughout her pamphlet she consistently employs the technique of demonstrating the deficiencies of male logic, which she sees as directly related to male power: she continually quotes their words of wisdom only to demolish their case with cool confidence. 'It is a very great absurdity, to argue that learning is useless to women, because, forsooth, they have no share in public offices', she states, for example, for 'Why is learning useless to us? Because we have no share in public offices. And why have we no share in public offices? Because we have no learning' (ibid., p.27). Such an inconsistency may not strike men, she argues, because they arrange the world on the basis of suiting themselves without reference to the implications for those who are not men, but women cannot escape the consequences of men's arrangements, and yet their differing reality is given little or no credence by men.

In propagandist style, she asks (not at all innocently) why men have insisted on the validity – and justice – of their own *false* reasoning: 'Why are they so industrious to debar us that learning we have an equal right to with themselves?' and then she provides the answer: 'for fear of our sharing with them in those public offices they fill so miserably.' She goes on to say that it is: 'The same sordid selfishness which urged them to engross all power and dignity to themselves, prompted them to shut up from us knowledge which would have made us their competitors' (ibid., pp. 26–7).

The analysis provided by 'Sophia' is one which has recently been put forward in contemporary educational circles (see Smith, 1978, and D. Spender, 1981a, 1981b and 1982a); it has been treated as a new conceptual framework for evaluating women's position in education. It is understandable that we should have been deprived of 'Sophia's' work – what would the consequences have been in a male-dominated society if we had been working on these insights for almost 250 years and they were familiar to all members of the society?

'Sophia's' concluding remarks in this chapter suggest that she does not share men's positive opinion of themselves or the structures they have created. She does not want to become one of them, but to change society so that the power, position and prestige of women and men is drastically altered in the interest of equality. 'I could easily forgive them the usurpation by which they first took the trouble of public employments off our hands', she says, 'if their injustice were content with stopping there. But . . . vices seldom go single, they are not satisfied with engrossing all authority into their own hands, but are confident enough to assert that they possess it by right, because we were formed by nature to be under perpetual subjection to them' (ibid., p. 28). And we all know where that idea comes from!

As with many feminists today, 'Sophia' understood the power of images, and models, in socialisation and sex-stereotyping, and argued convincingly that because men 'are so accustomed to see things as they now are, that they cannot represent to themselves how they can be otherwise' (ibid., p. 36). What they have not experienced they cannot admit exists. It is their limitation that they cannot conceive of women as the head of government, pleading causes in counsel, administering justice in court or teaching rhetoric, medicine, philosophy or divinity as university professors. And, she adds scathingly, if 'the *Men* had been so little envious and so very impartial to do justice to our talents, by admitting us to our right of sharing with them in public action; *they would have been as accustomed to see us filling public offices, as we are to see them disgrace them*' (ibid., p. 37: my italics).

'How many ladies have there been, and still are,' she asks, raising a question no less relevant today, 'who deserve place among the learned; and who are more capable of *teaching* the *sciences* than those who now fill most of the university chairs?' (ibid., p. 38). Women's legal rights in some cases may have been won, but the claim which 'Sophia' made in 1739 for women's intellectual autonomy and capability is in many respects no closer to being realised now than it was then, despite the 'right' to engage in 'men's education' (see D. Spender, 1981b). Perhaps we have been misled in believing that change would come when we gained what appeared to be the same institution-based 'rights' as men. 'Sophia' suspected that the power basis was elsewhere – in men's ability to decree the value system – and that in some ways the institutionalised power merely reflected and did not account for men's so-called superiority. This is an understanding forged from a woman's experience of the world, from the experience of being suspicious of the logic which generated explanations of power, and institutions, as well as women and men.

It is this suspicion which leads 'Sophia' to introduce a debate which seems to have changed little, over time, that of the relationship of women and men to knowledge which men have classified as 'medical'. 'Sophia' states that women seem more capable of practising physic, 'to restore health to the sick, and preserve it to the well[11] . . . we can invent, and have invented, without the help of *Galen,* or *Hippocrates,* an infinity of reliefs for the sick, which [men] in their blind adherence could neither improve nor disapprove. An *old woman's receipt,* as it is termed, has often been

---

[11] Contemporary medicine under male control seems to have lost sight of the 'well' – but women medical practitioners have established 'Well Woman Clinics'; see Katy Gardner, 1981.

known to remove an inveterate distemper which has baffled the researches of a college of graduates' (1739, p. 41). Prophetic words? It took a long time for their implications to be explored.

But men have made a contribution, 'Sophia' admits fairly, for 'we must yield to them in the art of inventing hard names,' with puzzles in terms of the names and the number of cures, 'as well as adding to a patient's grievance with the costliness of remedies' (ibid., p. 41). Her assessment, while radical, would still be considered pertinent today; it is related to male control which still persists but which might have been more successfully undermined if there had been a 250-year campaign directed towards the elimination of such control.

Despairing of the intellectual advantages which men have organised for themselves and contemptuous of the pathetic use they have made of them, echoing many a contemporary sentiment, 'Sophia' states: 'I hardly believe our sex would spend so many years to so little purpose as those *Men* do, who call themselves philosophers. . . . I believe we could point out a much shorter road to the desired end' (ibid., p. 42). In line with Aphra Behn's evaluation, 'Sophia' mocks male scholarly pretention.

Writing at the time she did, 'Sophia' could not ignore the role played by religion in justifying women's exclusion from power (and religious institutions were a centre of power as Mary Astell had found in the case of Bishop Burnet). While accepting that women are excluded from full and equal participation in religious rites by divine edict, she manages to give this argument quite a novel twist: 'God undoubtedly knew the tendency of the *Men* to *impiety* and *irreligion*', she says, 'and therefore why might he not confine the functions of religion to that sex?' It is because men are in greater need of instruction in virtuousness and justice (a point she has been making throughout the entire pamphlet) that God made them responsible for religion: a most irreverent suggestion, but typical of 'Sophia' who has the audacity and confidence consistently to formulate explanations which are not flattering to men and which therefore are rarely heard and even more rarely tolerated in a male-dominated society where male explanations prevail.

'Sophia' also takes up the most-modern question of women's equality in the military and allows that there is no factor which prevents women from equalling men's performance: 'The military art has no mystery in it beyond others, which *Women* cannot attain to', she says. 'A woman is as capable as a man of making herself by means of a map, acquainted with the good and bad ways, the dangerous and safe passes, or the proper situations for encampment. And what should hinder her from making herself mistress of all the stratagems of war, of charging, retreating, surprising, laying ambushes, counterfeiting marches, feigning flights, giving false attacks, supporting real ones . . .?' (ibid., pp. 49–50). There is nothing mystical about warfare to 'Sophia', she sees it as rather a shabby business and is not at all impressed; nor is she impressed by the contention that women are not strong enough for such activities: 'Are not the *Women* of different degrees of strength, like the *Men*? Are there not strong and weak of both sexes?' she asks, and then adds, just to clinch the argument anyway,

'*Men* educated in sloth and softness are weaker than *Women;* and Women become hardened by necessity, are often more robust than *Men*' (ibid., p. 50). If this is arranging arguments to suit one's own interest, it is no less than men have habitually done, but men's are given the stamp of approval while women's are treated as testimony of their irrationality.

'Sophia' goes on to quote *Boadicea* and 'the maid of Orleans' to prove that women are equally competent and asks: 'Need I bring *Amazons* from *Scythia* to prove the courage of women?' (ibid., p. 54). But having established to her own satisfaction that women can perform all the feats men deem necessary (and having indicated that this is not inordinately difficult), she raises the question of whether women would wish to use their energies in this way. 'The real truth is', she says, 'that humanity and integrity make us abhor unjust slaughter' (ibid., p. 51). Unable to resist a 'parting shot', however, she also explains why it is that men go off to battle while women stay at home, and again her explanation clashes with conventional patriarchal ones where men are portrayed in a positive light: 'As sailors in a storm throw overboard their more useless lumber, so it is but fit that *men* should be exposed to the dangers and hardships of war while we remain in safety at home'. Here she touches upon what Adrienne Rich (1981) has suggested is the most fundamental threat to males and a rationale for the construction of patriarchy – the possibility that men are dispensable. 'They are, generally speaking, good for little else but to be our bulwarks' (ibid., pp. 55–6) 'Sophia' states; and reveals unapologetically that she stands beyond the patriarchal frame of reference which is predicated on the belief that men are necessary to women, hence women's dependence on them. For such a stance are women abused and ridiculed, harassed and vilified, and 'Sophia' was no exception. Such 'heresies' are dangerous and have to be purged; *Woman not Inferior to Man* was no exception.

'Sophia' was perfectly aware that men made up the meanings of society, and, while she does not use the terms *double standard* or *double-bind* (which are the product of exclusive control by one sex, arranging the world in its own interest), these concepts are articulated throughout her book. 'When they wish to stigmatise a *Man* with want of courage', she says, men 'call him effeminate, and when they would praise a *Woman* for her courage they call her manly' (ibid., p. 51), for men have ensured that they and the characteristics they have appropriated are perceived positively. 'Sophia' recognises the operation of the double standard and the double-bind for women are rated negatively if they do *not* have courage, as it is a quality prized in males, but rated negatively if they *do* have courage for their 'womanliness' is called into question – they are *manly*, and this is intended disparagingly. She rejects this value system. She proposes instead to *reverse* it, to make women the positive reference point, and men the negative (a process she has implicitly engaged in throughout the book), to give them a taste of their own medicine and to see how they like it. 'When a *Man* is possessed of our virtues he should be called *effeminate* by way of the highest praise of his good nature and justice', she asserts, 'and a *Woman* who should depart from our sex by exposing the injustice and cruelty of *Man's* nature, should be called a *Man*' (ibid., p. 51). Maleness and femaleness are not biological constructs but social ones in Sophia's analysis. Mary Wollstonecraft (1792) made the same point about 'masculine women' (in Kramnick, 1978, pp. 80–1), and today terms such as 'male identified' are still used to make this point. We have not come as far as some would have us believe.

If there has to be a value judgement about which sex is the better sex (and today we may be more sophisticated in our understanding that difference does not necessarily mean deficiency), then 'Sophia' has no hesitation in declaring it to be the female sex, for, she says, 'I believe no one will deny but that at least, upon the most modest computation, there are a thousand *bad men* to one *bad woman*' (ibid., p. 59). And in her book, it is power that is to be held responsible.

In her analysis it is male power which is the root of evil and injustice, for men have gone to evil and unjust lengths in the attempt to protect that power and to preserve their primacy. It is clear, she argues, that men have created 'superior' men and 'inferior' women but women do not have to accept the organisation and the values that men have created – they are not immutable but can be undone and replaced. When she demands education for women, however, as a means of 'deconstructing' what men have done, it is by no means just a demand to share in the education men have designed for themselves; she is not arguing for the 'right', as women were to do later, to have access to the institutions men had created (the right to enter *their* educational establishments, to be equal before *their* laws, to participate in *their* political structures). She is demanding that women be free to develop their own reason, their own logic, their own intellect, free from abuse and harassment and *on the basis of their own experience*. What value is the right to equal representation if men continue to count more than women – for after all, women are equally represented in the population and yet are inferior. She demonstrates that women's ideas, women's ways of making sense of and explaining the world are qualitatively different from men's while women are subordinate – and that men's will be qualitatively different if and when women are equal and must be taken into account. They would no longer be the sole *authorities,* the only arbiters. They would have to partake of the experience of *not* being able to impose their meanings on the world (an everyday part of women's existence) without reference to those on whom they were imposed. 'Sophia' argues for a different view of the world in which men are not superior (and for institutions which will reflect this) and then the social structure which she has described in her pamphlet – patriarchy – would no longer prevail.

'Men,' she says, 'by thinking us incapable of improving our intellects, have entirely thrown us out of all advantages of education: and thereby contributed as much as possible to make us the senseless creatures they imagine us' (ibid., pp. 56–7); their beliefs have 'come true' by means of the social system they have arranged, so that the reality of patriarchy is superior men and inferior women. 'If the truth be spoken', she states in her conclusion, 'the blame lies chiefly and originally in the Men' (ibid., p. 57).

'Sophia's' book could be published today and with the aid of a few minor editorial changes could pass as a contemporary feminist analysis of patriarchy. Inside feminist circles it could be perceived as radical – outside them as 'outrageous' and cause no doubt for the abuse and harassment typically heaped upon women who dare to assert such reasons in a male-dominated society. Her sanity would be called into question before her intellectual contribution was acknowledged.

Be it philosophy, sociology, psychology, or any of the other branches of the humanities or social sciences, which have since been shaped in modern mould, *not one of them* has incorporated into its framework the fundamental intellectual questions and perspective introduced by 'Sophia'. None has incorporated women's ideas on power, and its inherent sexual dimension into the stock of accumulated wisdom and transmitted it from one generation to the next. Education is still male controlled, the seats of learning still occupied by men, the disciplines still owned and operated by men, the ideas generated still justifying the interests of men, despite the gains in access to institutions (see D. Spender, 1981a, 1981b and 1982a) and in many respects women are no more free today to assert the authenticity of their own experience, and the validity of their reasoning, which emerges from that experience. The male version of the world is still passed off as the human version and women are still deviant, still required to deal daily with the double standard and the double-bind, and are still the scapegoats, being blamed for the actions of women and men, over which they have no control. It is a mark of male control that *Woman not Inferior to Man* is not a basic text in educational institutions, for it could be such empowering knowledge for women – but in present (patriarchal) terms it would be 'emasculating' for men.

4 Grub Street

There is no doubt that after Aphra Behn (and her relative financial success) there were women who sought to follow her example and who tried to 'sell' their ideas to a public audience; by the eighteenth century some women perceived a choice of occupation between the 'oldest profession' and the 'newest profession', and the reason for engaging in either was usually necessity.

One reason that women took to earning their living by the pen was that men found it difficult to stop them, particularly if they descended to such deceitful depths as using a male pseudonym, adopting a male persona, or remaining 'anonymous'. Unlike the male professions where men were indubitably in control and could readily deny women entry, the world of letters proved to be harder to maintain as a peculiarly male preserve. True, women were denied the systematic education which men claimed as a prerequisite for becoming a 'man of letters', but many women had acquired the rudimentary skill of reading – and of writing – and some of them were sufficiently improper and impertinent to 'intrude upon the rights of men' – as Anne Finch expressed it (see Goulianos, 1974). That women's skills at times appeared to suffice – and were even sufficient to excel – in the face

of the more elaborate and more expensive preparations men had made for
their own occupancy of the literary world was exceedingly galling to a
number of men who prided themselves on their own ability and who
declared that the world of letters, like all other public forums, was theirs
by virtue of their superior intelligence, learning and aptitude, and that
women, even when they did 'attempt the pen', were well below standard.
As Mary Astell (1700) said, men, 'having possession of the pen, thought
they also had the best right to it' (In Rogers, 1979, p. 43); they were hostile
to women's entry to the literary ranks and consistently engaged in harassing
behaviour which was designed to discourage and disparage women, and to
force them to retire. For, after all, this was not just a theoretical debate
about whether a woman writer could reach the standards men had deemed
appropriate for themselves, it was on many occasions a practical matter of
livelihood, with women competing for 'men's' jobs.

Without exception, men have for the last few hundred years resisted
women's attempts to enter *paid* work which men have reserved for themselves; a fundamental tenet of a male-dominated society has been that
women must have no resources of their own but must look to men for
support. This is one of the ways male dominance is maintained and one of
the reasons that women who earned their living by the pen were more
often than not treated as transgressors and punished for their 'crime'.

Into this volatile context came women like Eliza Haywood (1693–
1756); Mary de la Rivière Manley (1672–1724) and Mary Pix (1660–
1720) to name but a few. They were bold, they were courageous, and they
were pioneers; they were (and when referred to, which is rare, still are)
abused and ridiculed as women and as writers.

It might be assumed – mistakenly as it transpires – that women writers
who challenged the dominant male view of the superior male would understandably reap a relevant reward, but that women who *supported* male
values and massaged male egos would fare somewhat better. This is not
the case. The women who were pioneers in earning their living by the pen
had to *sell* their ideas in order to live. They had to gain the approval of
male publishers who perceived then, as they usually do today, that the
audience (the reading or viewing public) is predominantly male. (Even in
the case of the Women's Page in newspapers, the argument is often used
that because males read it, it is males who must not be offended; see Crystal
Eastman, 1927, quoted in Blanche Wiesen Cook, 1978, p. 96. This is but
another example of the deeply entrenched belief that male experience and
male values are more important and the prime market consideration.)

So the women who entered the fray did so in a male-dominated society
and if they wished to survive – literally – they were under considerable
pressure to *supply* material that males found pleasing. Most men do not
find material which challenges them and their position at all pleasing and
most women who have written – from Aphra Behn to Virginia Woolf and
Adrienne Rich – have appreciated this. Many of the early pioneers had no
choice but to comply.

I have included here a brief discussion of the work of Eliza Haywood
not because, like Mary Astell and 'Sophia', she was to some extent free to

question and criticise male power, but because she was not, and because she too disappeared. Without doubt, Haywood tried to present a female view of the world, but a view that men could concur with. However, instead of finding favour for her acceptance of woman's place, she found that she was mocked for the limitations and silliness of her view. Eliza Haywood, when placed with Mary Astell, helps to substantiate the thesis that women are damned either way; women who cultivate the attributes men decree desirable (and stay in their place) are despised along with women who do not. It is the sex that is the 'crime' and which allows their writing – regardless of merit or topic – to be devalued.

Writing in the 'Introduction' to a selection from Eliza Haywood's 'political' periodical (1744–6), J. B. Priestley, a prominent 'man of letters', stated in 1929 that 'Nearly two centuries have gone by since Eliza Haywood, having tried her hand at many things – acting, adapting plays, novel writing – decided to become an Addison in petticoats and bring out a *Female Spectator*. It was the second attempt to produce a periodical for women, but the first to actually be written by a woman' (p. vii). He then proceeds to comment on the inadequacy of her behaviour – and her literary style – and quotes 'a chokepear of a sentence', adding, 'It is astonishing to reflect that the author of those ponderous phrases was generally held to be a lady who was no better than she ought to be, one of a fast set. Instead of tripping on the scene, this *Female Spectator* comes lumbering up like a pantechnicon' (ibid., p. viii).

If no interest has been displayed in Eliza Haywood since these memorable statements, it is not difficult to determine why, and the fact that she was the first woman to produce a periodical for women, gets lost in the rhetoric of devaluation (It is interesting to note that this selection of Haywood's work was made by a woman, Mary Priestley, but that 'J. B.' wrote the introduction. Presumably Mary thought it worth reprinting Haywood's contributions; one assumes from the introduction that J. B. Priestley did not.)

Given that Priestley also grants that the *Female Spectator* could be regarded 'as the ancestress of all those women's magazines we have today' (ibid., p. vii), there can be little doubt about what he thinks of women (who are expected to be dainty and frothy, to 'trip' and not to 'lumber'), or of women's magazines. Although in his restrained and masculine style he says that the *Female Spectator* was 'wildly different from anything we know now' (ibid.), it cannot be said that there have been wildly different changes among men's attitudes towards women and their writing: Priestley betrays the same patronising, if not hostile, attitude to Eliza Haywood's contribution as that which she encountered in her own time.

Not that one would expect the *Female Spectator* to provoke wrath, if it is just the ideas that are important, for there is nothing remotely radical about it in today's terms. It is a woman's comment on the manners and mores of her time. There is much concern with the horrors of seduction and the tricks to which men may resort, and this is intended to serve as a warning to women to be wary. When women's work is marriage and income secured through the acquisition of a husband, then issues of chast-

ity, in a woman's world, are issues of marketability; what men have sometimes termed women's gossip is to women tantamount to dealings in the
business world. This is why a woman's magazine – then and now – takes
issues such as love, marriage, and seduction – as seriously as men take
stocks and shares, and why 'a fall' for a woman is perceived to be as
calamitous to females as 'a fall' on the stock exchange for males.

The pages of the *Female Spectator* are not particularly complimentary
to a certain 'type' of man and it is interesting to note that while Astell and
'Sophia' conceptualised men as a single entity in their analysis of sexual
inequality, Eliza Haywood divides them definitely into two groups – good
and bad men. (Her husband deserted her and left her with two children to
raise.) The 'good' ones are not a problem and reinforce the idea of fulfilment
in marriage for women; it is the bad ones that create the difficulties.[12]

The sad tale of 'Erminia, How Ruined' is a case in point. Erminia
attends a masquerade ball, chaperoned by her brother, loses him in the
crowd, then catches sight of his costume and pleads with the 'occupant' to
take her home. He obliges, takes her to a strange house and removes his
mask. It is not her brother.

'Never was surprise and terror greater', writes Haywood, 'than that
which now seized the heart of the unfortunate young lady: she wept, she
prayed, she conjured him up by everything that is called sacred, or worthy
of veneration, to suffer her to depart; but he was one to whom, had she
been less beautiful, her innocence was a sufficient charm; he satiated, by
the most barbarous force, his base inclinations' (in Priestley, 1929, p. 22).

Erminia is ruined and, despite the generous offer from her sweetheart
still to marry her, decided that she could not support the shame of *his*
condition and nobly goes off to live with an aunt in a remote part of the
country.

The 'injustice' is all here; it is but a small shift in perspective to see
how it impinges on women. This is to some extent the same 'evidence' used
by Mary Astell and 'Sophia'; it is the arrangement of social conditions for
the convenience of men, the double standard whereby *he* commits the
crime, and *she* bears the punishment. Whether Haywood actually ever
challenged men about this, rather than cautioned women, is difficult to say
but, even if this was a source of anger and resentment in her life, it was
probably an idea she could not give expression to in her writing – if she
wanted to sell her wares. Of one thing we can be sure, J. B. Priestley made
no such connection between the accounts provided by Haywood, and
injustice.

The dangers of seduction are repeatedly spelled out in the *Female
Spectator* (and implicitly the message is there that women can do little to
protect themselves, for even the most careful often get caught) and these
stories could well have proved to be popular among women for whom such
events were a life-and death issue. Priestley, however, finds the subject
boring, almost beneath his (male) interest and says 'The ensnaring of
innocent maidens, frequently a very long and (to our minds) tedious busi-

---

[12] There are contemporary parallels here.

ness appears to have been almost the chief pastime of the eighteenth century gentleman, the one to which he devoted most of his time, energy, skill and patience. The fact is not really a tribute to the beauty and initial virtue of the eighteenth century maidens', he adds in superior tone, making his only concession to women's existence in this otherwise male-oriented discussion. 'It is explained, I fancy, by the lack of resources for the idle man of that century. With no golf, no bridge, no cars, these gentlemen had to pass the day somehow, and if they did not care for hunting, drinking, politics or literature, they had to go seducing out of sheer boredom.' In equally offensive manner, he continues, 'I suspect they were careful, like good sportsmen, to choose the most difficult subjects, so that the end would not come too quickly' (ibid., p. xii).

Priestley's literary reputation remains; Eliza Haywood's has been ridiculed. 'Mrs Haywood offers us some good specimens of the Seducer', says Priestley, patronisingly, 'but of course she does not understand them. She thinks it a question of unbridled desire, and does not see that these long pursuits and elaborate stratagems argue an intellectual interest' (ibid., p. xii). Nor would any other woman of sound mind, no matter how convincingly the case may seem to men.

Veiled though the hostility may be it is none the less present in Priestley's view of Haywood as 'lumbering', petty and ignorant. 'She fails to convince *us*,' he says (ibid., p. ix), she has but 'empty pomp and ceremony of phrase' (ibid., p. x) and in a manner most significant he reserves his praise – in this the 'Introduction' to Eliza Haywood's work – *for men and their activities*! It is Steele, Goldsmith, Fielding and Sterne who are the genuine writers deserving of admiration. It is an article on natural philosophy in the *Female Spectator* which is singled out for positive endorsement, for it is a 'contribution from a gentleman, one of the sterner sex' (ibid., p. xi). It is Haywood's references to golf and tennis which Priestley finds refreshing and entertaining. His 'politics' could not be more explicitly stated.

Haywood's view of the world is no more tolerated, understood, or respected than that portrayed by Astell or 'Sophia'; her ideas are no more valid although they may have been less frightening. It does not matter whether she confronts men or cautions women, however, for in the end she is a woman and it is this that has determined her treatment by the critics.

Mary Pix – who challenged much more than Eliza Haywood appears to have done – has none the less received much the same treatment. She was primarily a dramatist with more than a touch of impudence, who wrote in the dedication of one of her plays (thereby preempting the customary criticism) 'I am often told, and always pleased when I hear it, that the work's not mine' (quoted in Fidelis Morgan, 1981, p. 45).

Fidelis Morgan – in her excellent anthology of women playwrights of the Restoration – lists some of the plays known to have been written by Mary Pix; *Ibrahim, the Thirteenth Emperor of the Turks* (1696, Drury Lane – revived 1702, 1704 and 1715); *The Spanish Wives* (1696, Drury Lane, a bustling and amusing comedy of intrigue); *The Innocent Mistress*

(1697, Lincoln's Inn Fields); *The Deceiver Deceived* ('Mary Pix showed this play to Queen Mary, and "Her Royal Highness showed such a benign condescention as not only to pardon [her] ambitious daring, but also encouraging [her] pen" ', Morgan, 1981, p. 47); *A heavy English Tale* (1698, Lincoln's Inn Fields); *The False Friend* (1699, Lincoln's Inn Fields); *The Beau Defeated* (1700, Lincoln's Inn Fields, 'a very funny comedy', ibid.); *The Double Distress* (1701); and within days, a tragedy attributed to Mrs Pix, *The Czar of Muscovy* (Lincoln's Inn Fields); *The Different Widows* (1703, 'a hilarious comedy'); *The Conquest of Spain* (1705, the new Queen's Theatre, Haymarket); *The Adventures of Madrid* (1706, Haymarket). In 1696 she wrote her only novel, *The Inhuman Cardinal, or; Innocence Betrayed* and in 1704 she translated the eighth novel of the second day of *The Decameron* into verse, and published it under the title, *Violetta, or: The Rewards of Virtue* (ibid., p. 49).

Twelve plays? One novel and one translation? And still women's contribution to the world of letters in general and to the drama in particular is denied. And still new members of society are initiated into a tradition of male dominance which takes away women's resources and women's achievements, and insists that it is only men who are worthy of consideration. And still we wonder how this has happened and are even naïve and misguided enough (at times) to ask ourselves whether it may have been an 'accident' instead of asserting that it is a systematic process which helps to ensure that males retain their image – and the material advantages – of the superior sex.

It isn't necessary to look far to see how it's done. Before women's writing is even published or performed, the male experts declare that women are incapable of literary feats (and have established an education system which they hope facilitates this end). When the writing is published or performed its value is denied, its merit mocked; and because the edict is that only men can achieve success, then a woman's work that *sells* must 'logically' be the work of a man, or else there is something wrong with the woman, for the possibility that women are intellectually competent and have their own literary resources cannot be admitted. And when the records are written up, some, if not all, of these masculist judgements find expression.

In the case of Mary Pix, her biographer (in the *National Dictionary of Biography*) is quick to eliminate any favourable impression that may have been gained from the listing of her plays, by declaring that her first play, which was entitled *Ibrahim; the thirteenth Emperor of the Turks*, was a mistake, discovered too late for rectification; it should have been *Ibrahim the Twelfth* – but then, what else could be expected? The woman was uneducated, as she herself admitted in her dedication in *The Spanish Wives* for 'while she had an inclination for poetry, she was without learning of any sort. . . . Her tragedies were intolerable. She had not the most superficial idea of the way in which blank verse should be written, pompous prose, broken irregularly into lengths, being her ideal of versification' (Stephen and Lee, 1973, p. 1276).

Twelve plays? One novel? One translation? And she is uneducated, *without learning of any sort*, intolerable as a tragic dramatist and a fool when it comes to writing verse? In this biographer's mind, Mary Pix's achievements are not going to be allowed to interfere with the belief that women cannot write. And Mary Pix's work is not going to be left around for anyone to get the wrong ideas for themselves: 'The writings of Mrs Pix were not collected in her own age, nor have they been reprinted since' (ibid., p. 1276). One does not need to ask who is responsible for collecting the writings and keeping the records.

The result is that Mary Pix has disappeared, retrieved only by feminists seeking women's past that men have buried. Little is known about her; Fidelis Morgan has included *The Innocent Mistress* in her anthology and has stated that about all that we do know is that she didn't make much money from her writing and that she was fat, a characteristic the record makers *are* likely to record for posterity. She was independent, outspoken and articulate – this we can tell from her plays, as we can also tell that she was a target for much abuse because she was obliged frequently to defend herself in her prefaces. She was also one of a *group of women* who made their presence felt in the theatre in their own day and who supported and defended each other, and who were satirised for daring to compete for men's jobs. Along with Catherine Cockburn and Mary de la Rivière Manley, Mary Pix was ridiculed and mocked in a play of the time – *The Female Wits or the Triumverate of Poets*. Pix's biographer says that she was 'Mrs Wellfed' in the play – in honour of her love of food and wine.

Fidelis Morgan says that *The Female Wits* was written anonymously by a group of men precisely because the women playwrights *did* provide each other with mutual support and praise and the male dramatists found this insufferable. 'What had been expected was a cat-fight' among the women, says Morgan, and when the men 'did not get a squabble in reality... [they] *made one up* and presented it as *The Female Wits*' (1981, p. 391; my emphasis). Morgan includes the play in her anthology to show what the women were up against. It is vicious. Pix's biographer (Stephen and Lee, 1973), says 'innocently' that *The Female Wits* is the main source of information on Mary Pix. This is the way the records are invented, and we are fooled.

Of Mary de la Rivière Manley (Morgan refers to her as Delarivier), a little more is known. Fidelis Morgan has pointed out, however, that what is known about her cannot necessarily be relied upon – and not for the usual reasons. In this case I think it characteristic of Manley that she is the one whose 'interpretation' should be called into question because she herself wrote some of the records and she provided more than one version! When she heard that Charles Gildon 'was about to start on a biography of her, she anticipated the possibility of its being scandalous or even too near the truth for comfort and wrote her own, *The Adventures of Rivella* [1714]' (in Morgan, 1981, p. 32). In her audacious (and inspiring) way she gave herself a pseudonym (Sir Charles Grandlover) and in the process she also gave herself opportunities for certain 'liberties', says Morgan, but there can be no disputing the 'philosophy' behind the description she provides of herself. 'Her virtues are her own', says Manley of Manley, and 'her vices occasioned by her misfortunes; and yet, as I have often heard her say: if she had been a man, she had been without fault. But the charter of that sex being much more confined than ours, what is not a crime in men is scandalous and unpardonable in woman, as she herself has very well observed in divers places, thoughout her own writings' (ibid.).

Joan Goulianos (1974) says that Manley described herself as a 'ruined woman' which was the reason she took to writing (the life of a mistress proving to be predictably precarious) and why she wrote with such compassion about ruined women. She consistently 'attacked the double standard', states Goulianos, 'by which women are condemned for acts which men are free to commit, and she spoke out for women and women writers. Her own life seems to have been marked by the qualities she gave her female characters – strength, insight born of hard experience, passion and desperate courage' (1974, p. 103).

In 1688 Manley was drawn into a false marriage with her cousin, John Manley of Truro, whose wife was then living. He soon left her. She turned to writing as a means of support. In 1696 she published *Letters Written on a Stage Coach Journey to Exeter* and also in 1696 her first play, *The Lost Lover; or, The Jealous Husband* was performed at Drury Lane. The play was not all that successful (although Morgan considers it to have merit and quotes extensively from it) and Manley herself was not insensible to what was happening: 'I am satisfied the bare name of being a woman's play damned it beyond its own want of merit', she said (Morgan, 1981, p. 36) and she was convinced that men meted out severe criticism to a woman playwright – not on the basis of the work but on the basis of sex. Almost three hundred years later this point has to be made again – and again – and it can be readily discerned, again and again, that the men who do the criticising can disclaim complicity in the process. But we have three hundred years of evidence that men *do* discredit and bury women's work on the basis of their sex, and the question I ask myself repeatedly is how much more evidence do we need before we defiantly assert that men's treatment of women's intellectual and creative contributions is consistent and systematic and constitutes sexual harassment, whereby women are treated on the basis of their sex and not their work?

Manley's next play, *The Royal Mischief*, was performed soon after in 1696 at Lincoln's Inn Fields and this time the major objection to the play would have given Aphra Behn cause to commiserate; it was too 'warm'; in contemporary vernacular too 'hot'. 'In her preface to the play Mrs Manley points out that the same members of the audience "sit attentively and unconcerned" at equally passionate moments in plays written by men, and suggests that "when the ladies have given themselves the trouble of reading it and comparing it with others, they'll find the prejudice against our sex" ' (ibid., p. 39). As Charlotte Brontë was to find, if written by a man it was acceptable – even brilliant – but if written by a woman it was a disgrace. Thus have men retained their territory for themselves.

Almyna was performed in December 1706, and Morgan says of it that 'Like all Mrs Manley's work, the play has strong feminist undertones, and her plot revolves around her own pet grievance; that it is possible for a man "after accumulated crimes to regain opinion, when (women) though often times guilty but in appearance are irretrievably lost" ' (ibid., p. 40). In 1717, *Lucius the First Christian King of Britain* was performed at Drury Lane and, like *The Royal Mischief*, it was quite successful; she was paid six hundred guineas for it.

But she didn't just write plays. In 1705 her first attempt at political satire was published; *The Secret History of Queen Zarah and the Zarazians*. Goulianos (1974) is pleased to draw attention to its originality and achievement, but Manley's biographer (Stephen and Lee, 1973) is not! Of this work he says: 'The species of composition, though new in this precise form in England, had for some years been familiar in France' (p. 921). Pettiness! We are not to be deceived into thinking she was creative!

This was followed in 1706 by an epistolary novel, *The Ladies Paquet Broke Open* and in 1709 by her scandalous accounts in her *Female Tatler* (begun in July 1709) under the name of Mrs Crackenthorpe.

Her most famous book – *Secret Memoirs and Manners of Several Persons of Quality of Both Sexes from the New Atlantis* – was published in 1709; it passed through seven editions and was translated into French. Morgan says that it is 'a clever blend of fact and fiction, romance, politics, scandal and autobiography' (1981, p. 40) but Jonathan Swift (a great satirist) said that it seemed as if Manley 'had about two thousand epithets and fine words packed up in a bag and that she pulled them out by handfuls, and strewed them on her paper, where about once in five hundred times they happened to be right' (Swift to Addison, 23 August 1710; quoted Stephen and Lee, 1973, p. 921). If her success could not be completely denied, then at least it could be attributed to *accident* in the minds of the great literary men.

While Mary de la Rivière Manley was careful not to offend male Tories with her political satire, she was quite ready to focus on those with 'Whiggish proclivities' and 'impudently slandered many persons of note' with the result that 'on 29 Oct 1709 she was arrested with the publishers and printers of the book' and was questioned as to the source of her information, which was evidently quite accurate. With considerable spirit and defiance she declared, 'that if there were indeed reflections on particular characters, it must have been by inspiration' (Stephen and Lee, 1973, p. 921).

Lady Mary Wortley Montagu could not conceal her impatience to get a copy of this book. She also wanted to know what happened to 'the unfortunate authoress', and wrote that: 'people are offended at the liberty she used and she is taken into custody. Miserable is the fate of writers! If they are agreeable they are offensive, and if dull they starve' (Thomas, 1893; quoted in Morgan, 1981, p. 41).

Once the Tories were back in power, Manley's position was more secure and after collaborating for some time with Swift, she succeeded him as editor of the Tory publication, the *Examiner*, in 1711. Swift, it seems, had a lot to say about her and if we today are prepared to evaluate her positively there were times when he was not. He took it upon himself to provide heartfelt assurances that some of the political pamphlets published in her name were *entirely* her work (it must be remembered he had a formidable reputation as a satirist) and when 'she was ill with dropsy and a sore leg', he expressed sympathy and stated: 'she has very generous principles for *one of her sort*, and a great deal of good sense and invention; she is about forty, very homely and fat' (Stephen and Lee, 1973, p. 922; my emphasis). That 'fat' is a feminist issue (Orbach, 1978) is beyond dispute.

It is important to restate that in 1711 Mary de la Rivière Manley took over from Swift as editor of the political periodical, the *Examiner*. (Were there no male candidates with access to the inner circle of power? With education and contacts? This is an astonishing feat.) Manley was a remarkable woman and a talented writer. Fidelis Morgan says that Manley 'is perhaps the most fascinating of the women playwrights of her time. At once an example of decaying gentility and of a sort of swashbuckling feminism . . . (captured by Erica Jong in *Fanny*, 1980) . . . at the same time as she snubbed her nose at popular opinion she was upset that people did not approve of her behaviour' (1981, p. 43). This is not unusual; we have a centuries-old tradition of women writers feeling the conflict between their ideas of women's oppression and their 'womanliness' in a male-dominated society. This conflict has been explored by Anne Finch, Elizabeth Barrett Browning (*Aurora Leigh*), Virginia Woolf ('The Angel in the House'), Tillie Olsen (*Silences*) and Adrienne Rich – to name but a few – and it is a conflict which not coincidentally confronts women with 'the double-bind'. They are damned if they express their challenging ideas (for it is 'unwomanly') and damned if they do not (for there is little literary merit to savour in being a 'womanly writer').

But Mary de la Rivière Manley wrote more than plays and political satires. Joan Goulianos (1974) refers to Manley's extensive documentation of women's lives in, for example, *The Cabal* and *Corinna*, where women's sexuality is made a central concern. In *The Cabal* (which is comprised exclusively of women) we are given an account of sexual relationships among women with the accompanying sardonic statement that women who give themselves to men are 'criminal' but so too are women who give themselves to women so, 'Alas, what can they do?' (Manley quoted in Goulianos, 1974, p. III.)

In this rare literary account of lesbianism, Manley shows no compunction about mocking men, and suggests that it is possible for women to create a small space – free from men – in a male-dominated world. Men are excluded from the women's assignations; there is a reversal in that it is the married women who are the objects of sympathy and the single women are portrayed positively. While it is acknowledged that it is economically necessary for most women to marry, it is considered possible for women to reserve their hearts and amity for each other and to treat men as 'irrelevant' in the circumstances. In making such statements as these, Manley is being most subversive, for she is establishing an area of autonomy for women where they may function outside the influence of men, and define themselves and each other, rather than being defined by men and only in relation to men.

It is difficult to know how much significance should be attached to Manley's account of love between women. As Lillian Faderman (1981) has indicated, lesbianism has not always constituted the threat that it does today – there have been times when women have engaged in lesbian activities with impunity; it depends entirely on how men have defined it. There have been periods, says Faderman, when as long as the women 'appeared feminine, their sexual behaviour would be viewed as an activity in which women indulged when men were unavailable or as an apprenticeship or appetite-whetter to heterosexual sex' (1981, p. 17). In other words, while women were still available to men, attractive to men, their relationships with each other considered a 'substitute' which did not inconvenience them or their inheritance arrangements by the production of an heir, then men did not take lesbianism seriously. Faderman suggests that it 'was not the sexual aspect of lesbianism as much as the attempted usurpation of male prerogative by women who behaved like men that many societies appeared to find so disturbing' (ibid.).

I think, however, that there is another element involved; it is when women start to act as complete in themselves, when they find men irrelevant to their existence (when men are concerned with being the centre of women's universe) that men may find lesbianism threatening. I think this is Adrienne Rich's (1981) thesis and I think it was part of Manley's. She was not counselling women to behave like men. Rather she portrayed a context in which women were free of men (albeit for only short periods) and were happy with the arrangement. This seems to me to be very subversive.

I don't know if it was this aspect of Manley's writing that so incensed B. G. MacCarthy (1944) and produced such a vitriolic response, or whether it was something else, but I do know that if I had read the following evaluation of Mary de la Rivière Manley I would not (as I did with Goulianos's and Morgan's account) want to know more. Writing of Manley, MacCarthy stated that: 'Fate kicked her down into the field at first. Thereafter she was the sport of many, and she gathered mud all the way' (1944, p. 215). Commenting on Manley's satire, MacCarthy says: 'From gathering mud to throwing it is an easy transition. Mrs Manley collected filth with the relentless energy of a dredger, and aimed it with the deadly precision of a machine gun. It was her revenge in a condemnatory world' (ibid., p. 216). An embittered woman, I suppose.

Since Manley wrote her satires, MacCarthy notes, 'These scandals have found sanctuary in the tomb, and it is strange that in recording them Mrs Manley should at one stroke have secured for herself notoriety and for her pen oblivion – both unending' (ibid., p. 218). Her 'words are those of a scolding woman' (ibid.), her creativity – non-existent: 'some delusion of intellectuality betrayed her into an elephantine style, heavily sentimental, dully ironic, enlivened only by highly absurd bursts of ranting' (ibid., p. 219). 'Mrs Manley and Mrs Haywood', says MacCarthy, 'succeeded in debauching . . . prose fiction to an almost incredible extent. Their artificial and poisonous concoctions were doomed to perish by their very excesses' (ibid., p. 204). Here speaks the voice of moderation and impartiality.

This is how it is done. There are no secrets about it. This is why

Manley's contemporary and fellow satirist Jonathan Swift has been 'immortalised' and why she has disappeared, when her achievements, it could be readily argued, were (and are) much greater than his. Women are slandered and slated and systematically silenced – and all so that men may appear superior. Men have set up these 'rules' for valuing the sexes but women have learnt them and frequently and distressingly apply them in their own (understandable) quest for approval – and survival. This is why I think it a fundamental *political* activity to find in favour of women; it can be no less *accurate* than the male practice of finding in favour of men anc against women, and it suits women's purposes more. Of course, men do not have to *find* evidence that women are the first to find fault with other women but they need and like such evidence so much they can always construct such myths as those embodied in *The Female Wits* and thereby invent their own false records.

Given that women are damned anyway in a male-dominated society, we should at least work on the principle of doing what we find advantageous, useful, and enhancing – for it seems the consequences are the same, no matter what we do: vilification, abuse, burial. Besides, it is not such a big challenge to view women positively as it has been for men to view them negatively. And men's word has been accepted for centuries; it is our turn!

5 The Bluestockings

In contrast to the women of Grub Street, the Bluestockings did not seek to earn their living by the pen (although Hannah More, one of their number, is reputed to have earned £30,000 from her writing and Fanny Burney was able to support herself – at times – from her writing). These women sought to raise their status, and the status – and extent – of some of the activities that ladies were permitted to engage in in a male-dominated society. They used the private realm, their skills as hostesses, their hospitality, their manners, and their learning, literary and artistic talents to enlarge the space that respectable and wealthy women were permitted. They even used their attributed qualities of 'higher' and 'purer' morality: they justified the expansion of their role as a direct means of counteracting what had become one of the most popular social activities in their set – that of card-playing for money which they saw as barbarous. They introduced a new form of enlightening and civilised entertainment – with themselves at the centre.

In general, the Bluestockings have gone down in history with little praise from men – or feminists: men have devalued their activities and feminists have been critical of their conservatism. The term itself (about which there has been considerable debate as to its origin, see Seon Manley and Susan Belcher, 1972, and Edith Rolt Wheeler, 1910) has become a derogatory term, and, almost predictably, a label for women with intellectual pretentions (and who therefore lead embittered and sterile lives). Susan Conrad (1976) states that: 'First used in the 1750's, the term referred to men and women of wit, knowledge and advanced opinions who frequented houses where the social display of knowledge was cultivated as a fine art, . . . To "wear your blues" became a metaphor for an evening of brilliant conversation, and the term was soon used for women who held salons, and for the female members of these cultural coteries' (p. 17). Once the term became associated with women, however, particularly knowledgeable and witty women, its fate as an abusive term was virtually sealed (see D. Spender, 1980). We can be sure that if a term were ever coined to refer to a circle of witty men, it would not become derogatory.

One hundred years after the introduction of the word to the language 'even the staunchest advocates of women's rights blanched at that word' (Conrad 1976, p. 20) as it acquired connotations of 'misfit' (which is in some senses an apt depiction of an intellectual woman in a male-dominated world) and the Bluestockings are therefore in the somewhat unenviable position of being devalued by men for their presumption, and by feminists for their caution.

There were really two generations of Bluestockings with Mrs Delany (1700–1788), Mrs Carter (1717–1806), Mrs Chapone (1727–1801), Mrs Montagu (1720–1800), Mrs Thrale (later Mrs Piozzi, 1741–1821) and Mrs Vesey (1715–1791) among the older generation, and Fanny Burney (1752–1840) and Hannah More (1745–1833) among the younger members[13] and much of what is known about them comes from Fanny Burney's diaries and letters, and Hannah More's poem 'Bas Bleu'.

Despite the negative image they have acquired, there are some very interesting features of the Bluestockings: they were a group of women who in general seem to have been very good friends. Edith Rolt Wheeler (1910) in her book *Famous Bluestockings* says 'they were all probably acquainted with one another' and quotes a newspaper paragraph of 1781 which states that 'Miss Burney, the sprightly writer of the elegant novel *Evelina*, is now domesticated with Mrs Thrale in the same manner as Miss More is with Mrs Garrick, and Mrs Carter with Mrs Montagu'. There is some evidence that, at that time, such a newspaper report would not have been intended to flatter the women concerned, or to enhance their good names (see Lillian Faderman, 1981 and Elizabeth Mavor, 1971). Wheeler adds that the account is not quite accurate, anyway, for 'the ladies so coupled, though not primarily living under one roof, were bound by ties of intimacy and affection. Mrs Carter, whose attachments were strong and lasting was also the friend of Mrs Chapone and Mrs Vesey; while Mrs Vesey and Hannah More were linked in tender association. Mrs Delany, who belongs to an older generation, knew Mrs Montagu well and was thrown into familiar contact with Fanny Burney' (Wheeler, 1910, pp. 13–14).

In the past, the very, very few who have wanted to portray the Bluestockings positively have tended to gloss over the relationships among the women, but it is precisely in the interest of portraying them positively today that I want to draw attention to these 'friendships' among them. In the absence of a particular word to convey the meaning I intend (such friend-

---

[13] It is interesting to note that it was the two younger women who were the more professional writers, earning money; perhaps the others helped to 'pave the way'.

ships among women hardly being a phenomenon men would wish to elaborate enhancingly), I am obliged to refer to their affection, warmth, support – none of which is an adequate term – to describe the way they related to each other in their predicament of exclusion from the male-defined world of letters and ideas. They established their own alternative, intimate, and self-sufficient circle.

These women by their very existence challenged male dominance; they deliberately cultivated an intellectual life, looked to each other to validate their ideas, and demonstrated their competence – in men's terms. Their energies and emotions went into their work, and each other; it is no wonder they have been erased from the mainstream and presented, where they are registered at all, as most unattractive women. It is no wonder that their name has become a term of abuse even today. It seems that most of them had little to contend with by way of a husband who restricted their activities or demanded their services, and if there is an image of them as deprived, embittered or lonely, it does not come from their own pens.

Hannah More and Elizabeth Carter were single (and references to them as *Mrs* can be misleading now that *Mrs* has come to be associated with marital status and is not a parallel term with *Mr*, for adulthood, as it used to be[14]). Mrs Delany, Mrs Chapone and Mrs Montagu were widows: Mrs Chapone's husband died ten months after marriage and Mrs Montagu's husband was twenty-nine years older than she, but neither seemed to provide evidence that their intellectual activities were a substitute – nor did they show any inclination to enter matrimony again. Fanny Burney was forty-one when she married in 1793, and by then the Bluestocking era was virtually at a close. Mrs Vesey was married, but Wheeler states that her husband took little or no part in her intellectual activities.

Mrs Thrale was the only exception: Mr Thrale was a brewer whose wealth was a recent acquisition and he wished to improve his cultural standing in the community and enlisted the services of his more cultivated wife to this end. (She had 'received an excellent education. Hebrew, Greek and Latin were among her acquisitions. . . . In every branch of learning she made extensive advances,' Tillotson, n.d., p. 185). There are many accounts in print about Mrs Thrale and Dr Johnson (who was invited to stay with them in 1766 and who remained for fifteen years, and, 'Boswell represents this as a happy event for the great lexicographer: "He had . . . all the comforts and luxuries of life; his melancholy was diverted, and his irregular habits lessened, by association with an agreeable and well ordered family" ' ibid., 185–6), which intimate that Mrs Thrale was in awe of her distinguished house guest, flattered by the presence of his enlightening company, and gratified that he should choose to remain. This pretty – patriarchal – picture is rather spoiled by the information that upon Mr Thrale's death, she is supposed to have expressed relief that she would not have to wait on Dr Johnson again ('his bearish rudeness was insupportable,' ibid., p. 186), and with the only breath of scandal that ever touched the Bluestockings, proceeded to marry her daughter's music master, Mr Piozzi. Dr

[14] Mary Astell adopted the title Mrs on maturity as did Harriet Martineau.

Johnson wrote reprimandingly to her (she was upon widowhood a woman of independent means) declaring he had been betrayed, and her reply indicates that she probably, enjoyed putting him in *his* place (Wheeler, 1910).

That the Bluestockings were artistic, literary, *and intellectual*, is beyond dispute. Mrs Delany was admired for her artistic ability, she invented the art of paper mosaic, was an artist who used crayons and oils as well as needle and thread, and who excelled in the art of spinning. These, however, rank among the traditionally feminine arts (more often derogatively labelled as 'accomplishments' to distinguish them from their prestigious male counterparts) and therefore do not normally figure in a list of creative achievements. But even these 'accomplishments' (particularly the paintings) had the potential to provoke the ire of men, as Edith Rolt Wheeler well understood when she stated in 1910 that the undoubted originality which Mrs Delany brought to bear upon her work was unresented because she kept within strictly defined limits. Her work was never exhibited, she painted only for her friends and herself, says Wheeler, and, because she did not come into competition with men, she remained inoffensive and was even admired (1910, p. 85).

Before commenting on Hester Chapone's written work, Mary Hays (1803) states that: 'The married life of this lady, which was short, appears not to have been happy,' and, 'Her circumstances when left a widow were scant and limited (vol. 3, p. 284). She turned to writing: 'although she did not have an acquaintance with classical learning, the style of her compositions was elegant and correct', and, as she was acquainted with the modern languages, 'she made some translations of the French'. She was also 'fond of conversation, and possessed considerable powers, with an occasional talent of humour' (ibid.). Mrs Chapone wrote on education for women and Mary Wollstonecraft found many of her ideas useful.

Elizabeth Carter, a 'linguist, a translator, a poet and an excellent conversationalist and noted wit' (Judy Chicago, 1979, p. 178) was the author of a translation of the works of Epictetus, the Greek stoic philosopher, and Mrs Montagu wrote essays on Shakespeare (which Dr Johnson dismissed without reading, see Wheeler, 1910, p. 37) as well as satire and many other works.

Virginia Woolf called Fanny Burney the mother of the English novel, acknowledging the contribution of *Evelina*, *Cecilia*, *Camilla*, and *The Wanderer or Female Difficulties*. Burney's entry to the world of letters was accomplished with much secrecy, for she had been instructed by her stepmother, at adolescence, to burn all her 'scribblings' on the grounds that it was most unseemly for a young lady to engage in such activity. So Fanny Burney wrote during the night, and her first novel *Evelina* was published anonymously, without her father's knowledge, which helps to underline Burney's courage, determination and astuteness, for it is unlikely that her father would have granted permission for publication, constrained as he was by his notion of 'lady-like' behaviour, and his assessment of his daughter's ability. In 1910, Edith Rolt Wheeler lamented the loss of Fanny Burney's play, *The Witlings*, which her father and 'the Burney mentor, Mr Crisp of Chessington' decreed inappropriate for performance, being as they were 'concerned with the possible effect of failure on the sensitiveness of the author' (p. 20): they could give their advice now that the 'author' was known, and known to be but a woman.

However, as an aside, in 1978, Ellen Moers rewrote the record when she stated that *The Witlings* is alive and well, in manuscript form only (for the opposition of Mr Burney prevented it from being published). She stated that it is very funny, quite stageworthy, and that when she read it she shattered the calm of the splendid chamber in the New York Public Library 'where the manuscript is currently housed' (p. 178). Burney wrote three more plays: one, at least, significantly 'an *unpublished master*piece' (ibid.).

I suspect that there are many, many more facts on the record, which need to be rewritten, particularly in relation to the Bluestockings. *The Witlings* is a satire on the Bluestockings, and Hannah More also wrote about them, though not generally in satirical form (see 'Bas Blue', for example); she also wrote religious, moral and educational treatises, and in her younger days, wrote for the theatre (Manley and Belcher, 1972, pp. 92–4).

What we know about these women has generally been heavily edited, and not just according to random rules but on the basis of the systematic repudiation of women's intellectual capacity and contribution (see Lynne Spender, forthcoming). The Bluestockings have not appeared attractive to feminists today and little has been done to 'reclaim' them, but it might be more in our interest to direct our critical energy to the sources of our information rather than against these women themselves; at least it will make for a pleasant change.

When I realise that, despite the range and volume of her work, Hannah More is probably best known for her condemnatory comment on Wollstonecraft's book – that the title *A Vindication of the Rights of Woman* was so ridiculous she would not dream of reading it – I find it no great mystery why this particular piece of information should be 'selected' for transmission from one generation to the next. When one woman condemns another, it serves patriarchy well; in this case not only does it give substance to the belief that women cannot get along with each other, it also 'proves' that Mary Wollstonecraft was unrepresentative of her sex – if she did represent her sex, then Hannah More would of course agree with her. (There are no such interpretations for men who, fight though they might, are still supposed to 'bond'.)

Mary Wollstonecraft is 'isolated' by Hannah More's comment, but it isolates Hannah More as well, for, well-quoted though it may be, it is not a comment which deserves respect for its intellectual substance. No doubt Hannah More gained male approval (for a short time) for her retort; it is precisely the sort of point which is pleasing in a patriarchal system and a perfect quote for the record. But . . . Dr Johnson is not known for his dismissal of Mrs Montagu (and even if he were, in a society where there is one rule for men and another for women, his unreasonable behaviour could well be used as evidence of his good sense, precisely because he did not take the ideas of a woman seriously). When the two sexes are not equal, their behaviour is not judged equally.

By portraying Hannah More and Mary Wollstonecraft as 'enemies', it becomes easy to ignore their similarities — and there were some, particularly in relation to their ideas on women's education. Judging from some of Hannah More's writing, *after* the death of Wollstonecraft (including *Strictures on the Modern System of Female Education*, 1799) one would assume that she was familiar with Wollstonecraft's work. But such comparison has usually been preempted because we have been led to believe that Hannah More condemned *all* of Mary Wollstonecraft's work, and that Mary Wollstonecraft had no time for More's.

This is not to suggest that all contributions made by women are equally valuable, or even that Hannah More deserves a modicum of praise (some of the statements she ostensibly made make me flinch) but it is to suggest that we should not simply accept the 'accumulated wisdom' when it contains such negative evaluations of women and when these evaluations have served male dominance so well. Regardless of whether women were supposed to have supported or challenged male-dominated society, their fate is often much the same, anyway, and what we must keep in mind is that all women in recent history at least have argued, analysed, explained and written in a male-dominated world. This has affected not only what they have to say, as they strive to 'accommodate' and survive, it has also affected the way their ideas have been treated. It is within this context of male dominance that women should be assessed, and reassessed.

The portrayal of the Bluestockings as pretentious, elitist and ultimately vacuous is a useful image of 'intellectual' women in a male-dominated society. When I read Boswell's patronising statement that Bluestocking gatherings were places where 'the fair sex might participate in conversation with literary and ingenious men, animated by a desire to please' (see Wheeler, 1910, p. 53), it is not their 'desire to please' which attracts my attention, for this is a condition of women's existence in a male-dominated world, it is that these women found a way into the society of 'literary and ingenious men' when society had been organised to exclude them. The ingenuity, to my mind, lies not with the men.

Formally debarred from politics, from the law, from education and from employment, completely excluded from the centres of power and the realm of (male) ideas, these women had few other resources than themselves, 'private study', and in a few cases, money. Yet through their own initiative and efforts they created a forum where there was some dialogue between those who had power and those who ostensibly did not, and, unsatisfactory as it may have been, it is the fact that the dialogue existed at all that is remarkable. For how can we explain the complete 'powerlessness' of women and at the same time accept that they were able to act, and to influence the social customs?

It has become quite acceptable to dismiss ladies who held 'salons' and to subscribe to the belief that their ostensible learning was nothing other than mere affectation. This does them a grave injustice; it also helps to suggest that there have not been any genuinely intellectual or learned women. The work of the Bluestockings indicates that without benefit of systematic education, without entry to the public sphere for employment, experience, or stimulation, many of these women became serious scholars and artists. They took a radical stance and defied the deeply entrenched conviction that women were not intellectually competent and could not *master* the classics, and letters, and made a claim for women's intellectual capacity; they created a context in which their learning was not only demonstrated, but developed. Their achievement should not be underestimated.

We do not know what, if any, price they paid, but in terms of the steps they took to establish the case for women's education, perhaps we should take into account Matina Horner's (1974) thesis on the 'avoidance of success' among women *today*, where she claims that women pay such a high price for intellectual success (in terms of the stigma associated with an intellectual *woman*) that it produces conflict which can be resolved by *avoiding* intellectual success. If such a theory is valid, then it is feasible that the conflict was even greater for the women of the eighteenth century, where there was less 'evidence' than today of women's ability while women were not permitted employment in the professions or allowed to hold public office.

Descriptions of the Bluestockings as 'decorous, learned and loquacious women' (Kramnick, 1978, p. 37) leave me feeling uneasy, partly because any woman who wants to talk – particularly seriously – in a male-dominated society can be perceived as talking too much (D. Spender, 1980). Stating that they were 'unwilling to jeopardize their own precarious hold on convention' and that they 'accepted without cavil the traditional notions about a woman's limited rational capacity and her proper domestic sphere' (ibid., p. 37) also seems to be open to question. When Emily Davies opened the first women's college at Cambridge, she was uncompromising in her belief that women students had to conform rigidly to the rules of ladylike behaviour precisely because they were challenging the fundamental idea of women's intellectual inferiority. It is not beyond the bounds of possibility that the Bluestockings may have succumbed to similar pressures and asserted that they did not wish to challenge men or the limits of a woman's sphere – while they proceeded to do so. Assuming that they did adopt such a position, it could well have been a mistake, but then we are hardly in a position to outline the successful alternative.

What little has been written about the Bluestockings is a constant source of frustration to the reader who locates them in a patriarchal context. When it is stated – disparagingly – that some women would not join Mrs Montagu in her scheme to found a women's college, I do not jump to the conclusion that women could not or would not support each other but, instead, am fascinated that the proposal has come up yet again (and continues to come up again and again) and wonder what these women knew about Mary Astell and her *Serious Proposal to the Ladies*. Did they too want to be independent of men? For there are signs that they thought this a positive state.

Dorothy Gardiner (1929) says of them that these women 'with much mental conflict were now beginning to acquire a wider outlook; to visualize the place of women not merely in the home, but in human society; they pondered over the causes of feminine inadequacy, and they drew conclusions from experience within their own knowledge' (p. 454). She sees them as the predecessors of Wollstonecraft; I see that there is a lot I do not know. I do not think it mere coincidence that women who were moving towards the claim for intellectual competence and who wished to exchange ideas did so frequently in the company of other women and with little regard for men. The two are so often linked together.

' "Miss Talbot is absolutely my passion; I think of her all day, dream of her all night, and one way or other introduce her into every subject I talk of." What time of day is it?' asks Elizabeth Mavor (1976): '1741. And who is speaking? Is it perhaps some lover of Miss Talbot's? . . . it is Miss Carter (or Mrs Carter), twenty-two, a clergyman's daughter, fated to be the learned translator of Epictetus, and to be revered by Dr Johnson for her intellect. Miss Carter who reads and writes eight to twelve hours a day, takes snuff and binds a wet towel round her head and another around her stomach, and chews green tea to help her keep awake; Miss Carter who has a pack thread running from a bell on her bed-head into the garden below, where it is twitched at four each morning by the sexton to awake her and prevent the wastage of precious hours in sleep' (p. 81).

Anna Seward, another noted intellectual of her time (called The Swan of Lichfield) was well known for her friendships with women and was admired by Lady Eleanor Butler and Sarah Ponsonby, who eloped together in order to lead self-sufficient, creative, intellectual (and physical) lives. Mrs Piozzi (Mrs Thrale) wrote about the phenomenon (not always approvingly) and when it came to passionate correspondence 'Even the impeccable Mrs Delany, as a girl, conducted one with her friend Miss Kirkham, whom her father had forbidden her to meet, considering Miss Kirkham "too free and masculine", although he revised his opinion later, when the over-free Miss Kirkham married and turned into excellent Mrs Chapone' (Mavor, 1976, p. 23); for a while, anyway.

How are we to make sense of this loss of our heritage? We know that during the eighteenth century there was a group − or there were groups − of women who wanted to be educated, who wanted to read and write, to talk and exchange ideas; and we know they were excluded from all areas where such activities were legitimated. We know that they provided each other with intellectual and emotional support, and that they rarely sought the attention of men (if their marital arrangements were representative of the population, then there would have been some justification for a concern that society would not continue). We know that they found their lives full and complete, even stimulating and exciting. We know that they constitute one of the initial claims for women's right to education, to a life of the mind, to being reasoning human beings; perhaps we should know more. Perhaps we should know that they did not see themselves in a ghetto, that they did not see their lives deficient in any way, that they had no desire to join the 'mainstream' and that they would be at home today in women-only, Women's Studies courses. This is at least better knowledge (and more accurate and better substantiated) than that we have inherited. I should not mind arguing that since Mary Astell women have been insisting on the necessity of women-only education in the interest of intellectual equality; I should not mind encompassing the Bluestockings in any submission for Women's Studies. I should not mind making a virtue of their relationships with each other. Of course, I understand why such 'ideas' would not be received with enthusiasm and why my objectivity would be called into question, but as it is called into question NO MATTER WHAT I DO, I think I should at least like to enjoy the 'truths' I generate.

While the 'Ladies of Llangollen' (Lady Eleanor Butler and Sarah Ponsonby) were engaging in their 'studious retirement of fifty years (1779–1829) in the Vale of Llangollen' (Gardiner, 1929, p. 424; see also Lillian Faderman, 1981 and Elizabeth Mavor, 1976) other women in other places were also making a claim for intellectual competence for women and it is a mark of our current intellectual confinement that we know so little about the women of ideas in mathematics and science. Caroline Herschel (1750–1848) and Mary Fairfax Somerville[15] were in the face of incalculable resistance demonstrating women's intellectual existence; Caroline Herschel was sweeping the heavens with her telescope by night (although most of her achievements were in support of her brother) and Mary Somerville was 'studying the stars at her bedroom window, and mastering abstruse mathematical treatises, the mere names of which filled her friends with dismay' (Gardiner, 1929, p. 432).

All of these women were trying to find a way into 'a man's world', which probably distinguishes them in part from Mary Astell, and 'Sophia', for example, who were more intent at times on exposing its inadequacies. All of them, however, had experience of the world as belonging to men and all of them wanted some of it for women. Perhaps it took Astell and 'Sophia' to conceptualise the problem before the others could begin to work for change, but all together, these women formed a growing circle from which *A Vindication of the Rights of Woman* grew. By Wollstonecraft's time the concept of women as intellectual beings had more substance and was more real than it had been in Astell's time. It was a concept however that was still a threat, and one which has still to be fully realised.

6 Revolution and rebellion

While in England the Bluestockings were attempting to build bridges between the private world of women and the powerful world of men, women in the new world were also 'testing their wings' and making critical statements (sometimes to a limited and private audience) about sexual inequality, its causes and effects. Abigail Adams (1744–1818), using one of the few means available to women to enter a dialogue with men, wrote to her husband John Adams, in a letter[16] which has since become famous and in

---

[15] For further details see Lynn Osen, 1974, and the section on Mary Somerville, p. 168.
[16] How many other women there might have been writing similar statements, is not known. This is one of the problems of 'information' in the private realm.

which she called on him to 'Remember the Ladies' while he was making the new laws.

The letter, dated 31 March 1776, reveals Abigail Adams's awareness of sexual inequality and its manifestations. It also indicates that she is *not* trying to gain approval from her husband, but on the contrary, is prepared to introduce a threatening overtone if he does not heed her 'advice'. 'Remember the Ladies', she writes, 'and be more generous and favourable to them than your ancestors. Do not put such unlimited power into the hands of Husbands. Remember all Men would be tyrants if they could' (Adams in Rossi, 1974, p. 10).[17] These are hardly 'wooing words' and Abigail Adams continues: 'If particular care and attention is not paid to the Ladies we are determined to foment a Rebellion, and will not hold ourselves bound by any Laws in which we have no voice, or Representation' (ibid., p. 11).

From Adams's statement it seems that the ladies have been talking together, that they are not at all pleased with existing conditions, and that there will be trouble if this new opportunity for formulating new laws (on the principle of '*No* taxation *without* Representation') is not taken. As their spokesperson, Abigail Adams anticipates Mary Wollstonecraft's demand – that what constitutes justice for men also applies to women. The claim for 'individual liberty', formulated by men in relation to themselves, is being generalised to women, by women, using the arguments that men provided.

Abigail Adams continues her letter to her husband on a more conciliatory note: 'That your Sex are Naturally Tyrannical is a Truth so thoroughly established as to admit of no dispute, but such of you as wish to be happy willingly give up the harsh title of Master for the more tender and endearing one of Friend. Why then, not put it out of the power of the vicious and the Lawless to use us with cruelty and indignity with impunity. Men of Sense in all Ages abhor those customs which treat us only as vassals of your sex' (ibid., p. 11).

But in this case, it seems, the flattery got her nowhere. John Adams replied (14 April 1776): 'As to your extraordinary Code of Laws, I cannot but laugh' (ibid.). If Abigail Adams's reference 'tender and endearing Friend' were intended for her husband, then her friend did not take her very seriously. The idea that a woman should be treated more justly, although a 'saucy' one, was absurd. 'We have only the Names of Masters', says John Adams coyly, 'and rather than give up this, which would completely subject Us to the Despotism of the Peticoat, I hope General Washington and all our brave Heroes would fight' (ibid.).

This is the brand of 'male reason' that was 'Sophia's' target. On the one hand John Adams protests that men have only the name of *Master*, a title without substance, but then he goes on to argue that men will use all the might and power at their disposal to keep what is but a name!

Upon receipt of this letter, Abigail Adams wrote to her friend, Mercy

[17] I am enormously grateful to Rossi for her book *The Feminist Papers* which not only served as a catalyst for this work, but made the task immeasurably easier.

Otis Warren (27 April 1776) and said that her husband had sent a 'saucy' reply to her List of Female Grievances. She suggests to Warren that they petition Congress, currently in the process of formulating the new laws: 'I ventured to speak a word on behalf of our Sex, who are rather hardly dealt with by the Laws of England which gives such unlimited power to the Husband to use his wife Ill,' she says, and having examined her husband's disinterest and virtue on this matter, 'when weigh'd in the balance have found it wanting' (ibid., p. 12).

It is understandable that Abigail Adams should be looking to the *law* as a solution for the problem of male power within marriage. That the law was not preordained or immutable was perfectly obvious to her as she found herself surrounded by the fervour that accompanied the formulation of the new code. What was less obvious to her perhaps (at least, going on the letters available) was the possibility that male and female roles were also neither preordained nor immutable. Adams's understandings do not comprise an analysis of patriarchy, but a generalisation of the arguments – and strategies such as 'rebellion' – used by men, to improve the position of women, even though men would probably not be impressed by her behaviour or her 'logic'.

Despite her assurances to Mercy Otis Warren that she is going to continue to assert her logic to her husband, Abigail Adams responds to him fairly deferentially. As Rossi (1974) states: 'From her original prediction of rebellion she has moved to a passive assertion of women's "sway"; thus an early skirmish over women's rights to representation ends on this tame note' (ibid., p. 8). But there can be no doubt that the concept of 'women's rights' was in the air. Abigail Adams did not find it necessary to offer Mercy Otis Warren any explanation of the 'List of Female Grievances' and she refers to the 'Ladies', implying that her ideas were not confined to herself, or to her friend.

The issue of *rights*, at this stage, distinguishes the old world from the new in many respects, for while there were women in England who had argued for the equal *worth* of women (with 'Sophia' going so far as to assert they were *worth* more, and were indeed superior), and others, such as the Bluestockings who were intent on demonstrating that worth, none had – as yet – made use of the concept of individual and inalienable rights as they related to women.

Abigail Adams could describe sexual inequality in her letters, she could offer accounts of her own experience – and the injustice of it, as she did when writing to Isaac Smith (20 April 1777), a friend who was visiting London. She says how much she would have liked to travel, and how if she had been a man she would have done so, but as a woman she must stay at home, for 'the many dangers we are subject to from your Sex, renders it almost impossible for a Single Lady to travel without injury to her character. And those who have a protector in a Husband, have generally speaking obstacles sufficient to prevent their Roving' (ibid., p. 9). Adams knows that single or married, women cannot win when it comes to travelling, but she does not translate this into any theoretical explanation (in her letters).

Adams also experienced educational disadvantage and was concerned that women should be better educated (see Stanton et al., 1881, vol. I, p. 33) and, although neither educated like men, nor allowed to travel like men, she was aware of some of the events taking place outside her own country. In the last paragraph of her letter to Isaac Smith she asks him to find out everything he can about Catherine Macaulay. 'One of my own Sex so eminent in a tract so uncommon naturally raises my curiosity', she says (in Rossi, 1974, p. 10).

In the last few decades of the eighteenth century, women in the old world and the new were beginning systematically to question sexual inequality and to take a variety of steps towards bringing about change. And as a woman of systematic ideas, Judith Sargent Murray (1751–1820) played a part in developing the understanding for the need for change. Born in Massachusetts, into a prosperous and liberal family, she seems to have had the opportunity to reflect and to write, and she seems to have arrived at some of the ideas that are currently acceptable. Like other educated women of her time and place (and like the Bluestockings in England), she was effectively excluded from circles of social, political and economic power by reason of her sex, but she was not debarred (although she may have been discouraged) from taking up her pen. She wrote essays, verse and plays: ('She is the first native-born woman dramatist in America to have her plays professionally performed', ibid., p. 16).

She was fortunate enough to share the educational facilities provided for her brother (brothers sometimes being a most useful resource in this respect), at least, until he went off to Harvard.

It is difficult to determine the actual combination of circumstances that led to Judith Sargent Murray's development of ideas on the relations of the sexes, and instead of assuming that she was the *only* woman to hold such ideas, we can be grateful that she was a woman who had access to publication and who has therefore left us a record of what one woman thought about women's position.

Judith Sargent Murray was not only able to describe sexual oppression – her own and others – she was also able to formulate ideas about its source outside the framework of divine ordination. She used her personal experience to illustrate the discrepancy between the male version of women's existence and her own lived reality as a woman. For Judith Sargent Murray there was the definite knowledge – outside male experience – that the characteristics of women which men would have as 'natural' were most assuredly acquired and learnt. Drawing on her personal experience leads her to make links with other women who share that experience: she makes women's experience and understanding of the world the 'norm' for explaining women, and in the process rejects the male norm and takes the simple steps into a feminist framework.

In 1790 her essay 'On the Equality of the Sexes' was published in the *Massachusetts Magazine,* and, not only is her case strikingly similar to Wollstonecraft's (not yet written), but there are reasons for believing that for Murray it was not entirely new. She provides a footnote to her essay which is very interesting, for she assures the readers that the essay existed in manuscript form in 1779 and that she cannot therefore be accused of plagiarism. The possibility of plagiarism could only exist if there were other writers saying the same thing, so it is reasonable to assume that Murray wasn't the only one advancing the cause. As with so many other women who have written, particularly on this topic, Judith Sargent Murray published under a pseudonym, in this case 'Constantia'.

In her essay, Murray launches straight into the crux of the matter – the intellectual worth and competence of women. However, she will not argue in the terms which men have laid down and attempt to prove that women are as capable as men. She too turns the argument round and questions men's definitions of themselves (and not just women) and asks if it is really a fact that half the human species has 'so unquestionable a mental superiority?' (in Rossi, 1974, p. 18). It is men's reason and logic which is under attack, not women's.

She examines some of the definitions of women and shows how false they are: ingeniously she exposes the contradictions within men's beliefs for at the same time as they would have women devoid of creativity and imagination they would also crown them the 'undoubted sovereigns of the region of fancy' with creative talent for slander. Murray's intellectual agility is to be admired: on the one hand she takes what have been seen as women's *vices* and offers them as proof of *virtue,* while at the same time acknowledging that 'fancy' and 'slander' are vices which are the consequence of men confining women to the domestic sphere. She uses the same techniques that men have used, but she uses them in the women's interest.

The needle and the kitchen, says Murray, are just not enough to keep a woman intellectually occupied, and because they have no intellectual outlet, and because they are intellectually endowed, women are obliged to use their creative talents for less than constructive ends. The needle and the kitchen, she says, are *mindless,* they are 'those very departments' that 'leave the intelligent principle vacant, and at liberty for speculation' (ibid., p. 19). That such speculation takes the form that it does is because men will not permit them to put their minds to constructive use. The 'scapegoat' principle is introduced again as Murray states that women are blamed by men for not possessing the qualities men will not permit them to have: 'Are we deficient in reason? We can only reason from what we know, and if opportunity of acquiring knowledge hath been denied us, the inferiority of our sex cannot fairly be deduced from thence' (ibid.).

Murray moves into the realm of the personal as political, and asserts that housework is mindless (that it is *shitwork* and that women are required to do it for all human beings, and men for none) and puts forward a point that was one of the early tenets of the modern women's movement. To those who would say: 'Your domestic employments are sufficient,' says Murray, she would reply that women are degraded when 'allowed no other ideas, than those which are suggested by the mechanism of a pudding, or the sewing of the seams of a garment' (ibid., p. 20). 'At length arrived at womanhood', says Murray, predating Betty Friedan (1963) by almost two hundred years, a woman 'feels a void, which the employments allotted to her are by no means capable of filling' (ibid., p. 19). It is understandable that men might want to think that this is what women need, argues Murray, but it is undeniable that women know more on the question than men.

Having shifted from 'divine' explanations for inequality (albeit by invoking the argument that God would not have granted women souls if it were intended that they be degraded in this way, the same case used by 'Sophia' before and Wollstonecraft after), Murray begins to examine the means by which inequality materialises, and notes, from the position of a woman who must live with the architecture of society as distinct from being one of its architects, that there are observable and different lessons taught to females and males. She introduces issues of 'expectation', of socialisation and sex stereotyping.

'Will it be said that the judgement of a male of two years old is more sage than that of a female's of the same age?' asks Murray pointedly, and defies readers to assert that the sexes are *born* unequal. But, she continues, 'from that period, what partiality! how is the one exalted and the other depressed, by the contrary modes of education that are adopted! The one is taught to aspire and the other is early confined and limited' (ibid.). It is a salutary lesson to recognise that Murray's ideas, formulated almost two centuries ago, have not as yet become 'mainstream' in the social sciences; think of what might have been if for 200 years there had been research on the preferential treatment provided for boys! As it is, women educationalists today are arguing as she did then, that their experience is one of being 'depressed', 'confined', 'limited' (see D. Spender, 1981a, 1981b). That men may state that, for them, education is a process of encouragement, of growth and development, confirms, not contradicts, women's thesis, but the limited logic of men who accept their view of the world as the human view will not permit them to understand that it may be very different for half the human population.

In a statement that could stand as a rationale for current projects aimed at reducing the male monopoly on science, Murray says: 'As the years increase, the sister must be wholly domesticated while the brother is led by the hand through all the flowery paths of science. Granted that their minds are by nature equal, yet who shall wonder at the *apparent* superiority, if indeed custom becomes *second nature,* nay, if it taketh the place of nature, and that it doth the experience of each day will evince' (in Rossi, 1974, p. 19).

Fundamental to the 'nature' argument is not only the assertion that males are more intelligent, but that they are stronger, and Murray takes up this as well and turns it back upon men (as 'Sophia' had done). Murray makes men's strength and their claims of superiority problematic, rather than trying to prove that women are as strong as men. How is it, she asks, that men can account for brilliant and gifted men who are *small, weak,* or even *deformed?* If the male argument about the significance of male strength is to stand up to scrutiny, then surely there should be a relationship between strength *and* intellectual ability seeing that men's claims for superiority rested on both. But this is not the case: 'I fancy Mr Pope, though clogged with an enervated body, and distinguished by a diminutive stature, could nevertheless lay claim to greatness of soul' (ibid., p. 22), she argues. Murray quite readily admits that males share certain characteristics with 'the lion, the tiger, and other beasts of prey' (ibid., p. 23), but even here she reverses patriarchal values by refusing to rate this positively.

As with 'Sophia', once the possibilities of re-evaluating inherited concepts about weakness and strength and female and male are opened up, Murray beings to speculate on the plausibility of females being superior: 'were we to grant animal strength proved anything, taking into account the accustomed impartiality of nature we should be induced to imagine that she had invested the female mind with superior strength as an equivalent to the bodily powers of men' (ibid., p. 22). Again, Murray is revealing the traps which men fall into by accepting only their own experience of themselves as superior, without reference to the inconsistency which women's experience provides.

While speculating that women might be more intelligent, even superior, Murray indicates that she does not want to make the same mistake as men: 'But waiving this however palpable advantage,' she says, 'for equality only we wish to contend' (ibid., p. 22). But Murray cannot help but follow this line of reasoning in the attempt to explain the aspects of male behaviour and male logic that she has witnessed. She adds an addendum to her article, in the guise of a letter to a friend, in which she states 'Strange how blind *self-love* renders you men: were you not wholly absorbed in a partial admiration of your own abilities, you would long since have acknowledged the force of what I am now going to urge' (ibid., p. 23) and she proceeds to dismantle the 'divine' arguments that men have so readily advanced as a justification for women's subordination.

In a manner which anticipates Elizabeth Cady Stanton and Matilda Joslyn Gage one century later, and Mary Daly almost two, Murray points to the logical fallacies in men's account of the human fall from grace. Eve, says Murray, ate of the apple in her search for *knowledge,* and it was 'a laudable ambition which fired her soul', but Adam? He could not plead the same case: Eve stood before him as the testimony of the consequences of such action. Adam had knowledge which Eve had not possessed and she had not achieved 'that wisdom which she fondly hoped to obtain'. So 'What then could be his inducement', she asks, 'to burst the barriers, and to fly directly in the face of that command, which *immediately* from the mouth of Deity *he* had received, since, I say, he could not plead the fascinating stimulus, the accumulation of knowledge' (ibid., p. 23). It is not Adam, she argues, whom we should hold up as a model of sagacity and courage; that men can continue to insist that he be seen this way simply shows the deficiencies of their own reasoning, brought about by their partiality for themselves and their sex.

Judith Sargent Murray directed her attention to the rules of society, and the originators of those rules. She saw that it was men who were responsible for them and that they made them in their own interest with little regard for women, or for the *logic* which they held in such high esteem and had appropriated for themselves. That men could argue that their beliefs were logical was to Murray evidence of their presentation of themselves as superior. There is little in her analysis that would need to be

revised 200 years later. Again, this is probably the reason for the disappearance of her work. Alice Rossi states that: 'Murray's essay stands as the
earliest example of this argument that I have found in my search of the
American feminist literature. This is its first republication since its 1790
appearance' (ibid., pp. 17–18). No doubt there were more such analyses
– many of them unpublished – no doubt it would have been different if for
the last 200 years women had been refining, developing, elaborating the
ideas that Murray put forward, and which she was keen not to be seen as
'borrowed' from other writers on the topic. Women are interrupted and
silenced in a male-dominated world – not that men can be expected to
vouch for the veracity of this, for it is outside their experience, and it is
their experience which is accepted as real.

7 The French connection

As a radical, interested in liberty, Mary Wollstonecraft turned to France
for ideas, experiments and models, and she found a rich source of inspiration. She did not always like what she found (and in *A Vindication* was
more than critical of her French contemporaries, Madame de Genlis (1746–
1830) and Madame de Staël (1766–1817)), but in France there were *visible*
women, advocating reform. In many respects, both de Genlis and de Staël
have their contemporary counterparts, and probably promote a comparable
contemporary response from feminists for we are led to think that de Staël
'believed in the rights of the exceptional individual but was quite uninter-
ested in the condition of the majority', while 'Madame de Genlis went so
far as to ridicule the spectacle of women joining in the debates at the
Société fraternelle (a mixed club with a petty bourgeois membership)'
according to Claire Tomalin (1977, p. 199). But it is interesting to note
that what little we know about them is so unflattering. After not having a
single good word to say about de Genlis's contribution to girls' education,
Dorothy Gardiner (1929) ends on a semi-triumphant note when she says
de Genlis's biographer stated that she avowed in later life (having gone to
England as a refugee from the French Revolution) 'that she would have
done better to advocate for her pupils an elementary knowledge of common
law' (p. 442).

    But if Wollstonecraft was critical of these women, she was also critical
of Rousseau (some uncharitable persons might say – eventually) and exposed both the absurdity and the convenience of his double standard which
led him to think it reasonable and logical to educate boys for their own
sake and to educate girls for the sake of boys! Rousseau, de Genlis and de
Staël were undoubtedly influential for Mary Wollstonecraft, even if they
only served as a catalyst at times for her critical opposition. More positive,
however, in their influence were the activities of Madame Roland (1754–
1793), the ideas and activities of Olympe de Gouges (1745–1793) and the
theories of one man, Condorcet.

    To begin with the man: Condorcet was an intimate friend of Thomas

Paine, (in turn a close friend of Mary Wollstonecraft's) and, while it is not established that they ever met, it is not unlikely that Wollstonecraft was aware of his theories on women's equality which were published in 1787 and 1790 – before her own. Tomalin says that 'Mary herself was either wholly ignorant of his work (in spite of Paine) or preferred not to mention it' (1977, p. 135). This assessment seems surprising for, given that Wollstonecraft was a member of a lively circle in which the ideas from France were constantly discussed, it is far more likely that she *did* know of his work, than that she did *not*.

In Tomalin's terms, Condorcet gave 'unequivocal support for a programme of immediate advancement of women to equal rights' (ibid., p. 132) and dismissed as 'irrelevant' many of the reservations that are still advanced today (for example, 'Condorcet dismissed menstruation as of no more account than fluctuations in the general health of men', ibid., p. 133). He had broken from 'divinely ordained' explanations of the social order and held men, not God, accountable for sexual inequality.

In his essay *Sur l'admission des femmes au droit de Cité* (1790), he stated that 'Either no member of the human race has real rights, or else all have the same; he who votes against the rights of another, whatever his colour, religion or sex, thereby abjures his own', and, adds Tomalin, he argued that, 'if women tended to put personal considerations before general social justice', then it was 'the result of their deficient education and social conditioning.' There were few fallacies in his logic, except perhaps for the idea that 'personal' consideration was of less value and significance than 'social justice' when the personal applied to women (men's personal considerations *being* social justice). It seems that Condorcet's argument was not new, nor the 'usual response' to it unknown, for 'He invited serious replies to his claims on their behalf: he had had enough of the jokes and the ranting that were the usual response' (ibid., p. 135).

While recognising the usefulness and the value of Condorcet's contribution, it does seem unfortunate that Tomalin should state that: 'There is no doubt that Condorcet's ten pages pack more logic than Mary's three hundred' (ibid., pp. 135–6), for it is this sort of gratuitous and *completely unsubstantiated* remark[18] which helps to support the erroneous belief that men have a monopoly on intelligence and logic.

Condorcet continued to write on the issue of women's equality until the last day of his life and among some of his work is the statement that: 'As far as general happiness is concerned, one of the most important advances in human thinking must be the total destruction of the prejudices which have established differences in the rights of the two sexes (a difference which harms the favoured sex too).' Condorcet argues that: 'There is no justification for these differences, either in the physical nature of women, their intelligence or their moral sensibility' and, he adds derisively, 'The

---

[18] I am convinced that I could 'prove', and that it wouldn't be difficult, that even in the terms that are acceptable to men the three hundred pages contains *more* logic than the ten; *more* logic is itself a problematic concept which could be assuredly used to advantage.

only basis for inequality is the abuse of brute strength, and all the sophistry that has been brought to bear on the subject cannot alter the fact' (ibid., p. 206). It would seem that neither then nor now is it mandatory that males should see only in terms of their own interest. Whether or not Wollstonecraft knew Condorcet, these ideas were part of the intellectual climate in which she wrote.

Another of the French connections was Madame Roland, whom Wollstonecraft met when she went to Paris (*after* the publication of *A Vindication*) and to whom she was introduced by Thomas Paine. In this case it is clear that Wollstonecraft did know about Madame Roland long before she met her, because Wollstonecraft was passionately interested in the French political scene, and Madame Roland was at its centre for quite some time. Roland was in the anomalous position of being a female contender for political power and this contradiction was overcome by the ruse of using her husband. When Mary Wollstonecraft arrived in Paris 'Madame Roland and Danton were opponents in the struggle for power. They were the outstanding figures in the Convention, although of course Madame Roland worked behind her husband's name. But the truth was known; most of the pamphlets, appeals and warnings which Roland signed were the work of his wife' (Edna Nixon, 1971, p. 102). (No doubt if *she* had signed them they would not have been classified as 'political' – then, or now; she might even have been criticised for putting her time into intellectual issues rather than doing anything 'practical', such is the nature of the double standard and women's culpability.)

If Madame Roland did devote any of her energy to an analysis of the position of women, this aspect of her life has been lost by the consideration of her as a participant in the male political arena. She did write: 'I am much annoyed at being a woman. On every hand my spirit and heart find the shackles of opinion, the iron of prejudice, and all my strength is wasted in vainly shaking my chains' (quoted in Nixon, 1971, p. 105). But if the ambivalence of her position as a woman with power (be it masked) was wasted on her, it was not lost on Mary Wollstonecraft, who had great faith in women's potential, which could be released when the chains were broken. Madame Roland existed as a model for Wollstonecraft and highlighted some of the limitations, and frustrations, with which women had to deal.

The other woman who could have served as a model for Wollstonecraft (though a model of a different sort) was Olympe de Gouges. She was a Parisian playwright and pamphleteer, an uneducated one who held women's education dear, and she was very well known. She founded women's clubs and tried to break down the exclusion of women from politics through discussion in these clubs and through her own writing and pamphleteering. As a woman, however, in line with the traditional classification and division of women, and politics, her interests have not often been perceived as political. 'She was indefatigable in composing appeals for good causes; the abolition of the slave trade, the setting up of public workshops for the unemployed, a national theatre for women' (Tomalin, 1977, p. 200). What does a woman have to do to be seen as political?

In 'Nine hundred and Ninety Nine Women of Achievement' (Chicago, 1979) it is said of Olympe de Gouges that: 'She demanded equal rights for women before the law, and in all aspects of public and private life. Realizing that the Revolutionaries were enemies of the emancipation of women, she covered the walls of Paris with bulletins – signed with her name – expounding her ideas and exposing the injustices of the new government.' She was sentenced to death by Robespierre, and guillotined, but not before she demanded to know of the women in the crowd, 'What are the advantages you have derived from the Revolution? Slights and contempt more plainly displayed' (p. 177).

Evidently, she was quite troublesome. In 1791, in response to the Declaration of the Rights of Man, she produced her own Declaration of the Rights of Women (a strategy closely paralleled by Wollstonecraft's work and later by the women at the first Woman's Rights convention in Seneca Falls, 1848) and, 'Taking the seventeen articles of the *Declaration des Droits de l'Homme* and replacing whenever she found it the word man by woman, she demanded that women should have the same political and social rights as men' (Nixon, 1971, p. 81). It was also one of her convictions that marriage had failed as a social institution and should be replaced by a more just and appropriate arrangement. 'All this lit a flame in Mary', says Edna Nixon, 'if indeed she read it' (ibid.).

It is unlikely that Mary Wollstonecraft remained oblivious to the activities and ideas of Olympe de Gouges partly because her sex and her style (so 'inappropriate' for her sex) attracted so much publicity, and her name was so well known. Had she been a male, starting clubs for women and workships for the unemployed, campaigning for the abolition of slavery, urging the emancipation of women whenever and wherever she could, writing slogans, rewriting the manifesto of liberty and pointing to its contradictions and abuses, and being guillotined for her efforts, she would no doubt have been perceived as a 'politician' – of significant stature no less and with a thorough and firm grasp of social and political issues. As a woman, however, the verdict is different: 'Olympe's mixture of flamboyance and courage *might have made her a good politician,* irritating and eccentric. Later militant feminists have shown similar traits and deployed them successfully' (Tomalin, 1977, p. 200, my emphasis). If by 'irritating' Tomalin is referring to 'irritating to men' and by 'eccentric', 'eccentric in men's terms', then one should expect nothing less from women while men continue to dominate. One should celebrate, not condemn, the later militant feminists, and Olympe de Gouges, for their logical and laudable stand. But, all too frequently, it is men's terms which determine how women are portrayed – and women who do not conform to male definitions are not portrayed positively.

There is no doubt that the feminist issue had arisen in France before Mary Wollstonecraft wrote *A Vindication* and there is no doubt that Mary Wollstonecraft *knew* France, although her exact relationship to these individuals and their ideas is not clear. Tomalin states: 'The subject was in the air and needed an outspoken champion in England: why should Mary not produce *Vindication*[19] for her own sex?' (1977, p. 132); after all 'she knew the subject from the inside' (ibid., p. 135).

There is little in Mary Wollstonecraft's book that was not said before (but much that was said before which is not in *A Vindication*) but, while traditionally, great pains have been taken to expose the 'unoriginality' of women's intellectual contribution, by documenting all the precedents, by quoting all those who spoke or wrote on the matter prior to the particular woman's entry, this has not happened to Wollstonecraft. One should be grateful for small mercies, that Wollstonecraft has been spared this specific, and perhaps only, form of disparagement, but it does raise the question of why in the face of so much contrary evidence she has been presented as 'alone'. I suspect that it is because Wollstonecraft has more value as an *isolate* than she does as 'part of a movement' in a patriarchal society.

8 Two is a crowd: Catherine Macaulay (1731–1791)

That Catherine Macaulay's work – particularly *Letters on Education* (1790) – should have disappeared in the interest of the preservation of patriarchy is understandable, because she was a persuasive feminist writer, but that the same work, on the same grounds, should not have been reclaimed by women poses something of a problem. Not only was *Letters on Education* significant in her own time, exerting a fundamental influence on Mary Wollstonecraft (to the extent that if either of them had published *Letters* or *A Vindication* anonymously it would no doubt have been attributed to the other, on the basis of 'internal' evidence, for at times the similarity is great), but much of her analysis could still stand today at the centre of feminist educational theory.

There are few references to Macaulay in some of the nineteenth-century guides written by women to celebrate women's achievements, with Mary Hays (1803) being one of the few exceptions. When she is referred to it is often in disparaging terms so that although, for example, Dorothy Gardiner (1929) says that she was a pioneer among the Bluestockings, she makes no mention of her as an educationalist and only passing mention of her 'less than passable ability' as an historian: 'Mrs Macaulay made a great though temporary reputation as an historian: her writings were spoiled for any permanent value by their partisan character' (p. 454).

In commenting on Macaulay's disappearance, Florence Boos (1976) noted that at that time there was only one article on Macaulay's work in print,[20] entitled 'The Celebrated Mrs Macaulay' by Lucy Martin Donnelly (1949), it asserts that her work is unreadable (a comment not designed to promote a flurry of interest in it), particularly the *Letters on Education* –

---

[19] Thomas Paine had already of course written *A Vindication of The Rights of Man*, in 1790.

[20] Florence Boos states that the situation could be remedied: in 1974 Garland Publishers issued a reprint of *Letters on Education* (edited by Gina Luria) and Barbara Schomenberg of North Carolina University was working on a biography of Macaulay.

written 'late in life' – with all the negative connotations such a statement has in relation to a woman. That Macaulay's work is now only found in the British Museum appears to Donnelly to be quite justified.

This is quite surprising, for it was not just Mary Wollstonecraft who acknowledged her debt to Macaulay – a 'woman of the greatest ability, undoubtedly, this country has ever produced' – (Wollstonecraft, in Kramnick, 1978, p. 206), but also Elizabeth Cady Stanton, Susan B. Anthony and Matilda Joslyn Gage (1881), who made much of her contribution. In *History of Woman Suffrage* (vol. I) they acknowledge the lively interest Mrs Macaulay took in the American struggle and state that her 'writings aided in the dissemination of republican ideas' (and it was because she was 'biased' towards republicanism no doubt that Dorothy Gardiner judged her a poor historian); so useful and influential were Macaulay's ideas, state Stanton et al., 'that after her death a statue was erected of her as the "Patroness of Liberty".' (1881, p. 32).[21] But this was not all: 'During the whole of the revolutionary period, Washington was in correspondence with Mrs Macaulay, who did much to sustain him during those days of trial,' and she actually wrote books such as *An Address to the People of England, Scotland and Ireland on the present Important Crisis of Affairs*, which were 'designed to show the justice of the American cause' (ibid.) to those in the home country.

Doris Stenton (1977) says that: 'She was the first to attempt the writing of history on a large scale, based on materials, in manuscript as well as in print,' and that: 'Over a period of twenty years she published eight massive volumes concerning the history of England from the accession of James I to the coming of the Hanoverian kings. Her narrative is supported with ample footnotes, giving the sources of her information and extracts from them' (p. 306). W. E. H. Lecky, commenting a century later on Macaulay's work, said that she was 'the ablest writer of the New Radical School' (1883–87, vol. III, p. 256).

Macaulay's links with George Washington are also mentioned by Stenton: 'in 1784 Macaulay sailed for America to see for herself the new republican state. She and her husband spent ten days with George Washington in 1785, and she corresponded with him until her death' (1977, p. 309). In turn, states Stenton, Washington accepted her as a representative of radical opinion in England and confided in her his hopes for the future happiness of his country (ibid., p. 310).

Catherine Macaulay then was a person of note in her own time; it seems that she had even achieved a measure of social and political influence in spite of the limitations imposed on her sex (for correspondence with Washington could be construed as such, and would be, if she had been a man). Yet as Dorothy Gardiner (1929) has said, her reputation was but temporary. Different explanations have been provided for her disappearance.

Florence Boos (1976) provides a 'rational' explanation in terms of Macaulay's own writing and position: she was a radical and there was a

---

[21] I have been unable to locate the whereabouts of this statue, assuming it still exists.

reaction against radicalism with the beginning of the nineteenth century; she was 'an isolated figure in intellectual history, despite conversations with distinguished writers and politicians, in large part because no other Enlightenment theorist held feminist views' (p. 65); she could not be revived or reclaimed as an early romantic as Wollstonecraft could when romanticism came into vogue; and finally, in the case of *Letters*, the structure of the book itself could have contributed to her 'demise' for it was really a combination of three books, 'each well written and unified but unlikely to appeal to the same reader' (ibid.).

While these reasons may all sound plausible, I suspect, however, that it is because the *Letters* is 'Among the most significant early feminist documents' (ibid.) that it disappeared, and that the apparent 'isolation' (and disappearance) of Macaulay is a convenient patriarchal reconstruction and not necessarily an accurate representation of her life. Mary Wollstonecraft's claim to being representative of her sex looks much stronger if Catherine Macaulay is seen to present almost the same case at the same time; one of them had to go if it was to be accepted that there was but a *lone* voice asserting the feminist case.

Alice Rossi (1974) has a different explanation from Boos for Macaulay's disappearance. She outlines Macaulay's achievements, her immense popularity as an historian before she published her treatise on education, her 'eight volumes of . . . *History of England*, published between 1763 and 1783' which 'were acclaimed in England and France' (p. 29). 'Macaulay and her book were warmly greeted in Paris, translated into French, and reputed to be the inspiration of Madame Roland, who wanted to do a similar history of France' (ibid., pp. 29–30). But, says Rossi, 'a critical reason for public neglect is a familiar one' (ibid., p. 30) or, at least, it *is* for women. Macaulay offended public taste by her private morals and, in the nineteenth century, 'the written work of those whose personal morality was in question became the object of a powerful sanction exercised by public opinion – neglect' (ibid.).

Between the publication of the early volumes of *History of England* and that of the *Letters on Education*, a significant event took place: Catherine Macaulay was widowed and then remarried. 'Her unforgivable "sin" in the eyes of her contemporaries was to marry "beneath her".' In 1778 'at the age of forty-seven, she married William Graham, aged twenty one. This in itself was clearly a violation of "accepted behaviour",' states Rossi, for 'to become the wife of one twenty six years her junior was extremely "improper". Furthermore, Graham was the brother of a quack doctor and was himself a "surgeon's mate". There was a stormy response in the social world that had previously admired her' (ibid.).

Perhaps this does help to explain her absence in the nineteenth century. Mary Wollstonecraft suffered a similar fate, but her 'improprieties' were probably more difficult to accommodate (a lover, an illegitimate child, another conceived out of wedlock). Mary Wollstonecraft, however, has been reclaimed, although great pains were taken to ensure that her behaviour was not condoned (see the centenary edition of the *A Vindication* published in London 1891 by Millicent Fawcett).

Neither Boos nor Rossi satisfactorily explain Macaulay's disappearance: neither of them suggests that what happened to Macaulay is representative of what has happened to most women who have raised their voices in protest against 'male tyranny'. I think it perfectly possible that these two women whose ideas so closely resembled each other's (with Macaulay even using the phrase 'the vindication of female nature') were just too close together. Between them (and along with other women such as Mary Hays who wrote *Appeal to the Men of Great Britain in Behalf of the Women* (1799) see page 101) they might have been construed as the 'beginning of a movement' and it would be very unproductive, in patriarchal terms, to support the idea that the women's movement has a 200-year history – and is *still* fighting the same battles. Better that there are only 'occasional', unrepresentative voices making unreasonable demands – better still, if such voices can be repressed completely and protests about male tyranny, or sexism, can be perceived as 'new' in each generation which gives rise to them.

The only surprising feature about Macaulay's disappearance is that it represents a lost opportunity for discrediting Wollstonecraft: Wollstonecraft could have been accused of plagiarism, of unoriginality, of saying nothing which had not been said before and even said better. But then there was much other evidence available to 'discredit' her in terms of her personal life – more 'damning' evidence than in the case of Macaulay; this cannot be discounted as irrelevant.

In *Letters on Education*, Macaulay established the parameters for *A Vindication of the Rights of Woman*; she outlined what had come to be accepted as the differences between the sexes, but, far from taking them as *natural*, she adopted what appears to be the unprecedented stand of asserting that there were *no* natural or innate sex differences, and that sexual inequality was constructed entirely by man; 'all the vices and imperfections which have generally been regarded as inseparable from the female character', she states, 'do not in any manner proceed from sexual causes, but are entirely the effects of situation and education' (1790, in Luria, 1974, p. 202). As Florence Boos (1976) declares, this was most definitely not the usual interpretation of her time (nor for that matter, after her time), and that, indeed 'Macaulay's environmentalism led her to a position maintained by almost no one else till the twentieth century' (p. 72).

Having established the source of difference – education and situation – Macaulay then proceeds, in a well-informed, satirical (and to my mind, entertaining) manner to expose the means by which this feat is accomplished, and the means by which it can be changed, and her focus is largely upon education. She acknowledges the individuals who have influenced her thinking, and not only is it significant that there is only one woman to whom she declares her indebtedness, it is also important that she (Madame de Genlis), and Macaulay, are the only two among these educationalists to have actually reared children and who have combined their theories with *personal experience*.

In Macaulay's writing there is little suggestion that she is seeking male approval, that she is attempting to flatter men in order to obtain a hearing.

She readily admits that some women are forced to find favour with men by telling them what they want to hear, for as an oppressed group women have few options open to them for survival. But she is adamant that this need not be the case, that if the two sexes were treated the *same*, they could become *equal* and then there would be no reason for women to be dependent on men.

Macaulay herself is confident and assertive: she makes male reasoning problematic and not only argues theoretically for women's intellectual competence, she also *demonstrates* it. She was aware, even bitterly aware, of the severe restrictions placed on women's intellectual growth and development, and the extent to which their ideas could still be devalued if they did manage to overcome the obstacles placed in their way and went on to produce critical and creative work. She saw the reason for this arrangement as *male vanity* (in Luria, 1974, p. 205) and suggested that it was because men wanted to appear superior that they handicapped women, denied them educational opportunities and disparaged their ideas, in order to ensure that they *were* perceived as superior.

Macaulay refers to the invidious practice of labelling a critical, creative and competent mind as *masculine* (ibid., p. 204), a practice which persists to this day, and which is used to maintain a male monopoly on the intellectual realm. Obviously, Mary Wollstonecraft shared Macaulay's anger and frustration on this issue, for she too repudiated the belief that ideas belong to men, but she found it more difficult to describe, convincingly and positively, the intellectual capacity of women. In the case of Macaulay herself, Wollstonecraft states in *A Vindication* that: 'I will not call hers a masculine understanding, because I admit not such an arrogant assumption of reason', but, she continues, struggling to articulate a concept which virtually lies beyond the social classification scheme of her own day and ours, 'I contend that it was a sound' understanding and 'that her judgement, the matured proof of profound thinking, was a proof that women can acquire judgement in the full extent of the word' (Wollstonecraft, in Kramnick, 1978, p. 206).

The willingness to divide society into women and men, into powerless and powerful, slave and master, to assert the existence of women as an autonomous entity, and to present the opposing and conflicting nature of the interests of these two different and unequal groups, is one of the features of Macaulay's analysis which allows her to speak to us readily and relevantly today, in the framework in which we are currently functioning. She grasps and deals derisively with the basic but erroneous premise that men can be relied upon to act in women's best interest – an argument which men frequently advanced and used as a rationale for many social arrangements and which Macaulay reveals as ridiculous. Men, she suggests, are committed to acting in their *own* interest so if and when there is a conflict of interest with women it is resolved in favour of men. The proposition that women's interests were best served when men's interests were served, that happiness for women lay in happy men, was for Macaulay totally untenable; she could see that while men were served, women were slaves.

To Macaulay, *femininity* was a social construct, a state to be worked for and attained, and while it might be in the interest of men to have docile, delicate and dim women, this arrangement certainly had little to recommend itself to women. She examines the attributes that are found desirable in women – particularly as they relate to beauty – and declares them to be the product of men's minds projected onto women's minds – and bodies – and which demand that women distort themselves in order to be desirable. While Macaulay's terminology may be different from that used today, her meanings are not far removed from many of our own.

Making one of the links made by Mary Daly (1978) in *Gyn/Ecology*, Macaulay refers to the then current practice of confining girls' feet in tight shoes and says 'if littleness alone . . . constitutes the beauty of feet, we can never pretend to vie with the Chinese, whilst we presume the privilege of walking' (1790, p. 44) and she emphasises the way women are required to disfigure themselves in the effort to become attractive to men. She also comments on why men may find such disfigurement and deformity 'attractive': it enhances their images of themselves as strong, intelligent, and superior. The attempt to appear small, delicate, fragile, and foolish, put upon women to promote the superiority of men, leads women to engage in the most appalling practices, states Macaulay. They are 'obliged to lisp with their tongues, to totter in their walk, and to counterfeit more weakness and sickness than they really have, in order to attract the notice of the male,' and, echoing the words of Mary Astell of almost one hundred years before, says that men *admire* excellence, but *love* those they despise. So much for 'romance'; she has few illusions about the relationship between the sexes.

She also recognises that men cannot see what she describes while they have only their own experience as a reference; but *her* experience of being required to be 'attractive' gives her full knowledge of the demands that men are making on women, while they are prepared to insist that nature is responsible. She rails against the conditions imposed upon women which drive them to being dishonourable, and which therefore can become another entry in the inventory of women's unworthiness. She does not argue that women are 'pure' and 'good', but like Wollstonecraft accepts the evidence that they are 'debased', and then goes on to attribute the cause not to women, but to men. The only 'standard' required of women, asserts Macaulay, is fidelity to one man (for predictable reasons): 'let her only take care that she is not caught in a love intrigue, and she may lie, she may deceive, she may defame, she may ruin her own family with gaming, and the peace of twenty others with her coquetry, and yet both preserve her reputation and her peace' (1790, in Luria, 1974, p. 210). This is what happens when the two sexes are treated differently, states Macaulay, when there is one standard for men and another for women, and the solution is to be found in treating both sexes the *same*! For this reason she advocates co-education, where girls and boys receive *identical* (not 'different' but 'equal') treatment (a point made by Eileen Byrne, 1978). Virtue and knowledge are the same for both sexes, argues Macaulay; there can be no double standard, for what is good for one sex is good for the other.

But she does not fall into the trap of assuming the superiority of male experience and of advocating that girls receive the same (unchanged) education as boys. Unlike some of the women who followed her in the nineteenth century, who insisted that the practice of providing girls with the same education enjoyed by boys constituted equality, Macaulay urged a re-examination of boys' education, which she found exceedingly problematic. She stated that she would rather see her pupils, girls and boys, 'engaged in the innocent employment of forming a button, than in spending whole days hunting down a harmless animal, both at the hazard of their necks and at the expense of their benevolence' (1790, p. 65). (In this, she is mocking Rousseau's educational philosophy which encouraged males to go hunting as a means of evading the allurement of women.)

Macaulay asserts the value and worth of the female sex: 'my pride and my prejudices lead me to regard my sex in a higher light than as the mere objects of sense' (ibid., p. 62) she states, as she argues for the value and worth of traditionally female skills, which are to be acquired by *both* sexes. Not that she sees the problem of sex inequality completely overcome by education. She argues for education as a means of equipping the sexes equally, and as a means of changing attitudes (a rationale which is still popular) but she recognises that the social and political laws are made by men and that these too will need revision. She emphasises how powerless women are when she says they are totally excluded from every political right and 'have hardly a civil right to save them from the grossest injustices' (ibid., p. 210). This makes them ready victims, in sexual matters as well, where women are blamed for men's actions, yet where men keep them ignorant in order to facilitate opportunities for their own advantage.

When women are as worthy as men, as they will be with the same education as men, argues Macaulay, they will be in a better position to change the social and political structures which work against them. Establishing women's autonomous value (and ending men's apparent superiority) came before political and legal reform in Macaulay's view of the world.

Overall, *Letters on Education* contains a well-developed critique of patriarchy and Macaulay raises many of the issues that still burn today. She testifies from her own personal experience and clearly outlines the consequences for women of men's self-interested assertions and beliefs about women. But men were and still are in a position to arbitrate on *her* value and it seems that their self-interest was served by silence. Were Macaulay allowed to coexist with Wollstonecraft in our understandings of the past, and of women's protest about male domination in the past, the two women could look suspiciously like a crowd. Wollstonecraft was isolated, and Macaulay lost.

9 Mary Wollstonecraft (1759–1797)

Mary Wollstonecraft spent considerable time engaged in discussion and debate on the topics of her day, and one of those topics was feminism. The question could well be – where did Catherine Macaulay forge *her* ideas, for there is no doubt that many of Macaulay's ideas were taken up by Wollstonecraft and shaped to become her own. Wollstonecraft acknowledged her debt to Macaulay and indicated that she deeply regretted her death: 'when I first thought of writing these strictures', says Wollstonecraft in relation to *A Vindication*, 'I anticipated Mrs Macaulay's approbation, with a little of that sanguine ardour which it has been the business of my life to depress,' but, she adds, I 'soon heard with the sickly qualm of disappointed hope, and the still seriousness of regret – that she was no more' (1792, in Kramnick, 1978, p. 207).

I can find no mention of the influence of Mary Astell or Lady Mary Wortley Montagu, for example, in Wollstonecraft's writing, or in accounts of her life (although my search has by no means been exhaustive) but, none the less, it was a small world. Henry Fuseli – with whom Mary Wollstonecraft tried to initiate an affair and whose opinion of his own greatness she came close to accepting – was the German translator of Lady Mary Wortley Montagu's letters. Fuseli and Mary Wollstonecraft talked often and long, and it is perfectly in character for a woman to ask a man questions about his work, and it was perfectly in character for Fuseli to provide every impressive detail. Is it possible that Wollstonecraft who had such a thirst for knowledge and such a commitment to the analysis of the position of women in society did not also share some of the feelings that are common among women today – the pressing need to know what went before, to uncover and understand the past in relation to women? Is it possible that she did *not* find out about Lady Mary (and then of course, about Astell who wrote the preface to the letters), and did not read their work?

My only hesitation in declaring this impossible is the knowledge – personally experienced – of how quickly and completely women's ideas can disappear: forty years after Virginia Woolf and twenty years after Simone de Beauvoir, I reached adulthood and gained a university degree in history and literature, without knowing about their ideas on women. *Woman not Inferior to Man* was published sixty-three years before *A Vindication*.

However, I do hold the view that Mary Wollstonecraft was *not* alone, that her ideas were formed in a community of women, a community created by the spoken and written word. There is the evidence of the women she knew – Catherine Macaulay, whose work she had read, and Mary Hays, whose friend she was. Apart from writing the six volumes of *Female Biography* (1803), Hays also wrote *Appeal to the Men of Great Britain in Behalf of the Women* (1797), partly as the sequel to *A Vindication* intended by Wollstonecraft, but unwritten at her untimely death. Hays's book was issued anonymously by the same publisher who had published *A Vindication*, 'and it must have been a very small edition, since no copies appear to have survived,' states Claire Tomalin (1977), and if it were not for a review and summary of it in the *Analytical*, 'its contents would be quite lost' (p. 296). (It has since been reprinted, see Luria, 1974.)

There is also the evidence from Wollstonecraft's writing itself. It is primarily personal experience she offers as evidence, it is her experience of the world *as a woman* from which she generalises and which she asserts is representative, and in a male-dominated society where such evidence has little currency, a woman requires support to assert such a view. I suspect that it would be extremely difficult to put such a case clearly and confidently without confirmation from other women. It depends so much on the appreciation that one's personal experience is not idiosyncratic, but shared by other women, and the only way to reach such an understanding is by sharing experience with other women.

Mary Wollstonecraft knew that what she was asserting was outside male experience and she knew what the response was likely to be (although she could not be expected to have predicted the extent to which it would go after Freud added his little bit) and it is difficult to accept that she would have so defiantly asserted the validity of women's personal experience without checking with other women for validation. She was a serious writer, a philosopher, concerned with *reason*, engaged in the (precarious) activity of earning her living as a thinker and critic. Even if she had overcome her doubts about the public response, how could she have overcome her *self-doubts*? This is a problem which plagues women even today as they attempt to describe as 'real' what society – in male hands – has decreed unreal; it is the problem which *still* very often leads women to explain the structural difficulties of oppression in terms of their own inadequacies rather than in terms of the structure.

That Wollstonecraft does understand that what is problematic for men becomes the 'problems' of society, while what is problematic for women remains the responsibility of the individual women, is reflected throughout *A Vindication*, and it is partly her connection between the personal and the political for women, which makes her work so valuable and appropriate today. She confirms the current experience of women in a male-dominated society in a way in which I suspect her own experience had to be confirmed. That women's experience today enjoys little more validity (and possibly even less) than it did then (given the Freudian influence) reveals what it is women share in a male-dominated society.

This is one of the reasons that Wollstonecraft (and Astell, 'Sophia', Murray and Macaulay) devoted so much time to discussing the deficiencies of male reasoning. Mary Wollstonecraft begins *A Vindication* with a 'Dedication' to Talleyrand, and states: 'I am confident you will not throw my work aside, and hastily conclude that I am in the wrong, because you did not view the subject in the same light yourself' (1792, in Kramnick, 1978, p. 85). In doing so, she makes explicit one of the conditions of women's existence – being in the wrong, on the basis of sex, which has been a focus in the work of women such as Virginia Woolf, Simone de Beauvoir and Sheila Rowbotham, this century. 'I plead for my sex, not myself,' adds Wollstonecraft to Talleyrand.

Why is it, asks Wollstonecraft, that men are in a position to decide what is valid and what is not: 'Who made man the exclusive judge', she asks, 'if women partake with him the gift of reason?' (ibid., p. 87). By what authority do men judge what is best for women? Why is it that the term *women's reason* is virtually a derogatory one? Because men are tyrants, men have power, and 'women are excluded without having a voice' (ibid., p. 88), she states. Reason has been 'perplexed and involved in error' (ibid., p. 91) because it is confined to male experience and 'built on partial experience' and on 'narrow views' (ibid., p. 92). 'For man and woman, truth, if I understand the meaning of the word, must be the same', argues Wollstonecraft, and yet the truth which men put forward, in relation to women, has 'no other foundation than utility, and of that utility men pretend arbitrarily to judge, shaping it to their own convenience' (ibid., p. 139).

Men's experience is one of appearing superior, and reason and truth, argues Wollstonecraft, are but tools used by men to bring about and justify that superiority and power. While she demands a return to an absolute truth, not this *false* truth men have propounded for their own purposes (a position which would be difficult to maintain today) there can be no doubt that her analysis of the way men have used the concepts of truth and reason to reinforce their own position as arbiters of truth and reason, is a fundamental part of her protest. Women's experience, which is qualitatively different, which is based on different assumptions, and which therefore can give rise to different truths, is not considered as a serious alternative in a male-dominated society.

This accounts in part for Wollstonecraft's discussion of the masculine woman, a 'hybrid' who breaks and threatens the classification scheme which demands a dividing line, with on one side women, emotion, sentiment and irrationality, and on the other men, reason, logic and truth. While the classification scheme continues and men have a monopoly on reason, then women of reason must have either their womanliness or their reason – or both – called into question – according to male reason!

Wollstonecraft begins in a mocking tone: 'From every quarter have I heard exclamations against masculine women, but where are they to be found? If by this appellation men mean to inveigh against their ardour in hunting, shooting and gaming, I shall most cordially join them in the cry,' she says, indicating that things 'masculine' do not necessarily have positive connotations as men would like us to believe. But then the tone changes, and she adds, 'but if it be against the manly virtues, or more properly speaking, the attainment of those talents and virtues, the exercise of which enables the human character' that men wish to discourage women from acquiring, then they will get no support from the writer, who says 'all those who view them (women) with a philosophic[22] eye must, I should think, wish with me that they may every day grow more and more masculine' (ibid., p. 80).

'Sophia' (1739) had turned around the concepts of *effeminate* and *manly* (see page 103), and Wollstonecraft indulges in a similar twist when she admits the existence of a masculine woman, but then changes the nature of those who qualify. There are women, she says, who 'argue in the same

[22] Where philosophic meant – ideally – impartial, objective, even the forerunner of scientific.

track as a man', who subscribe to male ideas about female inferiority, 'and adopt the sentiments that brutalise them, with all the pertinacity of ignorance'. These are the masculine women who allow their reason to be coopted by men, and use it to burnish rather than snap their chains (1792, in Kramnick, 1978, p. 202).

In order to expose the deficiencies of male reasoning, Wollstonecraft employs the useful device of allowing men to speak for themselves. Chapter Five is entitled 'Animadversions on Some of the Writers who have Rendered Women Objects of Pity, Bordering on Contempt' (ibid., p. 173) and in it Wollstonecraft quotes extensively from the male authorities, and then comments critically and caustically on their case (as Kate Millett was to do 180 years later, in *Sexual Politics*). Rousseau, and his theories on women's education, provide her with some of the best evidence for her analysis of the corruption of power on male reasoning.

'I shall begin with Rousseau, and give a sketch of his character of woman in his own words', she says, 'interspersing comments and reflections. My comments, it is true, will all spring from a few simple principles' (ibid., p. 173), she adds, recognising that it takes only a slight shift to call into doubt the whole belief system constructed by males and in which they appear in a superior light. Wollstonecraft begins where Rousseau begins – with the assumptions about desirable behaviour in women – but, unlike Rousseau, Wollstonecraft questions the origin and nature of these assumptions. 'Woman ought to be weak and passive,' states Rousseau, and from this he then 'infers that she was formed to please and be subject' to man, and that 'it is her duty to render herself *agreeable* to her master – this being the grand end of her existence' (ibid., p. 173). The task of exposing the inadequacies of this particular line of reasoning and of pointing to the 'wishful thinking' contained in it is by no means difficult. One could wonder why the glaring deficiencies were not apparent to a man of such intellectual stature as Rousseau, or indeed why they have not become obvious to the critical educationalists who have continued in the tradition established by Rousseau.

'For this reason', continues Rousseau, 'the education of the woman should be always relative to the men. To please, to be useful to us, to make us love and esteem them, to educate us when young and take care of us when grown up, to advise, to console us, to render our lives easy and agreeable – these are the duties of women at all times, and what they should be taught in their infancy' (ibid., p. 175). Wollstonecraft has chosen her illustrations well (not a difficult exercise, as so many of them abound in Rousseau's writing), and lets Rousseau himself demonstrate how he only defines women in relation to men, how he grants them no other existence apart from serving men's needs; he makes no mention of the way boys should be taught from their infancy to meet the needs of women – on the contrary, he assumes that women have no needs of their own. As Sheila Ruth (1980) has pointed out, the fact that Rousseau's theories of liberty depended upon the enslavement of over half the population has not prevented him from being proclaimed by the rest as the champion of liberty, for, after all, he did represent *liberty* to the male half of humanity, and their error lies – as Wollstonecraft indicated – in assuming that the experience of their *half* equalled the *whole*.

At times one can sense Wollstonecraft's anger as she outlines Rousseau's outrageous case which did, and does, enjoy such favour. In what must be one of the most ridiculous statements made on the subject, Rousseau authoritatively asserts as a male that: 'The first and most important qualification in a woman is good nature or sweetness of temper: formed to obey a being so imperfect as man, often full of vices, and always full of faults, she ought to learn betimes even to suffer injustice, and to bear insults of a husband without complaint; it is not for his sake', says Rousseau deceptively, 'but her own that she should be of a mild disposition' and he proceeds to provide the standard patriarchal explanation for men's violence against women – it is women's fault! 'The perverseness and ill nature of the woman only serve to aggravate their own misfortunes, and the misconduct of their husbands' (1792, in Kramnick, 1978, p. 179–80).

There can be few better examples of the arrogance and absurdity of male explanations for the oppression of women than this one of Rousseau's, singled out by Wollstonecraft. Women must learn to be pleasing, he argues, because it suits men, and if therefore men are not suited the explanation is to be found in terms of women not being sufficiently pleasing, with the result that women deserve any censorious measures men may take against them. If women were to suggest that men's existence should be governed by the whim of women, that men were to have no identity apart from their relationship to women, no needs but the need to serve women, that therefore they must learn to please women, to expect punishment if they fail to do so, and to blame no one other than themselves for their own inadequacies, such advocates would be condemned as irrational, would no doubt be accused of *man-hating*, and certainly of *emasculating* men. But while men make such statements about women, their rationality can be applauded and their woman-hating perceived as perfectly acceptable. The only difference between the two is the *worth* attributed to the sexes in a male-dominated society.

Wollstonecraft has captured the essence of the arguments men use to keep women in the place men want them to be. Unlike Mary Astell, 'Sophia' and Catherine Macaulay, however, she does not always draw out and emphasise the way in which women can be blamed for actions which men commit. At times, she recognises that women are the *scapegoats*, but frequently her refutation of male arguments consists of exposing the fallacies, and the injustices, rather than elaborating on the role women play in exonerating and absolving males in a patriarchal society. She recognises that Rousseau has set up a male *aristocracy* (ibid., p. 185) and has made women slaves, but she is not going to take his advice and be pleasing, passive and polite in the attempt to earn his approval. She declares that she has no intention of being agreeable or of subscribing to his self-interested edicts about women, and men. 'Educate women like men', says Rousseau, and any power they currently have over men, they will lose, for in his view of the world women have no other existence apart from men. 'Stupid man' one can almost hear Wollstonecraft say, as she exposes the fundamental flaw in his argument: 'This is the very point I am at. I do not wish them to have power over men, but over themselves' (ibid., p. 154).

Herein lies the crux of the matter: Wollstonecraft is asserting the autonomy of women, the right of women to define themselves and their world from their own position, and to place men in relation to women. This is a concept that Rousseau (as a representative of mankind) cannot or will not admit. As Adrienne Rich (1981) has suggested, this concept prompts fear among many men, the fear that if women are independent men might be irrelevant. It was a concept that 'Sophia' had not been averse to using, and one that Wollstonecraft implied on occasion.

While men have been in charge of explanations they have consistently argued that because women are not as capable as men of learning, they should be further handicapped by not being given the same opportunities; because they are passive they should be prevented from engaging in activities that might lead to independence, etc. Even in their own terms, this is *false* logic and few have been the feminists who have not identified this particular flaw in male reasoning. If men have any deficiencies this constitutes grounds for 'remedial' action to improve their performance, but if women have 'deficiencies', then, according to men, this constitutes grounds for reinforcing them.[23] This double standard permeates most of the pronouncements made by men on the nature of the sexes and Wollstonecraft systematically exposed its operation.

Wollstonecraft demonstrates how men have made women financially and emotionally dependent, so that marriage for women becomes an economic necessity; it is 'the only way women can rise in the world' (1792, in Kramnick, 1978, p. 83), she says, and when women are without resources, it becomes a matter of urgency to 'rise' and obtain some. But these power relations between the sexes are well camouflaged; women are urged to believe that it is not economic necessity that leads them to marriage, but the promise of fulfilment, the prospect of love, and for this they are prepared to degrade themselves, to cultivate weakness and foolishness which men find attractive in women, and to which they will respond. In words which echo Macaulay's and which are still relevant today, Wollstonecraft says: 'I once knew a weak woman of fashion who was more than commonly proud of her delicacy and sensibility', and who 'thought a distinguishing taste and puny appetite the height of all human perfection' (ibid., p. 130). So many women abuse themselves in this way, argues Wollstonecraft, and like Mary Astell she deplores not only the wastefulness, but the uselessness, for it does *not* lead to the enhancement of their lives. Do women not notice, asks Wollstonecraft, how eager men are to degrade the sex from whom they pretend to receive the chief pleasure in life? (ibid., p. 166). Women are being deceived and she cannot understand why so few of them realise it.

---

[23] This same argument still applies in educational circles today: where boys are thought to have a 'deficiency', remedial education is provided as in remedial reading facilities in Britain and Australia where the students are predominantly male. But when girls are thought to have a deficiency — such as in science, for example — no such remedial facility is provided. Instead it is used to 'prove' that girls cannot do science.

In words which must have sent a shiver of apprehension up the spine of many a man, Wollstonecraft declared 'I wish to persuade women to endeavour to acquire strength, both of mind and body, and to convince them that the soft phrases, susceptibility of heart, delicacy of sentiment and refinement of taste', in short, those attributes which men have deemed necessary as femininity, 'are almost synonymous with the epithets of weakness, and that those beings who are only the objects of pity, and that kind of love which is termed its sister, will soon become objects of contempt' (ibid., pp. 81–2).

In 1970, Broverman et al. carried out a study in which they found that women were only considered normal and acceptable when they acquired the characteristics that men found undesirable for themselves; women had to adopt and adjust to non-prestigious forms of behaviour in order to be perceived as 'healthy' and 'attractive' in a male-dominated society. This is the point that Wollstonecraft made in 1792 – and which Mary Astell had made before her, in 1694.

Why is it that women cannot see the purpose of 'those pretty feminine phrases that men use to soften our slavish dependency'? (1792, in Kramnick, 1978, p. 82) asks Wollstonecraft, for to be flattered by being informed that one is weak and foolish is absurd; it indicates how far women have come to believe in men's images of women at the expense of their own. 'I lament that women are systematically degraded by receiving the trivial attentions which men think it manly to pay to the sex, when in fact, they are insultingly supporting their own superiority' (ibid., p. 147).

Wollstonecraft lists all the qualities men think desirable in a woman (making use of Rousseau, in this respect), from passivity, weakness, lassitude and dependency to frivolity, a fondness for dress, and a dislike of serious purpose, and declares that if such qualities are indeed *natural*, then women could simply be left alone to allow them to unfold. But this is not the case; on the contrary, women are subjected to rigid discipline in order that these qualities can be cultivated. Wollstonecraft knows this – and Rousseau and other men do not – for this is her own *lived* experience as a female, reared in a male-dominated society. Against male 'beliefs' she asserts the full weight of her own personal concrete experience and says, 'I have, probably, had an opportunity of observing more girls in their infancy than J. J. Rousseau' (whose own children, incidentally, were sent to a foundling home), and 'I can recollect my own feelings'. They lead her to very different conclusions, for what may appear to an 'outsider' as natural, effortless behaviour, is for women, Wollstonecraft states emphatically, something which must be *acquired*, and which entails a considerable struggle. 'I will venture to affirm', she says, generalising from her own childhood and her observations of girls, 'that a girl whose spirits have not been damped by inactivity, or innocence tainted by false shame, will always be a romp and the doll will never invite attention unless confinement allows her no alternative' (ibid., p. 129).

To argue in this way was to challenge the deeply entrenched beliefs that nature was divinely ordained, and like Murray and Macaulay before her – and Gage, Stanton and Daly after her – Wollstonecraft was prepared to examine the 'religious myths' that were used to justify women's subordination. She looks at the story of creation and declares it poetic. No one who 'bestowed any serious thought on the subject ever supposed that Eve was, literally speaking, one of Adam's ribs', argues Wollstonecraft, and such 'a deduction must be allowed to fall to the ground, or only be so far admitted as it proves that man, from the remotest antiquity, found it convenient to exert his strength to subjugate his companion, and his invention to show that she ought to have her neck bent under the yoke, because the whole creation was only created for his convenience or pleasure' (ibid., p. 109).

These are daring and defiant words: Wollstonecraft is committing the most serious of sins in a patriarchal society – she is correcting men in public, she is exposing their limitations in an area in which they have great pride in their authority and achievement – that of *logic*. She is showing them to be governed by self-interest; to be base, not noble. In short, she strips them of their 'superiority' and leaves them standing naked and vulnerable. Predictably, men would hit back and make every effort to regain their status and strength, and predictably (particularly if Wollstonecraft's analysis has substance), many women, in general, would help them in their task.

It is possible to continue outlining the feminist frame of reference which Wollstonecraft helped to codify: numerous books could be written on *her* work – as books are written of course, on *male* philosophers and thinkers of note – and it is significant that so little reference is made to Wollstonecraft's arguments and ideas in contemporary feminist literature. But it is perhaps understandable that many women have been discouraged from studying her work when almost without exception *A Vindication* is described as poorly written, rambling, difficult to read. (The exception is Kurtz and Autrey, 1937, who in *Four New Letters of Mary Wollstonecraft and Helen M. Williams* say of *A Vindication* that it 'remains today one of the sanest and best written documents in the feministic movement. In reality a plea for the economic independence of women and for an equal education of the sexes by the State, its plain language in attacking the assumption that woman is the plaything and solace of man produced a furor of criticism. The author at one bound achieved celebrity on both sides of the Atlantic. Her book and her character became a subject of both extreme commendation and fascinated objurgation' (pp. 23–4).)

This stands in marked contrast to most other assessments of Wollstonecraft's work. Josephine Kamm (1966) for example, in one of her three references to Wollstonecraft, states that *A Vindication* is a 'rambling book which shows every mark of having been hurriedly put together. . . . *The Vindication*, like its author, is flamboyant, passionate and sentimental' (p. 19) and in one of the other references, that John Stuart Mill's theme in the 'famous' *The Subjection of Women* (1869) 'resembles Mary Wollstonecraft's *Vindication*; but Mill expressed it with less heat and superior clarity and logic' (p. 29). Edna Nixon (1971) says: 'Her book is not well planned. She reiterates her arguments without strengthening them, suddenly returning on her steps to insist on some point which previously she had not sufficiently stressed' (p. 97), and Claire Tomalin (1977) says the 'book is without any logical structure' (p. 136). Miriam Kramnick (1978) states that: 'Too many have apologized for the style and lack of coherent organization in the *Vindication*. It doesn't seem important any longer, since what she had to say was clear enough' (p. 41). In part, I agree, what she had to say *was* perfectly clear, but I cannot accept that the issues about the way she said it are not important, for this typifies the way women's ideas are discredited and dismissed.[24]

The grounds are impossible to substantiate (see earlier discussion on Claire Tomalin's assessment of Wollstonecraft's lack of logic, page 91) but very difficult to refute, yet substantiation is rarely called for and refutation almost always is. This is one of the most commonly used techniques for maintaining and reinforcing the myth that women are not intellectually competent and it is a myth which must be dislodged if women are not to defer to men.

To be sure, Wollstonecraft's style was *different*, deliberately so, but it is crucial that feminists do not accept the patriarchal classification scheme that ordains that women's *differences* constitute their *deficiency*. Kramnick states that *A Vindication* 'was written hastily in six weeks' and what might be construed as a sign of genius in man becomes a reason for failure in women for there 'are many digressions in the text, with the arguments turning suddenly from one subject to another' (1978, p. 41). But, adds Kramnick, 'Wollstonecraft would probably have been somewhat defensive about her digressions . . . for she says in Chapter 2, when a train of thought invited her to digress on standing armies, that she would follow the associations that sprang to mind, as if, we may assume, they were some kind of emanation from the well springs of a natural order' (ibid., p. 41). In Wollstonecraft? Whose whole argument is based on questioning the natural order?

Why, when it would be just as easy to argue that Wollstonecraft's book constitutes a logical, coherent, well-presented and highly readable argument – and I am convinced that it would be relatively easy to present such a case, particularly after having been initiated into the skills of literary criticism and having practised them on so many of the masters – why, argue *against* Wollstonecraft? I am *not* suggesting that her book is a perfect model which should be emulated, only that a case could be made *for or against* her literary skills, and that it is almost always made *against*.

My own personal experience will not permit me to accept as fair or just some of the criticisms that are levelled (often by feminists) at Wollstonecraft, because they so closely resemble the criticisms that are made of contemporary feminist writers and thinkers who do not follow the established conventions. Conventions are but man-made agreements, they are not sacred nor are they absolute. Be they conventions of style, order, argumentation, they are limited, and it could be because they have their

---

[24] The modern counterpart, familiar I am sure to most feminists, takes the form of 'I agree that your argument is sound but you *spoil* it by your presentation – i.e. too emotional, irrational, man-hating, humourless'. It is an excuse for not dealing with the ideas.

origins in male subjectivity (a point made more recently by Virginia Woolf and Adrienne Rich) that feminists find them overly constraining, and elect to dispense with them. But when conventions are not followed by women, it is almost always assumed that it is because they are incapable – that they do not come up to standard – rather than that they may be seeking to find new forms for expressing their ideas – developing standards of their own.

It seems to me quite reasonable that Mary Wollstonecraft, who was insisting on the validity of personal experience, should argue that if her ideas did not conform to conventional patterns of arrangement, she would not apologise. Many feminist writers today – myself included – will *not* apologise for their 'departures from the norm'. But why should this not be seen as *innovative*? Why should it be a weakness about which we are defensive?

It is very depressing to read the assessments of Mary Wollstonecraft's contribution, because she has been so consistently devalued by feminists and non-feminists. Berenice Carroll (1981) has documented the way women's ideas are negated, and one woman, unfortunately, makes use of most of them in relation to Mary Wollstonecraft. According to (she who will remain anonymous) Wollstonecraft is 'unreliable' because of her exaggeration; she hands out 'excessive praise' to Catherine Macaulay; she is not sufficiently circumspect and objective. 'Given to exaggeration as it was' says Anon. of *A Vindication*, 'by taking exceptional abuses as though they typified the experience of all women, it had rhetorical power and persuasiveness'. Women are cast in the role of popularisers and publicists, according to Carroll, given little credit for their insights and rarely deemed to have engaged in any arduous process in arriving at them, and this is the way Anon. treats Wollstonecraft. 'There is no gradual build-up of either argument or feeling. Ideas, like people, are the objects of spontaneous enthusiasms in the life of Mary Wollstonecraft: the rights of man, the rights of woman, the French revolutionary cause were ideas spontaneously and enthusiastically accepted with much the same immediacy as persons, whether Fanny Blood, the Clares, Tom Paine, or Gilbert Imlay and William Godwin.' I am sure Mary Wollstonecraft would have objected to this portrayal just as much as I do. It suggests that she is flighty, effusive, without the desire or the capacity to engage in serious intellectual activities, and the fact that such a perception of woman persists – in the face of enormous evidence to the contrary and after so many hundreds of years – indicates how limited is the distance we have travelled since Mary Astell, 'Sophia' and Mary Wollstonecraft asserted that women were intellectual beings, and were not accepted as such because it was in the interest of men to deny them this standing.

There are countless subtle ways in which women are devalued. One way, guaranteed to light the fire of my own anger (and to lead to damaging consequences for the book concerned) is to open a book ostensibly devoted to a woman and to find that it is concerned with the role played by a man. Such men are usually so supportive, encouraging, and helpful in the way that they assist women to form their ideas and live their lives, and the reader is left with the distinct impression that the woman *would have been nothing without him* and that *lucky she was to get him*. I am heartily sick of the good, self-sacrificing William Godwin (among others) who, it must be remembered, when he first met Mary Wollstonecraft 'records that he had not read any of her work, and that he found her insistence on talking when he wanted to listen to Paine irritating' (Tomalin, 1977, p. 131); and who was married to her for but a few months. But Alice Rossi does spend a considerable time talking about Godwin, in her discussion of Wollstone-craft, and also chooses to quote from Ralph Wardle (1951) and on the topic of Wollstonecraft's (unfortunate) influence on Godwin! 'As Wardle put it', she says, ' "though he was a better man for having been Mary's husband, he was a worse philosopher" ' (Wardle, 1951, p. 323, quoted in Rossi, 1974, p. 38). What does Wardle mean, and how does he know, and why does Rossi choose to include this unsubstantiated and grossly deni-grating comment?

So many of these comments have their origin in a male frame of reference which flatters the male and assumes the universality of male experience, and, while women function within this framework, it is almost inevitable that we will simply generate more information about women in terms that are acceptable to men, and which do little to establish the autonomous and positive nature of women. For example, quite a few of Wollstonecraft's critics have noted that she was the first person to apply the phrase *legal prostitution* to marriage (Tomalin, 1977, p. 137), that she saw wife and prostitute as equally oppressed, and tried to work out the connection between the two (Margaret Walters, 1976), that she recognised that selling their bodies was a form of *work*, for women, and that: 'Necess-ity never makes prostitution the business of men's lives' (Wollstonecraft, in Kramnick, 1978, p. 165). But this woman-centred conceptualisation of women's work and women's pay, developed more recently by Adrienne Rich (1981) and Lisa Leghorn and Kathy Parker (1981), is again criticised for its failure to conform to the conventions of economics as formulated by men, rather than praised for its achievement in making women's ex-perience central and legitimate. The suggestion that Mary Wollstonecraft did not analyse the economic basis of society is not an uncommon one, but it is an inaccurate one. What should be said is that *she did not use the economic framework constructed by men*, which explains their own behav-iour and from which women's work and pay were, and still are, excluded, but instead constructed an economic framework for women, in which the relationship between women's sexuality and financial remuneration is ex-plored. To Mary Wollstonecraft, prostitution *in* and *out* of marriage was work, and work which was forced upon women as a means of obtaining the necessary financial resources for survival. It was not asylums that were required for fallen women, nor generosity and goodwill from husbands, if women's needs were to be met, she argued: 'It is justice, not charity that is wanting in the world' (Wollstonecraft, in Kramnick, 1978, p. 165).

It was male power which for Wollstonecraft was the root cause of all the many problems. Margaret Walters (1976) says of her that she had real insight into the nature of sexual oppression and she saw that 'sexual relations are power relations, each partner manouvering for advantage'

(p. 319), an understanding which *still* has not undermined the belief in 'romantic love'. At almost every point at which women's experience departs from male prescriptions, Wollstonecraft discerns the nature of the issue and insists that 'the oppression of women is personally experienced, that their protest springs out of a deep personal sense of injustice and wrong', says Walters (ibid., p. 306) and her stance is both significant and challenging. Wollstonecraft urges women to adopt one of the strategies most threatening to patriarchy – to articulate and validate their different personal experience, to do away with their deference, politeness and silence which is so pleasing to men and so useful. 'Women must talk for themselves, tell their own life stories, however absurd and trivial they may seem to men ... (or however dangerous). ... It is only by articulating their denied feelings, their wrongs, they will find the strength to protest,' says Margaret Walters (ibid., p. 328), summarising Wollstonecraft's appeal. It is only by insisting on the validity of what men neither know nor understand that women will come to gain their full rights; so it was with Wollstonecraft – so it is today.

It was not her recommendations for a system of national, equal, co-education, or even her argument that an educated woman is a better wife and mother (and these were and are still good arguments which are useful on occasion), which a male-dominated society found so offensive. It was not her style – personal or literary – which posed a real threat, although both could be readily used against her. It was the fact that she disputed male authority, that she was unimpressed by the intellectual machinations of a male-dominated society, that she saw through male ruses and insisted on being visible, on presenting the evidence they so conveniently omitted, that constituted her offence. She demonstrated her intellectual competence; she denied the existence she had been allocated; she refused to conform to the image she was supposed to find natural, and even called into question the man-made definition of natural. She generated a great deal of knowledge which men sought to 'lose' as soon as possible – and that is why she was personally attacked.

Because of the way the dominant sex has structured the world, women who are not deceived by men's explanations, who persist in articulating the limitations of those explanations in a way not accessible to many men, are not accepted as starting with different assumptions and constructing an equally valid but different world view; they are seen as an abomination.

What is often not appreciated is that in Wollstonecraft's own time there were many who applauded and celebrated her work. Anna Seward thought it was 'wonderful. ... It has, by turns, pleased and displeased, startled and half-convinced me that its author is oftener right than wrong' (quoted in Sunstein, 1975, p. 215). Sunstein adds: 'As conventional a young woman as Maria Holroyd wrote her aunt that she not only had read Mme. Roland's *Vie* without being tarnished, but added, "I should like you also to read Mrs Wollstonecraft's *Vindication of the Rights of Woman*. There are many sensible and just observations." A thoughtful American girl, Elizabeth Drinker, noted in her diary that she thought Mary Wollstonecraft "a prodigious writer. In many of her sentiments, she ... *speaks my mind,* in some others I do not altogether coincide with her – I am not for quite so much independence." Aaron Burr heartily agreed with the book, and adapted his daughter's education to its principles. Many progressive intellectuals and writers were deeply interested' (ibid.). We are not familiar with such praise, although few people who have heard of Mary Wollstonecraft have not heard that Horace Walpole described her as a 'hyena in petticoats' or that Hannah More said her book was ridiculous.

Miriam Kramnick (1978) is one of the few commentators on Wollstonecraft who outlines the nature of the ridicule she was subjected to and the significance of this form of sexual harassment. Wollstonecraft was the recipient of 'barely printable insults', states Kramnick. 'Her own contemporaries called her a shameless wanton, a "hyena in petticoats", a "philosophizing serpent" or wrote jibing epigrams in the *Anti-Jacobin Review*, like

> For Mary verily would wear the breeches
> God help poor silly men for such usurping b------s

Twentieth-century readers have called her an archetypal castrating female, "God's angry woman", a man hater whose feminist crusade was inspired by nothing more than a hopeless, incurable affliction – penis envy' (ibid., p. 7).

Even feminists have been careful about associating with her and: 'The name "Wollstonecraft", once considered synonymous with the destruction of all sacred virtues, disowned by the feminist movement as it marched for votes or pressed for admission to universities, became an obscure reference indeed' (ibid., p. 8). When women sought to convince men that they were honourable, respectable, and deserving of equal representation in the institutions men had created for themselves, there was little room for Wollstonecraft, who had challenged those institutions and who had gained a 'reputation'.

Like many of the reviews of Aphra Behn, some of the reviews of Wollstonecraft's work and life, on her death, were vicious. Her work should be read, declared the *Historical Magazine* (1799), 'with disgust by any female who has any pretensions to delicacy; with detestation by everyone attached to the interests of religion and morality, and with indignation by anyone who might feel any regard for the unhappy woman, whose frailties should have been buried in oblivion' (vol. I, p. 34). This was about as far as critics could go in the pre-Freudian days, but once he had made his priceless contribution, the attack on women who did not conform to the precepts dictated by men assumed a new and greater ferocity.

'Mary Wollstonecraft was an extreme neurotic of a compulsive type,' argue Ferdinand Lundberg and Marynia Farnham (1959) in *Modern Woman: The Lost Sex*. 'Out of her illness arose the ideology of feminism, which was to express the feelings of so many women in years to come. Unconsciously . . . Mary and the feminists wanted . . . to turn on men and injure them. . . . Underneath her aggressive writings, Mary was a masochist like her mother, as indeed all the leading feminist theorists were in fact.

. . . By behaving as she did Mary indicated . . . that she was unconsciously seeking to deprive the male of his power, to castrate him. . . . It came out . . . in her round scolding of men. The feminists have ever since symbolically slain their fathers by verbally consigning all men to perdition as monsters' (pp. 159–61). Really?

With the framework formulated by Freud, it again became easy to ridicule and harass women who developed any analysis of patriarchy, to dismiss them without having to refute their ideas. The scientific dogma took over from the religious dogma which had been seriously discredited (by women like Wollstonecraft) and both these male-decreed belief systems have been used ruthlessly against individual women and against women collectively. In her own day Mary Wollstonecraft was maligned for her moral sickness; with the advent of Freud it was her mental sickness. The principle is the same and it was a principle that Wollstonecraft herself identified and discredited – the principle that if women do not *cheerfully* confine themselves to the place to which men have relegated them, then there is something wrong with the women rather than the place they are expected to occupy. Mary Wollstonecraft understood that women would continue to be perceived as abnormal while the limited experience of men was treated as the sum total of human experience. One of her main protests was that men did not know how the world looked to women and, while they insisted that it looked no different from the way it looked to men, women were without space to discuss, share and confirm their feelings and ideas. And in this, Wollstonecraft is one of a long line of women who have come to understand the significance of male power to name the world and to say what is and what is not important, valuable, and 'logical'.

Wollstonecraft used Rousseau to demonstrate the inadequacies of the assumptions with which males began; had she lived this century, she could have used Freud. There are many reasons for suspecting that men will continue to create frames of reference in which women are held responsible for the ills of the world which men control, as the need arises. There are many reasons for suspecting that such a need is making its presence felt at the moment – not just because of the mindlessness and stupidity which characterises the current state of affairs, but because feminists today, like Mary Wollstonecraft and many other women of yesterday, are exposing those absurdities. The women's movement today is not as strong as it was earlier this century, and we have no grounds for believing that our gains are any more permanent. What we do know, however, and should constantly keep in mind, is that men can always use their inventive logic to find new and increasingly more sophisticated means of discrediting our protest and damning us and our ideas. We have not established our claim as intellectual, thinking, rational, responsible and authoritative beings – despite Wollstonecraft's pleas and documentation – and we are therefore, very vulnerable.

PART TWO

1800-1850
THE SILENT YEARS?

In some ways Mary Wollstonecraft marks the turning point, not the beginning, of a particular feminist tradition, a tradition of the 'disagreeable' woman – that is, a woman who will not try and gain a hearing by being agreeable to men. While we know more about more nineteenth-century, women involved in the movement for women's liberation and their claims for intellectual, social and political rights, there is often a greater emphasis on directing their arguments towards men (particularly towards the end of the nineteenth century), with all the inherent limitations this implies, for not only were there many things men could not or did not want to hear, there were also many forms in which they did not want to hear them!

This move is understandable. Men held all the power (so they said) and, short of a full-scale revolution – a most unlikely eventuality then or now – one of the most sensible strategies was to convince men (a) that they were being unjust, and (b) that women were worthy of a share in their institutions which they had, until then, reserved for themselves. If one believes that the emancipation of women could have been achieved in one 'short, sharp, burst', then the activities of many of the women during the nineteenth century could be viewed as time-consuming, and not particularly effective. But again, before making such an assessment we should look more closely at our own assumptions, at the framework we are using to make sense of the world, at the origins, and purposes of our value system. Many contemporary feminists are extremely suspicious of the assumption that change is accomplished by revolutionary activity: not only do they suspect that this may be an explanation which arises from male experience of the world and which has been used to justify and explain male behaviour, past and present, they also think it destructive and not a very effective method of procuring change.

Elizabeth Sarah (1980), for example, talks of *ejaculatory politics* as a means of labelling men's understanding about change, and suggests that women are not concerned with change based on the premise that 'might is right' but on gaining consensus. She suggests that women are more concerned with *consciousness,* with developing collective understandings (partly because of their experience in developing and maintaining social relations which helps them to understand how human beings change, and what sort of change is enduring). Women are much less likely to *impose* their ideas, partly because they have the experience (often gained through child-rearing or other inter-personal relationships) that this can be counterproductive. (Ruth Platt, forthcoming, also looks at this issue in her account of women's collectives.)

Certainly women placed great faith in the potential of education to bring about enduring and englightening change and it may be that to evaluate the nineteenth-century women's movement pejoratively as a reform movement is to evaluate it according to a male-defined standard (which not coincidentally discredits it); it might be more productive to assess the movement in terms of women's 'standards'. Although I can appreciate the sense of impatience which goes with seeing how long it has taken women to move men so little, I can also appreciate that I have inherited the positive results of many of those reforms. Women may still not be recognised as intellectually competent, one woman may still not equal one man in our current society in which men hold power and in which they engage in all manner of tricks to keep it that way, but I prefer to challenge their monopoly from the basis of technically available rights to equal education, employment, political participation, divorce, etc. We owe much to the nineteenth-century women even if at times we prefer not to look too closely at some of their 'explanations' (Caroline Norton, for example, being a case in point). It is not whether 'revolution' or 'reform'; as we know them in a patriarchal context, are desirable – it is what is of assistance to women in both the long and the short term.

It is my personal preference which leads me to wish that there had been a few more women of the disagreeable sort in the nineteenth century, but I am mindful of the fact that in relative terms many of the women who fought for women's rights during the Victorian period were probably every bit as disagreeable as many of those before or after them. Barbara Charlseworth Gelpi (1981) provides chilling documentation of the restrictions under which girls were reared and of the rigid rules which bounded their lives, and confined to the same extent no doubt Lady Mary Wortley Montagu and Mary Wollstonecraft would have become a little more polite and deferential in overall terms, while still appearing outrageous in their own.

While men continued to distort and discredit the women and their efforts for liberation during this century, women also played a part, and not just by condemning the feminists. Reading through some of the biographies written during the nineteenth century by women on other women can become a most laborious task for one like myself who admires the disagreeable woman, for repeatedly their biographers have tried to 'compensate' for any offence their subjects might have given and to present them in a 'flatteringly feminine' light. Catherine Birney's (1885) biography of Angelina and Sarah Grimké is of this ilk, as is Mrs Fenwick Miller's (1884) of Harriet Martineau. While it makes a change to have their 'womanliness' praised, rather than their 'manliness' condemned, it is at times no less distorting, and in a patriarchal world, ultimately no less discrediting: they are women and damned either way. This, however, is also part of our heritage.

1 Frances Wright (1795–1852)

One woman who did continue in Mary Wollstonecraft's disagreeable trad-ition, who flaunted just about every precept laid down for desirable and decorous behaviour in women, and whose biographers have not added a feminine 'veneer' to her life (partly because there is a notable absence of biographers) is Frances Wright. Born in Dundee, Scotland, two years before Mary Wollstonecraft's death, she and her name became associated with a number of outrageous activities.

The second child in a prosperous family, Frances Wright was orphaned at an early age and she and her sister Camilla were reared by a most conservative and un-liberal aunt; they also spent some time with their great-uncle, James Milne, professor of moral philosophy at Glasgow Col-lege and he and the college library are given the credit for Wright's edu-cation. Evidently Frances Wright was quite rebellious even at an early age and as soon as she was no longer subject to legal guardianship, she and her sister set sail for America (1818), which had always held considerable fascination for her. From her early travels she wrote *Views of Society and Manners in America* (1821) which is in many respects an endorsement of most things American, and, while she feels that the position of women in America is better than it is for women in Europe, she indicates her concern for women – and for all forms of oppression – and gives promise of the radicalism that is to come.

Already she was aware of the nature of power and its consequences and stated: 'The lords of creation receive innumerable, incalculable advan-tages from the hand of nature, and it must be admitted that they everywhere take sufficient care to foster the advantages with which they are endowed' and, she added: 'Love of power . . . is . . . more peculiarly the sin of little than of great minds.' For those who might disagree, she states: 'In what consists the greatness of a despot? In his own intrinsic merits? No, in the degradation of the multitude who surround him' (Wright, in Rossi, 1974, pp. 105–6).

Wright does not need to be told what the objections are to her argu-ment – she anticipates them: ' "But what," I hear you ask, "has this to do with the condition of women? Do you mean to compare men collectively to the despot . . .?" Why not? The vanity of the despot . . . is fed by the folly of their fellow men, and so is that of their sex collectively soothed by the dependence of women; it pleases them better to find their companion a fragile vine, clinging to their firm trunk for support, than a vigorous tree with whose branches they may mingle theirs' (ibid., p. 106).

After the publication of this book, which Alice Rossi states 'was her passport out of obscurity to some considerable public attention' (ibid., p. 89), Wright came to the notice of influential people – Whigs who were delighted with her enthusiasm for America and Tories who were angered by her disparagement of England – and even secured the admiration of General Lafayette. At this stage of her life she had done little to invite condemnation – Catherine Macaulay had even set a precedent for Wright's behaviour in many respects – but as Macaulay's 'personal life' was called into question, so too was Wright's in relation to Lafayette. She spent much time at his home and acted as a courier for him between Paris and England (1821–3), and Rossi devotes considerable space in her discussion of Wright (one of the few reasonably available discussions which still exists) to her unorthodox relationship with Lafayette, which was evidently a matter of some discomfort to his family. 'The complex friendship was clearly modeled on a tender and intellectually stimulating father-daughter relationship', states Rossi, 'yet there were at least undertones, perhaps unclear to the two partners, that suggested something more than paternal and filial tenderness' (ibid., p. 90).

I do not think such (Freudian) innuendo necessary: it serves no useful feminist purpose – although clearly it serves a patriarchal one! I would prefer to know more about Fanny Wright's *reading* habits, and the intellectual circles in which she moved, given the range and radicalism of her later ideas. But – and it becomes wearyingly monotonous – this is not the only way in which her almost incredible contribution has been called into question.

In 1824 Frances Wright returned to America and was no longer quite so enthusiastic; she saw it almost with new eyes and began to formulate sweeping criticisms of American society and to advocate both a revolution of ideas and a reform of social arrangements. Her concept of *oppression* was applied to the powerless – across the categories of race, sex and class – and it was *all* forms of oppression that she claimed should cease in this new country which had the potential for creating equal human beings, but which was in practice creating rulers and the ruled. She emphasised the discrepancy between the ideology and the reality.

One form of oppression which Wright would not close her eyes to was that of slavery. In what must be one of the greatest understatements, Miriam Gurko (1976) summarises the role Wright played in demonstrating the way in which the problem might be dealt with, when she 'bought a large number of slaves and about two thousand acres of land near Memphis, Tennessee. There she set up a colony called Nashoba where she hoped to prepare the slaves for living as free men (sic). But the colony soon expanded its aims, tried to accomplish too much and eventually failed' (p. 32).

To evaluate Wright and her work in this way may be perfectly consistent with the image of women in a male-dominated society, but not consistent with the context in which Wright was functioning. Strictly speaking, some of these bare bones are accurate enough but they camouflage the courage – and the obstacles. 'Two decades before the sermons and the public lectures of modern abolitionists' (Rossi, 1974, p. 99), Wright gave vent to her repugnance of slavery and conceived of practical measures aimed at overcoming some of its more horrendous abuses. She believed that it would be irresponsible to free slaves without helping them to cope in the 'free market' and it was for this reason she purchased them, and the land, and began the co-operative community geared to preparing them for economic independence.

Her efforts in this regard have been discredited. The opinion of Frances Trollope is usually cited to substantiate the allegation that Wright was irresponsible in her undertaking. Significantly (as is too often the case when women criticise other women), little effort seems to have been made to establish the reliability of Frances Trollope's indictment of Wright. Frances Trollope left England to find suitable employment in America for her son, and was enthused by the prospect of Nashoba – although Wright tried to dissuade her and suggested that she might not find the place to her liking. Frances Trollope, however, remained undaunted and, according to her biographer Johanna Johnston (1979), although she was given descriptions of Nashoba, 'erected a little English village in her imagination' (p. 84). She was therefore quite devastated when she encountered the colonial reality.

For someone who found the American habit of spitting almost more than she could bear, who was distressed by the custom of dining publicly in hotels instead of in one's room, in private, who deplored the lack of civilised conversation at such dinners, and who was disquietened by the practice of finding her manservant seated not only at the same hotel dining table but 'as close to the head of the table as she was' (ibid., p. 81), it is hardly surprising that the primitive colonial existence – be it Nashoba or anywhere else – should have proved to be traumatic. But it seems a bit much to blame Frances Wright for the climate, the malaria, the failure of the planted crops to grow, the unfinished buildings, the moral laxity, the difficulty of communications, and the fact that 'since she was a publicist and a reformer at this period, the pitiful little effort at Nashoba was widely known from her writings and was thought to be far more successful than it actually was' (Rossi, 1974, p. 92).

Again we are confronted with a woman's apparent ineptitude: she was over-enthusiastic, she exaggerated, she was a publicist and a reformer (as distinct from a visionary and responsible human being who attempted to put into practice some of her own plans which might help to ameliorate some of the problems for some slaves and serve as an example). We have an eye-witness account of Wright's 'incompetence' from Frances Trollope – yet, ten years later when Harriet Martineau also visited America, Frances Trollope represented for her precisely the model she did *not* want: 'She had been forewarned by the example of Frances Trollope's *Domestic Manners of the Americans*', Valerie Pichanick (1980), her biographer, states, who 'was proud rather than critical of her own country, and she regarded with impatience any deviation from the standards and morals to which she was accustomed. . . . Mrs Trollope was unwilling to adapt to the conditions of the country' (p. 75). But Mrs Trollope's assessment of Nashoba is used against Frances Wright.

How readily are the 'deficiencies' of women constructed without reference to the reliability of the records, or acknowledgement of the enormous bias against women. In the case of Nashoba, I have not seen it mentioned that most co-operative ventures – past or present and on a small or large scale – have been abandoned. Wright is condemned for the collapse rather than commended for the commitment.

Nashoba was not the only venture Wright engaged in; she also undertook a series of public lectures – at a time when this was a disgraceful thing to do – and on topics that were unlikely to win friends in high places.

Stanton, Anthony and Gage (1881, Vol. I) have acknowledged the contribution she made in this respect: 'Her radical ideas on theology, slavery and the social degradation of women, now generally accepted by the best minds of the age, were then denounced by both press and pulpit, and maintained by her at the risk of her life' (p. 35).

Wright – vehemently – attacked slave-holders, legislators and the clergy, classifying them all as a ruling elite imposing their own self-interest on others. She was strongly supportive of the working-class struggle (to the extent that the workingmen's movement of the 1820s which evolved into a political party 'was often referred to as the Fanny Wright Party', Rossi, 1974, p. 99). With Robert Dale Owen, she edited a newspaper 'in his Utopian colony of New Harmony in the Indiana frontier country: later they were joint publishers and editors of the *Free Enquirer* in New York' (Eleanor Flexner, 1979, p. 27).

Miriam Gurko (1976) says that: 'It was as a lecturer – a female lecturer – that Fanny Wright made her greatest impact on the United States. She was the first woman to speak in public here, and this as much as her radical ideas created a sensation' (p. 32). In outlining the topics that Wright dealt with, Gurko says they were 'daring' and included 'equality for women, emancipation for slaves, the political rights of workingmen, free religious inquiry, free public education for everyone, regardless of sex, race, or economic status. She even advocated birth control and equal treatment of illegitimate children. These topics drew large audiences, both male and female, but aroused immense hostility. . . . She was denounced as a "red harlot", a "Fallen and degraded fair one," a "disgusting exhibition of female impudence." She was accused of the twin horrors of atheism and free love . . .' (ibid., p. 33).

As Eleanor Flexner (1979) says, Fanny Wright's ideas were 'strong meat' and the easiest way to dispose of them – and Fanny Wright – was to fall back on accusations of atheism and free love: 'her reputation became such that later woman's rights advocates were tagged "Fanny Wrightists" as the worst kind of abuse' (p. 27).

Fanny Wright might have made an impression on society, but it must not be forgotten that there is a big price to pay for being disagreeable, and society's recriminations and abuse also made an impression on her. 'In speaking of her persecutions she said: "The injury and inconvenience of every kind and every hour to which, in these days, a really consistent reformer stands exposed, none can conceive but those who experience them. Such become, as it were, excommunicated, after the fashion of the old Catholic Mother Church, removed even from the protection of law, such as it is, and from the sympathy of society, for whose sake they consent to be crucified" ' (Stanton et al., 1881, p. 36). Fanny Wright was a very serious and very courageous woman: any other portrayal of her is purely patriarchal (see Perkins and Wolfson, 1939).

There are many ways in which I see Frances Wright as one of the founding mothers of *women's studies* for, while she does not use the same terms we use today, she recognises that women are *invisible* in encoded knowledge, that they simply cannot be *added on,* that women must participate in the construction of knowledge and not be the mere recipients of knowledge encoded by men and which serves men's interest. Her term was *free enquiry*, but the phenomenon she was describing is the one often being addressed in women's studies today.

During her second visit to America, Wright surreptitiously secured an old Methodist church hall which she renamed the 'Hall of Science' and in which many public lectures were given – including her own. Here the emphasis was on free enquiry, on examining the source of ideas and beliefs, on discerning the assumptions on which knowledge was based, on examining the way in which it was used. She firmly believed that all human beings could be *knowledgeable* (a most radical idea) and that it was necessary to test and forge personally credible – and useful – knowledge. Her ideas translate readily into the theoretical framework for contemporary women's studies.

Wright recognised that knowledge was power, and that ruling elites used knowledge to strengthen their power: men 'come selfishly and not generously to the tree of knowledge,' she states. 'They eat but care not to impart of the fruit to others,' and, she asserts there will be no *just* knowledge until both sexes can engage equally in the work of enquiry (Wright in Rossi, 1974, p. 109). 'Do not the rich command instruction?' she asks, and 'they who have instruction, must they not possess the power? and when they have the power, will they not exert it in their own favour? I will ask more I will ask *do* they not exert it in their own favor?' (ibid., p. 110).

'There is a vulgar persuasion', says Wright, 'that the ignorance of women, by favoring their subordination, ensures their utility' (ibid., p. 115) and then she proceeds to demonstrate the origin of such a 'persuasion', how it could only be put forward by those to whom it does not apply, and how destructive and wasteful such a belief is. Women, she acknowledges, have been the victims of this persuasion, they have come to accept their own subordination, instead of examining it in the spirit of free enquiry. She urges her audience to action: 'Go, then! and remove the evil first from the minds of women, then from their condition, and then from your laws' (ibid., p. 115). *Consciousness* comes first in Wright's list of priorities: she wants all women to begin with *themselves* – not men – and to analyse what we know, how we know it and whether we should begin to know very different things.

For Wright one of the greatest evils in society was that of the ethic of competition, and she argued that knowledge was used for *competitive* purposes rather than to explain and improve the world. Men acquired knowledge, she stated, in much the same way as Virginia Woolf was to do one hundred years later, for its 'trimmings', its status, for the edge it gave them over others. This form of knowledge was not what she wanted for the oppressed: she mocked much of the knowledge men had made and said, 'all the branches of knowledge, involved in what is called scholastic learning, are wrapped in fogs of pompous pedantry' (ibid., p. 116) and are of little use to women. In words which have not lost their resounding ring, Wright urges the oppressed to 'break our mental leading strings' (ibid., p. 117) and to examine closely where our ideas come from, and why it is we know what we know. She advocates that we be suspicious of what we have learnt about ourselves and our society and her words of wisdom would be appropriate introduction in any women's studies classroom today.

It is not possible to do justice to the range and richness of her ideas, which were radical then and in many cases remain so today. She tackled almost every question that has been raised in the last ten years in feminist circles, and, unlike some of the women who followed her in the nineteenth century, she was not silent on issues of sexuality; she made the links between women's sexuality and money. (One criticism Frances Trollope made of Wright and Nashoba was in relation to the moral laxity of the place.)

In 1831, Frances Wright returned to Paris, and married Philquepal D'Arusement, and there are a few references to her inadequacy as a wife. Evidently, she continued to travel and to lecture to support her family, while her husband took charge of their daughter. She was left an inheritance (which removed the need for travelling and lecturing) over which she retained control and it appears that her husband attempted to contest this.

There is no shortage of derogatory references to Frances Wright. They vary from the enraged responses of those whom she threatened in her own time to the more subtle inferences about her credibility in our time. Why, I ask myself, has it been necessary to state that in the case of Frances Wright, Lucretia Mott was 'the only woman she knew and liked'? Of course it is readily believed in our society that women do not like each other – to the extent that Virginia Woolf devoted considerable attention to the phrase 'Chloe liked Olivia' in *A Room of One's Own* (1928) because the statement was so unusual – but is it necessary that we continue to give substance to this belief and to participate in the construction of this particular reality? Would it not be better to do as Wright suggests, to examine the origin of this belief, the uses it serves, and, if it is not in women's interest, to forge new beliefs? With patriarchy relying on divisions among women we need to be subversive, not conformist.

Without quoting references, Alice Rossi states that: 'Like radical women much later in American history, Fanny has little sympathy for the middle class women's movement that grew up in America' (1974, p. 97). Is it inevitable that we must choose between Frances Wright and an organised women's movement? That Frances Wright could be very disagreeable and many of the members of the nineteenth-century women's movement felt that being agreeable was the way to accomplish their ends could simply indicate that women have not been free to *choose* their own strategies while men hold the power.

The means for undermining women's protests have not been much modified over the centuries. Today attempts are still made to discredit women's efforts to gain independence with the clichéd but sanctioned accusation that the women's movement is nothing but a middle-class, bourgeois 'luxury' or 'distraction'. *I* do not know how such critics can *know* this; it is a charge I cannot substantiate (and one that will not stand up to the sort of scrutiny that Frances Wright urged). But it is a charge that suits patriarchy.

'Sophia' (1739) warned against accepting assertions about women's deficiencies by those who had a vested interest in promoting such deficiency, and her advice is no less pertinent today. There can be no question that men stand to gain if women's struggle for liberation can be represented as lacking seriousness or significance. And this is the case regardless of the reasons used for discrediting the women and the movement.

Given that there is no convincing evidence that the diverse women's movement is composed of anyone other than women, given the absence of documentation for a case for or against the movement being divided along lines men have formulated in relation to themselves, why should women not insist that we have more in common than we have to divide us? Why should we not construct our own explanations *in our own interest* and disregard the explanations provided by men – *in their own interest?* We would be doing no less than many of our foremothers have done, Frances Wright among them.

We would, however, be doing something rather different from Harriet Martineau.

2 Harriet Martineau (1802–1876)

Harriet Martineau most certainly did not continue in the disagreeable and passionate tradition of some of the women who went before. She was even critical of this tradition and stated that it was in women's interest that the women who presented the case for women's rights 'must be clearly seen to speak from conviction of the truth and not from personal unhappiness,' for: 'The best friends of the cause are the happy wives and the busy, cheerful, single women, who have no injuries of their own to avenge, and no painful vacuity or mortification to relieve' (Martineau, 1877, vol. 1, p. 401). Fortunately, while this may have been Martineau's professed ideal, it was not always her practice.

Harriet Martineau was born in Norwich, the sixth of eight children, in a Unitarian family, which believed in the education of girls, as well as boys. Her childhood was miserable, she felt ugly and rejected, she became deaf, and from her own accounts appears to have been consistently troubled and distressed. Some biographers have labelled her as neurotic. The love of her life was her younger brother James with whom she shared many of her intellectual interests. Some biographers also have labelled her as a 'latent homosexual'.

At the age of 24 she was (briefly) engaged to a young man and experienced conflict; she was expected to marry to find fulfilment but she understood that marriage would restrict her life. *She* did not have to resolve the conflict; *he* died. There were no further flirtations with feminine fulfilment. All of her biographers raise questions about her sexuality; evidently it is problematic.

Alice Rossi says that, although Martineau was never married, 'she showed no regrets on this score' (1974, p. 121). Why should she? In her own words she stated that: 'The older I have grown, the more serious and irremediable have seemed to me the evils and disadvantages of married life as it exists among us at this time' (1877, vol. 1, p. 101). One of the few possible disparaging comments missing from the inventory for Martineau is masochism. There can be no doubt that she saw marriage as a form of bondage for most women, that she recognised that they entered it from ignorance, or economic necessity, or both, and that she counted herself fortunate that she had been able to create a choice for herself and that she was able to gain a reasonable amount of emotional and financial security from her work.

Her nineteenth-century biographer, Mrs Fenwick Miller, cannot, however, leave open the possibility that Harriet Martineau was a spinster because no man would have her (and she gives no evidence that she entertained the possibility that Martineau might have *preferred* the single state). She tries to show that Martineau did taste the joys of love: 'such a love, once filling a woman's soul, sweetens it and preserves it for her whole life through. Pity the shrivelled and decayed old heart which were not thus embalmed in youth! Harriet Martineau did have this precious experience; and her womanliness of nature remained fresh and true and sweet to the end of her days because of it' (Miller, 1884, p. 51).

It is possible that Mrs Miller did not read many of Martineau's cryptic comments about marriage – she makes no reference to Martineau's feminism throughout the entire 224 pages (quite an achievement given Martineau's numerous publications on the topic) and continues with: 'there are many like Harriet Martineau, who are single in life, but whose hearts have been mated, and so made alive. I do not know that she would have gained by marriage, in any way, except in the chance of motherhood, a yet greater fact than love itself to a woman' (ibid., pp. 51–2).

Rather than 'condemning' Mrs Miller for the 'selection' she makes in order to present Martineau positively in accordance with the prevailing values and beliefs, I quote this to show the way women are required to operate in a male-dominated society. Miller was trying to portray Martineau *in the most flattering terms she could find* in order that she would be accepted. The only difference between the process Miller engaged in and the one I engage in now is that I neither know nor care whether Martineau is acceptable – *to men*. I am writing for women. I write from within the confines of a male-dominated society, but I am more than prepared to dispense with male approval (having secured a publisher, *first*, of course).

One of the traditions in which feminists have often consciously operated is that of knowing that the audience and the critics are male. This exerts a powerful influence over women's ideas and the forms in which they are presented (see Cheri Langdell, in press). I suspect that this was a major source of conflict to Harriet Martineau. It was a source of anger to one of her contemporaries, Harriet Taylor (1807–58), who summed up one of the problems for women in the nineteenth century (a problem which still persists in the twentieth century and is discussed by Virginia Woolf and Adrienne Rich) and made the constraints under which women thought and wrote patently clear. Women, she said, are required 'to profess what-

ever opinions they expect will be agreeable to men', for: 'They depend on
men's opinion for their literary as well as their feminine success; and such
is their bad opinion of men, that they believe there is not more than one
in ten thousand who does not dislike and fear strength, sincerity or high
spirit in a woman' (Taylor, quoted in Rossi, 1970, p. 119).

Harriet Martineau did not receive unqualified male approval – not in
her own lifetime nor since her death – and there are reasons for suspecting
that she lived the contradiction of trying to be a woman and a serious
thinker/writer, with the result that she experienced a threat to her self-
esteem as a woman, *and* as an intellectual being. At different times she
attempted to resolve this conflict in different ways and it is almost impossible to set either her theory or her practice (and she was one of the first
feminists to make such a distinction – partly I think as a result of the
conflict she experienced) in 'aspic'. (See Gaby Weiner, 1982b, for further
discussion.)

When she was 27 (and after her father had died) what might have
constituted a tragedy for some members of the family was for Martineau
a 'blessing in disguise' – the family fortunes were ruined. As she said: 'I
who had been obliged to write before breakfast, or in some private way,
had henceforth liberty to do my own work in my own way; for we had
lost our gentility . . . but for that loss of money, we might have lived on in
the ordinary provincial method of ladies with small means, sewing and
economizing, and growing narrower each year' (Martineau, 1877, vol. 1,
p. 142).

Not that Martineau was completely free to write or to pursue a 'literary' career; she was still required to prove her dexterity with a needle
(and to fulfil other appropriate domestic duties not all of which were
necessary but which were proof of her womanliness). When she visited
London in 1829 to establish 'contacts', and stayed with her aunt and uncle,
her aunt wrote without her knowledge 'to Mrs Martineau advising that
Harriet had much better content herself with earning a certain living by
the needle rather than indulge her vainglorious ideas of success in the
masculine world of literary London. Her mother immediately upon receipt
of this missive ordered Harriet's return to Norwich. Despite her mature 27
years, the would-be author returned meekly home,' though, adds Valerie
Kossew Pichanick (1980), Martineau's most recent biographer, 'The old
habit of obedience prevailed, but beneath it there burned a deep resentment
at being remanded "to a position of helpless dependence, when a career of
action and independence was opening up before me" ' (pp. 31–2).

After this initial disappointment, however, Harriet Martineau planned
her *Illustrations of Political Economy,* which helped to establish her reputation as a professional writer. Stanton et al. (1881) see a direct line
between Martineau and Wollstonecraft and say that after Wollstonecraft
'came Jane Marcet, Eliza Lynn and Harriet Martineau, each of whom in
the early part of the nineteenth century, exerted a decided influence upon
the political thought of England. Mrs Marcet was one of the most scientific
and cultivated persons of the age. Her "Conversations on Chemistry"
familiarized that science both in England and America and from it various

male writers filched their ideas. It was a textbook in this country for many years. Over one hundred and sixty thousand copies were sold, though the fact that this work emanated from a pen of a woman was carefully withheld. Mrs Marcet also wrote upon political economy, and was the first person who made the subject comprehensive to the popular mind. Her manner of treating it was so clear and vivid, that the public to whom it had been a hidden science were able to grasp the subject. Her writings were the inspiration of Harriet Martineau, who followed her in the same department of thought at a later period.' (vol. 1, p. 34).

The series was immensely popular: by 1834 it 'was selling ten thousand monthly copies while by contrast John Stuart Mill's *Principles of Political Economy* (1848) sold a mere three thousand copies in four years' (Pichanick, 1980, p. 50). However, we could be forgiven for assuming that this 'success' of a woman writer in a new and closely guarded male sphere was of little consequence. 'The simplicity and ease of Martineau's style was one of her greatest assets, and it accounted in part for her success as a journalist. Nevertheless it is difficult for the modern reader to readily appreciate the reasons for the success of her Illustrations' (ibid., p. 53). Besides, she herself 'never laid claim to the title of economist and she was aware that she was merely the popularizer of other people's ideas. Her knowledge of economics was superficial, impressionistic, and often ill-digested' (ibid., p. 49), *but* (and note the contradiction) 'meticulously basing her diligent little volumes on the principles set out in James Mill's *Elements of Political Economy* and on standard works like *The Wealth of Nations* and Malthus *Essay on Population,* she conscientiously included in her narratives every aspect of her subject. She utilized government blue books and the library of the House of Commons, and she relied on the advice of friendly experts like Francis Place, Joseph Hume and William Tait' (ibid., p. 53).

As at this stage there was no formal training available in economics, no degree course or institution devoted to its study, it remains a mystery to me how one could have become an economist by any means other than those used by Harriet Martineau. What claim to fame did these other 'economists' have, John Stuart Mill included, that Harriet did not, apart from their sex? Because they are male they are economists; because she is a female, 'the derivative sex', she is but a publiciser of their ideas.

What Harriet Martineau was doing, that the men were not – and I think it is most significant – was trying to make much of this new and powerful knowledge generated by men, which until that time had been kept within the confines of a small privileged circle, to invest it with her own 'original' refinement, and to make it available to all who could read. She got rid of the 'trimmings' so condemned by Frances Wright and made her own contribution to the social sciences in the process. But, as Wright asserted (and as many feminists today appreciate), little respect is given to those who do not play the 'mystifying' game and who instead insist on the *knowledgeability* of all human beings and who attempt to make knowledge accessible to them.

Not even Harriet's mother was impressed by the sales, the remuneration, or the accolades that Harriet achieved. In a sense they were an embarrassment because they so widely advertised the 'unfeminine' nature of her daughter, for femininity demanded that women recede into the background and not be prominent figures in the foreground. Perhaps trying to compensate for the absence of feminine graces, Mrs Martineau insisted that Harriet still engage in the frequently superfluous but approved tasks of the dutiful daughter. Harriet Martineau faced a double-bind: instead of gaining security with her success, she was further challenged and she resolved this in part by insisting that she should be judged in the same way as a man. In her *Autobiography,* she says that she wrote to her mother from London: 'I fully expect that both you and I shall feel as if I did not discharge a daughter's duty, but we shall both remind ourselves that I am now as much a citizen of the world as any professional son of yours could be' (1877, vol. 3, p. 91).

This intellectual and creative contribution of Martineau's deserves careful consideration. Had she been a male and made a contribution of this nature she would probably have been accorded an important place among the founders of social science. Her life and her work would no doubt have been well known and, as a distinguished intellectual, she would have attracted considerable scholarly attention – which in itself helps to perpetuate a reputation – and today there would be debates about her ideas and their contemporary relevance. But, because a woman, she has almost disappeared.

It is not just that she was a woman, however, but a woman for whom woman's position in society was fundamental to her philosophy and central in her conceptualisation of society and its workings. It could be said that at the dawn of sociology, a woman was there, helping to shape the discipline and helping to establish the visibility and centrality of women in any analysis of society. But she – and her ideas – have disappeared. The modern social sciences have managed to render women invisible – despite the contribution of Harriet Martineau. It could never be argued that the founding fathers were ignorant, that they did not know about women and the intellectual and social questions their subordinate position posed. They did know. Harriet Martineau could not be ignored in her own lifetime even if she can be in our own (see Weiner, 1982b). She was ousted.

Had Martineau's thesis on women been taken up, explored and refined within the social sciences – as many of her other theses have been appropriated but without due recognition as to their origin – over the last 140 years, we would not today be required to confront exclusively male-controlled and defined disciplines which are passed off as pertaining to the human condition (see D. Spender, 1981a). This is one point in our history where we can state that women's issues were placed at the forefront in a new and developing body of knowledge; it may have been an accident that they made their presence felt at that time but it is no accident that they disappeared.

One of the problems of dealing with Martineau's work is that although she was such a prolific and versatile writer the absence of scholarly attention has meant that there has been little systematic collation of her material. Her feminist writings are scattered through hundreds of newspaper articles.

For years she wrote the leader in the *Daily News* (Gaby Weiner, 1982b, states that in her time with the *Daily News*, Harriet Martineau wrote 1,642 articles) 'It is interesting to turn the yellowed sheets of the old files and pick out leader after leader on every imaginable subject, all bearing the hall-mark of that richly informed perspicacious mind. The range of subjects is truly remarkable, including as it did many essays . . . on America; on India; on Haiti and San Domingo; on the Lancaster cotton trade; on industrial strikes; on Sidney Herbert; on Mrs Beecher Stowe; on Java; on the Duchess of Kent; on domestic servants; on cheap food; on nepotism in cathedral cities; on the advertisement tax – "Town criers are not taxed, so why advertisements in papers,"; on emigration; on dwellings; on lighthouse dues; on the abuse of the money left by Edward Alleyn for Dulwich College; on Parizzi and the British Museum; on architecture . . . on sanitary reform – "deep ditches filled with the accumulated filth of centuries in the Clapham Road" . . .' (Wheatley, 1957, pp. 324–5). As Margaret Walters (1976) has said, Martineau 'worked hard as a professional writer, pouring out a stream of articles, pamphlets, books on social problems, histories, travel accounts, as well as an autobiography, novels and children's stories. The sheer range of her interests is extraordinary' (p. 332).

Her first published article was on women, 'Female Writers on Practical Divinity' (1821) for the Unitarian *Monthly Repository*, as was her second, 'On Female Education', and women and education was a topic she was to return to again and again. On both occasions she used a male pseudonym (a most sensible strategy at the time, although perhaps unnecessary from the point of view of those at the *Monthly Repository* which consistently carried feminist articles and with which Harriet Taylor and John Stuart Hill were also associated). Her most sustained writing on the position of women is found in *Society in America* (1837).

She began by saying: 'If a test of civilisation be sought, none can be so sure as the condition of that half of society over which the other half has power, – from the exercise of the right of the strongest'. Unlike Frances Wright, who on her first visit to America compared American women favourably with their European counterpart, Martineau compares the reality for American women with the professed ideology of the country, and finds that women have gained little if anything in the new world. 'Tried by this test,' she says, 'the American civilisation appears to be of a lower order than might have been expected from some other symptoms of its social state' (in 1974, Rossi, p. 125).

She stated that men controlled American society – in the same way that they did in Europe – and that they defined a narrow sphere for women. Women, argued Martineau, should define their own sphere and it should be as great as their natural abilities – expressed by themselves – would permit. Martineau quickly cut through the hypocritical and self-interested sentiment put forward by men and exposed the absurdity of their assumptions: 'While women's intellect is confined, her morals crushed, her health ruined, her weakness encouraged and her strength punished, she is told that her lot is cast in the paradise of women,' she argued bluntly and in tones reminiscent of Mary Astell stated, 'there is no country in the world where there is so much boasting of the "chivalrous" treatment she enjoys. That is to say, – she has the best place in stage coaches: when there are not chairs for everybody, the gentlemen stand' (ibid.). 'In short', says Martineau of women in America, 'indulgence is given her as a substitute for justice. Her case differs from that of the slave, as to the principle, just so far as this; that the indulgence is large and universal instead of petty and capricious. In both cases, justice is denied on no better plea than the right of the strongest' (ibid.).

She was adamant that men had organised society so that: 'Nothing is thus left open to women but marriage' (ibid., p. 126) and so that men's interests could consistently be catered for. This pattern 'must remain while women continue to be ill educated, passive and subservient; or well educated, vigorous and free only upon sufferance' (ibid., p. 130), she argued. She objected to the virtually compulsory nature of marriage and the limitations it imposed on women, but had a word of praise for the more liberal divorce laws in America (in contrast with the disgraceful laws in England). It must be noted that later in the nineteenth century the issue of divorce was often shelved because it was considered too sensitive and promoted too much bad publicity for the women's movement (Elizabeth Cady Stanton proving to be an 'embarrassment' on this score to some of her colleagues), yet in 1837 Martineau openly and freely advocated liberal divorce. (She also advocated birth control – and I would like to be able to say, in the interest of women controlling their own bodies, but it was because she subscribed to the belief that it was *economically* necessary.)

Martineau documented the consequences of narrow education and opportunity for women and said that they were ready prey for religious fervour (because it could break the monotony and vacuity of their existence) or else they became 'more or less literary' in the attempt to save their minds from vacuity. Among American women, she said, 'Readers are plentiful: thinkers are rare' (ibid., p. 140). But she did not blame women for this.

She was scathing in her attack on male chivalry which made it impossible for women to be economically self-supporting. Such 'chivalry' could only persist while the plight of working women was kept invisible, and she argued that 'the condition of the female working classes is such that if its sufferings were but made known, emotions of horror and shame would tremble through the whole of society' (ibid., p. 141).

As an economist (I refuse to portray her as 'not the real thing' by virtue of her sex), Martineau made the links between men's arguments that women *should not* or *could not* work and the pitifully low pay women received as workers. She was appalled by the low wages women received as needlewomen or governess, labourer or teacher. In a most unsentimental manner she declared that: 'Teaching and training children is to a few, a very few, a delightful employment notwithstanding its toils and cares. Except to these few it is irksome: and when accompanied with poverty and mortification intolerable.' The 'scanty reward of female labour in America remains the reproach to the country' she declared (ibid., p. 142).

If Martineau's insights had ever been made the substance of economics it is unlikely that today economics would comprise a discipline devoted to men's work, men's pay, and men's conditions while women's work and absence of pay, or low pay, does not constitute an issue. This arrangement, detected by Martineau, was not merely an oversight on the part of men, she argued, but a necessary condition for the maintenance of female subordination. Men were obliged to make women's work in the home invisible, obliged to pretend that working women did not exist, for their arguments that women were moral creatures whose place was on a pedestal simply would not stand up to the evidence of women's work. And, of course, while it remained non-existent, there could be no crude, crass arguments about its monetary value.

Martineau suspected then, as Ann Oakley (1974) does now, that if men were to apply to women the same standards as they applied to themselves in relation to pay and conditions, they could simply not afford women's work. So they solved the problem by acting as if it did not exist.

While directing many of her arguments to men, and assuming (mistakenly as we can see in retrospect) they could understand their import and would be prepared to change their ways, Martineau also addressed herself to women and outlined a programme of action which, although superficially dated, is fundamentally still applicable. 'All women should inform themselves of the condition of their sex and of their own position,' she advised. 'It must necessarily follow that the noblest of them will, sooner or later, put forth a moral power which shall prostrate cant, and burst asunder the bonds (silken to some but cold iron to others) of feudal prejudice and usages. In the meantime', she added, 'is it to be understood that the principles of the Declaration of Independence bear no relation to half of the human race? If so, what is the ground of this limitation?' (ibid., p. 143).

That Martineau urged women to 'inform themselves of the condition of their sex and of their own position' should not be underestimated. She too wanted women to practise 'free enquiry', to engage in consciousness-raising, to ask themselves how it was they came to believe what they did about themselves, about men, and about the relationship between the two. She was aware of the origins of the idea about women's place, and, despite her disclaimers about passionate protest and bitter personal experience, she insisted that women should document their oppression for she was sure that it would galvanise them into action once women's reality was encoded. But because of the contradictions of her own life, and because she was trying to function within the framework of that oppression, Harriet Martineau also addressed herself to men.

Martineau had great faith in the power of reason and assumed that once the arguments against women's inferiority and subordination were clearly put the justice of the case would be undeniable, and men – who continually portrayed themselves as just, as one of their justifications for holding power – would take steps to remove the injustices that were perpetrated against women. One would have thought that this assumption would be seriously threatened by the response she received to her reasons.

First of all Harriet was advised to leave women out of her book on America: 'William Empsom, who had favourably reviewed the political tables for the *Edinburgh Review* . . . begged Harriet not to embark on the thorny topic of American women' (Wheatley, 1957, p. 176) and she responded with a most spirited declaration of her own independence and integrity. But after publication, 'Scorching letters arrived by every post . . . she had not anticipated such taunts and insults she received – particularly those concerning her deafness' (ibid., p. 177). It was not just the private post, however, but the public reviews which were aimed at harassing her.

'The *American Quarterly Review* described her tour as an "espionage" and her criticisms as an "insolence", and ostentatiously thanked heaven that it knew of no woman who would "get up at a public meeting and make an abolition, an amalgamation, or a Malthusian speech"

> Excepting it be Fanny Wright or Harriet Martineau there is not a sane woman in the world, much less the United States, who has a desire to enlarge her sphere of action beyond the limits of her domestic home (*American Quarterly Reivew*, Sept 22: 1837: 21–53)

The *New York Review* expounded in similar vein, attacking her Unitarianism along with her abolitionism and her feminism. But it was especially the latter which shocked her critics, and the American press pejoratively called her "masculine", and "Amazonian" along with such epithets as "incendiary", "radical", "amalgamationist" and "pitiless". . . . One anonymous reviewer inferred that as the author under review was neither a wife nor mother, she had failed to fulfill woman's *natural* role and therefore had no *natural* right to demand' (Pichanick, 1980, p. 100).

In England the *London and Westminster Review* (under the proprietorship of John Stuart Mill) had great praise for *Society in America* as 'incomparably the best' book on the United States, and William Johnson Fox at the *Monthly Repository* was predictably positive. 'But conservative critics like *Fraser's* called her a "female Quixote" whose utopian, unrealistic visions had succeeded only in proving the impracticability of democratic institutions. She was, it said, as manifestly wrong in assuming that all men were created equal as she was in assuming that men and women could even be equal. It described her as one who "had grown old (she was then thirty-five) in single blessedness" and was therefore incapable of appreciating the joys of feminine dependency' (ibid., p. 101).

Benjamin Disraeli, reviewing the book in *The Times*, said she was much too concerned with her pet schemes for her sex instead of providing accurate descriptions for her readers, and the reviewer in the *Athenaeum* said:

> She allows herself to indulge in ascetic reflections upon the tyranny of man, in denying woman that independence which woman, as a class, would refuse if it were offered to her, as being inconsistent with her nature; and affects to look down upon and despise, as incompatible with the existence of the intellect, that softness and tender susceptibility which is the chief charm of the sex, but which incapacitates alike her body and her mind for independent

action. . . . If Miss Martineau, therefore, or any other maiden
malcontent, should again venture to assert the equality of man and
woman, our only advice to whomsoever that lady may be, is to turn,
before sitting down to her task to the book of Genesis (*Athenaeum*,
Dec, 1840, pp. 958–9).

Her arguments are not dealt with: instead male authority is invoked. Many
current feminists get comparable snide and patronising reviews. Unfortunately, such a system works.

Too readily today the pressure that women such as Harriet Martineau
worked under is quickly dismissed. Few would be the contemporary feminists, I suspect (myself included), who could withstand the harassment, the
taunts, the jibes, the abuse, that were par for the course for feminists in
years past. I am sure they took their toll, and perhaps it is why some of
them elected to present a public and not a personal face to the world.
Perhaps that is why Harriet Martineau, as a woman, still remains elusive
because, despite all her writing, there are still many aspects of her which
to me remain inexplicable.

It is not difficult to find criticism of her (in the few contemporary
discussions on her) in terms of her insistence that the case for women's
rights should not be *personal* but based on calm reason. Yet she herself
made many personal and passionate statements at times and much of what
she wrote made *personal* connections for other women. Walters (1976)
says that after the publication of *Society in America* she did not only receive
abusive post: 'dozens of women wrote to her complaining of how the "law
and custom" of England oppressed them' (p. 334) and in her *Autobiography*
she says: 'Some offered evidence of intolerable oppression, if I could point
out how it might be used. Others offered money, effort, courage in enduring
obloquy, everything, if I could show them how to obtain, and lead them
in obtaining, arrangements by which they could be free in spirit, and in
outward liberty to make what they could of life' (1877, vol. 2, p. 104).

But, states Walters, 'she let the opportunity evaporate. Deeply attracted
to other women and sympathetic to their troubles, she was nervous about
identifying with them. Though at one point she was involved with plans
for a periodical to further the cause of women, she held the emerging
women's movement at arms length' (1976, p. 334).

Certainly she experienced conflict about making her way to the *centre*
of man's world in the early nineteenth century; certainly she lived a contradiction when the world was divided so rigidly into 'masculine' and
'feminine' and when she was seen – and saw herself – variously as both,
or neither. Certainly she found respite at times by 'dropping out'. For
example, at the age of 35 – she found herself under enormous pressure,
when apart from everything else she was offered the editorship of a new
economics periodical. Is it surprising that she should have experienced a
crisis of confidence? She declined the offer, and instead wrote a novel (a
writing activity, but one which could be more readily reconciled with the
feminine role) and then took to her bed where she stayed for the next five
years.

'After expecting an early death until it was too late to die', she says, with honest self-mockery, she turned to mesmerism and obtained a dramatic cure. Thus she does not represent the ideal, strong, autonomous, uncompromising feminist that many of us today would like to discover and reclaim. But if she had been such a figure, much of our feminist analysis would no longer apply. That she tried – within the framework of patriarchy – that she saw what she did, explained what she did, argued as she did, indicates that there has been a feminist tradition and that it has been powerful. The limitations are not hers, but society's.

There are aspects of her life that I can so readily identify with. I have visited her house in the Lake District (which she planned and built and which is one of the few dwellings of a feminist of the past that remains intact) and have appreciated the sense of security and warmth that she experienced there, as she wrote, farmed, walked, wrote, trained girls, mended her clothes, wrote, and smoked 'her cigars like any "man of business"' (Walters, 1976, p. 351). But in some ways she remains an enigma.

Many of the questions that arise in relation to Harriet Martineau are concerned with her sexuality, and Harriet Taylor – where she is discussed at all – usually suffers a similar fate, although in her case, the questions are narrower in range. They revolve around her relationship with John Stuart Mill.

3 Harriet Taylor (1807–1858)

Alice Rossi (1970) says that: 'John Mill and Harriet Taylor were in their early twenties when they first met. Harriet was at the time a young married woman with two young children, but within a year the relationship between Mill and Mrs Taylor was one of intellectual and spiritual intimacy. For the next twenty years Mill continued to live at home with his mother and younger siblings, while Mrs Taylor remained in her husband's household, yet it is clear that the unconventional relationship they enjoyed with each other was the very core of their lives. It was not until 1851, two years after her husband's death, when they were in their forties and suffering very poor health, that they married' (p. 6). Rossi also says that: 'Tradition has it that Mill and Harriet Taylor met at a dinner party at William Fox's home in the summer or fall of 1830. . . . Harriet Martineau, known personally by Fox since the 1820s was also a member of the party, and it was she who was very fond of telling and embroidering upon the occasion of John and Harriet's first meeting' (ibid., p. 20).

Some of the so-called scholarly work which centres on Harriet Taylor is of the speculative order of did-she-or-did-she-not-sleep with John Stuart Mill during their twenty-year pre-marital intimacy; most of the rest of the so-called scholarly work (with the exception of Alice Rossi, 1970, and Constance Rover, 1970) on Harriet Taylor, centres on the role she played in John Stuart Mill's intellectual life. It is difficult to say which of the two areas I find more offensive! Only an obsession with genital heterosexuality could produce the former and only a deeply engrained contempt for women and women's intellectual ability the latter.

One of the 'problems' for scholars of Mill has been that he was most emphatic about the positive role that Harriet Taylor played in the shaping of his ideas and his prose: the 'problem' is that Mill is eulogised for his accurate and dispassionate assessments (a common criticism being that this was almost to the extent of the exclusion of emotion), and yet if he is to be taken at his word on this count, not only must the intellectual stature of Harriet Taylor be acknowledged, but the possibility that Mill's work is at times a collaborative effort must be entertained.

If the image of John Stuart Mill was to be preserved, then the image *he* presented of Harriet Taylor had to be discredited, but this had to be accomplished without tarnishing *his* reputation. It was therefore productive – and plausible in a patriarchal society – to tarnish *hers*. First of all it was established that this was one of the few areas where John Stuart Mill's judgement was not reliable; even Alice Rossi (1970) thinks he was a little lavish and extravagant in his praise of Harriet Taylor (p. 32). (As is so often the case in such instances, I suspect that these are completely unsubstantiated value judgements. I find nothing excessive in his evaluation of Harriet Taylor and would be perfectly prepared to argue – with no less 'proof' – that he understated the role she played.) A veritable arsenal of weapons exists in our society to be used against an 'intellectual woman' and in the case of Harriet Taylor many of them have been employed so that it has been possible to demonstrate that not only was she not an intellectual, she was also not an acceptable woman.

She has been portrayed as stupid, as an 'ogling' woman, as both frigid and yet capable of ensnaring the great man, as empty-headed and a plaything who repeated prettily everything that John Stuart Mill said; these are the considered and dispassionate assessments of scholars, of course. Stillinger (1961) has said that the 'Harriet of the incomparable intellect' as presented by Mill, 'was largely a product of his imagination, an idealization according to his peculiar needs, of a clever, domineering, in some ways perverse and selfish invalid woman' (p. 34).

If any evidence is needed that she was treated more harshly after Freud introduced his science, or that women have at times colluded with men to discredit other women (sometimes in the hope of obtaining approval and acceptance for themselves), Diana Trilling (1952) certainly provides it. (I quote here from Rossi having decided that I have better things to do with my time than trace such 'original' sources.) 'John Mill had characterized Harriet as his "intellectual beacon," but Mrs Trilling suggested she had in fact "nothing more than a vest-pocket flashlight of a mind . . . one of the meanest and dullest ladies in literary history, a monument of nasty self-regard, as lacking in charm as in grandeur," whose correspondence shows a "fleshless, bloodless quality" full of "injured vanity, petty egoism and ambition." Mrs Trilling then exhibits the standard of femininity by which she assesses Harriet Taylor . . . Harriet Taylor had "no touch of true femininity, no taint of the decent female concerns which support our confidence in the intelligence of someone like Jane Carlyle" ' (Rossi, 1970, p. 35).

Apart from the fact that feminists (Virginia Woolf among them) have often suggested that the world would have been a much better place if Thomas Carlyle had done the housework and Jane Carlyle the writing – a possibility which would probably have offended Diana Trilling's sense of order – I think I can state without fear of contradiction that there is more evidence of malice on the part of Diana Trilling than she had evidence of deficiencies in Harriet Taylor. Alice Rossi points out that the very aspects of Harriet Taylor's behaviour which were found so terrible by Trilling were the same qualities which in a man – in the nineteenth or the twentieth century – would be cause for commendation. She was a serious, and at times single-minded intellectual: she 'was no shrinking violet, no soft and compliant woman. She had, after all, lived against the grain of Victorian London in an unconventional liaison with John Mill for twenty years . . .' (ibid., pp. 35–6).

There is every reason to believe that Harriet Taylor would not have provoked such vicious attacks if she had been less threatening, that is, if she had been more of a passive provider of comfortable working conditions for Mill, rather than an active participant in a joint intellectual endeavour. We have, after all, a 'tradition' of women servicing intellectual and creative men, of providing everything from domestic to secretarial services (in the manner which Jane Carlyle did, see also Marion Glastonbury, 1979), of having their own creative and intellectual efforts 'appropriated' by men, treated as 'raw data' which is transformed into the polished product with the flourish of a male-held pen (sometimes, just by adding a signature, see Hilary Simpson, 1979). Had Harriet Taylor conformed to this more appropriately feminine image, she might have been accorded more patronising praise.

As it is, her reputation has been severely undermined – sometimes by the simple technique of attributing some of her writing to John Stuart Mill! In July 1851 an article 'Enfranchisement of Women' appeared in the *Westminster Review* and it seems that many people – including Harriet Martineau – attributed it to John Stuart Mill. In a letter which Martineau wrote to Paulina Wright Davis (3 August 1851) to thank her for the *Report of the Proceedings of the Woman's Rights Convention* (held in Worcester, October 1850) she states: 'I hope you are aware of the interest excited in this country by that Convention, the strongest proof of which is the appearance of an article on the subject in *The Westminster Review* (for July), as thorough-going as any of your own addresses, and from the pen (at least as it is understood here) of one of our very first men, Mr John S. Mill. I am not without hope that this article will materially strengthen your hands, and I am sure it can not but cheer your hearts' (Stanton et al., 1881, vol. I, p. 229).[1]

---

[1] This was not the first article to appear on this topic in the *Westminster Review*; there was one by an anonymous woman in 1831 and another in 1832 by a Member of Parliament, see Josephine Kamm, 1966, p. 22.

By Harriet Martineau and Harriet Taylor's time there is no longer any need to speculate about whether or not such women stood alone, for there is ample evidence that they were 'among friends'. But the practice of anonymous reviews and articles was not without its difficulties, even among friends.

Stanton, Anthony and Gage (1881) have no doubts about the authorship of the article: 'From her letter', they say, 'we find that Miss Martineau shared the common opinion in England that the article in the *Westminster Review* on the "Enfranchisement of Women" was written by John Stuart Mill. It was certainly very complimentary to Mrs Taylor, the real author of that paper, who afterward married Mr Mill, that it should have been supposed to emanate from the pen of that distinguished philosopher' (vol. I, p. 231).

In attributing 'Enfranchisement of Women' to Harriet Taylor, Alice Rossi says that she does so not just because in 1849 Harriet Taylor had drafted a pamphlet on this topic, but because the ideas contained in it are identifiably Harriet Taylor's – she was very much more radical in many respects than was John Stuart Mill. Taylor objected – vehemently – to the idea that women's education should serve to make them fit companions for men: she wanted every career open to them, she wanted them educated for their own sake, and she certainly didn't think marriage and motherhood disqualified them from doing anything else. Mill, on the other hand, thought that women should be educated, but that if they *chose* marriage and motherhood, they should treat it as a full-time occupation, forgo any possibilities of other employment, and be 'equal' companions to their husbands! It is the former philosophy which provides the parameters for 'Enfranchisement of Woman' and not the latter.

One of the reasons that Harriet Taylor's superb case for women's rights is so little known is the bias which surrounds the selective study of the works of John Stuart Mill, for even *his* writing on women has not received the same attention in scholarly circles as his writing on rights and liberty – as they relate to men. It is to men of little consequence that *The Subjection of Women* would probably not have been written without Harriet Taylor's influence, and, by Mill's own admission, certainly would not have taken the form that it did without her – and later her daughter's – collaboration. 'All that is most striking and profound' in the book, said Mill, 'belongs to my wife; coming from the fund of thought which had been made common to us both, by our innumerable conversations and discussions on a topic which filled so large a place in our minds' (quoted in Rossi, 1970, p. 57).

Like Martineau, Mill made 'the woman question' a central part of his analysis in the emerging framework of the social sciences; unlike Martineau, his name lives on, is even revered, but his work on women and the priority he gave it, has suffered a similar fate to hers. *No* social science discipline materialised, devoted to *this* topic, whereas almost every other issue raised by Martineau and Mill has been incorporated into the bodies of knowledge of various social sciences. While the pro-feminist aspect of Mill's work is 'glossed over', so too, is his Harriet, and her intellectual and creative existence. Yet Harriet Taylor's influence also extended to other areas of Mill's writing. 'Mill refers to many of his publications from 1840 onward as "joint productions" of Harriet and himself,' states Rossi (1970, p. 39) and this includes *Principles of Political Economy* and *On Liberty*. Mill describes the process whereby they together went over every sentence and carefully weeded out any faults in thought or expression, and he says that sometimes the sentences were taken straight from her lips (see ibid., p. 40). This of course raises the question of why these books were not published in joint names, and, apart from patriarchal explanations where women's resources are made available to men (see Glastonbury, 1978, 1979, and Simpson, 1979), there is also the practical consideration that it might have proved even more embarrassing for Harriet Taylor — and her husband — if this had been the case.

But Mill's acknowledgement of Harriet Taylor's role, his praise of her, and his positive evaluation of her has often proved to be embarrassing for his publishers and devotees. In 1873 when Mill's friend and biographer Alexander Bain read the proofs of Mill's *Autobiography* he tried to prevent the publication of the excessive praise of Harriet Taylor Mill on the grounds that Mill outraged all credibility in his descriptions of her 'matchless genius', and he himself resolved the 'problem' of Harriet Taylor Mill by suggesting that 'she' stimulated Mill's intellectual faculties by 'intelligently controverting' his ideas (see ibid., p. 32).

A few, like Francis Mineka (1944), have been more open to the possibility that Mill was accurately portraying the role Harriet Taylor had played in his life: 'there can be no doubt that she was the saving grace of his inner life', states Mineka, and, 'without her John Mill might well have been a different person, but one can doubt that he would have been as fine, as understanding, or as great a man' (pp. 274–5).

Alice Rossi (1970) points to the peculiar habits of scholars in relation to John Stuart Mill and his work. Prior to the relationship between Mill and Harriet Taylor, they were each members of different political groups — Harriet Taylor was primarily a member of the Unitarian Radical set, while Mill was a member of the Philosophic Radicals, and therefore, perhaps, it comes as no surprise to find that those who were 'very critical of Harriet belonged to the Philosophic Radical circle. . . . These were all persons who disapproved of Mill's involvement with Harriet and with the Unitarian Radicals' (p. 37). Indirectly indicating one of the reasons men have preferred to study each other (and have ignored women), Rossi goes on to say that: 'Scholars are more apt to do research on people whose thinking they find attractive than on people whose thinking they dislike and disapprove,' and this is why 'one observes a division among modern scholars in their opinions of Harriet which reflect the divisions of the Philosophic Radicals and the Unitarian Radicals themselves' (ibid.). The members of John Mill's set — right down to those who identify with it today — are frequently explicitly critical of Harriet Taylor, but also implicitly suggest that she was the 'ensnaring woman' who lured John Stuart Mill away from the fold.

But this 'division' and devaluation has had other advantages for Mill scholars as well: most conveniently, any aspect of John Stuart Mill's work which scholars do *not* like or which may no longer be acceptable, can be attributed to Harriet Taylor Mill! She is damned for not being the intellectual influence that Mill made her out to be, but damned for being an intellectual influence – when it suits.

Overall there has been a systematic devaluation of Harriet Taylor and, while it is interesting to see what form this devaluation has taken, the reason for this treatment is not, in the end, a matter of divisions between Unitarian Radicals and Philosophic Radicals – it is a matter of male supremacy, particularly as it relates to the intellectual realm. I concur wholeheartedly with Rossi, who states that 'the hypothesis that a mere woman was the collaborator of so logical and intellectual a thinker as Mill, much less that she influenced the development of his thought, can be expected to meet resistance in the minds of men' (1970, p. 36). To accept Mill's evaluation of Harriet Taylor would be to accept the intellectual competence of women. Of course many men will resist such acceptance and will find a deficiency in Harriet, rather than in their own scheme of patriarchal values.

Despite the way she and her work have often been portrayed, Harriet Taylor's 'Enfranchisement of Women' is a delight to read. Actually, in the discussion of her work there are few of the customary criticisms usually levelled at feminist writers about 'the style', and this could be partly because there has been so little discussion, or partly because the essay has so often been attributed to John Stuart Mill, in which case of course, the standards for evaluation have been so different.

In her essay, Taylor addressed herself to both women and men, but to women and men who are capable of 'reason', who are not bound by prejudice, who are not frightened of what is new or unknown, and who would not stoop to using the argument that 'it has always been so' as a justification for existing social arrangements. As she says: 'That an institution or practice is customary is no presumption of its goodness' particularly when another 'cause can be assigned for its existence' (in Rossi, 1970, p. 99).

Her presentation is confident, cool and concise: she does not suffer fools gladly and is clearly contemptuous of those who cannot or will not follow her case. In this stance she portrays some of the elements of a disagreeable woman – and this is probably what irked Diana Trilling so much. Taylor has no hesitation in dividing humanity into two discrete, opposing and unequal forces and says, 'we are firmly convinced that the division of mankind into two castes, one born to rule over the other, is in this case as in all cases an unqualified mischief' (ibid., pp. 97–8), with those who insist on its rightness and necessity being those who benefit from the arrangement. Those who make the rules, she argues, would not wish to be the recipients of the treatment they hand out to those they rule. They take for themselves the prerogative of political liberty and personal freedom and disdainfully pass by the few options they provide for the dependent class (ibid., p. 97).

With curiously contemporary perception, Harriet Taylor puts the case that, having deemed that women are not to possess certain qualities, men are then able to insist that such qualities do not exist. She is aware that men define the world in relation to themselves and on the basis of their own experience, that they will not acknowledge any reality which is not consistent with their own experience and that by this means the rich range of female understandings and forms of operating in the world are denied and made invisible (ibid., p. 101). She assumes that men have been able to appropriate power, because they are physically stronger, and that this ethic of might is right – of which she is highly critical – underlies most aspects of social organisation: 'that those who are physically weaker should have been made legally inferior', she argues, 'is quite conformable to the mode in which the world has been governed' (ibid., p. 99).

As 'Sophia' (1739) argued for women's definitions of motherhood, and against men's, so too does Harriet Taylor when she says that: 'It is neither necessary nor just to make imperative on women that they shall either be mothers or nothing; or that if they have been mothers once they shall be nothing else during the whole remainder of their lives. . . . To say that women must be excluded from active life because maternity disqualifies them for it, is in fact to say, that every career should be forbidden them in order that maternity may be their only resource' (ibid., pp. 103–4).

Harriet Taylor is not puzzled as to the origin of this peculiar arrangement: women have been denied access to every form of power or possible independence, and restricted to the realm of administering to men and their needs, and 'the only reason that can be given is that men like it. It is agreeable to them that men should live for their own sake, women for the sake of men' (ibid., p. 107). And women, unfortunately, have come to believe and accept men's wishes; as 'subjects' they have come to acquire the qualities 'which are agreeable to rulers' and the male rulers have 'succeeded for a long time in making the subjects themselves consider' these qualities 'as their appropriate virtues' (ibid.).

Men have discouraged every form of growth and development in women, asserts Taylor, in order to channel them into marriage, maternity and maids for men, and have insisted that they passively conform to this oppressive role, for 'a man likes to have his own will, but does not like that his domestic companion should have a will different from his' (ibid., p. 108). And it is simply not enough, she argues, to suggest that women should be educated in order that they can become better companions for men; she indicates that she is completely against such *reform* (despite the fact that it was a position held by John Stuart Mill). These people say: 'that women should be, not slaves, nor servants, but companions: and educated for that office,' and, exposing the double standard that exists in this respect, adds in parenthesis 'they do not say that men should be educated to be the companions of women' (ibid., p. 111).

Male experience is not the sum total of human experience, claims Taylor, and men are not the yardstick for humanity; the world does not exist simply to meet their needs, although they have managed to impose such an arrangement upon it. But women do not have to accept male explanations, or arrangements devised by men to justify and reinforce male power. She urges women to change – to become disagreeable! Women, she says, 'are told from infancy that thought, and all its greater applications, are other people's business, while theirs is to make themselves agreeable to other people' (ibid., p. 112) and she demands that women become thinking, responsible beings, making their own decisions, defining their own exist- ence, advancing their own explanations, claiming their own creative intelli- gence – despite the fact that there will be a conflict of interest, that many men will not like what it is that women say, and will even go so far as to dispute their ability and their authority to say it.

She exposes the absurdities of the male reasoning process when she says – in what I see as 'classic feminist style' – that if men are so sure that nature intended women for marriage, motherhood and servitude, why then do they find it necessary to erect so many barriers to other options, why are they required to force women to be restricted to this role? For if women's 'preference be natural', she says, 'there can be no necessity for enforcing it by law' and it has never been considered necessary in any other area 'to make laws compelling people to follow their inclination' (ibid., p. 118). With great confidence in the potential of women to describe, explain, and assert the validity of their own experience, when permitted the oppor- tunity, she argues that: 'if education took the same pains to form strong minded women which it takes to prevent them from being formed' (ibid., p. 112), then it would soon be found that the ruling caste had little justification for their supremacy.

There is no limitation within women which debars them from enjoying the full legal, financial, social, and *political* rights which men claim for themselves, argues Harriet Taylor; the only obstacle to this realisation lies within men who hold the power. But she is not demanding the right for women to act in the same way as men: 'Concerning the fitness, then, of women for politics, there can be no question', she says categorically, 'but the dispute is more likely to turn upon the fitness of politics for women' (ibid., p. 103).

She also makes short shrift of the argument that men have often used that women do not want to be responsible, independent, thinking human beings, that they are happy, even fulfilled in their servitude, and that there are sufficient women who will attest to this: 'It requires unusual moral courage as well as disinterestedness in a woman, to express opinions favour- able to women's enfranchisement, until, at least there is some prospect in obtaining it,' says Taylor. But apart from this, a woman's survival – social and economic – will 'usually depend on the good-will of those who hold the undue power' so that if she wishes to survive, she must cultivate the good will of a man, she must be agreeable, she must even oft agree that she is content with her own oppression. And foolish are the men, says Taylor, who take such statements as accurate, or voluntary: they are the statements of an oppressed group and they are made to please the masters on whom women depend.

Many of the ideas presented in 'Enfranchisement of Women' are dis- cussed by Harriet Taylor in her letters to John Stuart Mill (and her letters help to substantiate Mill's conceptualisation of her as a women of great intellectual stature who was an inspiration for him, see F. A. Hayek, 1969). That she was more radical than Mill – on many issues – is obvious from her letters, and that she spoke and reasoned from the depths of *personal* experience is apparent on every page. Perhaps it was personal experience that made her so angry about marriage arrangements – 'in the present system of habits and opinions, girls enter into what is called a contract perfectly ignorant of the conditions of it, and that they should be so is considered absolutely essential to their fitness' (Hayek, 1969, p. 77) – and so disposed towards liberal divorce laws (see also Constance Rover, 1970).

She acknowledges that *divorce* is seen as *failure* (and that women are often assumed responsible even though it is the actions of men that may be untenable) and speculates on how such a value judgement could be changed: 'Suppose instead of calling it a "law of divorce" it were to be called "Proof of affection" ', she suggests, 'they would like it better then' (Hayek, 1969, p. 77).

But even Hayek, who has edited the collection of letters of John Stuart Mill and Harriet Taylor, cannot accept that Harriet Taylor is intellectually competent, so great is the prejudice against women that it outweighs any contrary evidence. He notes that during the 1830s the *Monthly Repository* contained many feminist articles, particularly by W. J. Fox and W. B. Adams, 'and their arguments often so closely resemble some of Mrs Taylor's manuscript drafts of the period that one wonders whether it was merely that she imbibed her ideas from them or whether her somewhat unpolished drafts did not perhaps serve as the basis for the articles of the more skilled writers' (ibid., pp. 28–9). Either way, her intellectual work existed only in relation to men! I have not seen the 'unpolished drafts' of Harriet Taylor, but I do know that to many men all feminist arguments look much the same (a common manifestation of prejudice), and I do know that it was perfectly possible that Harriet Taylor, in her own terms, was writing and thinking for *herself*, and not for men.

One thing that her correspondence does make clear is that it is not impossible for men to hear and accept as valid what women are saying, although it does necessitate that they abdicate from their role of 'sole authority' and follow the way through experience which is not their own and to which they have no direct access. This correspondence of Taylor and Mill reveals that there are no biological restrictions, that a man can come to accept as real, some experience that is different from his own, and that he can come to appreciate the limitations of his own assumptions and his own knowledge. He can also take account of that different experience and include it in his own frame of reference. Not that I would want to suggest that John Stuart Mill has access to the same knowledge as Harriet Taylor; there is a qualitative difference, for hers is derived from her own experience and his is derived from her explanation.

Like so many of her predecessors (and her contemporaries and successors), Harriet Taylor's work has almost been lost, despite her 'connection' with John Stuart Mill, which must keep her existence 'alive' to some extent while ever he is studied. But even where a woman has been placed firmly in the foreground – as John Stuart Mill placed Harriet Taylor – it is not beyond the capacity of a male-dominated society, and male-dominated knowledge, to eliminate her from consideration, to deny her intellectual existence even where it is demonstrated. Alice Rossi's book on Harriet Taylor and John Stuart Mill (1970) is an excellent attempt to 'reclaim' Harriet Taylor and perhaps, in time (I am eternally optimistic in some respects) Harriet Taylor will be as well known, as affectionately esteemed, and as well studied among women, as John Stuart Mill has been among men. We might even be able to confound the belief that *he* was responsbile for *her* intellectual growth and that he acted as her mentor; we might even be tempted to put the case that he wasn't the superior influence she thought him to be. But that would necessitate the establishment of Harriet Taylor as an intellectually autonomous woman, and such an entity is still an ideal, and not a reality; it would mean that women would have to be able to control their own resources, rather than have them appropriated by men.

While Harriet Taylor has suffered at the hands of the knowledge makers, her treatment seems not so harsh when compared with that received by Margaret Fuller (1810–50). Both women and men have thought, described, explained, discussed, reasoned, written and published (although with reference to publication the ratio is about four times as many men as women, see Lynne Spender, forthcoming) and yet the tradition that we have inherited is almost exclusively concerned with men.

If we can understand the precise way in which Frances Wright, Harriet Martineau, Harriet Taylor and Margaret Fuller were relegated to marginal positions which resulted in denial and obscurity – despite their considerable reputations and visibility in their own times – we may be able to take counteractive measures. To do this, however, we need more detailed documentation of the male-controlled 'image-making-processes' which help to establish a consensus that particular women are 'not up to standard', that their contributions are not of central significance, and that their ideas – if they are to be entertained at all – are to be treated as of only minor importance.

4 Margaret Fuller (1810–1850)

Because Marie Mitchell Olesen Urbanski (1980) has done an intensive study of the making of Margaret Fuller's reputation, I have drawn heavily on her documentation. I am enormously grateful for some of the insights that she has provided and I suspect that more studies of this nature, on a variety of women, would reveal that there are some tried-and-true-techniques for eliminating women's voice from our culture and knowledge, in a patriarchal society. Urbanski begins with a summary of Margaret Fuller's life and work: 'She is the most important woman of the nineteenth century – its best literary critic, the first editor of the *Dial*, a nurse in an abortive Italian revolution (a precursor of both Florence Nightingale and Clara Barton), a woman who recognised the complicated emotional needs of women and men during the early stages of the repressive Victorian era, a foreign correspondent of the daily *New York Tribune*, and the author of numerous works, the most important of which is *Woman in the Nineteenth Century*, the intellectual foundation of the feminist movement' (1980, p. 3).

The question is, by what means was this woman and her work banished from the mainstream of our cultural heritage?

Born in Cambridgeport, Massachusetts, Margaret Fuller was rigidly educated by her father, with a daily routine that was astonishing. She herself said that she would rise before five in the morning, walk for an hour, practise the piano till seven, read French until eight and study philosophy until nine thirty when she departed for a school, to read Greek until twelve. She then returned home, recited and practised until dinner at two, after which she sometimes spent half an hour in conversation – but this was a rare luxury. In the afternoon she tried to read Italian for two hours but was often interrupted. At six she would go for a walk or a drive and she would sing for half an hour or so before going to her room at eleven when she would do exercises and write in her journal on her day's work! (Wade, 1940, pp. 13–14). Her health broke down; at fourteen she was sent away to school; she appeared strange to many of her peers, was ridiculed and felt rejected (Rossi, 1974, p. 146). In 1835 her father died and she assumed responsibility for the family. She went teaching, first in Boston (at the school headed by Bronson Alcott), then in Providence, Rhode Island. In 1839 she moved back to Boston and joined an intellectual group who called themselves the Transcendental Club.

She was acutely aware of the narrow education which women received, and in a way that we would readily associate with *women's studies* today, attempted to do something about it by setting up an educational programme for women, *outside* the institutions controlled by men. She started her *Conversations*. Women (primarily from intellectual families) paid twenty dollars to attend a series of conversations on a wide range of topics. Alice Rossi (1974) says that: 'Fuller provided an important circle of Boston women with skill in public speaking, in defending their viewpoints, in marshalling evidence' (p. 149). She helped women make the transition from the 'private' to the 'public' realm in some respects.

She also became editor of the *Dial* from its inception in 1840 until 1842 and it was in the *Dial* in 1843 that her first major feminist essay was published. Entitled 'The Great Lawsuit – Man versus Men. Woman versus Women', it was later expanded into *Woman in the Nineteenth Century* (1845). After the publication of her book *Summer on the Lakes* she was invited to be the literary critic on the *New York Tribune*, an extraordinary achievement for a woman at that time, and during her period in New York, 1944–6, she wrote numerous essays on a range of topics.

In 1846 she left America for England and Europe where she spent a year meeting with many intellectual and political figures (including Georges Sand) and then she went to Italy, a country which she loved dearly. In Italy she not only participated in an abortive revolution, she also married Angelo Ossoli and gave birth to a son. Returning to America in 1850 with her husband and son, she was drowned on 19 July, off the shore of Long Island, during a storm.

From the moment of her untimely death and the decision to publish her *Memoirs* the process of misrepresenting Margaret Fuller began. Whereas during her lifetime Margaret Fuller was known as both an intellectual woman *and* a woman of personal magnetism and charm, after her death, in what appears to be a fairly consistent pattern for the construction of images of women who have been visible and who have been accorded some status, her personality, and *not* her intellectual accomplishment, became the focus of attention on her. But emphasising personal qualities at the expense of intellectual ones is not the only *bias* apparent in the representation of Margaret Fuller, or for that matter, any other woman of comparable note. A particular personal profile, which may bear little resemblance to the reality of the woman's life but which proves to be productive in patriarchal terms, frequently emerges.

In the case of Margaret Fuller, it was the *Memoirs of Margaret Fuller Ossoli* published in 1852 and edited by such reputable men of intellectual stature as Ralph Waldo Emerson, William Henry Channing and James Freeman Clarke, which began the printed distortion of her personality. As Urbanski says, 'This work became the literary canon that established Margaret Fuller as an "arrogant old maid", aggressive and ugly, the archetypal feminist whose need for attention was channeled into the feminist movement. In fact', she adds, 'this depiction of Fuller established the feminist archetype that remains today' (1980, p. 4).

Margaret Fuller's life has been the subject of many books and biographies, and the *Memoirs*, edited so soon after her death by men of distinction who knew her, has usually been accepted as an authoritative source. The emphasis and values inherent in it have been built upon, elaborated and amplified by subsequent scholars without necessarily being questioned. But the pattern which the editors set for the interpretation of Margaret Fuller was one in which her conversational ability was prominent, and one in which her writing – where included – concentrated on her *literary* rather than her *social* criticism; little attention is paid to her feminism or to *Woman in the Nineteenth Century*. Unfortunately, says Urbanski, the editors did not merely publish Margaret Fuller's letters and journals; they used their position as gatekeepers not just to select, but to *change*, her writing. They constructed an image of Fuller that does not have its origins in her work or her life. A comparison between the accounts in the *Memoirs* and the original documents reveals not only that much of the material was 'destroyed and defaced' by the editors, but that they 'also rewrote Fuller's work, *changing her writing style*' (ibid., p. 5, my emphasis).

And if this isn't enough, let it be noted that they then *criticised that writing style!*

Urbanski is not revealing some previously unknown scandal; this aspect of the fabrication of Fuller has not been entirely a secret in 'scholarly' circles, though of course, it has by no means constituted an 'issue'. There has been some debate about the motives of the editors of the *Memoirs* with Perry Miller, a notable and 'objective' scholar (who has himself taken comparable 'liberties' with her work) excusing the behaviour of the editors on the grounds that in days past the standards of scholarship were not nearly so exacting, and that, distorted and unsubstantiated though the image of Margaret Fuller may be, it can be attributed to accident and a consequence of ignorance (a likely story).

Unlike the 'men of letters', however, Urbanski is outraged that: 'Under the façade of reproduction of actual letters and a journal, the editors rewrote history. What emerges then, is not Margaret Fuller (except in fragments) but the archetypal feminist' (ibid., p. 5). Yet this is not an isolated case. When the male dramatists of the Restoration could find no evidence to support their negative and nasty views of women, they too invented it in the form of *The Female Wits* which has also become an authoritative source on the women it claims to depict.

While women are defined as negative within the society, while their intellectual and creative force is denied, while their resources are seen to be available to men and while their literary work is often perceived as the unfinished or raw data which needs a man to transform it into the polished 'work of art' (a point made clearly by Hilary Simpson, 1979, in relation to D. H. Lawrence and F. Scott Fitzgerald for example), then it is to be expected that men may find it perfectly logical to *rewrite* women's words, while steadfastly denying any intention of misrepresentation. The reverse does not apply; any group of women editors who attempted to rewrite the words of an eminent man, to present their rewritten version as authentic, and then proceeded to castigate him for being what they had created, would be labelled as fraudulent, deceitful and malevolent – and their behaviour would no doubt be cited as evidence of the emotional and unreliable nature of their sex.

According to Urbanski it was the highly reputable and reliable Emerson who was the major architect of the distortion of Fuller, as he presented her as arrogant, aggressive and – predictably – unattractive. She is portrayed as sexually unhappy, as extremely emotional and egocentric, and while she could not write, he says, she could certainly talk! These are the lengths to which the objective sex will go (I would argue, habitually,) to deny women's contribution. This is the literary and historical harassment which works to consign women to their male-decreed sexual identity, thereby repudiating their work.

It is Emerson who is largely responsible for the words attributed to Margaret Fuller which have helped to make her appear not just unattractive, but repellent. In his section of the *Memoirs*, for example, Fuller is reputed to have made the statement: 'I now know all the people worth knowing in America and I find no intellect comparable to my own.' Instead of using this statement to dismiss Margaret Fuller (and I am sure countless women have decided not to proceed further with a study of her, after encountering this sentiment which is usually prominently presented), we have to begin to accept that we cannot trust *any* of the evidence handed to us, while men control knowledge. It is my firm belief that *all* women must be presumed innocent – no matter what the evidence – until we can satisfy ourselves as to the origin of the knowledge about them in a male-dominated society.

So blatant is the misrepresentation of Margaret Fuller in the authoritative records, and so readily has this misrepresentation been accepted (or excused where exposed), that it is possible to dismiss completely any claims of objectivity or veracity, or even fairness, and to argue that male fantasies abound in what we have been led to believe are unchallengeable sources. The image constructed of Margaret Fuller suggests that men may invent anything they choose and pass it off as truth. We are worse than gullible if we take their truths at face value – particularly when they portray women negatively.

Emerson claims that Margaret Fuller was a 'Mountainous ME', a domineering, ugly woman with a nasal voice; so repellant was she, people 'did not wish to stay in the same room with her' (Urbanski, 1980, p. 6). He adds – tellingly – that he was in terror of this Bluestocking. But it is very interesting to note that Emerson also reveals his fascination with Fuller's sexuality, and guardedly hints that he was attracted to her – at the same time he declares that he was puzzled as to what other men could possibly see in her, and her 'burly masculine existence'! (ibid.). Besides, she had many passionate friendships with girls and women (and this not meant as a compliment), and was frustrated in her attempts to gain the love she sought from men, according to him. Contradictory though these images of her may be, and revealing though they may be of Emerson rather than Fuller, one thing that cannot be denied is that they were unlikely to promote a warm response, and to invite women to identify with and seek to know more about Fuller.

In his criticism of Fuller, Emerson stated that she allowed her personal feelings to colour all her judgements – to which I would add that he should know a great deal about the process – and that really she couldn't write at all – her 'pen was a non-conducter', he says (ibid., p. 7). Urbanski points out that the overall impression he gives of Fuller is not just one of an emotional and unstable woman, but one 'whose greatest power was not in her reason but in woman's traditional weapon – her tongue' (ibid.).

Emerson was familiar with Fuller's feminist writing (he was editor of the *Dial* when the first version of *Woman in the Nineteenth Century* was published, and even agreed at one stage to write the introduction to the expanded version), but he completely omits any consideration of her feminist writing in his discussion of her and her work. More than this, he goes so far as to provide a picture of Fuller which seems nothing other than a figment of his own imagination when he suggests she willingly confined herself to female circles and was content with female accomplishments! As *all* 'of Fuller's writing in one way or another', says Urbanski, 'expresses her frustration with the limitations that society placed on women', this depiction is absurd and completely without foundation.

The image Emerson presented, however, was added to by Clarke and Channing, his fellow editors, and then built upon by subsequent commentators who added their own equally derogatory embellishments. Nathaniel Hawthorne was one who not only insisted that Fuller's husband was an ignorant, illiterate, boor but that Fuller, being so unattractive, was fortunate to get him (this in the guise of 'literary criticism', I might add). His opinion, whilst distasteful for me to reproduce here helps to establish the brutal contempt in which many reputable men hold women; 'Tragic as the cata-strophe was', he wrote in relation to Margaret Fuller's death, 'Providence was after all kind, in putting her and her clownish husband and their child on board the fated ship' (quoted in Urbanski, 1980, p. 19). And there is more of the same.

In the long line of detractors, there is also a woman, Sarah Josepha Hale, editor of the *Ladies Magazine*, an opponent of enfranchisement for women. In *Women's Record*, 1855, she said of Fuller that: 'Whatever she might have done, we are constrained to add, that of the books she has left, we do not believe they are destined to hold a high place in female literature. . . . Her fame, like that of a great actor, or singer, was dependent on her living presence, – gained more by her conversational powers than her writing' (p. 667, quoted in Urbanski, 1980, p. 33). There can be little better evidence that the myths about women, about their creativity and intellectual ability, when put forward by women themselves, carry considerable weight; and while such 'sound' judgements may meet with approval from men, they do little to help women.

James Russell Lowell, aspiring poet and editor of the *Atlantic Monthly*, 'laid the groundwork for the myth of the spiteful, egotistic feminist through his bitter satire against Margaret Fuller' (ibid., p. 33). Her brother, Arthur, persisted with the pronouncement that her writing was not matched by her conversation in his introductions to the posthumous edition of her work, and as an ordained minister he felt obliged to present her as a devout Christian. 'Not recognizing the irony of the fact that he was writing a preface to a feminist manifesto', says Urbanski, 'Fuller's brother was at pains to reassure his readers that despite his sister's intellectual accomplish-ments, she did not neglect a woman's domestic duties, no matter how humble' (ibid., pp. 33–4).

Even Julia Ward Howe – 'a member of the Radical Club in Boston, an editor with her husband of the antislavery paper *Commonwealth*, and a lecturer on women's suffrage, prison reform, and international peace' (ibid., p. 34) – who could have been expected to make much of Fuller's feminism in her biography, elected instead to distance herself from the ostensible scandal of Fuller's marriage, and from her feminism, and emphasised her personality rather than her writing.

In the twentieth century, the picture of her has too often been a magnification of the one generated in the nineteenth, with even the most sympathetic accounts concentrating on her personality and ignoring her writing. 'In a July 1949 issue of *Harper's Magazine*, Edward Nicholas published an article with a title that reveals its context: "It is I: Margaret Fuller".' He portrayed her as egotistic and audacious and 'wondered why Ossoli was attracted to "the American woman with the sad plain face, ten years older" ' (ibid., p. 37).

Perry Miller, who excused the rewriting of the record by the editors of *Memoirs* on the basis that 'scholarly methods' were insufficiently estab-lished in 1850, demonstrates that scholarly methods did not change much over the century. He was undoubtedly a scholar, with impressive creden-tials, a professor of American literature at Harvard. The tenor of his treatment of Fuller is also evident from the title he gave one of his articles; 'I Find No Intellect Comparable to My Own'. 'He selected the most derogatory descriptions of Fuller's appearance that he could find to quote', says Urbanski, 'and changed former descriptions of her full figure to "angular and ailing", descriptions of her abundant hair to "not quite blond, stringy and thin" and asserted that she was "phenomenally homely".' He stated that she had no sense of humour and that her style was as verbose as her emotions chaotic (ibid., p. 37). Typical!

'The temptation to make Margaret a great liberal, a champion for the splendid proposition that women have a right to possess and use intelligence, and to shed tears over her untimely death is too often offset by the suspicion', says Miller, 'that much of the ridiculous was mixed up in her tragedy. The long neck, the near sighted arrogance, those qualities which put her in the galerie of the bluestockings of that age . . . prevent us from erecting memorials' (Miller, 1957, p. 99, quoted in Urbanski, 1980, p. 37).

To him, Fuller was ridiculous, ludicrous and ugly and while he offers little (or no) substantiation for his scholarly evaluation, it is patently clear (as Urbanski points out and as the similar treatment of so many women makes obvious), there is no room in a patriarchal society for acceptance – let alone positive recognition – of women's intellectual and creative existence. Fuller's treatment is standard; she is isolated and portrayed as repellant, her ability and worth is denied, she is pushed to the periphery of serious consideration so that the shift into oblivion is barely perceptible and leaves only a lingering shadow of someone who was neither likable nor laudable. Women's traditions are again interrupted and silenced; with few traces left behind of the wisdom and wit of the woman, and with only the surface evidence to go on that she was without personal or intellectual merit, who is going to pursue a study of Margaret Fuller?

This is part of our common heritage; 'James Russell Lowell, Ralph Waldo Emerson, Nathaniel Hawthorne, Oliver Wendell Holmes' – all men of letters and men who control the knowledge we inherit – 'all reacted to Margaret Fuller in an unwitting conspiracy of outrage', says Urbanski. 'Threatened, they used their pens like a chorus to denigrate Fuller as an intellectual and a writer' (ibid., p. 39). I do not think they are unrepresentative of their sex; nor is their behaviour either irrational or surprising in a patriarchal society. Their actions reflect the systematic treatment of women and their ideas, where men are in control, and where they are intent on maintaining their power.

A study of *Woman in the Nineteenth Century* suggests just how much 'tampering with the evidence' was necessary for Margaret Fuller to be accorded the image that for so long has justified her exclusion from our cultural tradition. *Woman in the Nineteenth Century* is an attempt to provide a feminist symbolic framework in which women's existence can be located and made meaningful: it is a panorama of women and their lives with a sub-text which argues for their equality. In a patriarchal society where women's existence and reality is systematically denied, made invisible, and consigned to the realm of non-data, myths are introduced and created to give substance and significance to women's lives. Throughout the book there are references to individual women, to female writers and female characters, all introduced to serve as models and to make women's cultural presence visible and real. From Mary Wollstonecraft to Anna Jameson and Harriet Martineau, to Maria Edgeworth, Mary Somerville, Queen Elizabeth I, Queen Isabella and Georges Sand, Madame Roland and Madame de Staël, to mention but a few who people the pages, Fuller constructs a tradition as she introduces one woman after another and presents the individuality yet shared commonality of women's humanity.

And she cogently argues for the acceptance of her symbolic panorama. Human beings, she says, cannot own or have rights over other human beings: 'As the friend of the negro assumes that one man cannot by right hold another in bondage, so should the friend of woman assume that man cannot, by right, lay even well-meant restrictions on women' (1845, p. 26). No amount of rationalisation about chivalry or protection will justify the restrictions placed on some women, or eliminate the hypocrisy while others are exploited. 'Those who think the physical circumstances of woman would make a part in the affairs of national government unsuitable are by no means those who think it impossible for the negress to endure field work, even during pregnancy, or the sempstresses to go through their killing labours', she says, and 'as to the pen, there was quite as much opposition to woman's possessing herself of that help to free agency, as there is now to her seizing on the rostrum or the desk' (ibid., p. 24).

For those men who argue that women are content, or that they are well provided for, there is, she says, an acid test of their conviction: 'early I perceived that men never, in any extreme of despair, wished to be women. On the contrary, they were ever ready to taunt one another at any sign of weakness, with, "Art thou not like the women, who" – The passage ends various ways, according to the occasion and rhetoric of the speaker,' says Fuller (ibid., p. 30).

Women are held in such low esteem – despite protestations to the contrary – that any woman who is admired by a man is inclined to be labelled as 'above her sex' (ibid., p. 30). And a woman who is proud to be a woman, and who, if required to choose, decides it is *better* to be a woman – as Fuller does – is an oddity indeed.

Like her feminist foremothers, Fuller pinpoints one of the fundamental features of patriarchy – that men have claimed for themselves the qualities they perceive as positive and imposed on women the qualities they regard as negative, and which they seek to avoid. With little concern for the evidence, men have appropriated for themselves such attributes as creative energy and intellectual accomplishment; but the world will not always fit into their framework and women, on occasion, and despite the obstacles, demonstrate that they too possess creative and intellectual ability. And how is this contradiction then overcome, asks Fuller? Not by men admitting that their male definitions are inadequate, but by treating the woman as unusual, as atypical of her sex. 'She has a masculine mind' (ibid., p. 31). In such a way, male *ownership* of creativity and intellectuality is not challenged, nor is the definition of woman challenged, but the individual woman who is supposed to receive such a statement as a compliment is being asked to deny the competence of her own sex and to accept as flattering that she is a pseudo-male. Again, she is damned if she does not have a masculine mind – the only sort of mind that is valued in a male-dominated society – and damned if she does, because she is no longer perceived as a *full* member of either sex. 'A masculine mind' may find this arrangement logical and satisfactory, but Margaret Fuller does not.

Having stipulated that women do not possess these prestigious quali-ties, men then go to great lengths to ensure that their beliefs come true, argues Fuller, and in what could be called prophetic words she says that 'women are so overloaded with precepts by guardians who think that nothing is so much to be dreaded for a woman as originality of thought or character', that women themselves begin to believe what they are daily told, with 'their minds impeded by doubts till they lose their chance of fair and free proportions' (ibid., p. 29).

What woman needs, says Fuller, is 'to live freely and unimpeded', to have 'the free and full employment of her talents', to define herself, for herself, and without reference to men (ibid., p. 27). But, she adds, there is not one man in a hundred million who 'can rise above the belief that woman was made *for man*' and who can accord woman her autonomy (ibid., p. 25). She asks why it is that men feel the necessity to define women in this way, and concludes that part of it is vanity, part power, for 'each wishes to be lord in a little world, to be at least superior over one' (ibid., p. 32). This need, and this reality, distinguishes men markedly from women.

Fuller comments on some of the methods men have used in order to construct and maintain their 'supremacy'. Rather than having lost their relevance, some of the insights she presents are currently being used as the basis for research in such areas as sexual harassment, and the preferential treatment boys receive in mixed sex schools (see Dale Spender, 1982a). We have thought these ideas new and we are only beginning to appreciate that we are just catching up in some instances to where Margaret Fuller left off almost 150 years ago. Think what we might know today if for 150 years we had been systematically developing the ideas she put forward.

She did not believe that men were innocent and that the whole edifice of sex inequality was a terrible accident. She focused on what men were doing and firmly stated, for example, that the male does not use his greater opportunities and advantages to help women, but to hinder, 'he often discourages with school boy brag: "Girls can't do that: girls can't play ball" ' (1980 reprint, p. 33) and he protects and defends the territory he has claimed for himself. (See the work of Elizabeth Fennema, 1980, for the way in which boys today make use of this technique to keep women out of mathematics.)

But girls can, and often do, show themselves to be equally competent, regardless of self-interested male opinion to the contrary. It takes courage though, sometimes enormous courage, for a woman to persist in demon-strating that competency which men insist they do not have, for 'let anyone defy their taunts, break through and be brave and secure, they rend the air with shouts' (ibid.). Men, argues Fuller, engage in the intimidation of women, by a variety of means, so that women will not move out of that narrow and servile space that men have decreed is woman's natural sphere. Nature plays no part in it – it is *force* that keeps woman in her place.

In more recent times the demand for women's autonomy has often led to a 'backlash' and the protestation that there are also many restrictions placed on men. In a patriarchal society, explanations are ready-made to 'blame' women and some of the debates on stereotyping have helped to suggest – erroneously – that *both* sexes have this problem inflicted on them (and usually, that the fault lies with the mother!). Clearly, Margaret Fuller would never have accepted such an interpretation. She could be quoted verbatim in many a contemporary context and her words would not have lost their radical sting: 'It may be said that man does not have his fair play either; his energies are repressed and distorted by the interposition of artificial obstacles. Aye, *but he himself put them there*' (ibid., p. 37, my emphasis) and if he does not like them, he has the power to remove them. Woman possesses no such power, the obstacles for her are not self-imposed, nor does *she* impose obstacles on men! Let men show their good will, their sense of justice and honour, argues Fuller, by ceasing to intimidate women, by removing the barriers to women's full humanity which they as men have erected.

She also tackles the age-old argument put forward by men that women *like* the role men have ordained for them, and that they are happy with their lot. Fuller does not deny that women might agree – indeed, it is fundamental to her case that a measure of women's subordination is the extent to which they are prepared to be agreeable to men, to be self-effacing and deny their own known capacity, in order to please their masters. 'Ye cannot believe it, men', she says, 'but the only reason why women ever assume what is more appropriate to you, is because you prevent them from finding out what is fit for themselves' (ibid., p. 51). Women usually have no choice *but* to agree.

Fuller's analysis ranges across the whole spectrum of contemporary feminist issues, and her theoretical framework is consistent throughout; it is men who are in charge of what we know with the result that we know only what is convenient and enhancing for them. Only a man, she suggests for example, could take prostitution, which is *degrading* for woman, and call this *civilization* (ibid., p. 119). Only men could be responsible for the belief that a boy child is to be preferred to a girl child (ibid., p. 145). Only a man could instigate the idea that a woman's happiness lies in serving and pleasing a man (ibid., pp. 143–4). For, she says 'men do *not* look at both sides' (ibid., p. 108); they see only their own side and they are determined that women agree to see *only* that as well.

And what is the consequence for women? 'The life of woman must be outwardly a well-intentioned, cheerful dissimulation of her real life' (ibid., p. 145). Men require her to be happy with her lot. She must feign fulfilment, pretend passivity and pleasantness, repudiate her own resources. But women must stop, says Fuller; they must understand that they have been deceived, that they will not feel better if they simply try harder to achieve the ideal of femininity. 'I would have woman lay aside all thought, such as she habitually cherishes', says Fuller, 'of being taught and led by men.'

Woman must lead herself, define her own capacities and determine her own destiny. 'I would have her free from compromise, from helplessness', she says, 'because I would have her good enough and strong enough to love one and all beings, from the fulness, not the poverty of being' (ibid., p. 107). Like Wollstonecraft, Fuller wanted women to be strong, and to have control over themselves.

I could quote some of the comments which abound on the deficiencies of Fuller's *style*; I would not want to suggest that *Woman in the Nineteenth Century* is written in a style that is common or familiar today. It has some features that are characteristic of its time and place – but so too do Shakespeare and Milton, and I have not often noticed that they have been handicapped by this, nor that explicatory footnotes which help us to understand what they mean are perceived as a weakness. I *would* want to suggest that there is much in *Woman in the Nineteenth Century* which is useful for us today and which is an integral part of the feminist tradition which we have *not* inherited but which we are reconstructing.

Bell Gale Chevigny (1976) says that: 'Fuller, in her early twenties was living a problem the more impressive and insidious because she could not name it' (p. 3) and one of the factors which must constantly be kept in mind in dealing with women's ideas on women's position is the *absence* of concepts and words to make meaningful women's experience (see D. Spender, 1980). We have no ready-made vocabulary, no shorthand, and we are – still – required to describe and explain with analogy, anecdote, myth. Margaret Fuller did this very well. More than most other feminists she tried to create a whole frame of reference for women, in which those concepts and words were painstakingly brought into existence and on which other women could build, giving shape, substance and meaning to women's lives – if they had been permitted to do so.

Until Margaret Fuller, the feminist protest was predominantly one of exposing the limitations, the absurdities, and the self-interest of the patriarchal frame of reference that men had devised. While it was a necessary initial task to respond in the terms laid down by men, to counteract their claims about society, about women and men, it was not a freely chosen feminist task. The autonomy of women does not consist of *reacting* to the prescriptions of men (although, while men hold power this must be a part of it) but demands that women also begin to encode their own reality, without reference to male definitions of the world. Such a feat is not achieved overnight (it is not achieved over a decade, as the last ten years indicate, for even the most radical of us still have one foot firmly planted in that patriarchal frame of reference in which we were initiated as Mary Daly (1978) indicates), but Margaret Fuller took one of the first steps towards constructing a feminist framework and towards laying the foundations for future exploration.

There are many possible explanations for this particular development within the feminist intellectual tradition, but it is probably no accident that it should originate in America where the contradictions experienced by women were more pronounced in the first part of the nineteenth century. Margaret Fuller was reared on an ideology of freedom only to find as an adult that it did not apply to women: as Bell Gale Chevigny (1976) says, 'Margaret Fuller's problem was the problem of all American women who wanted to *realize* in their adult life an ideology of freedom which was intended simply to be a plaything of their youth' (p. 5). She had the dream of self-determination and rather than abandon it when informed it was not for her, she tried to give it substance, to forge its meaning, to turn her vision into a reality.

The experience of North America seems to have encouraged and facilitated this growth of confidence in women (inadvertently, of course). Harriet Taylor is one of the few feminists of this time not to have been exposed to its direct influence. One woman who did become increasingly more daring – by the standards of the day – after her visit to America and Canada, was Anna Jameson.[2]

5 Anna Jameson (1794–1860)

'Anna Brownell Murphy', says Ray Strachey (1928), 'had been born in Dublin in 1794, and after going through the usual governessing experiences she had married in 1825 a Mr Jameson, who seems to have been a plausible but selfish man, and turned out to be a very unsatisfactory companion, so that after several years of unhappiness his wife separated from him' (p. 90). She took to writing, to support herself: she wrote travel books, art books, literary criticism and implicit protests against women's position in society (see Moers, 1978, p. 285). She was often harassed in her own day and demeaned in ours.

Little has been written about her: her niece Geraldine MacPherson wrote Jameson's *Memoirs* in 1878; some of her letters were edited in 1915 by Mrs Stewart Erskine and in 1939 G. H. Needler published her letters to her friend Ottilie van Goethe. Clara Thomas (1967) has written a biography of her, which begins on the first page of the Preface (in a manner that has become depressingly familiar) with the statement that an authority, 'John Steegman adds a solid testimonial to her importance: "She was rather a compiler than a thinker, perhaps" ' (p. vii).

She kept good company: numbered among her friends were Harriet Martineau, Elizabeth Barrett Browning, Lady Byron, Fanny Kemble – and in her later years she was the adopted 'aunt' of Barbara Bodichon, and Emily Faithfull (ibid., p. 209).

Anna Jameson was earning her living by her pen and this meant that there were restrictions on what she could say, if her living was to be a viable one. Clara Thomas says of her that: 'She was never a radical, though

---

[2] Jacquie Mathews (1981) has pointed out just how many feminists travelled and lived abroad, and sees this as a crucial factor in both their independence and their ability to challenge the taken-for-granted assumptions of their own society. She poses the question of whether these women sometimes defied convention and broke with expected family ties to travel, or whether travel made them question convention and family ties. Harriet Taylor of course travelled extensively in Europe.

a woman writer in her day was open to that suspicion' (ibid., p. 50) as she gained some measure of economic independence in a field reserved primarily for men. 'Her attitudes were those which society in her day expected of her; they assured her of admirers and readers and of a market for all she could produce' (ibid., p. 51). Her feminism, which was fundamental, was usually concealed behind 'a policy of wide-scale appeasement' (ibid., p. 60).

For example, she wrote *Characteristics of Women* (1832), in which the female characters of Shakespeare are treated as 'models' and in this book her purpose and her text work at more than one level. 'It is in its own way a masterful piece of fence sitting,' says Thomas. 'Any serious criticisms which might be levelled at its author are silenced by her statement that she was writing about women, not Shakespeare,' and therefore she could not be considered presumptuous or an intruder in male territory, while 'the many who might carp at a feminist crusade are silenced by the scholarly prestige of the magic word "Shakespeare" ' (ibid.). Thomas adds that there 'is a considerable amount of feminist propaganda' in her writing and while 'the pills have been well-sugared with inoffensiveness they may have been nonetheless effective' (ibid., p. 61).

Anna Jameson tries to be very agreeable; her policy of appeasement is very different from that of Margaret Fuller's (or some of the earlier feminists) but in the long run appears to have been no more acceptable in a male-dominated society. It wasn't enough to satisfy Harriet Martineau either, for she felt that Jameson went too far, that she allowed her *personal* feelings to intrude too much (presumably, in a patriarchal society Jameson could be perceived as possessing a 'grudge' because of the unsatisfactory nature of her own marriage), and Martineau remarked that less personal passion would have rendered her claims for equality more effective (see Margaret Walters, 1976, p. 336).

Some of her letters (which may have permitted a freer forum for her feminism) are very appealing. In January 1837 she wrote from North America to her friend Ottilie van Goethe about the advantages of wedding an Indian chief, and after providing a satirical but none the less horrific account of life for such a wife, she concludes that: 'on the whole good husbands and faithful lovers are not *more* common in savage than in civilized life, as far as I can learn' (see Thomas, 1967, p. 116). Ultimately, however, she was to be even more critical of European practices, which was one of the reasons she was taken to task by most American critics.

As with all women writers, Jameson was a target for the critics and in 1829 'Christopher North' in *Blackwoods* reviewed her book *Loves of the Poets* and said: 'Is there, or is there not such a thing in nature as an ugly woman – not comparatively, but positively? We do not scruple to answer – yes. We saw her – this very day. Red hair – a mouth that – But, to the surprise of Dr Knox, let us run away from the subject . . . That the authoress of "The Loves of the Poets" is a beautiful woman, using that epithet in any one of its million meanings you choose, we lay no claim to a particular fine tact in having discovered from the nature of her volumes' (quoted in Thomas, 1967, p. 52). What on earth does 'Mr North' (John Wilson) mean? Apart from being a load of pretentious 'nonsense', this is just a blatant statement that Anna Jameson is to be associated with ugliness, without any reference to Jameson. It is disparagement by (unfounded) association but none the less acceptable as valid criticism among 'men of letters'. It is a total denial of Jameson's contribution: plain misogyny – but probably perceived as witty and clever; not picked up as evidence that by men's standards women were not permitted to be serious writers, to have any autonomous creative existence, or to be considered in any other way except as sex-objects.

Ten years later the criticisms are less by association. After the publication of *Winter Studies and Summer Rambles in Canada* (1838) – which was likened to Mary Wollstonecraft's 'Letters from Norway,' the record of the travels of another 'disappointed woman' – Anna Jameson receives raps on the knuckles because of her feminism. From the reviews, says Thomas (1967), it is obvious 'that Mrs Jameson has, finally, overstepped the fine-drawn line between permissible criticisms of the education of and role assigned to her sex and the highly suspect field of feminist propaganda. Her writings on the "Woman Question" had formerly been prettily disguised as light reading for ladies; now, she was speaking frankly of and for her own sex – women, not ladies' (p. 141).

However, it is Jameson's later activities which are fascinating from a feminist perspective. 'Anna's most direct influence on the "Rights of Women" movement', says Thomas, 'came through her encouragement of a group of young women, friends and associates of Adelaide Proctar, the daughter of her old friend' (ibid., p. 209). These were the women of the Langham Place group, and they were encouraged by Jameson to make their head-quarters her stopping place. 'She was their patroness and she called them her "adopted nieces". She suggested the idea of the Englishwoman's Journal, a periodical which was designed to open new avenues for women' (ibid.). And, says Thomas, 'The correspondence of Anna's last years was much concerned with the affairs of her "nieces" ' (ibid., p. 210).

Ray Strachey (1928) gives Anna Jameson an honourable mention in her account of the history of the women's movement and says that: 'In 1855 and 1856 this lady gave two drawing-room lectures which were entitled "Sisters of Charity" and "Community of Labour," which created a real sensation in literary and philanthropic London' and which gave impetus to the cause (p. 89). When she 'came forward as the champion of the new cause', says Strachey, 'the effect was prodigious' (ibid., p. 90). For Strachey, Jameson marks the beginning of organisation – with a periodical – in the women's movement.

Across the Atlantic, Angelina and Sarah Grimké also began with 'drawing-room lectures', but the stir they created was not confined to literary and philanthropic circles.

6 Angelina Grimké (1805–1879) and Sarah Grimké (1792–1873)

Born and bred in an upper-class slave-owning family in the deep south, the sisters Sarah Grimké and Angelina Grimké spent many frustrated years trying to find an acceptable outlet for their opposition to slavery. But for them there was little opportunity for effective action. Raised, as they were, in the rigid and restrictive religious and moral code of their time, there was little means of justifying any little action they did engage in. Their protest, which was inextricably tied in with their abhorrence of slavery, and their assertion of human rights, was not born so much of *self*-demand, or the deliberate intention of being disagreeable (although this is how it may have been interpreted), but of deep moral and religious convictions of the sinfulness of slavery. They began to fight against the oppression of others and quickly confronted the reality of their own. In many respects their demand for *women's* rights was thrust upon them, for they found that they had to establish their right to their own voice before they could raise it against slavery, and they found that the right of self-determination which they were claiming for others was a right which they themselves had been denied.

The Grimké sisters are more in the mould of 'missionaries', but the religious and moral dimension of their struggle in no way made it less radical and in many ways served them well, for it constituted a powerful resource which protected them and helped them withstand some of the intense harassment they were often subjected to.

Theoretically, it is unlikely that two much less politically astute women, unwise in the ways of the world, could be found; practically, their political, social and intellectual contribution was considerable. They had led very sheltered lives and the extent of their audacity – not to be underestimated by any means – was their move to Philadelphia and their conversion to Quakerism. Alice Rossi (1974) and Gerda Lerner (1971) both document the isolation of their lives in terms of the social and intellectual issues of their day and Rossi says that they were unaware for example of the work that Frances Wright was engaged in during these years: 'had they read Wright's work or heard her speeches, they might have been spared many years of intellectual struggle, for many of the points they painfully worked out on their own a few years later had been developed and advocated by Fanny Wright several years previously' (1974, p. 285). But Fanny Wright was certainly not required reading in the Quaker circles in which they moved in Philadelphia.

Angelina started it all with a letter to the abolitionist, Garrison, who published it in *The Liberator* – without seeking her permission. 'Her orthodox Quaker friends were furious at the strong public stand Angelina had taken,' says Rossi, and 'her refusal to withdraw the letter was the symbolic act of Angelina's emancipation from the past' (ibid., p. 285). The notoriety was embarrassing to the Quaker community and their censure cost her (and Sarah) some anguish, but when faced with the choice of recanting and working to regain the approval of the community, or of coming out and working to oppose slavery, she – and Sarah – chose the latter.

This *choice* 'seemed to free both sisters for a rapidly escalating aware-ness of the many restrictions upon their lives. Their physical and intellectual energies were soon fully expanded, as though they and their ideas had been suddenly released after a long period of germination,' says Rossi (ibid.). Angelina was galvanised into writing her *Appeal to the Christian Women of the South* (1836).

Angelina's argument was based on the premise that it was God to whom she owed her allegiance, not man-made laws, and in God's terms slavery was sinful; no number of man-made laws could disguise this or make the institution more acceptable. And it was to the women of the south that she appealed for the acknowledgement and denunciation of this evil practice. She assumed that they were moral and responsible beings who had force and could resist, and, while she recognised that women had no formal political power, she did not see them as powerless or unable to end their complicity or unable to take action. Catherine Birney (1885), biographer of the Grimké sisters, says of Angelina's *Appeal* that: 'The chief point she took was this: "The denial of our duty to act in this cause is a denial of our right to act; and if we have no right to act, then may *we* well be termed 'the white slaves of the North' for like our brethren in bonds, we must seal our lips in silence and despair" ' (p. 172).

As a southern woman, Angelina Grimké could draw on the personal experience of white women in the south, *and* understand the experience of slave women. This appeal, as Rossi states, of one woman to other women is unique in the context of the abolition movement. It is no accident that Angelina Grimké urged women to *speak out* against slavery wherever and whenever they could.

Her *Appeal* was widely circulated and its potential for promoting change recognised, and Angelina and Sarah Grimké were soon invited further north to talk to women in private homes and sewing circles about abolition, and under the semi-official support of the Anti-Slavery Societies. But they began to draw larger crowds, to need more than private homes to accommodate their audiences, and to attract men to their lectures. Whether or not they realised it, they were committing 'Fanny Wrightism' and reaped appropriate rewards. There was great hostility to them – particularly from the clergy – and Gerda Lerner (1971) quotes Oliver Johnson, a friend and close co-worker of Garrison who said that: 'The women at that day . . . were the strongest allies of the clergy and in many things their main reliance. The ladies from South Carolina were making a very deep impression on their sex whenever they went, and proslavery ministers felt that some strong measures must be taken to counteract their influence . . . I believe they were more afraid of those two women than they would have been of a dozen lecturers of the other sex' (p. 188).

The clergy, however, were not the only ones to harass the Grimké sisters: Lerner herself says that: 'Most frequently the judgement of press and public did not go beyond a disapproving awareness of their "notoriety" and sniggering speculations as to their motivation in abandoning respectability and its comforts. They were described as old maids anxious to attract men, abnormal creatures lusting for the degenerate pleasures of "amalgamation", embittered spinsters venting their frustrated emotions by public attacks on the sacred and time-honored institutions of society, or simply and most frequently as "cranks". Historians of a later time have, generally, not gone beyond that contemporary judgement' (ibid., p. 226). Personally, I should think that the press and the public went quite far enough!

Catherine Birney (1885) says that: 'the newspapers had not spared them. Ridicule, sarcasm and pity were liberally bestowed upon the "deluded ladies" by the press generally, and the *Richmond Whig* published several editorials about "those fanatical women, the Misses Grimké" ' (p. 170). Birney sees this as little, in comparison to what the clergy had to say about them: 'The feeling grew very strong against them. They were setting public sentiment at defiance, it was said: they were seeking to destroy veneration for the ministers of the Gospel; they were casting contempt upon the consecrated forms of the church; and much more of the same kind' (ibid., pp. 184–5). The clergy felt that their power was being usurped and that they had to take swift and severe action in order to reclaim it; individually and collectively many ministers responded by launching a tirade against women and reminding them that their only power (conveniently), lay in dependency.

What with the clergy, the press, and the public, the sisters felt some obligation to defend themselves and were drawn more into the issue of women's rights in order to justify their stand. And this did not please the abolitionists: the 'woman question' became a divisive issue in the abolition movement.

Theodore Weld – later to become Angelina Grimké's husband – and at this stage the quasi-employer, and advisor of the Grimké sisters, felt that 'as did most of the leaders of the Anti-Slavery Society, the woman's rights issue threatened the concentration of reformers on the anti-slavery cause. Weld regarded the subject in the same light as he might the "peace" issue or the Graham diet – as a side issue which the enemies of abolition might seize on, in order to distract reformers from their main goal' (Lerner, 1971, p. 199).

Characteristic of the response to women's protest across the centuries is the assertion that the time is not yet ripe, that there are other issues that are more important, and that the 'woman question' will be settled after this particular revolution, or war! Women have consistently been urged by men to abandon the 'luxury' of fighting for the female half of humanity in order to fight for the more pressing problems of the male half. Even the problem of slavery was considered a male problem, with female slaves sharing the same fate of invisibility as their sisters.

While Weld – generously – admitted the justice of the cause and unequivocally stated that women could participate in the public realm, he deeply regretted that the sisters had taken to talking and writing about women's rights for: 'Writing of this sort was something any woman could do. But in their function as female anti-slavery speakers they were unique.

He asked them to let others do the lesser work (that is, women's rights work) let *them* do the work they were best qualified to do' (ibid., p. 200).

Given that they had antagonised the south by their opposition to slavery, and the north by their accusations of race prejudice, that they had upset the Anti-Slavery Society, were a source of unease to the public and the press, and a major threat to the clergy, one wonders who comprised the constituency for the Grimkés – if one leaves out women, of course, as a male-dominated society is prone to do.

So incensed were the clergy by the behaviour of the sisters that they issued a Pastoral Letter (1837) which was an attack on 'disagreeable' women in general but on the Grimké sisters in particular, and the best thing that can be said about it is that it provoked Sarah Grimké to write her *Letters on the Equality of the Sexes*: 'Attacking the Bible argument, which was the strongest point of those who claimed women's inferiority was God-given, she held that the Scriptures had necessarily reflected the patriarchal society which had produced them. . . . "I ask no favors for my sex",' she said, ' "All I ask our brethren is, that they will take their feet from off our necks, and permit us to stand upright on the ground which God has designed us to occupy" ' (ibid., p. 192).

In her *Letters on the Equality of the Sexes and the Condition of Woman* (1838) – and signed significantly, I think, 'Thine in the bonds of womanhood' – Sarah Grimké draws together most of the feminist issues that are still current today. Because of the attack by the clergy, and because the *Letters* were an attempt to put forward the alternative view, understandably much of her discussion is devoted to the religious arguments that were put forward to legitimate women's inferior status. By the time Grimké has finished, few are the clerical arguments that are left standing. Even Catherine Birney (1885) – whose biography is ever so modest and ladylike – says that Sarah Grimké 'showed in the clearest manner the unsoundness of [the Pastoral Letter's] assertions, and the unscriptural and unchristian spirit in which they were made. The delicate irony with which she also exposed the ignorance and shallowness of its author must have caused him to blush for very shame' (p. 186). If only it were so!

Judith Sabrosky (1979) is quite misled when she says that Sarah Grimké 'was the first feminist to counter male arguments supporting female inferiority by proving the arguments false themselves' (p. 61), for while she undeniably 'beat them at their own game', she was by no means the first to do so. I think it could be said that Sarah Grimké was one of the contributors to the feminist intellectual tradition which is built on the assumption that male reasoning is restricted because it relates primarily to male, and not human, experience. Women possess different evidence which, when put alongside male logic, renders the male version false.

Surprisingly, perhaps, Sarah Grimké is also part of the feminist tradition of disagreeable women in that she does not ask, she demands; she does not flatter, she decries; she does not appease, she defies. She makes no allowances for male pride or vanity, but instead frequently indulges in an exposé of them and holds them up to ridicule.

Sarah Grimké begins her first letter by stating that women need to be emancipated from 'the traditions of men', for they have been constructed by men to reinforce their own power. She mocks and derides these traditions and says that the Pastoral Letter is part of the same pattern which permitted judges to sit 'on the trials of witches, and solemnly condemn nineteen persons and one dog to death for witchcraft' (in Rossi, 1974, p. 306). While ridiculing and condemning the stance of the clergy, however, Grimké still makes the connection between their power and their violence against women. The basis of their case has been, she says, that women are dangerous, but it is not women who are dangerous, for the danger lies in 'those who, having long held the reins of *usurped* authority, are unwilling to permit us to fill that sphere which God created to move us in, and who have entered into league to crush the immortal mind of woman' (ibid., p. 307). Men have displaced women from their rightful sphere, she argues, and they have stooped to deceitful means to effect and justify this state of affairs.

'The New Testament has been referred to', writes Grimké, 'and I am willing to abide by its decisions, but must enter my protest against the false translation of some passages by the MEN who did that work, and against the perverted interpretation by the MEN who undertook to write commentaries thereon. I am inclined to think', she adds, 'when we are admitted to the honor of studying Greek and Hebrew, we shall produce some various readings of the Bible a little different from those we have now' (ibid.). In this she sets the stage for the work of Elizabeth Cady Stanton (*The Women's Bible*) and Matilda Joslyn Gage.

A woman is no longer kept in her place by the sole use of brute force, Sarah Grimké argues, but is coaxed into believing that the place men have allocated her is appropriate. She is urged to be 'private and unobtrusive', informed that 'her light is not to shine before man' and that 'she is passively to let the lords of the creation, as they call themselves, put the bushel over it, lest peradventure it might appear that the world has been benefitted by the rays of *her* candle' (ibid., p. 308). Men have convinced women to remain backstage so that only they have the limelight – and then they have dared to assert that their presence front stage proves their superiority and its divine origin!

Referring to the Pastoral Letter, Sarah says: 'we are told, "the power of woman is in her dependence, flowing from a consciousness of that weakness which God has given her for protection." If physical weakness is alluded to, I cheerfully concede the superiority: if brute force is what my brethren are claiming, I am willing to let them have all the honor they desire; but if they mean to intimate that mental or moral weakness belongs to woman, more than man, I utterly disclaim the charge. Our powers of mind have been crushed, as far as man could do it, our sense of morality has been impaired by his interpretation of our duties; but no where does God say . . . (even given that men have been the editors and translators of the bible) . . . that he made any distinction between us, as moral and intelligent beings' (ibid., p. 309).

It is totally without foundation in scripture, she argues, 'that what is virtue in man is vice in woman' (ibid., p. 310) and it is perversity and blasphemy on the part of men to suggest that arrangements they have made for their convenience – which is precisely what the *double standard* is – are sanctified by God. This double standard, so espoused and lauded by men, feels very different when one is a woman: 'Ah, how many of my sex feel in the dominion, thus unrighteously exercised over them, under the gentle appellation of *protection*, that what they have leaned upon has proved a broken reed at best, and oft a spear' (ibid., p. 311). Not only are men's arguments false, states Sarah Grimké, but men cannot even begin to live up to the definitions they have of themselves and their own prescriptions for their own strength and importance.

Bit by bit Sarah Grimké dismantled the elaborate religious edifice built up by men and exposed the self-interested and false foundations on which it was built. With some spirit, she points out that if women were to behave towards men in the way required by men, they would be breaking the commandments, for women would be practising idolatory! She demonstrates, repeatedly, that there is no scriptural evidence for the subordination of women, that both sexes are *equal* in the eyes of God, to the extent that there is no reason women should not be ordained, if they so choose. (This was familiar territory, given that the Quakers accepted that women could be 'ministers', as indeed, Lucretia Mott was.) She even goes so far as to reprimand women in sewing societies, whose industry is used to support and educate young men for the ministry, and suggests that if they 'were to withdraw their contributions to these objects, and give them where they are *more needed*, to the advancement of their *own sex*, in useful learning, the next generation might furnish sufficient proof, that in intelligence and ability to master the whole circle of sciences, woman is not inferior to man' (ibid., p. 318). In urging women to stop supporting men, to stop helping them acquire their superiority which they would later use against women, Sarah Grimké is advocating a feminist revolution, which goes even further than Mary Wollstonecraft's strategies for change. Grimké could not have done anything which could have been considered more heretical (and threatening) by the clergy then to demand publicly that women cease helping men to become clergymen, and to put their energy and resources into establishing their own alternatives.

Grimké wants women to stop looking to men for guidance and confirmation for their existence. She wants them to look to themselves, to support each other, to promote opportunities for their own sex instead of giving their allegiance to opportunities for the opposite sex. Emphatically she states that men cannot be relied upon to provide disinterested advice; they see women in relation to themselves and their own self-defined needs, and therefore advise women accordingly.

Men prevent women from being educated, from becoming moral and responsible beings by the simple means of convincing them that such full humanity is unattractive in women and by arranging the world so that a woman's survival depends upon being found attractive by a man. Women 'seldom think that men will be allured by intellectual acquirements, because they find, that where any mental superiority exists, a woman is generally shunned and regarded as "stepping out of her appropriate sphere," which in their view, is to dress, to dance' and 'to set out to the best possible advantage, her person' (ibid., p. 311). If Grimké's argument had not changed substantially from that put forward by 'Sophia', 100 years before, it is also accurate to say nor have subsequent arguments shifted significantly in the 150 years that have elapsed since she made her statement.

One of the issues which she raises and which is no less relevant (and little altered) today, is that there is 'a disproportionate value set on the time and labor of men and women' (ibid., p. 313) and she looks not only at unequal pay for the same work, but *unequal work* – and *no pay* for women! Central to her analysis of women and work and pay, is the female slave, and Grimké points out that women slaves are required to engage in additional services for their masters. That women are 'owned' in a way that men are not is an issue not often raised in abolition literature but one which is fundamental to Grimké's frame of reference. 'Our southern cities are whelmed beneath a tide of pollution,' she says, 'the virtue of female slaves is wholly at the mercy of irresponsible tyrants, and women are bought and sold in our slave markets, to gratify the brutal lust of those who bear the name of Christians' (ibid., p. 314). She appeals to white women to understand this powerlessness, violation and abuse of their sisters and to act in the name of sisterhood: 'Can any American woman look at these scenes of shocking licentiousness and cruelty', she asks, 'and fold her hands in apathy, and say "I have nothing to do with slavery"? *She cannot and be guiltless*' (ibid., p. 315).

Repeatedly, Sarah Grimké urges women to be responsible for their own lives and to cease putting their faith in men and their opinions: 'I do earnestly entreat my sisters to lay aside their prejudices, and examine these subjects for *themselves*,' she says, 'regardless of "the traditions of men" ' (ibid., p. 317). She has much less faith in the capacity of men, however, to put aside their prejudices: they, she says, 'may reject my doctrine, because it runs counter to common opinions, and because it wounds their pride' (ibid., p. 316). It also undermines their power base.

I think that Sarah Grimké is especially interesting for the (modern) way in which she deals with that wearisome question – 'how did it all begin'. 'Now,' she says, 'whether our brethren have defrauded us intentionally, or unintentionally, the wrong we suffer is equally the same' (ibid., p. 317) and, while she does not openly advocate a 'conspiracy theory', she was not suggesting (as many feminists since have done) that the structure of patriarchy was an 'accident' or a necessary stage in the progress of humanity. I like her politics!

Evidently, however, my partiality is not widely shared. One of the most striking features in reading about the Grimké sisters (and I know of no separate treatment of them), is the prominence given to Angelina; the second most striking feature is the prominence given to Angelina's husband, Theodore Weld. (In my notes on the Grimké sisters I can see my own expression of anger as on seven occasions I have actually written some form of expostulation against the great god Theodore whose pronouncements most assuredly fail to capture my imagination.)

Some of Angelina Grimké's insights are no less valuable than Sarah's and her assessment of Catherine Beecher could well be used in a number of contexts today. Catherine Beecher worked long and hard for women's education – not so women could be independent, but so they could more competently fill the position which man had assigned them. Yet with her 'public' role, her own 'career', Beecher could hardly have been said to practise what she preached, and this contradiction – among others – angered Angelina Grimké. (Beecher's views on ending slavery – by a process of gradual elimination – was no less irksome to Angelina, who thought that Beecher did not comprehend the daily realities of the lives of slaves, and women.) Writing to her friend, Jane Smith, Angelina Grimké said that: 'Catherine's arguments are the most insidious things I have ever read, and I feel it my duty to answer them; only I know not how to find language strong enough to express my indignation at the view she takes of woman's character and duty' (quoted in Birney, 1885, p. 198). But answer them she did (her reply is reprinted in Rossi, 1974, pp. 319–22).

Even Catherine Birney sees the contradiction in Catherine Beecher's stand: 'With independence, striking individuality and entire freedom from timidity of any sort it would appear perfectly natural that Catherine should espouse the Woman's Right's reform, even though opposing that of abolitionism. But she presented the singular anomaly of a strong minded woman, already successful in taking care of herself, advocating women's subordination to man, and prescribing for her efforts at self help, limits so narrow that only the few favoured as she was could venture within them' (1885, p. 197). My only disagreement with this statement is that Catherine Beecher was probably not quite so 'singular' as Birney suggests; the same argument was also used by Queen Victoria, who from a very privileged position deplored the presumption of women's rights (see page 321), and neither Catherine Beecher nor Queen Victoria were the last in this line.

One of the features of the life of Angelina and Sarah Grimké which is responsible – at least in part – for what appears to be a peculiar emphasis in their biographies is the fact that their revolutionary activities were in the main condensed into a two-year period. There were many years before and after which have to be accounted for and in some respects the detail of their earlier and later life makes disappointing reading. Before their public speaking and writing, their energy was expended primarily in a religious struggle with which it is difficult to identify today, and after their venture into the public realm the documentation of their confined domesticity suffers in contrast.

If Angelina started it all, so too did she end it, with her wedding, although that had never been the intention. On the contrary, Theodore Weld was determined that she should continue her public role and help prove that marriage did not disqualify women from office. But three days after the wedding (16 May 1838) Angelina Grimké Weld, Theodore Weld and Maria Chapman (Harriet Martineau's friend) were to speak against slavery at the newly opened Pennsylvania Hall which had been built for the specific purpose of providing a place for free speech. There was mob violence even while Angelina Grimké spoke, and the next day the four-day-old building was burnt to the ground. It was the last public speech she gave for many years (she did make a speech in support of women's suffrage at a much later date) and Sarah Grimké gave no more either, although no biographer seems to think this absence on Sarah's part requires an explanation.

Catherine Birney (1885) says: 'Angelina Weld never again appeared in public. An accident soon after her marriage caused an injury of such a nature that her nervous system was permanently impaired, and she was ever after obliged to avoid all excitement or over-exertion' (p. 241).

Gerda Lerner (1971) throws some light on this subject: Catherine Birney, she says, accepted the vague and unscientific explanation offered by Theodore Weld for his wife's 'invalidism' and it has never been re-evaluated, but: 'There is no reference to any kind of accident during this early period. . . . A more plausible explanation is offered by several references made by Sarah years later, which indicate that "accident" is a euphemism for "female condition", which may have occurred between the first and second pregnancies and which, apparently, was greatly aggravated by succeeding pregnancies following quickly one upon the other. . . . Sarah referred to this condition as a prolapsed uterus, so severe that at times it protruded externally, causing great pain. This condition, which with modern medical knowledge is easily corrected, was incurable during Angelina's lifetime' (p. 289–90). The second 'injury' which Weld refers to was either a miscarriage or a hernia condition which developed later.

Alice Rossi (1974) provides a thoroughly feminist explanation for Angelina Grimké's existence after marriage: 'There are no letters from Angelina to tell whether she was pleased, displeased or ambivalent about Weld's firm insistence that she continue her involvement in reform', she says, when he 'discussed the social significance of their marriage, warning her that people think her utterly spoiled for domestic life, so that thousands will be watching their "experiment".' Angelina Grimké was required to be *superwoman*: 'Poor Angelina!' says Rossi. 'Like generations of women to follow, she is expected to meet impossible standards: she must continue her contribution to reform in the larger world, maintain a home and a happy marriage, and in due time, bear and rear children. In Angelina's case, a Southern background that provided her with few domestic skills and little interest in acquiring them up to this juncture in her life, a realistic expectation of a meager income, and no contraceptive devices whereby to control the number or spacing of children – none of these are auspicious indices that she could become the paragon of perfection and boundless energy Weld held out to her' (ibid., p. 291). But in a rather surprising statement, Rossi continues and says: 'It is a credit to Theodore that he applied the same stern standard to himself' (ibid.). It was hardly the same situation, and I for one would forgo the opportunity to give him a pat on the back.

What did Angelina and Sarah (who lived with the Welds) do? Initially, they spent part of the time helping Theodore write a book on slavery – *American Slavery as it is: Testimony of a Thousand Witnesses*. Catherine Birney says that: 'In the preparation of this work, Mr Weld received invaluable assistance from his wife and sister. Not only was the testimony of their personal experience given over their own names, but many piles of southern papers were industriously examined for such facts as were needed and which Mr Weld arranged' (1885, p. 257).

Sarah Grimké knew this was work, and hard work. In 1839 she wrote: 'I do not think we have labored more assiduously for the slave than we have done this fall and winter, although our work is of the kind that may be privately performed, yet we find the same holy peace in doing it which we found in the public advocacy of the cause' (quoted in ibid., p. 258).

Mr Weld was grateful:

The fact is those dear souls spent six months averaging more than six hours a day, in searching through thousands upon thousands of southern newspapers, marking and cutting out facts of slaveholding disclosures for the book. . . . After the work was finished, we were curious to know how many newspapers had been examined. So we went up to our attic and took an inventory of bundles, as they were packed heap upon heap. When our count had reached *twenty thousand* newspapers we said: 'There let that suffice' . . . (ibid., pp. 258–9).

Weld's task was to arrange the material the 'unpaid research assistants' provided; *the book appeared solely in his name.* It was Sarah Grimké who herself said women must abandon their faith in men; they could not begin to understand the issues that related to women, and it seems Weld was no exception. This is blatant appropriation of women's resources and a denial of their intellectual being.

But what about Sarah Grimké? I find it difficult to accept the picture presented of her – the spinster aunt, who 'interfered' too much with the children, who could make Angelina feel inadequate because Sarah took over so much of the responsibility of child care; the suggestion that she disturbed the harmony of an otherwise happy 'nuclear family'. I find it easier to accept the way she plunged herself (along with Angelina) into teaching, in order to earn a living. But were there no other feminist protests from 1838 until 1870 when she joined Lucy Stone in the attempt to vote in the town election, or 1871 when at the age of 79 she went travelling through the country on foot to obtain signatures for a petition to Congress on woman suffrage? For in those thirty and more years feminist theory had given place to a feminist movement.

When I first began this task it was 'conventional wisdom' that while there had been some call for women's rights in the late eighteenth century – represented in the main by Mary Wollstonecraft – this was but an aberration, and the first part of the nineteenth century had witnessed a 'return to normal' with little or no feminist agitation and the implication that women were content with their lot. My survey – which is little more than a tentative exploration of the first layer below the patriarchal surface – suggests that the 'conventional wisdom' has much of the patriarchal convention about it and very little wisdom, from a feminist perspective.

Many were the women who were writing and talking about oppression and injustice (and it must always be kept in mind that the written, published, and preserved record to which this study is of necessity confined represents but the tip of the iceberg); some were doing it more directly than others, and some more disagreeably than others, but it is a gross misrepresentation – although predictably patriarchal – to suggest that feminism did not exist in the first half of the nineteenth century (see also Part III, (b), p. 279).

7   Mary Somerville (1780–1872)

Mary Somerville was also part of that tradition and it is nothing short of an indictment of us as feminists that we tend to omit her and her *mathematical* contribution from our own efforts at reclamation.

Mary Fairfax was born in Scotland; and her father was in the navy, and therefore away from home for long periods. It has been suggested that the absence of patriarchal authority was one of the reasons Mary Fairfax was allowed to grow up as a 'savage', living a carefree life, exploring the coast and moors that bordered her home, and haphazardly if at all educated – 'by the age of ten she could scarcely read' (Lynn Osen, 1974, p. 97). Upon his return her father despatched her to boarding school. Mary Fairfax hated the school 'and even in her old age, her writings continued to reflect the horror of this experience' (ibid.). 'She wrote of the stiff stays with steel busks that were placed in the front of her dress; heavy bands pressed her shoulders back so that her shoulder blades met. A steel rod with a semicircle supporting her chin was clasped to the steel busk in her stays, and in this constrained state she was expected to prepare her lessons' (ibid., pp. 97–8).

But she began to read, and when she returned home for the holidays, the verdict was pronounced that she read too much and sewed too little and in yet another attempt to make her conform to the restricted role of women, she was sent to a sewing school. Not surprisingly, she was – as were many other women of her time not required to engage in paid work in order to survive – extremely bored, and it was out of boredom that she took to studying the stars by night (an activity which could remain undetected) and to teaching herself Latin. When in her mid-teens she attempted to obtain a more formal and systematic education, her aspirations met with fierce family resistance and even greater effort was expended in forcing her to fill her time with domestic duties – not all of which were necessary or contributed to the maintenance of the household but which were seen as proper – albeit superfluous – activities for a young woman. She could have exchanged some words of advice with Harriet Martineau.

Her introduction to mathematics occurred at a tea-party, where she noticed some algebraic symbols in a magazine. 'At the end of the magazine', she wrote later, 'I read what appeared to me to be simply an arithmetical question, but on turning the page I was surprised to see strange looking lines mixed with letters, chiefly Xs and Ys, and asked, "What is that?"

"Oh", said the friend, "it's a kind of arithmetic; they call it Algebra; but I can tell you nothing about it."

And we talked about other things; but on going home I thought I would look if any of our books could tell me what was meant by Algebra' (quoted in Margaret Tabor, 1933, p. 98).

Lynn Osen says that even if Mary Fairfax had had access to someone who knew about the things she was interested in, she would probably have been too fearful to pursue her enquiries because her efforts would have met with ridicule and abuse from her family. She did one day overhear a conversation in which it was suggested that Euclid's *Elements of Geometry* was significant, but obtaining a copy presented enormous difficulties for it simply wasn't on for a young woman to walk boldly into a bookshop and ask for the book. Eventually, however, she did manage to get a copy and while she impressed her brother's tutor with her understanding, she promoted her family's wrath: 'Her mother was appalled and ashamed by such aberrant behavior, and the servants were instructed to confiscate Mary's supply of candles so that she could not study at night. However, by this time, Mary had gone through the first six books of Euclid' (Osen, 1974, p. 102).

In 1804 she was married to her cousin, Samuel Greig, but he had little sympathy for her study and even less for intellectual pretention in women. She had two sons (one of whom died in infancy) and then in 1807 her husband died. Although she was depressed after these events, she also found that as she was *financially independent* she could for the first time in her life indulge her desire to study mathematics. 'By this time', says Osen, in a statement which is not meant to be humorous but which I find quite entertaining, 'she had mastered plane and spherical trigonometry, conic sections, and J. Ferguson's *Astronomy* on her own. She had also attempted to study Newton's *Principia*, although she found this latter extremely difficult at first reading' (1974, p. 103).

Then she won a prize for a solution, in a popular mathematical journal, and with advice from some experts began to acquire a background in mathematics. 'I was thirty three years of age when I bought this excellent little library of mathematics books,' Mary wrote, and 'I could hardly believe that I possessed such a treasure when I looked back on the day that I first saw the mysterious word "Algebra," and the long years in which I persevered almost without hope. It taught me never to despair. I had now the means, and pursued my studies with increased assiduity; concealment was no longer possible, nor was it attempted. I was considered eccentric and foolish, and my conduct was highly disapproved by many, especially by some members of my own family. They expected me to keep a gay house for them, and in that they were disappointed. As I was quite independent, I did not care for their criticism' (quoted in Tabor, 1933, p. 107). Mary Somerville deserves a lot more attention – in terms of both her mathematical and feminist theories.

Mary Somerville lived as a feminist and supported women's issues –

including suffrage although she did not write explicit feminist theory (or none that I have discovered). She was a woman of great intellectual stature who produced an impressive amount of creative work. One wonders how many more women there might have been in mathematics, or in the arts (see Germaine Greer, 1979 and Rosika Parker and Griselda Pollock, 1981), if they had been financially independent and able to cater for their own interests, rather than those of men.

In 1812, Mary married another cousin, William Somerville, who supported her work and 'helped her to search libraries, read proofs, and check manuscripts' (Osen, 1974, p. 105). Once she moved to London (and the Royal Institution of Great Britain where she could continue her studies), Mary Somerville associated with some of the greatest mathematicians of the time. In 1826 she presented a paper to the Royal Society on 'The Magnetic Properties of the Violet Rays of the Solar Spectrum' and in 1827 she was approached to write two books – one on Pierre Laplace's *Mécanique céleste* and one on Newton's *Principia*. Confronted with this request, Mary Somerville experienced those self-doubts that are so characteristic of women in a male-dominated society. She had no 'crisis of confidence', however, and had already dealt with the 'fear of success' syndrome (for she no longer seemed to be worried as to whether or not she was suitably feminine) and she consented to write the books, with the safeguard that the task should be kept secret until they were completed and that the manuscripts should be destroyed if she failed in the endeavour.

But like so many women – Elizabeth Gaskell among them (see Anna Walters, 1980) – she found it difficult to call her time her own, and to concentrate on her work 'I rose early and made such arrangements with regard to my children and family affairs that I had time to write afterwards;' she wrote, 'not, however, without many interruptions. A man can always command his time under the plea of business; a woman is not allowed any such excuse.' Unlike Mary Astell, who over one hundred years before had encountered the same problem, Mary Somerville, it seems, was unable to engage in subterfuge to ensure that her time was her own: 'At Chelsea I was always supposed to be at home when friends and acquaintants came out to see me; it would have been unkind not to receive them. Nevertheless, I was sometimes annoyed when in the midst of a difficult problem someone would enter and say "I have come to spend a few hours with you" ' (quoted in Tabor, 1933, p. 106).

Mary Somerville did not just translate Laplace's work; she presented her 'own very valuable opinions' which were not only accepted, but praised (Osen, 1974, p. 108). Her book was entitled *The Mechanisms of the Heavens*, and, with aims that were very similar to those that Martineau was to adopt in her *Illustrations*, Somerville tried to explain her work in terms that were accessible to lay people. (The wonder of it is, of course, that Somerville was not dismissed as a 'populariser' but perhaps this is because so little attention has been paid to her and her work.) When today practitioners of women's studies insist that there must be no mystification, when they argue that all people are capable of knowing and understanding, they are not doing something new, but are continuing in a tradition established by such women as Mary Somerville, Frances Wright, and Harriet Martineau.

'After the publication of *The Mechanisms of the Heavens* in 1832, she was raised to the first rank among scientific writers of the time', says Osen (1974), and 'distinctions were showered on her. The British Royal Society ordered her bust by Chantry to be placed in their great hall; a civil list pension was awarded to her; and her work became a required textbook for the honor students at Cambridge' (p. 110). The irony of the latter was undoubtedly not wasted on Mary Somerville who was, of course, not permitted to attend Cambridge (women were not admitted there as full students until 1948, see Rita McWilliams-Tullberg, 1975) and who was well aware of the arguments put forward by men that women were not capable of serious study, particularly scientific study. Her 'ideas' in this case could be used by patriarchy, and were duly taken – without any modification to the basic thesis of the denial of women's intellectual ability.

In 1834 she published *The Connection of the Physical Sciences* in which she stated in the preface that it was her intention 'to make the laws by which the material world is governed, more familiar to my country-women' (Osen, 1974, p. 113) and, while this publication was a source of immense satisfaction to her, 1834 was also a year of intense disappointment – in one respect. It was the year of the new comet and at the time she was in Italy, where the only observatory which had the required facilities for sighting it was a Jesuit one – where no women were allowed. To many, this deprivation is seen as a symbol of Mary Somerville's life – she was excluded over and over again from those communities which nurtured and informed her work. It must always be remembered that not only was she 'self-taught' – a remarkable achievement in mathematics and the sciences – but that she was self-taught in the face of fierce resistance and hostility on many occasions.

She continued to produce her creative and intellectual work. *The Connection of the Physical Sciences* was followed by *Physical Geography* and numerous papers and monographs. *Molecular and Microscopic Science* was published in 1869 when Mary was eighty-nine years old. It was a summary of the most recent discoveries in chemistry and physics. Among her other works were several treatises on subjects related to physics, such as the unpublished *The Form and Rotation of the Earth*. . . . She also wrote *The Tides of the Ocean and Atmosphere*.

She did receive some honours in her lifetime – a Victoria gold medal of the Royal Geographical Society in 1869, distinctions from the Italian Geographical Society – but, apart from Somerville College at Oxford and the Mary Somerville mathematics scholarship for women at Oxford, few are the reminders of her fame and achievement. She too has virtually disappeared, and so extensive has the repudiation of her been that it is still possible for people to assert that women are prevented from participating fully in mathematics and science because of some defect in their make-up. Women are still prevented from doing mathematics and science – and in the same way as Mary Somerville was – by being excluded from the circles in which such knowledge is nurtured and generated (for further discussion see Dale Spender, 1981b, and 1982a).

During the first half of the nineteenth century, contrary to 'conventional wisdom', women were challenging the limitations imposed on them, in a variety of ways. Some, like Mary Somerville, simply persisted in a relatively quiet but stubborn way to disregard both the boundaries which circumscribed women's existence, and the sanctions that were used against those who practised defiance. While she by her very existence and intellectual achievements made a mockery of men's stipulations that women were intellectually inferior (Dr William Whewell, Master of Trinity, said of Mary Somerville that she 'shows herself in the field in which we mathematicians have been labouring all our lives and puts us to shame', Tabor, 1933, p. 112, and of course her book was the text at Cambridge), there were other women moving on other frontiers and presenting comparable evidence of their intellectual competence.

Jane Austen had written her novels which not only revealed the women's world through women's eyes (see Judith Newton, 1978) but which in terms of technique and style commanded respect from the male literati, and the Brontë women (partly through the use of 'deceit' and male pseudonyms, of course) had used their pens and their experience as women to show how the structures imposed on women resulted in consequences not envisaged by men. The Brontës too helped to subvert the belief that women were incapable of intellectual or creative activity.

In Italy, Elizabeth Barrett Browning was making a more explicit feminist protest, particularly in the form of *Aurora Leigh*, where she not only challenged men's ostensible superiority on the grounds that as they had more advantages they were more likely to achieve, she also argued that they were more likely to achieve in a world of their own making, where their own standards prevailed (see Cora Kaplan, 1978).

Across the Atlantic, by the mid-nineteenth century Lucretia Mott and Elizabeth Cady Stanton had organised the first Woman's Rights Convention in 1848 and Paulina Wright Davis had organised a follow-up, in Worcester, in 1850. Lucy Stone and Antoinette Brown had graduated from Oberlin College and registered many a feminist protest in the process, as Lucy Stone set her sights on being a public speaker on behalf of her sex, and Antoinette Brown looked towards ordination in the ministry.

8 George Eliot (1819–1880)

And in England, during the early 1850s George Eliot was meticulously piecing together some of the recorded fragments of women's experience and was trying to construct a meaningful pattern for women's lives.

In 1855 she published an essay entitled 'Margaret Fuller and Mary Wollstonecraft', drawing together the lives and the ideas of these two women and attempting to provide a conceptual framework which could form the foundation of a feminist tradition. She built on the work of

Wollstonecraft and Fuller and attempted to make links between their lives and her own. Needless to say, this is not an essay for which she is famous. The essay was only reprinted once from the time it was first published until Thomas Pinney's (1963) selection of her essays.[3]

It was not so surprising that George Eliot should have identified strongly with Margaret Fuller and Mary Wollstonecraft — there is a large element of common experience among them, for George Eliot too 'had faced and defied almost every contemporary manifestation of masculine oppression' (Nicholas McGuinn, 1978, p. 193) and was intent on living her own life *outside* the boundaries laid down for women. Like Wollstonecraft and Fuller, she too made heartfelt claims for the intellectual existence of women; she too was trying to earn her living by her pen, and she too encountered criticism and hostility about the way she conducted her life — particularly her personal life. What is significant is that, despite the undoubted vulnerability of her position, George Eliot was prepared to risk public identification with these women — and consequently, to risk (more) public abuse, *and* her livelihood.

Why was she prepared to take such a big step? Part of the answer lies, I think, in the way in which Eliot appreciated that the three of them were not just three individual women, but were representative of women's struggle in a male-dominated society. She saw not just 'interesting coincidences' among the three of them, but a pattern. She was not content to see women's problems as *individual* but instead used the collective experience, ideas and explanations as the substance for a thesis on women and women's traditions. This comes through in her essay, not just in the words themselves but in some of the 'meanings between the lines'. Working on two levels, she tries to achieve the contradictory aims of reclaiming Wollstonecraft while protecting herself.

In 1855 there was no 'professional' reason for George Eliot to write about Mary Wollstonecraft; there was not even an immediate reason why she should write about Margaret Fuller, for *Woman in the Nineteenth Century* had been published almost ten years before, Fuller had died in 1850 and the *Memoirs* had been published in 1852.[4] Why then would she choose to write such an article as this?

Whereas it might have been relatively safe to present some information on Margaret Fuller — who still enjoyed an element of esteem in some quarters — it was not at all safe to try and bring Mary Wollstonecraft back into the literary fold from the wilderness to which she had been virtually banished after Godwin's edition of her *Memoirs*. Nicholas McGuinn (1978) says, why indeed 'should she introduce the name of Mary Wollstonecraft into the review, compare her work with *Woman in the Nineteenth Century*, devote so much space in an already short article to quotations from *A Vindication of the Rights of Woman*, and, as a climax to the essay, add

---

[3] Because there are biographies and critical works on George Eliot available I have not included the personal details of her life nor an evaluation of her fiction.

[4] George Eliot had expressed her wish to write a full-scale article on Margaret Fuller in 1852, but it was not written, see Pinney, 1963, p. 99.

her voice to the pleas of the two authors, if it was not George Eliot's intention here to advance the idea of a growing tradition of feminist theory, to reacquaint the reading public with the work of Mary Wollstonecraft, and use the opportunity provided by her review of two feminist works to make a personal statement on the oppression of women?' (p. 195).

George Eliot knew that Mary Wollstonecraft was in grave danger of disappearing and she attached particular significance to this. She knew that it was not Wollstonecraft's ideas that had been discredited – they had virtually not been seriously addressed – but her 'womanliness', her 'morals', her conformity to male-decreed standards which was the weapon used against her. Eliot knew that the process had already begun with Fuller and was likely to extend to herself, and she determined to make some effort to alter this course of events. But even as she registered her protest she found herself in the same compromising position as her foremothers. She was not free boldly to proclaim what it was that men were doing. Instead she is forced to function in the same deferential framework, and not just in terms of using a male pseudonym and at times adopting the more prestigious form of the male persona, but by feeling obliged to employ a particular style and tone – which is acceptable to men – to ensure that she can continue to have a public voice at all.

The tone adopted by George Eliot in this essay, says McGuinn, 'belies all that has been said before about her style of essay writing. The frankness, self confidence and "fierce gusto in denunciation" so characteristic of her other pieces are replaced in "Margaret Fuller and Mary Wollstonecraft" by subtly-planned rhetorical strategies and a sense of caution that is almost ingratiating' (ibid., p. 195). George Eliot finds herself confronted with the same contradiction experienced by both Fuller and Wollstonecraft (and Aphra Behn too), the very contradiction she is indirectly addressing, of trying to declare her endorsement and support for women, while at the same time retaining her reliability and respectability. Like them, she compromises on many issues. She makes her concessions to her male readers (and employers) but she also manages to insert a few barbs of her own on the way. Perhaps she left the way open for them to suggest, patronisingly, as Thomas Pinney does in 1963, that the interest in these women on George Eliot's part can be explained in terms of a 'melancholy attraction' for 'such anomalous women' basically on the grounds of her impressionable youth (ibid., p. 199)!

Eliot *was* fascinated with Wollstonecraft: she made references to her throughout the course of her life and the attempted suicide of Mirah in *Daniel Deronda* closely parallels Wollstonecraft's attempted suicide. But her fascination is not just with the individual, but with what she represents to Eliot. In the absence of an established tradition of creative, intellectual, and respected women philosophers and writers, George Eliot – like Virginia Woolf was to do in *A Room of One's Own* in 1928 – constructed a heritage, a context, in which to locate herself, her ideas, and her writing.

In writing her article on the two women, Eliot recognises that, while it is important that she present their ideas, men are not going to find them at all pleasing. But she will not allow the possibility of dismissal on the customary grounds – that is, that women are intellectually inferior, incapable of reasoning, unable to present a serious and substantiated argument. Eliot is concerned to show – beyond any possibility of doubt – that Margaret Fuller and Mary Wollstonecraft are rational and serious, that their arguments are sound and of substantial intellectual calibre – and that if men do not find them acceptable, then it must be for some other reason.

In commenting on *Woman in the Nineteenth Century* (and in the process, indirectly commenting on her own position), Eliot says that the book contains no 'injudicious' statements, but is 'a calm plea for the removal of unjust laws and artificial restrictions, so that the possibilities of (woman's nature) may have room for full development' (ibid., p. 200). Who could find such a stand objectionable?

Once she has established that Margaret Fuller's case is fair, just, reasonable – and intellectually competent – Eliot feels that the ground is sufficiently prepared to introduce Mary Wollstonecraft. It is interesting, she says, to compare Fuller's work 'with a work on the position of women written between sixty and seventy years ago – we mean Mary Wollstonecraft's *Rights of Woman* . . . the comparison, at least in relation to strong sense and loftiness of moral tone is not at all disadvantageous to the woman of the last century' (ibid., pp. 200–1). Eliot then provides a clever explanation for the disappearance of Mary Wollstonecraft – clever because it too is designed to remove the grounds for the usual male objection to this thesis and to appeal to a sense of superiority. 'There is in some quarters', she states, 'a vague prejudice against *Rights of Woman* as in some way or other a reprehensible book, but', she advises, 'readers who go to it with this impression will be surprised to find it eminently serious, severely moral' (ibid., p. 201). She makes it very difficult for the book to be discredited on moral grounds (the basic rationale for its banishment).

However, although Eliot is definitely addressing herself to men, she still insists on including the basic dimensions of the argument; she still wants to state why it is when the case is so convincing it has been dismissed. 'Anything is more endurable', she writes, 'than to change our established formulae about women', and, despite the fact that she uses a male persona, she adds forcefully 'or run the risk of looking up to our wives instead of looking down to them' (ibid., p. 205). She continues with characteristic causticness and says, 'men say of women, let them be idols, useless absorbents of precious things, provided we are not obliged to admit them to be strictly fellow beings, to be treated one and all with justice . . .' (ibid.). To Eliot the crux of the matter is that men will not treat them seriously, they will not allow women to be thinking conscious human beings – with a different experience of the world.

In relation to Wollstonecraft, Eliot deals only with her book and her ideas (which were little known) instead of her personal life (which was well known, caricatured, and discredited). Nicholas McGuinn suggests that this is because there are too many parallels between Wollstonecraft's life and Eliot's own, and she does not want to draw attention to their similarities in case they both end up being 'tarred by the same brush'. But surely this is also because George Eliot is constructing a pattern of the way women thinkers and writers have been treated in a male-dominated society. She recognises – even if McGuinn does not – that it has been a much-used strategy to condemn a woman's personal life so that it removes the necessity to address her ideas, and so she treats Fuller's and Wollstonecraft's ideas very seriously in order that they may become the substance of debate. For Eliot there is simply no need to focus on how many children these writers had, or under what circumstances; it has never been necessary for men to know these things in relation to their own sex, as a basis for assigning credibility to men's ideas.

That it is men who have the vested interest in the status quo, that it is men who are benefiting from denying women's intellectual existence and that it is men who are insisting that what is best for them is best for women too, are not the only aspects of feminist theory that George Eliot shares with her predecessors and that she left as a legacy to her successors. She understands some of the (current) complexities of the interaction between expectation and reality, and the way men have made use of it against women. 'On the one side', she says, 'we hear that women's position can never be improved until women themselves are better: and on the other, that women can never become better until their position is improved' (ibid., p. 205). This is used in the way that 'Sophia' indicated – so that women are denied opportunities for 'improvement' and then blamed for not 'improving'.

One statement she makes – which might prove to be not at all popular but which none the less does point to some of the 'inconsistencies' in some forms of feminist analysis today – is on the danger of arguing that while existing conditions pertain, women are superior. Such a position, states Eliot, reinforces male justification for the status quo, for if it can be substantiated that oppression produces a 'superior' being, 'then there would be a case in which slavery and ignorance nourished virtue, and so far we would have an argument for the continuance of bondage' (ibid.).

Eliot is perfectly aware that masculinity is prestigious because men have power. She is also aware that the male perspective on the world – while prestigious – is not necessarily desirable, for it ignores much, distorts much, and yet is not open to challenge or change because of the power of men. 'Men pay a heavy price for their reluctance to encourage self help and independent resources in women' (ibid., p. 204), asserts Eliot, emphasising that there is much which men cannot or will not see.

But it is not so much what she says as what she does to establish the visibility of women's traditions that makes this (understandably much-neglected) essay so significant. Her validation of Margaret Fuller, her reinstatement of Mary Wollstonecraft as well as her own feminist statement – all made in a context of male domination and all made with the consciousness that her words and her life might be subjected to the same processes as her predecessors – all help to construct the basis of the feminist tradition as it has existed in a male-dominated society.

Nicholas McGuinn sums up this essay and says much with which I concur: ' "Margaret Fuller and Mary Wollstonecraft" merits particular attention because it is the first attempt of any length by a woman of feminist sympathies to rescue *A Vindication of the Rights of Woman* from fifty years of public obscurity, and again because it affords a fascinating insight into George Eliot's thoughts regarding the position of women on the eve of that literary career in which this theme was to feature so prominently' (ibid., p. 202–3). But George Eliot is not – as McGuinn implies – an isolated example of a woman who is forced to couch her ideas in a form acceptable to men – for the recognition that this is not an individual experience but the reality for women under patriarchy is very much a concern in her essay.

Says McGuinn, this 'essay shows how a woman of proud spirit and great mental power is obliged to humiliate herself intellectually – by cajoling and hinting when she has just cause to speak with frankness and anger: by tailoring her arguments to suit the prejudices of her audience' (ibid., p. 203). This is outrageous – but it was not and is not just the fate of George Eliot. Cajoling and hinting, tailoring arguments to suit the prejudices of the dominant group, masquerading as 'feminine' to obtain a hearing, being interrupted and silenced, are demands that are made on women while they are subordinate and are by no means peculiar to George Eliot – as she knew. Nor is this attributable to women: it is not women's fault as McGuinn also implies.

George Eliot was trying to establish part of the tradition of women in a male-dominated society and she included herself in that tradition. She felt obliged to phrase her case in a form acceptable to men (particularly in her essays – although she had more freedom in her fiction), but she cannot be held accountable for that, for it was *realistic* on her part to recognise that men controlled resources – and she was trying to earn her living. But she knew that women were without intellectual credibility, and that her efforts, no matter how cautious or circumspect, were unlikely to promote change. She would not have been surprised to learn that this essay should also have virtually disappeared, for by the mid-nineteenth century women were becoming increasingly aware of what happened to women and their ideas.

PART THREE

BACKWARDS OR FORWARDS?

(A)

NORTH AMERICA

1 The failure of the women's movement

In 1855, seven years after the first woman's rights convention in the United States (Seneca Falls, 1848), Elizabeth Cady Stanton (1815–1902) and Frances Dana Gage (1808–84) were obliged to defend the women's movement against the accusation of *failure*, made by one Gerrit Smith.

If this strategy of declaring the women's movement to be 'over' sounds familiar, so too does the feminist stance taken by Stanton and Gage, who in the repudiation of the charge, raised virtually every issue that concerns the modern women's movement. This similarity between the past and the present is not just an interesting coincidence, for what we need to know – and what we have been diverted from discovering – is that this pattern of accusation (and response) has recurred again and again over the last 130 years.

When we are informed today (as many of us are) that the women's movement has run its course and has been unsuccessful in achieving its aims (and it has even been put to me that it has been downhill all the way since 1977, although the precise date was not volunteered), then we are being little short of self-destructive if we treat such declarations seriously. But we are beyond being intimidated – and perhaps even being demoralised – if we treat such statements with the dismissal they deserve, and instead of apologising for our supposed failures, instead of feeling guilty and resolving to change ourselves and to try harder, we securely assert that this is but a tired old technique which hasn't worked before and isn't going to work now. This was the advice of Elizabeth Cady Stanton in 1855 and when she gave it she drew on the advice and counsel of her foremothers, women such as Mary Astell, 'Sophia' and Frances Wright, who all insisted that women must examine the source and the purpose of these ideas, and must remember that men have a lot to gain if women begin to believe that they are powerless and incapable of changing the social arrangements.

And it is not just the advice offered by women like Elizabeth Cady Stanton that we can turn to – it is the testimony of their own lives. For almost fifty years after Gerrit Smith's statement that the women's movement had failed, Elizabeth Cady Stanton went on living, working, speaking writing against male dominance. If part of the purpose of declaring the women's movement to be a failure was to send Stanton back to the kitchen, then it was spectacularly unsuccessful.

Hundreds of women like her comprise our cultural heritage – women for whom the issue of male dominance was of central concern and who made a life-long commitment to changing it. For Lucretia Mott (1793–1880), Susan B. Anthony (1820–1906), Lucy Stone (1818–93), Matilda Joslyn Gage (1826–98), Emma Goldman (1869–1940), Olive Schreiner (1855–1920), Josephine Butler (1828–1906), Millicent Fawcett (1847–1929), Charlotte Perkins Gilman (1860–1935), Crystal Eastman (1881–1928), Mary Ritter Beard (1876–1958), Virginia Woolf (1882–1941), Winifred Holtby (1898–1935), Vera Brittain, and Rebecca West, Dora Russell and Simone de Beauvoir – *to name but a few*, their passionate ideas about women were *not* a passing phase but part of their entire existence. It is a male myth – possibly the product of wishful thinking – that has led us to believe that the women's movement has come and gone on a few occasions. Since 1855 (and earlier) there has been a 'women's movement' and there have always been women who have analysed the social arrangements and who have protested, resisted, argued, challenged, contested, struggled, consolidated, and fought to change those arrangements and to end male power. *Their* efforts have been sustained and *uninterrupted*. That we have inherited a history of silences and interruptions indicates the extent to which men have written – and falsified – the records. It also points to the oppression that women have been resisting but which still in many respects, remains.

Had Elizabeth Cady Stanton – and Frances Dana Gage – known just how long and hard the struggle was to be, they might not have been quite so confident in their rebuttal of Gerrit Smith's case, but whereas their optimisim was based on *faith*, faith in women to go on, we have the *evidence* that they did. We also have the evidence that many of the issues of 1855 are the issues of the 1980s as well.

Gerrit Smith's letter (printed in Frederick Douglass's paper, see Stanton et al. 1881, vol. I, pp. 836–9) stated that the women's movement had failed in 1855, primarily because it was 'not in the proper hands' (p. 836), and, because the wrong hands also wore the wrong dress. He was a supporter of dress reform, and his daughter, Elizabeth Smith Miller, had visited Elizabeth Cady Stanton in Seneca Falls in 1852 'dressed somewhat in the Turkish style – short skirt, full trousers of fine black broadcloth; a Spanish cloak, of the same material, reaching to the knee' (Stanton, 1898a, p. 201) and its advantages were not lost on Elizabeth Cady Stanton: 'To see my cousin with a lamp in one hand and a baby in the other, walk upstairs with ease and grace, while, with flowing robes I pulled myself up with difficulty, lamp and baby out of the question, readily convinced me that there was sore need of reform in women's dress, and I promptly donned a similar attire. What incredible freedom I enjoyed for two years! Like a captive set free from his ball and chain, I was always ready for a brisk walk through sleet and snow and rain, to climb a mountain, jump over a fence, work in the garden, and, in fact, for any necessary locomotion' (ibid.).

But only for two years.

The costume became known as the bloomer – as a result of Amelia

Bloomer using her paper the *Lily* to advocate its adoption – and the issue was then taken up by the press in general 'and much valuable information was elicited on the physiological result of woman's fashionable attire; the crippling effect of tight waists and long skirts, the heavy weight on the hips, and high heels, all combined to throw the spine out of plumb,' wrote Elizabeth Cady Stanton in *Eighty Years and More* (ibid.). 'But, while all agreed that some change was absolutely necessary for the health of women, the press stoutly ridiculed those who were ready to make the experiment' (ibid.).

Elizabeth Cady Stanton says that quite a few sensible women adopted the bloomer costume, as did skaters and gymnasts and 'Paulina Wright Davis, Lucy Stone, Susan B. Anthony, Sarah and Angelina Grimké, Mrs William Burleigh, Celia Burleigh, Charlotte Beebe Wilbour, Helen Jarvis, Lydia Jenkins, Amelia Willard, Dr Harriet N. Austin . . .' (ibid., p. 203), but after two years the experiment was abandoned among the women in the women's movement. And why?

Because so 'many laughed it to scorn and heaped such ridicule on its wearers that they soon found that the physical freedom enjoyed did not compensate for the persistent persecution and petty annoyances suffered at every turn. To be rudely gazed at in public and private, to be the conscious subjects of criticism, and to be followed by crowds of boys in the streets, were all, to the very last degree, exasperating. A favorite doggerel that our tormentors chanted, when we appeared in public places, ran thus:

> "Heigh! ho! in rain and snow,
> The bloomer now is all the go.
> Twenty tailors take the stitches,
> Twenty women wear the breeches.
> Heigh! ho! in rain or snow,
> The bloomer now is all the go."

The singers', adds Stanton, 'were generally invisible behind some fence or attic window' (ibid.).

Today, we would call this form of behaviour harassment. It has its modern counterpart in women who have objected to the way women's bodies have to be 'laced' and marketed to find favour among men, and the ridicule heaped upon women who abandoned the lacing of the bra and took to more comfortable clothing. But the 'bloomer wearers' – a media image – became a caricature in the same way as the 'bra burners', and because of the adverse publicity – and because women were obliged to defend their dress at the expense of articulating their ideas – many women, like Stanton, returned to the conventional and restrictive costume of the day.

There was so much hostility towards the bloomer, that it was decided that it simply was not worth preserving: it was not only uncomfortable for the women, says Stanton, but for any men who accompanied them. 'People would stare, many men and women make rude remarks, boys followed in crowds, with jeers and laughter, so that gentlemen in attendance would feel it their duty to show fight, unless they had sufficient self-control to pursue the even tenor of their way, as the ladies themselves did, without taking the slightest notion of the commotion they created' (ibid.).

Gerrit Smith accompanied his daughter, encouraged and supported her and she 'bravely adhered to the costume for nearly seven years, under the most trying circumstances', ibid., (p. 202), but when some of the prominent figures in the women's rights movement gave up the bloomer, he announced that the movement had failed. The crux of the matter, argued Smith, was chivalry. Men behave as they do towards women because women dress as they do and 'were woman to throw off the dress' then man 'would confess her transmutation into his equal' with the result that tyranny 'would have passed away' (Stanton et al., 1881, vol. I, p. 837). It was not sufficient for women to urge their claim for equal rights, stated Smith, no matter how ably this was performed, for 'in the case of woman, the great needed change is herself' (ibid.).

As usual, in a male-dominated society, we are asked to accept that there is something wrong with women; there is no hint that part of the fault may lie with men; instead male behaviour is accepted as unproblematic – even as reasonable under the circumstances – and the case rests on the (patriarchal) assumption that it is women who must make the change.

As a side issue, Smith acknowledged that part of the problem was that women were without material resources – 'That women are helpless is no wonder, so long as women are paupers' (ibid., p. 838), but this, too, was their fault, and could also be remedied by a change in their dress. 'The next "Woman's Rights Convention" will, I take it for granted, differ but little from its predecessors,' he argued, and therefore 'it will be, as has been every other Woman's Rights Convention, a failure' (ibid.). He said, in a style characteristic of a male-dominated society where women are held to be 'at fault' no matter the issue nor the degree of control: 'Woman must first fight against herself. . . . And when she has succeeded there, an easy victory will follow. But where shall be the battleground for this indispensable self-conquest? . . . I tell her, that her dress, aye, her dress, must be that battle-ground. . . . I add that her triumph there will be her triumph anywhere; and that her failure there will be her failure everywhere' (ibid., p. 839).

Elizabeth Cady Stanton was quick to refute Smith's case and used what is today a fundamental tenet of the women's movement: women will speak for themselves, and no man who has but the limited experience of being a man in a male-dominated society will tell women what to do, or provide prescriptions of what is good for them. In a tone which is by no means conciliatory, she declares that women 'alone, whose souls are fired through personal experience and suffering can set forth the height and depth, the source and center of the degradation of women; they alone can feel a steadfast faith in their own native energy and power to accomplish a final triumpth over all adverse surroundings (ibid., p. 839–40). And Stanton proceeds to show how limited is the reasoning behind Smith's assessment of the women's rights issue as a matter of dress.

Of course, she argues, women want and need more sensible dress; of course there are advantages in donning male attire: 'Disguised as a man, the distinguished French woman, "Georges Sand" has been able to see life in Paris, and has spoken in political meetings with great applause, as no woman could have done. In male attire, we could travel by land or sea; go through all the streets and lanes of our cities and towns by night and day, without a protector' (ibid., p. 841), she says, making the point that women's mobility is curtailed by intimidation. But to Stanton, there is a great deal that is problematic about the male-norm. She is not going to concede that men have got it right and that all will be well when women dress and behave like men: 'We have no reason to hope that pantaloons would do more for us than they have done for man himself' (ibid.), so that dress is hardly a desirable focus for women's energy. But with mounting anger she derides the idea that women's position in society could be reduced to the issue of dress. 'Dress is a matter of taste, of fashion; it is changeable, transient and may be doffed or donned at the will of the individual', she argues, 'but institutions, supported by laws, can be overturned but by revolution' (ibid.); and it is revolution that Elizabeth Cady Stanton seeks.

She is equally contemptuous of the argument about chivalry. 'Talk not to us of chivalry', she said, for 'that died long ago. Where do you see it? No gallant knight presents himself at the bar of justice to pay the penalty of our crimes,' for breaking laws which we had no part in making; and she proceeds with a devastating account of man's violence against woman which makes a mockery of the case of chivalry. It is not just that women are obliged to work for longer hours and less money than men – hardly a chivalrous arrangement – but that even in their own homes, common is the man who 'will permit his aged mother to carry pails of water and armfuls (sic) of wood, or his wife to lug a twenty pound baby, hour after hour, without ever offering to relieve her' (ibid., p. 842).

Women are abused physically, psychologically and materially every day, in their own homes, by those designated as their chivalrous protectors, and those who are supposed to act in women's best interest. 'Yes, sir,' says Stanton to Smith, 'there are women, pure and virtuous and noble as yourself, spending every day of all their years of their existence in the most intimate association with infamous men, kept so by that monstrous and unnatural artifice, baptized by the sacred name of marriage. I might take you through many, many phases of woman's life' into the reality, not the myth, 'where woman feels her deepest wrongs, where in blank despair she drags out days, and weeks, and months, and years of silent agony. I might paint you pictures of real life so vivid as to force from you the agonized exclamation, How can women endure such things!' (ibid., p. 840). This is the side of woman's life that man does not experience, argues Stanton, and which he therefore assumes does not exist.

What right have you to speak of chivalry and dress, asks Stanton, when forty thousand women in the state of New York are forced to live with and be dependent on drunkards who subject them to every kind of abuse and against whom they have no redress? What right have you to assert that donning trousers will put an end to women's exploitation, she asks, when so many men in the blind gratification of their passions force excessive maternity on women, and when this is likely to continue 'so long as man continues to write, speak and act, as if maternity were the one and sole object of a woman's existence'? (ibid., p. 841).

'Did it ever enter the mind of man that women too had an inalienable right to life, liberty and the pursuit of her individual happiness?' demands Stanton (ibid., p. 840). 'You', she says accusingly to Smith, 'who suppose the mass of women contented, know but little of the silent indignation, the deep and settled disgust with which they contemplate our present social arrangements' (ibid.), but about which they are forbidden to speak. Men have insisted on women's silence in these matters in order that the myth that women are content in serving their masters, can be preserved. She knows that many women have broken the taboo, she knows that they have spoken out and suffered for it; she also knows that while women have no official recognition, their voices have too often gone unheard.

Imagine yourself to be a woman, she urges Smith, interested in the welfare of her country and in all the great questions of her day – and Stanton places women's rights at the centre of the great questions of the day – and yet in neither Church nor State, the two social institutions that govern people's lives, do you have a voice. 'Little men, with little brains, may bring forth their little sentiments by the hour, in the forum and the sacred desk, but public sentiment and the religion of our day teach us that silence is most becoming in a woman' (ibid.). If we speak out, says Stanton, it is *we* who are condemned, before our ideas can ever obtain a hearing.

And unlike men, she continues, we can take little solace from the past for when we turn to literature we do not find ourselves represented as strong and positive beings, instead 'the philosopher, the poet and the saint, all combine to make the name of woman synonymous with either fool or devil.' To Smith she says: 'What measure of content could you draw from the literature of the past' if you were a woman? (ibid.). The philosopher, the poet and the saint are male; their ideas about women have predominated in the interest of men and at the expense of women. It is time for women to give voice to their ideas about men, argues Stanton, to describe men the way women see them and not as men have insisted they want themselves to be seen. They are not chivalrous, they are not benevolent, they do not act in women's interest or make laws for women's protection. They act in their own interest and protect themselves, she says, by oppressing women.

Obviously, Elizabeth Cady Stanton is not looking for male approval when she gives voice to this critique of Smith's argument. She is aware that she is breaking the taboos against women's voice (even at this stage she had endured sufficient harassment to last a lifetime) but she was convinced that the time had come for women to speak out. 'You say you have but little faith in this reform', she addresses Smith, 'because the changes we propose are so great, so radical, so comprehensive; whilst they who have commenced the work are so puny, feeble and undeveloped.' Well, she continues, 'the mass of women are developed at least to the point of discontent, and that in the dawn of this nation was a most dangerous point in the British Parliament, and is now deemed equally so on a Southern plantation' (ibid.).

'As to the cause of women', says Stanton, 'I see no signs of failure' (ibid., p. 841) and she goes on to list some of the male-erected hurdles that have already been crossed and to warn of the changes which are to come. 'Judge by yourself, then,' she urges Smith, 'how long the women of this nation will consent to be deprived of their social, civil and political rights: but talk not to us of failure', for there is no room for it (ibid., p. 842). In Elizabeth Cady Stanton's terms, the world could no longer afford the high price to be paid for male supremacy.

She concludes her case by addressing Gerrit Smith's charge that the women's movement is in the wrong hands: 'Go to those aged widows who have reared large families of children alone and unaided,' and, taking them as representative of many women, says, 'ask them on whom they depended. They will tell you on their own hands.' 'It is into hands like these – to these who have calmly met the emergencies of life – who, without the inspiration of glory, or fame, or applause, through long years have faithfully and bravely performed their work, self-sustained and cheered,' she writes, acknowledging the enormous amount of emotional repair work that women do and men see fit not to notice or credit – it is into hands like these 'that we commit our cause. We need not wait for one more generation to pass away, to find . . . women . . . to assert the humanity of women, and that is all we claim to do' (ibid., p. 841).

It may seem that Elizabeth Cady Stanton said it all – or most of it anyway – but Frances Dana Gage responded to the same article of Gerrit Smith, with the same efficacy as Stanton, but not necessarily with the same points, nor in quite the same style.

'Dear Sir', begins Frances Dana Gage, 'In your issue of Dec 1st, I find a letter from the Hon. Gerrit Smith to Elizabeth C. Stanton, in reference to the Woman's Rights Movement, showing cause, through labored columns, why it has proved a failure. The article, though addressed to Mrs Stanton, is an attack upon everyone engaged in the cause. For he boldly asserts that the movement "is not in proper hands, and that the proper hands are not yet to be found" . . . I do not propose to enter a full criticism of Mr Smith's long letter. He has made the whole battle-ground of the Woman's Rights Movement her dress. Nothing brighter, nothing nobler than a few inches of calico or brocade added to or taken from her skirts, is to decide this great and glorious question – to give her freedom or to continue her a slave' (ibid., pp. 842–3), writes Frances Dana Gage, who adds that the only reason Mr Smith is to be taken seriously is because he is 'the almost oracle of a large portion of our reformers' (ibid., p. 843) and a supporter of women's rights. (A reminder of the contemporary parallels is probably superfluous.)

Gage continues with some satirical comments designed to demonstrate that there is little relationship between one's attire and one's love of liberty, and cites Romans in their togas, and even Christ in his dress, as proof that it is not her dress which debars women from enjoying full humanity – although Gage herself adds that she would not want to say one word in defence of women's dress. But dress is *not* the issue: 'We *must own ourselves under the law first*, own our bodies, our earnings, our genius and our consciences', she states, outlining the priorities, 'then we will turn to the lesser matter of what shall be the garniture of the body' (ibid.).

The 'side issue' of Gerrit Smith's – that women are paupers and have only themselves to blame – is taken up angrily by Gage; she made central the issue of the appropriation of women's resources. It is not women's fault that they are paupers, says Gage, but men's, for men have made the law that appropriates the fruits of women's labour and gives all of women's 'earnings into the hands of manhood' (ibid.). Women work long and hard, she argues, but men have chosen not to pay them for their labour. 'Do not the German women and our market women labour right earnestly?' she asks 'Do not the wives of our farmers and merchants toil? Is not the work of the *mothers* in our land as important as that of the fathers?' (ibid.).

'Mr Smith says', she continues, ' "That women are helpless, is no wonder, so long as they are paupers"; he might add, no wonder that the slaves of the cotton plantation are helpless, so long as they are paupers. What reduces both the woman and the slave to this condition? The law which gives the husband and the master entire control of the person and earnings of each: the law that robs each of the rights and liberties that every "free white male citizen" takes to himself as God-given' and, she continues, 'Truth falling from the lips of a Lucretia Mott in long skirts is none the less truth, than if uttered by Lucy Stone in short dress, or Helen Maria Weber[1] in pants and swallow tail coat.' Where there might be some contemporary disagreement with the ideas of Frances Dana Gage would be in her assertion that: 'I can not yet think so meanly of manly justice, as to believe it will yield simply to a change of garments' (ibid.) for some of us today might be forgiven for asserting that there *is* no manly justice, and that man will not yield at all to logic, no matter how irrefutable, or convincing the ideas and arguments for women's equality may be.

'Let us assert our right to be free', says Gage. 'Let us own ourselves, our earnings, our genius; let us have power to control as well as to earn

---

[1] 'In Leipsic, in 1844, Helen Maria Weber – her father a Prussian Officer, and her mother an English woman, – wrote a series of ten tracts on "Women's Rights and Wrongs" covering the whole question and making a volume of over twelve hundred pages. . . . These essays were strong, vigorous and convincing. Miss Weber also lectured in Vienna, Berlin, and several of the large German cities' (Stanton et al., 1881, vol. 1, p. 41). To the Worcester Convention on Woman's Rights (1850) Helene Marie Weber sent a letter (reprinted in ibid. pp. 822–3) in which 'She contended that the physical development of women was impossible in her present costume, and that her consequent enfeebled condition made her incapable of entering many of the most profitable employments in the world of work. Miss Weber exemplified her teachings by her practice. She usually wore a dress coat and pantaloons of black cloth; on full dress occasions, a dark blue dress coat, with plain flat gilt buttons, and drab-colored pantaloons. Her waistcoat was of buff cassimere, richly trimmed with plain flat gilt buttons, exquisitely polished; this was an elegant costume, and one she wore to great advantage. Her clothes were all perfect in their fit, and of Paris make; and her figure was singularly well adapted to male attire. No gentleman in Paris made a finer appearance' (ibid., p. 225)

and to own' and when all this has been achieved, 'then will each woman adjust her dress to her relations in life' (ibid.).

She readily acknowledges that there is a long way to go, and that women have only begun to appreciate their own strength, but in the name of the women's movement of 1855 she makes many of the same claims that we do today: 'No movement so radical, striking so boldly at the foundation of all social and political order, has ever become before the people', she asserts, 'or ever so widely and rapidly diffused its doctrine' (ibid., p. 844). The women's movement has not failed, she says in 1855, for there are conferences, conventions, members, newspaper articles, debates, which testify to its growing significance and certain success. 'Shall we talk of failure, because forty, twenty, or seven years have not perfected all things?' (ibid.). Would she have been so courageous had she known that 130 years would pass, when, far from all things being perfected, the basic problem remains much the same?

2 *History of Woman Suffrage*

The exchange of views quoted here, between Gerrit Smith, and Elizabeth Cady Stanton and Frances Dana Gage, occupies but 8 $\frac{1}{3}$ pages of the 876 pages that comprise Volume I of *History of Woman Suffrage*; there are six volumes in the series. With its mass of detail and documentation – by no means confined to the women's movement in the United States – which covers the period up to the turn of the century and the passage of the woman suffrage amendment in 1920 and which ultimately drew in a 'younger' editor, Ida Husted Harper, it is no exaggeration to state that every page of *History of Woman Suffrage* contains at least one item worthy of note, and it would take a series of series to document the relevance, significance, and inter-relationship of the women and their ideas quoted within the pages of this unique and valuable record.

There is no doubt that the three women who began this task of compiling the *History* were well aware of the significance of their undertaking, for each in their own way fully appreciated that women and their contributions were systematically made invisible in a male-dominated society, and they were determined that the great movement for which they all worked should not too pass into oblivion. In looking around in the 1880s, and seeing the number of women who had entered the movement, and the number of activities, publications, reports, hearings, that the movement had given rise to, they were not lulled into a false sense of security, they did not see themselves as qualitatively different from the women who had gone before, even though they believed that there was a quantitative difference.

So these three women, Stanton, Anthony and Gage took on the arduous task of writing the record, and, for reasons that are discussed later, we have much more information on the working relationship of Stanton and Anthony than we have on Gage. For Stanton and Anthony, the *History* was part of a partnership that existed for almost fifty years, and that they complemented each other is a suggestion often made by Elizabeth Cady Stanton herself, as she recounts the details of their relationship in the *History*.

'It is often said by those who know Miss Anthony best,' says Stanton, 'that she has been my good angel, always pushing and guiding me to work, that but for her pertinacity I should never have accomplished the little I have; and on the other hand, it has been said that I forged the thunderbolts, and she fired them' (Stanton et al., 1881, vol. I, p. 458). Stanton readily acknowledges that with the demands of a large family to meet it would have been very easy to have found little or no time to participate in the women's movement, but because Susan constantly called on her for assist- ance and prompted her to action (usually by some account of injustice) the family was often required to wait. Susan B. Anthony's 'description of a body of men on any platform, complacently deciding questions in which women had an equal interest, without an equal voice, readily roused me to a determination to throw a firebrand in the midst of their assembly,' says Stanton. 'Thus, whenever I saw that stately Quaker girl, coming across my lawn, I knew that some happy convocation of the sons of Adam were to be set by the ears, by one of our appeals or resolutions' (ibid.).

Defying the conventional wisdom that women cannot work together, Stanton proceeds to show just how close was her relationship with An- thony: 'We were at once fast friends, in thought and sympathy we were one, and in the division of labor we exactly complemented each other. In writing we did better work together than either could alone. While she is slow and analytical in composition, I am rapid and synthetic. I am the better writer, she the better critic. She supplied the facts and statistics, I the philosophy and rhetoric, and together we have made arguments that have stood unshaken by the storms of thirty long years: arguments that no man has answered. Our speeches may be considered the united products of our two brains,' says Stanton (comparing their relationship to 'husband and wife' and asserting categorically that there has never been jealousy, envy, or a break of one hour in their friendship). 'Night after night', she continues, 'by an old fashioned fire-place we plotted and planned the coming agitation, how, when, and where each entering wedge could be driven, by which woman might be recognized, and her rights secured' (ibid., p. 459).

Few and far between are the references in literature to the bonds between women, yet they are described on page after page of *History of Woman Suffrage*, and this deep friendship and commitment among women is not just confined to Stanton and Anthony. But it was Stanton and Anthony who together appreciated how important it was that women's lives and activities and ideas be described from the perspective of women and 'handed on' to future generations who would then receive an important gift, which they themselves had not inherited.

That the records of women and their struggle should be secured to posterity had always been a concern of Susan B. Anthony, says Ida Husted Harper, in the preface to Volume IV (1902), in which she outlines the history of the *History*. With the aim of handing on the information, Anthony 'had carefully preserved as far as possible the letters, speeches, and newspaper clippings, accounts of legislative and congressional reports' (Anthony & Harper, 1902; vol. IV, p. v) and Elizabeth Cady Stanton (1881) explains that for the four years prior to 1876 these efforts were increased: 'In addition to the domestic cares which a large family involved', says Stanton, 'Mrs Gage, Miss Anthony and I were busy collecting material for "The History of Woman Suffrage" (sic). This required no end of correspondence' (Stanton et al., 1881, vol. I, p. 323) as everyone who had ever participated in the movement was traced, contacted, asked to provide copies of correspondence, copies of speeches, newspaper clippings, reports, minutes of meetings, photographs, autographs, personal impressions, re-collections of people and events, reminiscences of those deceased.

None of the women had foreseen the magnitude of the task, says Ida Harper, (and I have some idea of how they must have felt) for 'they made a mutual agreement to accept no engagements for four months, expecting to finish it within that time, as they contemplated nothing more than a small volume, probably a pamphlet of a few hundred pages. Miss Anthony packed in trunks and boxes the accumulations of the years and shipped them to Mrs Stanton's home in Tenafly, N. J., where the two women went cheerfully to work.' (Anthony and Harper, 1902, vol. IV, p. v).

But if they had not understood the magnitude of the task to begin with, they soon began to appreciate the dimensions of what they had undertaken. Writing in *Eighty Years and More* (1898a), Elizabeth Cady Stanton says: 'I had never thought the publication of a book required the consideration of such endless details. We stood appalled before the mass of material, growing higher and higher with every mail, and the thought of all the reading involved made us feel as if our life-work lay before us. Six weeks of steady labour all day, and often until midnight, made no visible decrease in the pile of documents. However, before the end of the month we had our arrangements all made with publishers and engravers and six chapters in print. When we began to correct proof we felt as if something was accomplished. Thus we worked through the winter and far into the spring, with no change except the Washington Convention and an occasional evening meeting in New York City' (pp. 326–7).

Co-operation and teamwork were the order of the day, says Ida Harper in commenting on this period: 'Mrs Stanton was the matchless writer, Miss Anthony the collector of material, the searcher of statistics, the business manager, the keen critic, the detector of omissions, chronological flaws and discrepancies in statement such as are unavoidable even with the most careful historian. On many occasions they called to their aid for historical facts Mrs Matilda Joslyn Gage, one of the most logical, scientific and fearless writers of her day' (Anthony and Harper, 1902, vol. IV, p. v).

Harper emphasises that in the enormous task these three women set themselves they had no assistance in terms of research assistants, stenographers or typists. The authors themselves 'were amazed at the amount of history which already had been made and still more deeply impressed with the desirability of preserving the story of the early struggle', with the result that 'a labor which was to consume four months eventually extended through ten years and was not completed until the closing days of 1885. The pamphlet of a few hundred pages had expanded into three great volumes of 1,000 pages each and enough material remained to fill another' (ibid., p. vi).

'And so together, for a long decade', says Harper, 'these two great souls toiled in the solitude of home just as together they fought in the open field, not for personal gain or glory, but for the sake of a cause to which they had consecrated their lives' (ibid.). During that time the big boxes of documents made many journeys from the home of one to the other, there were complications with those gathering data, trials with publishers, financial difficulties, criticisms to contend with, 'delays, disappointments and vexations,' but 'all interspersed and brightened with many humorous features' (ibid.).

We are fortunate that they persisted. As Harper says, 'Had it not been for their patient and unselfish labor the story of the hard conditions under which the pioneers struggled to lift woman out of her subjection, the bitterness of the prejudice, the cruelty of persecution, never would have been told. In all the years that have passed no one else has attempted to tell it, and should anyone desire to do so it is doubtful if, even at this early date, enough of the records could be found for the most superficial account. In not a library can the student who wishes to trace this movement . . . obtain the necessary data except in these three volumes, which will become still more valuable as the years go by . . . ' (ibid., pp. vi–viii).

Stanton, Anthony, Gage – and Harper – needed no lessons on the topic of women's invisibility. They knew that women were absent from the records not because women had not led interesting, significant, active, useful lives, but because women's contribution was 'eclipsed', blocked out by the men who were officially and ostensibly responsible for writing, and transmitting the records. They were determined this should not happen to this particular period of women's history, but they encountered many obstacles, not the least of which was the hard work, or the capacity of a male-dominated society to consign such records, or sections of such records to oblivion, even *after* they had been written and published.

Many challenged their work; some said it was too soon (women's suffrage had still not been achieved); some said it was too late, too presumptuous, too diverting. 'We had numberless letters from friends and foes,' writes Stanton 'some praising and some condemning our proposed undertaking, and, though much alone, we were kept in touch with the outside world. But so conflicting was the tone of the letters that, if we had not taken a very fair gauge of ourselves and our advisers, we should have abandoned our project and buried all the valuable material collected, to sleep in pine boxes forever' (1898a, p. 327).

It is characteristic of Elizabeth Cady Stanton when she comments on a letter received from a reverend gentleman – who, in keeping with the spirit of her response, shall remain nameless – who criticised Stanton for using one of *his* anecdotes on Lucretia Mott, without giving him due credit. 'I laughed him to scorn', she writes, 'that he should have thought it was my duty to have done so. I told him plainly that he belonged to a class of

"white male citizens" who had robbed me of all civil and political rights;
of property, children and personal freedom; and now it ill became him to
call me to account for using one of his little anecdotes that, ten to one, he
had cribbed from some woman. I told him that I considered his whole class
as fair game for literary pilfering. That women had been taxed to build
colleges to educate men, and if we could pick up a literary crumb that had
fallen from their feasts, we surely had a right to it.' With a final flourish,
she adds: 'Moreover, I told him that man's duty in the world was to work,
to dig and delve for jewels, real and ideal, and lay them at woman's feet,
for her to use as she might see fit,' for after all, was not this what men
were urging as the proper pedestal for women and the desired relationship
between the sexes, and therefore, should he not 'feel highly complimented,
instead of complaining, that he had written something I thought worth
using?' (ibid., pp. 327–8).

Other difficulties were financial: knowing who controlled resources
and what priorities they had, it was Susan B. Anthony's long cherished
desire 'to put this History free of charge in the public libraries', for only
then could she be certain that the records were secured to posterity and
available (Anthony and Harper, 1902, vol. iv, p. ix). But the bigger the
project grew, the longer it took, the more volumes it extended to, the more
money was needed; and Ida Husted Harper spells out the implications of
this commitment for Susan B. Anthony. 'Miss Anthony began this work in
1876 without a dollar in hand for its publication', says Harper (ibid.,
p. vii), but resolved to spend everything she had on it (and determined to
try and raise more) rather than not publish the *History*. Some women were
generous patrons and contributed to the project. 'The first volume of the
History had been issued in May, 1881, and the second in April 1882. In
June 1885, Mrs Stanton and Miss Anthony set resolutely to work and
labored without ceasing until the next November, when the third volume
was sent to the publishers. With the bequest ($24,125 from Mrs Eliza
Jackson Eddy of Boston – gained after being contested by an indirect heir)
Miss Anthony paid the debts that had been incurred, replaced her own
fund, of which every dollar had been used, and brought out this last
volume' or what had been envisaged as the last volume (Anthony and
Harper, 1902, vol. iv, p. vii).

The expenses associated with the publication of the *History* were
considerable and not just confined to paper – and other materials – which
were currently expensive. There were the steel engravings ($5,000 alone),
the salaries of proof readers and indexers, and even, for seventeen years,
the storage costs on the earlier volumes and the plates. But it did mean
that she was able to give away the *History*, and not just to public libraries:
'In addition . . . she has given it to hundreds of schools and to countless
individuals, writers, speakers etc., whom she thought it would enable to do
better work for the franchise' (ibid., p. viii).

The publication of the third volume marked the completion of the
original task – but much history had been made while Elizabeth Cady
Stanton, Susan B. Anthony and Matilda Joslyn Gage had been putting
together the *History*, with the result that to Susan B. Anthony there was

more yet to be done. 'From the time the last volume [vol III] was finished it was Miss Anthony's intention, if she should live twenty years longer, to issue a fourth containing the history which would be made during that period, and for this purpose she still preserved the records,' writes Ida Husted Harper, who joined Susan B. Anthony as co-editor in this undertaking. 'As the century drew near a close, bringing with it the end of her four score years, the desire grew still stronger to put into permanent shape the continued story of a contest which already had extended far beyond the extreme limits imagined when she dedicated to it the full power of her young womanhood with its wealth of dauntless courage and unfailing hope. She resigned the presidency of the National Association [National American Woman Suffrage Association] in February, 1900, which marked her eightieth birthday, in order that she might carry out this project' (ibid.).

Conditions were not the same as they had been in 1876 when the project initially began: 'Mrs Gage passed away in 1898,' says Harper, and although 'Mrs Stanton is still living as this volume goes to the publishers in 1902, and evinces her mental vigor at the age of eighty-seven in frequent magazine and newspaper articles, she could not be called upon for this heavy and exacting task' (ibid., p. ix). And Harper knew just how demanding and time-consuming the task could be: as Susan B. Anthony's biographer, she had witnessed, first hand, what was required, and has even tried to convey some impression of the magnitude of the work involved.

Documentation from fifty States and Territories – as well as documentation from other countries – was needed, and the task was complicated by the fact that it was not just routine archivist work that was required, for it was a *woman's* movement that was the subject and therefore 'a movement for many years unnoticed or greatly misrepresented in the popular press' and besides, 'its records [were] usually not considered of sufficient value to be officially preserved' (ibid., p. x). Countless women 'have spent weeks of time and labor, writing letters, visiting libraries, examining records, and often leaving their homes and going to the State capital to search the archives. All this has been done without financial compensation,' says Harper, acknowledging the great efforts of many women who contributed (and who amassed the data that the editors were required to sift) and 'to give an idea of the exacting work required it may be stated that to obtain authentic data on one particular point the writer of the Kansas Chapter sent 198 letters to 178 city clerks' (ibid., pp. x–xi).

It is little wonder that Ida Husted Harper was reluctant to accept Susan B. Anthony's invitation to be co-editor, for she had 'a full knowledge of the great labor and responsibility involved', and she readily confessed that commitment to the women's movement, of its own, would have been insufficient to persuade her and that it took 'personal devotion to a beloved and honored leader' (ibid., p. ix) to outweigh all other considerations, and take on the task. However, having become involved, it seems that she herself became convinced that such effort should continue: she took up where Susan B. Anthony left off so that in 1922 Volumes V and VI appeared edited solely by her, and covering the period 1900–1920.

That the vote was a primary goal of the women's movement, from

Seneca Falls (1848), and that *History of Woman Suffrage* – at least in name – emphasised that important symbol (while still recording many other issues that were addressed) does not, however, completely explain the *absence* of documentation of the women's movement *after* Harper's publication of Volumes V and VI. It is the very *absence* of such a record which helps to give rise to the assumption that the nineteenth and early twentieth-century women's movement concentrated on the vote, and disintegrated once it was won. As Elizabeth Sarah (1982a) has pointed out, not only is such an assumption unjustified, but it serves predictable ends in a patriarchal society.

The existence of the *History of Woman Suffrage*, and the absence of any systematic documentation by women about women's activities, after 1922, also has considerable implications for us today for we can see the contrast clearly. Without *History of Woman Suffrage* our belief in the women and their struggle of the past might be little short of an act of faith, for we would never be able fully to substantiate our belief – no matter how concerted current archivist attempts may be, for much of the data would simply have disappeared. We would be required to argue – as we are often obliged to do in reference to the period *after* 1922 – that there were many, many women, thinking, writing, arguing and protesting about male power, but because of the biases in historiography we know nothing about them.

Is it possible that a history of the women's movement of the 1920s, or 1930s, or 1940s, would have provided us with the same overwhelming evidence of women's activities as does the *History of Woman Suffrage* with its six volumes of approximately one thousand pages each? If a record had been kept from 1920 to 1960, would we today be able readily to 'prove' that women were working to end the oppression of women? We would be in a very different position if we could.

And what lessons should we learn from the past? Obviously, it simply isn't enough to have best-selling books on contemporary issues and on the development of the modern women's movement, for these too were written in the nineteenth century, and early twentieth century, and too often disappeared. One of the ways we have 'discovered' them and reclaimed them is through the *History*. The *History* stands as overwhelming contrary evidence to the patriarchal myth. We have benefited enormously from its existence – yet it is unlikely that we shall bequeath such a concrete legacy to our successors, for we are making no comparable attempt to document our existence in such detail and to 'secure it to posterity'. And, if anything, we are better informed than were some of our foremothers on the invisibility of women and the way in which it is realised. We have been lulled into a sense of security which might prove to be false, for frequently we assume that we are different and that it simply would not be possible to make the current women's liberation movement 'disappear' to future generations.

Just these four women – Elizabeth Cady Stanton, Susan B. Anthony, Matilda Joslyn Gage, and then Ida Husted Harper – and what a difference their analysis and efforts have made. This by no means minimises the countless woman-hours of the hundreds of women who helped to collect all the necessary data, but it does emphasise the importance of the foresight these four displayed (and the dedication they demonstrated) when they insisted on the significance of what was often – then – a thankless task. They well understood the political and subversive nature of the *History*. While they were all engaged in what has traditionally been termed 'political activism', giving speeches, organising conventions, demonstrations, petitions, conducting test cases, there were still times – months and years – when the public realm gave way to the tedious, isolated, and no less politically active task, of collecting, collating, and publishing information about women and women's ideas.

Although primarily concerned with the American scene, the *History* is by no means confined to it. As Harper states in the *Preface* to Volume V, the *History* 'covers to some degree that of the whole world. The chapter on Great Britain was prepared for Volume VI by Mrs Millicent Garrett Fawcett', and accounts from other 'countries come from the highest authorities' (1922, p. 111). With the existence of the *History* it simply is not possible to assert that the women's movement of the past was only a single-issue movement, that it was confined to a small group or even a middle-class group, that it was uneventful, fundamentally just reformist, lacking in political analysis, and parochial. The *History* tells a very different story from what we have been led to believe in a male-dominated society. They are women's voices, and women's ideas that come to us through the pages.

Elizabeth Cady Stanton knew well what she was doing when she addressed the reader in Volume I: 'In gathering up these individual memories of the past', she said, 'we feel that there will be an added interest in the fact that we shall thus have a subjective as well as an objective view of this grand movement for woman's enfranchisement' (Stanton et al., 1881, vol. I, p. 171). Given the contemporary analysis, that objectivity is the name men allocate to their own subjectivity thereby endowing it with authority and prestige (Rich, 1980; D. Spender, 1980, 1981a, 1982b). Stanton is intimating in terms not dissimilar to those used today that this *History* has the added *interest* of containing women's view of women's experience. She becomes even more explicit as she continues. 'To our older readers, who have known the actors in these scenes, they will come like the far-off whispers of by-gone friends; to younger ones who have never seen the faces of the noble band of women who took the initiative in this struggle, it will be almost as pleasant as a personal introduction to have them *speak for themselves*' (Stanton et al., 1881, vol. I, p. 171, my emphasis).

And the editors are right – it is almost as pleasant as a personal introduction to have Lucretia Mott (1798–1880), Ernestine Rose (1810–92), Paulina Wright Davis (1813–76), Lucy Stone (1818–93), Sojourner Truth (? – 1883), Antoinette Brown Blackwell (1825–1921), and many, many more speak for themselves. Letters from Harriet Martineau, Frances Power Cobbe, Mary Somerville, Emily Faithfull, Josephine Butler, are quoted and discussed. But it is more than pleasant, it is *political*, to hear the voices of these women. Had it been left to those who are officially and ostensibly concerned with the writing of human history we would now encounter only a void, a silence, instead of these rich and ringing voices. Now, we can listen to each of these women of the past, 'in her own peculiar style recount the experiences of those eventful years' and, without risk of 'wearying the reader with much repetition' (ibid. p. 171), precisely because Stanton, Anthony, Gage and Harper took the history of women and their ideas into their own hands, in the hope that it would be preserved, in the hope that we would not have to spend the enormous amount of energy necessary to recover and reclaim our foremothers, in the hope that for future women the record would be set straight, in the hope that we would inherit a tradition they had been required to construct. We have a long way to go to equal their achievement.

Tracing the development of women's ideas in a male-dominated society becomes a very different — but no less problematic — task for the period 1850–1920, for, while in one sense it becomes much easier (with all that information available), it also becomes more complex. There *is* a record, but first of all it is only *one* record, and much of importance may have been omitted, for many reasons; but secondly, as has already been indicated it would be beyond the scope of any one book, even if exclusively devoted to the topic,[2] to begin to summarise the nature and significance of all the women, their ideas, and their reception, over the period encompassed in the *History*. While on the one hand I recognise the futility of trying to outline the ground covered in the *history*, I cannot simply assume that women today are familiar with its existence. Nor can I just make passing reference to it as if it were readily accessible. Although there is a record of some aspects of women's history for this period, because it is *women's* history it has not become part of the mainstream, is unlikely to be readily known or readily available, and to omit discussion of the period is therefore to risk leaving a considerable *gap* in this chronological outline of the development of women's traditions. Because the *History* is a product in a male-dominated society, it must be assumed that the values of society, of male dominance, prevail, and that, despite the existence of the *History*, it remains for many *invisible*, and therefore requires some documentation and discussion. But the question is — how to do justice to this wealth of material?

Recognising that any attempt to provide a comprehensive coverage would be impossible, I have decided to select a few of the more visible women to serve as illustrations. From the outset, however, it must be acknowledged that there are problems with such selection — not the least of which is that it perpetuates and reinforces some of the divisions between visible and invisible. In the interest of organisation I have also decided to treat the women of different countries as different groups, to avoid crossing

---

[2] Little scholarly work has been undertaken on *History of Woman Suffrage* on the nature of its significance or the scope of its selection (although there were criticisms, past and present of the biases inherent in it and there is an enormous need to examine the biases it sought to correct). There is of course *The Concise History of Woman Suffrage*, 1978 (Mari Jo and Paul Buhle), and I am indebted to Leslie Wheeler for bringing it to my attention.

and recrossing the borders and the oceans, but this approach, too, has limitations, for it maintains national boundaries and masks the international exchange that continually occurred. With these reservations – and with the conviction that the *History* is something which every woman should see (and read part of) for herself – it is, however, possible to suggest what some of the women of the time were thinking and doing in a patriarchal society, and the way in which their thoughts and activities were greeted.

3 Elizabeth Cady Stanton and Susan B. Anthony

Elizabeth Cady Stanton and Susan B. Anthony have already made their presence felt, but there are many other aspects of their lives, their work and their friendship which merit further consideration.

Elizabeth Cady Stanton

Born in 1815, Elizabeth Cady herself says that from a very early age she developed a strong sense of injustice about the devaluation of her sex; she also learnt some fundamental principles that were to influence her understandings for the rest of her life. When she was 11 years old, she says, an event occurred which changed her life: her only brother came home to die (Stanton, 1898a, p. 20). 'We early felt', she explains, 'that this son filled a larger place in our father's affections and future plans than the five daughers together', and her father's behaviour, on the death of his only son, confirmed this belief. In her attempts to comfort her father, Stanton climbed on his knee and 'he mechanically put his arm round me,' and after a while 'heaved a deep sigh and said: "Oh my daugher, I wish you were a boy!"' (ibid.).

Temporarily paralysed by the knowledge that 'a girl weighed less in the scale of being than a boy' (ibid., p. 21), Stanton then resolved to be to her father all that her brother had been, and with considerable acumen deduced that this meant being able to manage a horse and study Greek. She immediately began to put her resolution into effect. She also made rapid progress. 'I learned to drive, to leap a fence and ditch on horseback,' she says, and 'I taxed every power, hoping some day to hear my father say: "Well a girl is as good as a boy after all." But he never said it' (ibid., p. 22).

Indeed, the more she proved she was as competent as a boy in the activities usually reserved for boys, the more her father regretted that she was *not* a boy. When she went so far as to win a prize in Greek, she tells of how one thought alone filled her mind – that her father would now be satisfied with her – and with this anticipation she ran to his office and laid the prize, a new Greek Testament, on his desk: 'He took up the book,' she says, 'asked me some questions about the class, the teachers, the spectators, and evidently pleased, handed it back to me. Then, while I stood looking and waiting for him to say something which would show that he recognised the equality of the daughter with the son, he kissed me on the forehead and exclaimed with a sigh, "Ah, you should have been a boy!" ' (ibid., p. 23).

That no matter what women do they are not seen as the equals of men was an understanding forged early for Elizabeth Cady Stanton. The recognition that it was neither the horse riding, nor the Greek, but the sex, which was the source of value, was one of the foundation stones of her analysis and one of the reasons that she was later perceived as a radical. While some of her contemporaries thought that equal treatment of the sexes would lead to equal performance, and an end to women's subordination, for Stanton this line of reasoning was never acceptable; she knew that even where women could perform as competently as men – be it sport or work or study – nothing necessarily changed. For her, the problem, and the solution, lay elsewhere. From a very early age, Stanton appreciated the necessity of law reform, but equality before the law – while a principle she held dear – was insufficient of itself as far as she was concerned, to end the oppression of women, with the result that there were other areas which demanded her energy and insight as well. This, however, did not preclude her from being one of the most passionate, persuasive and powerful advocates of women's rights.

Her interest in law also began during her childhood when she spent time in her father's law office, listened to the clients, talked with her father's students, and read the laws that related to women. 'The tears and complaints of the women who came to my father for legal advice touched my heart', she says, 'and early drew my attention to the injustice and cruelty of the laws. As the practice of the law was my father's business, I could not exactly understand why he could not alleviate the sufferings of these women. So, in order to enlighten me, he would take down his books and show me the inexorable statutes' (Stanton, 1898a, p. 31). It was her father who said that when she was an adult, she should go and make a speech to the legislators to pass new and more just laws – advice he might, of course, have given to a son – but Stanton adds that when she attempted to *follow* precisely this advice later in life, she found her father to be one of the bitterest opponents to her public appearances and demands (ibid., pp. 32–3). This provided another example that for girls ideas about freedom and justice, and the possibility of acting to promote change, are meant to be but the playthings of youth and to be abandoned on adulthood (see Bell Gale Chevigny, 1976).

In her father's law office Stanton also found how men may act towards women who do not just accept their subordination. Her father's students, 'observing my interest' in women, she says, 'would amuse themselves by reading to me all the worst laws they could find' (1898a, p. 31) and she describes the other forms of behaviour – euphemistically called 'teasing' – which they engaged in. Such behaviour is still often characteristic of boys today and its occurrence in mixed-sex schools has been extensively documented in Australia, Britain, Sweden and the United States (see Fennema, 1980 and D. Spender, 1982a). It is sexual harassment and is employed by males with the intention of undermining the confidence of females, so that they will withdraw, and thereby become 'subordinate'.

Elizabeth Cady Stanton found herself 'continually squabbling with the law students over the rights of women. Something was always coming up in the experiences of everyday life', says Stanton, 'to give us fresh topics for argument. They would read passages from the British classics quite as aggravating as the laws. They delighted in extracts from Shakespeare, especially from "The Taming of the Shrew" ' and 'would recite with unction the famous reply of Milton's ideal woman to Adam: "God thy law, thou mine." The Bible, too, was brought into requisition' (1898a, p. 34). But, says Stanton with characteristic wit and irreverence, while 'it seemed to me that every book taught the "divinely ordained" headship of man . . . my mind never yielded to this popular heresy' (ibid.).

But the customs of the time were observed: Elizabeth Cady watched her male classmates go off to college, while she was confined to home. On 10 May 1840, she married Henry B. Stanton, an active abolitionist, and their wedding journey was a trip to London to attend the World's Anti-Slavery Convention. For Elizabeth Cady Stanton it proved to be a most eventful journey.

Outlining in the *History* some of the causes of the women's movement, the editors give the Anti-Slavery struggle as the cause 'above all other causes' (Stanton et al., 1881, vol. I, p. 52). 'In the early Anti-Slavery conventions,' in America, they say 'the broad principles of human rights were so exhaustively discussed, justice, liberty and equality so clearly taught, that the women who crowded to listen, readily learned the lesson of freedom for themselves' (ibid., p. 52). But the women who took on the role of public speaking in the struggle for abolition also learnt: 'Sarah and Angelina Grimké and Abby Kelly, (sic), in advocating liberty for the black race, were early compelled to defend the right of free speech for themselves' (ibid., p. 53).

The role of women – and the issue of women's rights – within the Abolition movement, precipitated a division in 1840 in the ranks of the Anti-Slavery Society, for, as Stanton et al. comment, 'Many a man who advocated equality most eloquently for a Southern plantation, would not tolerate it at his own fireside' (ibid.). For the World's Anti-Slavery Convention in London, an invitation had been issued to all Anti-Slavery organisations in America and accordingly, say Stanton et al. 'several American societies saw fit to send women, as delegates, to represent them in that august assembly' (ibid.). If the issue of woman's rights had split the Anti-Slavery societies of America, it was to be no less divisive and disturbing at the Convention in London.

After going three thousand miles, say the editors, 'it was discovered that women formed no part of the constituent elements of the moral world. In summoning the friends of the slave from all parts of the two hemispheres to meet in London, John Bull never dreamed that woman, too, would answer his call. Imagine then the commotion in the conservative anti-slavery circles in England, when it was known that half a dozen of these terrible women who had spoken to promiscuous assemblies, voted on men and measures, prayed and petitioned against slavery, women who had been mobbed, ridiculed by the press and denounced by the pulpit . . . were on their way to England' (ibid., pp. 53–4). And imagine what happened when on 12 June 1840 the women[3] arrived to present their credentials – 'The excitement and vehemence of protest and denunciation could not have been greater, if the news had come that the French were about to invade England' (ibid., p. 54).

The issue of whether or not to admit women was debated at length (and is well covered in the *History*, vol. I, pp. 54–61, and not only makes for enlightening reading but puts paid to the notion that the battle for women to appear in public was peculiar to America). One man on the committee, who had issued the invitations, said: 'As soon as we heard the liberal interpretation Americans had given to our first invitation, we issued another as early as Feb 15, in which the description of those who are to form the Convention is set forth as consisting of "gentlemen" ' (ibid., p. 55). 'The Rev. J. Burnet, an Englishman,' state the editors, 'made a most touching appeal to the American ladies, to conform to English prejudices and custom, so far as to withdraw their credentials, as it never did occur to the British and Foreign Anti-Slavery Society that they were inviting ladies. It is better, said he, that this Convention should be dissolved at this moment than this motion (to admit women) should be adopted' (ibid.).[4]

Many of the arguments advanced for the exclusion of women were put forward by the clergy of both Britain and America, and after lengthy – and often ludicrous debate – finally, 'the vote was taken, and the women excluded as delegates of the Convention, by an overwhelming majority' (ibid., p. 60). They were forced to sit in the gallery, where they were fenced off behind a bar and a curtain. Wendell Phillips, who had supported their admission, was however 'gracious in defeat', and implied that women would no doubt follow the proceedings with as much interest from behind the bar and the curtain (ibid.). Stanton expresses her outrage at his failure to understand the women's position and says it is important to mention 'that it is almost impossible for the most liberal of men to understand what liberty means for woman' (ibid., pp. 60–1).

That men's experience, and men's vision, was limited and that they were unable to comprehend the significance of what women were thinking and demanding, was a central thesis of Stanton's. Throughout the fifty years in which she wrote and talked about the way the world looked from the perspective of woman, she made frequent reference to the idea that men

---

[3] Among them were Lucretia Mott, Sarah Pugh, Abby Kimber, Elizabeth Neal, Mary Grew, Ann Green Phillips, Emily Winslow and Abby Southwick.

[4] In *The Cause: A Short History of the Women's Movement in Great Britain*. Ray Strachey (1928) says that the non-admission of the American women delegates to the Anti-Slavery Convention was 'a most painful affair' (p. 41) but, while it prompted the American women to return to their country and hold a Woman's Rights Convention, 'In England . . . things did not proceed so openly. The new idea spread quietly about, creeping from one person to another and slowly undermining the enemies' defences; and in this process the happenings of the World's Convention of 1840 were an undoubted help' (p. 42).

could not see what women saw, could not feel what women felt, and that a fundamental right of woman was to describe the world, in her own terms, and to have her description treated as valid.

To Stanton, there were many aspects of the Anti-Slavery Convention of 1840 that were humiliating. Not only was there the failure of male supporters to understand, there was also this 'sacrifice of human rights, by men who had assembled from all quarters of the globe to proclaim universal emancipation,' and they had offered it up 'in the presence of such women as Lady Byron, Anna Jameson, Amelia Opie, Mary Howitt, Elizabeth Fry, and our own Lucretia Mott' (ibid., p. 61). And to crown it all was the indignity of finding 'that unwittingly, I was by marriage on the wrong side' (ibid., p. 420), for Henry B. Stanton was a member of a society that did not support the admission of women – despite the fact that he, personally (so he claimed), stood for women's rights.

The two redeeming features for Elizabeth Cady Stanton were the actions of William Lloyd Garrison, one of the leading abolitionists in America, and the presence of Lucretia Mott. 'William Lloyd Garrison, having been delayed at sea, arrived too late to take part in the debates' on the admission of women delegates, say the editors, but: 'Learning on his arrival that the women had been rejected as delegates, he declined to take his seat in the Convention; and, through all those interesting discussions on a subject so near his heart, lasting ten days, he remained a silent spectator in the gallery' behind the bar and curtain, with the women (ibid., p. 61).

By the time Elizabeth Cady Stanton met Lucretia Mott she hardly knew what to expect. First of all she had been warned by James G. Birney – with whom she had travelled from America and who was one of the leaders of the anti-women, anti-slavery societies – that Mott was one of those dreadful 'women who had fanned the flames of dissension, and had completely demoralized the anti-slavery ranks' (ibid., p. 419). Secondly, because Stanton was the only woman among the 'Birney faction' – by virtue of her husband – Stanton thought that it was quite possible that Lucretia Mott would be hostile to her: Thirdly there was the fact that Lucretia Mott was a Quaker. With candour, Stanton admits that she had never spoken to a Quaker before and that she was disposed to find Lucretia Mott 'a being above ordinary mortals, ready to be translated at any moment' (ibid., p. 420). That their meeting would be the beginning of a lifelong friendship was not a possibility that occurred to Stanton under the circumstances.

They met – along with other delegates – in the hotel in Great Queen Street, and after dinner, the conversation turned to women's rights, with several Baptist ministers making their sentiments known to Lucretia Mott. Says Stanton, 'As I had thought much on this question in regard to the laws, Church action, and social usages, I found myself in full accord with the other ladies, combatting most of the gentlemen at the table. . . . In spite of constant gentle nudgings by my husband under the table, and frowns from Mr Birney opposite, the tantalizing tone of the conversation was too much for me to remain silent' (ibid.); and the behaviour of Lucretia Mott was too much for Elizabeth Cady Stanton to remain unimpressed. 'Calmly and skillfully Mrs Mott parried all their attacks,' says Stanton, 'now by her quiet humor turning the laugh on them, and then by her earnestness and dignity silencing their ridicule and sneers' (ibid.). It was important to Elizabeth Cady Stanton that Lucretia Mott *knew* she had support in the face of this assault from these 'humane' and 'civilised' men and Stanton says, 'I shall never forget the look of recognition she gave me when she saw by my remarks that I fully comprehended the problem of woman's rights and wrongs. How beautiful she looked to me that day' (ibid.).

For Stanton, Lucretia Mott became a 'model'; she 'was to me an entire new revelation of womanhood', she says, and 'I sought every opportunity to be at her side, and continually plied her with questions, and I shall never cease to be grateful for the patience and seeming pleasure with which she fed my hungering soul' (ibid.). Stanton recounts how they spent some of their days and says that, 'on one occasion with a large party we visited the British Museum', and, 'On entering, Mrs Mott and myself sat down near the door to rest for a few moments, telling the party to go on, that we would follow. They accordingly explored all the departments of curiosities, supposing we were slowly following at a distance; but when they returned, after an absence of three hours, there we sat in the same spot, having seen nothing but each other, wholly absorbed in questions of theology and social life. She had told me of the doctrines and divisions among "Friends", ... of Mary Wollstonecraft, her social theories, and her demands of equality for women. I had been reading Combe's "Constitution of Man" and "Moral Philosophy" ... and Mary Wollstonecraft, though all tabooed by orthodox teachers, but I had never heard a woman talk what, as a Scotch Presbyterian, I had scarcely dared to think' (ibid., pp. 420–1). Elizabeth Cady Stanton states that she found in her new friend, Lucretia Mott, 'a woman emancipated from all faith in man-made creeds, from all fear of his denunciations' (ibid., p. 422) and for Stanton this represented a form of liberty; it was this model and this analysis that she adopted.

Stanton saw that Mott could not be intimidated by abuse, ridicule or ostracism. During their stay in London, Stanton saw first hand the pressure that Mott was subjected to, particularly from Quakers who disapproved of the sect she belonged to (and Elizabeth Fry was among those who felt it her duty to dissociate herself from Lucretia Mott, see ibid., p. 423). To Stanton, Lucretia Mott was both rational and wise. 'And yet this pure, grand woman', she says, 'was shunned and feared by the Orthodox Friends throughout England' (ibid.). While readily acknowledging that in her own lifetime Lucretia Mott was too much persecuted ever to indulge in the persecution of others, Stanton herself is not quite so ready to 'turn the other cheek' and does not hesitate to document and condemn the pettiness and the bigotry that were encountered by Lucretia Mott. 'While in London', she says, 'a rich young Quaker of bigoted tendencies who made several breakfast and tea parties for the American delegates, always omitted to invite Mrs Mott. He very politely said to her on one occasion when he was inviting others in her presence, "Thou must excuse me, Lucretia, for not inviting thee with the rest, but I fear thy influence on my children!!" '

(ibid.). Adds Stanton, 'How hateful such bigotry looks to those capable of getting outside their own educational prejudices' (ibid.).

And what did Elizabeth Cady Stanton and Lucretia Mott decide to do? As they wended their way arm in arm down Great Queen Street, 'they agreed to hold a woman's rights convention on their return to America, as the men to whom they had just listened (at the Anti-Slavery Convention) had manifested their great need of some education on that question. Thus a missionary work for the emancipation of woman in "the land of the free and the home of the brave" was then and there inaugurated' (ibid., p. 62) and I detect Elizabeth Cady Stanton's touch in the following statement from the *History*: 'As the ladies were not allowed to speak in the Convention, they kept up a brisk fire morning, noon, and night at their hotel on the unfortunate gentlemen who were domiciled at the same house. Mr Birney, with his luggage, promptly withdrew after the first encounter' (ibid., pp. 61–2).

Another eight years were to elapse before the first woman's rights convention was to be held, and in some respects this had its positive features, for the experience of Elizabeth Cady Stanton changed within that time from being a young bride in cosmopolitan London to being a careworn mother in relatively isolated Seneca Falls. On her return to America, Stanton lived in Chelsea 'with beautiful views of Boston Bay' (Stanton, 1898a, p. 136), and here where she had *good servants* and good company – and only two children – she was somewhat unsympathetic about the drudgery of housework, as she herself states. 'I tried to give an artistic touch to everything', and she proceeds to outline the details of her domestic accomplishments – right through to the floral arrangements! 'I put my soul into everything, and hence enjoyed it. I never could understand how house-keepers could rest with rubbish all round their back doors . . .' (ibid., p. 137).

The similarities with our own time should not go unnoted; it seems that even in the 1840s the intellectual arguments were not always sufficient protection against the seductive myth of marriage and motherhood, and if today some assert that entry to the women's movement is by way of disillusionment with domesticity, Elizabeth Cady Stanton would readily have accepted the validity of such an explanation. 'In Seneca Falls [where she and her family moved in 1847] my life was comparatively solitary,' she says, 'and the change from Boston was somewhat depressing' (ibid., p. 145). The house was old, had been unoccupied for a few years, was in need of repairs and had a very overgrown garden; it was on the outskirts of town, there were no footpaths ('sidewalks') and the road was often muddy. 'Mr Stanton was frequently away from home, I had poor servants, and an increasing number of children. To keep a house and grounds in good order, purchase every article for daily use, keep the wardrobes of half a dozen human beings in proper trim, take the children to dentists, shoemakers and different schools, or find teachers at home, altogether made sufficient work to keep one brain busy, as well as all the hands I could impress into the service.' Besides, she adds, 'the novelty of housekeeping had passed away, and much that was once attractive in domestic life was now irksome' (ibid., p. 145).

'I now understand the practical difficulties most women had to contend with in the isolated household', says Stanton, and the phrase 'a healthy discontent is the first step to progress' assumed new significance for her. 'The general discontent I felt with woman's portion as wife, mother, house-keeper, physician, and spiritual guide, the chaotic conditions into which everything fell without her constant supervision, and the wearied, anxious look of the majority of women impressed me with a strong feeling that some active measures should be taken to remedy the wrongs of society in general and of women in particular. My experience at the World Anti-Slavery Convention, all I had read on the legal status of women, and the oppression I saw everywhere, together swept across my soul, intensified now by many personal experiences. It seemed as if all the elements had conspired to impel me to some onward step. I could not see what to do or where to begin – my only thought was a public meeting for protest and discussion' (ibid., pp. 147–8).

And then she received an invitation to visit Lucretia Mott who was staying nearby. Elizabeth Cady Stanton went to see her friend and, in recalling the experience, says: 'I poured out, that day, the torrent of my long-accumulating discontent, with such vehemence and indignation that I stirred myself, as well as the rest of the party, to do and dare anything' (ibid., p. 148). They decided then and there to call a 'Woman's Rights Convention' and published an announcement the following day in the *Seneca County Courier*, giving but five days' notice of the meeting to be held on 19 and 20 July 1848. The chief 'movers and managers' were Lucretia Mott, Mary Ann McClintock, Jane Hunt, Martha C. Wright (Lucretia Mott's sister) and Elizabeth Cady Stanton.

Three days before the Convention, the women met in Mary Ann McClintock's parlour 'to write their declarations, resolutions and to con-sider subjects for speeches,' but they were unsure where to begin, and, admit the editors of the *History*, 'the humiliating fact may as well now be recorded that before taking the initiative step, those ladies resigned them-selves to a faithful perusal of various masculine productions' (Stanton et al., 1881, vol. I, p. 68). 'They knew women had wrongs, but how to state them was the difficulty' (ibid.). Then someone took up the Declaration of 1776 – the principles and the justification for rebellion against the tyrant, 'King George' – and it was agreed that this with some significant changes and an additional eighteen grievances would be the document adopted for the 'Woman's Rights Convention'.

There was only one problem on the day of the Convention – what to do with the men! 'It had been decided to have no men present, but as they were already on the spot' when the women arrived, something had to be done. The conventional picture of the 'woman's rightists' that we have inherited suggests that many of the nineteenth-century 'reformers' were not committed to an 'autonomous women's movement' (and this is often put forward as a contributing factor for their ostensible failure) but it seems that, despite the comparatively more rigid restrictions placed on the women in the middle of the nineteenth century, many of them were still intent on establishing a movement *of their own* and were prepared to restrict or preclude male participation. But at this first convention, a compromise was reached: 'it was decided in a hasty council, round the altar that . . . they should remain', but that they should make themselves useful undertaking some of the chores at which women had little or no experience (ibid., p. 69). James Mott was made president and the way he conducted the meeting was scrupulously studied for future reference by some of the women for whom this was to be a 'training ground'.

In this instance, no other reference is made by the editors as to the verbal behaviour of the men, whether or not they dominated the discussion or used it as a forum to protect and promote their own self-interest, but it is chastening to note that in the respect of the relationship of men to the women's movement (see Elizabeth Sarah (ed.), 1982b *The Problem of Men*) the issues have changed but little over 130 years.

The Declaration – with amendments – was read at the Convention by Elizabeth Cady Stanton, discussed, and adopted. In essence, the amendments were quite simple but none the less very radical, and consisted of substituting *man*, for the tyrant 'King George'. For example, the Declaration stated

> We hold these truths to be self evident; that all men and women are created equal; that they are endowed by their Creator with certain inalienable rights that among these are life, liberty and the pursuit of happiness . . . The history of mankind is a history of repeated injuries and usurpations on the part of man toward woman, having its direct object the establishment of an absolute tyranny over her. To prove this, let facts be submitted to a candid world.

And the Declaration proceeded to list the facts (published in full in Stanton et al., 1881, vol. I, p. 70–1) which ranged from woman's exclusion from the franchise, the compulsion to submit to laws she had had no part in making, the construction of her civil death upon marriage, the theft of her property, the status of woman as an irresponsible being required to promise obedience to her husband and being bound to submit to his chastisement, the formulation of divorce laws in the interest of men, taxation without representation, the exclusion of woman from 'all the avenues of wealth and distinction which he considers most honorable to himself', scanty remuneration for woman, denial of education, the double standard which operated to the advantage of men, to the monopolisation of the Church, and 'usurpation of the prerogative of Jehovah himself, claiming it as his right to assign for her a sphere of action, when that belongs to her conscience and her God' (ibid., p. 71). As well as this, stated those women over 130 years ago, man 'has endeavoured, in every way that he could, to destroy her confidence in her own powers, to lessen her self-respect, and to make her willing to lead a dependent and abject life' (ibid., p. 60).

Had that declaration been read to me in 1968 when I was searching for some way of naming the problem, it would no doubt have been a revelation; but it might also have been too radical for me to accept! For it was revolution that these women were demanding, and justifying, as woman's responsible duty; they were demanding the autonomy of women, a concept that is still radical, and still resisted in a male-dominated society.

Not much was left out of the list of grievances and there can be no doubt at whose door women laid the blame for the oppression of their sex. This is no reformist document, but a categorical 'naming of the enemy', a systematic analysis of his assaults, and a resounding call for rebellion. The women who were responsible for the wording of the Declaration were well aware that it was in the power of men to bring about change. If the prevailing situation were unsatisfactory to men, they could do something about it and unless and until they did 'put their own house in order', women were justified in claiming that the oppression of women suited men, that men were nothing other than tyrants, regardless of the account they gave of their own behaviour.

From Stanton's point of view, the convention was an immense success. The problem had been named, the issues articulated, the demands formulated, the work had begun, and therefore, she states: 'No words could express our astonishment on finding, a few days afterward, that what seemed to us so timely, so rational, and so sacred should be a subject for sarcasm and ridicule to the entire press of our nation. With our Declaration of Rights and Resolutions for a text it seemed as if every man who could wield a pen prepared a homily on "woman's sphere." All the journals from Maine to Texas seemed to strive with each other to see which could make our movement appear the most ridiculous ... so pronounced was the popular voice against us, in the parlor, press, and pulpit, that most of the ladies who had attended the convention, and signed the declaration, one by one withdrew their names and influence and joined our persecutors. Our friends gave us the cold shoulder and felt themselves disgraced by the whole proceeding' (Stanton, 1898a, p. 149).

The process of harassment and discrediting had begun, and for Elizabeth Cady Stanton there were to be many occasions over the next fifty years when she would recall the example of Lucretia Mott, and refuse to be intimidated by derision or denunciation.[5] She departed from Mott's example in one respect, however, and rather than excusing or forgiving her 'enemies', she used their behaviour as confirmation of her suspicions about the mechanics of male power, and became even more determined – and defiant. But in looking back over her life and the heavy toll that was exacted by the harassment directed against her, she says: 'If I had had the slightest premonition of all that was to follow that convention, I fear I should not have had the courage to risk it' (ibid.). But just one month later, another convention was called in Rochester, and, though 'it was with fear

---

[5] In many ways, Lucretia Mott was like Angelina and Sarah Grimké, convinced that it was 'God's will' that women should be equal, and looking not to man for sanction and approval, but to her own personal god. This was a form of protection against ridicule and harassment.

and trembling that I consented to attend', she plunged into the women's rights movement which she had helped to usher in.

There is no adequate way to convey the contribution that Elizabeth Cady Stanton made: she talked and wrote volumes, and Alice S. Rossi (1974) has said of her that: 'There was probably not another woman in the nineteenth century who put her tongue and pen to better use than Elizabeth Stanton' (p. 382). Fundamental to her beliefs was the insistence that women must abandon the mentality of oppression in which they had been socialised; they must learn to value themselves, to insist on their own needs, to repudiate self-effacement and sacrifice, which they *could* do without jeopardising their strength of being able to provide emotional support.

That women should give up guilt was one of her tenets, that they should learn to express their justifiable anger was another. 'She was not a woman easily threatened by new experiences', says Rossi (1974) and among her prescriptions for a healthy womanhood was one she clearly followed herself, but which it would take many decades for medicine and psychiatry to learn. She insightfully put her finger on an important cause of hysteria and illness among the women of her day, in an 1859 letter to a Boston friend: 'I think if women would indulge more freely in vituperation, they would enjoy ten times the health they do. It seems to me they are suffering from repression' (Stanton and Blatch, 1922: II, 73–74 (Rossi, 1974, p. 381)).

To Elizabeth Cady Stanton, women's anger was not only valid, and necessary, but rational: 'I am at boiling point,' she once wrote to Susan B. Anthony, and, 'If I do not find some day the use of my tongue on this question I shall die of an intellectual repression, a woman's rights convulsion' (Theodore Stanton and Harriet Stanton Blatch, 1922, vol. II, p. 41).

She began her public lecturing (and writing) career in much the same spirited manner in which she was to continue, when, upon hearing that she was preparing to go on a lecture tour, her father came to ask if this were true. She told him that it was: ' "I hope", he continued, "you will never do it in my lifetime, for if you do, be assured of one thing, your first lecture will be a very expensive one" ' (for he would disinherit her). She replied: 'I intend . . . that it shall be a very profitable one' (ibid., p. 61). She could not be bought by male approval, or the promise of male rewards in return for good behaviour.

At no stage did she fall into the trap of believing that woman's position was the consequence of ignorance among men and that all that was necessary was for women to present their case, and men, instantly enlightened, would be won to women's cause. She had no delusions about male 'justice'. She understood that men held the power and that, short of women going off on their own and starting an alternative society (never an option for Stanton although she created her own female enclave from which she drew her emotional support), men had to be confronted, and coerced into giving it up. Because her style was not conciliatory, because she did not seek to persuade men that she was respectable and worthy, because she did not try to convince them that men themselves would be better off when women were enfranchised, and that nothing would change, for women would still continue to be the homemakers, child-rearers, and domestic servants, she was often considered unacceptable not only by men, but by many women who took a more cautious approach. She insisted on delivering her speeches criticising marriage as an institution, she insisted on advocating divorce law reform (despite the fact that she was branded, and discredited as, an advocate of free love), and her outspokenness, and her outrage were often a source of embarrassment to some of the women towards the end of the nineteenth century who were trying to allay and soothe the fears of men – in the hope that, no longer frightened, they would grant women the vote.

After the Civil War – during which much of the agitation for women's rights was put aside as the women put their shoulders behind the men, and proved their patriotism – the divisions within the women's movement were so great that two separate societies were formed, with Elizabeth Cady Stanton and Susan B. Anthony prominent in the more radical National Woman Suffrage Association. (Stanton and Anthony believed 'that it was largely due to the preponderance of men in the Equal Rights Association leadership that women's interests had been betrayed, and that the women who followed the men's lead – Mrs Stone, Mrs Howe, and others – had been misled or duped by them', Flexner, 1979, p. 155.)

Stanton and Anthony deplored the conservatism of those in the American Woman Suffrage Association, but the members of the 'American' equally deplored what they perceived to be the 'alienating' policies and practices of the 'National.' To members of the American, the fact that the journal of the National was to be called *Revolution*, when they were trying to establish their respectability, was most disturbing and some of them expressed their dismay. Writing to Susan B. Anthony about this, Stanton said: 'The establishing of woman on her rightful throne is the greatest revolution the world has ever known or will know. To bring it about is no child's play. You and I have not forgotten the conflict of the last twenty years – the ridicule, persecution, denunciation, detraction, the unmixed bitterness of our cup.' Stanton was not prepared to 'gloss over' the elements of confrontation, nor the naked operation of power; she wanted to force it out into the open rather than to mask it with a cloak of respectability: 'A journal called the *Rosebud* might answer for those who come with kid gloves and perfumes', Stanton said, 'to lay immortal wreaths on the monuments which in sweat and tears others have hewn and built; but for us . . . there is no name like the *Revolution*' (Stanton and Blatch, 1922, vol. II, p. 74–5). And for the American Woman Suffrage Association there was to be no association with the formulators of such sentiment for many years.

In *Eighty Years and More* Stanton says that she and some of her friends were frequently criticised for their behaviour – and often by women who were reaping the rewards of those fifty years of struggle. Such critics suggest, Stanton says, 'If these pioneers in reform had only pressed their measures more judiciously, in a more ladylike manner, in more choice language, with a more deferential attitude, the gentlemen could not have behaved so rudely for so long' (Stanton, 1898a, p. 167). But Stanton makes no apology for being unladylike – in her analysis, no one ever relinquished power because they were asked – no matter how nicely!

Like some of her predecessors, she was often frustrated by the actions of women, and like them, she refused to blame women for the circumstances over which they had no control. Yet she fervently wished that women would look to each other – and not to men – if it was approval they needed. Again and again she tried to make it clear that it should not be important to women to be acceptable to men and that if all women became 'unacceptable' and defined their own terms of their own existence, much of the battle would be won, because men would have no alternative but to 'accept' unacceptable women – or go without! She deplored the strategy of being 'feminine' to achieve women's rights, because she thought that it was ultimately self-defeating. Not only would it *not* achieve the desired aim (partly because the more 'feminine' women acted the more evidence they provided of their unfitness for public office – which was where men started, to begin with), but such masquerading and repression also did violence to oneself. There was no self-esteem to be gained as far as Stanton was concerned, from acting in a 'feminine' fashion; it left one feeling shabby.

Her unashamed intention was at times to frighten men, to insist that they would have to change, to demand that their privileges and their images of themselves should go. Her verve, her mockery and her wit are constantly present and she was not at all reluctant to make a joke at the expense of a man (behaviour that is customarily called man-hating in a male-domi-nated society where men make up the rules and do not see themselves as 'funny'). That she did sometimes on the most public of occasions make a man and his foibles the butt of the joke is no doubt one of the reasons she was called a man-hater (see Gail Parker, 1975), but it is one of the reasons I enjoy some of the incidents she recounts.

One such incident occurred in 1869, when, after addressing a conven-tion in Lincoln, Nebraska, some of the members called on Stanton to discuss the points of her speech. 'All the gentlemen were serious and respectful with one exception', says Stanton, and he tried 'at my expense to be witty and facetious. During a brief pause in the conversation he brought his chair directly before me and said, in a mocking tone, "Don't you think that the best thing a woman can do is to perform well her part in the role of wife and mother? My wife has presented me with eight beautiful children: is not this a better life work than that of exercising the right of suffrage?" I decided', says Stanton 'to give him an answer not soon to be forgotten: so I promptly replied to his question, as I slowly viewed him from head to foot, "I have met few men, in my life, worth repeating eight times" ' (Stanton, 1898a, pp. 300–1). Resolved that she would not be subdued by psychological intimidation and harassment, Stanton per-sisted in defying the constantly reiterated injunction that she should retreat to her proper sphere.

Reading just some of the things that Stanton said and wrote, it becomes impossible to believe that there is anything *new* in the modern women's movement. For my own part I have spent a number of years engaged in research on the talk of women and men, and have been convinced – at least at one stage – that I was on the brink of valuable new insights, when I began to appreciate that, contrary to conventional wisdom, it was men who talked more, that they dominated talk, and that they were likely to

suffer anything ranging from resentment to apoplexy when they were prevented from talking and were required to be silent and to *listen*. It thus
came as something of a shock to realise that Elizabeth Cady Stanton had
known this (without benefit of a research degree) a century before.

In 1850 the first woman's rights convention in Ohio was held in Salem
and this convention 'had one peculiar characteristic. It was officered entirely
by women; not a man was allowed to sit on the platform, to speak or vote.
Never did men suffer so. They implored just to say a word; but no – the
President was inflexible – no man should be heard. If one meekly arose to
make a suggestion he was at once ruled out of order. For the first time in
the world's history, men learned how it felt to sit in silence when questions
they were interested in were under discussion' (Stanton et al., 1881, vol. I,
p. 110, original emphasis).

The final touch in this paragrph – a role reversal – is characteristically
Stanton, when she recalls the way women have been treated, and suggests
'It would have been an admirable way of closing the Convention, had a
rich banquet been provided, to which the men should have had the privilege
of purchasing tickets to the gallery, there to enjoy the savory odors, and
listen to the after-dinner speeches' (ibid.).

In relation to this event it is important to remember that some actions
that are more acceptable today would have been outrageous in 1850.
Women were allowed to speak to each other; it was the presence of men
that was the overriding factor, as Sarah and Angelina Grimké had found
out when they began to talk on abolition. Women were not permitted to
speak in the presence of men, as Lucy Stone had found at Oberlin College
(see page 254) and Elizabeth Cady Stanton had found at the World's
Anti-Slavery Convention in London. Therefore for women to meet and talk
with each other (often perceived as a radical move today) was not nearly
as great an act of rebellion in 1850 as it was *to have men present, and to
have only women speakers*. Permitting men to attend but not permitting
them to speak was one of the most radical moves that could have been
taken and an unambiguous declaration of woman's rights and woman's
autonomy.

From marriage to motherhood to divorce; from women's work to
women's pay; from the control of her earnings to the control of her body;
from sexuality to religion; from the male monopoly of medicine, philosophy
and literature to male control of education and the law, Elizabeth Cady
Stanton's intellectual energy was boundless as she analysed, and criticised,
and formulated alternatives, and few are her ideas that are not applicable
today. She emphasised the man-made nature of knowledge and, following
in the footsteps of her predecessors (women like 'Sophia' and Frances
Wright), she stated that: 'When women understand that governments and
religions are human inventions; that Bibles, prayer books, catechisms and
encyclical letters are all emanations from the brain of man, they will no
longer be oppressed by the injunctions' delivered so readily by *men*, in the
guise of divinely ordained authority (ibid., p. 285). To Stanton, women
must be responsible for generating their own knowledge, for valuing it and
themselves, for only then would women be socially valued.

Nowhere is this philosophy more manifest than *The Woman's Bible* (Stanton, 1898b). The clergy, and the habit among many of them of incessantly quoting the scriptures to justify women's subordination, were anathema to Elizabeth Cady Stanton, and clerics and their practices were often her target for scathing attack (another feature of her behaviour that did not endear her to those seeking respectability). Throughout her public life she made the division (articulated to her originally by Lucretia Mott, in London, see Stanton et. al. 1881, vol. I, p. 422) between religion and theology, where religion was a virtue, but theology – and the uses to which it had been put by some unscrupulous clergy – was a vice. The Bible in its existing form, and the way it was interpreted, was for Stanton a particular source of anger, for, as she observed, 'when those who are opposed to all reforms can find no other argument, their last resort is the Bible. It has been interpreted to favor intemperance, slavery, capital punishment and the subjection of women' (Stanton, 1898b; p. vi). Stanton wanted to revise the Bible: 'particularly those texts and chapters directly referring to women, and those also in which women are made prominent by exclusion' (ibid., p. 5). And why not?

With the assistance of seven other women, including Matilda Joslyn Gage, Stanton (who had won the Greek prize over fifty years before, and who also knew Latin) studied the original texts and came to the conclusion that they had not been translated or interpreted accurately. But even more than that, says Miriam Gurko (1976), 'she wanted to convince women that the Bible was not the direct Word of God, but a series of writings, by men, a compilation of Hebrew mythology and history. The position of women as laid down in the Bible was not divinely ordained; it was only the reflection of ancient patriarchal attitudes, which men had used ever since to reinforce their male authority. Women were under no obligation, moral or otherwise to accept these dictates' (p. 286).

Stanton wanted women to think for themselves, to see the world in relationship to themselves and not themselves in relationship to men: 'She wanted them to stop thinking along purely traditional lines and explore the real relationship between the sexes; to examine with a fresh, uncluttered eye the institution of marriage, the controversial subjects of divorce and birth control. She wanted them to shake off the restrictive influence of religious thought' (ibid., 282) – and this at a time when 'suffrage' had become more acceptable, and respectable, and had attracted more 'religious' women.

'The Bible position of women briefly summed up' was, according to Stanton, the means of keeping woman in her 'divinely ordained sphere'. 'The Bible teaches that woman brought sin and death into the world', she states in her Introduction, 'that she was arraigned before the judgement seat of Heaven, tried, condemned and sentenced. Marriage for her was to be a condition of bondage, maternity a period of suffering and anguish, and in silence and subjection, she was to play the role of a dependent on man's bounty for all her material wants, and for all the information she might desire on the vital questions of the hour, she was commanded to ask her husband at home' (1898b, p. 7).

Such a set of injunctions were not only irrelevant in Stanton's eyes, they were positively harmful (and besides, they had always been false) and so she organised the revision of the Bible. Such 'revisions' were not so unusual, as the Church of England had appointed two groups of scholars as recently as 1870 to undertake such a revision. But predictably Stanton and her Revising Committee came up with a very different set of interpretations and were greeted in a very different manner from those on the official committee of the Church of England. There was great opposition and hostility to Stanton's undertaking, but she met the objections with characteristic defiance: 'One correspondent conjured us to suspend the work as it is "ridiculous" for "women to attempt the revision of the Scriptures",' she says, but 'I wonder if any man wrote to the late revising committee of Divines to stop their work on the ground that it was ridiculous for men to revise the Bible. Why is it more ridiculous for women to protest against her present status in the Old and New Testament, in the ordinances and discipline of the church, than in the statutes and constitution of the state? Why is it more ridiculous to arraign ecclesiastics for their false teaching and acts of injustice to women, than members of Congress and the House of Commons? ... Women have compelled their legislators in every state in this Union to so modify their statutes for women that the old common law is now almost a dead letter. Why not compel Bishops and Revising Committees to modify their creeds and dogmas?' she asks (ibid., p. 10).

To Elizabeth Cady Stanton, it was beyond comprehension that women could develop as responsible and autonomous beings while they accepted the ideas – including the ones supposedly justified by religion – men had of them. She could not understand how women could at the same time be self-sufficient *and* self-sacrificing (as the Bible enjoined them to be), how they could develop self-respect and confidence and at the same time accept that they had brought sin into the world and were therefore obliged to spend their lives in remorseful atonement. To her, independence was a much more embracing concept than 'the vote'; the vote was but a symbol. To her it was vitally important that women cease to be the people that men had defined and started to be the people women defined. Some men, she said, tell us 'that we must be womanly. My friends, what is man's idea of womanliness? It is to have a manner which pleases him – quiet, deferential, submissive ...' (Stanton, 1890, quoted in Gurko 1976, p. 281). Such a manner pleased Stanton not at all, and was a source of frustration and anger when she saw it deliberately and inflexibly cultivated among respectable women, who wanted the vote.

She shows little patience with the cautious: 'Forty years ago it seemed as ridiculous to timid, time serving and retrograde folk for women to demand an expurgated edition of the laws, as it now does to demand an expurgated edition of the Liturgies and Scriptures,' and adds, 'Come, come, my conservative friend, wipe the dew off your spectacles, and see that the world is moving.' Addressing herself to women, she says: 'Whatever your views may be as to the importance of the proposed work, your political and social degradation are but an outgrowth of your status in the Bible,' and there is no doubt in Stanton's mind that the pernicious arguments advanced by previous male editors and interpreters of the Bible can and will be repudiated and 'expurgated'.

For those who may believe that feminism can be but a passing phase, that our history is one of short feminist bursts, of the fleeting commitment of a few women who are then 'burned out', and who then withdraw (to domesticity?), it is well to remember that Stanton was 83 when this was published and, not only did she show no signs of giving up, she showed no signs of becoming conservative in her old age either!

She was still prepared to fight: there are those, she said, who say, 'it is not *politic* to rouse religious opposition. This much-lauded policy is but another word for *cowardice*. How can woman's position be changed from that of a subordinate to an equal, without opposition. . .? For so far-reaching and momentous a reform as her complete independence, an entire revolution in all existing institutions (of which the Church was a major one) is inevitable' (1898b, pp. 10–11). And a revolution she proceeded to promote either despite the fact that, or because, her publication was offensive to the clergy. Her actions caused considerable division within the women's movement and a substantial effort was made to 'disown' her.

Over the last century the influence of the Church has waned somewhat (perhaps the actions of Stanton and Matilda Joslyn Gage who was equally outspoken and who wrote *Woman, Church and State* (1893) were contributory factors, although, as current feminist efforts indicate, while the Church may be less powerful 'outside' little has changed 'within') and one of the statements Stanton makes in her *Introduction* may be relevant to even more women today than it was when first written. 'Again there are some who write us that our work is a useless expenditure of force over a book that has lost its hold on the human mind,' says Stanton, for, 'Most intelligent women, they say, regard it simply as the history of a rude people in a barbarous age, and have no more reverence for the Scriptures than any other work.' But, she proceeds, 'so long as tens of thousands of Bibles are printed every year, and circulated over the whole habitable globe' (and, one is tempted to add, so long as the White House is inhabited by 'born again Christians') 'and the masses in all English-speaking nations revere it as the word of God, it is vain to belittle its influence' (ibid., p. 11). I suspect that few would disagree with her rationale.

There is no doubt that *The Woman's Bible* caused a stir in its own time – and is enjoying considerable popularity in our own – and one must ask, again, where it went in the intervening years. There is no doubt that Elizabeth Cady Stanton could provide a most acceptable explanation. Her publication of *The Woman's Bible* in the face of immense opposition, much of which was mounted by women in the woman's rights movement, indicates to me just how very 'disagreeable' – and therefore likeable – she could be. She had an 'openness of intellect' (Rossi, 1974, p. 381), an ability to change, to rethink and reanalyse, that was evident even in her later years, and she had a well-developed sense of self-esteem. 'Self development', she said, 'is a higher duty than self-sacrifice and should be a woman's motto henceforward' (Stanton, 1898b, p. viii).

In 1892 Elizabeth Cady Stanton gave an address to the Senate Committee on Woman Suffrage, entitled 'The Solitude of Self' (Anthony and Harper, 1902, vol. IV, p. 189–91), in which she stressed the human, individual and solitary nature of woman, and summed up much that she had been saying for many years: 'The isolation of every human soul and the necessity of self dependence must give each individual the right', she said, to choose their own surroundings. 'The strongest reason for giving woman all the opportunities for higher education, for the full development of her faculties, her forces of mind and body; for giving her the most enlarged freedom of thought and action; a complete emancipation from all forms of bondage, of custom, of dependence, of superstition; from all the crippling influences of fear – is the solitude and personal responsibility of her individual life. The strongest reason', she adds, for our demands for equality 'is because of her birthright to self-sovereignty; because as an individual she must rely on herself . . .' (ibid., p. 190).

Turning her attention to the role man had played in denying woman self-sovereignty – and in justifying his sovereignty over her, Stanton says: 'How the little courtesies of life on the surface of society, deemed so important from man towards woman, fade into utter insignificance in view of the deeper tragedies in which she must play her part alone, where no human aid is possible. . . . Nothing strengthens the judgement and quickens the conscience like individual responsibility. Nothing adds such dignity to character as the recognition of one's self sovereignty', she said. 'The talk of sheltering woman from the fierce storms of life is the sheerest mockery, for they beat on her from every point of the compass, just as they do on man, and with more fatal results, for he has been trained to protect himself, to resist . . .' (ibid., pp. 190–1).

Like Mary Wollstonecraft who wanted women to control their own lives, like Margaret Fuller who wanted women to define their own sphere, like 'Sophia' and Frances Wright who wanted women to generate their own knowledge, Elizabeth Cady Stanton wanted all this for woman. She is so much part of that tradition of women – in many respects she represents the synthesis of what had gone before. And she stood there and demonstrated the positive gains for women who persisted in defying male-decreed reality.

There was little about her that was self-sacrificing (it would have been self-sacrificing to her to adopt a 'feminine' and conciliatory role in the struggle for women's rights but the way she fought was, to her, self-affirming). When it came to marriage and maternity she was not reticent about registering her protest, and was perfectly capable of expressing – without guilt – that she wished to be free of house and children for a while, in order that she might have time to read and think and write. The only area where she seems to display reservation – rather than defiance and anger – is in relation to her husband and, if the absence of women is obvious in history, then the absence of Henry B. Stanton is obvious in the written records of Elizabeth Cady Stanton! Although they were married for forty-six years, Elizabeth 'clearly received only shallow emotional support and no political support for her convictions from Henry Stanton', says

Rossi (1974, p. 385). It was the women in her life, particularly Lucretia Mott and Susan B. Anthony, who were her source of support.

Again, in a letter to Susan B. Anthony, Stanton reveals a glimpse of the domestic scene when she writes, 'the pressure on me now is just too great. Henry sides with my friends, who oppose me in all that is dearest to my heart. They are not willing that I should write even on the woman question. But I will both write and speak. I wish you to consider this letter strictly confidential', she states to Anthony. She concludes: 'Sometimes, Susan, I struggle in deep waters' (Stanton and Blatch, 1922, vol. II, p. 60).

But what is the assessment of Stanton? In reading about her, one of the things I found striking was the number of times that I was assured that 'Mrs Stanton did not really hate men', that 'Mrs Stanton was not really interested in a sex-war'. Though there are exceptions, it appears that even today there are those who feel obliged to 'qualify' some of Stanton's explicit statements about the self-interested role men have played in the construction of society, and the sexes. Some who have written about her have done so in a manner that is hardly consistent with Stanton's own politics: she was never conciliatory; she never sought to be portrayed flatteringly and in a 'feminine' light. Yet in presenting her to us today, there are some writers who try to introduce an ostensibly flattering and feminine overtone; there are others who present a more complex portrayal.

Gail Parker (1975), for example, in her Introduction to *Eighty Years and More: Reminiscences 1815–1897*, certainly detects the independence of spirit and healthy self-esteem that I do in Stanton, but does not exactly portray her in the positive light in which she has been presented here. She recognises the radical nature of Stanton's demands (if not her intellectual contribution) and her reluctance to settle for respectability, her refusal to accept the authority of the clergy. 'Mrs Stanton's confidence that the suffragists were superior to others of their sex in their lack of concern for what people would say, was disappointed as woman's rights became a socially acceptable enthusiasm,' says Parker, and while 'She may not have converted the majority of suffragists to her belief that to be eternally politic and polite was to do violence to yourself and your own deepest needs as a human being . . . she managed in her own life to know the satisfactions of a healthy self-esteem' (p. xvi).

Is there a suggestion here that Parker does not approve?

Parker quotes a letter of Stanton's to Lucretia Mott, an innocuous letter in which Stanton tells of the birth of her first daughter, and an uncharacteristic letter in some respects because Stanton presents birth as problem-free and even takes some pride and satisfaction in having given birth somewhat effortlessly. But does it tell us about Stanton – or about Parker – or about the patriarchal context in which women's ideas are formulated, when Parker follows this letter – directly – with the statement: 'This is not, in the end, a letter of a castrating feminist, singlemindedly out to destroy men and the male prerogative' (ibid., p. xvii).

I quote this, because it is beyond me to see how castration comes into it: I cannot even make the preliminary link between an account of a relatively easy childbirth and the destruction of men. But I can see why it is relevant to disparage *any* account of Elizabeth Cady Stanton's life; I can see the reason (based on fear, not 'logic') for branding a woman who protests as *castrating* – no matter what else she does. While to women it may seem that there are no links at all between an 'indecently short time' to give birth, and the potential to be castrating, there are many 'emotional' links in a male-dominated society where a 'defiant' woman has her perceived emasculating power projected on to *all* her activities – partly so that her defiance and the ideas that inform it can be discredited and dismissed.

Parker has little praise for Stanton; she even manages to render some of Stanton's positive features quite unattractive: 'There is unquestionably something repellant about Elizabeth Cady Stanton's superiority complex', she says. And, 'I cannot help but wish that she had manifested a less invidious sisterly love for her sex and that her championship of the slaves, and later of the working classes, had been marked by a genuine feeling of involvement with their fate, instead of a vicarious pleasure in being able to share in their rebellious feelings' (ibid., p. xviii). What is the source of this value judgement?

Parker makes fleeting reference to Stanton's intellectual contribution – she 'was the philosopher and chief publicist of the radical wing of the woman's rights movement' (ibid., p. v). No mention is made of the mammoth task of editing the *History of Woman Suffrage*, the reasons for its existence or the extent of its significance. She is portrayed as something of a 'scold', lecturing to those who will not understand, uncompromising in the sense of her own righteousness, and persistent in hammering home her message. And she is most definitely seen as having an abundance of self-love, a superiority complex, of being a radical elitist. Yet, says Parker, pointing to the extenuating circumstances, 'I am forced to wonder whether a more egalitarian Mrs Stanton would have had the ego strength, or whatever to explore her own passions and to express them so honestly. An egalitarian ideology, when it is backed up by social reality, by an actual sisterhood or brotherhood or comradeship, may instead of having a leveling effect on its adherents' (and *I* wonder where *this* idea comes from) 'give them the kind of support they need to develop their individual resources. But with only Susan B. Anthony to rely on, and no real prospect of setting up a cooperative household, it is hard to be too critical of Mrs Stanton's devotion to a creed of exceptionalism.' And just in case any reader is beginning to feel that Mrs Stanton's self-love was not as repellant as Parker found it, she continues directly, and in the same paragraph with: 'Toward the end of her life her self-love manifested itself in abundant flesh, and Susan Anthony, grimly spare to the last, admonished her to exercise and diet. But Mrs Stanton refused to go along with the refined masochism of the female physical culturists. She was more interested in celebrating her body than disciplining it' (ibid., pp. xvii–xix). Is this why she had so much energy, intellectual and physical, for so long?

Had I read Gail Parker's account of Elizabeth Cady Stanton *before* I had read anything else about her or by her, it is quite probable that I would not have found Stanton at all attractive, and quite likely that I would not have attempted to find out any more about her. We simply cannot afford to continue to collude in this practice of the denial and disparagement of women.

Of course I have presented a biased account of Elizabeth Cady Stanton – *this is all anyone can do!* The only unusual feature of it may be that it is biased in *her* favour, and this borders on being 'a cultural' or unreasonable in a patriarchal society. In the sum total of her life there are aspects which – even a century later – I prefer to 'gloss over', things she wrote and said which are no longer helpful or acceptable, but then, in my own relatively short lifespan, or for that matter, in the last decade, there are things which I have written and said which are now neither useful nor acceptable (and at times, even mortifying) and which I also 'gloss over'. I cannot afford to operate a double standard.

Besides, she also wrote and said what I have reported here; that cannot be denied.

There is so much about Elizabeth Cady Stanton that is today so affirming: the fact of her existence and her defiance is a rich resource for women. In a male-dominated society it is so easy to be reduced into devaluing the lives and works of women like Stanton, that it takes deliberate defiance to insist on and persist with the assertion that the women, and their contributions, are positive. There is no more evidence that Stanton was 'repellent' than there is that she was 'attractive', but there is a considerable amount of evidence that a patriarchal society wants women who have protested – like Stanton – to be seen as 'repellent', to be devalued and dismissed, by women as well as men. It is not mandatory that we follow patriarchal prescriptions.

Susan B. Anthony

One of the other biases in my selection of material on Elizabeth Cady Stanton has been to present her almost exclusively as an 'individual' when her life and her work were so interwoven with the life and work of Susan B. Anthony. In *The Feminist Papers* (1974) Alice Rossi says: 'it is fitting . . . to introduce these two remarkable women together in one essay and to focus on their friendship and the nature of their collaboration' because they were the 'two women most closely associated with the emergence of the woman's-rights movement in the nineteenth century' and from the time 'they first met, until Elizabeth's death in 1902 they were the most intimate of friends and the closest collaborators in the battle.' They lectured together, founded equal rights and suffrage associations, organised conventions and were co-editors of the *History*, says Rossi, and 'the contributions of these two pioneers are so intertwined that it is nearly impossible to speak of one without the other. They were in and out of each others personal lives and households for more than fifty years. Their friendship and shared commitment to the cause of women's rights were the solid, central anchor in both their lives. As Elizabeth wrote to Susan in 1869, "no power in heaven, hell or earth can separate us, for our hearts are eternally wedded together" (Stanton and Blatch 1922: II; 125)' (Rossi, 1974, p. 378).

Yet, for many reasons, it is slightly more difficult to get a sense of

Susan B. Anthony than it is of Elizabeth Cady Stanton. In part I suspect this is because Stanton was more extrovert, more flamboyant, more given to anger and rage where her personal characteristics are more readily revealed. But it is also partly because it was Stanton who was responsible for much of the written record with the result that a great deal of what is known about Susan B. Anthony comes not from herself, directly, but is filtered through Stanton – or Ida Husted Harper – and there is therefore a 'distancing' not present with Stanton.

But where there are direct impressions from Susan B. Anthony (in her letters and some of her speeches) it is clear that they both shared the same commitment to each other, and to the cause (although they often perceived 'the cause' differently). And their relationship was not just one of emotional support, but often of intellectual stimulation as well. In commenting on them, a 'mutual friend' stated 'that opposites though they be, each does not so much supplement the other's difficiencies (sic) as augment the other's eccentricities. Thus they often stimulate each other's aggressiveness, and at the same time diminish each other's discretion' (Stanton et al., 1881, vol. I, p. 457). This is more likely to have been applicable in the earlier than the later years when Susan B. Anthony became more conservative, but it seems they were quite a good team when it came to creating a movement.

Without many domestic responsibilities herself (for Susan's sister Mary Anthony cared for their aged mother), Susan B. Anthony was not one to concede that domestic responsibilities were mandatory, or even a priority in women's lives. Lucy Stone sensed Anthony's disapproval when she retired temporarily from public life after the birth of her daughter, Alice Stone Blackwell, and Ida B. Wells encountered a similar response after having taken her child to a number of conventions (Wells asked Anthony at one stage if she thought women should not marry, to which Anthony replied: 'Not women like you who have a special call for special work. . . . Since you've gotten married, agitation seems practically to have ceased. Besides, you're here trying to help in the formation of this league and your baby needs your attention at home. You're distracted over the thought that he's not being looked after as he would be if you were there, and that makes for a divided duty', Dorothy Sterling, 1979, pp. 100–1). Obviously it was not Anthony's way to let Stanton be overwhelmed by domestic duties and by a variety of means she pushed Stanton towards the public arena, and the struggle, in the early years.

First of all, there could be the plea for help. 'There is so much to say and I am so without constructive power' to say it, Anthony wrote to Stanton in 1856. 'So for the love of me and for the saving of the reputation of womanhood, I beg you, with one baby on your knee and another at your feet, and four boys whistling, buzzing, hallooing "Ma, Ma", set yourself about the work,' urged Anthony, and write me a speech, and – with characteristic encouragement – 'Do get all on fire and be as cross as you please. You remember Mr Stanton told how cross you always get over a speech' (Stanton and Blatch, 1922, vol. II, pp. 64–5). And Stanton put family responsibilities aside, responded – and usually got very cross!

But this was not the only tactic Anthony employed to get Stanton going; she would also come visiting, and as Stanton reports, her 'little portmanteau stuffed with facts was opened and there we had ... false interpretations of Bible texts, the statistics of women robbed of their property, shut out of some college, half paid for their work, the reports of some disgraceful trial, injustice enough to turn any woman's thoughts from stockings and puddings' (Stanton et al., 1881, vol. I, p. 458). And Anthony would share the child care and assume some of the domestic responsibilities while Stanton wrote.

According to Stanton, 'The children of our household say that among their earliest recollections is the tableau of "Mother and Susan" seated by a large table covered with books and papers, always writing and talking about the Constitution, interrupted with occasional visits from others of the faithful' (ibid., pp. 461–2).

We are usually asked to accept that the Stanton–Anthony relationship was one of 'opposites' (a portrayal encouraged by Stanton herself) and I am sometimes left with the sneaking suspicion that we are being asked to validate the premise that it takes the different but combined characteristics of these two women to constitute a sufficient influence to develop and sustain the issue of woman's rights. I am aware of no male leaders of any movement portrayed in this way. Stanton is the wife and mother while Anthony is the 'spinster' and many of their attributes are catalogued consistently under these headings: Stanton is perceived as more emotional, as exuberant, self-indulgent, even irresponsible, while Anthony is cautious, controlled, meticulous; Stanton is creative while Anthony is the critic, Stanton the philosopher while Anthony is the organiser and administrator. To accept these judgements without question is, I think, to do both women a disservice.

It leaves Anthony open to a particular form of devaluation: it helps to suggest that she substituted women's struggle for a full and satisfying personal life, that she was not creative or innovative, that she was concerned with collecting all the scraps of paper (for the *History*) and was the one who could be counted upon to undertake all the tedious details associated with the organisation of constant meetings. That Anthony was a shrewd and perceptive person (which was one reason she chose 'spinsterhood') is a facet of her that often tends to be blurred by the treatment that she has received from biographers and commentators. She was an excellent propagandist, who, had she been a man, would no doubt have been assessed as an astute, well-informed, highly capable statesman or politician, able not only to generate ideas for change but also to put them into practice. As a woman, however, she is often devalued as an ardent campaigner.

What may appear paradoxical is that this assessment of Anthony does not seem to have facilitated her 'disappearance'. Anthony herself noted that during her lifetime she moved from being 'the most hated and reviled of women' to one who appeared to be universally loved, but this is by no means a common occurrence for many of the other women who have fought against women's oppression. It didn't happen to Elizabeth Cady Stanton, who became *more* reviled in some respects, the older she got. But when Anthony resigned from the presidency of the Suffrage Association in

1900 and celebrated her eightieth birthday, there was considerable evidence
that she was accepted and admired, and that her spinsterhood was no
longer considered a mark of failure. The same papers 'that had once printed
grotesquely unflattering caricatures of Susan Anthony and had referred to
her as "this shrewish maiden" [now] warmly praised "The Napoleon of
the Woman's Rights Movement," and competed with each other in listing
her many virtues', says Miriam Gurko. 'One editorial said "there was an
element of tragedy in the fact that Miss Anthony," with all her worthy
accomplishments, had nevertheless "missed wifehood and motherhood, the
crowning honor and glory of a woman's life" ' (1976, p. 294), but she
seems to have been the recipient of 'sympathy' rather than abuse as a
consequence of her single state.

It is interesting to note that not even contemporary writers can resist
the temptation to offer reassurances about Anthony's single state. Miriam
Gurko (1976), for example, goes to some length to convince readers that
not only did Anthony have a full and satisfying personal life but also, that
she 'was both maternal and domestic. She loved children and young people,
and managed to practice a great deal of mothering: she was a second
mother to her own nieces and nephews, and to the Stanton children. . . .
As she grew older and the age gap between herself and the new recruits to
the suffrage movement widened, she assumed a maternal relationship to
the young women entering the association' (p. 295). When she retired and
moved in with her sister Mary, they 'set up a thoroughly domestic establishment' and, just in case there is still anyone left with any doubts about
Anthony's maternal and domestic traits, 'When Mrs Stanton came to visit
later that year, she found Susan "demurely seated in her mother's rocking
chair hemming table linen and towels for her new home" ' (ibid.).

Anthony herself never tried to 'rationalise' her unmarried state; she
was quite explicit that it was a choice, and a good one. In an interview in
1906 she stated: 'I never felt I could give up my life of freedom to become
a man's housekeeper. When I was young, if a girl married poverty, she
became a drudge; if she married wealth, she became a doll. Had I married
at twenty one, I would have been either a drudge or a doll for fifty-five
years. Think of it!' (quoted in Gurko, 1976, p. 291). She was also prepared
to 'use' the fact that she was not married for 'political' purposes. Elizabeth
Cady Stanton says that when Anthony was asked why she was not married
she used to respond with the declaration 'that she could not consent that
the man she loved, described in the Constitution as a white male, native
born, American citizen, possessed of the right of self government, eligible
to the office of President of the great Republic, should unite his destinies
in marriage with a poltical slave and pariah' (Stanton, 1898a, p. 172).

Anthony had no illusions about marriage; she knew how powerless
women were upon marriage and their 'civil death', and she knew the extent
to which they could be abused by their husbands without any possibility
of redress. She did not make the same scathing criticisms of marriage as
Stanton, but her actions on many occasions indicated that she shared the
same analysis (particularly in the early years) and perceived the same links
between male power and the belief that women were deviant. One such

occasion was in 1861 when, records Stanton, 'Miss Anthony had been instrumental in helping a fugitive mother with her child, escape from her husband who had immured her in an insane asylum. The wife, belonging to one of the first families of New York, her brother a United States Senator, and the husband a man of position, a large circle of friends and acquaintances were interested in the result. Though she was incarcerated in an insane asylum for eighteen months, yet members of her own family again and again testified she was not insane' (Stanton et al., 1881, vol. I, p. 469).

Miss Anthony was firmly convinced that the woman was a victim of conspiracy and under no circumstances would she reveal her hiding place. Day after day, pressure was placed on her to help return the woman to her husband – telegrams, letters, personal pleas from many influential men warning her that she was violating the law and that there could be dire consequences, but day after day with the support of the women who understood the implications for the woman (who would no doubt be returned to the insane asylum with the latest episode even further proof of her 'insanity'), Anthony remained implacable: she would not tell. She considered it just as important to help this woman escape from the power and control of her husband as it was to help a slave escape to Canada from the power and control of her master.

'Miss Anthony remained immovable,' says Stanton, 'although she knew she was defying authority and violating law, and that she might be arrested at any moment on the platform. We had known so many aggravated cases of this kind, that in daily counsel we resolved that this woman should not be recaptured if it was possible to prevent it' (ibid.). Stanton states that it was a wise decision – but it was Anthony who was instrumental in carrying it out; the woman in later years was never considered insane. 'Could the dark secrets of those insane asylums be brought to light', adds Stanton, 'we would be shocked to know the countless number of rebellious wives, sisters, and daughters that are thus annually sacrificed to false customs and conventionalisms, and barbarous laws made by men for women' (ibid.).

With the full and unromanticised knowledge of women's existence within marriage, the problem is not one of explaining why Anthony remained single, but why some of the women who shared the same understandings chose to be married. In the case of women like Anthony (and Elizabeth and Emily Blackwell, or in Britain, Mary Astell, Harriet Martineau and Lydia Becker) so much of the small space allocated to them in the annals of history has focused so extensively on their 'inability to form proper intimate relationships with men' that it becomes monotonous reading: why should women have chosen to make themselves potential victims? Why are they not praised for their sense instead of patronised for their peculiarities?[6] To praise the single state for women, to present it as a positive lifestyle would be to undermine some of the foundations of patriar-

---

[6] As Dorothy Jones and Jennifer Jones (forthcoming), indicate, there is virtually a total absence of positive portrayals of single women in the literature of English-speaking people.

chy. Susan B. Anthony knew this and willingly and defiantly presented herself as happily single.

Despite her unmarried state and her early radicalism, Susan B. Anthony has not only survived in many historical records (a factor which does require more examination and is treated later) but has enjoyed a reputation of some standing. Being presented as almost perfectly acceptable has had some drawbacks, for the element of wit and audacity – often present in Anthony's letters and speeches, particularly in her earlier years – tends to be overlooked. There is one instance, however, in which some of Anthony's positive qualities emerge very clearly – that of her trial in 1873.

Anthony had led a group of sixteen women to vote in the Presidential election of 1872, in order to test the rights of women and in the full knowledge that there were severe penalties for voting illegally. 'Miss Anthony was of course made the test case,' says Eleanor Flexner (1979) and she displayed her usual shrewdness when, 'In the weeks preceding the trial she took her case directly to the citizens (and prospective jurors!) of Monroe County, speaking in every one of the county's twenty nine postoffice districts. The tour attracted so much attention that the prosecuting attorney became alarmed and obtained a change of venue to Canandaigua in neighbouring Ontario County, where the trial was set for June 17, 1873' (p. 169). Undaunted, Susan B. Anthony proceeded to speak in twenty-one postal districts of Ontario County (while Matilda Joslyn Gage covered the other sixteen) and the basis of her argument was that because she considered herself legally entitled to vote, she could not be held guilty of criminal action or intent.

The trial which followed was blatantly irregular. Tried by Justice Ward Hunt who was 'trying his first case and anxious to produce the results desired by the Administration', says Flexner, 'his high-handedness was astounding' (ibid.). But at the end of the trial in which she was found guilty by the Judge (who had ruled that there was no role to play for the jury), the judge made a tactical error: 'he asked the defendent whether she had anything to say as to why sentence should not be served. She had; over his repeated admonitions, once he realised what he had unleashed, Susan Anthony gave Justice Hunt, the jury, and the packed courtroom, a blistering denunciation not only of the trial itself, but of the whole issue of women's disfranchisement' (ibid., p. 170).

Reading the speech that Susan B. Anthony delivered – and recognising the manner in which it was delivered – makes it difficult to accept that she was in entirety, cautious, cool, and a campaigner. There were times when she was also passionate, defiant, and very perceptive, and for these attributes she is generally too little praised. This aspect of her – along with others – has in part disappeared. I think, therefore, that it is fitting that some of her speech to the judge be included.

> *The Court:* The prisoner will stand up. Has the prisoner anything to say why sentence shall not be pronounced?
>
> *Miss Anthony* Yes, your honor, I have many things to say: for in your ordered verdict of guilty, you have trampled underfoot every

vital principle of our government. My natural rights, my civil rights, my political rights are all alike ignored. Robbed of the fundamental privilege of citizenship, I am degraded from the status of a citizen to that of a subject; and not only myself individually, but all of my sex, are, by your honor's verdict, doomed to political subjection under this so-called Republican government.

Judge Hunt: The Court can not listen to a rehearsal of arguments the prisoner's counsel has already consumed three hours in presenting.

Miss Anthony: May it please your honor, I am not arguing the question, but simply stating the reasons why sentence can not, in justice, be pronounced against me. Your denial of my citizen's right to vote is the denial of my right to consent as one of the governed, the denial of my right of representation as one of the taxed, the denial of my right to a trial by a jury of my peers as an offender against law, therefore the denial of my sacred rights to life, liberty, property, and –

Judge Hunt: The Court can not allow the prisoner to go on.

Miss Anthony: But your honor will not deny me this one and only poor privilege of protest against this high-handed outrage upon my citizen's rights. . . .

Judge Hunt: The prisoner must sit down: the Court can not allow it.

Miss Anthony: All my prosecutors, from the 8th Ward Corner grocery politician who entered the complaint . . .

Judge Hunt: The Court must insist – the prisoner has been tried according to the established forms of law.

Miss Anthony: Yes, your honor, but by forms of law all made by men, interpreted by men, administered by men, in favor of men, and against women; and hence your honor's ordered verdict of guilty, against a United States citizen for the exercise of 'that citizen's right to vote,' simply because that citizen was a woman and not a man . . .

Judge Hunt: The Court orders the prisoner to sit down. It will not allow another word.

Miss Anthony: When I was brought before your honor for trial, I hoped for a broad and liberal interpretation of the Constitution . . .

Judge Hunt: The Court must insist – (Here the prisoner sat down.)

Judge Hunt: The prisoner will stand up. (Here Miss Anthony arose again.) The sentence of the Court is that you pay a fine of one hundred dollars and the costs of the prosecution.

Miss Anthony: May it please your honor, I shall never pay a dollar of your unjust penalty. All the stock in trade I possess is a $10,000 debt, incurred by publishing my paper – *The Revolution* – four years ago, the sole object of which was to educate all women to do precisely as I have done, rebel against your man-made, injust unconstitutional forms of law, that tax, fine, imprison, and hang women, while they deny them the right of

representation in the Government; and I shall work on with might and main to pay every dollar of that honest debt, but not a penny shall go to this unjust claim. And I shall earnestly and persistently continue to urge all women to the practical recognition of the old revolutionary maxim, that 'Resistance to tyranny is obedience to God.'
(Stanton et al, 1881: vol. I, pp. 687–9).

The significance of this encounter was not lost on Elizabeth Cady Stanton, who, although in later years was to be critical of Anthony's conservatism, was at the time gloriously impressed with the 'unruly defendant', In *Eighty Years and More* (1898a), Stanton not only expresses her delight in Anthony's defiance and diatribe, but makes sure that the judge comes in for his share of condemnation. Allocating him a 'representative' status, Stanton says: 'Was it not an historic scene which was enacted there in that little court house in Canandaigua? All the inconsistencies were embodied in that Judge, punctilious in manner, scrupulous in attire, conscientious in trivialities, and obtuse on great principles' (ibid., p. 179). But it was not just Stanton who perceived the limitations of male reasoning and the contradictions in male behaviour – Anthony saw them too, and exposed them.

But if Stanton became more radical as she got older – particularly on matters of religion and sexuality – it appears that Anthony became more conservative. Stanton herself expressed this evaluation and indicated that she became impatient with Anthony on occasion. When Stanton first advocated franchisement for women in 1848, it was a most radical demand, so radical that there was considerable hesitation about including it in the resolutions. But by the end of the century votes for women may have been an issue which still met fierce resistance, but it was no longer a radical demand – particularly when put by so many respectable, Christian women. Stanton moved on: she even asserted that the vote would change nothing and that there were other aspects of oppression that demanded consideration and action.[7] But to Anthony, the vote was paramount ' "Miss Anthony" said Mrs Stanton, "has one idea and she has no patience with anyone who has two ... I cannot work in the old ruts any longer. I have said all I have to say on the subject of suffrage" ' (quoted in Gurko, 1976, p. 282).

There is no doubt that once the issue of the vote became 'respectable', so too did Susan B. Anthony. Those who 'moved on' to other issues associated with women's oppression also tended to 'move out' of the records we have inherited of woman suffrage. This raises the question of why Anthony is to some extent honoured while some of her sisters have 'disappeared'.

---

[7] In this, her argument has many parallels to that put forward by Margaret Stacey and Marion Price (1981) in the attempt to explain why nothing changed when women got the vote.

4 The third person: Matilda Joslyn Gage

There was one other woman involved in the 'triumverate' – as it has been called – a woman who has as yet had little mention and whose story casts a very different light particularly on Susan B. Anthony but to a certain extent on Elizabeth Cady Stanton as well: she was Matilda Joslyn Gage (1826–98). (See Wagner 1980.) Anthony's biographer and co-editor, Ida Husted Harper, makes but passing reference to Gage in the Preface to Volume IV of the *History* (1902): 'Mrs Stanton was the matchless writer, Miss Anthony the collector of material, the researcher of statistics, the business manager, the keen critic,' says Harper, while Mrs Gage was the one 'they called to their aid for the historical facts' (p.v). But Harper then adds some information which aroused my curiosity enormously: she says that Gage was one of the most logical and fearless writers of her day and that the first two chapters and the last chapter of Volume I of *History of Woman Suffrage* were written by Gage. I was aware that the last chapter had been written by Gage (she is listed as the author in vol. I, and I also knew she had written a book of the same title) but I was surprised to find that the first two chapters were her work – I had been under the misapprehension that Elizabeth Cady Stanton was their primary author. I went back to the first two chapters of 'matchless writing' which I had erroneously attributed to Stanton, and found that I agreed with Harper: they were logical and fearless, as was the last. Indeed, I decided, those three chapters were probably among the most creative, profound and radical chapters in the whole volume – this was partly why I had assumed that Stanton, the matchless writer, the philosopher, the feminist radical and intellectual, was the author.

This discovery presented me with a problem: when the last chapter is so impressive, why had I not linked the first two with Gage? Why had I assumed they were the work of Stanton? Fundamentally, my problem was one of why I was predisposed to 'fit' such work into my image of Stanton, and to 'ignore' Gage. Why did I know so little about Gage and her work? I wondered if I had been so careless in my reading that I had missed important references to Gage and I was determined to find out more about this woman who had developed such an amazing and impressive critique of patriarchy. So I went to some of my 'quick sources', looking for her name and for some 'leads'; but the issue became more complex when I realised that I had not been so careless, that my 'ignorance' was in some ways understandable, for in most of the standard books on that period little or no reference is made to Matilda Joslyn Gage. It is as if – for the most part – she had not existed.

In four hundred pages, Eleanor Flexner (1979) makes only two references to Gage (and her name is misspelled in one): she notes that Matilda Joslyn Gage helped Anthony in the weeks before her trial and that: 'Matilda Joslyn Gage, who, although tied for many years to a home and small children in an upstate New York town, became one of the most scholarly' of all the women in the woman's rights movement (p. 90). As there is no further mention made of this 'scholarship', the puzzle deepens.

Matilda Joslyn Gage is not in Rossi's selection of *The Feminist Papers* (1974), nor is she among the list of women whom Rossi states she would have liked to include if consideration of space had permitted. Miriam Gurko (1976) has one reference to Gage – in relation to her support of Anthony (p. 252) and there is no entry under her name in Judith Sabrosky's *From Rationality to Liberation: The Evolution of Feminist Ideology* (1979) nor are their extracts from Gage in Miriam Schneir's *Feminism: The Essential Historical Writings* (1979). Leslie Tanner does include a speech from Gage in *Voices from Women's Liberation* (1971) (and I had missed it, or not taken cognisance of it – but then it is so short and not a particularly memorable speech) and Wendy Martin has included Gage in *The American Sisterhood* (1972), but again, the biographical details and the extract from her work ('Argument for Woman Suffrage, 1886'), far from suggesting the incisive, creative and revolutionary nature of Gage ('the logical and fearless writer', 'the most scholarly of them all'), help to place her in the context of one of the many hard-working, sincere and dedicated reformers of her time.

But Matilda Joslyn Gage *is* mentioned, and at some length, in Mary Daly's *Gyn/Ecology* (1978) and her presentation by Daly is in stark contrast to the other sources, for Daly glows with praise and admiration for this woman who wrote with such 'impressive erudition and passion', with 'boldness, accuracy and pride of her *own* tradition' (p. 217). And Daly is virtually stunned by the recognition that this woman, who made such an enormous contribution to women's knowledge, understandings, and heritage, should have almost completely disappeared, and in such a short space of time. For some of us, says Daly, it has been 'shocking to come upon the work of Gage, and to read this very perceptive and learned woman's study.[8] It is infuriating to discover that this foresister, and others like her, had already gathered and analyzed materials which feminist scholars are just beginning to unearth again' (ibid., p. 216). Mary Daly quotes from Jane Caputi (significantly in an unpublished paper), who says: 'It is infuriatingly ironic to confront the erasure of Gage . . . [who] devoted the overwhelming portion of her energies towards reclaiming our past.' Daly proceeds to ask the questions which I have been asking throughout this book: 'How could we – especially women historians, educated and legitimated by "degrees" – have been kept in such ignorance of our own tradition?' and, she asks, will our work 'be as effectively concealed from our "educated" sisters of the future as the work of our foresisters has been hidden from us?' (ibid., p. 217).

It is this question which has become part of the daily reality of my life, for not only is Matilda Joslyn Gage in her disappearance 'representative', as distinct from an isolated case, not only is much of her work concerned with proving that women have always made a contribution and men have consistently made them invisible, not only was she intent on subverting male-controlled history by leaving a record of women's trad-

---

[8] Daly is referring to *Woman, Church and State* (1893) but there are many other writings as well.

itions – but she was also part of the very recent movement: her name is there on three volumes of *History of Woman Suffrage* and yet she has been almost totally eclipsed by Stanton and Anthony, even within feminist (and non-feminist) studies of our immediate antecedents.

Mary Daly went in search of information about Gage. She consulted *Notable American Women* (James, James and Boyer, 1971) and found in the case of Gage what Berenice Carroll (1981) found in general – she had been minimised, her work had been obscured. 'Since Gage's perspective was gynocentric, the reality and meaning of her work is erased by historians', says Daly. In *Notable American Women,* much space and much praise is given to her father for directing her education, and the 'entry devotes a long paragraph to the details of Gage's marriage but allots exactly eight illuminating lines to its description of her major work. . . . We are informed that Gage "never equaled the achievement" of Elizabeth Cady Stanton and Susan B. Anthony' and, adds Daly, 'Literally speaking, this is true. Gage was a revolutionary thinker who did not "equal" but rather outdistanced these reformers in the originality and creativity of her thinking . . .' (ibid., p. 219).

In the dedication to *Women, Church and State,* Gage writes:

> This Book is Inscribed to the
> Memory of My Mother,
> who was at once mother, sister and friend.

She makes no mention of her father and suggests there was a deep bond between herself and her mother. In contrast, in *Notable American Women* (where her father attracts so much attention) her mother is described diminishingly by Warbasse (1971) as 'a lady of refined tastes, whose handsome furniture and carpets enabled the Joslyns to begin housekeeping in comfortable circumstances'!

Why has Warbasse presented Gage in this way? Persumably she undertook some research on Gage and was familiar with the nature and extent of her writing, but why has it been given such peripheral and diminishing consideration? It is possible that Warbasse was continuing within a tradition of the devaluation of Gage, but it must also be stated that Warbasse was helping to construct such a tradition. Few of the readers of the entry are going to have their imaginations fired by the description of Gage and her work; they are unlikely to find her so fascinating and attractive that they feel compelled to find out more about her. I could have read such an entry and still not made the links between the woman being described and the woman who wrote the three chapters of the *History* (among other things), which, to put it bluntly, make Stanton look less than really radical, and Anthony positively reactionary.

Perhaps Warbasse was taking her cue from the pattern that was first laid down in *History of Woman Suffrage* itself. Whereas Stanton has considerable space in *History of Woman Suffrage* to provide much information about the personal details of her life, there is no such entry from Gage. It is Stanton who provides the scanty biographical details that are included on Gage – mostly in a footnote. Again, it is Dr Joslyn who is praised extensively for his worthiness, 'a man of learning and philanthropic tendencies', Mrs Joslyn is also included, but in a manner not calculated to inspire admiration. Gage, says Stanton, 'in a certain way' was no 'less indebted to her mother, a Scotch lady, belonging to the noble, old, and influential family of Leslie, a woman of refined and elevated tastes, universally respected and beloved. From this side Mrs Gage inherited her antiquarian tastes and habits of delving into old histories, from which she has unearthed so many facts bearing upon woman's degradation' (Stanton et al., 1881, vol. I, p. 466).

With the benefit of hindsight it is now possible to look back over the records in relation to Gage, to observe her 'erasure' and to see that some of the seeds for it were planted in those very volumes which bear her name as editor. In a very subtle way, Elizabeth Cady Stanton helps in the process of consigning Gage to oblivion. Stanton tells us about Gage's parentage, her unusual education for the time (to which she attributed her 'non-acceptance of masculine authority'), her predilection for libraries and old books, her natural reticence and yet her courage in overcoming it when the occasion demanded, *and her 'domestic responsibilities'*. Stanton says of Gage that she 'always had a knack of rummaging through old libraries, bringing more startling facts to light than any woman I knew' (ibid.) and that: 'Although Mrs Gage was surrounded with a family of small children for years, yet she was always a student, an omnivorous reader and liberal thinker, and her pen was ever at work answering the attacks on the woman movement in the county and State journals' (ibid.). But there is little else.

She suffered the normal trials and tribulations of women who were engaged in the struggle: 'In Manlius, where she lived some time after her marriage,' says Stanton, 'she was the sole representative of this unpopular reform. When walking the street she would often hear some boy, shielded by a dry-goods box or a fence, cry out "woman's rights" ' (ibid., p. 465) and there were social occasions at which there were burlesques 'on "strong-minded" women' and where there was much ridiculing of 'careers and conventions, and the many claims being made for larger freedoms' (ibid., p. 466). On such occasions, 'Every eye was fixed on her, as evidently the type of womanhood' being satirised and mocked, and while embarrassed, she usually gave a good and gracious account of herself and 'turned the laugh' on the author of such comment (ibid.).

This does not help to suggest Gage's intellectual stature and commitment: 'rummaging through old libraries' suggests an eccentric; defending oneself and deflecting jibes suggests a dilettante. Stanton does not in any substantial way refer at all to the analysis and understanding that Gage brought to the whole feminist framework of the movement. There are no eulogies of Gage as there are of Anthony, no descriptions of life and work together, no accounts of shared personal experience, no reference to the political vision which she and Gage shared (and which Anthony did not, for example in relation to their analysis of the role played by organised religion), no comment on their intellectual debate or their common isolation as the radical philosophers in a movement becoming increasingly conservative and concerned more exclusively with the vote. Even in *Eighty Years and More* (1898a), it is Gage's absence as a presence in Stanton's life which becomes strikingly obvious when one remembers how much time these two women spent together and how close their intellectual positions were.

There is one reference to Gage in *Eighty Years and More* which is perhaps significant. Stanton reports that there was an occasion when Gage accused her of taking one of Gage's statements without acknowledgement; she says that Gage felt unfairly treated. But it emerges that Stanton is being somewhat sarcastic, because the matter at issue is a sentence in an autograph book. One always hastily responds to demands from autograph seekers at the end of a lecture, says Stanton, and: 'In this way I unfortunately used a pet sentiment of Matilda's. So here and now I say to my autograph admirers from New York to San Francisco, whenever you see, "There is a word sweeter than Mother, Home or Heaven – that word is Liberty," remember that it belongs to Matilda Joslyn Gage' (ibid., pp. 328–9) and Stanton goes on to add that she hopes Gage will now be satisfied with this declaration and no longer feel unfairly treated.

The whole incident reported in this way helps to suggest that Gage is petty and unreasonable, while Stanton is tolerant and generous towards her. This is hardly a comprehensive – or accurate – portrayal of the relationship between Gage and Stanton. There is a sense of unease in the recognition that Stanton is leaving a lot out – and what she is putting in does not portray Gage in a flattering light. I have the distinct impression that I have observed this process at work before – but that it has been men who have employed it.

Stanton (or one assumes that Stanton is the writer) does refer to Gage's entry to the woman's rights movement at the Syracuse National Convention in 1852, and at the young age of 26. This was where Gage made her first 'public appearance' and, says Stanton, 'She pressed the adoption of some settled plan for the future – brought up many noted examples of woman's intellectual ability, and urged that girls be trained in self reliance. Although Mrs Gage ... had not before taken part in a Convention, yet from the moment she read of an organized effort for the rights of woman, she had united in it heart and soul, merely waiting for a convenient opportunity to publicly identify herself with this reform.' She adds that, as she was unacquainted with any of the leaders, 'it was quite a test of moral courage' for this young woman to come forward and speak. 'She consulted no-one as to time or opportunity, but when her courage had reached a sufficiently high point, with palpitating heart she ascended the platform ...' (Stanton et al., 1881, vol. I, p. 582). And what a speech: nothing quite like it had been heard before, and Lucretia Mott immediately insisted that it be printed and circulated as part of the movement literature.[9]

Her speech was an outline of women's past achievements – despite the obstacles that had been placed in their path – and, by presenting the information that she did, Gage not only indicated the enormous amount of archivist activity she must have already undertaken, but she changed many

---

[9] Part of it is reprinted as the extract in Tanner, 1971.

of the assumptions about history and about women. Until Gage's entry the discussion had been very much in terms of what women *might* do, once they were given the opportunity. Gage showed what they had done – without opportunity – and she challenged, fundamentally, the belief (held by Stanton as well) that history was a process of gradual improvement, an evolution towards a higher and more civilised goal, and that the time had now arisen for women to take their steps and to become full members of the civilised community. Suggesting that there had been women in the past who enjoyed more freedom and who had played a greater role in the running of society represented a startlingly new frame of reference for many, if not all of the women then involved in the woman's rights movement. Some excerpts from that first speech from a nervous, 26-year-old woman help to illustrate the extent of her erudition and the radical nature of her argument:

'Although so much has been said of woman's unfitness for public life, it can be seen from Semiramis to Victoria, that she has a peculiar fitness for governing. In poetry, Sappho was honored with the title of the Tenth Muse. Helena Lucretia Corano, in the seventeenth century, was of such rare scientific attainments, that the most illustrious persons in passing through Venice, were more anxious to see her than all the curiosities of the city; she was made a doctor, receiving the title of Unalterable. Mary Cunity, of Silesia, in the sixteenth century, was one of the most able astronomers of her time, forming astronomical tables that acquired for her a great reputation. Anna Maria Schureman was a sculptor, engraver, musician and painter; she especially excelled in miniature painting. Constantina Grierson, an Irish girl, of humble parentage, was celebrated for her literary acquirements, though dying at the early age of twenty-seven.

'With the learning, energy, and perseverance of Lady Jane Grey, Mary and Elizabeth, all are familiar. Mrs Cowper was spoken of by Montague as standing at the head of all that is called learned, and that every critic veiled his bonnet at her superior judgement. Joanna Baillie has been termed the woman Shakespeare. Caroline Herschell shares the fame of her brother as an astronomer. The greatest triumphs of the present age in the drama, music and literature, have been achieved by women, among whom may be mentioned Charlotte Cushman, Jenny Lind, the Misses Carey, Mrs Stowe and Margaret Fuller. Mrs Somerville's renown has long been spread over both continents as one of the first mathematicians of the present age' (ibid., p. 529).

To women who believed that the barriers against them in a male-dominated society had to be broken *before* women could begin to participate in the organisation and cultural activities of society – and there still are such women who accept that women are 'under-achieving' and that this will pass once the last discriminatory barriers are removed – Gage's documentation came as a revelation. Not only did it demand a reassessment of history as a form of systematic progress, it also raised the question of *why didn't they know* about these women and their impressive achievements? Her speech served as a source of strength, of pride, of confidence;

it repudiated the 'inferiority' of woman, and introduced the issue of how women came to know and believe what they did – who had told them?

In one instance in the *History* there is a summary of another speech that Gage gave and it can be used to illustrate the tenor of her arguments on numerous public occasions: 'Matilda Joslyn Gage spoke at length of the brilliant record of women in the past in every branch of human activity – in art, science, literature, invention; of their heroism and patriotism in time of war, and their industry and endurance in many equally trying emergencies in time of peace. Woman has so fully proved her equality with man in every position she has filled, *that it is too late now for clergymen on our platform to remand us to the subjection of woman of Corinth centuries ago. We have learned too well the lessons of liberty* . . . to accept now the position of slaves' (ibid., p. 384, my emphasis).

Gage was certainly getting her message across. With her 'non-acceptance of masculine authority', her insistence that what men believed and said about women was not true, and her evidence that the records men constructed were false, Gage chipped away at the foundations of patriarchy (her term was 'patriarchate'), revealing male authority as a myth invented by males.

Apart from her speeches, however, there are also the first two chapters of Volume I of the *History,* and the last chapter, and her book, *Woman, Church and State* (1893). In 'Preceding Causes' (Chapter 1, of the *History*), Gage presents part of her analysis of woman's subordination, and makes connections between women, work, and profits, which today are 'resurfacing'. 'Woman has been the great unpaid laborer of the world' (ibid., p. 28), she states and sets the scene for Charlotte Perkins Gilman (1899). 'Although woman has performed much of the labor of the world, her industry and her economy have been the very means of increasing her degradation' (ibid., p. 27) asserts Gage, and goes on to explain with clarity and precision that, because men *own* women's labour, the harder women work, the richer men get. This, says Gage, means that the financial distance between women and men increases as women work harder and display more initiative, for the women do not reap the products of their toil – the products go to men! This is the touchstone in Gage's analysis, that 'woman has always been robbed of the fruits of her own toil' (ibid., p. 28), and that the more she toils, the more men profit and in contrast, the more 'degraded' does woman appear.

And there is no doubt in Gage's mind, how this has been allowed to happen, how such a monstrous practice has been made 'acceptable' and seen within society as a reasonable and justifiable arrangement. The Church, says Gage, has provided the 'logic' and rationale for this gross inequality. Under male control, the church has declared woman to be inferior and men have then been free to steal woman's creative and physical energy. When women's resources have been taken away, then the Church stands vindicated for it is demonstrable that women are without resources and are therefore inferior! To Gage it was patently obvious that men – under the guise of religious legitimation – were constructing sexual inequality, were taking away women's resources and then blaming women because they had no resources.

Gage's documentation of women's past achievements was not just an interesting 'extra', but a fundamental part of her analysis; it was her 'proof' of male theft of female labour. Integral to her thesis was that men had not just deprived women of the fruits of their toil in the physical sense (in domestic terms, and in the pitifully low remuneration women received when they did engage in paid labour) but that men were stealing women's creative, spiritual and intellectual energy as well. This was why these women had disappeared – this was why women's creative and cultural contribution was not transmitted from one generation to the next – *it did not belong to women, it was not theirs to pass on!* It was taken over by men and used to further their own interests (which may have meant anything from suppressing it to passing off the ideas, contributions, as their own).

From Ancient Egypt to England in the seventh and ninth centuries, from Italy to America, Gage exposed the intellectual labours of women that had been stolen by men. Partly because it provides a salutary lesson and partly because it is a primary purpose of this book to outline what women have done, I have made an 'inventory' of some of the women to whom Gage refers in Chapter 1 (and who are not mentioned elsewhere) where she challenges the way men have described and explained the world in a manner which has helped them to accumulate resources – at the expense of women.

In the fourteenth century, begins Gage, there was a 'Christine of Pisa, the most eminent woman of the period' who 'supported a family of six persons by her pen,' and there was also Margaret of Angouleme, the brilliant Queen of Navarre who 'was a voluminous writer, her Heptameron rising to the dignity of a French classic' (ibid., p. 29). And in the sixteenth century, in Italy, which was 'then the foremost literary country of Europe,' there were 'many women of learning, one of whom, Lucrezia Morinella, a Venetian lady, wrote a work entitled "The Nobleness and Excellence of Women, together with the Faults and Imperfections of Men" ' (ibid.).

And in England, where the 'reign of Queen Anne [was] called the Golden Age of English Literature', says Gage, 'there were the remarkable Mary Astell and Elizabeth Elstob. The latter, speaking nine languages was most famous for her skill in the Saxon tongue', and she goes on to recount the story of Astell's plan for a Woman's College, Queen Anne's support and approval, and Bishop Burnett's objections and obstructions. She returns to the England of the ninth century – before the Conquest and to the Synod of Whitby, which 'was held in the convent of the Abbess Hilda, she herself presiding over its deliberations,' and to the seventh century when women took part in and signed the decrees of the great National Council at Baghamstead (ibid., p. 30).

Gage insists that the past has not witnessed a process of gradual development, up to the present day, and begins to suggest – in terms that become much stronger in *Woman, Church and State* – that women have possessed powers in the past, which were taken away from them, particularly with the introduction of christianity. 'In the reign of Henry III', she writes, 'four women took seats in Parliament, and in the reign of Edward I ten ladies were called to Parliament, while in the thirteenth century Queen Elinor became keeper of the Great Seal, sitting as Lord Chancellor in the *Aula Regia,* the highest court in the kingdom.' Going back even further, argues Gage, women are to be found in all manner of public offices, and acquitting themselves with merit: 'Running back two or three centuries before the Christian era, we find Martia, her seat of power in London, holding the reigns of government so wisely as to receive the surname of Proba, the Just. She especially devoted herself to the enactment of just laws for her subjects, the first principles of common law tracing back to her,' and, adds Gage significantly, 'the celebrated laws of Alfred, and of Edward the Confessor, being in great degree restorations and compilations from the laws of Martia, which were known as the "Martian Statutes" ' (ibid., pp. 30–1). The fruits of Martia's labour were also stolen: stolen by men who then presented the work as a product of their own effort and which therefore commanded respect and substantiated their claim for supremacy.

Gage then turns to America, to some of the women who displayed 'deep political insight' – Mercy Otis Warren, Abigail Smith Adams, Hannah Lee Corbin (ibid., p. 31), but where is their contribution acknowledged? And during that dramatic period of American history there was 'at least one woman who watched the struggle of America with lively interest, and whose writings aided in the dissemination of republican ideas. This was the celebrated Catherine Sawbridge Macaulay, one of the greatest minds England has ever produced' (ibid., p. 32). And has she been given due recognition?

She draws on Mary Wollstonecraft, Margaret Fuller, Jane Marcet and Harriet Martineau, revealing the extent of their creative and intellectual energy, and says that, while 'Eliza Lynn, an Irish lady, was . . . writing leading editorials for political papers,' let us remember that Catherine II, in Russia was expressing views of which 'the revolutionists of France and America fondly thought themselves the originators' (ibid., p. 35). Is this the light that Catherine II of Russia is customarily seen in? If women today are denied a political voice, argues Gage, women of the past died for possessing theirs: 'the eighteenth century was famous for the executions of women on account of their radical political opinions,' – Madame Roland and Charlotte Corday – 'while Sophia Lapierre barely escaped the same fate' (ibid.).

And what about pre-Christian times, asks Gage, what did women do then that they are not permitted to do today, what have women produced in the past but which is now owned by men? 'In Ancient Egypt', she says, 'the medical profession was in the hands 'of women, to which we may attribute that country's almost entire exemption from infantile diseases, a fact which recent discoveries fully authenticate. The enormous death rate of young children in modern civilized societies may be traced to woman's general enforced ignorance of the laws of life, and to the fact that the profession of medicine has been too exclusively in the hands of men. . . . Looking back scarcely a hundred years, we find science indebted to woman for some of its most brilliant discoveries.' In 1736 the first medical botany was given to the world by Elizabeth Blackwell, 'a woman physician' and there was 'Lady Montague's discovery of a check to small pox, Madame Boivin's discovery of the hidden cause of certain hemorrhages, Madame de Coudray's invention of the manikin' and these 'are among the notable steps which opened the way to the modern Elizabeth Blackwell . . .' and many others as well, and which are 'examples of woman's skill in healing arts' (ibid., p. 37).

There are names, names and more names of women who have worked long and hard and with considerable success, whose names may be meaningless to us today but whose efforts – where they have been considered desirable – have been taken over and passed off as the achievement of men. The work of women has 'vanished' and, without the expenditure of comparable effort, the achievements of men have been multiplied by this process. The men get richer, the women get poorer, no matter how hard women work, how creative they are, how profound their insights, no matter how much they contribute.

But we are beginning to understand how this is done, says Gage, and we have the resources – intellectually – to stop it. The chapter concludes with the following statement: 'The works of Georges Sand, Frederika Bremer, Charlotte Brontë, George Eliot, Catharine Sedgwick, and Harriet Beecher Stowe, in literature: Mrs Hemans, Mrs Sigourney, Elizabeth Barrett Browning, in poetry; Angelika Kauffman, Rosa Bonheur, Harriet Hosmer, in art; Mary Somerville, Caroline Herschell, Maria Mitchell, in science; Elizabeth Fry, Dorothea Dix, Mary Carpenter, in prison reform; Florence Nightingale and Clara Barton in the camp – are all part of the great uprising of women out of the lethargy of the past, and are among the forces of the complete revolution a thousand pens and voices herald at this hour' (ibid., p. 42).

It is one of the greatest tragic ironies that this woman who understood so much about the process, who put such energy into exposing and subverting it, should herself be the one to 'disappear', should have her work wiped away. Could it be that she was the most dangerous?

'Preceding Causes', the first chapter of *History of Woman Suffrage*, serves as an introduction to the issue of the oppression of women, but it also serves as an introduction to Gage's work. The basic principles of her analysis are present in 'Preceding Causes', but in *Woman, Church and State* – the chapter and the book of the same title – these principles are developed and explained in a way which demonstrates her astonishing breadth and clarity of understanding, as well as her daring. I am going to refer to the book, *Woman, Church and State* (1893) and not just because it is a more extensive analysis, but because the reprint (1980) contains both a 'Foreword' by Mary Daly and an 'Introduction' by Sally Roesch Wagner, and both help to provide some of the 'missing pieces' in the perplexing problem of the disappearance of Matilda Joslyn Gage.

In the first two paragraphs of the 'Foreword', Daly puts Gage into context. She is 'a major radical feminist theoretician and historian whose written work is indispensable for an understanding of the women's movement today,' says Daly, her work has transcended the barriers of time, being as relevant and significant now, as it was when first written. 'She made the connections which others feared to make. She prophesied, and she named the enemy', says Daly, and, 'Consequently, of course, her stature has never been acknowledged' (p. vii).

Daly tries to give some idea of her reaction to finding Matilda Joslyn Gage: 'The effect upon me', she says, 'was one of cumulative admiration, grief, rage and hope,' and she goes on to analyse and explain this range of responses: admiration for this extraordinary work, this 'tough creative vision'; grief at the horrors and the violence Gage describes as characteristic of and fundamental to patriarchy; rage that such work should be erased, and hope – a hope shared with Gage – that having unmasked patriarchy to some extent, there is the possibility of changing it. Obviously, this work which has left Daly so impressed (and demanded that I revise so many of my assumptions at this late stage of my research), requires some discussion and explanation.

In *Woman, Church and State,* Gage posits the existence of an ancient matriarchy ('matriarchate') and is the first feminist I know to do so. She provides the evidence based on meticulous and extensive research which indicates that women in past civilisations have possessed positive power and that they have been progressively and systematically deprived of that power, with the most accelerated assault being associated with the period in which christianity became a force. With clarity and precision, Gage asserts not just that christianity has been responsible for reducing women to subordination, but that christianity is only meaningful when women are oppressed. Take away women's subordination to man, she argues, and the whole fabric of the Christian religion collapses, or, to put it another way, christianity has been the means of justifying and legitimating the process whereby one half of humanity has plundered, ravaged, enslaved, the other half. Christianity, she argues, has not *led* to man's treatment of woman, but has *grown out of it,* reinforced it, extended it. It is a rationale produced by men in the attempt to explain and make acceptable their violent and barbarous treatment of women; if they did not treat women in this way they would have had no need of Christian ideology.

Step by step Gage shows how the ideology was constructed, how the more developed it became the more women were deprived of power – and full humanity – and the more leeway that was permitted for men to perpetrate atrocities against women. The male-controlled Church started this legitimating process and the male-controlled State – following the Church's example and sanctioned by the Church – perpetuated it. It is not a system of the past, Gage insists, but a system which continues to prevail, which is the basis of all those countries, such as America and Britain, which call themselves Christian civilisations.

If we are content to believe, argues Gage, that the Church was misogynist but that its influence has now waned, that things are 'better', that the outrages committed against women in its name are but features of the past, explained by reference to ignorance and superstition – then we are dangerously misled. The principles that informed the Church now inform the State; there has been a transfer of power from one patriarchal agency to another, but the fundamental premise that women are inferior, and that this calls for punishment – a premise given more substance during the ascendancy of the Church – has now been transferred, and is embedded with social sanction, in the principles of the State. For society in a 'Christian civilisation' takes much of its 'meaning' from the system and symbols constructed by the Christian religion. The practices, the fashions, the outward manifestations may have changed, argues Gage, but *not* the innermost belief.

In putting forward this thesis that the Church and the State are manifestations of patriarchy (with the Church providing the rationale for the functions of the State), Gage is bringing together those many strands which in a patriarchal frame of reference are usually perceived as unrelated. Taking woman as the central starting point and assessing historical practices in relation to her, and through her eyes, Gage is immediately able to make links between the sexual double standard, the appropriation of women's bodies, the enslavement of women, the practice of witch-hunting. Historical periods, practices, values, which when viewed by men have often seemed bizarre, inexplicable, unaccountable outbursts with no identifiable causes, become within Gage's framework the pattern of patriarchy, the systematised oppression of women.

Theft is a fundamental concept in Gage's work: women had power, and full humanity, says Gage (and provides example after example), and men seized it. Even in the early days of the Christian religion the Church was open to both sexes, but from the fourth to the ninth centuries groups of men progressively deprived women of these rights – they took away ordination, then deaconship, then forbade women to serve at the altar, and they robbed abbesses of all priestly functions. Their justification was that it was women who had brought sin into the world; this was the source of their inferiority and the reason they had to be punished.

But where does this idea of original sin come from, asks Gage, for in the early stages of the Christian religion the doctrine of original sin was denied. She traces its introduction to Augustine and shows how convenient it was for him to produce such a theory, and how quickly it was taken up by the fathers of the Church who found it a most attractive, self-enhancing, and profitable idea to promulgate. The belief 'snowballed' according to Gage. Once the 'contaminating' nature of woman was established, then it was but a small step to advocate that men who had no contact with women were 'purer', thus the clergy became celibate. Women, as the carriers of original sin, were a source of impurity and contamination; they were to be avoided, excluded, outlawed. Their sex became a crime, it was a disqualification for humanity. As the purer sex, closer to god, and exonerated from the burden of bringing sin into the world, it was the responsibility of man to make woman accountable to him; man defined himself in the same relationship to woman as god was to man.

This was what the male-controlled Church preached, asserts Gage, and *both* sexes accepted the division of humanity into two unequal parts. Therefore when the Church gave way to the State, the State simply persisted with what had become socially accepted beliefs. That was why, explains

Gage, it was relatively easy to introduce the system of 'Marchetta' or 'Marquette' – a form of female enslavement. Producing record after record, Gage shows how the Feudal lords established the 'right' to newly married wives for three days after the wedding, and how the eldest-born son was therefore considered the property of the lord. It was Christian countries – France, Germany, Prussia, England, Scotland – where this was practised, Gage says, because the Church provided the rationale which permitted such behaviour to be seen as logical and acceptable.

But even these details, and Gage's analysis and assessment of them, tend to pale into insignificance alongside her chapter on witchcraft – again, a belief system fostered by the Church but taken over by the State. People were put to death for their beliefs and for the fear they aroused long before the rise of christianity, argues Gage. But 'pagans unlike Christians, did not look upon women as more given to this practice than men; witches and wizards were alike stoned to death. But as soon as a system of religion was adopted which taught the greater sinfulness of women, over whom authority had been given to man by God himself, the saying arose "one wizard to 10,000 witches" and the persecution for witchcraft became chiefly directed against women' (ibid., p. 97). Teaching the extreme wickedness of women, to women and men alike, teaching that it was the duty of men to control wicked women, the Church laid the foundation for men to believe it was their right to persecute women – and for women to believe they had no rights, and no alternatives but to submit and endure. Suffering, self-sacrifice, penance, were expected of women and exacted by men, and rather than being a period of aberration, the witch-hunts, in this context, become a logical extension of existing beliefs.

Having established the logical base of witch-hunting under christianity, Gage proceeds to map the extent of the practice and the methods that were employed. Nineteenth-century woman she may have been, but 'Victorian' she was not, and she does not flinch from describing the horrors of this time. 'During the reign of Francis I more than 100,000 witches were put to death, mostly by burning, in France alone. . . . The Parliament of Toulouse burned 400 witches at one time. Four hundred women at one hour, dying the horrid death of fire for a crime which never existed save in the imagination of those persecutors and which grew in their imagination from a false belief in woman's extraordinary wickedness, based upon a false theory as to original sin' (ibid., p. 98).

They were usually burned, says Gage, because it was cheaper than boiling in oil, and she quotes the accounts from official records for expenditure on items of torture and death. No wonder Daly has described her as tough and daring. Gage addresses the fundamental questions of who these witches were, and why it became necessary to persecute them. She grimly states: 'When for "witches" we read "women," we gain fuller comprehension of the cruelties inflicted by the church upon this portion of humanity' (ibid., p. 127). There is no equivalent 'crime' for men, argues Gage: 'What was termed magic among men, was called witchcraft in woman. The one was rarely, the other invariably, punished' (ibid., p. 108). It was the sex that was the crime.

While evidence of witchcraft assumed many forms (attractive, wealthy, or old and infirm women all being likely suspects), it was *knowledgeable* women that the fathers of Church and State feared most and did their utmost to eliminate, argues Gage. The term witch used to mean simply a woman of superior knowledge, she says. It signified a wise and learned woman, and it was this idea of women possessing some knowledge and some power that men found so frightening. It was *outside* the *control* of men, it detracted from rather than contributed to male resources and for this reason it had to be seized from women and made the property of men.

Women had developed the art of healing; they knew much about herbs and remedies and cures. This gave them an area where they could *act*, where their work could be 'owned' by them and could be seen to influence the environment. For patriarchy, this was a danger. 'The church having forbidden its offices and all external methods of knowledge to woman, was profoundly stirred with indignation at her having through her own wisdom, penetrated into some of the most deeply subtle secrets of nature,' says Gage (ibid., p. 100), and it is no coincidence that 'at the time that witchcraft became the great ogre against which the church expended all its terrific powers, women doctors employed anaesthetics to mitigate the pains and perils of motherhood' (ibid., p. 104).

Not only were women able to own some knowledge, not possessed by men, not only were they able to act in a way in which their existence was unaccountable to men, but they were using their power to alleviate some of the pain which the Church insisted women must suffer as a form of penance. To the Church, this knowledge of women, and the uses to which it was being put, was intolerable subversion of the patriarchal world. Patriarchy is based on the appropriation of women's bodies and energy by men. Women have no independence, no autonomy, no way of acting in the world that does not produce wealth for men. Therefore women's energy can never be validated as an independent entity: the products of her labour must be invisible. Otherwise the whole system is challenged – for if women start to accumulate wealth and resources of their own how are they then to be controlled by men?

In *Gyn/Ecology* (1978), Mary Daly comments on this aspect of Gage's analysis. Gage named the problem accurately, says Daly, she recognised that 'the church feared and hated women's knowledge and power. She correctly named women *the* healers, who were therefore hated by the church and its sons' (1978, p. 217). The Church, adds Daly, 'had to erase women with the power to heal, not only by killing them, but by denying they healed *of their own power*' (ibid., p. 218). If women were seen to be a source of knowledge, power, and healing, then the only way to sustain the belief that women had no resources of their own was to insist that this power *originated in another source* – it must have come from the devil. If woman was not serving god/man – the two being conflated under christ-ianity – she must be serving the enemy, for she could not exist of her own, serving herself or her own needs; patriarchy has no such autonomous category for woman.

There were during the time of the witch-hunts other resources which

some women may have had and which could also arouse fear and indignation. Attractive women could be viewed with suspicion, as they could
perhaps ensnare men, assume power over men; and wealthy women who
may have had some means of independence were also targets. 'Uncommon
beauty was as dangerous to a woman as the possession of great wealth,'
says Gage, for it 'brought frequent accusations in order that the church
might seize upon the witch's property for its own use' (1893, p. 100). And
the woman did not have to be *independently* wealthy – it could be the
wealth of her father, husband, son: 'Trials for witchcraft filled the coffers
of the church, as whenever conviction took place' (and 'accusation and
conviction became convertible terms' ibid., p. 110) 'the property of the
witch and her family was confiscated to that body. The clergy fattened
upon the torture and burning of women' (ibid., p. 107).

It was not only the women who were *feared*, but also those who were
despised, who became ready victims: the old, the infirm, the mentally
disturbed. Gage explains this in terms of women only being tolerated while
they can function as sex-objects. 'We discover a reason for this intense
hatred of old women in the fact that woman has chiefly been looked upon
from a sensual view by christian men, the church teaching that she was
created solely for man's sensual use. Thus when by reason of declining
years she no longer attracted the sensual adulation of man, he regarded her
as having forfeited all right to life' (ibid., p. 117).

As I go over these words of Gage, again and again I have to try to
make sense of all the contradictions: Written in Victorian times? Encompassing some of the most radical insights of contemporary times? All that
scholarship? Why didn't I know? Why didn't Stanton even hint at it? The
extent to which I find her analysis challenging my assumptions? How do
I account for all this?

Her indictment of the clergy, and of men, is remarkable: 'The three
most distinguishing features of the history of witchcraft were its use for the
enrichment of the church; for the advancement of political schemes; for
the gratification of private malice' (ibid., p. 109). It created a whole industry
which provided jobs for men: the clerics who interpreted the scriptures, the
learned judges, the accusers, torturers, witch-prickers. At the same time as
the persecutions for witchcraft increased, the dogma of the celibacy of the
clergy was confirmed. And women were excluded from the emerging,
male-controlled, medical science. But it also gave husbands an option:
'Husbands who had ceased to care for their wives or by reason of their
sickness or for any cause found them a burden . . . now found an easy
method' of ending their marriages (ibid., p. 127): they accused their wives
of witchcraft. And fear was instilled in women: violence against women,
by men, from which there is no protection, no immunity. Women were
forced into their place that men have decreed, robbed of all their material
and psychological resources – enslaved to meet the needs of men.

In the last chapter of *Woman, Church and State*, Gage brings all these
strands together, under the title 'Past, Present and Future'; it is incredible.
'The most stupendous system of organized robbery known has been that
of the church towards woman,' says Gage, 'a robbery that has not only

taken her self-respect but all rights of person; the fruits of her own industry; her opportunities of education; the exercise of her own judgement, her conscience, her own will' (ibid., p. 238). 'The whole theory, regarding woman, under Christianity, has been based upon the conception that she has no right to live for herself alone. Her duty to others has continuously been placed before her and her training has ever been that of self-sacrifice. Taught from the pulpit and legislative halls that her position must always be secondary even to her children, her right to life has been admitted only insofar as its reacting effect upon another could be predicated' (ibid., p. 239).

This denial of women, argues Gage, is at the very core of social beliefs and organisation in Christian civilisations; it is the means by which the objects and events of the world are classified and invested with meaning. It is man who has generated this framework, which is a product of his own limited and biased experience, for: 'He is yet under the darkness of the Patriarchate, failing to recognize woman as a component part of humanity, whose power of development and influence upon civilization are at least the equal of his own' (ibid., p. 238).

The reason he cannot recognise the humanity of woman is because his own definition of the fully human is himself, and he therefore cannot make sense of woman's differences except by labelling them as signs of disqual- ification or deviancy: 'Of all circumstances biasing the judgement and restricting the sympathies, none have shown themselves more powerful than physical differences, whether of race, color or sex,' she states. 'When those differences are not alone believed to be a mark of inferiority, but to have been especially created for the pleasure and peculiar service of another, the elements of irresponsible tyranny on one side, and irremediable slavery upon the other, are already organized' (ibid., p. 240).

But the origin of this belief — that woman has been made for the pleasure and peculiar service of man — rests entirely with man, asserts Gage, justified on the grounds of religion and based on the theft of woman's physical and intellectual resources. Gage is one of the few women who categorically asserts that women have had their intellectual and creative energy stolen by men, and that it is the theft of their intellectual energy, as well as their physical energy, that is crucial in woman's oppression. 'Man has assumed the right to think for woman', she states (ibid., p. 239), he has 'robbed her of responsibility' and put himself in place of god: through the decisions of the patriarchal Church he 'has denied her independent thought, declaring her a secondary creation for man's use' (ibid., p. 241) and has insisted that it is to him alone that she is responsible.

This theft and denial cannot continue, asserts Gage: 'Woman herself must judge of woman' (ibid., p. 238). She is learning; she is beginning to challenge and to change. 'Woman is learning for herself that not self sacrifice but self development is her first duty in life: and this, not primarily for the sake of others but that she may become fully herself' (ibid., p. 239). It is women's intellectual resources which are needed she argues, it is women's perception and explanation of women, men and the world, which must be allowed to function, free from the control of men. Women must

use their intellectual resources in the interest of women, for the obtuseness
and emotionality of men are propelling the society towards destruction.

It is a pseudo-argument, she asserts, that women are emotional: 'To
one who has been present at four great presidential nominating conventions
and several large state conventions, knowledge upon this point is practical',
she says, departing from her usual historical sources. 'When one has seen
a cordon of police enforced by the mayor upon the platform, protecting
the officers of such a convention, while its members, standing upon seats,
stamped, shouted, gesticulated, threatened with revolvers, acting more like
uncaged wild beasts than like men, when one has witnessed the wildest
enthusiasm at the mention of a name, the waving of flags, of hats, of
handkerchiefs, the shaking of umbrellas, chairs, canes, with violent stamping, amid a hubbub of indistinguishable voices, all shouting . . . such
objections to woman's freedom as to her "emotions" fall to their lowest
value' (ibid., pp. 242–3), says Gage, and serve to indicate just how much
power men have to interpret their behaviour in their own favour. For,
when women own their own ideas, it appears as quite the reverse: 'In
Church and in State, man has exhibited the wildest passions, the most
ungovernable frenzy,' and has shown himself (from football matches to
war, from witch-hunting to rape) 'to be incapable of control by reason'
(ibid., p. 243).

She acknowledges that some people may find this difficult to believe
– it goes against everything society teaches, it is 'outside' the meanings and
assumptions of patriarchy: 'The superstitions of the church, the miseries of
woman, her woes, tortures, burnings, rackings and all the brutalities she
has endured in the church, the state, the family, under the sanction of
christianity would be incredible had we not the most undeniable evidence
of their existence, not alone in the past, but as shown by the teachings,
laws, customs of the present time' (ibid., p. 241), argues Gage. 'The careful
student of history will discover that Christianity has been of little value in
advancing civilization, but has done a great deal toward retarding it' (ibid.,
p. 243).

Despite what we may have been taught, argues Gage, the Church has
never been the leader in great reforms, has never advanced justice, equality,
or humanitarian concerns: 'the world has not grown wise' under christianity (ibid., p. 244). On the contrary, the patriarchal Church has been a
primary source of evil: 'Slavery and prostitution, persecutions for heresy,
the inquisition with its six hundred modes of torture, the destruction of
learning, the oppression of science, the systematized betrayal of confiding
innocence, the recognized and unrecognized polygamy of man, the denial
to woman of a right to herself, her thought, her wages, her children, to a
share in the government which rules her; . . . all these and a myriad more,
are parts of what is known as christian civilization' (ibid.).

Gage names men and their Church as the enemy, as a form of legalised
crime against women, and she is completely convinced that there can be no
'reform', there can only be overthrow and elimination. In words which
assume special significance for me today as I search for strategies, Gage

says: 'Woman will gain nothing by a compromising attitude,' by attempting to excuse the great wrong or by adopting leniency. 'On the contrary,' she says, 'a stern reference to the facts' keeping the world turned towards the crimes of patriarchy is the *duty of woman!* 'Wrongs of omission equal in magnitude those of commission' (ibid.). 'The woman who possesses love for her sex, for the world, for truth, justice and right will not hesitate to place herself upon record as opposed to falsehood, no matter under what guise of age or holiness it appears' (ibid., p. 245). This was what Gage herself did; she asks no more from others.

But she predicts that there will be conflict – 'looking forward, I see evidence of a conflict even more severe than any yet fought' (ibid.) as one half of humanity rebels against the other half and takes back its rightful resources. It is her own uncompromising attitude, her own insistence on men and their Church and their State (and to which I would add, their science), as the enemy of women, that made Gage unacceptable to many women in the woman's rights movement, for they were often intent on reform, on avoiding confrontation, bent on persuasion rather than rebellion, concerned with compromise not revolution; and many of them were committed Christians.

It could be argued that Gage gives too much emphasis to christianity, credits it with more power than it possesses and makes a 'bogey' of it. Mary Daly (1978), however, points out that while Gage concentrates on christianity in her critique of patriarchy she makes it perfectly clear that it is from patriarchy that such a religion has been able to develop, flourish, and interact with patriarchy, so that the two are mutually supportive (p. 218). She acknowledges the universality of patriarchy and accepts the possibility that man, in other places, may have constructed other patriarchal religions that serve the same purpose as christianity.

I am reluctant to discard the idea that the beliefs of christianity, in Christian civilisations, possess such a hold over our minds. I suspect that even when we actively reject religion, we do not escape its influence, but that the schemata that it has encoded has become part of the deeply embedded assumptions that form our taken-for-granted understandings of the way the world works.

The only way in which I would want to extend Gage's work – presumptuously to 'bring it up to date' – would be to remove 'science' from the positive place she accords it, as a form of hope for the future, and to add it on to Church and State. I would want to argue that Church, State, and science, are all male controlled, are all products of patriarchy, and all serve patriarchal interests; and all have been used against women. For my part, the only 'inaccuracy' in Gage's work was her vision of the future; she foresaw conflict and prophesied the end of women's subordination. She thought that the 'breakthrough' had been made and that women could begin to claim their psychological, intellectual and material resources for themselves, thereby destroying the relationship between women and men which maintained women's oppression. But like so many of the women she prised from the male vaults, Gage too was appropriated and buried. Stanton and Anthony may have been 'instruments' in the theft and erasure of Gage's work, but there can be little doubt that it has been patriarchy that has profited.

The life, work and 'disappearance' of Matilda Joslyn Gage is sketched in more detail in Sally Roesch Wagner's (1980) 'Introduction' to *Woman, Church and State*. From the first page the warmth and wit of the woman comes across as Wagner outlines Gage's 'public appearance' in the women's movement at the 1850 Convention and the battle she waged with a local cleric in the press, defending the convention and the movement. Denouncing the movement as 'satanic', the clergyman reserves his greatest condemnation for the bloomer dress. Gage quickly sent him back to his bible with the advice that he should practise what he preached; she pointed out that the bible enjoined ministers to wear robes trimmed with bells of gold, and a bonnet of fine linen, and that it expressly forbade men to shave and cultivate a resemblance to women. This 'ecclesiastical duel continued for several weeks in the local paper,' says Wagner, 'much to the delight of the Syracuse readers, especially when they discovered that the person who was running biblical circles around the minister was a woman!' (1980, p. xvi). When the minister insisted that man was made first and that meant he was superior, Gage responded with a 'joke' that is familiar today: 'some persons might think the order of creation would imply just the contrary', she said, 'for as we trace the progress of creation step by step, we perceive that the inferior were first made and each successive thing created, exceeded in rank the preceding one' (ibid.).

This humorous aspect of Gage certainly does not emerge in the *History*, where the predominant image of her is one of a scholarly woman confined to libraries by inclination, and to domestic responsibilities by necessity. The profile presented by Wagner, however, suggests that it is much more than Gage's humour which has been omitted in the official record. Wagner shows Gage to be both a grassroots activist, and a theoretician. Eleanor Flexner (1979) and Miriam Gurko (1976) each refer to Gage's support of Anthony prior to her trial, but Wagner gives even this a slightly different emphasis when she says, 'Gage was the only feminist' who went to Anthony's assistance, and that between the two of them they divided up the county, each giving a record number of speeches: Gage's speech, 'The United States on Trial, Not Susan B. Anthony' was based on the premise that governments could not *grant* rights, for they were a product of human existence, and that the United States government had *robbed* women of their rights; her lecture was one of the most closely reasoned arguments on the philosophical and constitutional nature of rights, that has been produced (Wagner, 1980, p. xviii).

Gage also produced other brilliant constitutional arguments which became the underlying theory for the National Woman Suffrage Association policy — and the basis for testing rights in the courts. And she backed up her theoretical analysis with courage and defiance when harassed. In 1876, during the centennial celebration, the NSWA held its convention in Washington and declared that it was the 'most sacred duty of the women of these United States to rebel against the injustice, usurpation and tyranny of our present government,' Wagner says, 'the government no doubt was a little unnerved by all this talk of revolution on their doorsteps. Gage was presiding, when the police arrived unannounced at one point, declared it an illegal assembly because the women had not procured the proper license, and threatened to arrest Gage if she continued the convention. Knowing that no license was required, and that this was simply harrassment, (sic) Gage continued the convention, declaring that if arrested, she would hold a woman's rights convention in jail. The crowd cheered their approval, and the police left' (ibid., p. xix).

There is no mention of this in the *History*.

From 1878 to 1881, Gage edited and published herself the *National Citizen and Ballot Box* (she gave it up to work on the *History of Woman Suffrage)*, which was the official paper of the NWSA, and which indicates the broad range of her feminist concerns. She saw co-operatives and collectives as the organisation of the future, she attacked the double standard in relation to prostitution and almost incredulously, for her time, discussed rape and the 'practice of non-conviction or pardoning.' She cited 'the state of Iowa, where in one year there were fifty seven rape trials and only four convictions' (Wagner, 1980, p. xxv). She decried the jokes about mothers-in-law, and in relation to marriage declared that 'no self-respecting woman will submit to being given away' (ibid., p. xxiv). She praised the work being undertaken with women prisoners and condemned the legal system which sent a woman, the mother of ten children, to prison for sixty days for stealing something to eat. Says Wagner, 'Gage, who had been earlier named an honorary member of the Council of Matrons of the Iroquois spoke out against the "oppression of Indians," and the government's breaking of its treaties with them.' Repeatedly she addressed the labour question, analysed women's work and women's pay (and absence of pay) and the accumulation of resources, by men (ibid.). It would take more than one volume to outline the diversity of Gage's activities and the breadth and depth of her underlying ideas.

But no woman could expect to put these issues so forthrightly and not be rebuked: Wagner reports that her writing earned her the reputation of being a 'man-hater' and the *Vineland Times* carried the following criticism of her paper:

> It is too aggressive and too bitter against men. It can say no good of them; it can hardly mention them with patience. We count no less than six paragraphs in a single half column, in each of which there is something ill-natured or bitter said or insinuated against the masculine half of humanity (quoted in Wagner, 1980, p. xxv).

Gage found this amusing: how else was one to treat the enemy?

But Gage's defiance went much farther than this and was – in her own time – so very effective. She was not just a scholarly woman who used some of her archivist discoveries to confound the truths of men; she was a political theorist and tactician who understood that while men had robbed women of the fruits of their work – physical and *intellectual* – they would not have been able to remove *all* incriminating evidence, and that one way woman could claim her intellectual energy for herself was to use it against men, to expose the theft men had engaged in on such a massive scale. Women could take back their energy, they could cease to allow men to act for them, talk for them, think for them, and start acting, talking, thinking for themselves, building their own independent and autonomous resources.

Her strategy for taking back women's energy (contemporary feminists would call it reclaiming) led her to specific and sensitive areas where subversion was more likely to be effective. She challenged the accepted belief that it was men who were the creative intellectuals, the artists, the philosophers, the respected rulers, and the inventors and military planners. In 1870 she published 'Woman as Inventor' and demonstrated that not only were women capable inventors who had been robbed of the recognition of their creativity, but they had also been robbed of the products and profits of their invention. (Autumn Stanley, 1981, supports this view.) In 1880, Gage published 'Who Planned the Tennessee Campaign of 1862?' (for it was widely known that this was a brilliant military strategy that had changed the course of the Civil War – which Gage had supported while it was fought to end slavery). Gage demonstrated convincingly that it was a woman who had planned this strategy, although the men claimed ownership and took credit for its success.

Over and over again she raised fundamental questions: if women could accomplish all these feats why were they branded as inferior and why were they not recognised? And over and over again the explanation came that it was in men's interest to have both sexes believe that women were inferior, because it allowed men to appropriate women's energy and to use it to substantiate their own claim of supremacy. Gage provided overwhelming evidence that men robbed women of the fruits of their labour: she returned to history (although in the case of inventions and military plans she was not going back very far) to make the case for the theft of women's creativity and intellectuality, but she also made it abundantly clear that it was not necessary to go to archives to establish that men robbed woman of the fruits of her labour: such evidence was available every day in the life of every woman, who was required to service men.

It is difficult to establish how familiar Gage was with the work of Marx (it is not at all difficult, however, to establish how familiar Marx was with the work of Gage!). Her analysis of the relationship between women and men is strikingly similar to Marx's analysis of the relationship *among* men, between worker and capitalist. In 1878, Gage introduced the following resolution to the NWSA Convention: 'Resolved, that the question of capital and labor is one of special interest to us. Man standing to woman in the position of capitalist has robbed her through the ages of the results of her toil. No just settlement of this question can be attained until the right of woman to the proceeds of her labor in the family and elsewhere be recognized, and until she is welcomed into every industry on the basis of equal pay for equal work' (Stanton et al., 1886, vol. III, p. 124).

It was at this convention that Gage also put forward her usual resolutions with regard to the role that the Church had played in this process – by providing the framework which would make this otherwise outrageous behaviour seem logical and acceptable. Some women were hesitant about passing the resolutions, concerned that the convention might be labelled as anti-Church, as had happened the previous year. Gage, like Stanton, was scornful about such caution. To Gage it was playing precisely into the hands of the 'patriarchate' to refrain from condemning patriarchal crimes; to allow the Church to go unchallenged and unchecked was to continue to allow men to steal women's ideas and energy. Wagner reports that Gage gave an impassioned speech asking whether 'things had come to the pass that a threat of the attacks of the clergy was to be held over the convention to deter it from doing its duty' (Wagner, 1980, p. xxx). The resolution was carried by a large majority and, although Gage's part in it is recorded in the *National Citizen and Ballot Box* (August 1878), which she edited, there is no reference to the role Gage played in *History of Woman Suffrage*, vol. III – only the inclusion of her name on a list of those who engaged in 'a prolonged discussion' (p. 125), and that is contained in a footnote.

Part of the reason that Gage's contributions are so infrequently mentioned in the *History* could well be Gage's own attitude. Wagner states that much of what we know about the nineteenth-century woman's movement clearly comes from Gage, from her newspaper articles (she acted as a correspondent for papers in New York and San Francisco as well as her home town; she also wrote an article on the woman's movement for an encyclopaedia) and her contribution to the *History*, yet she is not a very good source about her own work. 'It was not through any sense of false modesty that Gage played down her importance to the movement', says Wagner. 'Getting credit just does not seem to have been a very important concern of hers,' despite what Stanton may have implied in *Eighty Years and More*. 'For her, carrying on the struggle and letting others know of it were more important than who did it' (Wagner, 1980, p. xxvi).

Mary Daly (1980) has made a similar point, stating that it was more important to Gage that women should know and understand these ideas, that it was more important that the ideas be possessed by women than 'owned' by one individual woman: 'Matilda was not obsessively concerned about "credit" for her role as an activist in the annals of history' (pp. viii-ix).

To Gage, knowledge by and about women was definitely *power;* in her life and her work there were few distinctions between theory and practice, between intellectual and activist. Her archivist work, her writing, her theoretical arguments about the constitution and the Church, were just as much part of her activism as consciousness-raising and petition-gathering in her own home town. And while in part she may have contributed to her own 'erasure' by not categorically establishing ownership of her ideas, this is by no means the full story, and is perhaps an explanation given too much credibility. After all, what she did indisputably 'own' – the chapters of the *History,* and *Woman, Church and State* – comprise considerably more than some other individual offerings which have not been erased; but Gage's substantial work has been overlooked.

One of the major sources of Gage's disappearance is more likely to date from 1888, and for the account of her 'exclusion' from the 'mainstream' of suffrage activities I am completely indebted to Sally Roesch Wagner, without whose research Gage's disappearance would otherwise have remained a mystery to me.

In 1888, the 'National' sponsored the convention of the International Council of Women and issued 10,000 invitations to woman's rights workers all over the world. Many of them came, and many of them were women who would not normally have attended the 'radical' conventions that were the hallmark of the 'National'. Among the conservative visitors was Frances Willard – and other members of the Women's Christian Temperance Union which Willard represented.

There was at least one controversial incident at this convention: all the sessions began with a prayer, and the session Gage chaired began with a prayer to a female deity. Some women expressed outrage; Gage expressed dismay that women could believe themselves to be excluded from the deity and she went to considerable lengths to point out that the translations of the bible had been undertaken by (very) fallible men who had systematically eliminated women from the imagery of the deity in the attempt to enhance their own image of themselves as 'closer to god'. But, insisted Gage, women were equally part of the deity and it was their duty to assert their presence and visibility.

The members of the Women's Christian Temperance Union were neither amused nor impressed. Wagner sums up this union as one which 'under the banner "For God, Home and Native Land" represented a conservative army of "organized mother love" devoted to cleaning up the country's impurities' under the guidance of their leader, Frances Willard, who had 'received divine inspiration (she said) to work for suffrage. With the ballot in their hands, the mothers of America could legislate morality' (Wagner, 1980, p. xxxi). It was not a morality of which either Gage or Stanton approved, based as it was on the premise that women were spiritually and morally superior and had a duty to bring the government of America back to principles of christianity.

To say that Gage and Willard had little in common is an understatement: even their reasons for seeking the vote were virtually diametrically opposed. While to Gage it represented an extension of liberty, she saw that to Willard it represented an opportunity to impose a particular set of values and beliefs – derived from the scriptures – on the whole population. To both Gage and Stanton the Women's Christian Temperance Union with its insistence on conformity to a particular doctrine (which Gage and Stanton believed false, pernicious, a root of evil and the major source of woman's oppression) represented a considerable threat.

Anthony, however, liked Willard; she saw in her a potential ally, for after all Willard too was seeking the vote (and she had a lot of followers), and there are numerous references in many sources – even from Stanton herself – that all Anthony was concerned with, by this stage, was obtaining the vote. Besides, I think it fair to assert that while Anthony no doubt appreciated arguments put forward by Stanton and Gage in relation to religion, she did not necessarily share them, and at times even indicated considerable impatience with them.

But if Willard and Anthony were drawing together, and Gage and Stanton were remaining firmly with their analysis that the vote would change nothing unless the sources of woman's oppression – in the family, in the workplace, in Christian ideology – were changed, there were other forces at work in the late 1880s which were also to play a role in the isolation of Gage. Within the broad coalition of the women's movement attempts were being made – particularly by Alice Stone Blackwell (Lucy Stone's daughter) – to reunite the two suffrage associations that had split after the Civil War. Blackwell herself says: 'When I began to work for a union, the elders were not keen on it, on either side, but the younger women on both sides were. Nothing really stood in the way except the unpleasant feelings engendered during the long separation, and those could be overcome.' What she does not explain to my satisfaction is *why* such a union was considered. The only reason offered is: 'There was no longer any good reason for continuing two associations' (Blackwell, 1930; 1971, p. 229) which seems to me, patently absurd, given the differences – theoretically and practically – between the two associations.

These differences, while not given credence by Blackwell, were certainly obvious to Gage and Stanton, who, when they first heard of the overtures towards a union, thought the idea ridiculous, particularly after the 'American' aligned itself with the Women's Christian Temperance Union (and the dreaded Frances Willard).[10] Union was completely out of the question as far as Gage and Stanton were concerned, and not just because the 'National' concentrated at national level while the 'American' concentrated at state level – although these differences in analysis and strategy were fundamental and a source of constant antagonism – but because the 'National' regularly passed resolutions declaring the teachings of the Church to be the source of a woman's oppression and this left very little common ground for union with an association which wanted to make the teachings of the Church the basis of government.

But Gage, at least, reckoned without Anthony and her single-minded pursuit of woman suffrage. If one were to accept without question the version of the union provided by Alice Stone Blackwell, one could be forgiven for assuming it was a non-event. 'The American had all along stood for a delegate basis and a movable annual meeting. The National was ready to concede a delegate basis, and when, once that was adopted, an annual meeting made up of delegates from all parts of the country soon voted for the movable convention' (ibid., p. 239). Were the only obstacles that the 'American' organised itself around states, had delegates, and held its convention in different states while the National concentrated its efforts on the capital? An unlikely story, I think.

But what about the version in the *History* (which Blackwell consistently claims to be biased)? In Volume IV, edited by Susan B. Anthony and Ida Husted Harper, the union of the two societies is outlined, in entirety, in the following manner: 'The feature of this occasion [the convention of

---

[10] Stanton and Gage may not have been misrepresenting Willard: Ida B. Wells also distrusted and disliked Willard – and for good reason, see page 262.

1890] which will distinguish it in history was the formal union of the National and American Associations under the joint name. For the past twenty-one years two distinctive societies had been in existence, both national as to scope but differing as to methods. Negotiations had been in progress for several years toward a uniting of the forces and, preliminaries having been satisfactorily arranged by committees from the two bodies the officers and members of both participated in this national convention of 1890' (1902, p. 164).

Really? As simply and uneventfully as that? Here is the 'official' version of the National and an 'official' version of the American – but what happened to Matilda Joslyn Gage and Elizabeth Cady Stanton? Because these two women were vehemently opposed to a union with a 'single-issue', conservative, 'religious' movement, as they saw the American, and yet Stanton emerges as president of this union – and Gage disappears!

Sally Roesch Wagner provides a third – and astonishing – account of the union: it is a story of intrigue, duplicity and subterfuge which has to be read to be believed. It suggests that Anthony wanted union – at any price – because she saw it bringing woman suffrage closer, and she was more than prepared to sacrifice Gage and her radicalism, which was becoming increasingly embarrassing to Anthony, for the numbers and 'pressure' of many respectable women – and men!

Gage was not the only member of the National who awoke one morning to the incredible news that she and the other members of the 'National' had been unified with the 'American' – and the Women's Christian Temperance Union! There had been no prior warning, and anger at Anthony who had pushed the merger through was widespread. To Gage it seemed that the time had come to form the anti-Church association which she and Stanton had favoured and visualised for so long. Stanton agreed, although, while stating that she would talk whenever Gage thought it was necessary, she insisted that she would never hold office again because she was tired of political organisations. Says Wagner: 'We may never know what transpired behind the scenes but when the National American Woman Suffrage Association (NAWSA) convention took place four months later, Stanton gratefully accepted the office of President,' and also dissociated herself from the new association which Gage had formed, calling the group a secession from the woman suffrage movement. 'This casual betrayal of the political vision she and Stanton had shared and for which they had worked together for over twenty years was devastating to Gage. Years later she still carried the pain and anger from it' (1980, p. xxxvi).

And, of course, the differences between the two associations – including those represented by the analysis of the Church provided by Stanton – were to promote controversy and antagonism in the new union. Gage herself said that as it was only a union in name it would be counterproductive, and despite Alice Stone Blackwell's assertion that 'union strengthened the movement' (1930, p. 229), there is more reason to support Gage and her analysis than that of Blackwell on this issue.

Alice Stone Blackwell herself says that, 'Mrs Stanton was really more interested in attacking orthodox religion than in promoting equal rights for women', and proceeds to provide a most unflattering profile of Stanton as a trouble-maker whose only contribution was to equip the enemy (who was 'the enemy', I wonder?) with cudgels. 'In 1896 she brought out the so-called "Woman's Bible", a commentary on the Scriptures prepared by herself and a committee of friends, from a highly unorthodox standpoint,' says Blackwell (ibid., p. 230), and naturally it caused a scandal. The Association publicly disowned it (despite the protests of both Anthony and Stanton) because it was so difficult to obtain converts if people thought that the *Woman's Bible* was anything to do with the Association.

Gage was a contributor to that volume, but after the union of the two associations she was effectively isolated. Not that she was not active, but it was 'outside' the by-now-acceptable movement for the vote. While still maintaining many of the beliefs she had shared with Gage, Elizabeth Cady Stanton was in contrast more definitely centre-stage in the suffrage movement. Gage called the new, radical organisation she formed 'The Woman's National Liberal Union': Anthony denounced it as 'ridiculous, absurd, bigoted and too horrible for anything' (hardly cautious words), and Anthony wrote many letters to women all across the country forbidding them to attend the convention which Gage was organising (Wagner, 1980, p. xxxvi). But despite Anthony's warnings and threats, women came from far and wide to attend the *radical* convention which Gage organised (and which of course never merits a mention in the *History* of this period, edited by Anthony and Ida Husted Harper).

For her courage, her daring, her radical analysis and her inability to become conservative as she grew older, Gage paid dearly, says Wagner, for not only did she lose many of her friends and her community of forty years, she also 'lost her rightful place in history.' This was primarily, according to Wagner, because Anthony intentionally isolated and excluded her, and because Anthony – along with her friend and biographer Ida Husted Harper – was ultimately 'the one who told the story of the union' and who made Gage invisible in the process. As none of the dissenters (and Gage was by no means the only one) wrote up their side, 'Anthony's version stood, unchallenged, as the historically accurate account' (ibid., p. xxxviii). That this should have happened to Gage is not in itself surprising; this method of isolating and erasing 'disagreeable' and dangerous women is commonplace enough in the history of women. What is surprising is that it seems that on this occasion it was a woman, who was a leader of the woman's movement, who was concerned that the details of women's struggle should be 'secured to posterity' – it seems it was primarily Susan B. Anthony, who was responsible. It also seems that while Gage disappeared, Anthony secured a place in man's history. I do not think this coincidental.

The version of the struggle which Anthony and Harper provide centres on the vote and suggests that obtaining the vote was the over-riding concern of the women who were seeking their rights. As there were many other issues – most of which are raised today – which many other women considered even more important than the vote, this impression of a single-issue movement, a perfectly respectable movement, could only be sustained and justified by the elimination of every other consideration.

Once the vote was gained, suffrage for women could hardly have constituted a radical idea, and, particularly when there were no substantial
changes in the balance of power and the relationship between women and
men, it is easy to see how the 'steps' leading up to it (as distinct from the
'struggle' it had once been) became perfectly acceptable history, and fitted
readily into the schemata of linear and developmental history, the history
of 'progress' as it has been constructed in a male-dominated society. Without Gage and the ideas she espoused (ideas, which I would contend, were
far more dangerous to patriarchy), Susan B. Anthony and the history of
suffrage were ripe for male appropriation. She could be incorporated, and
patriarchy continues unchallenged. But in terms of Gage's thesis, both her
own physical and intellectual energy, *and that of Anthony,* were taken over
by men!

'Gage only becomes understandable by creating a new historical context,' says Wagner, for 'a study of her work gives us information with
which to rewrite our history' (ibid., p. xxxviii); it helps us to reclaim our
past by providing both the theoretical framework, and the examples.
'Through listening to Gage, we hear the story of a radical feminist movement which raised almost every issue of woman's oppression explored by
the current wave of feminism . . . the story ends in 1890, when the woman's
movement was replaced by a conservative caricature of feminism committed
only to achieving the vote' (ibid., p. xxxix).

If Lucy Stone's daughter, Alice Stone Blackwell, considered the union
to be a source of strength, Elizabeth Cady Stanton's daughter, Harriet
Stanton Blatch, returning to America from England in 1902 considered it
a disaster. She was appalled at what she found, saying that the suffrage
association 'bored its adherents and repelled its opponents' (Blatch and
Lutz, 1940, p. 92) and that there 'did not seem to be a grain of political
knowledge in the movement . . . A vital idea had been smothered' (ibid.,
p. 98).

Gage's worst fears were realised. Despite her analysis, her energy, her
actions, she has been negated and denied. Unable to *use* her ideas, patriarchy has elected to *lose* them. It is as if she had not existed. Yet it seems to
me from the few fragments I have been able to piece together, that she,
more than any other woman of the past (with the exception of Mary Beard,
1946), identified and understood the process of the denial of woman's
existence, the theft of women's being, in a male-dominated society.

5 The other side: Lucy Stone

It is irrefutable that those who write and edit the records select evidence
which confirms and justifies their own scheme of values: it is what men
have done from the bible to Margaret Fuller; it is what Susan B. Anthony
(with a little help from her friends) did to Gage; it is what I am doing here.
By such a process of selection, many individuals and activities that are
inconsistent with the values being put forward by the writers and editors

are omitted, and are in danger of becoming consigned to obscurity, if not oblivion.

This is one of the reasons I have chosen to include Lucy Stone in this record, because in writing her account of Lucy Stone's contribution, her daughter, Alice Stone Blackwell (1930) states that the *History of Woman Suffrage* is such a 'one sided account' that Lucy Stone (and the American Woman Suffrage Association) is misrepresented, but that during her lifetime Lucy Stone would not state her side of the case because 'to do so would have been to put weapons into the hands of the enemy' (p. 227).

Alice Rossi (1974) includes Lucy Stone in the section entitled 'the Blackwell Clan', which is in some respects a disservice to Stone, given the extent to which she went, and the harassment she endured, in order to retain the name Stone. Leslie Wheeler (1982) has suggested that the position Stone took on her name was probably the most radical one that she adopted (with the epithet 'Lucy Stoner' meaning 'a person who advocates the retention of the maiden name by married women', Wheeler, 1981a), for it seems that she too became increasingly conservative as she grew older. But it must be remembered that Lucy Stone, who was also called the 'orator' and the 'morning star' of the woman's rights movement, gave her first public lecture on the topic in 1847 – one year before Seneca Falls and many years before it was permissible for women to speak in public.

There is much about Stone that is admirable, and inspiring; that she is not held in as high esteem as Anthony, for example, is probably more a matter of who selected the material for the original history than a matter of the relative merit of the two women. And once the process of erasure begins it is readily compounded with Alice Stone Blackwell's biography (*Lucy Stone: Pioneer of Woman's Rights*, 1930), a fairly romanticised version I suspect, and Elinor Rice Hays (*Morning Star: A Biography of Lucy Stone*, 1961) being among the few accounts of her life and work until Leslie Wheeler's (1981b) *Loving Warriors: Selected Letters of Lucy Stone and Henry B. Blackwell, 1853–1893.*

Born in 1818, on what Flexner (1979) describes as a 'marginal farm' in Massachusetts, Lucy Stone learnt first hand that women worked very hard and that 'chivalry' was a myth. Alice Stone Blackwell (1930), says that Lucy 'was the eighth of nine children. Her mother, a farmer's wife, had milked eight cows the night before . . . When told of the sex of the new baby, she said sadly "Oh dear! I am sorry it is a girl. A woman's life is so hard!" ' (p. 3). And some of it, the product of 'father's will', needlessly so. The accounts of Stone's childhood and early years suggest numerous attempts to break her spirit and force her into submission. They make for distressing reading and one feels enormous empathy for this young woman who rather than become cowed became increasingly rebellious and determined, as her father insisted on the inappropriateness of education for girls, and insisted on Lucy's inappropriateness for marriage. 'Luce's face is like a blacksmith's apron: it keeps off the sparks' (Blackwell, 1930, p. 21), he taunted, while he controlled the purse strings and denied her mother access to money, and Lucy access to education and books. And what she didn't learn about patriarchy from the home, she soon found out from the Church.

The 'Pastoral Letter' directed at the Grimkés was read out in her own church, and Blackwell reports Stone's anger at the clergyman who, while it was being read, 'walked up and down the aisle, turning his head from side to side and looking up at the women in the gallery with an air that seemed to say, "Now! Now we have silenced you!" ' (ibid., p. 25). Stone herself said later: 'I was young enough then so that my indignation blazed. My cousin said that her side was black and blue with the indignant nudges of my elbow at each aggravating sentence; and I told her afterwards that if I ever had anything to say in public, I should say it, and all the more because of that Pastoral Letter' (ibid.).

Lucy Stone avidly followed the press reports on the Grimkés, and of Abby Kelley (another woman who deserves more attention for the contribution she made to both the Anti-Slavery and Woman's Rights cause), and read Sarah Grimké's essays on the 'Rights of Woman.' She wrote to her brother in 1838 and said that if *he* read Grimké's essays, 'I guess you would not think I was too "obstreperous". I tell you, they are first rate, and only help to confirm the resolution I had made before, to call no man master' (ibid., p. 37).

It was a burning desire of Stone's to go to college, partly to learn Latin and Greek and to check the translations of the bible which she believed to be false. But while her brothers were assisted in their education, it took her nine years to save enough money for a term at Oberlin (one of the first colleges to make no distinction for entry on the basis of colour or sex) where she went in 1843. Again she had to work hard – teaching in the preparatory department for two hours a day, and doing housework for the Ladies' Boarding Hall, as well as her studies, in order to support herself. And again she found that despite its relative liberality, Oberlin still operated a double standard for its women and men students.

In 1845, Antoinette Brown (later to become the first ordained woman minister and who also married a Blackwell) came to Oberlin, and she and Stone served as support for each other. Together, for example, they took on the college (particularly the Ladies' Board, designed to regulate the morals and manners of women students), initially over issues of debating.

'The young men had to hold debates as part of their work in rhetoric, and the young women were required to be present, for an hour and a half every week, in order to help form an audience for the boys, but were not allowed to take part,' reports Blackwell, but 'Lucy was intending to lecture and Antoinette to preach. Both wished for practice in public speaking' and they persuaded the head of the department to let them debate. 'Tradition says that the debate was exceptionally brilliant. More persons than usual came in to listen, attracted by curiosity. But the Ladies' Board immediately got busy, St Paul was invoked, and the college authorities forbade any repetition of the experiment' (ibid., pp. 60–1).

Undaunted, Lucy Stone organised a debating society among the women, although they were forced to meet clandestinely in the woods 'with sentinels on watch to give warning of intruders', because even at Oberlin it was considered outrageous for women to *practise* public speaking. When Lucy Stone did not waver in her determination to become a public speaker, on behalf of her sex, it can be seen that this was no small act of courage and defiance. Her first public speech was at Oberlin, at a celebration of the anniversary of West Indian emancipation. The day after she made her speech 'she was called before the Ladies' Board. All the texts commonly invoked against public speaking by women were quoted. Finally the president's wife said, "Did you not feel yourself very much out of place up there on the platform among all those men? Were you not embarrassed and frightened?" ' (ibid., p. 63).

Stone assured them that she was *not*; she knew she was meant to be both embarrassed and frightened, but that this was simply a form of intimidation designed to prevent women from speaking in public. If women were made sufficiently frightened they would not attempt to get *up* on the platform and seriously address men, and this was a far more satisfactory arrangement as far as men were concerned, than driving women *off* the platform, after they had arrived. But Stone was going to make sure that they had to drive her away, that her silence could not be bought in a discreet and ladylike way which helped to suggest that women did not want to talk, rather than that they were prevented from doing so.

There were two forms of courses at Oberlin, the literature course (usually undertaken by the women) and the regular classical course which led to the B.A. (and was usually undertaken by the men). Lucy Stone was in the regular course and at her graduation was appointed by the class to prepare one of the addresses, which would then be read by one of the men. Stone wanted to read her own address and prepared a petition to the Ladies' Board, requesting to do so. The petition was refused 'on the ground that it was improper for women to participate in public exercises with men' (ibid., p. 68). Stone refused to write the address.

Much pressure was placed on her to change her mind, to stop being 'disagreeable' and 'troublesome'. 'Mr Whipple came home with me,' she wrote home, 'and urged all the reasons he could think of to persuade me to write and let Professor Thome read for me. I told him that by so doing I would make a public acknowledgement of the rectitude of the principle which takes away from women their equal rights, and denies to them the privilege of being co-laborers with men in any sphere to which their ability makes them adequate; and that no word or deed of mine should ever look towards the support of such a principle, or even to its toleration' (ibid., p. 69).

Stone was uncompromising: she knew the principles that were involved: she knew why Antoinette Brown *was* allowed to read her paper on graduation. Brown had been taking the ladies' literary course and, despite the fact that the two courses 'had their graduating exercises on successive days, in the same auditorium, and before practically the same audience', there was a crucial difference, for 'when the graduates of the Ladies' Literary Course took their diplomas, the persons on the platform were all women, except the president; and when the students of the regular classical course received their degrees, the persons on the platform were almost all men. Hence on one occasion it was thought permissible for a woman's voice to be heard, while on the other it would have been considered a direct defiance of a divine command' (ibid., p. 73).

By such means is the visible supremacy and authority of men maintained and there was no way in which Stone would subscribe to it. At this stage of her life (and at this stage of the movement), when she defiantly declared that she would become a public lecturer, knowing full well the abuse and vilification that was in store for her, when she fervently declared '*Especially do I mean to labor for the elevation of my sex*' (ibid., p. 67), there were few issues in relation to women's oppression that Stone did not understand, and there were few steps she was not prepared to take in order to promote change. By any standards she was a most radical person when she began as a lecturer for the Anti-Slavery Society.

At a time when Abolitionist speakers were mobbed and murdered, Lucy Stone was engaged (in 1848) to lecture regularly for the Anti-Slavery Society, and soon found that she confronted many of the problems that the Grimkés had faced. She couldn't keep woman's rights out of her lectures, and the Anti-Slavery Society did not want woman's rights in. Having been told to refrain from mentioning women, Stone said: 'I was a woman before I was an abolitionist. I must speak for the women. I will not lecture any more for the Anti-Slavery Society, but will work wholly for woman's rights' (ibid., p. 90). But, adds Blackwell, 'The Anti-Slavery Society was very unwilling to give her up, however, as she had been one of their best speakers, and it was finally arranged that she should lecture for them on Saturday nights and Sundays – times which were looked upon as too sacred for any hall or church to be opened for a woman's rights meeting – and during the rest of the week she should lecture on woman's rights on her own responsibility' (ibid.).

It is sobering to read of the hardship and harassment Stone endured as she toured the country on her own lecturing against slavery and for woman's rights. She was thwarted and abused by many members of the clergy who obstructed her attempts to gain a hall in which to speak, she confronted mobs and jeering faces and was often greeted with a hail of spitballs. Missiles were hurled at her and, 'Once, in the winter, a pane of glass was taken out of the window behind her, the nozzle of a hose was put through, and she was suddenly deluged with cold water in the midst of her speech. She put on a shawl and went on with her lecture' (ibid., p. 80).

In the early 1850s when in England no respectable woman went about unaccompanied, and in America when no respectable woman spoke in public, Lucy Stone went, on her own, from state to state, under the most primitive of travelling conditions, and lectured on 'The Social and Industrial Disabilities of Woman', 'Legal and Political Disabilities' and 'Moral and Religious Disabilities'. It was a hazardous and isolated life. 'When I undertook my solitary battle for woman's rights', she said, 'outside the little circle of abolitionists I knew nobody who sympathized with my ideas. I had some hand bills printed, 12 x 10 inches. I bought a paper of tacks, and, as I could not pay for posting, I put up my bills myself, using a stone for a hammer. I did not take a fee at the door. But there was always the expense of hall and hotel. To cover this, at the close of my speech, I asked help for the great work, by a collection of expenses. Then I took a hat and went through the audience for the collection, for all were strangers to me' (ibid., p. 91).

Although determined never to marry, in 1853, Lucy Stone met Henry B. Blackwell and began to reconsider her decision. It has been suggested that it was partly because Blackwell was so persistent but also because he came from such an unusual family that Stone was even prepared to reassess her stance in relation to marriage. There were nine Blackwell children, as well as three women who married into the family, and together, states Alice Rossi (1974), they comprised a fascinating set of individuals. 'In the sibling set itself were the first two women to practice medicine in the United States to have earned American medical degrees – Elizabeth and Emily Blackwell.[11] Their older sister Anna was probably the first woman foreign correspondent. A younger sister Ellen was a talented artist and writer. Their younger brother Samuel married Antoinette Brown, one of the first American women to attend college and the first woman to be ordained and to hold her own ministry. Henry Blackwell, prominent in abolition and suffrage history in his own right, married Lucy Stone . . . Their daughter Alice Stone Blackwell became well known as a speaker, suffrage campaigner, and editor of the Boston *Woman's Journal*' (Rossi, 1974, p. 323).

That none of the Blackwell women ever married, as well as the fact that this was a closely knit family circle with all members (and spouses) drawing on each other for advice and support, has provided biographers and commentators with rich resources for theories of 'sublimation', 'inability to form intimate relationships with men', and 'neuroses'. I have not seen it stated anywhere that these five enlightened women saw marriage for what it was worth and chose to remain single.

In 1855 Lucy Stone and Henry Blackwell were married. There was much speculation in the press as to whether marriage would silence Lucy Stone (and there were similar pressures on Stone to 'prove' she was competent at two jobs, and not just one, as there had been on Angelina Grimké Weld) but, states Flexner (1979), the pundits were disappointed for 'the marriage made two advocates for woman's rights, where there had been one, and eventually three. Henry Blackwell, Lucy Stone, and their daughter, Alice Stone Blackwell, covered nearly the entire span of the woman's rights movement, from 1847 to 1920' (p. 70) and, like Harriet Taylor and John Stuart Mill, Stone and Blackwell began with a very radical declaration in regard to marriage.

Before their marriage service began they stood up together and read their Protest which began: 'While we acknowledge our mutual affection by publicly assuming the relationship of husband and wife, yet, in justice to ourselves and a great principle, we deem it a duty to declare that this act on our part implies no sanction of, nor promise of voluntary obedience to,

---

[11] There is further discussion of Emily and Elizabeth Blackwell in Rossi, 1974: see also Elizabeth Blackwell 1895; 1977, and accounts of women's entry to the medical profession.

such of the present laws of marriage as refuse to recognize the wife as an independent, rational being, while they confer upon the husband an injurious and unnatural superiority, investing him with legal powers which no honorable man would exercise, and which no man should possess', and which then proceeded to list many of the contemporary demands of the women's movement – beginning with a woman's right to her own person (Blackwell, 1930, p. 167). The protest gained wide publicity.

However, even more inflammatory, was Stone's decision to retain her father's name. Her daughter explains that 'Lucy looked upon the loss of a woman's name at marriage as a symbol of the loss of her individuality. Not believing in the thing, she would not have the symbol' (ibid., p. 171). As she was given legal advice that it was custom and not law that required a woman to take a man's name upon marriage, she retained the name Lucy Stone, and was warmly congratulated on her stand by Elizabeth Cady Stanton. Susan B. Anthony, however, did not regard Stone's actions in the same positive light and, although in 1856 Stone instructed Anthony that she simply wanted 'Lucy Stone' to appear on the list of names associated with the announcement of a forthcoming convention, Anthony ignored the request.

Stone was deeply distressed, and wrote to Anthony, 'At first it made me faint and sick until a flood of tears relieved me . . . O! Susan it seems to me, that it has wrought a wrong on me that it will take many years to wear out' (Stone to Anthony, 2 September 1856, Blackwell Family Papers, quoted in Leslie Wheeler, 1982).

Within the woman's rights movement this was probably the only occasion on which it was Stone who in the interest of respectability and avoidance of bad publicity was urged to modify her stand. It was argued that too many people thought she was not properly married and were intent on associating her and the movement with 'free love'. She was pressured – in a way in which she later pressured Elizabeth Cady Stanton on the issues of marriage, divorce, and the Church – to put aside her personal, controversial ideas, which were making it difficult to win respectable converts to the movement, for the sake of the movement as a whole. Stone would not compromise.

She does not seem to have been so ready, however, to allow the same latitude to other women in later years. She was very critical of Stanton's analysis of marriage (despite the fact that Stanton often only outlined the very conditions which Stone insisted did not apply in her own case and which she used as a justification for *not* taking her husband's name) and very apprehensive about divorce for, while she admitted that divorce should be considered as an option in the case of a loveless marriage, she fervently wished Stanton would not raise this irrelevant issue at conventions and, with all the attendant bad publicity, jeopardise the movement for woman suffrage.

Stone firmly advocated a woman's right to her own body and counselled male continence, and contraception. She was constantly concerned over women's economic dependence and sought better education and better jobs for women, to reduce such dependence. Initially disillusioned by organised religion, she became silent on the issue of the Church, in later years. She came to accept that the family – with some modifications – constituted the best context for women. She upheld the sanctity of hearth and home with the proviso that women had *some* money and *an* interest.

Given her own experience of married life and motherhood, this seems to have been a somewhat difficult position to hold – not that Henry Blackwell was not supportive. But Stone experienced considerable 'debility' from her role as a wife and mother, with some suggestions that at times she was on the verge of breakdown. And this was with support, with an outside career (she helped to establish the American Woman Suffrage Association after the Civil War, and founded and edited the suffrage paper *The Woman's Journal*, which continued uninterrupted for forty-seven years and was taken over by her daughter), and with some measure of economic independence and freedom from unwanted pregnancies.

That Stone did not write the history of the movement does to some extent help to explain why little is known about her (except perhaps that she was a good speaker and that she would not change her name), and that what little is known does such great injustice to her work, particularly in her earlier years. For while she did reduce her platform for change to a number of narrow issues, this should not detract totally from her earlier, magnificient contribution.

Conservatism, however, does not appear to be compulsory with the advance of years and it is not just Stanton and Gage who are testimony to life-long radical struggle. Ida B. Wells was another woman who maintained her radical stance throughout her life.

6 The experience of black women

Ida B. Wells

I am more than mindful of the difficulties involved in attempting to describe the experience of black women, for throughout these pages I have constantly reiterated two principles: (1) that the dominant group has excluded from the record all that does not advance its own interests, and (2) that I am selecting material in much the same way as those of whom I am critical. The dominance of white, middle-class men has meant the exclusion of women and I can speak authoritatively from the perspective of one who has been in that excluded category. But I have no such authority in relation to black women and am open to the legitimate charge that as a member of the dominant white group, I am excluding from the record all that about black women which does not advance my interest. But I am not prepared to construct the invisibility of black women. Even if I have unwittingly distorted black experience in my attempt to find common ground among black and white women, there will be debate, and not 'erasure'.

Ida Bell Wells was born in Mississippi in 1862 and was almost 3 years old when the slaves were emancipated. During her early years, spent in relatively secure circumstances which permitted her to attend school, she observed the Ku Klux Klan at work and knew of the many hundreds of blacks that were killed. When she was 16 her mother and father and youngest sibling died in a yellow fever epidemic and from 1878 to 1883 she supported her five younger brothers and sisters by teaching school. Then she went to Memphis to teach and attended Lemoyne Institute. Dorothy Sterling (1979) states that at the time, earning fifty dollars a month as a teacher 'Ida Wells was a member of the community's black elite' (p. 68). Dorothy Sterling reports that civil rights was not a burning issue to Ida B. Wells until, in the steadily deteriorating position of blacks which followed the 1883 Supreme Court ruling on the 1875 Civil Rights Act, Ida B. Wells was asked to leave her customary position on the train to work, and 'to move to the car ahead which was reserved for smokers – and blacks' (ibid., p. 72).

She refused. She also bit the conductor's hand when he forcibly tried to remove her. It took three men to push her out of the train at the next station. The passengers applauded the white men who threw her out. Convinced at this stage that the law would work in the interest of justice, Wells sued the railroad for damages, and won. 'While the railroad appealed the decision, Wells, flushed with victory, wrote an account of the case for *The Living Way*, a black church weekly. She had a simple point to make: if you stand up for your rights you will be able to keep them' (ibid., p. 73).

This marked her entry into journalism, and during 1884–91 she wrote for black newspapers across the country. Everywhere she travelled she found conditions for blacks worsening (another challenge to the thesis of history as a process of gradual evolutionary improvement), as 'legal' means were used to deprive blacks in the southern states of the few rights they had been granted after the Civil War. Segregation was everywhere becoming the rule in the south and was frequently enforced by violence.

Wells's faith in 'law' and 'justice' was further eroded when the appeal of the railroad was upheld, the verdict of the lower court reversed, and Wells ordered to pay costs. Rather than accepting that the law would protect blacks, she began to examine the possibility that it was being used against them, and when one of her close friends, Tom Moss, was lynched for *economic* reasons, Wells was not prepared to accept the 'cover-up' of rape. In an editorial in *Free Speech* (a paper in which she had bought an interest), she bitterly condemned the lynching and demanded the arrest of the murderers – but she quickly became aware that no attempt was made by the law to apprehend the murderer of a black man.

Wells knew that the lynching of Tom Moss was not isolated and she set out to investigate how systematic the lynchings of blacks had become. 'Reviewing the figures, Wells found that 728 black men and women had been lynched during the past ten years. Some had been shot or hanged, others burned alive or savagely dismembered. Often whole towns turned out to watch the executions and to cheer on the mob. The white press described these victims as "burly brutes" who had committed the unspeakable crime – rape of a white woman. It was necessary to kill them a Memphis paper explained, because there was no other way to restrain "the brute passion of the Negro" ' (ibid., p. 81). But Tom Moss had not been a rapist, and it was indisputable that many others who had shared an equally vicious fate were equally innocent.

After a week in which eight men were lynched, Wells wrote an editorial for *Free Speech*. She stated categorically that no one any more believed the threadbare lie that black men were being killed because they raped white women. Before the editorial was typeset Wells, wisely, left town. In Philadelphia she was handed a copy of the *Daily Commercial* which added to the reprint of her editorial:

> The fact that a black scoundrel is allowed to live and utter such loathsome and repulsive calumnies is a volume of evidence as to the wonderful patience of southern whites. But we have had enough of it.
>
> There are some things that the Southern white man will not tolerate and the obscene intimations of the foregoing have brought the writer to the very outermost limit of public patience. We hope we have said enough.
>
> (quoted in Sterling, 1979, pp. 82–3)

The offices of *Free Speech* were ransacked and type and furnishings were destroyed. Instructions were issued that incoming trains were to be watched and if Wells were found, she was to be hanged in front of the court house.

Wells made the link between systematic violence, oppression, and an ideology which made it acceptable. It was a similar link to the one made by Gage in relation to witch-hunting. In newspapers in New York she began a crusade against lynching, and, signing herself 'Exiled', she presented names, dates, quotations, which demonstrated that no black was immune from the possibility of lynching, and that lynching was a form of intimidation, of systematic violence against blacks, and designed to keep them in their 'proper place'.

Gerda Lerner (1981) states that Wells organised an anti-lynching campaign, and, 'Her constant theme was to expose lynching as an integral part of the system of racial oppression, the motives for which were usually economic or political. She hit hard at the commonly used alibi for lynchings, the charge of "rape" and dared bring out into the open the most taboo subject of all in Victorian America – the habitual sexual abuse of black women by white men. Thus, she expressed what was to become the ideological direction of the organized movement of black women – a defense of black womanhood as part of a defense of the race from terror and abuse' (pp. 85–6).

Wells stood at the centre of the complex intersection of two forms of oppression – race and sex – and saw clearly that while sex was the basis of the 'availability' of women to men, it was race that was at the crux of which women were available to which men; black women were 'available' to white men, but so great was the power of white men that they could use the unavailability of *their* white women as a pretext for the murder of black men.

In 1893 and 1894, Wells toured Britain, and reported on lynching and the segregation imposed on Negroes. Evidently, the British too had come to accept that a woman could be permitted to speak in public; she was well prepared, she spoke well, and thousands heard her. The difficulties she encountered were in two forms: financial – and Frances Willard (who had also been in England for two years as the guest of her British counterpart in the Women's Christian Temperance Union, Lady Henry Somerset).

Lady Somerset's opinion of Willard is not difficult to establish. She wrote the 'Introductory' to Anna Gordon's biography, *The Beautiful Life of Frances E. Willard* (1898), in which she stated that Willard was the greatest woman philanthropist of the time and that she, Lady Somerset, was 'persuaded that, when the annals of the nineteenth century are written, when the record of the modern movement that has metamorphosed the position of woman comes to be told, Frances Willard's name will stand pre-eminent as the one who saw with a keen prophetic eye ahead of her time, who realized the dangers, who steered clear of the rocks and shoals that beset any great change, and who furnished the women, not only of a great continent but the world over, with a just realization of their rightful position, and with that safe-guarding gospel, "Womanliness first – afterward what you will" ' (p. 13).

Perhaps Lady Somerset knew something about Willard that I don't, although I would not want to dispute that she put considerable energy into gaining the vote (see Flexner, 1979, pp. 186–8), but I would want to add that, like Lady Somerset, I too see Willard as cautious, conservative and reactionary in many respects and ultimately assisting to keep woman in her proper place – but with the vote! I do not find this reason for commendation, nor do I find her racism something which can be overlooked.

Sterling reports that when in America, and visiting the south ('entertained there by upper-class white ladies'), Willard had shown herself to be sympathetic to the plight of the white women. 'In an interview in the New York *Voice*, a temperance paper, she spoke of "great dark faced mobs". "The colored race multiplies like the locusts of Egypt. The grog-shop is its center of power," she said. "The safety of woman, of childhood, of the home is menaced in a thousand localities so that men dare not go beyond the sight of their own roof tree" ' (1979, pp. 90–1).

It could be that Willard was trying to win white southern ladies to the cause of suffrage, or convince society of the evil power of drink, but either way, there is no disguising her racism. Her comments had angered Ida B. Wells, who had armed herself with a copy of the *Voice* and who quoted from it whenever she was asked in Britain where Willard stood on the issue of lynching. And one white, British lady, Lady Somerset, was not at all amused, and tried to use her influence to discredit and stop Wells; her campaign against her, however, was unsuccessful. Wells returned to America praised by many of the establishment figures in Britain, even if it was in part only because she was so frequently, virulently condemned, by so much of the press in America.

While Wells is not indexed in the *History*, Sterling reports that when she spoke in Rochester, she was invited to stay with Susan B. Anthony who, for the sake of expediency asked Wells to tone down her criticism of Willard. Although Wells valued highly her time spent with Anthony, she was not willing to compromise. She probably did not endear herself to Anthony either, believing and openly stating as she did that while she completely supported woman suffrage, she did not think anything would change once women had the vote (ibid., p. 94). Wells had little faith in the political system, legal system, or justice, of white men: her attitude was the product of her own experience! In 1895, Wells was married to Ferdinand Barnett, a Chicago lawyer and editor, and her marriage was amazingly 'liberated' in its day. She became Ida Wells-Barnett, and she purchased *The Conservator* newspaper from her husband and his associates, becoming its editor, publisher and business manager. She also became involved in the organisation of black women, through clubs that were concerned with political action.

In 1896 the National Association of Colored Women was formed and this constituted a significant step in the organisation of black women. A convention was held in Washington with Wells-Barnett as chairwoman of one committee, while Mary Church Terrell − another woman active in civil rights and the woman suffrage movement (see Dorothy Sterling, 1979, pp. 118–57) − became president. At this convention Harriet Tubman received a tremendous reception in acknowledgement of the major and courageous role she had played in the Underground Railroad and for her stand on the rights and dignity of black women.

In attending this convention, Ida Wells-Barnett typified the problematic existence confronting women who wished to participate in public life, and who had children − in a society where provision was not made for such basic aspects of existence. Refusing to handle the problem so that it remained invisible (and therefore could continue *without* provision being made), Wells-Barnett took her child (at this stage, four months old) with her. In all she had four children and, while generally adopting the policy that her baby went with her whatever meeting she attended, there were times when the pressure got too great, and she temporarily 'retired' from public life.

Ida Wells-Barnett suffered the double oppression of racism and sexism and yet she did not give way. Within the black community and within the woman's movement she was frequently viewed as too radical, too 'hot-headed', too outspoken in her protests; she was a black woman who was not at all polite and deferential and she was often urged by both black men and white women to become more cautious and conciliatory. But she insisted on naming the issues, and on naming people, and for this she paid a high price. One wonders how she found the strength to cope, when, upon her appointment as financial secretary to the Afro-American Council, *The Colored American* carried an article which stated that, although 'a woman of unusual mental powers . . . the proprieties would have been observed by giving her an assignment more in keeping with the popular idea of woman's work and which would not interfere so disastrously with her domestic duties'; and, as a final insult; 'The financial secretary of the Afro-American Council should be a man – the best that can be found – and one who is not barred from meeting on amicable terms the leaders of the two races, North East, South and West' – this being a reference to her lack of conciliatory tactics (quoted in Sterling, 1979, p. 102). At the same time Ida Wells-Barnett, who had been a member of the white-led Women's Suffrage Association since she went to Chicago (and who had organised black women voters after women were permitted to vote in local elections), was asked by the officers of the National American Woman Suffrage Association not to march in one of their protests on Washington, 'lest her dark-skinned presence antagonize southern white women' (ibid., p. 110). In typical style, and with the backing of the Illinois delegation, she marched anyway.

Ida Wells-Barnett was not the only woman to encounter such treatment from some of her white sisters in the suffrage movement. This was in stark contrast to the early days, when Angelina and Sarah Grimké had come to acknowledge their oppression as women *through* their anti-slavery activities. Gerda Lerner (1981) states that 'most of the early feminists came to their convictions because of their interest in abolition. Elizabeth Cady Stanton, Susan B. Anthony, Lucy Stone, Abby Kelley, and scores of others found that if they wished to work for reforms in general, they would first have to fight for their right as women to engage in public political activity' (p. 98). Although in general many of the anti-slavery women had shown a much greater awareness and refusal to condone racism, that was in the days when the demand for suffrage was itself a radical issue, when both black women and white women who claimed their rights had *together* been vilified. By the end of the nineteenth century, and into the twentieth century, women who were working for suffrage were not necessarily radical at all, but at times were even the pillars of the respectable community, who endorsed many of the values of the status quo – including racism – in most respects, except those which related to the position of *white* women. The argument that upper- and middle-class white women were denied the vote while immigrant and black men were not was not an uncommon one, as an illustration of injustice. And the premise that association with black women would be harmful in the attempt to secure the vote also had its adherents – particularly when it was believed that southern white men would support the enfranchisement of white women – but not black women – precisely because it would help to strengthen white supremacy.

Stating that the passage of the federal amendment for woman suffrage was so close that nothing should be done to jeopardise it, Ida Husted Harper asked Mary Church Terrell to withhold the application from a federation of black women's clubs which sought affiliation with the National American Woman Suffrage Association (Sterling, 1979, p. 146). The suffrage movement had shifted from identifying *with* the cause of blacks, to trying to ensure that there were *no* links between the suffrage movement and blacks.

It was this position – and many, many actions which reflected it, that led Josephine Ruffin to take a stand.

Josephine Ruffin

'A suffragist, one of the first of her race to become a member of the New England Women's Club, and editor of *The Woman's Era*' (Flexner, 1979, pp. 193–4), she made a direct challenge to white women who were excluding black women from associations. She returned to the position that many of the earlier feminists had adopted prior to the Civil War when there had been solidarity among many black and white women. (As Gerda Lerner, 1981, p. 98, states, there were then integrated meetings, resolutions were passed condemning racism, and it was because black and white women 'linked arms as they marched out in pairs through a furious mob' that public prejudice was so incited and the newly built Pennsylvania Hall was burnt down after Angelina Grimké Weld's speech in 1838.)

Speaking on behalf of black women in Boston in 1895, Josephine Ruffin clearly stated the white image of black women, its false, pernicious and divisive nature, and asserted that the time had come 'to stand forth and declare ourselves and our principles, to teach an ignorant and suspicious world that our aims and interests are identical with those of all good, aspiring women. Too long have we been silent under unjust and unholy charges,' she said. 'Year after year southern women have protested against the admission of colored women into any national organisation on the ground of the immorality of these women, and because all refutation has only been tried by individual work, the charge has never been crushed, as it could and should have been at first. . . . It is to break this silence not by noisy protestations of what we are not, but by a dignified showing of what we are and hope to become, that we are impelled to take this step, to make of this gathering an object lesson to the world. Our woman's movement is woman's movement in that it is led and directed by women for the good of women and men,' Ruffin stated, and implored that no 'color-line' be drawn (quoted in Flexner, 1979, p. 194, from quotes in Elizabeth L. Davis, *Lifting as They Climb*, 1933, and Gerda Lerner, *Black Woman in White America*, 1973).

Flexner (1979) reports that 'Mrs Ruffin's appeal for cooperation was not reciprocated by organized white club women, although efforts were made by individual clubs to break down the color line' (p. 195), for in 1900 she presented her credentials from *two* clubs at the General Federation of Women's Clubs. When it was realised that one club – the New Era – was composed of colored women, 'the uproar was not confined to verbal exchanges: efforts were made on the convention floor to snatch Mrs Ruffin's badge: she resisted stoutly, and the fracas was widely headlined' (ibid.). (Flexner also states that within the Women's Christian Temperance Union, black women were admitted, but in their own separate units, ibid., p. 196.)

Sojourner Truth

Within the suffrage movement much had changed since that day in May 1851, at the Akron Woman's Rights Convention, when Sojourner Truth, representing in her presence and her speech the common cause of blacks and women, had earned the respect and admiration of an audience in which many were hostile to the issues of both blacks and women. At that state, the principles established by Angelina Grimké Weld, and Sarah Grimké, and given unwavering support by women like Lucretia Mott, Stanton and Anthony, were firmly upheld. Both Grimké sisters 'were radical, even among abolitionists' says Lerner (1981), 'in their total acceptance of black women and in their emphasis on combating racism' (p. 97). Angelina Grimké had written of the slaves: 'They are our countrywomen, they are our sisters,' and it was in this tradition that Sojourner Truth spoke.

Recording that event in her 'Reminiscences' (Stanton et el., *History of Woman Suffrage*, 1881, vol. I, pp. 115–17), Frances Dana Gage tried to point to the viciousness of that prejudice, but by the turn of the century that 'overlap' in the causes of blacks and women had been to a large extent lost, along with the 'lesson' presented by Gage. Gage reports on the reception that Sojourner Truth received from some in 1851, when she entered the Church Hall in which the convention was being held: 'A buzz of disapprobation was heard all over the house, and there fell on the listening ear, "An abolition affair!" "Woman's rights and niggers!" "I told you so!" "Go it, darkey!" ' (ibid., p. 115).

Gage continues: 'There were very few women in those days who dared to "speak in meeting"; and the august teachers of the people were seemingly getting the better of us, while the boys in the galleries, and the sneerers among the pews, were hugely enjoying the discomfiture, as they supposed, of the "strong minded." Some of the tender-skinned friends were on the point of losing dignity, and the atmosphere betokened a storm. When, slowly from her seat in the corner arose Sojourner Truth, who, till now, had scarcely lifted her head. "Don't let her speak!" gasped half a dozen in my ear. She moved slowly and solemnly to the front, laid her old bonnet at her feet, and turned her great speaking eyes to me. There was a hissing sound of disapprobation above and below. I rose and announced "Sojourner Truth," and begged the audience to keep silence for a few moments' (ibid., pp. 115–16).

Sojourner Truth, according to Gage's description, was very tall, with piercing eyes, and she spoke in deep tones which reached every part of the Church Hall. And once she started talking in her pointed, witty and solemn way (ibid., p. 116), she changed the course of the meeting. Gage tries to convey some of what Sojourner Truth said: ' "Dat man ober dar say dat womin needs to be helped into carriages, and lifted ober ditches, and to hab de best place everywhar. Nobody eber helps me into carriages, or ober mud puddles, or gibs me any best place!" And raising herself to her full height, and her voice to a pitch like rolling thunder, she asked, "And a'n't I a woman? Look at me! Look at my arm! (and she bared her right arm to the shoulder, showing her tremendous muscular power). I have ploughed and planted and gathered into barns, and no man could head me. And a'n't I a woman? I could work as much and eat as much as a man – When I could get it – and bear de lash as well! And a'n't I a woman? I have borne thirteen chilern, and seen 'em mos' all sold off to slavery, and when I cried out with my mother's grief, none but Jesus heard me! And a'n't I a woman?" ' (ibid.).

Says Gage, 'Rolling thunder couldn't have stilled that crowd, as did those deep, wonderful tones, as she stood there with outstretched arms and eyes of fire' and got stuck into the men who were claiming that women had no rights, because Christ wasn't a woman!

'Raising her voice still louder, she repeated, "Whar did your Christ come from? From God and a woman! Man had nothin' to do wid Him." Oh', says Gage, 'what a rebuke that was to that little man' (ibid.) and regretful that she cannot remember all the details of that magnificent speech, she quotes Sojourner Truth's closing statements: ' "If de first woman God ever made was strong enough to turn de world upside down all alone, dese women togedder (and she glanced her eye over the platform) ought to be able to turn it back, and get it right side up again! And now dey is asking to do it, de men better let 'em" ' (ibid.).

The cheering was loud and long, says Gage: there was deafening applause at the end of almost every sentence as Sojourner Truth neatly stripped away the façade of men's rationale to expose women's oppression. 'She returned to her corner', says Gage, 'leaving more than one of us with streaming eyes and hearts beating with gratitude. She had taken us up in her strong arms and carried us safely over the slough of difficulty . . .' (ibid., pp. 116–17).

In September 1853, at the convention in New York – named the 'Mob Convention' because it was interrupted throughout by the mob who harassed speakers – Sojourner Truth spoke again. Her appearance on the platform 'was the signal for a fresh outburst from the mob; for at every session every man of them was promptly in his place at twenty five cents a head . . . Sojourner combined in herself, as an individual, the two most hated elements of humanity. She was black, and she was a woman, and all the insults that could be cast on color and sex were together hurled at her; but there she stood, calm and dignified, a grand wise woman, who could neither read nor write, and yet with deep insight could penetrate the very soul of the universe about her' (ibid., p. 567).

Again Sojourner Truth's speech was direct. She began by saying that she could see the spirit of the audience: 'I see that some of you have got the spirit of a goose, and some have got the spirit of a snake' (ibid.), and she referred to their hissing. Women want their rights, she said 'and they don't get 'em,' and she exposed the falseness of the belief that women were held in reverence as mothers. 'When she comes to demand 'em, don't you hear how sons hiss their mothers like snakes, because they ask for their rights; and can they ask for anything less?' Referring to the scriptures, Sojourner Truth stated: 'I do not want any man to be killed, but I am sorry to see them so short-minded. But we'll have our rights; see if we don't; and you can't stop us from them; see if you can. You may hiss as much as you like, but its comin'. Women don't get half as much rights as they ought to; we want more, and we will have it' (ibid., p. 568).

Kathryn Taylor (1971) has provided a brief biographical sketch of this amazing woman who was a 'wandering lecturer' (who walked up and down the eastern seaboard several times). She had had her autobiography published in 1850 (*Narrative of Sojourner Truth: a Northern Slave*),[12] which, along with the eight entries in the *History*, is one of the reasons that she is 'visible' and that something is known about her. After the Emancipation Proclamation freed southern slaves, Sojourner Truth devoted much of her life to helping them establish themselves, even to petitioning Congress to give ex-slaves free land and tools. Says Taylor, 'no one had the foresight to see the intelligence of what she was proposing' (1971, p. 12).

Lecturing on non-violence and woman's rights (and abolition, prior to the Civil War), Sojourner Truth was really a remarkable woman. In her, states Gerda Lerner (1981), 'the fusion of the abolition and woman's rights movements seemed personified' (p. 99).

In 1867 the first annual meeting of the American Equal Rights Association was held in New York: among the speakers were Elizabeth Cady Stanton, Frances Dana Gage, Mary Grew, Ernestine L. Rose, Lucy Stone, Rev. Olympia Brown, Susan B. Anthony, and Sojourner Truth. Lucretia Mott introduced Sojourner Truth (who was greeted with loud cheers), and her speech is reported in the *History* (1882, vol. II, p. 193).

'My friends, I am rejoiced that you are glad,' Sojourner Truth began, 'but I don't know how you will feel when I get through. I come from another field – the country of the slave. They have got their liberty – so much good luck to have slavery partly destroyed; not entirely. I want it root and branch destroyed. Then we will all be free indeed. I feel that if I have to answer for the deeds done in my body just as much as a man, I have a right to have just as much as a man. There is a great stir about colored men getting their rights, but not a word about the colored women: and if colored men get their rights, and not colored women theirs, you see the colored men will be masters over the women, and it will be just as bad as it was before. So I am for keeping the thing going while things are stirring; because if we wait till it is still, it will take a great while to get it going again ... I want women to have their rights. In the courts women have no right, no voice; nobody speaks for them. I wish woman to have her voice there among the pettifoggers. If it is not a fit place for women, it is unfit for men to be there' (ibid., p. 193).

And she continued, giving in her speech the basic outline of the case for equal rights – including equal economic rights: 'I have done a great deal of work; as much as a man, but did not get so much pay. I used to work in the field and bind grain keeping up with the cradler; but men doing no more got twice as much pay: so with the German women. They work in the field and do as much work, but do not get the pay. We do as much, we eat as much, we want as much. I suppose I am about the only colored woman that goes about to speak for the rights of the colored

---

[12] Gage also mentions the narrative of Sojourner Truth without apparently noting the contradiction: she is in other places described as illiterate. As illiteracy has been one means of keeping many out of the historical record, the publication of Sojourner Truth's narrative – by whatever means she employed – was both subversive and beneficial.

woman. I want to keep the thing stirring, now that the ice is cracked. What we want is a little money. You men know that you get as much again as women when you write, or for what you do. When we get our rights we shall not have to come to you for money, for then we shall have money enough in our own pockets; and maybe you will ask us for money. . . . You have been having our rights so long, that you think, like a slave holder, that you own us. I know that it is hard for one who has held the reins for so long to give up; it cuts like a knife' (ibid., p. 194).

Out of the experience of double oppression Sojourner Truth made many of the links between the two, and helped to expose many of the limitations, contradictions and falsities in the standard white-male justification for white, and male, supremacy. Stating that women were the slaves of men when one had been a black slave of whites was not only radical, but very forceful. There are few points raised among feminists of the time that Sojourner Truth does not understand or use, and some that she gives extra weight and power to. While acknowledging, however, that she is probably the only black woman appearing at such conventions, and arguing the case for women's rights – the right to own themselves, their own labour, and the fruits of their own labour – she does not seem to find her solitary black protest on such occasions sufficiently unusual to warrant explanation. She saw herself as being old ('I have been forty years a slave and forty years free, and would be here forty years more to have equal rights for all' (ibid., p. 193), and 'I am old enough to be the mother of all that is here' (ibid.)), and as having wisdom associated with age. She saw herself as having a role to play: 'I suppose I am kept here because something remains for me to do; I suppose I am yet to help to break the chain' (ibid., pp. 193–4). But it seems that she did not bring other black women with her. Is it right that she was almost a solitary black voice addressing white women and men?

Well aware of the ramifications of having 'rights' (she had once sued and won damages of $125 from a newspaper which called her a 'Black Witch' – see Taylor, 1971, p. 12), she spoke again on the second day of the 1867 convention and, in humorous vein, stated how she would like to go to the polls herself, and how women who worked and paid taxes as she did would find it no effort to vote. If women can dig up stumps, she said, 'they can vote. (Laughter.) It is easier to vote than dig stumps. (Laughter.) It doesn't seem hard work to vote, though I have seen some men that had a hard time of it' (Stanton et al., 1882, vol. II, p. 225).

After this convention, Sojourner Truth stayed at the Stanton household and asked the children to read to her all the accounts of the convention and the speeches in the papers for, as she said to them, 'I don't read much small stuff as letters, I read men and nations. I can see through a millstone, though I can't see through a spelling book. What a narrow idea a reading qualification is for a voter! I know and do what is right better than many big men who read. And there's that property qualification! just as bad. As if men and women themselves, who made money, were not of more value than the thing they made' (ibid., p. 926).

This record comes from Stanton, who on Sojourner Truth's instructions, wrote a letter to the Editor of the *World* on the press coverage of the convention. In it Stanton also reports Sojourner Truth as saying, 'Yes children, I am going to rouse the people on equality. I must sojourn once to the ballot box before I die ... Now, the first time I vote I'll see if a woman's vote looks any different from the rest – if it makes any stir or commotion' (ibid., p. 928). Confiding to the editor that Sojourner Truth *smoked*, Stanton ends the letter with a postscript, that 'She says she has been sent into the smoking-car so often she smoked in self defense – she would rather swallow her own smoke than another's' (ibid.).

Sojourner Truth's complete disregard for 'propriety', her shrewd analysis of power, her understanding of 'economics', her absence of deference or guile, make her to me a very attractive figure. She may have been a token figure among some of the white workers for woman's rights (was she the only black woman who came forward, or the only one 'adopted'?) or, perhaps even worse, she may have been tolerated for the 'character' that she lent the early movement (although so many of these women were so severely harassed for their views it seems unlikely that they would have sought any other form of 'novelty'), but I am grateful that she existed and that her presence was documented. It is symptomatic though, that there is some confusion about her age: Taylor gives the dates of her life as 1797–1883 (which would make her 86), but Sojourner Truth herself stated in 1867 that she was over 80, and in Volume III, *History of Woman Suffrage*, it is stated that there was proof that she was over one hundred years old and that she 'was a long resident and laborer in reform in Michigan, from which state she went out to the District of Colombia to befriend her people, as well as to other distant fields. She went to help feed and clothe the refugees in Kansas in 1879–80, and in reaching one locality she rode nearly a hundred miles in a lumber wagon. She closed her eventful life in Battle Creek, where she passed her last days, having reached the great age of one hundred and ten' (pp. 531–32).

She, too, seems to have evaded the injunction that one should become conservative with age.

Gerda Lerner has emphasised again and again that the oppression of women across cultures, classes, races, is not experienced in the *same* way, that black women experienced oppression differently from white women, and organised differently.[13] Their analysis of oppression, their strategies for change, had to take account of racial oppression in a way that white women did not. Throughout history, black women defined themselves first and foremost as members of an oppressed race, says Lerner, and, 'Expressions by black women concerning the priority of race oppression are numerous.' Frances Ellen Watkins Harper, for example, represented this position when she stated in 1870 'after all, whether they encourage or

---

[13] I share Lerner's reservations about simple generalisations, but I do, of course, think that there are many aspects of women's experience of oppression that cut across divisions of culture, ethnicity, class, and while I would not want to argue that such experience is the *same*, identical in every respect, I would want to assert that there are elements (e.g. availability to men) which are common to women under patriarchy and constitute a framework of shared experience. (*Actually – rereading this at 'proof' stage and now adding this comment – this looks repetitious: apologies for going on and on.*)

discourage me, I belong to this race . . . and when it is down, I belong to a down race; when it is up, I belong to a risen race' (Lerner, 1981, p. 68). No black women could ignore racial oppression when, even if they had tried to assert the fundamental nature of women's oppression, they came face to face with the racism of many of the white suffrage societies. As Lerner says, 'the constant compromise of suffrage leaders with the Southern viewpoint on the race issue inevitably led to discriminatory practices and racist incidents' (ibid., p. 104), and black women had to take on the extra burden of challenging the racism of their white sisters, and of educating them. As Ida B. Wells confronted Frances Willard, so too, says Lerner, did many black women continue 'to agitate this issue and to confront white women with a moral challenge to their professed Christianity' (ibid., p. 109).

From the outset I have not accepted the premise that if there is no evidence of women's activities in a particular area, it can be concluded that women were not active. There are many reasons in a male-dominated society why women's actions are 'erased' and many reasons in a white-dominated society why the actions of blacks are erased. That there are so few black women represented in this context of protest against male domination *may* mean that male domination has not demanded the same degree of active protest as race domination, but it can also mean – as the hundreds of examples quoted within this book help to suggest – that there were many black women, protesting vehemently about their double oppression – but they have disappeared.

7 Clues and curiosity

In the earlier rather than later stages of the nineteenth-century American woman's movement, there were many other women who made their own unique intellectual contribution and whose names are scattered – tantalisingly – through the pages of the *History of Woman Suffrage*.[14] Many of these women deserve greater attention and visibility; maybe more Matilda Joslyn Gages will be reclaimed.

Among those about whom I have questions is, for example, Paulina Wright Davis (1813–76), a wealthy woman who used some of her resources from 1853 to publish *The Una*, a journal devoted to the enfranchisement of women. She wanted women to know and understand more about their own bodies and to rethink the links and implications of modesty and ignorance. As early as 1844 she was giving lectures to women on women's physiology and anatomy with the aid of a human model (called a 'manikin',

---

[14] In the later stages of the nineteenth century the more dynamic and radical intellectual debates took place – understandably – outside the suffrage associations. So Emma Goldman, for example, is not mentioned in the *History* and there is no reference to Charlotte Perkins Gilman in the first four volumes (up to 1902), even though *Women and Economics* was first published in 1898.

the origins of the term displaying patriarchal influence). Davis had a long way to go to overcome the deeply engrained belief among women that they should not validate their own bodies – many of them used to swoon at her lectures.

Davis was the president at the first national woman's rights convention in Worcester in 1850, and expressed her sadness at the death of Margaret Fuller, and the loss this represented to the newly formed movement, for Davis stated that she herself had hoped that Fuller would have been president at the convention and that a letter asking her to accept the office had been sent to her before her death.

There is also Ernestine Rose (1810–92), who arouses my curiosity considerably. Born in Pyeterkow, Poland, she was outrageously rebellious for the time, rejecting at the age of fourteen the teachings of her rabbi father. As a young woman she travelled widely in Europe, visiting England and becoming acquainted with Elizabeth Fry and Robert Owen (whom she met in 1832 and whose principles she 'warmly espoused', Stanton et al., 1881, vol. I, p. 96). She married William Rose in England and in 1836 they went to New York where: 'Soon after her arrival she commenced lecturing on the evils of the existing social system, the formation of human character, slavery, the rights of woman, and other reform questions' (ibid., p. 97). Her ideas – if not her manner of implementation and lifestyle – were very similar to those of Frances Wright, whom she greatly admired and to whom she paid tribute at the Tenth National Woman's Rights Convention in New York in May 1860.

She lectured widely in America; according to all reports she was an excellent speaker whose clear and thoughtful analysis was much admired by those within the movement. She was, of course, consistently harassed. Her concerns ranged far beyond woman suffrage: she was an abolitionist, a 'free thinker', an advocate of a more equitable distribution of wealth and a defender of religious freedom. The *History of Woman Suffrage* (vol. I) states that she 'was sustained in her work by the earnest sympathy of her husband, who gladly furnished her with the means of making her extensive tours, so that through his sense of justice she was enabled to preach the Gospel of Woman's Rights, Anti-Slavery and Free Religion without money and without price' (ibid., p. 98).

When requested by letter by Susan B. Anthony to furnish some of the details of her life and her work for the *History*, Ernestine L. Rose wrote from London in 1877 and said that, much as she would like to, she was unable to do so, partly because she suffered so much from neuralgia but 'especially as I have nothing to refer to' (ibid.). She wrote that as she had never intended to publish anything about herself, and as she had never spoken from notes, she had no records. 'I had no other ambition except to work for the cause of humanity, irrespective of sex, sect, country or color' (ibid.), she declared, and, 'all that I can tell you is, that I used my humble powers to the uttermost, and raised my voice in behalf of Human Rights in general, and the elevation and Rights of Woman in particular, nearly all my life' (ibid., p. 99).

But there were some things she could remember: 'Yet in spite of hardships, for it was not as easy to travel at that time as now ... I look back to that time, when a stranger and alone, I went from place to place, in high ways and by-ways ... I can mention from memory the principal places where I have spoken. In the winter of 1836 and '37, I spoke in New York, and for some years after I lectured in almost every city in the state,' and she goes on to list state after state, and city after city, until 1850 when 'I attended the first National Woman's Rights Convention in Worcester, and nearly all the National and State conventions since, until I went to Europe in 1869. Returning to New York in 1874, I was present at the Convention in Irving Hall, the only one held during my visit to America' (ibid.).

Four years before Elizabeth Cady Stanton and Lucretia Mott met in London and decided to hold a woman's rights convention, and twelve years before it took place, Ernestine L. Rose − 'a stranger and alone' − was speaking on woman's rights in America. Many of those who heard her over the next thirty years were very impressed with her ideas. She was recalled as being a 'matchless speaker' with well-developed skills of argument and repartee: 'As a speaker she was pointed, logical and impassioned. She not only dealt in abstract principles clearly, but in their application touched the deepest emotions of the human soul' (ibid., p. 100). Despite the fact that many of her speeches are reported, and scattered throughout the *History*, little seems to be known about this remarkable woman. There has been little or no systematic study of her work that I know of, no collection and analysis of her speeches, and even trying to establish some of the most elementary details of her life is no easy task (particularly when one is in Britain).

Ernestine Rose felt that changes had been made during the time she was involved in women's rights and, looking back over her life in 1877, she wrote: 'I sent the first petition to the New York Legislature to give a married woman the right to hold real estate in her own name, in the winter of 1836 and '37, to which after a good deal of trouble I obtained five signatures. Some of the ladies said the gentlemen would laugh at them; others, that they had rights enough; and the men said the women had too many rights already. Woman at that time had not learned to know that she had any rights except those that man in his generosity allowed her; both have learned something since that time which they will never forget.' In commenting on how what was once radical becomes respectable, Rose says: 'I continued sending petitions with increased numbers of signatures until 1848 and '49, when the Legislature enacted the law which granted to women the right to keep what was her own. But no sooner did it become legal than all the women said, "Oh! that is right! We ought always to have had that" ' (ibid., p. 99).

Ernestine L. Rose is just one of the many who 'appear' in *History of Woman Suffrage* and then 'disappear' in any discussion of the period. Another woman who makes an entry and arouses interest but who proves to be elusive when attempts are made to follow some of the clues she leaves behind is Elizabeth Oakes Smith. Stanton et al. state that at the second National Convention in Worcester, in 1851, 'Mrs Elizabeth Oakes Smith made her first appearance on our platform. She was well known in the literary circles of New York as a writer of merit in journals and periodicals. She defended the Convention and its leaders through the columns of the *New York Tribune,* and afterwards published a series of articles entitled "Woman and her Needs." She early made her way into the lyceums and some pulpits never before open to women. Her "Bertha and Lily," a woman's rights novel, and her other writings were influential in moulding popular thought' (ibid., p. 231). And at the National American Convention of 1894, Anthony and Harper (1902) report that 'Elizabeth Cady Stanton (N.Y.) sent an eloquent tribute to the memory of Lucy Stone . . . Elizabeth Oakes Smith and Elizabeth Peabody' (p. 227). In between, Elizabeth Oakes Smith made some stirring speeches (and did some passionate writing) which indicated that she was a woman of many ideas one of which was what the reception was likely to be for women with ideas.

'My friends, do we realize for what purpose we are convened?' she asked in 1852 at the Syracuse National Convention, 'Do we fully understand that we aim at nothing less than an entire subversion of the present order of society, a dissolution of the whole existing social compact? . . . We are said to be a "few disaffected, embittered women, met for the purpose of giving vent to petty personal spleen and domestic discontent." I repel the charge; and I call upon every woman here to repel the charge', and she went on to urge that women should have their own journal so that they were not at the mercy of the male-controlled press, which mocked and misrepresented them. But she acknowledged that there were problems: 'We should have a literature of our own, a printing press and a publishing house, and tract writers and distributors, as well as lectures and conventions; and yet I say this to a race of beggars, for women have no pecuniary resources' (Stanton, vol. I, et al., 1881, pp. 522–4). Little has changed; the reason for women having control over their own words and images remains, as does the reason that such control is – with some few exceptions – beyond our grasp.

This speech of Elizabeth Oakes Smith was followed almost immediately by one from the Reverend Antoinette Brown, a woman who Alice Rossi (1974) states, 'is the least well known but in my view the most interesting of these early pioneers in the woman's movement in the nineteenth century. She had a far more finely honed intellect than most of the early leaders, as sharp in purely intellectual reasoning as Elizabeth Cady Stanton's was in political and ideological thinking' (pp. 343–4). What little is known about Antoinette Brown (later Blackwell) is fascinating – and impressive – but it is significant to note that the only source of her quoted by Rossi is an unpublished manuscript of 1909, by Sarah Gibson. Antoinette Brown has obviously attracted little attention, scholarly or otherwise.

Yet many of her ideas are fundamental to the modern women's movement, some of them being but fairly recent 'rediscoveries'. Crucial to her analysis was the concept of men having decreed themselves as representative of humanity and of men having taken their own experience as the totality of human experience, thereby rendering the whole realm of women's experience as non-existent. This understanding emerges in part in the speech

Antoinette Brown gave after Elizabeth Oakes Smith, on the law, in which she said: 'Man cannot represent woman. . . . The law is wholly masculine; it is created and executed by man. The framers of all legal compacts are restricted to the masculine standpoint of observation; to the thought, feelings and biases of man' (Stanton et al., 1881, vol. I, p. 524). Her development of the concept of male-as-norm is, however, even more definitive in her later critique of Darwin and Spencer and the theory of evolution, and while it might be expected that someone with the theological training of Antoinette Brown may have been critical of Darwin and evolution, on theological grounds, this was not the substance of her analysis or her objections; she came to be critical of both theology and evolution on feminist grounds!

Her feminist response to theological teaching was evident from the outset in that she defied the traditional ruling that women could not be ordained in the Church and used the scriptures to support her stance. At Oberlin College, where she deliberately sought out the 'disreputable' Lucy Stone, Antoinette Brown continued to challenge the interpretation of the bible provided by men, and Rossi (1974) says that her 'senior class essay, later published in the *Oberlin Quarterly Review*, was an exegisis of the biblical injunction "let women keep silence in the churches" ' (pp. 341–2). At this stage and for a few years afterwards, Antoinette Brown registered her protest within the framework of conventional religion, but Rossi reports that during the winter of 1853 Brown read Darwin and Spencer and that this was no doubt a contributory cause to her loss of faith and her resignation from her parish in South Butler, New York. She went to work for Horace Greeley as a reporter and writer.

In 1875, after her marriage to Samuel Blackwell (and seven pregnancies), she published *The Sexes Throughout Nature* and it is in this that her account of the male-as-norm – as it is manifested in the new sciences of evolution and sociology – is made crystal clear. In a manner taken up by Elaine Morgan (1972) and Ruth Hubbard (1981) over a century later, Antoinette Brown Blackwell asks why it is that men should decree that only men have evolved. Men have 'interpreted facts by the accepted theory that the male is the representative type of the species – the female a modification preordained in the interest of reproduction,' she states, and because of this they have developed and justified a concept and theory of man as the primary line of evolution (quoted in Rossi, 1974, p. 357). (This point was also taken up later by Frances Swiney, 1908.)

Men have argued that woman's development has been arrested by reproductive functions, states Antoinette Brown Blackwell, but they have never thought of woman being complete in herself, and have never looked to see whether there has been equivalent development in woman; because she is different from them she has just been dismissed (Rossi, 1974, p. 357). Mr Spencer may explain it scientifically in terms of the female being *subtracted* from the male, and Mr Darwin may explain it scientifically in terms of the female being *added on to* the male, but either way, argues Blackwell, the male remains the norm in the minds of these men, while the female is measured only in relation to them and is perceived as 'inferior'. What is required is for women to begin their own study, starting with the premise that woman is a complete human being whose experience is valid: 'Only a woman can approach the subject from a feminine standpoint; and there are none but beginners among us in this class of investigations. However great the disadvantages are, these will never be lessened by waiting . . .' (quoted in Rossi, 1974, p. 360).

This was the rationale for the beginning of women's studies in the late 1960s and early 1970s. Waiting for 'experts' to teach the courses and undertake research was not considered a very practical idea because it was only *in* the teaching and the research that women began to understand the extent to which we had been misled by the male-as-norm knowledge constructed by men (Roberts, 1976; Spender, 1981a). Antoinette Brown Blackwell perfectly understood this; she understood the way in which women's ignorance could be used against them as an intimidatory weapon to prevent them from constructing their own knowledge, and to keep them in their ignorant and 'manageable' state. But her insights were not available as guidance for those early ventures in women's studies; she too has been erased so that we have been deprived of our heritage.

There was also Louisa May Alcott (1832–88) who, while she was never a committed member of the organised woman's movement, was none the less committed to achieving the same aims, and used much of her writing to present the possibilities and the difficulties of women's existence. In 1873 she wrote to Lucy Stone and said: 'I am so busy just now proving "woman's right to labor", that I have no time at all to help prove "woman's right to vote" ' (Stanton et al., 1882; vol. II, p. 831), and in 1873 *Work: A Study of Experience* was published. Sarah Elbert (1977) has said of *Work* that it is 'an expression of Alcott's feminist principles and a major effort toward synthesizing in popular, readable form the broad set of beliefs encompassing family, education, suffrage, labor and the moral reform of social life that defined feminist ideology in the nineteenth century' (p. x).

Alcott had herself sampled the problems of being a working woman – being employed as domestic servant (albeit dignified with the title of 'companion' but being nothing other than a 'galley slave'), nurse (during the Civil War), seamstress and laundress, but then, like Harriet Martineau (whom she admired), she found herself not only financially supporting herself and her family, once she had become an established writer, but was expected (and appears willingly to have agreed) to provide all those services to the family required of middle-class nineteenth-century daughters. Her life is a series of shuffles, says Elbert, from writing to domestic commitments. She 'continued to hold herself responsible for the domestic chores associated with women's role even as she pursued a serious literary career', and she was at the one time acting as an editor of a children's magazine, writing her stories, nursing her ailing mother and sewing for the family (ibid., p. xvii). Although at one stage she managed to move to Boston, she was constantly interrupted and recalled to home: 'Until the end of her life, Louisa's room of her own was only a temporary one in which to escape family pressures and labor for their support' (ibid.).

Her diary entries help to suggest the pressures on women who had modified their role sufficiently to be able to engage in meaningful and rewarding work, but who had not managed to modify the demands still placed on women within the family:

May 1973

D F wanted a dozen little tales and agreed to pay $50 a piece, if I give up other things for this. Said I would as I can do two a day and can keep house between times. Cleaned and grubbed and didn't mind the change. Let head rest and hands and feet do all the work . . .   Cold and dull but the thought of May . . . (her sister whom she was supporting in Europe) . . . free and happy was my comfort as I messed about (quoted in Elbert, 1977, p. xx).

There is some evidence that Louisa May Alcott was more concerned with extending women's sphere than in challenging the origin of women's role (with her acceptance of the 'double shift' and her constant concern over her father's dignity – and comfort – being two illustrations of this), but there can be no doubt about her commitment to the woman's cause – it was a major part of her life and her work, says Elbert. Her feminism demands more attention, as does that of Maria Mitchell (1818–89), another woman who worked outside the suffrage movement (and of whom no mention is made in the *History*) and who experienced from 1865 till 1888 at Vassar many of the problems that women confront today in the academic community. An astronomer, the first woman admitted to the American Academy of Arts and Sciences, a member of the Association for the Advancement of Science *and* president of the Association for the Advancement of Women (1874), she was the most distinguished member of staff at Vassar. She realised, on the death of the founder, Mathew Vassar, that the position women had won within the college was rapidly being undermined, as men were favoured in the new appointments. She toured America and lectured on astronomy, and on women's rights and wrongs, and demonstrated that it was a fallacy for women to believe that things would gradually improve: because men's attitudes about women's 'inferiority' had *not* changed, there was always the danger that men would take back some of women's hard won gains. And because men still possessed the power, women were not in a position to stop them.[15]

This is not the only parallel with contemporary times: Maria Mitchell also came up against the establishment because of her attitude to teaching and learning and her reluctance to promote competition – and failure. Kathryn Taylor (1971) says that: 'She refused to grade, feeling you couldn't judge a human mind in terms of a letter grade' (p. 47). She was an extremely successful, inspiring, and unorthodox teacher who appears to have had

[15] This has its parallels in contemporary abortion law reform as well where women cannot assume that reforms, once passed, will endure. In most Western countries consistent attempts are made to modify the laws and women are constantly having to defend them against erosion, having to fight to preserve a legal 'status quo' which challenges the unequal social 'status quo' of the sexes.

little difficulty in drawing students from their beds at night to 'sweep the
skies'.

These – and many, many more women – are part of our relatively
recent heritage, yet they have been erased from the traditions into which
most of us have been initiated. Their disappearance constitutes no puzzle
– on the contrary, it is perfectly predictable in a male-dominated society
where men, as the 'representatives' of humanity, have considered only what
suits them as knowledge worthy of transmission. And so men sustain the
system they established, decreeing that women's experience is unworthy of
inclusion in the record, and that because they are not in the record, women
are unworthy. This has been their scientific base for objective knowledge,
as Antoinette Brown Blackwell pointed out; it has been the means by which
men have appropriated the fruit of women's intellectual toil, as Matilda
Joslyn Gage pointed out; it is the means which women are exorcised from
history, as Elizabeth Cady Stanton, Susan B. Anthony, Matilda Joslyn Gage
and Ida Husted Harper appreciated, and determined to change. But I
suspect the process is at work just as much today as it was when these
women formulated their ideas about its existence and operation.

We have been robbed of the intellectual and creative energy of all these
women in the same way that Matilda Joslyn Gage describes herself as
robbed of the labours of her foremothers. And we have witnessed how the
theft is carried out. We have seen the harassment that these women were
subjected to and we can observe the results. The barrage of accusations
and threats and acts of violence which were directed against them – the
charge that their efforts were futile, their movement had failed, that they
wore the wrong clothes; the taunt (which could only come from a male
perspective in which the male was considered central and that without
'male' there was 'nothing') that they were unable to get a man because of
their (significantly) 'strong-mindedness', and the dismissal of them as embittered and frustrated; the threat against them of patriarchal (and hence
divine) authority; the verbal and physical abuse. All this helps to confirm
Gage's thesis of ungovernable male frenzy and emotionality, for it seems
that the male has done almost anything rather than take the female and
her ideas seriously.

(B)

GREAT BRITAIN

1 Objections that did not cease: Anna Wheeler (1785–?)

Although we may have been led to believe that women in Britain were perfectly content with their lot and made no protests about male power during the first half of the nineteenth century, this reveals more about the process of 'selective' history than about women's activities, for there was a steady stream of objections during the first fifty years, which built up into the more widespread and popular protest of the second half of the century. But while women both sides of the Atlantic (and across the Pacific as well) were questioning the social arrangements, challenging men's view of themselves and the world, analysing the relationship between the sexes, resisting the prevailing orthodoxy and reconceptualising human possibilities, there were some differences between Britain and America in terms of the experience of women and the ideas for change that they generated.

America was a 'new' country where the possibility of change had been realised and where there was faith that the future would be even greater than the glorious and recent past; Britain had traditions that were looked to for guidance and where the past (or parts of it) was combed for illumination. This different ethos in each country led to some differences in analyses, and arguments for change. If there were differences, there were also similarities; the problem was much the same in both countries. Women in both countries were not untouched by reform movements and, while Chartism and the Corn Law League did not constitute the same searching and searing issue as the abolition of slavery, they were sufficient to make some women in Britain aware of the extent of their own oppression. They also helped to provide some women with practical political experience in organising, canvassing, petitioning, etc.

But there does not seem to be a British equivalent to the decision of Lucretia Mott and Elizabeth Cady Stanton to hold a woman's rights convention, and no single act – such as the holding of that convention – to mark the beginnings of a woman's movement. From the records that have been preserved and which are accessible, however (for there is no equivalent, either, to the *History of Woman Suffrage*[1]), it is obvious that a

---

[1] The absence of a single source such as the *History* is offset to some extent by the

number of written protests were made, in a variety of forms, and that this could be taken as an indication that for many women, the position of their sex – and the position of the male sex – were in need of drastic change.

The framework in which British women operated, in which they assessed the relationship of the sexes, and in which they sought explanations and solutions, varied considerably from their American counterparts, for in turning to past traditions for insights they quickly came to recognise that their legal and political position, far from improving over the centuries, had deteriorated (see Charlotte Stopes, 1894). Whereas Matilda Joslyn Gage's assertion that women had once enjoyed political rights and had been systematically robbed of them was a startlingly new perspective for many American women reared on the doctrine of progressive freedom, the existence of *ancient rights*, some of which still survived, was known and accepted by many in Britain. It was relatively easy to establish that under these ancient rights women had enjoyed many and extensive powers (as Gage had demonstrated), even as recently as the seventeenth and eighteenth centuries, and that it was *custom* and not *law* which prevented women from exercising such rights in the nineteenth century.

For some women in Britain, then, the position was perfectly clear; the rights which they had once enjoyed, and which represented a more equitable distribution of power between the sexes, had been taken away from them and they wanted them back. They were not demanding something *new*; they were reclaiming something *old*. It was probably the fact that some of the ancient rights survived, and were somewhat anomalous, that made British women more disposed to think of the explanation and solution to the existing problem of sexual inequality in these terms, for the persistence of *some* of these ancient rights made the restoration of *all* of them seem more plausible and more possible. Helen Blackburn (1902) has pointed out that, while it might have been rare for a woman to be the head of state, custodian of a castle, hereditary sheriff, or to be called upon to attend the monarch in council or camp, grant charters or vote for the knights of the shire, women *did* perform these functions, 'they were facts that actually

---

availability of a few sources provided by some who were involved in the movement and who had different perspectives and different backgrounds: while by no means an exhaustive list, there is for example Helen Blackburn's account, *Women's Suffrage* (1902) and Millicent Fawcett's *Women's Suffrage* (1911), as well as such personal accounts as Emmeline Pankhurst's *My Own Story* (1914), Sylvia Pankhurst's *The Suffragette Movement* (1931), Annie Kenney's *Memories of a Militant* (1924) and Hannah Mitchell's *The Hard Way Up* (1977). Ray Strachey's *The Cause: A Short History of the Women's Movement in Great Britain* (1928) attempts to evaluate the whole process from the position of one involved for only part of the time and from a particular perspective, and Josephine Kamm has surveyed the period in *Rapiers and Battleaxes: The Women's Movement and its Aftermath* (1966). Roger Fulford's account, *Votes for Women* (1958), is from the point of view of one who was not involved. There have also been studies of particular aspects of the period – for example, Antonia Raeburn's *Militant Suffragettes* (1974), Constance Rover's *Women's Suffrage and Party Politics in Britain, 1866–1914* (1967), and *Love, Morals and the Feminists* (1970) and Andrew Rosen's *Rise Up, Women! The Militant Campaign of the Women's Social and Political Union 1903–1914* (1974). Nearly all those who have studied the period, however, lament the paucity of scholarly activity, the number of primary sources that remain unsorted and unstudied.

happened; when they did happen there was nothing extraordinary or exceptional about them; they were incidents in the natural order of things' (p. 4).

In America, where such ancient rights had not been preserved in the constitution, they did not happen; it was not part of the natural order of things for women to enjoy such political power – no matter how rare. So what was considered natural, and put forward as divinely ordained, varied somewhat from one continent to the other – not that this made any substantial difference to the problem, or to the resistance to change. British women did not have to look back very far to document the evidence of rights once enjoyed and since removed. For example, Helen Blackburn (1902), quoted the case of Anne Clifford (1589–1675), Countess of Dorset, Montgomery and Pembroke, who was one of 'the last women of the old traditions', who had 'upheld her lawful claim as hereditary Sheriff of Westmorland against King James I. himself, and she defended her castles against the troops of Cromwell' (p. 7). Of the same woman, Roger Fulford (1958) says, that when asked by one of the Secretaries of State in the reign of Charles II to use her influence in favour of a particular candidate, she replied: 'I have been bullied by an usurper (Cromwell): I have been ill-treated by a court (Charles II) but I won't be dictated to by a subject. Your man shall not stand' (p. 16).

Apart from individual women who had exercised considerable political power, there was also the law, which had been tested in 1733 when, in a local election, Sarah Bly was elected as sexton of one of the city churches, primarily because forty *women* householders had voted for her, while only twenty-two had voted for her opponent. So her opponent tried to have her election ruled invalid 'on the grounds that women voters should have been excluded' (ibid., p. 17). After much procrastination, Lord Chief Justice Lee ruled that there was no law which positively excluded women from voting or which confined it to men. While American women had used the same argument that there was no law which excluded them from citizenship and therefore from the right to vote, British women were in a stronger position with this ruling of Lord Chief Justice Lee. But this too was taken away from them with the 1832 Reform Act, which specifically stated – for the first time – that voting was confined to male persons. With this Act British women were in much the same position as American women (where the word 'male' was inserted in the constitution for the first time in 1868 with the Fourteenth Amendment) and were required to change not just *convention*, but the *law*, in order to reclaim the rights they had once enjoyed and which symbolised the political equality of the sexes. This is why many women in Britain looked to parliament as a means of regaining the rights they had lost and which they believed, once restored, would make a difference to their status.

That many people had much to say about the oppression of women at the beginning of the nineteenth century is demonstrable. *The Feminist Controversy in England 1788–1810*, edited by Gina Luria (1974), contains forty-four titles, reprinted in eighty-nine volumes, among which is Mary Hays's (1798) *An Appeal to the Men of Great Britain in Behalf of Women* and Mary Ann Radcliffe's *The Female Advocate or an Attempt to Recover the Rights of Women from Male Usurpation (1810)*. Roger Fulford (1958) mentions another publication of 1825, *An Appeal of One Half the Human Race, Women, against the Pretensions of the Other Half, Men, to Retain them in Political, and thence in Civil and Domestic Slavery: In Reply to a Paragraph of Mr Mill's Celebrated Article on Government*. Discussing this book, and its implications, Fulford tells a most interesting tale, although he does not always discern the significance of his own statements. In *Votes for Women* Fulford dates the feminist protest and the demand for the restoration of political rights – to his mind one and the same thing – from this 1825 publication. (He does acknowledge the existence of Mary Woll-stonecraft as the *only* earlier protester, but dismisses *A Vindication of the Rights of Woman* partly because it is not a demand for the vote, but partly because it is derived from 'the revolutionary outpourings of Tom Paine', 1958, p. 19; evidently her 'ravings' were not even original.) The struggle began, says Fulford, with this book by one William Thompson, and Fulford deplores the fact that for so long Thompson has been overlooked, for he was a brilliant philosopher, evidenced not only by this particular treatise but by the fact that he was 'in reality the teacher and inspiration of Karl Marx' (ibid., p. 20) (which, given Thompson's feminist sympathies and Karl Marx's absence of them, suggests that Marx did not learn everything his teachers taught!). Thompson, this great thinker who instigated the demand for political rights for women, has not been treated at all fairly, laments Fulford, and he was even omitted from the *Dictionary of National Biography* until included by Leslie Stephen in the three additional volumes of 1901. And women who owe him so much have also treated him badly, for *he* was never featured on the banners of the women suffrage marchers, even though they ostensibly depicted the individuals who had made a contribution to the cause.

But then Fulford mentions that there was a 'co-author'. Needless to say, there is not the same concern shown for *her* disappearance. Her name was 'Mrs Wheeler'; she is described disparagingly; her contribution commented on but by no means commended. We are informed that she came from Ireland, that she was the daughter of a highly respected archdeacon, that she married an Irish squire who 'possibly irritated by her opinions, took to the hunting field and the bottle' (ibid., p. 21), that her daughter (nameless) married the great novelist (named) Bulwer Lytton, that she was the great-grandmother of the later suffragette Lady Constance Lytton; that she left her husband, 'bolted' from Ireland and threw herself on the pro-tection of an uncle – and, if this is not enough – that she is to be remembered for the influence she had over the philosopher, Thompson, and for the way in which 'dukes, diamonds and dinner parties, captured her shallow mind' (ibid.).

There is no doubt in Roger Fulford's mind about the importance of 'Mrs Wheeler'. Outlining some of the background to the book in which Anna Wheeler is acknowledged as a co-author, Fulford explains that in 1823 James Mill (the father of John Stuart Mill) wrote an article on government for the *Encyclopaedia Britannica* in which he stated that

women had no genuine interests of their own which necessitated independent political representation, but were adequately represented through men.
Says Fulford, 'The feelings of Mrs Wheeler – a lady of powerful, volatile
but injured spirit, can be imagined as she read these fateful lines. The
memory of all her wrongs must have come flooding back, the child-bride
of fifteen, the succession of dead babies, the grey remorseless rain of Ballywire, County Limerick, with her husband Francis Massey (sic) Wheeler
roaring in the background' (probably because, as has already been stated,
he was provoked by her opinions), *she*, 'to depend for her political rights
on the roistering squire of Ballywire! She poured her tribulation into the
receptive ear of Philosopher Thompson and together they concocted an
answer to Mill' (ibid., p. 22).

This portrayal bears no resemblance to the one provided by Thompson
himself, to the one provided in Bauer and Ritt, 1979 or the one provided
by Richard Pankhurst in *William Thompson (1775–1833): Britain's Pioneer Socialist, Feminist, and Co-operator* (1954), but it bears many resemblances to the standard portrayal of women in a male-dominated society,
and a striking resemblance to the portrayal of Harriet Taylor, another
acknowledged co-author with a male of intellectual stature.

Fulford himself is not oblivious to the similarities, even if their significance eludes him. He notes that the relationships of John Stuart Mill
and Harriet Taylor, and that of William Thompson and Anna Wheeler,
have something in common, for in their strange way 'both Mill and Thompson believed that they were merely the amanuenses for ladies gifted with
minds of singular force' (ibid., p. 23) and that as Mill had conveyed a false
image of Harriet Taylor as a woman of intellectual standing so too it was
'the devotion of Philosopher Thompson [which] made him also magnify
the tricklings of a "suburban mind" into the "calm stream of argument"'
(ibid.). That men *steal* women's creativity and intellectuality for their own
ends is a thesis admirably substantiated by Fulford's endeavours, and that
women's resources of their own are insignificant, of no value, and readily
available for use and transformation by profound men, is so much part of
Fulford's taken-for-granted-reality, he is not even aware of the distortions
and misrepresentations he so assiduously constructs.

Thompson – who claims to be committed to the principle of woman's
full humanity and to the establishment of the recognition that women have
resources of their own which they must be free to use in their own interest
– leaves no doubt as to who has been his instructor in these matters. The
book begins with an 'Introductory Letter to Mrs Wheeler' and the statement
that he has tried to arrange the 'expression of those feelings, sentiments,
and reasonings, which have emanated from your mind' and while he cannot
speak for women, or with a sensibility equal to Anna Wheeler's – because
he is a man – he can state the plain facts and reasons of the case; he can
prove that it is impossible for women to be represented through men. But,
'to separate your thoughts from mine were now to me impossible,' he says
to Anna Wheeler, for 'so amalgamated are they with my own' (1825, pp.
v–vi); the work is a collaborative one.

Thompson continues with: 'I love not literary piracy any more than any other species of piracy: I wish to give everything to its right owner,' which is why he insists that Anna Wheeler's contribution be acknowledged. He would have preferred *her* to write the book, so he states, for she has proved that she could do so in the many articles which she has written under a feigned name (unfortunately, he does not say what her pseudonym or pseudonyms were, so this remains for me just another fragment of tantalising information). But circumstances will not permit her to do so, and he therefore has taken on the task of presenting the shared ideas of two individuals, of voicing 'the protest of at least one man and woman' against the so-called system of morals which is nothing other than a mass of hypocrisy, preached but not practised by knaves, enforced by blood and fear, and designed to keep women as slaves in blind, uninquiring obedience (ibid., pp. vi–x).

The analysis of inequality which he presents makes relevant reading almost a 160 years later. Individual competition, he says, leading to the accumulation of individual wealth, 'is the master-key and moving principle of the whole social organization,' and while it remains 'it seems impossible – even were all unequal legal and unequal moral restraints removed, and were no secret current of force or influence exerted to baffle new regulations of equal justice – that women should attain to equal happiness (as measured by equal wealth) with men.' For women – by virtue of time out for gestation and rearing of infants – would never be able to compete on the same terms as men and would never, therefore, be as successful in acquiring wealth (and happiness); while individual competition prevails women are doomed to inequality.

Leaving aside his (and her) failure to question the social arrangements with regard to child-rearing, Thompson is nevertheless declaring that men have made up the rules on terms that are convenient for them and that women cannot expect to compete successfully: women must set their own terms and they must not be based on individual competition and the accumulation of wealth (ibid., p. x). 'Though in point of knowledge, talent and virtue', he says, women might become men's equals, 'in point of independence *arising from wealth*, they must under the present principle of social arrangements, remain inferior' (ibid., p. xi). Now, 157 years later and with the advantage of the United Nation's (conservative) statistics that women own less than 1 per cent of the world's wealth, it is no doubt in order to say that William Thompson (and Anna Wheeler) had a point when they stated that women would be unsuccessful if they tried to compete with men on men's terms for wealth; 157 years after their prophetic words, however, we are no closer than they were to realising an alternative.

Not content with their *natural* advantage, argues Thompson, men have made even more terms designed to ensure that women are eliminated from *competition* and unable to acquire financial resources. They have set up 'the existing system of marriage: under which for the mere faculty of eating, breathing and living, in whatever degree of comfort husbands may think fit, women are reduced to domestic slavery, without will of their own, or power of locomotion, otherwise than as permitted by their respective masters' (ibid., p. xi).

Apart from Mary Astell, I think the critique of marriage as embodied in the *Appeal* is the most scathing I have ever encountered. I have often argued that if tomorrow every woman – in London, for example – were financially independent, few would be the marriages or heterosexual relationships that would last to the following day. Thompson makes the same point, stating that the true test of the relationship between women and men is that of *unbought and uncommanded* affection, and that if women had no need to be bought and no necessity to be commanded, men might find themselves confined to each others' company (ibid., p. xii). He makes short shrift of the argument that women freely enter marriage.

Men have set up the terms of marriage purely and simply for their own convenience, he argues, for, 'From regulating the terms of this pretended contract, women have been as completely excluded as bullocks, or sheep, or any other animals subjugated to man, have been from determining the regulations of commons or slaughter houses. Men enacted, that is to say, *willed* the terms, let women like them or not: man to be the owner, master and ruler of everything, even to the minutest action, and most trifling article of property brought into the common stock by the woman; woman to be the moveable property, and ever-obedient servant, to the bidding of man' (ibid., p. 57). It is absurd to suggest in this context that women may choose to marry or not to marry, he argues: if they do not, they will starve for, by creating the laws, by 'depriving women of knowledge and skill, excluding them from the benefit of all judgement and mind-creating offices and trusts, cutting them off almost entirely from the participation, by succession or otherwise, of property, and from its uses and exchanges – are women kindly told, "they are free to marry or not". Things are so arranged, knowledge, property, civil as well as political exclusions, man's public opinion, that the great majority of adult women must marry on whatever terms their masters have willed or starve' (ibid.).

Finding this book – rather late in my research efforts, I am afraid – has proved to be extremely disconcerting, for most of the tenets I subscribe to today are outlined and developed within its pages; it provides a synthesis of most of the fundamental feminist arguments, past and present, and until relatively recently I did not even know of its existence. How many more are there, I wonder, and how long must we go on conceptualising the case only to 'lose' it, instead of building upon it? To me, the *Appeal* deserves at least as much if not more attention than *The Subjection of Women*, and I cannot help but ask whether the relative visibility of one and the invisibility of the other is related to *socialism*; I can certainly answer the question to my own satisfaction!

Like Astell, Thompson emphasises that men allocate to women the qualities they despise in themselves and expediently insist that women cultivate intellectual, moral, financial – and even physical dependence. Men will not allow you strength, he says to women, they call it *unfeminine* in you, for strength 'would cause you to approach too nearly to those high prerogatives in your masters, with whom to aim at equality is the summit of female audacity if not wickedness' (ibid., pp. 190–1). You are systematically and deliberately robbed of every intellectual and moral quality, he states, which is then 'sacrificed at the shrine of man's all devouring jealousy, of his most immoral love of superiority', for only by robbing woman of all her intellectual and creative resources can man protect his usurped power. He will not even let you speak, he argues passionately, particularly not in public, or to other women, for the public arena which is a source of influence and intellectual improvement has also been monopolized by man' (ibid., p. 191). And when you protest at this injustice, he warns, will not 'men pleasantly tell you to be patient, to continue submissive, lest these chains should be rendered more galling'? Do not believe them, he urges women, for 'That they are not more galling is entirely owing to man's calculation of his own interest, not your happiness. . . . For *his own sake* man is restrained; he dare not, he cannot render your chains more galling' (ibid., p. 194).

These are not the aspects of the book chosen for emphasis by Roger Fulford, who concentrates on the 'forthright' treatment of sexuality. According to him, the book is 'powerfully argued and splendidly written. On sexual matters there are no feeble beatings about the bush but the author plunges straight in forcing the reader's attention over and over again to the horrors and dangers of what he calls "the shared pillow". Marriage is merely a superstition called in aid by men when they wish to admit women to the high honour of becoming their "involuntary breeding machines and household slaves" ' (Fulford, 1958, p. 23).

The origin of this particular description of Thompson's marriage is *woman*; marriage is described and explained from the perspective of those who are dominated and therefore stands in stark contrast with the conventional view of marriage which emanates from those who do the dominating. Fulford notes only that the description is *different* and *dramatic* and asks not how Thompson came to perceive the view of someone who is available, who is bought, and who is commanded. 'The recurring theme of this book', says Fulford, 'is that married women are slaves', that home is the eternal prison house of the wife, that the husband paints the picture of home as a haven of calm bliss while for the wife it is a form of hell, where the house and everything in it is his, 'and of all the fixtures most abjectly his is his breeding machine, the wife' (ibid.). But Fulford makes no connection between this thesis of the reputable and admirable philosopher Thompson, and the plight and flight of Anna Wheeler. She – and the position of the married woman – remains gloriously unlinked in his intellectual framework. This is obviously not what Thompson intended; it was the personal experience of Anna Wheeler *as a wife* that informed his thesis, and it was her descriptions and explanations – made available to him – that allowed him to formulate and develop it.

I can find very little about Anna Wheeler. Roger Fulford kindly provides a footnote for those interested in pursuing the details of William Thompson's life (he refers to Pankhurst, 1954), which does yield some information about her. Richard Pankhurst says that Anna Wheeler was born in 1785, 'the youngest daughter of the famous Irish Protestant divine, Archbishop Doyle' (1954, p. 70). She married at the age of 15, and 'Her marriage was to prove a disastrous failure. Massy Wheeler was a dipsomaniac and degenerating rapidly' (ibid.). Their home was falling into decay, he was in a nightly drunken stupor, and within twelve years she gave birth to six children, four of whom died. 'Nevertheless,' adds Pankhurst, 'endowed with remarkable tenacity and strength of character, she persevered with a systematic study of social and political philosophy, obtaining by post from London the works of the foremost exponents of egalitarian democracy, among them the still heatedly debated writings of the pioneer feminist revolutionary, Mary Wollstonecraft' (ibid., p. 71).

'Local opinion', adds Pankhurst, 'commiserated Massy Wheeler on account of his wife's absorption in study, for despite his own alcoholic failing it was held that her duty as a married woman was to immerse herself wholly in the interests of her spouse.' Her daughter Rosina later complained that Mary Wollstonecraft's writings had warped her mother's mind (ibid.). She left her husband (who died in 1820) to live with her uncle, Sir John Doyle, the Governor of Guernsey, and from then on she moved within the foremost intellectual circles of her day. She was a friend of Robert Owen, of Jeremy Bentham, of Charles Fourier and of Flora Tristan; she was the centre of a Saint-Simonian circle and was referred to as the 'Goddess of Reason' and 'the most gifted woman of the age' (ibid., pp. 73–4).

She 'became widely known in the metropolis where she took an important place in the Co-operative, Feminist, and Saint-Simonian circles. Disraeli described her as "something between Jeremy Bentham and Meg Merrilies, very clever, but awfully revolutionary." George Jacob Holyoake records that she was a frequent writer in Co-operative periodicals and delivered "well-reasoned" lectures which "attracted considerable attention" ' (ibid., p. 74).

She was a critic of organised religion (she referred to Christ as 'our Eastern philosopher') and an even more passionate critic of patriarchy. 'Society, she concluded, considered women should have no feelings of any kind but should "pretend to an overwhelming degree of admiration for their respective masters, whether wise or foolish, cruel or kind" ' (ibid., p. 72). 'She urged women "not to leave the bitter inheritance of ignorance and slavery" to their daughters . . . Were she to die without a sign expressive of her "horror, indignation and bitter contempt" for the "masked barbarism" of "so-called civilized society" her regret at having lived only to serve and suffer in the capacity of "slave and woman" would be complete' (ibid., p. 74). She thought it her duty to be thoroughly disagreeable.

But she flits in and out, and leaves behind only questions: who was this woman who wrote and spoke in this manner at a time when I am informed (by good patriarchal authority) that there was only silence, when the voice of Mary Wollstonecraft had disappeared, and where absolutely nothing was happening in Britain in relation to the 'woman question'? Pankhurst says that Thompson 'considered the championship of the emancipation of women was basically interrelated to opposition to private property, the State and organized religion,' and that, 'Marriage was the legalized prostitution by which man seized upon woman for his pleasure, taking advantage of her dependence to force her into virtual slavery' (ibid., p. 68), and that his position 'was undoubtedly intensified by his close friend and collaborator, Anna Wheeler, whose forceful personality and bitter experiences added poignancy and emphasis to his writings' (ibid., p. 70). I suggest she also added a great deal more!

Whether or not many women knew at the time about Anna Wheeler (and it would be surprising if her contribution were not widely known), there were numerous individual women who also registered their protests against patriarchy in the first half of the nineteenth century – when absolutely nothing was happening! In 1832, through the services of 'Orator' Hunt, Mary Smith, a Yorkshire woman of considerable means, lodged a petition in the House of Commons, requesting that as a property owner she be permitted to exercise her right to vote. In 1840 Lady Morgan published *Woman and her Master*, and in 1843 Mrs Hugo Reid published *A Plea for Women*, which listed the inconsistencies in women's position, for while they were permitted 'to vote for an East India director' – literally the governor of the country – (and while there was not, she added, 'the faintest hint of any inconvenience resulting from the practice'), and while they were allowed at times to vote at local elections, they were not allowed to vote for the governors of England (quoted in Blackburn, 1902, pp. 14–15). In 1832, William Johnston Fox (Member of Parliament for Oldham) had written an article entitled 'A Political and Social Anomaly' for the *Monthly Repository* in which he had pointed to the foolishness of the inclusion of the word 'male' in the Reform Act, and in 1845, at a meeting in Covent Garden, Richard Cobden stated unequivocally that it was ridiculous that women had been deprived of their right to vote.

In 1847, Anne Knight, 'an aged Quaker lady of strong political opinions', published a leaflet advocating the vote for women and in an accompanying letter (April 1847) wrote, 'I wish the talented philanthropists in England would come forward in this critical juncture of our nation's affairs and insist on the right of suffrage for all men and women unstained with crime . . . in order that all may have a voice in the affairs of their country' (quoted in Blackburn, 1902, p. 19; there is also a facsimile reprint included of the original leaflet).

Then, of course, in 1851, Harriet Taylor's article on the 'Enfranchisement of Women' appeared in the *Westminster Review*, and in 1855, there appeared 'a lucid and able pamphlet, *The Right of Women to Exercise the Elective Franchise*, by "Justitia" . . . later that pamphlet was reprinted by the National Society for Women's Suffrage with the name of the author, Mrs Henry Davis Pochin' (ibid., p. 20).

2 The lady without the lamp: Florence Nightingale (1820–1910)

While there is this published evidence that women were questioning the restrictions placed upon them and were seeking to regain their political rights, there were also many private battles being fought as women tried to rebel and change some of the circumstances of their own lives within the family. One such woman was Florence Nightingale and, as Ray Strachey (1928) points out, she is not usually seen in this role, for 'her real feeling towards the position of her sex' has never yet been fully stated. It has been assumed that her interest in the oppression of women – if it existed at all – was only peripheral. 'There is much indeed to give colour to this view,' says Strachey, 'for though she was a feminist of sorts, and signed petitions and believed in Women's Suffrage . . . she openly declared that she did not "expect much from it". . . . Everyone knows, too, that she shared with Harriet Martineau an active distaste for the feminist writing and propaganda which was multiplying so rapidly during her lifetime' (1928, pp. 23–4). But this is only part of the story – and yet it is by no means a coincidence that it is the part we are familiar with.

Florence Nightingale unflinchingly described the everyday reality of women's oppression in the wealthy stratum of society; she also formulated a vision of what women could and might do if men were not their masters (and according to Strachey, this is one of the reasons she did not marry, and one of the reasons she was able to accomplish what she did and to transform her vision into reality). In 1852, Florence Nightingale wrote down her ideas on the woman question and these along with her thoughts on religion 'were later amplified into three large volumes entitled *Suggestions for Thought to Searchers after Religious Truth*, a book which was printed in 1859 but was not published' (ibid., p. 26) and, says Strachey, there can be no doubt about its importance in terms of understanding the woman herself, or aspects of the woman question in general.

Unfortunately, Strachey also provides what I have come to consider a stereotypical assessment of women's philosophic contribution: Nightingale's book 'is very long, its arrangement is very confused, and it is a highly wearisome book to read. It is full of repetitions, and of things apparently irrelevant, and there is much in it which is not original' (ibid., p. 27). However, among the many chapters 'there is one remarkable fragment, an essay which she has called "Cassandra", which is . . . a terrible piece of writing, a scornful indictment of society against which there is no possible defence' (ibid., p. 29). Because it is not available, and because Strachey considers it such an integral and illuminating facet of the women's movement, she prints 'Cassandra' in full in her short history of the women's movement, declaring that it completes the explanation for the stirring of female discontent (ibid.).

Florence Nightingale was subjected to a 'ladylike' upbringing of enforced idleness with the most constructive activities allowed being those of company and visits, (Strachey says she was not even permitted to read to herself, but was read to, a practice which Nightingale describes as 'like lying on one's back and having liquid poured down one's throat' (ibid., p. 19).) It was against the uselessness and the despair of such an existence that Nightingale revolted and engaged in a continual battle with her parents. Her mother, who insisted on Nightingale's vacuousness in order that she might be marriageable, relented slightly as Nightingale grew older, rejected proposals, and passed the acceptable marriageable age. It was this relaxation of control, as well as Nightingale's determination, which led to her being able to break out from her suffocating existence and to pursue what she perceived as her vocation. But before she was able to make her move, she had to endure for more than thirty years the repressive regime of a 'leisured' and unmarried woman, 'shut up tight within the conventions which forbade independent action to a woman' (ibid.). It was from this experience that she wrote about and analysed the position of women.

Florence Nightingale recognised that men insisted that women should be happy, and that women therefore were required to assert that they *were* happy – no matter what the circumstances of their lives – for men took it as a personal offence if the women whom they 'supported' declared themselves unhappy, with the result that women who wished to continue to be supported continued to state that they were happy even when they were most miserable. (This is a point taken up by Jessie Bernard in *The Future of Marriage* (1972), though, of course, she does not suggest that this is a fairly old idea and one put forward by Florence Nightingale.)

That it is obligatory for a woman to be happy, to present a contented and cheerful disposition to her master in order that he can feel satisfied with the arrangement and secure in the knowledge of his own psychological (as well as financial) indispensability, is a lesson that mothers unwaveringly teach their daughters, argues Nightingale. The only way such a lesson can be taught successfully is by the systematic denial and removal of *passion* from women. If emotion were allowed to reside in women, says Nightingale, women could not bear their lives, so women go round teaching 'their daughters that "women have no passions." In the conventional society, which men have made for women, and women have accepted, they *must* have none, they *must* act the farce of hypocrisy, the lie that they are without passion – and therefore what else can they say to their daughters, without giving the lie to themselves?' (Strachey, 1928, p. 396).

And the daughters, taught to deny the existence of any passion, to deny the existence of any will or force in themselves to cultivate a smiling, serene veneer, which reinforces men's images of themselves, try to find amusement, fulfilment, meaning, in the most 'escapist' activities. This is why women read novels, states Nightingale, for in a novel, 'the heroine has *generally* no family ties (almost *invariably* no mother), or, if she has, these do not interfere with her entire independence' (ibid., p. 397); and the reader can dream. Women thus 'wish their lives away' because their daily existence denies them purpose, meaning, commitment, aspirations and action. They simply exist to cater for the psychological and physical needs of men and are permitted no life of their own. 'Passion, intellect, moral activity – these three have never been satisfied in a woman', says Nightingale. 'To say more on this subject would be to enter into the whole history of society, of the present state of civilisation' (ibid., p. 398), for women are given neither time, opportunity nor sanction to develop their own resources for themselves. (Mary Beard, 1946, had a great deal more to say on this subject.)

'Women are never supposed to have any occupation of sufficient importance *not* to be interrupted, except "suckling their fools",' she continues, 'and women themselves have accepted this, have written books to support it, and have trained themselves so as to consider whatever they do as *not* of such value to the world or to others, but that they can throw it up at the first "claim of social life". They have accustomed themselves to consider intellectual occupation as a merely selfish amusement, which it is their "duty" to give up for every trifler more selfish than themselves' (Strachey, 1928, p. 401).

So she continues, explaining why it is in a sense, women do not exist as individuals, why it is that women cannot pursue any intellectual activity, systematically, why it is that women's time is not considered valuable, and why it is that they do not have any. 'Women never have half an hour in all their lives (excepting before or after anyone is up in the house) that they can call their own, without fear of offending or of hurting someone' (ibid., p. 402), for they must always be *available*. And 'for a married woman in society, it is even worse. A married woman was heard to wish that she could break a limb that she might have a little time to herself. Many take advantage of the fear of "infection" to do the same' (ibid.).

Florence Nightingale gives every indication that she understands why the two sexes are required to behave in the manner that they do, and why it is that women's loss is men's gain. If it was this aspect of the woman question that she had in mind when she stated that she didn't expect much from the vote, her assessment was completely justified and her conventional portrayal as anti-feminist is then cast in a very different light. The changes that she sought (and which to some extent she managed to procure for herself – as did Harriet Martineau) were so radical that there was little likelihood that the vote would have been of much assistance in bringing them about.

I have always thought that one of the crucial features of the analysis of John Stuart Mill was his assertion that it was insufficient for women to be slaves, but that they must be *willing* slaves if patriarchy is to continue. Florence Nightingale makes a similar point when she says that: 'Women have no means given them, whereby they *can* resist. . . . They are taught from their infancy upwards that it is wrong, ill-tempered, and a misunderstanding of "woman's mission" (with a great M) if they do not allow themselves *willingly* to be interrupted at all hours' (ibid., p. 403). If women are not *willing*, they are not automatically available to men, and the whole system, therefore, could be challenged. (This is not to dispute that numerous 'weapons' may be used to procure their 'willingness'.) Hence women must protest that they *are* happy, that their lives are made complete by the presence of a man, that they are fulfilled by meeting his needs and would willingly and happily sacrifice their interests to *him*. To Nightingale, this was how the system worked, and when she showed that she was not willing, that she would not sacrifice her resources for the sake of a man, that she existed with her own human will and force she also proved – to her own satisfaction – that the system, rigid and constraining as it was, could not contain her. She was, of course, in the position of not being forced to find a man for financial support.

It is easy to see why Virginia Woolf (as well as Vera Brittain) was attracted to Nightingale's ideas, and was perhaps influenced by them, for Florence Nightingale states that for women, 'In every dream of the life of

intelligence or that of activity, women are accompanied by a phantom' –
(Woolf called it 'The Angel in the House'), 'the phantom of sympathy
guiding, lighting the way – even if they do not marry . . . Behind *his* destiny
women must annihilate herself, must be only his complement. A woman
dedicates herself to the vocation of her husband; she fills up and performs
the subordinate parts in it. But if she has any destiny, any vocation of her
own, she must renounce it, in nine cases out of ten' (ibid., p. 407). A
married woman's resources are used by the husband, and the phantom, the
'Angel in the House', hovers around persistently to ensure that this is so,
and to ensure that women willingly and happily hand over all their resources to men.

The lives of women says, Nightingale, how frivolous, how unworthy
they are, once women make available all their sexual, emotional, intellectual, verbal resources to men. There is nothing left but the constant lie that
they are happy, the constant denial of their own humanity. And why is this
so? Why must one sex sacrifice itself, while the other profits? It is because
men have made the world and they have made it to their liking; they enjoy
the benefits it bestows. It would be less beneficial for them – even inconvenient – if women were to cultivate any interests of their own. It would
also be psychologically disturbing for a man if he were not the sole centre
of a woman's existence. So available to men are women, so without resources of their own, says Nightingale, they cannot *study* anything, not
even their own lives; they are too busy, too much in demand, too immured
in smiling self-sacrifice.

There are some women, says Nightingale, 'who wish for something
better and try to create it' (ibid., p. 398) – a concept not inconsistent with
current feminist philosophy – and she adds there is a desperate need for
such women to come forward. Revealing her religious context and her
feminist insights, she states: 'The next Christ will perhaps be a female
Christ' (ibid., p. 416).

3 Why not for women? Barbara Bodichon (1827–1891)

Florence Nightingale did create a new context and new possibilites for
women in general but she also exercised (indirectly) some influence over
one woman in particular, her first cousin, Barbara Leigh Smith (who is
referred to more commonly by her married name, Barbara Bodichon). If
Barbara Bodichon experienced the private mental anguish of Florence
Nightingale, I can find no trace of it (which does not for a minute suggest
that she did not share Nightingale's assessment of the relationship between
the sexes, only that there is no readily accessible *record* of this). What she
did share was a conviction that women should enter the public arena and
that all forms of discrimination which existed to prevent them from doing
so should be removed. In public, Bodichon was more radical than Nightingale – she was one of the feminists seeking a political solution for the
problem of men.

According to many sources, Barbara Bodichon was the major force behind the founding of the nineteenth-century women's *movement*. 'In 1855', says Strachey, 'the first regular feminist committee came into existence and the person who took the initiative in this matter was a remarkable young woman whose name' . . . (surprise! surprise!) . . . 'is now little remembered, but whose share in the first organization of the Women's Movement was of the utmost importance' (ibid., p. 71). Ray Strachey made this statement in 1928; Barbara Bodichon is even less well known today and it has been inordinately difficult trying to find out more about her.[2] Some of her writing (and art) still survives (in pamphlets preserved by the Fawcett Library and paintings preserved by Girton College), and arouses interest and curiosity, but, as for details of her personal life, as for any illuminating information on her relationship with Florence Nightingale (or Harriet Martineau or George Eliot who was a very close friend), I have found little of value. There is one biography of Barbara Bodichon (Hester Burton, 1949), an unpublished manuscript by Margaret Cruikshank, and a forthcoming commentary of Jacquie Mathews. Both Josephine Kamm (1966) and Barbara Strachey (1980) make ever such discreet references, however, to what could possibly have been one of the most influential factors in Barbara Leigh Smith's life – she was illegitimate. What did she make of the fact that her highly principled and reform-minded father did not marry her mother, the ravishing 17-year-old milliner that he seduced?

Barbara Bodichon is a fascinating woman. She was born into a radical family that worked for abolition and parliamentary reform, and Elizabeth Cady Stanton and Lucretia Mott were among the guests entertained in her home when she was in her teens. Harriet Martineau, Mary Somerville and Mary Howitt were also frequent guests (even if Florence Nightingale was not), and, according to Jacquie Mathews, Bodichon's correspondence with George Eliot 'reveals the depth of a friendship that was central to their lives for twenty-five years'. (Ray Strachey mentions this relationship: 'There seems to have been something particularly vigorous and vivid about Barbara Leigh Smith who was taken by George Eliot as a model for *Romola*', 1928, p. 71).

Barbara Bodichon was engaged in a wide range of activities – law reform, women's rights, art, education, journalism. She is almost invariably portrayed (in the few sources that exist) as a woman of glowing strength, active intelligence, warmth, understanding, and energy; and as the initiator of the first feminist collective in England. Mathews says that Barbara Bodichon *lived* her ideas, that she was alert and daring. Interestingly, she says that Bodichon's insistence on creativity and her devotion to her art are currently being reappraised for, far from being an 'accomplishment', Bodichon's art – recently 'rediscovered' on Girton College walls, the college she helped to found and which she financially supported – is now beginning to be taken very seriously (see Mathews, 1982).

---

[2] I must thank Jacquie Mathews for first drawing my attention to Barbara Bodichon's contribution and significance – but I won't thank her for failing to warn me of the frustrating task I was taking on.

It was partly her insistence on the role of creativity that also led her to found (and to teach in) the progressive school, Portman Hall. She was one of the first students of Bedford College, a vehement feminist, and had a somewhat mysterious marriage. Given these bare bones of biography, why is it that Barbara Bodichon should not have attracted enormous interest?

Whatever else Barbara Leigh Smith's father did or did not do, however, he provided her with an independent income when she came of age (£300 per year) and, as Virginia Woolf so sagely said in relation to £500 a year, an independent income often leads to an independent mind; Barbara Bodichon could well have been a model for Woolf's thesis.

Looking back on their friendship in 1891, Bessie Rayner Parkes (Madame Belloc) said of Barbara Bodichon that even as a child she was involved in public movements, 'she was actively associated [with] the great Anti-Corn League struggle of Cobden and Bright', and, says Parkes, when she first met Barbara 'in 1846, that struggle had just been won. She was then a beautiful active girl of nineteen, ardent in every social cause. . . . It was in 1854 that she began her work by collecting in a pamphlet all the laws specifically relating to women, a pamphlet very thin and insignificant looking, but destined to prove the small end of the wedge which was to change the whole fabric of the law' *(Englishwoman's Review,* 1891, July, p. 149; quoted in Blackburn, 1902, pp. 48–9).

The pamphlet was a *Brief Summary in Plain Language of the Most Important Laws concerning Women,* and Ray Strachey reports that it had an immediate and wide sale. It was what it claimed to be, a simple compilation of the laws that related to women, and when they were all brought together in this way, there was no need for any comment, for they spoke for themselves; the position of women and the esteem in which they were held by men was perfectly clear if the laws enacted by men were any index.

To have elected to undertake such a task was in itself quite unusual – after all, at the same time as Barbara Bodichon was doing this, Florence Nightingale was deploring the fact that it was impossible for women to engage in any systematic study, or to take themselves and their intellect seriously. And it must have been (for it still is) a difficult and daunting activity to sift through the laws of the land to find those that related to women. This was serious research, and while Barbara Bodichon did attend Bedford College, it offered only a glimpse of the possibilities of women's research rather than practical training in how to do it (see Strachey, 1928, pp. 62–3).

She was brought up in a home where parliamentary reform was not only considered feasible but, after the 1832 Reform Act and the Anti-Corn League struggle, considered successful, and this perhaps helps to explain why she turned towards the law and to parliamentary reform as a possibility for changing the position of women. But what she actually thought about the laws she so systematically examined, whether she was angered by the evidence she accumulated, whether she was optimistic, or whether she thought parliamentary reform was the whole or only part of the answer, remains to me something of a mystery. (Jacquie Mathews reports that there is a wealth of primary sources – some at Girton, which have never been studied.) What is more certain is that having documented the oppression of women in this concrete way, she was determined to change the laws – and practices – of society, so that women could enter the public arena.

She gave her pamphlet on the laws of the land as they related to women to a family friend, Davenport Hill, who placed it before the Law Amendment Society and the following year a report was drafted, on the basis of the pamphlet, which aimed to remove some of the most severe liabilities placed upon women: it proposed to give married women property rights and allow them to make wills. A public meeting was held (and there were many women present), and a 'resolution supporting the proposed reform was of course passed, and a petition was drafted by Miss Leigh Smith and circulated for signature. Other meetings followed, other petitions were set on foot, and within the year, 26,000 men and women had given their approval to the reform' (ibid., p. 73). In 1857 the petition was presented to both Houses.

It received a hostile reception. Today, when we take it for granted that women are permitted to own property, and when we point to the fact that they own very little as an index of inequality, we have to make a conscious effort to appreciate what it was like, when by law married women were *not* allowed to own property; we have to try to understand just how radical was the demand that women were making. They believed that once women were allowed to control their own financial resources, the inequality of the sexes would be undermined, and they had every reason to believe this because men believed it, said it, and therefore resisted any moves that were made by women to obtain this 'right'.

When the petition requesting the right for married women to own property was presented to both Houses, the opposition inside and outside parliament was at times quite fierce, and suggests just how threatening many men found this reform. 'It would disrupt society, people said: it would destroy the home, and turn women into loathsome, self-assertive creatures no one could live with; it was an intolerable idea' (ibid.). In the *Saturday Review* it was stated that: 'So long as the petticoat rebellion was confined to a mistaken petition of a few literary ladies . . . we really had not the heart to say anything about it,' but the proposals of Barbara Leigh Smith, put forward to the Law Amendment Society, and treated seriously 'set at defiance the experiences of every country in Christendom and the common sense of mankind. . . . There is besides, a smack of selfish independence about it which rather jars with romantic notions of wedlock (quoted by Hester Burton, 1949, pp. 68–9; requoted by Josephine Kamm, 1966, p. 90).

In the process of obtaining signatures for the petition, Barbara Bodichon had gathered round her a group of like-minded and enthusiastic friends, who continued to meet and to talk even after the petition had been presented (and who continued to offer each other support after they had been abused and ridiculed by the press). The group consisted of Bessie Rayner Parkes (1828–1925), Adelaide Anne Proctor (described as Margaret Maison, in *The Listener,* 29 April, 1965, as 'Queen Victoria's favourite poet), Mrs Fox, Mrs Howitt (the writer of tales and poems), and, of course, Anna Jameson (who in February, 1855 had delivered her lecture 'Sisters of Charity', and later, 'Communion of Labour' and which together had helped to form a basis for the discussion of women's potential).

Between the time that the petition was presented and the Married Women's Property Bill failed, Bessie Rayner Parkes noticed a periodical 'edited by ladies for ladies', for sale, and put to the group the idea of purchasing it so that they could have a forum for discussion of the issues that concerned them. The idea was greeted with enthusiasm, and the un-married and 'the most influential and wealthy of the Group . . . Barbara Leigh Smith, whose many friendships brought her into touch with the world of journalism and literature' was able to seek advice from Harriet Martineau and George Eliot, among others, and the business of buying and running the paper was begun. But it took some time to be completed, and in the interim, almost burning with the need to state the case and to improve the position of women, Barbara Leigh Smith wrote another pam-phlet, this one entitled *Women and Work* (see Fawcett Library Pamphlets).

In it she argued that women could be and should be anything they wanted. She derided the idea that woman was only made for man, and that marriage was her vocation – not just on the grounds that no man would settle for such limited horizons and therefore why should a woman – but also on the more pragmatic grounds which were revealed by her own research. It was patently ridiculous to treat women as existing only in marriage when 43 per cent of the women in the country over the age of 20, were not married (1857, p. 10).

She claimed that the practice among men of exchanging women, of allowing only men financial resources and obliging women to be dependent on them, was prostitution, and was degrading to women: 'Fathers have no right to cast the burden of the support of their daughters on other men,' she wrote. 'It lowers the dignity of women; and tends to prostitution, whether legal or in the streets' (ibid., p. 11). If women were to make equal unions with men, stated Bodichon, they must have equal resources, and this meant that they must have paid work. But, she added, women who are performing unpaid work, in the home, in the interest of the family, should also be seen to be *working*. 'Women who act as housekeepers, nurses and instructors of their children, often do as much for the support of the household as their husbands; and it is very unfair for men to speak of supporting a wife and children' (ibid., p. 12).

'Do you think women are happy?' (ibid., p. 13) she demands, and breaks the taboo that would have all women content in their oppression. Using a combination of clearly stated facts, and personal letters of testimony from women who are trying to earn their living, but who are being out-rageously exploited, she presents a cogent case for opening up *all* areas of work to women and for paying them decent wages. She wants women to do the same work as men and to receive the same education and training as men, and says that things would be very different 'if fathers would help their daughters as they help their sons' (ibid., p. 15).

Anticipating the arguments that women who work for money are unfeminine, Bodichon says, 'to think a woman is more feminine because she is frivolous, ignorant, weak and sickly, is absurd: the larger natured a woman is, the more decidedly feminine she will be; the stronger she is, the more strongly feminine' (ibid., p. 18). To Barbara Bodichon, if *femininity* was to mean anything, it was to mean something positive and it was to be defined by women. From her perspective, strong women *were* feminine women and she had no intention of being swayed by men's interests which dictated that it was desirable that women be weak, without resources, and powerless.

She puts her finger on the fundamental issue when she says that, 'there is a prejudice against women accepting money for work' (ibid., p. 47), for she states quite plainly that *men are not in principle against women working*, what *they are against is women being paid for it* in any way for it might allow women to accumulate resources of their own and might facilitate their independence from men. She concludes with: 'To sum up. Women want work both for the health of their minds and their bodies. They want it often because they must eat and because they have children and others dependent upon them – *for all the reasons that men want work*. They are placed at a great disadvantage in the market of work because they are not skilled labourers, and are therefore badly trained. They rarely have any training. It is the duty of fathers and mothers to give their daughters this training' (ibid., p. 51).

Equal education and equal work (and implied, though not specifically stated, equal pay) may not constitute a radical demand today (although 125 years later it has still not been achieved) but it *was* a most radical demand in 1857. It was based on Barbara Bodichon's assumption that women would not be equal until they had equal financial resources and were therefore economically independent of men; on her belief that change was possible and that it could be procured by public agitation (meetings, publications, petitions) and parliamentary reform.

In commenting on *Women and Work*, Josephine Kamm (1966) provides a summary dismissal when she says it is 'badly arranged and badly written', and, to my surprise, that it 'clearly lacked the guiding hand of Davenport Hill' (pp. 92–3). Perhaps Kamm's assessment was influenced by the response the pamphlet received at the time.

Confronted with the assertion that women should do any paid job they wanted to do, 'the world mocked and even howled at the absurdity of the idea', says Strachey. 'Had they quite forgotten that a woman's job was to get married?' (1928, p. 92).

' "If this is a fair sample of what a lady who boasts to have made the subject her own is likely to publish," wrote the *Saturday Review*, "we are afraid that the sex is not really so developed as we had supposed ... Married life is woman's profession; and to this life her training – that of dependence – is modelled. Of course, by not getting a husband, or losing him, she may find that she is without resources. All that can be said of her is, she has failed in business and no social reform can prevent such failures" ' (ibid.). To the writer on the *Saturday Review*, it could not have been simpler: all resources resided in men, and if women wanted to exist, their business was to trade their agreeable and dependent *selves* in exchange for board and lodging. That was how man had made the world, that was how men wanted it to stay, and women who didn't share the view had failed in business and were unable to find a buyer for their wares of mind and body. Barbara Bodichon did *not* like it, and with her £300 a year was in a position to say so.

Blackwoods Magazine lodged a very clear protest: 'it would be an excellent thing if all single women would get married as fast as they can, and the rest hold their tongues in a dignified manner' (quoted in the *Englishwoman's Journal*, 1858, vol. I, no. 1, p. 12).

The more serious press, says Strachey, responded to Barbara Bodichon's argument that there were many more women than men (and therefore it simply was not practical to enjoin every woman to marry as a means of earning her living) and addressed the problem of *redundant* or *superfluous* women. (It is probably *superfluous* to point out that only in a society where males were considered central, where women were defined in relation to them and where men were the ones formulating the terms, could women ever be labelled *redundant* or *superfluous* when they outnumbered men.) Given the current prevailing orthodoxy which would have us believe that men are better at mathematics than women, the position of the serious press (which Strachey states 'was frivolous in the extreme', 1928, p. 92) seems to be one where the simple rules of addition and subtraction seem not to apply, for the argument was that if women were redundant, 'it was because the silly creatures would not marry' (ibid.). Perhaps the possibility of polygamy was being entertained.

Summing up the case against Bodichon's argument, as put forward in the serious press, Strachey says that it decreed that, 'if, after all, women really were found to be too thick on the ground, let them be exported to marry overseas! It needed only a little courage and a big scheme, and all the redundant ones could be landed in the colonies, and a good thing too! *Away with all this nonsense of trying to make the single life remunerative and pleasant for women!* Its only upshot would be to make marriage a matter of "cold philosophic choice", and then, of course, it would be "more and more frequently declined." And, what would happen to the home? Besides, why could they not become domestic servants? These happy creatures "fulfil both essentials of woman's being; they are supported by and they minister to the comfort of men . . . Nature has not provided one too many" ' (ibid., pp. 92–3).

My blood boils as I read and write these statements. I would feel less enraged if I could believe they were the arguments of the past, but they are arguments that are still used – and effectively – today. As Jessie Bernard (1972) and Lynne Spender (forthcoming) have so clearly demonstrated, there is a fundamental fear (and rightly so) among men that if women *can* lead a *single* life without severe penalty, they will *choose* to do so! But instead of men being prompted to re-evaluate marriage as it affects women (so that, for example, it might become more 'attractive' with a more equitable allocation of work within the relationship), they have insisted that women who lead single lives be penalised. Many of the penalties are psychological: men have decreed that they themselves are necessary to women, and women who cannot make themselves sufficiently agreeable to attract the interest and support of men have failed. They are 'old maids', 'spinsters', figures of fun and ridicule – from the perspective of men who see themselves as essential to a woman's existence. Dorothy Jones and Jennifer Jones (forthcoming) have claimed that in all the mainstream literature of the English-speaking world, fiction and non-fiction, there are almost no positive images of the single woman. It is a dangerous image and therefore one which I think should be actively encouraged.

(A little 'off the track', but I have just read some 'reviews' of women writers and in 1982 almost the same arguments that were used against Barbara Bodichon are being used yet again; my wonder is that men have not found a more novel dismissal for surely by now such tired old arguments are transparent!)

But the group of women – called the Langham Place Group by virtue of their meeting place – supported each other in the face of jibes and taunts from the press and public. Ray Strachey reports that they were not untouched by the ridicule and mockery (which may have had more power to harm and hurt in Victorian times than today) yet while their 'reputations' were besmirched and they were called strong-minded *and* foolish, they decided 'duty was more important then reputation, and reform could not be achieved in secret' (ibid., p. 94). The work went on: the first number of the *Englishwoman's Journal* appeared in 1858; they were joined by more women; their work expanded.

Once the *Journal* was published, women outside London could not only read about the issues raised by the Langham Place Group, they could also identify a location. Many wrote letters to the office, others arrived to help with the work. Jessie Boucherett was one such woman and Helen Blackburn (1902) reports that Boucherett 'was consuming her soul in solitary desire to help women to better economic conditions when one day she caught sight, on a railway bookstall, of a number of the *Englishwoman's Journal*. She bought it, attracted by the title, but expecting nothing better than the inanities commonly considered fit for women. To her surprise and joy she found her own unspoken aspirations reflected in its pages. She lost no time in repairing to the offices of the journal' (p. 50), where she met not the embittered, strong-minded, humourless women the press would have her believe but the enthusiastic, optimistic and joyful women who not only envisaged change but were in the exhilarating process of creating it. Jessie Boucherett stayed, and along with Adelaide Anne Proctor (evidently noted for her sense of humour, her jokes, and her 'fun') established the Association for the Promotion of the Employment of Women.

Josephine Kamm (1966) recounts the same story, but with a slightly different twist. Having already stated that 'Barbara and Bessie' were a bit outrageous (travelling alone in Europe, Barbara daringly in blue-tinted spectacles and Bessie outrageously in heavy boots), she proceeds with the statement that 'the girls were at one in their hatred of fashionable habit of tight-lacing and corsets, both electing to wear loose, comfortable and shapeless garments' (p. 94). So when Jessie Boucherett entered the offices of the

English Woman's Journal (sic) and reported Bessie Rayner Parkes as 'a handsome young woman dressed in admirable taste', and Barbara Bodichon as 'beautifully dressed, of radiant beauty, with masses of golden hair', Kamm concludes that Boucherett 'must also have belonged to the no-corset, shapeless-garment brigade' (ibid., pp. 94–5). What malice! We simply cannot afford it.

In 1857, the National Association for the Promotion of Social Science was founded and from the outset women were admitted and welcomed as members. Florence Nightingale contributed a paper at the first meeting, Isa Craig (a member of the Langham Place Group) was appointed assistant secretary to the Association. Initially the women were under some constraint in this public arena (which to a certain extent may have been 'self-imposed' by considerations of propriety or lack of confidence), but within a couple of years they were functioning as full members, writing and reading their own papers, participating in the discussion of the major philosophical, humanitarian and political issues of the day. Still excluded from the universities (for Queens College, established 1848, and Bedford, established 1849, were 'special', designed primarily to remedy the deficiencies of women's education and to equip them to be governesses or teachers), this opportunity to be involved in serious intellectual discussion was extremely valuable. It was access to a circle that had been denied to the Bluestockings almost a century before; it was also, as Ray Strachey points out, access to patrons who could support some of the new ventures which extended from Langham Place.

After the Association for the Promotion of the Employment of Women there was 'the Ladies Institute with its reading room and small club, out of which grew classes for governesses, book keepers and secretaries' (ibid., p. 94). All these ventures were supported by the Social Science Association and were fully discussed in the *Journal*. The *Journal* endorsed, agitated for, and reported on, the movement for women's higher education; it argued for women doctors, reported on the workings of the new Divorce Act, and it brought many women to its doors.

Many, many of the women who came, however, told of exploitation, of cruelty, of helplessness and despair, of the lack of education and money, and they 'brought their "culpable resignation" to the Employment Office', says Strachey, trying to show how difficult it was for the secretaries at Langham Place to break the bonds which tied women to the restricting roles deemed 'proper'. Some of the women 'were so timid they often refused to give their names and they shrank back in horror from the notion of seeking new work. *If a woman did anything at all to earn money she lost caste;* and the women who found their way to Langham Place were terribly anxious about this. As governesses they felt some little rags of their gentility remained to them. But as physical instructors, or wood carvers, or lecturers, they must surely cease to be ladies. And after years of the severest privations in the sacred cause of keeping up appearances they could not understand the new ideal and the new hope which was presented to them. Again and again they turned away and went back to their hopeless tasks' (ibid., p. 98, my emphasis).

It was not *just* governesses who arrived at the door, although they were well represented and their plight was well known: in *Women and Work* Barbara Bodichon had included a Letter to the Editor of *The Times* from 'A Poor Governess' under the heading of 'White Slavery'. In the letter the governess told of how, having walked for many miles to be interviewed (to save expenses) fifty women arrived, overcome with fatigue, and she herself, 'After having been kept standing in a cold, draughty hall more than an hour . . . at last obtained an interview with the lady, and learnt that the duties of the governess would consist in educating and taking the entire charge of the children, seven in number, two being quite babies, to perform for them all the menial functions of a nurse, make and mend their clothes; to teach at least three accomplishments, and "fill up the leisure hours of an evening by playing to company." For these combined duties the magnificent sum of 10/- [ten shillings] per annum was offered' (1857, p. 17). The governess also ascertained that there were two domestic servants in the household – one was paid 10 shillings per annum and the other 12 shillings.

The Langham Place Group in which Barbara Bodichon was the guiding light made none of the usual class distinctions about work. It was *women's* work which they examined and tried to change. It was the shocking conditions of needlewomen which aroused their ire and they recognised that it was partly because there were so many of them that they were readily exploited and discarded.

They fought for women to be trained and properly paid as clerks, shop assistants, doctors, nurses, teachers, hairdressers, watchmakers, wood carvers, hotel managers, house decorators, and they met much fierce resistance. When it seemed that there was no way women would be allowed entry to the printing trades to become compositors, Emily Faithfull (1835–1895), one of their number, not only went out and founded the Victoria Press, which from then on printed the journal (and trained women in the process), she also got the backing of Queen Victoria.[3]

Langham Place was a centre of activity and initiative, but it was not the only one. In 1865 the 'Kensington Society' was formed, and its members

---

[3] In reading about Emily Faithfull and the Victoria Press I came across the suggestion that Emily Faithfull was cited as a lesbian correspondent in a divorce case and that this was the reason that Queen Victoria withdrew her support for the Press. Knowing the old story that the reason lesbianism is not illegal in Britain is because Queen Victoria is supposed to have said that as women did not engage in this behaviour there was no necessity to pass a law against it, I wanted to pursue these conflicting clues. Where to start? I wrote to Patricia Staton in Canada (these are the ways of women's research) and asked her about it, as I knew she was working on Emily Faithfull. She graciously responded and said that the source from which I had obtained my information was incorrect. (The source was a man who shall remain nameless – as many of them are throughout this book, just so they might appreciate the 'benefits' of reversal and so that it will be women's names that are visible; as I am finding, it is a fairly easy path to follow if one sticks to the patterns men have used for centuries.) It was a personal friend of Emily's, Helen Codrington who was divorced, and Emily was called to give evidence on her behalf. Helen lost the case, says Staton, and her husband kidnapped her daughters: she sued but did not regain custody.

I hope Pat Staton does put the record right about Emily Faithfull: it would be good to see male publishers inundating her with requests for manuscripts. Ho hum!

were primarily interested in opening up education for women. Helen Black-burn has said that these women were truly a remarkable group, and she goes on to list their names: Barbara Bodichon and Emily Davies, the founders of Girton; Miss Beale (founder of Cheltenham Ladies College) and Miss Buss (founder of North London Collegiate School); Elizabeth Garrett (later Dr Elizabeth Garrett Anderson); Elizabeth Wolstenholme (later Elmy), Jessie Boucherett and Helen Taylor (daughter of Harriet Taylor and step-daughter of John Stuart Mill).

This society was interested in higher education for women *and* women's suffrage. In 1865, just after John Stuart Mill had been elected for Westminster (and after Barbara Bodichon had campaigned for him), the question for discussion was: 'Is the extension of the parliamentary franchise to women desirable, and if so under what conditions?' (Blackburn, 1902, p. 52). They decided that it was and Mill was approached by Barbara Bodichon to see if he would present a petition for women requesting the franchise. He agreed – as long as it was substantial; at least one hundred names, he suggested – if it was to carry any weight.

Barbara Bodichon knew about petitions. Along with Jessie Boucherett and Emily Davies she drafted it, got Mill's approval, and proceeded to collect signatures. In just over two weeks, 1,499 signatures were collected, and among them were the names of many prominent women – Frances Power Cobbe, Harriet Martineau, Florence Nightingale, Mary Somerville, Maria Grey and Emily Shirreff (leaders in the Girls' High School Movement, see Ellsworth, 1979), Josephine Butler, Sophia Jex-Blake, Viscountess Amberley, Lady Anna Gore Langton, Caroline Ashurst Biggs, and many more. On the day the petition was to be presented, Barbara Bodichon was 'unwell', and Emily Davies and Elizabeth Garrett went to Westminster Hall, where, self-conscious about their petition, they asked the applewoman near the entrance to hide it beneath the table of her stall. Mill arrived and asked for the petition which was quickly produced and he, 'on seeing it, exclaimed, "Ah, this I can brandish with effect." It was presented on June 7th (1866) the day the House went into Committee on the Representation of the People Bill' (Blackburn, 1902, p. 56).

The petition committee – of Barbara Bodichon, Jessie Boucherett, Emily Davies and Elizabeth Garrett – was the first of its kind in Britain, but it was quickly followed by others. In 1866 when the Social Science Congress met in Manchester, Barbara Bodichon gave a paper – *Reasons for the Enfranchisement of Women*, and among the audience was Lydia Becker. There was nothing outrageous in Bodichon's case for women's suffrage; she stated quite simply, 'that under a representative government, any class which is not represented is likely to be neglected. Proverbially, what is out of sight is out of mind, and the theory that women, as such, are bound to keep out of sight, finds its most emphatic expression in the denial of the right to vote' (1866, p. 3). While only men were represented, she argued, the views and values of men prevailed and they were not necessarily the views and values which served the interests or met the needs of women. Where only men are represented the 'tendency prevails to post-pone the claims of women to those of men' (ibid., p. 4). These same reasonable arguments are still used by women today in relation to work, education, law, etc., where it is still predominantly men who reign in the circles of power.

'What is treated as of no value is apt to grow valueless' (ibid., p. 6), argued Bodichon, claiming that women would become more serious beings when they were accorded more serious status, and when their ideas and opinions were treated as worthwhile. If women were treated as 'inferior' and retarded human beings, it should be no surprise that they began to behave as such, but if accorded value and dignity (as represented by the right to vote) they would respond positively: 'The mere fact of being called upon to enforce an opinion by a vote, would have an immediate effect in awakening a healthy sense of responsibility,' she stated (ibid., p. 7). 'When we find among the disfranchised such names as those of Mrs Somerville, Harriet Martineau, Miss Burdett Coutts, Florence Nightingale, Mary Carpenter, Louisa Twining, Miss Marsh . . . [all women of distinction] . . . and many others scarcely inferior to these in intellectual and moral worth, we cannot but desire, for the elevation and dignity of the parliamentary system, to add them to the number of electors' (ibid., p. 10).

To Barbara Bodichon it was a perfectly simple case and she could see no reason that the vote — and the many other radical reforms she was claiming should not be granted. That there was enormous opposition to her stand helped to reinforce her belief that the vote, and equal education, work and pay, would revolutionise women's position in society. Such opposition was heartening — it suggested that real and substantial change was being ushered in and was being resisted; it was not discouraging, for there had been opposition before, on other issues, and *it* had been overcome.

For not recognising that this was a different issue, that the relationship between women and men was *not* the same relationship as that between 'pro' and 'anti' corn-law factions (who were not required to live together, have their union blessed by the Church or procreate, etc.), Barbara Bodichon and the Langham Place Group have often been criticised. They were naive when they did not suspect that it would take over 50 years for their demands to be met. They were optimistic, says Strachey, and it was natural enough that they should be. 'They had never before done any political work, and being intelligent and disinterested themselves' (an assessment with which I disagree) 'they assumed that if a cause was just, and demonstrably just, as this was, it must quickly prevail. . . . They did not know that thousands upon thousands of their fellow countrymen honestly regarded their cause as impious and immoral. They did not understand that the more clearly they represented their vision of a free new world for women, the more surely they arrayed against them the selfish and self-interested among men . . . They did not realize how preposterous and subversive their whole conception seemed, but continued to believe that because it was just it must soon be popular. And so they were filled with hope' (1928, pp. 109–10).

It may not have been popular but it certainly had considerable appeal to many women, among whom was Lydia Becker.

4 Justice and patience are not enough: Lydia Becker (1827–1890)

Born in Manchester in 1827 (the eldest of fifteen children), Lydia Becker showed herself to be extremely interested in reading and learning, and the assessment of her as someone who could sift and store information, and pass it on, was shared within the family. According to her sister, Lydia Becker provided the intellectual life of the family (who were all almost entirely educated at home and one can imagine the role she played as 'teacher' as the eldest of fifteen) for she 'was always a great reader, and always remembered what she read, so that she was the universal referee when information was wanted, no matter what subject. She had a wonderful way, too, of getting at the kernel of a book in a very short time ... she seized on the salient points' (quoted in Blackburn, 1902, p. 25).

The picture of her as serious, as a bookworm, as a mine of information, is reinforced by her uncle, who wrote to her family in 1845 when Lydia Becker was staying with him in Germany. 'She is fond of learning and of everything that touches mental faculties and a clever understanding,' he wrote. 'She is sharp and keen in her intellect, clever in judging matters, fond of knowledge, has an excellent memory' (ibid., p. 27).

As an adult, Lydia Becker showed a continued commitment to the pursuit of knowledge, in 1864 publishing her first book, *Botany for Beginners*, and in 1867 becoming the president of the Manchester Ladies Literary Society. These women at the society met regularly, prepared and discussed papers on the issues of the day, and attempted to keep themselves well read and well informed in a society which denied them any intellectual role and prevented them from entering higher education. The meetings of the Bluestockings, the 'Conversations' of Margaret Fuller, the debates of the Kensington Society, the gatherings of the Manchester Ladies Literary Society (and even some women's studies courses today) were all attempts *by women* to create their own intellectual context, where they could engage in structured and purposeful reading, and exchange informed opinions. They were women's 'alternatives' to men's education and when they are portrayed mockingly and disparagingly it is worth considering whose interests are being served.

As president of the Manchester Ladies Literary Society, Lydia Becker was concerned that the members should be exposed to an educational experience of intellectual substance, and in her address in 1867 (reprinted in full, in Blackburn, 1902, pp. 31–9) she made a plea for the intellectual life of women and outlined the advantages of a trained and disciplined mind. Revealing some of her own wide reading in the process, she encouraged women to persist in their pursuit of knowledge and she directed them towards philosophy and science, urging them to read and understand, to take their own intellectual growth seriously in order that women would be taken seriously.

This was the woman who attended the meeting of the Social Science Congress in Manchester in 1866 and heard Barbara Bodichon advocate the franchise for women: 'Mme Bodichon's paper was "an era in her intellectual life" ' says Strachey (1928), 'and from that moment until the very day of her death she remained plunged wholly in the Cause in which . . . she became a very central figure' (p. 106).

The women in London had not disbanded after Mill had presented their petition but had formed themselves into a committee prepared to present more petitions and to work for women's suffrage. Emily Davies withdrew, however, because she believed that any association of the franchise for women with the move for higher education for women might prove to be disadvantageous (she seems to have been an exceedingly cautious soul from all accounts), and she elected to put her energies into women's education. After Barbara Bodichon went to Manchester (and no doubt talked about what the women in London were doing) the women of Manchester formed their own committee (January 1867), with Lydia Becker as their secretary.

Lydia Becker brought her many skills to the task of promoting women's suffrage. She was an able and efficient organiser, but she was also determined, dedicated, and a person who could sort and store information, and pass it on. She was the one who looked closely at parliamentary procedure, who assessed the members of parliament (who, frustratingly kept changing with each election) who took the measure of their preferences, prejudices and reliability, and who determined what particular wording would be acceptable in a bill: she was the one who studied what course a bill on women's suffrage would have to take in order to be successful and she devised and executed many strategies for helping such a bill on its way.

She wrote to members of parliament testing their sympathy, seeking their support, requesting information, volunteering drafts in her campaign to get a bill through the House. It was in this capacity that she wrote to Mr Eastwick on 4 March, 1874 (after the General Election in April in which some of the champions of the bill had been defeated, Mr Eastwick among them) about Mr Forsyth, the new champion, who was proposing to modify the draft bill: 'I earnestly hope Mr Forsyth does not wish to alter the wording of our Bill,' she wrote. 'It would be a fatal error, as it seems to me. We should limit ourselves strictly to the disabilities of *sex* and leave the marriage question alone. We ought not to introduce the matter of marriage into the electoral law. If married women cannot vote under the Municipal Franchise Act of 1869, it is nothing in the wording of the Statute which disqualifies them, but the common law disabilities of marriage. It would be very unwise to raise the question of the expediency of maintaining these disabilities in a debate on the question of removing the disabilities of sex' (quoted in Blackburn, 1902, p. 135).

Without benefit of higher education, without access to the parliamentary world, without training or experience in law or politics (all of which men took for granted for themselves), Lydia Becker made herself an expert on constitutional law and parliamentary procedure. Women, of course, at that time, lost all civil rights upon marriage in what was termed 'coverture' but this was enshrined in the common law and it was Becker's considered opinion that it would be best to avoid the introduction of this issue into the bill. Let women be granted the vote as women, she argued, and then we can address ourselves to the other forms of disqualification that they may be subjected to: let us pass a bill which says nothing about women's marital state but grants *women* the right to vote: this would be the 'thin edge of the wedge'.

She had a sound basis for her judgement. In 1867 for some inexplicable reason the name of Mrs Lily Maxwell was placed on the list of voters. Lydia Becker had recognised the significance of this 'error' and escorted Mrs Maxwell to the polling booth, where the Returning Officer had no choice but to accept the vote of Mrs Lily Maxwell. Says Roger Fulford: 'The case of Lily Maxwell proved that once women were on the register there was nothing to prevent them from voting. If the belief was well founded in law that there was no legal provision against women being placed on the register except in those new constituencies created by the 1832 Bill, the point of attack must be concentrated on the right of women to be admitted to the register as the law then stood' (1958, p. 56).

Richard Pankhurst was one of those who contributed to the task of testing the law. Lydia Becker played a vital role in organising the women and 5,000 women in Manchester alone applied for their names to be placed on the Parliamentary Register being prepared for the 1868 General Election. Some officials simply struck out the women's names on their own initiative and authority, 'but the majority of them left the matter to the revising court, presided over by a member of the Bar. Most of the revising barristers struck off the women, but a few of the learned men decided that they only had the power to strike people out where an objection was made. Therefore, where no objection was raised by the representatives of the political parties, the women remained' (ibid., p. 58).

The law was in a real tangle. There was an appeal to the High Court in 1868 (with Richard Pankhurst helping to present the case for the ancient rights of women), but the judges ruled that any rights which women were claiming from ancient times were non-existent. Justice Willes stated that it was a privilege for women to be exempted from voting. 'While the judges were happily mouthing out these historic rotundities of phrase they were perhaps unaware of the figure of Lydia Becker intently listening to their judgement. As soon as the case was over, she slipped out to the nearest telegraph office and sent off a telegram with the cryptic words of command "Post your letters." Immediately afterwards the 800 candidates for the General Election, then being fought, received a letter from Miss Becker asking if they would support a Bill giving women the vote' (ibid., pp. 58–9).

Lydia Becker was convinced that the strategy should be to have the 'privilege of exemption' removed by an Act which granted women the right to vote. Thirteen women had survived the objections in Manchester and were still eligible to vote, and on election day she drove round collecting them all and accompanying them to the polling booths (helping to prove that the world did not end when women cast their vote). None of these women could have been married, because married women were not entitled to possess property, and property was the qualification for voting. But a married women's property act would alter this, and, after all, they were working for it too, and it did not seem such a distant possibility. But Becker did not want to put *together* the issues of a married woman's right to own property, *and* women's right to vote, for she thought they would be used against each other. This was what Mr Forsyth did not seem to understand.

Working with men who held the power and decreed the rules did of course have its disadvantages, apart from the fact that the members kept changing, and kept changing the wording of the bill and disregarding advice. Helen Blackburn relates some of the trials and tribulations of Lydia Becker's life in this respect, and although I appreciate that Blackburn is trying to present Becker in a favourable light, I do at times wish that she did not consider self-sacrifice and patience such positive features leading to ultimate rewards.

One example of this philosophy which I find particularly galling is her account of Lydia Becker's admission to one enclave of male power. Those members of parliament who were also members of the National Societies for Women's Suffrage formed their own committee which met regularly to discuss and plan strategies, and as the liaison officer between the MPs, and the suffrage societies, Lydia Becker was to keep the women informed of the parliamentary state of play. Yet she was never admitted to the meetings of the all-male committee of MPs. 'Many a time', says Helen Blackburn, 'the present writer has waited with her in the corridor, till the Committee was over, and the secretaries came to deliver their minutes into her keeping' but things are better now, and we have much to be grateful for, as these days, 'all the delegates from the Societies in the National Union of Women's Suffrage Societies, have been allowed to attend, and they have been asked to give their opinions on the points under deliberation' (1902, p. 174). Be grateful for small mercies in a male-dominated society? It is obvious that Helen Blackburn held Lydia Becker in high esteem and wished to convey the most positive interpretation possible of her life and work, and of this I am not at all critical; my unease lies with what Blackburn considers to be positive.

Lydia Becker's achievements were substantial, and in many respects speak for themselves. She was a guiding force in the constitutional movement for women's suffrage; she was a strategist and organiser who helped to create a network and shape a movement. She was a veritable genius when it came to collating, interpreting and distributing information, as indicated by the pages of the *Women's Suffrage Journal*, which she started in March 1870 and which she edited 'with loving care and strenuous exactness during the rest of her life' (ibid., p. 101) and which ceased with her death in 1891. Roger Fulford (1958) has said that: 'The history of the decades from 1860 to 1890 — so far as women's suffrage is concerned — is the history of Miss Becker. In addition to her routine activities — organizing the Manchester society, travelling to London to guide the National Society and supervising all parliamentary work together with an unrelenting programme of lectures and speeches,' she conducted the *Women's Suffrage Journal* which 'is an astonishingly careful record — interrupted neither by explosive argument nor by bitter asides —' (presumably what one would expect of a woman), 'of every speech in and out of Paliament and every development which seemed to favour the women getting the vote' (p. 67). (He goes on to add that her feminine mind is displayed in the tidiness and neatness of every paragraph, and it was after all a bit humourless, she did exaggerate, and 'she did not hesitate to dress her window with obvious trifles,' but nevertheless, it was a worthy effort.)

Lydia Becker's efforts were also appreciated by many of her contemporaries, apart from Blackburn. On Becker's death, Arabella Shore said: 'The women's cause owes *everything* to her – she was the leader of the vanguard at the beginning and the chief supporter of it through all its first difficult years . . .' and Frances Power Cobbe said: 'One has hardly time to yet think of the loss she will be to the cause of women but it is *immeasurable*' (quoted in Blackburn, 1902, p. 187). Blackburn herself stated: 'To members of Parliament, to the general public, to workers in the Colonies and the United States, and indeed in every place where the question was alive, Miss Becker had been the visible head of the British movement' (ibid., p. 188).

Helen Blackburn was 'biased'; in relation to the women's suffrage agitation in Great Britain, Lydia Becker was to her 'the woman who will stand forth to after times as the leader whose personality was impressed on its early work, whose forethought and judgement moulded its policy' (ibid., p. 23). Blackburn subtitles her book on women's suffrage 'Biographical Sketches of Miss Becker' and throughout the pages it would be difficult to separate the suffrage movement from Lydia Becker. But even allowing for this 'bias' (which is present in *all* biographical treatment no matter how vehement the claim for 'objectivity'), it seems strange that this woman who was the 'visible head' of the movement for over twenty years, who was 'respectable', who was a gifted strategist and organiser, who was known to influential men, who had a sympathetic biographer – indeed, who had many of the qualities and advantages of Susan B. Anthony – should have faded into such obscurity.

The treatment of Lydia Becker after Helen Blackburn's biographical sketches leaves no doubt as to the image of her which has been constructed and transmitted – and which helps to explain why she has not 'attracted' further researchers and biographers. Ray Strachey (1928) acknowledges Becker's contribution, but treats it summarily and without any glow of enthusiasm. By 1958 Roger Fulford is making positive comments about her contribution, but adding a note of sarcasm as well. For example, he states that she was the first woman in Britain to speak in public on the issue of women's rights (Manchester, 14 April 1868, in the Assembly Room of the Free Trade Hall) and he commends her for her courage, and concludes with the significant information that 'the joke spread that human beings were now of three sexes – masculine, feminine and Miss Becker' (p. 63).

If 'Miss Becker was, by nature, quarrelsome and impatient of rivalry,' he says (and search as I might I can find no such suggestions, and as Fulford fails to state where he gets his information I cannot follow up his sources), 'such shadows across her character fade into insignificance in contrast with her qualities. Severely dressed, with thick hair plaited and placed on the top of her head and wearing narrow, metal spectacles, she looked somewhat grim, and the public, encouraged by *Punch*, occasionally flocked to her meetings to enjoy the inane pleasure of sniggering at the speaker. All this she endured superbly – perhaps comforted by the reflection that it was better to face this transitory ridicule than to live surrounded by . . . "gig-gledom" as a governess, or to undergo the melancholy grumbles of old ladies as a companion. There were virtually no other employments for the Victorian spinster' (ibid., p. 69).

Writing in 1966, Josephine Kamm said: 'Lydia Becker who was dis-tressingly plain and wore ugly steel rimmed spectacles had hitherto devoted her considerable powers of intelligence to the collection of scientific and botanical information. But botany and science seemed dry as dust in com-parison with the enthralling cause which she now proceeded to adopt with all her Germanic emotion and efficiency' (p. 131). Of course, says Kamm, 'There were moments when her starved emotional nature betrayed her into a wave of hysteria,' and she never achieved the stature of 'Millicent Fawcett, who had found fulfilment in a happy marriage' and who 'had many of the personal graces which Lydia Becker lacked' (ibid., p. 136). Why, oh why, are such comments made by one woman against another? Who is Josephine Kamm trying to impress?

By 1977 David Mitchell has turned this distressingly plain woman into 'a dedicated spinster who split the movement yet again by suggesting the exclusion of married women from the franchise' (p. 10) which, to my mind, constitutes a wilful but patriarchally useful misrepresentation of Lydia Becker's stand on the issue of married women and the franchise; it is, however, perfectly consistent with his statement that Becker's 'unprepos-sessing looks lent credence to the quip that "Women's Rights are Men's Lefts" ' (ibid.). This, there is no need to state, is pure historical analysis, based on his considered judgement, as is his later contribution that, in the case of Lydia Becker, Dr Pankhurst 'was said to have been the object of her unrequited passion' (ibid., p. 14). Who said? Mitchell quotes no source.

This is how women are destroyed, how they are robbed of their intellectual being and reduced to figures of fun in men's version of the world and men's version of their own importance. It is literary and histor-ical sexual harassment which denies women any existence other than that of sex-object; and women who protest about men, and who have lived without men, are prime targets for male abuse.

In writing about Emmeline Pankhurst (in a manner that must take the prize for misogyny, misrepresentation, malice and male fear) Piers Brendon (1979) says that, 'at the age of fourteen she attended her first suffrage meeting, addressed by Lydia Becker' and apropos of nothing – except harassment – continues with the information that, 'Miss Becker was sub-sequently to utter the bitter cry of outcast spinsterdom: "Married women have all the plums of life" ' (p. 143). No source is quoted; Brendon shows not the slightest insight into a women's movement which was arguing – as Barbara Bodichon had done with her pamphlet on the laws affecting women and her attempts to have a married women's property bill enacted – that marriage, far from providing women with plums, took away their legal, financial and emotional rights. Only a man could have generated the idea that marriage was a good state for women, and only in a society where men formulate the rules for making sense of the world could Lydia Becker have been condemned for her choice to live without a man. Her contribution has been taken away and twisted into a grotesque representation which reinforces patriarchy.

5 Murder and matrimony: Frances Power Cobbe (1822–1904)

Frances Power Cobbe's contribution, however, just seems to have been taken away. There are three minor references to her in Ray Strachey's book, two in Josephine Kamm's (both times in relation to someone else) and none in Roger Fulford's; there is also a recent unpublished dissertation of Helen Caskie's (1981). And yet what little information I have been able to glean about her (without benefit of an exhaustive or exhausting search) suggests she was a most remarkable women whose ideas are relevant and illuminating for the contemporary scene.

Born in Ireland in 1822, she was in her twenties when she moved to England after her father's death. 'By her views on social problems, philosophical and religious questions she challenged much current belief and practice. Inspired by Mary Carpenter, she worked in Bristol amongst girls released from prison, inmates of work houses, prostitutes and unfortunates. Later in London, by pen and on public platforms, she supported many reforms advocated by women or for women' (Nightingale, 1962, p. 24). As early as 1861, at a meeting in Ireland, she was reporting on her work in Bristol. Involved in the movement for higher education for women, she gave a speech (jeered and ridiculed by the press) advocating university degrees for women at the Social Science Congress in 1862; committed to the enfranchisement of women, she was on the executive council of the London National Society for Women's Suffrage from 1867.

Her letter sent to Paulina Wright Davis in 1870 expressing her regret at not being able to attend the Second Decade celebration of the woman's rights movement is quoted in *History of Woman's Suffrage* (1882, vol. II, p. 438) – and was one of the first items that made me curious about her. As part of the suffrage campaign in Britain a number of women were asked to write the reasons women wanted and needed the vote – the essays being collated into a pamphlet in 1879 and distributed to all members of parliament prior to a debate in the House – and Frances Power Cobbe's spirited contribution is reprinted in part in Caroline Ashurst Bigg's chapter (Stanton, Anthony and Gage, *History*, 1886, vol. III), on Great Britain.

In it Cobbe is uncompromising. It is crucial that women have the vote in order to protect their interests, and any woman who claimed otherwise lacked either sense or responsibility. 'I have scarcely ever known a woman possessed of ordinary common sense,' wrote Cobbe, 'who did not earnestly wish for it. The women who gratify these gentlemen [the members of parliament] by smilingly deprecating any such responsibilities, are those who have dwelt since they were born in well-feathered nests,' and, she says, continuing her metaphor with no reduction in force, it is utterly absurd for members of parliament 'to argue from the contented squawks of a brood of these callow creatures, that full grown swallows and larks have no need of wings, and are always happiest when their pinions are broken' (ibid., pp. 865–6).

No attempt seems to have been made by Frances Power Cobbe to avoid the epithet of 'strong-minded'; she was obviously not concerned with men's evaluation of her suitability as a servant for them. She was far more concerned with *their* unsuitability as leaders and lawmakers, and made many caustic and challenging comments about the limitations of male logic, the tyranny and injustice of male rule, and the flagrantly self-interested way men had organised society to make women available to them. The custom of marriage, and its enslavement of women, particularly attracted her attention and she was adamant in her assertion that men had deliberately and systematically arranged marriage so that women were deprived of all resources and that men could 'do with them what they will' – and this *frequently* meant they could use violence against women – with impunity.

In 1868 she published a pamphlet with the provocative title, *Criminals, Idiots, Women and Minors. Is this Classification Sound?* In it, she begins by adopting a technique, not unknown to feminists today, of trying to view the practices of society through the eyes of someone who does not share society's assumptions; Cobbe uses a 'visitor' from a distant planet for this purpose and a 'guide' explains to him the custom of marriage. Because it makes interesting reading, I quote the 'allegory' she uses:

> 'Ah,' we can hear him say to his guide, as they pass into a village church, 'What a pretty sight is this! What is happening to that sweet young woman in white, who is giving her hand to the good looking fellow beside her? . . . She is receiving some great honour, is she not?'. . .
>
> 'Oh yes,' would reply the friend; 'an honour certainly. She is being Married.' After a little further explanation, the visitor would pursue his inquiry:
>
> 'Of course, having entered this honorable state of matrimony, she has some privileges above the women who are not chosen by anybody? I notice her husband has just said, "with all my worldly goods I thee endow." Does that mean that she will henceforth have control of his money altogether, or only that he takes her into partnership? . . .'
>
> 'By our law it is *her* goods and earnings, present and future, which belong to him from this moment.'
>
> 'You don't say? But then of course, his goods are hers also?'
>
> 'Oh dear, no! not at all. He is only bound to find her food; and truth to tell, not very strictly or efficaciously bound to do that.'
>
> 'How! do I understand you? Is it possible that here in the most solemn religious act . . . every husband makes a generous promise,

which promise is not only a mockery, but the actual reverse and parody of the real state of the case: the man who promises giving nothing, and the woman who is silent giving all?'

'Well, yes; I suppose that is something like it, as to the letter of the law. But then, of course, practically –'

'Practically, I suppose few men can really be so unmanly and selfish as the law warrants them in being. Yet, some I fear, may avail themselves of such authority. May I ask another question? As you subject women who enter the marriage state to such very severe penalites as this, what worse have you in store for women who lead a dissolute life, to the moral injury of the community?'

'Oh the law takes nothing from them. Whatever they earn or inherit is their own. They are able, also, to sue the fathers of their children for maintenance, which a wife, of course, is not allowed to do on behalf of *her* little ones, because she and her husband are one in the eyes of the law.'

'One question still further – your criminals? Do they always forfeit their entire property on conviction?'

'Only for the most heinous crimes; felony and murder, for example.'

'Pardon me; I must seem to you so stupid! Why is the property of the woman who commits Murder, and the property of the woman who commits Matrimony, dealt with alike by your law?' (pp. 3–5).

Since Cobbe's time there have been changes in the law which were designed to remove the anomaly that permitted 'immoral' women from enjoying 'advantages' not available to wives. As Zoë Fairbairns (1979a), has pointed out, the 'cohabitation rule' was introduced with the explicit aim of ensuring that 'single' women on welfare would not be in a better financial position than their married counterparts. Perhaps as more exposés like those of Frances Power Cobbe's appeared, and women were more aware of the arguments *against* marriage, men were obliged to find some remedies in order that they could continue to have wives; in Thompson's words, the chains had to be less galling in *man's interest*.

For Cobbe certainly suggests in her article that foolish is the woman who enters marriage. In her introduction she wittily and amusingly satirises and exposes the absurdities of marriage customs in a non-threatening and impersonal way, but she then goes on to state the case against men and marriage in a thorough and more threatening manner. It is real women she is talking about and she gives their names, the conditions of their personal existence, and the legally sanctioned theft and violence to which they were subjected is described. From her pamphlet it is clear that she does not concur with men's good opinion of themselves. It is also clear that her concern is not confined to the psychological and emotional aspects of women's oppression (as outlined by Florence Nightingale, for example). Frances Power Cobbe focuses on violence against women and sees marriage customs arranged to permit rather than pre-empt such violence.

Her basic premises are that men desire to have authority over women and that they have organised social customs to secure and safeguard that authority. They will go to great lengths – to illogical, unjust and violent lengths – she argues, to preserve the power they have seized, and which they maintain in one of two ways – by the stick or the purse! In each household men contend there can be only one ruler, says Cobbe, and that: 'If somebody is to rule it can only be the husband, who is wiser, stronger, knows more of the world' . . . according to men . . . 'and in any case has not the slightest intention of yielding his natural dominance. But to give a man such rule he must be allowed to keep the purse. Nothing but the power of the purse – in default of the stick – can permanently and thoroughly secure authority' (ibid., p. 8). This is why men have seen fit to deprive women of any property upon marriage, for by making women totally dependent economically, a man can be reasonably sure that he will be the authority in the relationship, and reasonably sure that his authority will go unchallenged. Robbing women of any economic base ensures their agreement and co-operation.

That this is the purpose behind the practice, however, is not freely admitted, says Cobbe, for if men were to acknowledge that marriage is designed to deprive women of their resources, in order that men might have more, perhaps not as many women would *willingly* enter such a state of bondage. But men, instead of admitting what they have to gain from marriage, says Cobbe, hypocritically insist that it is all arranged in women's interest, rather than their own. Once women are without resources, they are vulnerable, argues Cobbe; they can so easily be made 'victims.' Men have taken many measures to ensure women are without resources, with the result that many women *are* victims. It is not just property which men have taken from women, in order to protect their own position, but legal rights as well. Women, deemed by men legally to not-exist upon marriage, are powerless economically and legally, and are without any possibility of redress for maltreatment. So what is to stop men maltreating women? Nothing.

She argued that men made the laws on the basis of the limited experience of men, that they thought only of themselves and were concerned primarily with enhancing and consolidating their position of power. Upon marriage, she protested, they take everything a woman has and oblige themselves to give nothing in return, for if husbands are unable to provide food and shelter for their wives – even if it is through the fault of drinking or gambling – *the laws men have made have not one word to say against such men.*

The laws have been used to rob women of their resources but they have not been used to enforce the responsibility of men. Such laws, she argues, could only have been made by men with no thought for the position of women and with every thought for their own protection: 'The legal act by which a man puts his hand in his wife's pocket, or draws her money out of the savings bank, is perfectly clear, easy, inexpensive,' she says. But, 'the corresponding process by which the wife can obtain food and clothing from her husband when he neglects to provide it, where may it be? Where is it described?' (1868, p. 11). Support for women is unattainable through men's laws – but the theft of women's resources by men is made legal. Cobbe is stunned by the total one-sidedness and illogicality of men's laws and declares that they could only have been made by those who were immune from the penalties that were imposed. If men were 'ever to ask themselves how such an existence' as a wife 'would suit *them*,' she says, 'they might perhaps be startled with the reflections which would suggest themselves' (ibid., p. 25).

Would a man think it logical and just to be in Mrs Seymour's position, she asks, and quotes a horrific case of the consequences for women of men's laws? In Lincolnshire, 'a parish surgeon wrote thus to the clergyman of the parish, who was also a magistrate:-

> Dear Sir, – I have today seen Mrs Seymour. I found her in a wretchedly weak state. She is nursing a baby, which office she has not been able to perform effectually from her exhausted condition. Her husband, she says, does not allow her the necessaries of life, which he, in his position, could find if he liked. Without some means being taken to provide her with good diet, etc., or to make her husband do so, she must die of starvation at no very distant period. If you could, in your official capacity, help the poor creature, you would confer a great blessing on the poor woman, and oblige yours faithfully,
>
> J. C. Smallman'

Quoting from *Illustrations of the Operations of our Laws*, Cobbe continues: 'The clergyman found, however, that he had no power as a magistrate to take cognisance of the case, unless the guardians would give the wife relief, and prosecute the husband; and this they declined to do. In vain did the poor half-starved wretch appear before them, and pray to be admitted into the workhouse. She was refused admission on the ground that her husband earned good wages; and so she went home, and after lingering a while, probably fed now and then by her neighbours, she died. The husband escaped without any punishment whatever. The jury who tried him (*men* of course!) gave him the benefit of a doubt as to the cause of his wife's death, and acquitted him' (ibid., pp. 12–13).

What do men suggest that women do under these circumstances, demands Cobbe? Do they suggest that women take action – protest, resist, defend themselves? Or do they suggest that women should quietly and passively permit themselves to be legally murdered? It is demonstrable that they prefer the latter, she argues, for there are cases where women have rebelled against male tyranny, where they have retaliated, and it is perfectly clear what can happen to them. Women who have earned their own money to support themselves and their children, who are then legally robbed of it by their husbands, have few alternatives available then, and she quotes the case of a woman whose 'lawful tyrant came home as usual, drunk with the spoils of her starving children' and who rather than starve quietly, in desperation 'took up some wretched relic of their ruined household and smote him to death'. Under men's laws, says Cobbe, 'She was a murderess.

In former times she would have been burnt alive for "petty treason" for killing her lord and master' (ibid., p. 14).

There is Susanna Palmer, she says, quoting a case before the public at the time; what does it tell us about men's laws and the value men place upon women? 'Susanna Palmer was indicted on the 14th January, 1869, at the Central Criminal Court, for wounding her husband in a struggle, in which it appeared he had, while drunk, endeavoured to wrench a table knife from her hand at supper. The evidence, which has since been carefully sifted and amply corroborated, showed Susanna Palmer to be a most industrious and sober woman. For twelve years since her marriage with James Palmer she has managed to support herself and her four children, having received from him during that period the sum of *five shillings* for the purpose. He has been four or five times in gaol for beating her, knocking out her teeth, and nearly killing her boy. Each time he returned from prison only more brutal and rapacious, and seized whatever money or furniture she had managed to obtain, breaking up her home over and over again. She applied to the magistrates at Clerkenwell for a Protection Order, to enable her to retain her earnings, but was refused it as her husband had not "deserted" her; and, of course, had not the slightest intention of doing so' (ibid.).

Little has changed: Cobbe sees violence against women not as the aberrant behaviour of a few isolated males but as an extension of a system of laws and practices – encoded by men – which decree that whatever women have is available to them as of right. And it is because such behaviour is part of the sanctioned social system that men will not 'intervene' in such circumstances, that they will not 'come between a man and his wife', between a 'master and his slave', for the master *owns* the slave as the man *owns* his wife, and can do with her what he will. This, decree men, is a 'private' arrangement and beyond the jurisdiction of the law – while men are in charge of the law, anyway.

But there are instances, says Cobbe, when it is no longer possible to deny male violence against women, where it intrudes on the public conscience and will not go away, and what do men do about it then? Do they consider changing the laws? No, she says firmly, by some strange twist of logic they argue that men are honourable, and the *particular* male who has committed an offence is exceptional – and the law cannot be made for exceptions!

Perhaps there is a contradiction here, suggests Cobbe, because in other circumstances men are very quick to enact laws on the basis of exceptions: 'The greater number of people are honest, and neither steal their neighbour's goods nor break into their houses. Yet the law takes pretty sharp account of thieves and burglars' (ibid., p. 15). There is no contradiction here, however, argues Cobbe, if we look at the laws in terms of property and the way men protect the property they claim as their own. Men can pass laws against thieves to protect their property and they can fail to pass laws which provide assistance for women – to protect their property! The laws, she argues, exist to protect men and to give them legal access to women's resources and no amount of 'rationalisation' on the part of men changes this: it is not women who are the object of male concern, it is men themselves. This can be readily demonstrated by example after example.

Any other segment of the community seen to be disadvantaged (such as children who work in factories) has their position strengthened by protective legislation. But it is quite the reverse for women. Bending logic to meet their own ends, men have argued that *because* women are *inferior* they cannot have legal rights or protective legislation: 'it is the alleged helplessness of married women which, it is said, makes it indispensable to give all the support of the law, *not* to them, but to the stronger persons with whom they are unequally yoked' (ibid., p. 16). Men start off with the advantages and they use their laws to increase those advantages, and they have the temerity to offer the absurd explanation that it is only women they are thinking of!

Helen Caskie (1981) says that Frances Power Cobbe was a woman of powerful intellect who could express her ideas in a vigorous manner: 'Hers is a punchy style, full of amusing asides and satirical comments, which are impossible to describe but a delight to read. Her open but combative nature shines out in her writings, yet the seriousness of purpose and the lucid arguments cannot disguise her deep understanding and her desire to be just' (p. 32). Not that she was seen in this positive light in her own time, for, despite being cited frequently in the then current literature, the references to her were not always flattering! She was the first woman, says Caskie, 'to have written so prolifically and profoundly on the actual question of womanhood' (ibid.), and while this may not be accurate (given how many 'firsts' there are supposed to have been), her contribution was indeed most significant.

Defiantly, Frances Power Cobbe contends that men have made the world to suit themselves and to serve their interests and they have *forced* women to fit into their scheme. They have fooled themselves with a poetic vision of marriage which they find pleasing and, without reference to the demands and denials it exacts from women, have proceeded to act as if their vision were true. They have created a structure in which they are made strong and have asserted 'that a woman's whole life and being, her soul, body, time, property, thought and ease ought to be given to her husband; that nothing short of such absorption in him and his interests makes her a true wife' (1868, pp. 18–19). Only men could propose such a reality, asserts Cobbe; only men who took no account of women as part of humanity would have the gall to suggest that this was a satisfactory arrangement.

Frances Power Cobbe's analysis is astute and bold: the centrality which she gives male violence against women makes her views very much contemporary and the scorn which she pours on male logic places her firmly in the tradition of women who have for centuries seen that men attempt to pass off their own interests and views as human interests and views. But the same old question arises – where did she go? What has happened to this daring and disagreeable woman who repudiated the male version of reality, who rebelliously asserted her independence of men and their approval, who for thirty years lived with her female companion, Mary Lloyd, who mocked male authority and exposed the ludicrousness of male logic and the limitations of male intellect? How was it that an unmarried woman, in Victorian times, found the confidence and courage to assert her autonomy and to ridicule the idea that a sensible woman would want to make a man the centre of her universe and find herself content to be legally robbed and raped? What influences were at work which allowed her to so clearly see that men took women's soul, body, time, property, thought and ease and used them for their own advantage?

And what does it mean for us today when *both* deferential Lydia Becker *and* defiant Frances Power Cobbe have disappeared? To me it suggests that while women do not control their own resources it doesn't much matter whether we try and seek men's approval for our actions or not – there is no evidence that seeking male support makes achievement of our goals more likely, for we are damned if we do, and damned if we don't, and I think Frances Power Cobbe probably gained more self-esteem from her defiance than Lydia Becker did from her deference. For my part, I do not think I will ever again accept the validity of the argument that caution, conciliation and male approval are either desirable or necessary. Given that men rob women of their resources, I'm not going to make it easy for them: I'm not going to be *willing*.

Frances Power Cobbe challenged male authority and, unlike Lydia Becker, saw some positive results for her efforts. Partly in response to her public protests magistrates were empowered in 1878 to grant separation orders which afforded women some small protection from violent husbands. But her work was not consolidated over the next century, and in 1978 women were fighting many of the same battles again, having to 'prove' as she had done, that 'wife battering' and 'wife torture'[4] was not confined to the exceptional few (who probably did something to provoke it), but was a widespread pattern of behaviour among men, and was likely to remain so while men accorded themselves the right to appropriate women's resources of mind and body for their own unaccountable use.

6 Let him claim the copyright on this! Caroline Norton (1808–1877)

There was another woman, almost a contemporary of Frances Power Cobbe's, and who could even have been one of her 'case studies', who confronted the injustice and the cruelty of the legal non-existence of women, and who fought to change it. She was Caroline Norton (who was George Meredith's model for *Diana of the Crossways*), and though in some respects she was concerned with the same problem as Cobbe, most available records suggest she had very different ideas about women, society and change.

Daughter of the dramatist Thomas Sheridan (who had died without leaving his wife and family endowed with financial resources and therefore

---

[4] She wrote a pamphlet *Wife Torture*, see Caskie, 1981.

with little likelihood of entertaining free and independent opinions), Caroline Sheridan at the age of 19 married George Norton,[5] who proved to be violent, vindictive, and an extremely poor provider. Drawing on her female talents of wit and beauty – and all those attributes which comprise the repertoire of a successful social hostess – Caroline Norton gained entry to some of the most select London circles (despite her husband, it seems, see Janet Courtney, 1933, p. 76) and made use of some of her 'contacts' when she found it necessary to support herself (and at times, her husband), by writing. Among her social contacts was the prime minister, Lord Melbourne.

That Caroline Norton was concerned with her 'appearance' in fashionable society (for it was her 'currency') is indicated by a comment of Janet Courtney's, when she says that Caroline Norton had an aversion to her sister-in-law, Augusta Norton, who 'was eccentric, wore closely cropped hair, bloomers and short skirts,' and, 'Caroline shrank from taking her about' (ibid., p. 81). I would be interested in knowing more about Augusta Norton but no more information is forthcoming.

Some of the deatils of Caroline Norton's married life are quite dreadful: her husband was violent, he was foolish, he could not keep a job which kept him in the manner to which he wished to become accustomed. She ran away (more than once) and took refuge with her family, but she consistently sought reconciliations – even after he had advertised in the newspaper that he was not responsible for her debts. But one of the reasons she sought reconciliations was because Norton had the children (as he had every right to) and she wished to be with them. Caroline Norton experienced the penalties imposed on married women by the law, first hand; her husband had not provided for her, he had beaten her, and she had left to find that she was penniless, had no rights to her children and no redress against her husband. She even recognised that if she continued to write and to support herself, her husband could claim for himself every penny she earned and leave her completely destitute.

When biographers state that George Norton was vindictive they have considerable grounds for their assertion. While Caroline Norton was staying with her sister to escape his violence, while he was in no way contributing to her upkeep and was denying her any access to her children, he brought an action against Lord Melbourne for 'criminal conversation' with his wife (Strachey, 1928, p. 35). The case against Melbourne (and Caroline Norton) was so weak, however, that: 'Counsel for the defendant Premier did not even trouble to call his witnesses' (Courtney, 1933, p. 83), yet while Caroline Norton was vindicated – she also *lost*. She 'lost' her good name (necessary to her in the circles in which she moved and which helped to provide her literary success and her livelihood), she lost her children, and she lost the possibility of a future divorce – for after the unsuccessful suit brought by her husband he would not have a claim for divorce – and Caroline Norton, having no legal existence, could not sue for divorce herself!

[5] Ray Strachey (1928) refers to him as Richard Norton.

Strachey (1928) states that after the court case, her husband sent the children away to Scotland and for a long time Caroline Norton did not even know where they were: 'Her husband refused all her pleadings, refused to give her any allowance, and retained, as was his legal right, the furniture and all the property that was hers' (p. 35). Faced with such mammoth injustice, Caroline Norton decided to fight; the means available to her were not only few, but virtually unthought of in the cicles in which she moved. She began to write pamphlets about *Mother's Rights*, which were widely circulated and proved to be influential (although such activity was not compatible with the image of a 'lady').

Among the statements that she makes about the injustice of men's laws as they relate to women is one defiant statement issued to her husband who rightfully can rob her of anything she earns: after a savage indictment of the laws and the way they are used by some men, she concludes: 'My husband' has a legal lien (as he has publicly proved) on the copyright of my works. Let him claim the copyright of THIS . . .' (quoted in Strachey, 1928, p. 37). Such defiance was also extremely clever for, by giving utterance to her own version of reality and the unflattering place that some men in general and her husband in particular occupied within it, Caroline Norton makes a dramatic point that women can use their own resources for themselves and make it at least embarrassing, and at most impossible, for men to seize them and make them their own.

While this is one very good example that when women cease being quiet and seeking approval and start being disagreeable and defiant there can be a positive outcome, unfortunately according to what I can find, it seems to be a single instance of desperation on Caroline Norton's part, rather than a planned strategy. While she fought for custody provision for mothers and later women's right to divorce, all accounts of her motives suggest that not only was she *not* interested in challenging male dominance, but she was hostile to those who were. In relation to the Divorce Bill, Strachey (1928) says that Caroline Norton had no interest in its wider implications, 'and like so many others, she ridiculed the wider reforms of which some people were thinking. She repudiated the "ill-advised public attempts on the part of a few women to assert their 'equality' with 'men'," and made fun of the "strange and laughable political meetings (sanctioned by a chairwoman) which have taken place in one or two instances." All she wanted was to secure that if a woman was obliged to leave her husband she might resume possession of her own property' (p. 75). If this was Norton's analysis, her dependence on male approval for her living goes a long way towards explaining it.

One thing Caroline Norton does do (albeit unintentionally) is provide illuminating insights into some of the ways women can be divided and ruled by men. At the same time she was writing her pamphlets in the attempt to change the custody and divorce laws, Barbara Bodichon was conducting her campaign for reforms relating to married women's property, and the two acts, with two different sponsors, were used in some measure to counteract each other. By 1857 there were two women's bills being debated, says Strachey, 'both dealing with the innermost sanctuary, the home, and to a certain extent they were used to destroy each other. The larger aspirations of feminists were freely used as an argument against both proposals, and the struggle over the Divorce Bill was intense. "Some loose notions have been thrown out of women's intellectual equality with men," ran a horrified pamphlet of the day, "and of their consequently equal right to all the advantages of society . . . these are speculative, extravagant, and almost unnatural opinions" ' (ibid., p. 74).

Not surprisingly, it was the bill which Caroline Norton fought for which proved to be the one that gained favour: the 1857 Marriage and Divorce Act which was no part of the women's movement reflected the prevailing double standard of the time and, rather than eroding male power, simply attempted to remove some of the more blatant forms of injustice in order to make male power more acceptable (as in line with the thesis put forward by William Thompson). Basically it laid down that as it was natural and expected that men should be unfaithful this was to be acceptable and not culpable behaviour and therefore could not constitute grounds for divorce; but for a woman such behaviour was not natural (and besides, it threatened inheritance procedures and ran the risk of deceiving men about their heirs – although this of course was not explicitly mentioned), and therefore could constitute grounds for divorce. A woman must prove cruelty or desertion, as well as adultery, before she could claim a divorce from her husband. But once divorced, the reform also contained provision for possible maintenance for the wife, for possible custody of children, and for the right of the wife to possess any future earnings or inheritance.

Once this Act was on the Statute Book, says Strachey, even though it was far from any remedy envisaged by Barbara Bodichon, it was obvious that no further reforms relating to married women's property would be considered for many a day. This was partly the reason Barbara Bodichon turned to the issue of women's employment, because at least there was some prospect of change in this area (ibid., p. 76).

7 The Queen!

All the time that women were trying to bring about some small improvements in their status and position there was a fundamental irony that the most prestigious – if not powerful – position in the country was held by a woman. Queen Victoria, however, far from suggesting that because *she* was competent to fulfil the requirements of a powerful position, *other* women might be equally capable of conducting themselves with credit in a public role, actually went out of her way to decry the reform movement among women. One instance of this is the case of Lady Amberley (the mother of Bertrand Russell).

In March 1879 a suffrage meeting was held in Hanover Square Rooms, in London, and women were very much in evidence as they chaired the meeting and gave their talks, stating the reasons for women's enfranchisement. There was an outcry after this meeting – with accusations that women who talked in public 'unsexed' themselves (evidently quite a simple process) and Lady Russell afterwards wrote to her son, Lord Amberley, congratulating him on the fact that he had a wife who did *not* speak in public. Her congratulations were shortlived, for Lady Amberley very soon decided she should speak out on women's suffrage and she proceeded to do so at the Mechanics Institute at Stroud. 'But even worse than the flashes and cavernous roarings of Fleet Street were the horrified comments of that august personality withdrawn behind the walls at Windsor,' says Roger Fulford, for Queen Victoria wrote:

> The Queen is most anxious to enlist everyone who can speak or
> write or join in checking this mad, wicked folly of 'Woman's Rights'
> with all its attendant horrors, on which her poor feeble sex is bent,
> forgetting every sense of womanly feeling and propriety. Lady
> Amberley ought to get a *good whipping* (quoted in Fulford, 1958, p.
> 65).

While I am not uncritical of Queen Victoria and the hypocrisy of the position she adopted, I am even more critical of Fulford who rather enjoys pointing out that 'women are their own worst enemy', are irrational, and cannot be relied upon even to know their own best interest. It is undeniable that I have found his book useful in many respects, but it has also taken its toll as I exercise restraint: on the same page that he reports Lady Amberley's act of defiance, he also tells of Helen Taylor's support of her. Helen Taylor wrote to Lady Amberley saying it was better to be scandalous because of one's strong-mindedness than for any other reason, and Fulford adds – gratuitously and without a single shred of substantiation, 'There was, however, no great danger of Helen Taylor figuring in a scandalous story: she was not likely (even in slight mourning) to be the toast of White's' (ibid., p. 64).

Why has there never been a scandal about men who have such perverse opinions of their own importance and who have fabricated such perverse reputations for women? No prizes for shrewd guesses – those who have the power, have the power to decree the rules.

8 Traditional and non-traditional jobs?

During the second half of the nineteenth century many, many women came into the public arena and fought on a variety of fronts in Britain for women to own and control their own resources. The number of women who have analysed the social arrangements, identified male power as a central problem, and worked to undermine that power in any one of its many manifestations is too numerous for me to provide even a brief summary of their lives and work.

Among those who hold rich promise for further investigation are Esther Roper and Eva Gore-Booth. Both were involved in the suffrage movement, both were pacifists (and supporters of conscientious objectors) and both worked to organise barmaids in the effort to protect their jobs at a time when a moral crusade was being conducted to prevent them from working. While today we may take it for granted that women have a place serving in a male stronghold of club or pub, without the effort of these two women, we could today just as easily take it for granted that women were *excluded* from such male territory. While men were successfully pushing women out of many areas of employment – primarily on the spurious grounds that they were morally and physically unsuited to the work, despite the fact that in the coal mines, for example, it was demonstrable that women were performing the hardest and least desirable physical tasks – Esther Roper and Eva Gore-Booth fought to preserve this area of women's employment, and they were successful.

Eva Gore-Booth was also a poet of some acclaim and was among feminist friends in her own family; she was the younger sister of Countess Markievicz, who was the first woman elected to parliament in 1918 (but who did not take her seat, as her protest for Irish independence). Esther Roper was also the first woman, I think, to stand for election as a woman's suffrage candidate in a general election (this information contained in her obituary, *Manchester Guardian*, 1938).

Lady Byron (1792–1860) and her daughter Ada Lovelace (sometimes referred to as 'the only legitimate daughter of Lord Byron') made a considerable contribution. Generous with financial assistance, Lady Byron opened schools for the poor, was a close friend of Anna Jameson, much admired by Harriet Martineau and much maligned by her husband and his biographers. Her daughter Ada was encouraged to tackle every branch of learning and excelled in mathematics: Williams, *A History of Technology* (vol. VII, part II) actually states that it was Charles Babbage and his friend Lady Lovelace (I would of course have put it the other way around, thereby providing a different emphasis), who understood some of the principles of what would today be called computer programming. Ada Lovelace 'translated a paper describing the analytical engine (the forerunner of the computer) written by General L. F. Menebrea ... and in doing so added extensive translator's notes (in total more than twice the length of the original paper) which amounted to an explanation of the manner in which the machine would be programmed. ... She thus described what we would now call a "loop" and a "sub-routine" ' (p. 1178). That was in 1841; almost a century later in 1937 and then in 1946 her notes and ideas were built upon and extended to become some of the underlying principles of computer programming – and one of the more recent computer languages has been named in her honour.[6]

It does seem ironic that what we tend to take for granted this century (that women can readily be barmaids and that it has become a traditional area of employment, and that women have difficulty with mathematics, so a female mathematician is in a non-traditional job) should have been almost

---

[6] I am grateful to Dorothy Stein who originally brought Ada Lovelace to my attention and is currently writing a biography of her.

the reverse last century when Mary Somerville and Ada Lovelace were acknowledged as leading mathematicians but when women had to defend their right to be barmaids. Is it that women have been permitted to work as barmaids because this is not an influential position, and that as mathematics have become increasingly important women have been pushed out?

9 Hitting a nerve: women and education

Within the movement for women's education there were so many women, of so many varying beliefs, and with so many ideas about how to secure education for women, and so many hopes about what such education would bring. Nearly all of them shared the assumption that a basic reason women were not treated seriously and as intellectual beings was because they were not educated, and that once women enjoyed the *same* education as men (which was Emily Davies's uncompromising line even when it could be demonstrated that the education men were receiving was hardly helpful or useful), they would perform in the *same* intellectually competent way, and would soon be accorded the same treatment as intellectual beings. Some women even assumed that this would lead to women having the same job opportunities and the same pay and it was therefore a major focus for work for the elimination of inequality.

There was Elizabeth Garrett Anderson, the first woman doctor in Britain, close friend of Emily Davies and sister of Millicent Fawcett, who endured all manner of mockery and abuse and who was the last woman as well as the first woman to find a way through the old provisions for becoming qualified: after her, the 'loophole' was closed and Sophia Jex-Blake had to start again from scratch under a new set of rules.

Dorothea Beale and Frances Mary Buss have become almost a legend – but a legend of the spinster/headmistress type in which their intellectual contribution is almost denied and their radical vision of educated girls has been reduced to respectable and fairly insubstantial reform, now that secondary education for girls is no longer considered a threat to society and a challenge to male power. But when they conceptualised such an education, it *was* radical and they had every reason to believe that it would lead to significant changes in the relationship between the sexes, for many men believed this would occur and fiercely resisted their efforts to secure change. But so harmless have these two women been rendered that their individual personalities and considerable differences in analyses and strategy have virtually been lost as they have almost been blended together into a single entity. As Jill Lavigueur (1980) has remarked, the fact that they founded two very distinct traditions of education for girls is rarely noted (p. 181).

Dorothea Beale became headmistress of Cheltenham Ladies' College in 1858 and her aim was to 'provide an education which was worthy of comparison with the boys' public schools but which was specifically for girls' (ibid.). She wanted educated and accomplished 'ladies' who were morally educated and morally responsible, who could provide a worthy example for the future generation they would rear. To this end she introduced some academic work and intellectual training into the curriculum and, although it went beyond the limits previously permitted for girls and was considered radical and dangerous (see Carol Dyhouse's accounts (1977, 1981) of the assertions that such training for girls would lead to infertility, would inhibit lactation, would result in atrophy of uteri and nervous breakdowns, etc.), was none the less very different from boys' education in public schools, and was more definitely within the framework of what was appropriate for young ladies.

In adopting this educational model, Dorothea Beale was almost diametrically in opposition to the stance taken by Emily Davies who insisted that girls and women should pursue an educational course that was identical in every respect with that of their male counterparts.

Frances Mary Buss also had very different ideas from Dorothea Beale, and a very different philosophy of education, for rather than trying to make her female students fit into the existing social patterns (and providing a curriculum which would help to equip them for the role society had assigned them and preparing them for the traditional division of labour), she sought to educate young women who would change women's role, who would challenge the sexual division of labour and thereby change society. She wanted to train her girls for an independent life; she wanted them to have financial independence, to support themselves, and even have 'careers', and the two schools she founded (the North London Collegiate School and Camden Girls' School) reflected these values. Social and religious distinctions were abandoned to an almost unprecedented degree as she organised these schools so that they provided 'a basis for the pupils to initiate a new role for themselves in society' and a challenge to accepted conventions (Lavigueur, 1980, p. 182).

Both these women deserve far greater attention and admiration than they have received. The reasons they gave, the arguments they amassed, the case they mounted for education for girls in the face of hostile opposition (frequently from the medical profession who had objective scientific proof that it would be most damaging for girls to learn anything serious, even if they could, of course, and virtually fatal if they were to equip themselves with the same amount of learning (and incidentally find they enjoyed the same opportunities) as boys), their efforts on behalf of girls and their rebuttal of the medical profession and the establishment, deserve greater consideration.

Anne Jemima Clough (1820–91) also warrants more attention. Born in Liverpool in 1820, she then moved to Charlestown, South Carolina, and returned to England when she was 16. All her life she was concerned with women's access to educational circles and the growth and expansion of women's intellectual potential; all her life she was frustrated by the absence of opportunity for girls for such development, but she was never more frustrated than as a young teacher herself in Ambleside, where she started a school, after her father's death. She had a thirst and a passion for knowledge which was never satisfied, but she devoted much of her energy to trying to ensure that what she had missed would be available to women of future generations.

In 1861 she moved to London to live with her sister and found herself in the company of women who not only shared her ideas but were trying to put them into practice. She was caught up in the enthusiasm, the despair, and the defence of women who were helping Elizabeth Garrett fight the medical profession, and who were gathering round Emily Davies as she prepared for her struggle with Cambridge University.

In 1866, Anne Jemima Clough returned to Liverpool (where she met with Josephine Butler who was also active in the women's education movement) and tried to put into practice her plan for overcoming the weaknesses inherent in girls' schools as they were structured at that time. Basing her ideas on a principle very similar to that which underlies the current organisation of sixth-form colleges, Clough tried to bring together the senior girls from a range of small, poorly equipped and staffed schools, for lectures from highly qualified and experienced teachers. Establishing 'lecture tours' for visiting university staff members, she laid the foundation for what was to become the University Extension Lecture movement.

Out of her efforts to bring teachers to the girls, when the girls were not permitted to go to the teachers, emerged the North of England Council for Promoting the Higher Education of Women, with Anne Jemima Clough as secretary. By 1870 they had achieved the remarkable result of creating twenty-five lecture centres. When someone was required to supervise 74 Regent's Street, Cambridge – a house that had been taken to provide accommodation for young women in Cambridge in order that they might go to the teachers, instead of the teachers going to them, and attend some of the lectures – it was Anne Clough who was asked. She went in 1871 with the intention of staying but a short while, but remained until her death in 1891, and she supervised the residential scheme which grew into Newnham College.

As the woman in charge of Newnham, she was not Emily Davies's best friend. This was because Emily Davies (1830–1921) struggled long and hard to establish Girton on particular principles, and she thought Newnham was undermining everything she hoped to achieve. Rita McWilliams-Tullberg (1975) has said that from the very outset of the women's education movement there were two factions, 'those for whom education was an end in itself, and those for whom it was a particular end, proof of equality with men' (p. 25). Anne Jemima Clough was more sympathetic to the former while Emily Davies was unequivocally in favour of the latter. She argued strongly that 'women could only challenge men's intellectual dominance if they matched them at their own tests' (ibid., p. 26), and she most definitely wanted to challenge men's intellectual dominance so she therefore unyieldingly insisted that the women at Girton follow to the last letter and in every detail the tests which men had set up for themselves.

She was not to be persuaded that the tests were stupid, or that there were extenuating circumstances for females (who, for example, had often not enjoyed the same facilities or the same teacher expertise as their male counterparts), and it seems fair to say that she would have resisted to her dying breath any attempt to set up separate systems where women received one form of education and men another. To Emily Davies this would have achieved nothing in terms of changing the relationship between the sexes, for she believed that unless women's education was the same as men's it would not be considered valid and would make no difference to the intellectual status of women, who would continue to be denied intellectual competence precisely because they had *not* received the same education as men.

In some respects I think Emily Davies's analysis was accurate – there was no way men would treat women as serious intellectual beings while women undertook a different form of education, which was bound to be seen as a 'deficient' or 'lesser' form of education in a male-dominated society. What she omitted from her analysis, however, was the possibility that no matter what women did, men could continue to treat them as intellectually incompetent and that education was not the one and only rationale men might use. Men could still treat women as intellectually incompetent and inferior beings even if and when they had access to the same education!

Of course she had grounds for her argument. She had been closely involved with Elizabeth Garrett's campaign to gain entrance to the University of London, where the men certainly suggested by their behaviour that anyone who qualified in their terms as a medical practitioner was indeed a qualified medical practitioner and deserved to be treated as a proper medical practitioner. This was why no more women were permitted entry through the Apothecaries Society.

Emily Davies also encountered the frequent opposition of those who believed that if women were allowed to do the same examinations and courses as men, men would no longer hold such examinations and courses in high esteem. As this was precisely what Davies wanted, for men not to be able to laud an *exclusive* achievement over women, she pursued the goal of the *same* education for women with single-minded purposefulness.

Today, I would argue that she omitted another factor in her analysis: that the education that men had (and that women imitated) was designed by men, about men, for men, and that the battle for women's education was but a battle for women to find out in a systematic and legitimated way, just how prestigious and authoritative men are (and how inferior and deviant are women, in contrast). I would argue that it is because men control the construction and distribution of knowledge and because they have simply conceded to women the opportunity to partake of the knowledge they construct about themselves and the world, that women still do not have the *same* education as men. Women have no control over the knowledge which is generated, no control over what women learn, or what men learn: the authority of men remains unchallenged despite women's entry to the 'halls of learning' and because women are still excluded from the 'halls of power' (see D. Spender, 1981b). That is why the women in this book are not the substance of education, and will not become so while men remain in control. It is why the intellectual contributions of women past and present can be appropriated by men.

But if Emily Davies did not foresee this development, neither did the men who tried to prevent women from gaining access to the university. Rita McWilliams-Tullberg (1975) has given an excellent account of the resistance they mounted and the 'logic' that these illustrious dons used to defend their territory and retain their authority. Although, primarily through the efforts of Emily Davies, women had been attending lectures at Cambridge since 1872, their presence was based on a complicated system of private arrangements which could be revoked at any time, and in 1897 an attempt was made to formalise the situation and to have women accepted as official students who could be granted degrees. For six months before the vote was to be taken (by all men of course) a campaign was begun (for and against) and a veritable battle was waged in the press. Numerous were the men who adopted the position that every penny spent on women's education was a penny less spent on men's, and many were the men who indicated that they would fight any move women made to share in the government or privileges of the university.

Using the intelligence for which men are so famed, W. B. Skeat wrote of women's entry to the university that:

> If given the B.A., they must next have the M.A. and that would carry with it voting and perhaps a place on the Electoral Roll; a vote for the University Livings and all the rest. Even the B.A. degree would enable them to take 5 books at a time out of the University Library on a ticket countersigned by 'their tutor'. I am entirely opposed to the admission of women to 'privileges' of this character. And I honestly believe they are better off as they are (quoted in McWilliams-Tullberg, 1975, p. 89).

There were educated men – the cream of the intelligentsia and the custodians of authority – who expressed their bafflement that women should want education at all and who prophesied gloom and doom if it should come to pass. Women would be unsexed and men would be unable to control themselves they warned, seemingly unaware of the contradictions in their case. The abuse that was heaped upon women, and the vitriolic nature of much of it, suggests that men were quite frightened by the possibility that women might come to share their intellectual haven.

The vote was lost: women were not to be admitted (at Cambridge they were not to be admitted as full members for another fifty years). Some of the men celebrated by taking to the streets and rioting – in logical and objective manner, of course. 'The undergraduates began their celebrations by storming down to Newnham with the news' that the women had lost, says McWilliams-Tullberg (1975) and 'a student there remembers listening from the roof of one of the Newnham buildings, to the roar from the town which increased in volume as the attacking force gradually approached, to be finally held up by the closed College gates, with the (women) dons assembled beneath the archway. When their gentlemanly instincts were appealed to they left the women alone and returned to the Market Place for a night of wild celebration' (p. 139).

There was an extra-special edition of the *Cambridge Weekly News*, entitled 'The Triumph of Man', which told of the night's festivities – a bonfire in the Market Square fuelled by doors and shutters from shops, firecrackers exploded among the crowd and thrown into houses round the square, proctors mobbed, dogs terrorised. 'According to the report the police took a very sensible view of the whole demonstration and it was owing to their unfailing good humour and the way in which they kept their temper at critical moments that serious disorder did not occur' (ibid.). Some other papers brought out pictorial supplements of the events and referred to the 'high spirits' of the young men.

Too frequently today the women who fought for women's education are portrayed as cautious spinsters who plodded along diligently in the backwaters, gradually expanding an area that was deemed appropriate for women anyway. Such a presentation is far from the reality of the women who were involved in what was considered at the time to be a revolution. That we know so little about these women, or that what we know appears so dull and boring, is more likely to be evidence of what men have done with women's labour than it is to be evidence of the labour itself.

Some women were not in the front line; they did quietly and persistently enlarge women's sphere, but most of them who made any effort to widen women's educational opportunities at any level met hostility and harassment and had many an aspersion cast upon their personal life and aspirations.

Two very 'proper' women who were in their sixties before they took the 'plunge' (partly because, as I see it, by that time most of their family had succumbed to various illnesses and their services were no longer required for nursing) were the sisters Emily Shirreff (1814–97) and Maria Shirreff Grey (1816–1906) who, in the words of their biographer, 'laid the foundation of a national educational system for girls at the secondary level, a valid teacher-training pattern for that level of education, a revamped, in fact a new national system of early childhood education and the teacher-training structure to sustain it' (Ellsworth, 1979, p. 4).

These two sisters wrote 'major polemical works' (which for males would be 'major intellectual treatises') as well as novels. While not enjoying any great formal education themselves, they had a variety of informal experiences which probably endowed them with a better education than that given to the 'high spirited' Cambridge undergraduates. They travelled fairly extensively and had a wide circle of intellectual friends (Mary Somerville being a close friend) and were reasonably well read. There is much more to them than the conventional portrayal of philanthropic and benevolent Victorian ladies of the middle class who were concerned with civilising the poor.

While both evidently shared somewhat conservative assumptions early in their lives, in the later years (when they were in their seventies) Maria Grey moved more towards socialism and co-operative movements, as a consequence of her involvement in 'reform'. Emily Shirreff, who was not quite so ready to embrace this revolutionary cause, became mistress of

Girton in 1870. These women are part of our heritage; had they been men and contributed less, it is likely that we would still know more about them.

There were other branches of the women's movement apart from education: Octavia Hill (1838–1912) was at one stage a somewhat reluctant teacher, and an enthusiastic friend of Sophia Jex-Blake, and she later found her forte when she became a pioneer in housing reform. Josephine Kamm (1966) comments on the relationship between Octavia Hill and Sophia Jex-Blake (devoting more space to their relationship than housing reform) and indicates in the process how co-operation and friendship among women can be viewed through the prism of a male-dominated society to become distorted and distasteful: 'there sprang up one of those intense and passionate friendships', she says, 'which seem to have been common among the ranks of the "strong-minded" and which, though highly emotional, appear innocent' (1966, p. 107). Evidently I'm supposed to be reassured and to heave a sigh of profound relief.

Despite her involvement in reform, however, it seems that Octavia Hill – like a few other prominent women of her time – was not very interested in transforming society, only in modifying some of its more blatantly unjust practices. (Liz Stanley has since informed me that this is a most misleading view of Hill.) According to Kamm, she was concerned with inculcating a respect for property among the poor, and she was against women's suffrage – but I have no reason for taking this assessment of Octavia Hill at face value, and am more inclined to accept Liz Stanley's 'preliminary' research.

10 Organisation not legislation: Emma Paterson (1848–1886)

One woman who tried to break down some of the barriers of male dominance and who was interested in transforming the power base of society, who insisted – but who often went unheard – on women's autonomy, was Emma Paterson, trade unionism's forgotten woman, according to her biographer, Harold Goldman (1974). Whether the advantages of finding out something about her are outweighed by the disadvantages of having to see Emma Paterson through Goldman's eyes, I will leave to others to decide, but from the beginning of his account of Paterson's life, Goldman makes it quite clear that he has a certain amount of admiration for Emma Paterson, and that she is therefore not like other women: and she bears little resemblance to those other terrible women who fought for their sex. She is neither reticent nor bold, according to Goldman (although she made some errors of judgement on occasion and was a bit too obstinate in adhering to some of her less sensible ideas), but she was on the whole just the right mixture and was influential in bringing women into the trade union movement.

Her schoolmaster father provided her with a good education. On his death, when she had to support herself, she started out as a bookbinder's apprentice, but then later, at the age of 19, she acquired a post as assistant secretary to the Working Men's Club and Institute Union (July 1867) and it was in this context that she developed her passionate commitment to the autonomous organisation of working women. Into the discussion and debates of the time, says Goldman (1974), 'came the voice of a woman – not shrill and appealing as so often in the past' (and I wonder who he has in mind, for he refers to no one), 'but confident, firm and unyielding' (p.19).

It was at the Working Men's Club and Institute Union that she met Thomas Paterson, cabinet maker, her future husband, but his presence in the place did not deter her from applying for another job – that of the secretary of the Women's Suffrage Association. Goldman does not discuss the reasons that she changed jobs, nor even the attitude that she had to women's suffrage – or women's position in society – when she went there in 1872. All he says is that it was an unhappy affair, that the Women's Suffrage Association wanted 'fire and thunder' (and I think of Lydia Becker and ask *where* Goldman gets his information), and that she was not acceptable to the suffragettes. As the term 'suffragettes' did not even come into existence until 1906 (when the militants were given this name by the *Daily Mail*), I am not at all surprised. Has Goldman found some information that I have not, or does he just have a particular crude image of women who struggle for their sex as shrill, militant, 'fire and thunder', all lumped together under the term 'suffragette'? Emma, he assures us, did not get on with the fighting women in the suffrage movement because she 'was no natural agitator. She won people by her tact and quiet persuasiveness' and just in case we are still unconvinced of her 'womanly' virtues, 'her fist never hit the table' (ibid., p. 28).

From what I can deduce from Emma Paterson's own writings (which are quoted by Goldman), I wouldn't be at all surprised to find that if there was any friction between her and the Women's Suffrage Association it was more likely to be because she found some of the women there too timid and cautious, and unable to share her vision of autonomous, organised women.

After her brief encounter with the Women's Suffrage Association she married Thomas Paterson and they left for America, on a working honeymoon, where they were determined to study the organisation of labour as it had developed in the United States. On her return Emma Paterson began to work for the formation of an autonomous women's union, and to this end she gave a speech in London in 1874, urging women to organise themselves. Goldman concedes that she handled the issue well until she introduced the topic of protective legislation for women, where her ideas constituted a 'strange argument which led her to trouble and lost her support' (ibid., p. 37). She was against it!

At this stage she argued that it was both degrading and injurious to advocate protective legislation for women – degrading because women themselves were not consulted and injurious because it was another means of reducing women's wages. She suggested that women might not want their working hours reduced and that it was irresponsible for men's trade unions to proceed with this cause without even asking women workers what their preferences were; she also suggested that it was a manoeuvre on the part of men to push women out of their jobs.

Undoubtedly Goldman sees this as an error of judgement on Paterson's part, for she did not carry the men with this particular line of reasoning. I see it very definitely as a woman asserting women's independence of men, as a woman perfectly capable of seeing through the transparent arguments of men and of naming men's self-interest. I am not at all surprised that a male should not like this and decide it is an 'error of judgement'.

Much of Emma Paterson's speech in 1874 was directed against the trade unions which at that stage had been meeting for six years at the annual trades union congress, but without a single woman among them despite the enormous number of women in the workforce: 'At three successive annual congresses of leaders and delegates of trade unions', she said, 'the need of women's unions has been brought before them, and each time someone present has asserted that women *cannot* form unions. The only ground for this assertion appears to be that women *have not* yet formed unions. Probably they have not done so because they have not quite seen how to set about it' (quoted in Goldman, 1974, p. 38).

Emma Paterson made it quite clear that women and men had different interests, and that they each needed to organise around those different interests, while meeting annually (at the congress) on the basis of shared interests. So emphatic is she about this that Goldman feels obliged to protest that Emma Paterson was not interested in promoting that dreadful thing – 'a sex war'. Personally, I don't believe him.

The women bookbinders were the first to respond, and in 1875 the women dressmakers, milliners and mantlemakers joined; they were followed by women in the binding, sewing and trimming trades, the women upholsterers, and the women shirt- and collar-makers. Together they formed the Women's Protective and Provident League, with a central office; in 1876, a journal, the *Women's Union Journal,* was brought out under their auspices.

Numerous facilities were provided at the central office – lectures, meetings, a library, job information, assistance for women who were ill (or about to be released from gaol); excursions were organised, holidays arranged, swimming classes set up. The centre constituted a genuine meeting place for women and Emma Paterson was vehemently against the introduction of prayers or other 'virtuous activities', stating that: 'Wherever women go it seems to be thought the right thing to thrust needlework in their hands; no one has yet held a father's meeting at which work is carried on' (ibid., p. 101). The women's centre was for the women to organise in the way they felt fit and not for 'do-gooders' to come in and reform them.

The *Women's Union Journal* was extremely useful in helping to keep the women informed about employment and employment issues; cases of exploitation were reported and negotiations with employers commented upon. Other issues were also raised, such as that of dress reform, a measure to which Emma Paterson was personally committed.

There was much to be gained from having such a journal and it is interesting to note that while the women's union was formed later than the men's, and was much smaller, it had its journal before the men had theirs; Benjamin Pickard, writing from the Miners' Offices, Wakefield, said: 'I am struck forcibly with the idea that so far as being able to manage and support a trade journal the women are far ahead of the men. Many a time during the latter half of the nineteenth century have workmen essayed the issue of a trade journal, but I believe in every case they have failed miserably' (ibid., p. 94).

Three reasons can be put forward for women's success with the journal – one is that writing and reading is important to women (for, although no research has been undertaken in the area, I suspect that if it were, it would reveal that women in general read and write more on the average than men – including letters and diaries – and that this is partly because it is an activity not directly controlled by men); and secondly that women set up literally tens of journals in the late nineteenth and early twentieth centuries (see Elizabeth Sarah (ed.), 1982a,b,c). The other reason is Emma Paterson herself.

She was involved with Emily Faithfull in the planning of the Victoria Press (which printed the *Englishwoman's Journal*) and which was established primarily because of the resistance of men to women in the printing trades. Once the Victoria Press was under way (producing some of the best work in England despite constant attempts on the part of men in the printing trade to discredit it, or where its achievements could not be denied to declare – predictably – that the work was being done by men), Emma Paterson joined Emily Faithfull and learnt at the Victoria Press a trade she could learn nowhere else. Then in 1876 she founded the Women's Printing Society which printed the *Women's Union Journal* and which Emma Paterson edited until her death.

The printing trades were not the only ones, however, to oppose the employment (and organisation) of women. Emma Paterson fought hard and long to have the women's union admitted to the trades union congress, to have the word *women* included in the resolutions (particularly those relating to the appointment of factory inspectors where year after year the congress passed a resolution calling for more men, and Emma Paterson stood and requested that *women* also be included, until the president stated she was just being unreasonable and obstinate), and to have women's case presented. Harold Goldman is at some pains to explain the basis of this – from his perspective!

'There is no doubt that one of the main obstacles to women joining trade unions has been the attitude and open hostility of men in trade unions', he says, and with decided reasonableness adds, 'This cannot be dismissed as sheer bloody-mindedness, however, and it should not be thought that this exclusion was in any sense an objective of male trade unionists' (1974, p. 57). Why shouldn't it be thought men intentionally kept women out of trade unions because they thought it would be advantageous? Emma Paterson certainly thought this. It wasn't because they didn't want women, says Goldman, just that it took men a while to relax; they had fought so hard for their union, for it had really been a men's battle, and 'rights won by blood, mental torture and every sort of human privation were to be jealously guarded' (ibid., p. 58). Were only *men* involved, I ask myself?

I think Emma Paterson would have scoffed at Goldman's 'explanation' as she scoffed at many other 'explanations' put forward by male trade unionists in her own day. She did not try to disguise the issue that men were consistently trying to edge women out of employment – she had even been told at a trades union congress that the place for married women was in the home and not in the workplace taking 'men's jobs' – and that under the guise of protective legislation, men were trying to make women unacceptable as workers and thereby assure their own monopoly on employment. It is organisation, not legislation, that women need, Paterson protested defiantly, thereby failing to endear herself to male trade unionists (and committing another error of judgement in the process, as far as Goldman is concerned).

Over and over again Emma Paterson heard the male argument that because women would work for less and undersell them, men unionists would not work with women: over and over again Emma Paterson patiently explained that if women were organised, they would *not* work for less, and then there would be no problem. But her words fell on wilfully non-receptive ears, for Emma Paterson was arguing for equal pay for women, and few were the men whose dignity was not affronted (and whose value system was not threatened) by the suggestion that a woman's work was worth as much as man's. Only men who could see nothing beyond their own self-interest could insist that women be paid less, then complain that women were underselling them, and then proceed to insist that they would not work with women. It is the familiar scapegoat syndrome where men denied women the same pay and then blamed them because they received less pay. Emma Paterson knew this was the crux of the matter, even if Harold Goldman does not.

She was remarkably successful in her efforts, given that she started from scratch and built for a relatively short space of time a viable women's union. On her early death, her close friend Emilia Pattison (later Lady Dilke) took over leadership of the union until her death in 1904. If we need to know more about Emma Paterson, so too do we need to know more about Emilia Pattison, who was active in the suffrage movement and in women's trade unions, and who wrote a number of books about women and work. Of Emilia Pattison, Goldman says that she was 'a writer, art critic, outstanding intellectual . . . a friend of Ruskin' (not necessarily an advantage, given his position on women, and the fact that he wrote to the *Women's Union Journal* in 1878 to declare that Paterson was committing 'the definite error of endeavouring to make the sexes independent' and that 'the men of the country must maintain the women or they are worse than beasts', see Goldman, 1974, p. 95). Emilia Pattison was a friend of 'Robert Browning, and George Eliot who is said to have used at least some parts of Mrs Pattison's character in the drawing of Dorothea Brooke in *Middlemarch*' (ibid., p. 43).

Emma Paterson was primarily concerned with working women, with establishing a power base and a means of protection for women in the work force, and she insisted not on woman's weakness, but woman's strength. It is affirming but none the less dispiriting to find that many of the battles she fought 100 years ago are being played out again today; the arguments she put forward then are in many respects the same arguments that are put forward today, and I cannot help but ask – will they have the same effect? One thing I do know is that I want to spend much more time studying her ideas as they are reflected in the pages of the *Women's Union Journal* and not as they are presented through the filter of Harold Goldman.

11 Sexual economics: Josephine Butler (1828–1906)

We have inherited an image of the Victorian era which Martha Vicinus has aptly represented in the title of her book on that period – *Suffer and Be Still* (1973). I grew up with the conviction that 'Victorian' was a suitable term for designating denied and repressed sexuality, and with the firm belief that, with one notable exception, the Victorian period was for women an all-time-low in terms of the rigid restrictions imposed on their behaviour, and in terms of the extent to which they accepted the self-sacrificing and chaste place accorded to them. This is, of course, not an empowering image of one's past. Needless to say I have revised my image of the Victorian period and the Victorian lady, and not just because of the public stand (and the courage it entailed to take it) so many women adopted in the area of women's rights, but also because of the public and difficult stand many women took on the taboo issue of sexuality itself.

A *lady* was supposed to be unobtrusive, to attract no attention to herself, and to be 'innocent' (read 'ignorant') during the Victorian era. Josephine Butler broke all of these rules – and more – when for forty years from 1866 she was a prominent figure on the public stage and spoke openly on issues of sexuality. For her efforts she became not only a target for the ridicule and abuse that was the standard treatment handed out to 'strong-minded' women who placed themselves beyond the pale of men's protection, but also found reserved for her the even more vicious vilification thought 'fitting' for an 'impure' woman. A lady who was knowledgeable about sexual issues could provide no more clear indication that she was no longer a lady, and a lady who spoke about such issues in public was disgraced and damned beyond redemption.

Declaring that men divided women into two classes in order to preserve their own position and their own comfort, as Josephine Butler did, was not a new idea. It had been expressed by Mary Wollstonecraft and Harriet Martineau, by Frances Wright and Margaret Fuller, who had all claimed that the ideal of womanhood – based upon the *lady* who in return for her weakness was chivalrously protected – allowed the exploitation of working women to be denied and to remain invisible. But Josephine Butler gave a new and radical slant to this division of women, for she introduced *sexual economics* as a fundamental part of the issue. In so doing she not only broke the rules for the classification of women by being a lady who was not a lady, she exposed the rules and the reasons for them. Her public denunciation of this false division among women, her outright assertion that it was used to divide woman from woman and to make them sexually available to men, was a theat to the very foundations of male dominance and met with a characteristic response from men who believed they had much to lose if their arrangements – and their rationale – were disturbed.

William Acton was one such man: a medical practitioner, a specialist in venereal disease, editor of the *Lancet,* a 'scientific' man who waged war against 'prostitutes', he was outraged by the so-called 'ladies' who were critical of the measures being introduced to control immoral women, and he was at his most vindictive when condemning the impure and knowledge-able women who were sufficiently brazen and depraved to write and dis-tribute literature (as well as make speeches) about sexual economics, and who were spreading their noxious ideas through the population at large. Distressed but not deterred by the vitriolic abuse meted out by influential persons like Acton, Josephine Butler persisted in her efforts to make sex-uality a central issue in the explanation of women's oppression.[7]

From an early age she had protested at the divisions which had been structured among women, and the double standard that was an attendant part of such division. Born into a liberal family and surrounded as she said by a network of strong, supportive women – her mother, her beloved sister and her remarkable aunt, the 'strong-minded feminist' Margaretha Grey (who 'was so disgusted at finding she was not allowed to attend Parliament when her cousin was leader of the Whigs – there was no Ladies Gallery in either House at the time – that she made it a custom to obtain admission by dressing as a boy', Walkowitz, 1980, p. 115) – she was accustomed to solidarity and to shared interests among women. Encouraged to question social arrangements and to challenge the existing assumptions on which society was based, she was disposed to look beyond conventional arguments (particularly as they related to women) which were put forward in defence of inequality and exploitation. When in 1852 she went as a young wife with her husband George Butler to Oxford she was both astonished and angered by the intellectual limitations of the men she encountered there with their complete denial of the existence of women.

In *An Autobiographical Memoir* (1893)[8] she recounts this episode in her life where she was allowed to glimpse (and wait upon) the exclusively male circle which comprised the fellows of Oxford, for in 1852 she says, 'Oxford was not then what it is now under expanded conditions, with its married fellows and tutors, its resident families, its ladies' colleges and its mixed general social life' (p. 30). For centuries women had been banished from its precincts, and Josephine Butler quickly recognised the self-interest of the logic and intellectual debate of the all-male group it was her privilege

---

[7] I am grateful to Jenny Uglow for her information and insights on Josephine Butler.

[8] I am indebted to Sally Adams who found this volume for me – not in the protected and revered environs of a library, museum or antiquarian book shop, but at a jumble sale: ostensibly having nothing of value to contribute, its monetary value has not increased with the passing of time – it was five pence.

(as one of the few 'faculty wives') to serve and observe. 'A one-sidedness of judgement is apt to be fostered by such circumstances,' she wrote in 1893, 'an exaggeration of the purely masculine judgement on some topics and a conventual mode of looking at some things' (ibid., p. 30).

Josephine Butler viewed the world from a very different perspective from the men to whom she was obliged to listen: she was a subordinate, one who felt the consequences of male pronouncements and actions, not experienced by the men themselves. She saw what these men did not, and did not want to, see: 'In the frequent social gatherings in our drawing room in the evenings,' she says, 'there was much talk, sometimes serious and weighty, sometimes light, interesting, critical, witty and brilliant. It was then that I sat silent, the only woman in the company, and listened, some-times with a sore heart; for these men would speak of things which I had already resolved deeply in my own mind, things of which I was convinced, which I knew, though I had no dialectics at command with which to defend their truth. A few remarks made on these evenings stand out in my memory. They may seem slight and unimportant, but they had a significance for me, linking themselves as they did, to long trains of thought which for some years past, had been tending to form my own convictions' (ibid., pp. 30–1).

Josephine Butler lived the exclusion of women and women's experience from circles in which knowledge was generated and stamped with the sign of logic and legitimation. She lived the devaluation of women and the accompanying doubts about the reality and the validity of her own ex-perience, she lived the absence of words and reasons to substantiate the claim that the world looked very different from where she stood. And all these aspects of her experience, all these aspects of oppression, were drawn together by her to make a meaningful framework for interpreting the world and to propel her towards action to change it.

She gives an example (which in men's framework would be called a subjective female 'anecdote' but which is here treated as serious 'data') of the way she put the pieces together to form the whole, of the way she came to conceptualise women's oppression with sexuality as centrally significant. 'A book was published at that time by Mrs Gaskell,' she says (*Ruth* was published in 1853) 'and was much discussed. This led to expressions of judgement which seemed to me false – fatally false. A moral lapse in a woman was spoken of as an immensely worse thing than in a man: there was no comparison to be formed between them. A pure woman, it was re-iterated, should be absolutely ignorant of a certain class of evils in the world, albeit *those evils bore with murderous cruelty on other women.* One young man seriously declared that he would not allow his own mother to read such a book as that under discussion – a book which seemed to me to have a very wholesome tendency, though dealing with a painful subject. Silence was thought to be the great duty of all on such subjects' (ibid., p. 31, my emphasis).

But who benefited from such silence, asked Josephine Butler? Not the women; not the women who were kept in ignorance, and not the women who were cruelly exploited. Only the men who wished to preserve this distinction between women, who, because it suited them, divided women into those who were immoral (and available as 'prostitutes') and those who were ignorant (and available as wives). To Josephine Butler, this *division* was artificial; for women had in *common* their availability to men, their allocation of a role that was convenient for men. And besides, what was the origin of this belief that it was men who had sexual appetites and that women existed only to satisfy them?

It was to be almost fifteen years before Josephine Butler was publicly to challenge male authority, the male version of their own sexuality and that of women, but even at this stage of her life, her ideas about society, about the relationship between women and men, were emerging and developing. There was little that was spontaneous about her decision defiantly to lead a campaign which demanded that she break the most rigid taboo of her time. Her decision was the product of many years of intellectual debate, of many years of experience as a woman in which she tested the hypothesis that women's subordination was predicated on a link between sexuality and economics and that the relationship had been set up by men for their own profit.

By the time Josephine Butler spoke out she had conceptualised a framework for understanding and interpreting women's oppression. When even many of the women who were involved in the then radical issues of women's suffrage, women's education, women's employment and women's property, were at some pains to convince men that they were not intent on a sex-war, Josephine Butler had no hesitation in declaring that women and men constituted two different groups with conflicting interests, and that it was because men had power that men's interests prevailed. If there were to be changes, if women were to cease being the mere objects for male gratification, then men's interests must cease to prevail. Men would have to have their power taken away from them and if this was a 'sex-war', so be it, because it was unthinkable that there could be any alternative to the establishment of women as independent beings, accorded their own personal liberty and with the capacity to decree their own needs and to conduct their own lives without reference to men.

Barbara Bodichon, Lydia Becker, Emily Davies (all well known to Josephine Butler), and even Emma Paterson, were fighting for women's rights on the political, legal, employment and educational fronts in the expectation that equal rights would lead to financial independence and would provide a basis for women's independence of men. But to Josephine Butler, these reforms on their own were insufficient, for to her the denial of women's rights was not a *cause* of their oppression but a *manifestation* of it; to her there was a link between economics and sexuality, a link not discussed openly by other women who were working for women's emancipation.

Josephine Butler was committed to obtaining these rights – they were undeniably women's due. She signed the petition presented by John Stuart Mill, she campaigned for women's education and was president of the North of England Council for the Higher Education of Women (in which Anne Jemima Clough was secretary). But she firmly believed that this was not enough and that even the *achievement* of these rights would be no solution. She looked at marriage and the family, at the rationales that were given for their existence and the arrangements that were made to sustain this idealised version of human existence; she looked at the way women were coerced into marriage and the way those who did not comply (for all number of reasons) were made vulnerable. Her analysis of sexual economics in the latter half of the nineteenth century fits comfortably with Adrienne Rich's (1981) analysis of sexual economics in the latter half of the twentieth century, although Rich names it explicitly (as Butler did not) as *compulsory heterosexuality*. But both Josephine Butler and Adrienne Rich made men's definitions of their own sexual needs, their propensity for accumulating resources, and their unequivocal definition of women in relation to them-selves in gratifying those needs and replenishing those resources, the crucial features in women's oppression.

Fundamental to this form of organisation, argued Butler in 1882, is the division among women which must be overcome, for, while it persists, 'One group of women is set aside, so to speak, to minister to the irregu-larities of the excusable man. That section is doomed to death, hurled to despair, while another section of womanhood is kept strictly and almost forcibly guarded in domestic purity for his own exclusive use and peace of mind (quoted in Jenny Uglow, 1982, in press).

Far from seeing the history of the human race as a form of progress as men were wont to argue, Josephine Butler saw the position of women deteriorating at the same time as women were campaigning for civil rights. In *Personal Reminiscences of a Great Crusade* (1898), Butler explicitly states that conditions for women were made worse during the second half of the nineteenth century with the introduction of the Contagious Diseases Acts which created a slave class of women for the purpose of satisfying licentious men who *gave only their own word* that their sexual appetite was uncontrollable, that it was natural to satisfy it, and that women were to be organised to accommodate male sexual, economic and ideological needs.

This understanding came not as a sudden flash of insight to Josephine Butler but was formed gradually over a period of time and was drawn from a variety of influences. The Christian ethics of the gospels played a crucial role, for it was beyond her comprehension that anyone should read them and not come to the realisation that all human beings were of equal worth and had equal rights to personal freedom and dignity. She clung tenaciously to this scriptural justification for her stand, partly because, I think, without the conviction that she was part of a 'divine purpose', she would never have been able to withstand the onslaught. For it must be remembered that even the women working for women's rights believed in the main that it was best to dissociate themselves from her controversial and condemned campaign, otherwise the battle for the vote, and for education and em-ployment, might be endangered; so she was an 'outsider' in relation to the women's movement itself because of the radical position she took.

By the time she did take her stand she had in some small ways been prepared for it. Her father had been a vigorous opponent of slavery, she knew of many of the American abolitionists, and she and her husband were socially ostracised when they supported the north, and the anti-slavery position in the American Civil War. Of this experience she later philosophically commented that: 'It was good training in swimming against the tide ... the feeling of isolation on a subject of such tragic interest was often painful; but the discipline was useful; for it was our lot again more emphatically in the future to have to accept and endure this position for conscience sake' (1893, p. 45).

She had been at the forefront of radical reform movements for most of her life – listening to, if not participating in, the struggle; she was in touch with many of the women working for women's rights in America as well as being an early member of the Langham Place Group. She kept a close watch on European reform movements, particularly through her sister, Hattie, who married a liberal and intellectual Swiss banker. She was well read (and became herself a prolific writer) and mixed (at least initially) with some of the most thoughtful and socially conscious people of her time, receiving in effect the best possible education available for women – and perhaps, even, the best possible education. Virginia Woolf (1938), who scathingly condemned the education men had devised for themselves, certainly would have thought so.

These influential and intellectual circles, however, were not the only ones in which Josephine Butler moved and it was partly because she moved outside the stipulated sphere of a lady, and entered the ordinarily invisible world of poor women, that she came to see the shared facets of women's experience and to protest so passionately that the division between women should be removed. In a patriarchal framework which presupposes a linear ordering of experience it is not possible to determine which comes first – was it her interest in exploited women which led her to find out more about the conditions under which they lived, or was it because she became familiar with the horrors of their existence that she became so committed to women who were made victims? Fortunately, in a feminist framework, an answer is not necessary: she was interested in victimised women (taking into her home a woman who had committed infanticide, and women who were prostitutes), and through her involvement in their lives, she identified with them and fought to end women's oppression.

On the death of her 5-year-old daughter, she and her husband moved to Liverpool where she began to visit the workhouse which then accommodated 5,000 people. One biographer, Joseph Williamson (1977), says of this place that: 'There was on the ground floor a Bridewell for women, consisting of huge cellars, bare and unfurnished with damp stone floors. These were called the "oakum sheds" and to these came voluntarily creatures driven by hunger, destitution or vice, begging for a few nights shelter or a piece of bread, in return for which they picked their allotted portion of oakum. Others were sent there as prisoners. . . . Josephine begged admission to the gloomy vault crowded with more than 200 women and girls. She sat on the floor among them and picked oakum. They laughed at her "but while we laughed we became friends". Some jeered at this fine lady who would return home to her grand house and her good food. But

Josephine persevered in winning their friendship' (p. 18). And she listened to and accounted for the circumstances which had led them to this horrific place.

She knew that it was not the women's fault that they were in the workhouse; they had no alternative, there was nowhere else for them to go. The fault lay with a society organised along these lines and the blame for that organisation could lie with no one else but men! Everywhere she looked Josephine Butler encountered evidence of women's oppression which was structured on sexual economics and nowhere was this more blatant, or the hand of man more readily displayed, than in the Contagious Diseases Acts. These Acts were ostensibly introduced on 'sanitary' grounds and were designed to control the spread of venereal disease among enlisted men and they could only ever have been put forward as a logical measure in a society which found it acceptable for males to have access to females, but at the same time thought it reasonable that males – and only males – should be protected from venereal disease. When the justification given for these measures was 'to arrest venereal disease at its source', and when that source was seen to be women – particularly working women – it is not difficult to determine who is formulating the justification and implementing the measures!

That there was one rule for women and another for men was acknowledged by some of the men who were behind the Acts, but rather than seeing this as illogical (and unfair), they saw it as perfectly natural (and quite fair from their point of view). 'Thus', says Judith Walkowitz (1980), 'the Royal Commission of 1871 couched its defense' of the Acts, 'in the pseudo-scientific language of "spermatic economy" transforming a time honored male privilege into a physiological imperative;

> We may at once dispose of any recommendation founded on the principle of putting both parties to the sin of fornication on the same footing, by the obvious but not less conclusive reply that there is no comparison to be made between prostitutes and the men who consort with them. With the one sex the offence is committed as a matter of gain; with the other it is an irregular indulgence of a natural impulse' (Report of the Royal Commission on the Administration and Operation of the Contagious Diseases Act 1866–1869 (1871): quoted in Judith Walkowitz, 1980: 71).

This was the 'excusable man', and the slave class of women available to gratify his needs, to which Josephine Butler referred. In a climate of concern created by the medical profession over the spread of venereal disease among men, military authorities and government bureaucrats put forward the proposal of controlling women, and in July 1864, the first Contagious Diseases Act was passed in parliament. Although not actually making prostitution legal, it provided for a woman identified as a prostitute by a plainclothes member of the metropolitan police force in any one of eleven garrison or dock towns in England and Ireland to be forced to undergo a medical examination carried out by army and navy surgeons. Once identified as a prostitute (on the word of one plainclothes member of the metropolitan police force), a woman had no recourse but to submit voluntarily to the examination (and if found to be a 'source' of the disease she could be detained in hospital for up to three months), or be brought before a magistrate (and face all the accompanying publicity), and to be bound by his orders – which were invariably to insist that she submit to examination. The Admiralty and the War Office were the overseers of the Act. In 1866 it was extended and two more districts were included. Perhaps unaware of the significance of the links that were being made, the 1866 Act included the term *medical police* to describe those talented individuals who went around identifying prostitutes.

Many were Josephine Butler's objections to these Acts, but one which could be simply articulated was the issue of *who was a prostitute?* There was no statutory definition of such a person and, in the absence of a definition, the *proof* that such a person existed resided in the word of a medical policeman (hardly a state of affairs guaranteed to promote confidence, and one which has led me to conclude that it is possible to argue that prostitutes were the figment of the imagination of medical policemen, and I'm not being totally facetious). One reason that there was not – and is not – a definition of a prostitute seems to me to be because it would be difficult to formulate such a definition in a way that excludes wives, who also exchange sexual services in return for support. It is the fact that prostitutes and wives are obliged to engage in comparable behaviour – as *work* – that makes it difficult to definitively distinguish between them, and why I suggested that the distinction which a medical policeman could make was possibly a figment of his own imagination. *The difference between prostitutes and wives lies not within the women, but within the men,* and the role played by men is not and has not been open to investigation or indictment, while men have been in control. From Mary Wollstonecraft to Josephine Butler it had been pointed out that women's relationship to men – be it as wives or prostitutes – was comparable and shared many common features, for both were sexually available to men who had monopolised economic resources. This shared basis of oppression was lost on men, however, who wanted to divide women into two classes for their own convenience.

That this was what men were attempting to do becomes apparent from some of the defences they provided to the objection that a prostitute was not defined. William Harris, for example, the Assistant Commissioner of the Metropolitan Police, declared that in London, the definition of a prostitute was 'any woman who goes to places of public resort and is known to go with different men' (quoted in Walkowitz, 1980, p. 80). Basically this meant that the onus was on women to prove that they were not prostitutes by behaving in a manner which found approval among men – by staying within the home, being available to only one man, attracting no attention to themselves, and by being invisible and existing only to service an individual man; any behaviour to the contrary could be sufficient evidence that a woman no longer warranted male protection and that she was a 'source of disease'. This was blatant intimidation of women by men.

But women who were identified as prostitutes? What happened to them? Writing in the *Shield* (2 March 1870), Josephine Butler told what happened to these women and pointed explicitly to the hypocrisy of men and their laws. Relating the case of a woman committed to prison, Butler wrote that the woman had said: 'It did seem hard, ma'am, that the Magistrate on the bench who gave the casting vote for my imprisonment had paid me several shillings, a day or two before, in the street, to go with him.'

To Josephine Butler the popular sentimentalisation of marriage and motherhood was but a thin veneer for the distrust and contempt that men felt for women. It was prostitution and the laws men made in relation to it which was more indicative of the male attitude to women, for it was prostitution that 'served as a paradigm for the female condition' and which 'established the archetypal relationship between men and women' (Walkowitz, 1980, p. 128). 'It is men, men, only men from the first to the last, that we have to do with!' one woman told Josephine Butler who made public her story. 'To please a man I did wrong at first, then I was flung about from man to man. Men police lay hands on us. By men we are examined, handled, doctored, and messed on with. In the hospital it is a man again who makes prayers and reads the bible to us. We are had up before magistrates who are men, and we never get out of the hands of men until we die' (*Shield*, 9 May 1870).

And Jospehine Butler says that as this woman spoke she thought: 'And it was a parliament of men only who made this law which treats you as an outlaw. Men alone met in committee over it. Men alone are the executives.' She adds, 'when men of all ranks thus band themselves together for an end deeply concerning women', when they divide woman from woman, create two classes, 'and forbid the one class of women entrance into the presence of the other . . . it is time that women should arise and demand their most sacred rights in regard to their sisters' (ibid.).

It was in men's minds that the two classes of women were created and it was in men's minds only that the distinctions between them were clear. William Acton, the editor of the *Lancet*, stated that it was 'a remote possibility that any woman should be charged with being a common prostitute, unless her conduct was notoriously and openly bad' (quoted in Walkowitz, 1980, p. 17); the difference was perfectly obvious to him, a reputable medical man. And on all sides the weight of the male establishment was thrown behind the Acts. Initially put forward by the military – in the attempt to remedy the loss of man-hours incurred with endemic venereal disease among the troops – the acts were openly supported by the government (on the basis that prostitution was a threat to public order), by the police, by the medical profession, and by the Anglican clergy (on the basis that prostitution was a threat to morality), and so, with the astonishing logic which could only have been displayed by men, they proceeded to legalise prostitution. Such logic is only inconsistent, however, if women are to be taken into account.

In the course of my own life I have on occasion heard vague mutterings about the Contagious Diseases Acts, and the sexually repressed and prurient Victorian ladies who fought them. But until I came to read about Josephine

Butler (whom I almost dismissed originally, and predictably, on the basis that she was some zealous, prudish 'missionary' concerned with moral hygiene, for that is the predominant 'popular' image of her that has been constructed), I had no idea of the savage and blatant purpose behind these Acts and certainly no suspicions that they were an attempt to exert greater control over women at precisely the same time that women were throwing off some of the bonds that had enmeshed them, and were coming into the public arena to demand greater and full participation in the running of society.

I have no hesitation in accepting Josephine Butler's claim that things became progressively *worse* for women during the second half of the nineteenth century, and in trying to make sense of this I have thought about the thesis put forward by Ann Jones (1980). Jones argues that every time there is a feminist upsurge there is a male backlash and *harsher penalties are inflicted* on women in the courts, so that men can claim with some credibility (*but no basis*) that women are becoming more violent and therefore require greater control – and all this conveniently constructed and objectively 'proven' so that they can protect their own position of power and engage in harsh and repressive treatment of women which might otherwise be seen as unjustifiable and unacceptable.

The women involved in the campaigns for women's rights did not want to be linked in any way with the campaign against the Contagious Diseases Acts or with Josephine Butler and the Ladies' National Association who were conducting the campaign. This was not because they did not support the campaign against the Contagious Diseases Act. Many of them endorsed it – but not in public (Florence Nightingale and Harriet Martineau being among the exceptions – explained partly by their privileged position). Great care was taken to ensure that the two movements were kept distinctly separate because it was feared that the case for the vote, for education and employment opportunities for women, might be brought into disrepute if associated in any way with Josephine Butler and her denunciation of sexual economics.

Historically, the same distinction that operated at the time seems to have been preserved and the two very different campaigns against male dominance have been treated separately. Perhaps this is why I can find no suggestion that there might have been a relationship between the two. Could any of the women involved in either campaign have ever asked themselves whether it was their steadily growing success in the area of women's rights that was responsible for the desperate measure to control women as embodied in the Contagious Diseases Act? There can be no doubt that some of the men who were most resistant to the claims for women's rights, who were most vociferous in the House about the threats that such rights constituted to marriage, to the home, to the family, and to the position of males, were the very same men who passed the Contagious Diseases Acts.

Nor can there be any doubt that the Contagious Diseases Acts were virtually an archetype of sexual harassment. With no definition of a prostitute, the threat of being identified as a prostitute, examined and locked up, was one which was held over *all* women, used to intimidate them and make them conform to patterns of behaviour which were considered convenient by men. Even the most scientific and objective men of the day, such as William Acton, quite openly stated that a woman had nothing to fear if she behaved herself properly and modestly!

Women who did not gain male approval – for any one of a number of reasons – were labelled as prostitutes and provided by men with a set of distasteful and disturbing characteristics which then helped to justify the treatment such women received. The 'Ex-Constable of the Devonport Division', writing in a pamphlet at the time, stated that the female instinct to promiscuity was inherent and therefore had to be controlled, and that he would not accept the argument (put forward by Josephine Butler and the Ladies' National Association) that prostitution was *work*, and was forced on women in their effort to survive; he knew it to be a fact that it was pleasure and vanity that motivated prostitutes, and not economic necessity. He also knew that women of the lower classes who were attractive were uniformly of low character and almost without exception likely to engage in prostitution. 'In every large town', he wrote, 'where a woman has a chance of this course and runs no danger of serious loss or inconvenience, and possesses the means of deluding her friends she will embrace it', for it is inherent, it is 'natural'. The Acts were a deterrent; it was only the fear of detection and the fear of compulsory examination which kept these women from 'resorting to the streets when the day's work is done' (quoted in Walkowitz, 1980, p. 81). The crime was to be an attractive woman of the lower classes, a working woman who could delude her friends, a woman seen in public with a different man, a woman who behaved badly, a woman who was immodest: As with witchcraft, it was the *sex* that constituted the *crime* which led in this case – not to burning – but to forced physical examinations (which Josephine Butler had no hesitation in calling *instrumental rape*) and to being immured in a 'lock-up' hospital for up to three months at a time.

Josephine Butler recognised that the crime was to be female, and that in a society where men determined the rules, men were 'right' and women were 'wrong'. She recognised that prostitution and the way it was defined and treated by the Contagious Diseases Acts was a consequence of male power and that little would change until the power balance changed. (She also believed that the power balance *would* change to some extent once women achieved their rights, once they were represented in the circles of power and could have their voices heard and their experience taken into account. This was one of the reasons she was so determined that women should have the right to vote and why to *her* women's rights and the campaign against the Contagious Diseases Acts were interwoven.)

But if she believed that women would be listened to, that they would be accorded full humanity and treated with respect because their case was just, she also kept the evidence that men could be vicious and cruel to women at the forefront of her analysis. That men despised women and were contemptuous of them was no abstract thesis cultivated by her in the rarefied atmosphere of the Victorian middle-class drawing room but a reality that she confronted almost every time she entered the public arena. For me it has been a salutary lesson to come to terms with the fact that this woman who is portrayed as strikingly beautiful, as the epitome of women's greater grasp on morality and spirituality (Joseph Williamson's biography of her is entitled 'The Forgotten Saint'!), and as a middle-class philanthropist concerned with uplifting the values of the lower classes – and she is portrayed in all these ways which are unlikely to promote immediate enthusiasm for her and her work in a contemporary context – endured harassment that many of us today would find it impossible to contend with.

She was regularly threatened. She was attacked and abused. When visiting different towns in order to speak she could find no accommodation. The platform from which she was speaking was once set fire to. She was assaulted by a mob while the metropolitan police force who were supposed to be protecting her, looked on and lifted not a finger in her defence. She was jostled and jeered at meetings and frequently had to be smuggled out of windows in order to escape violence, and was generally assisted by local prostitutes with whom she often sheltered. Her clothes were smeared with excrement. And this was the 'missionary' intent on moral reform? For this was what I thought of Josephine Butler not many weeks ago.

She also knew that this violence towards women was not confined to uncouth, uneducated men; she encountered sexual harassment in the halls of the influential and great as well. When she gave evidence to the Royal Commission on the Contagious Diseases Acts, Joseph Williamson (who could not be said to put the myth of Josephine Butler as a prude and moral custodian to rest) says that: 'Twenty five men of the highest rank and ability made up the Royal Commission. They were free to rake up all they could to discredit Josephine and her cause, and they tried. They were all men and they did not spare her finer feelings' (1977, p. 31).

For Josephine Butler there were to be no divisions among women, and no divisions among men. She herself noted that there was an inherent contradiction in this stand, for some men elected to abstain from using the power which society accorded them. 'It seems strange', she said once, 'that I should have been engaged in taking up the cudgel against men when my father, brothers, husband and sons have all been so good' (quoted in Walkowitz, 1980, p. 121). And there is considerable evidence that her husband, George Butler, was good. He did support her and very much to the detriment of his own career; and as a man who lived with and did not condemn this 'strong-minded' and 'unsexed' feminist, he came in for his own predictable share of abuse. It was openly stated that he was a weakling who could not control his own wife and was therefore a poor example to and a bad influence on boys, and could not be trusted in his capacity as a headmaster.

But these positive qualities in the men around her did not alter Josephine Butler's analysis. She did not argue that they were *different* (a strategy familiar in many feminist circles today to justify alignment with males and which always leaves me wondering why it is that I have never met all these 'different' men), but rather that they chose not to make use of some of the powers that were theirs by right. It is a little like men doing domestic chores – no prizes or pats on the back for behaving *reasonably*.

Basically Josephine Butler's analysis was quite simple: men had the power and they had given themselves rights over women. They controlled the activities available to women, restricting their entry to employment, channelling them towards marriage and motherhood. Women who were in the 'legitimate' paid labour force were exploited and paid less than subsistence wages which, far from permitting independence, coerced them towards obtaining resources from men. So women's *work* was to 'trade' their bodies, on a casual basis (prostitute), a semi-permanent basis (mistress), or permanent basis (wife). This was *sexual economics*; men had the money and women had to work by sexual means to have access to it and to obtain support.

Because men were decreeing the rules, she stated, women were *scape-goats*: they were being punished under the Contagious Diseases Acts for satisfying a male demand when they were in absolutely no position to refuse. They were nothing short of slaves. Besides, she did not believe that this demand was inevitable, that it was *natural* for men to be unable to control their need for sexual gratification. She does not use the term, but her explanation of male sexuality approximates the explanation offered today, that it is *socially constructed*. Her explanation of female sexuality is of the same order and she rejects the biological model (which defines female sexuality in terms of reproduction), denies the existence of a maternal instinct, and states that women *can* live their own lives without reference to men or to children.

There was too much work to do, she argued, for every woman to think it was her duty to marry and rear children. The world was in need of women without domestic ties, women who could move freely into the public arena and represent women's interests so that male power did not continue to go unchecked. Once women could overcome their feeling that it was woman's destiny to be a wife and mother and that 'failure' to achieve this end was failure to live a full life – and women *should* overcome this feeling because it was certainly not in their own interest to retain it – then women would be breaking free of the sexual economics which had kept them in subordination.

There was one aspect of her analysis that George Eliot no doubt would have been uneasy with, for in some respects Josephine Butler *did* perceive women as superior. She wanted women to have complete equality with men – equal power, equal resources, equal sexual demands – but she did not want to abandon the positive aspects of women's culture which had evolved while women had been confined to their separate sphere. Judith Walkowitz says that: 'Butler's feminism combined two distinct tendencies – advocating sex equality while celebrating the virtues of a distinctive women's culture' (1980, p. 117). Her brand of feminism is not so far removed from that of today. I wonder whether with our current campaigns against pornography and violence against women, we will be portrayed to future generations as repressed, prudish missionaries?

12 And still there were more

In Judith Walkowitz's excellent book (*Prostitution and Victorian Society*) the name of Elizabeth Wolstenholme Elmy[9] crops up again. She appears – always briefly – in a number of records and in relation to a wide range of activities, yet despite some of the fascinating glimpses that are offered of her, no biography of her has been written. She lived a long and active life and in 1905 – 44 years after entering the fray ('As a schoolmistress she had been working since 1861 for higher education and better employment opportunities for women', Sylvia Pankhurst, 1931, p. 31) – she welcomed and joined the new militant suffrage movement. She seems to have lived a somewhat unconventional life – modelled on that of Mary Wollstonecraft.

Sylvia Pankhurst (1931) quotes the incident for which she was perhaps most famous – or infamous – in her own time. Because women lost so many rights upon marriage (and evidently because Mary Wollstonecraft had set a precedent), when Elizabeth Wolstenholme met Ben Elmy in 1875 she decided to live with him without benefit of the legal service of deprivation. 'When it was obvious that she was pregnant, there was much fluttering in the suffrage dovecotes, and eventually Mrs Jacob Bright induced the two to marry, on the plea that their continual refusal would be harmful to the suffrage cause' (p. 31). I would like to know more about this woman who in the name of women's rights refused to marry and for the sake of women's rights was persuaded to do so.

Sylvia Pankhurst gives a brief outline of Elizabeth Wolstenholme Elmy's activities: she worked for fifteen years for the Married Women's Property Acts of 1870 and 1882, for three years for the 1886 Custody of Infants Act; she worked with Josephine Butler and with Lydia Becker. Before the formation of the Manchester Suffrage Society she, along with Emily Davies, read a paper on women's suffrage in London to the Kensington Society. She personally collected three hundred signatures for the petition that John Stuart Mill presented to parliament.

Evidently she wrote an incredible number of letters, and Sylvia Pankhurst states that: 'For half a century no man or woman gained prominence in political and social work but was drawn into the enormous circle of her correspondence, receiving from her, if she could procure any hopeful response, a regular stream of information and exhortation' (ibid., p. 32). Trying to explain in 1931 why this woman who played such an active role over such a long period of time was not better known, Sylvia Pankhurst states that: 'Though a clear and voluminously informed speaker, Elizabeth Wolstenholme was never, I think, an orator, which partly explains the fact that her true worth has not always been recognised' (ibid., p. 33). It does only *partly* explain it; had she been a great orator there is no reason to believe that she would have been accorded any more visibility by male historians.

[9] David Doughan, assistant librarian at the Fawcett Library, has suggested that Elizabeth Wolstenholme Elmy should be the first priority for research into 'forgotten' women of the period.

But what happened to all those thousands of letters? In 1910 at the age of 76 she wrote to Sylvia Pankhurst and said that she was steadily going through all the many thousands of letters that she had kept, for she intended to put them together in a book which she was going to call *Some Memories of a Happy Life*.

However, besides all these positive features, Sylvia Pankhurst suggests that there was also a shadow over her life; that Ben Elmy never forgave the interference of the moral women of the suffrage movement, that he was violent to his wife, and that her son was sickly because there was never enough money to look after him properly or to provide him with the necessary material comforts. Pankhurst goes so far as to suggest that because Elizabeth Wolstenholme Elmy was so involved in questions of women's emancipation, her child was neglected. I am uneasy with this interpretation: obviously the myth of maternal deprivation has been around in some form for a long time and few efforts have been made to repudiate it. I wish Sylvia Pankhurst could have read Jane Ritchie's (forthcoming) article which indicates that women who work outside the home report more positive experiences in relation to their children (as do the children themselves) than mothers who do not; would she have re-evaluated Elizabeth Wolstenholme Elmy as a mother?

What were the ideas of Elizabeth Wolstenholme Elmy – about society, power, women and men, and motherhood? There is real loss in the fact that we do not know, and may never know.

Judith Walkowitz (1980) refers to another woman who immediately aroused my curiosity: Emilie Ashurst Venturi, who was Mazzini's literary executor, who was a cigar-smoking divorcee whose sister ran away to Paris to live like Georges Sand. She too played a role in the campaign against the Contagious Diseases Acts and she too seems to have missed out on biographical treatment (p. 123). But my editor is almost in despair, convinced that I will never finish this work, as every week I go off hunting for clues about yet another woman who appears fleetingly and tantalisingly as a sort of 'aside' in the records (and often in a footnote) and as much as I want to pursue these clues, I have to turn back to the task of trying to complete the overview of women of ideas – and what men have done to them!

13 A life of contradictions: Millicent Garrett Fawcett (1847–1929)

Millicent Garrett Fawcett is invariably presented as the cautious leader of the constitutional movement for women's suffrage; the predominant image that emerges of her is one of a dedicated and dull woman. Martin Pugh (1980) has said that even her accounts of the constitutional movement 'are largely bland and unremarkable' (p. 40) and there is no doubt that she has suffered in contrast with her more flamboyant contemporary, Emmeline Pankhurst. Mrs Pankhurst's efforts were considered worthy of recognition in the form of a statue in Victoria Tower Gardens, Mrs Fawcett's by two plaques added to the abbey memorial of her husband.

Most accounts of Millicent Garrett's life and work include the story of her entry to the suffrage movement at a very early age. Emily Davies, a close friend of Elizabeth Garrett's, went to stay with the Garretts at Aldburgh, and at night, says Ray Strachey (1928), Emily and Elizabeth 'sat talking . . . Millicent Garrett, then quite a small girl, sat nearby on a stool, listening but saying nothing. After going over all the great causes they saw about them, and in particular the women's cause, to which they were burning to devote their lives, Emily summed the matter up. "Well Elizabeth," she said, "it's quite clear what has to be done. I must devote myself to securing higher education, while you open the medical profession to women. After these things are done," she added, "we must set about getting the vote." And then she turned to the little girl who was still sitting quietly on her stool and said, "You are younger than we are, Millie, so you must attend to that" ' (p. 101). Josephine Kamm (1966) tells the same story with only one addition: she refers to 'dictatorial' Emily (p. 132).

Millicent Garrett Fawcett seems to have had a propensity for taking on onerous tasks at an early age. She married Henry Fawcett – a leading radical politican – in 1865, and was still too young in 1866 to add her signature to the great petition for women's suffrage presented in parliament by John Stuart Mill. It seems that many of her understandings and much of the framework for her analysis of women's position in society (and the strategies required for change) were formed directly and indirectly through her relationship with her husband.

Some attention has been given by feminists to the 'Rochester' syndrome (whereby Jane Eyre felt able to marry Rochester and enter a reciprocal relationship once he was blind and she became necessary to his existence) and, without commenting on the credibility or desirability of this rationale, I think it fair to say that Millicent Fawcett appears to have enjoyed a comparatively equal and reciprocal relationship with her husband, who was blind. She was necessary to his existence and she gained more than a sense of self-esteem from her indispensability, she gained the sort of political experience and insight not usually available to women of her generation, for she was virtually Henry Fawcett's private secretary. When women were completely excluded from the political process and its complexities, Millicent Fawcett had access to some of the innermost machinations.

It was neither tolerance nor indulgence on the part of Henry Fawcett, who was at the centre of many of the controversial political issues of the time, to engage in debate and discussion with Millicent Fawcett; together they frequently went through his post, weighed responses, formulated replies. Together they frequently planned campaigns and wrote his speeches. Nor could the involvement of Millicent Fawcett in any of these activities be labelled as dilettante as she combed newspapers for items of interest, read and summarised books and reports for her husband's benefit, and became for all intents and purposes a working (if unpaid and unacknowledged) politician.

If she literally shared Henry Fawcett's political experience, she also seems to have shared some of his values – she believed that women would get the vote, but that it would be difficult and it would take a long time (in this respect she was different from many of her contemporaries who were inclined to think that it would not take very long at all for men to see the justice of women's claim and to include them on the electoral roll). One of the fundamental tenets of Millicent Fawcett's analysis was that men would have to vote (in the House) to give women the vote, and that they would not do so until they could be persuaded that it was in their own best interest.

It was not, and is not, easy to convince men who are committed to tyrannous ways to accept that they will be better off when both sexes have equal access to resources. As far as men were concerned, on the *credit* side there are abstracts such as liberty, dignity, independence and self-determination for women, but these are not likely to hold sway against the materialist aspects of the *debit* side – such as for men cooking one's own meals, cleaning one's own clothes and premises, caring for one's children, managing one's own emotions and those of others, and ceasing to be the centre of someone else's universe! When Millicent Fawcett recognised that many men would have to believe that abstract advantages would outweigh what to them were material disadvantages, she knew it would take a very long time for them to be convinced. That she thought women would ultimately get the vote was probably a sign of supreme optimism.

'If we had votes', Millicent Fawcett used to say (as did Christabel Pankhurst later) 'it would be easy to get votes' (see Strachey, 1931, p. 154), but while women did not have votes, while they were completely excluded from political power and were in no way able to influence men, or men's events, the prospect for obtaining votes looked to her extremely remote and demanded for its success a public education programme aimed at converting men to the belief that it was for the social if not the individual good for women to be represented politically.

Apart from the fact that Millicent Fawcett found it offensive that women should be denied the symbol of equality which the vote represented, she had other reasons for seeking women's suffrage, and they were often the very same reasons that men put forward for denying women any participation in the public and political realm. In almost every aspect of daily life among the middle classes – right through to the withdrawal of the ladies after dinner – Millicent Fawcett saw that the two sexes were segregated and allocated their separate spheres, and one sphere was considerably more powerful and prestigious than the other sphere. It was her belief (and it arose from her experience) that a basic feature of this segregation lay in women's exclusion from political participation, that while women need not be courted by politicians, while their views were not sought nor their opinions considered significant (for their 'votes' were of no account), men had every reason to refuse to take women seriously, to insist that they could not contribute to important decision-making processes, and that they could therefore be dismissed from the male sphere. To her, it was perfectly clear that women were scapegoats, that they were denied political experience and access to serious discussion and then discounted because they had no political experience and no serious discussion.

Millicent Fawcett thought that having the vote would make a difference to women's position in society, not necessarily in terms of what women might do with the vote once they got it, but in terms of *what it would do for them* to have it. Once women could vote – and influence men's affairs (with reference particularly to party politics) – men would be more inclined to take women seriously, to seek their views and take account of them, and the barriers which divided women and men into separate and unequal groups would be undermined and would eventually collapse. And it was partly because many men believed that this would be the inevitable outcome of women having voting power that they resisted – and ridiculed – all the efforts made by women to find a way into the political arena. Once women slipped out of their separate sphere, their place that men had allocated them, then the sexist classification scheme which was the basis of society was challenged and in the minds of many men, chaos threatened.

When it came to 'men's politics' Millicent Fawcett was extremely astute and, while many have condemned her for being 'content' to work for women's suffrage for sixty years, it is too simple and too unsatisfactory to 'blame' her because it took so long to convince men that it was in their interest to vote for women to have the vote. The Pankhursts, of course, had very different ideas about the way into the political arena for women, and constructed their own power base apart from men's, and *then* engaged in confrontation (and were successful). But at the time when Millicent Fawcett entered the campaign, it is unlikely that she could have envisaged the Pankhurst tactics and even more unlikely that she could have won sufficient numbers of women to a militant cause, for it to have had any impact.

To her, the only way was through the existing system, and this was hazardous and daring enough. In the 1860s when she entered the fray, 'Pamphlets were printed, and petitions signed, and before long it became evident that public meetings would have to be held,' says Ray Strachey (1931) in her biography of Millicent Garrett Fawcett, and, 'This was regarded as a most terribly bold and dangerous thing in the 'sixties and 'seventies. Women hardly ever spoke in public, and it was thought dreadfully "advanced" and likely to be "unsexing": besides no one believed a woman's voice could be heard. All the committee members were afraid of this duty, and the Press howled with laughter at the mere idea' (p. 45).

To Millicent Fawcett it was her *duty* to work for women's suffrage and the elevation of the position of women, no matter how unpleasant the task may have been. That she justified her unpopular stand on the basis of *duty* has, however, allowed her and her values to be readily misrepresented. *Duty* is not a term that would be used today, conjuring up as it does an image of unquestioning allegiance to a code based on 'higher' principles associated with the moral censoriousness of the nineteenth century, but before dismissing Millicent Fawcett's 'duty' as no longer applicable, it is worth while asking whether she fits the image of the dry, dedicated and dreary 'duty-ridden' person that has often been portrayed under patriarchy.

To my mind, she does not; substituting the term *commitment* for *duty* renders her most acceptable.

She was unwavering in her commitment to women and could not be discouraged or dissuaded from her task. Distasteful though she found it on many occasions – for she too was harassed and vilified by the Press, although in her case it was more likely to be by the establishment newspaper *The Times* than the *Saturday Review* – and frustrating and wearying as she found the struggle over sixty years, with all its bitter disappointments, there could be no question of giving up. It was her *duty* to continue – and even to enjoy some of the incidents on the way.

In a letter to a friend (quoted in Strachey, 1931) Millicent Fawcett wrote of a 'well known member of parliament, Mr C. R., [who] referred publicly in the House of Commons to the appearance of Mrs Taylor and myself upon a platform to advocate votes for women, as "two ladies, wives of members of this House, who had disgraced themselves," and added that he would not further disgrace them by mentioning their names. It so happened that a very short time after this', she continues, 'my husband and I were spending the weekend in Cambridge, and . . . Mr James Porter . . . asked us to dine with him. What was my amusement to see Mr C. R. among the guests: this amusement was intensified into positive glee when he was asked to take me into dinner. I could not resist expressing condolences with him on his unfortunate position. Should I ask Mr Porter to let him exchange me for some other lady who had not disgraced herself? . . . After all, what he had said was very mild compared to Horace Walpole's abuse of Mary Wollstonecraft as "a hyena in petticoats" ' (pp. 63–4).

Millicent Fawcett saw herself as part of a tradition of women protesters who could expect to be abused by men. One of her strengths was that she rarely took such abuse personally but instead saw it as directed at women in general. This – as well as her concept of duty – afforded her some protection against the insults and harassment she was so frequently subjected to.

More than most other women involved in the nineteenth-century women's movement in Britain she seems to have had 'a foot in both camps' and to have lived a life of contradictions, without conflict. On the one hand she seems to have been concerned that a 'sex war' not be promoted (all those who have written about her have taken great pains to emphasise that engaging in sex warfare was *not* her intention), but she was unflinching in her condemnation of particular men – which is probably one of the reasons that so many assurances about her struggle being for both men and women are given. She looked to parliamentary processes for the improvement of the position of women while acknowledging that this all-male enclave was likely to be one of the last places in which men would be converted to women's cause.

She put her energies into parliamentary reform but would not give her allegiance to the male-party system, and even split the women's suffrage movement at one stage, with her insistence that women's issues be kept free from political party entanglement. She would not join, but none the less supported, Josephine Butler's campaign against the Contagious Diseases Acts, and the early stages of the Pankhursts' militancy. She was delighted that the militants had been able to break 'the conspiracy of silence' of the Press (there had been an agreement not to report on the activities of the women's movement) and she gave a firm lead when, in 1906, some of the militants were released from prison and she arranged a banquet for them at the Savoy and said: 'I hope that the more old-fashioned suffragists will stand by their comrades who in my opinion have done more to bring the movement within the region of practical politics in twelve months, than I and my followers have been able to do in the same number of years' (quoted in Kamm, 1966, p. 154). But she would not condone violence and, the more violent the militants became, the less she publicly endorsed them. Writing of 'The Progress of the Women's Movement in the United Kingdom 1900–1920' in *History of Woman Suffrage* (1922, vol. VI), she said: 'The fact that men under similar circumstances had been much more violent and destructive . . . did not inspire us with the wish to imitate them' (p. 729).

Millicent Fawcett advocated reform by constitutional means yet it was a revolution in the position of women that she sought. She was eminently 'respectable' and concerned with remaining so by her standards, yet at the same time she was considered a disgrace and a threat to the fabric of society. She was a woman excluded from the political realm, yet she had access to many political inner circles and, while she was diplomatic in her dealings with politicians and the establishment, she also gave many of their leaders – Gladstone and Asquith among them – an acerbic tongue-lashing not soon to be forgotten. She was concerned with the equality of the sexes but not, it seems, with the equality of all human beings, and if Josephine Kamm's account is to be relied upon was not averse to 'pulling strings' to obtain preferential treatment (particularly in prison) for friends and relatives. She was a cautious political strategist who condoned early militancy because she thought it would help bring about 'conversion' of the men. She was both a stern and a witty woman who lived to see women vote on the same terms as men.

At the end of the First World War limited franchise was extended to women, and it is usually suggested that this was because women had 'proven' themselves during the war (and there is no need to point to whose interests it serves to suggest that women were rewarded for putting their shoulders behind the men in this act of violence), and that their rights could no longer be denied. While not wanting to dismiss women's wartime contribution, Millicent Fawcett offers an alternative explanation which is not only fascinating but helps to reveal her ideas about society, particularly a male-dominated society.

'I do not believe we should have won the vote just when we did', she wrote, except for the fact that, 'it was absolutely necessary to introduce legislation in order to prevent the almost total disfranchisement of many millions of men who had been serving their country abroad in the Navy and Army, or in munition or other work which had withdrawn them from places where they usually resided . . . the most important qualification for the Parliamentary franchise . . . before 1918 was the occupation of premises, and before a man could be put on a register of voters it was necessary for its owner to prove "occupation" of these premises for twelve months previous to the last 15th of July. . . . Millions of the best men in the country had become disqualified through their war service by giving up their qualifying premises. . . . Therefore, by sheer necessity the Government was forced to introduce legislation dealing with the whole franchise question as it affected the male voter' (Fawcett, 1922, pp. 741–2).

In this context, states Fawcett, it was possible to raise the issue of women's suffrage which, after much manoeuvring (and because of fortuitous circumstances), was recommended on a limited basis: the 'household franchise' was introduced for women and, 'An age limit of thirty was imposed upon women, not because it was in any way logical or reasonable but simply and solely to produce a constituency in which the men were not outnumbered by the women' (ibid., p. 744).

Far from accepting that limited franchise was an inevitable ɛ ɪd logical outcome of women's participation in the war effort, Fawcett imṛ 'ies that the franchise could have been as distant in 1918 as it was during the nineteenth century and that it was the 'disarray' among the parties, and the fact that a whole new franchise bill had to be introduced for *men* that provided the circumstances for women to get one foot inside the door.[10] Her version makes more sense to me than most 'official' versions that I have read and indicates, once again, a significant discrepancy, and considerable difference in interest, between the explanations provided by women and those provided by men.

This, however, is not the only record that Millicent Fawcett left. She was a prolific writer and pamphleteer (as well as a frequent speaker, imposing on herself a limit of four speeches a week) and was concerned that women's voices be heard and their contribution in all aspects of life be recognised. This was partly why she wrote her series *Some Eminent Women of Our Time*, as well as her many accounts of the women's movement (including *The Women's Victory and After*, 1920) in the hope that women's view of women and their struggle would be preserved. Her contribution deserves to be seen in the same light.

Yet even placing the most positive interpretation possible on Millicent Garrett Fawcett's life and work, I still feel a keen sense of disappointment that I could begin this section on women in Britain in the nineteenth century with the revolutionary and radical stand taken by Anna Wheeler who

----

[10] It is worth noting that many women in America had been persuaded of the logic of the argument that if they could prove themselves by their patriotic efforts during the course of the Civil War, their contribution would be recognised by men and they would – afterwards – be rewarded by the vote. Many men encouraged this view. But after the Civil War, women were legally in a worse position as it was proclaimed to be the male 'Negro's Hour' and the word *male* was inserted in the constitution for the first time. Millicent Fawcett did not see a *logical* relationship between women's war effort and the franchise – to her, men's actions were 'capricious' and it was not women's contribution in time of war that was responsible for their enfranchisement. It is interesting to see how the 'historical authorities', however, have constructed this logical link and generated the suggestion that women are rewarded when they help men in wars – like they were rewarded for their efforts after the Second World War?

fundamentally questioned the competitive basis of society, who challenged the principle of the accumulation of wealth and insisted on the possibility of co-operative arrangements which made it practicable for all human beings to have equal access to resources instead of attempting to individually acquire them, and I have concluded with Millicent Fawcett, who seems to have simply wanted to improve women's position in a society which she basically found to be workable.

I do not want to suggest that it should be a case of either/or, that we should follow the precepts of Anna Wheeler *or* those of Millicent Fawcett; we need *both*. I have already stated that I have benefited from the reforms procured by people like Millicent Fawcett (and Emily Davies, etc.) and that I would rather be undertaking my present task from a position where I am allowed to claim my own earnings, have access to education (albeit, *men's* education) and obtain a divorce! But this does not alter the fact that I cannot see women's history and women's struggle as one of gradual development and improvement. To my mind it was downhill after Anna Wheeler. I cannot conceive of working for women to have a bigger share of the existing cake. It is a new cake I want and that seems as far away now as it did in 1825. The only difference is that I now have many models to turn to for guidance and insight and I have before me the constant lesson that women's resources are appropriated by men. Like Caroline Norton, I hardly expect many men to come forward and 'claim' this case!

PART FOUR

THE TWENTIETH CENTURY

(A)

SOCIAL REVOLUTION: PROCESS OR EVENT?

One does not customarily find Emma Goldman, Margaret Sanger, Charlotte Perkins Gilman and Crystal Eastman grouped together, but in some respects they shared certain characteristics – apart from the obvious ones of being concerned with women's position at the turn of the century. In varying degrees they sought a social revolution and stood in sharp contrast with many women who were then concerned with improving women's position within the existing system rather than changing the system. Developing (in general) more along the lines of Elizabeth Cady Stanton – and Matilda Joslyn Gage – rather than those of Susan B. Anthony, they saw that *equality* in legal terms in the *public* arena would count for little if the inequality of the *private* arena (the home) were to persist. In 1981, Margaret Stacey and Marion Price asked why it was that changes in political power and social organisation – which so many women had believed would accompany women's suffrage – were not forthcoming, and Stacey and Price conclude that it was primarily because *nothing else changed* when women got the vote, and *the vote itself was not an instrument for procuring change within the domestic circle.* If we were more familiar with our own history – steeped in the ideas of our foremothers and not just our forefathers – and if we were aware of the systematic doctoring of the records that men have engaged in, we would not be hailing Stacey and Price's explanation as new, and would not be just now suggesting that perhaps the earlier women's movement was not the 'single issue suffrage' movement we have too often been led to believe: we would *know* that there were many women who were perfectly aware that the vote was not *the* answer – and not necessarily even *an* answer. But what women such as Stanton, Goldman, and Eastman knew we have had to discover again for ourselves.

Because they were not looking to the vote as the panacea for women, they located the problem, and the solution, elsewhere and turned their attention – as Mary Astell, Mary Wollstonecraft and Sarah Grimké had done – to the institution of marriage and the oppression of women within the private confines of the home. They were all concerned with the economic dependence of women and the way this was exploited by the economic structures set up by men for themselves. They sought psychological and economic independence from men and for this reason were advocates of birth control and both proponents and exponents of a reorganisation of the division of labour among women and men – with Goldman, Gilman and Eastman, for example, demonstrating acute aversion to chores domestic.

All four women repudiated the existing economic basis of society and fought for drastic changes in the distribution of wealth; but they fought in different ways and for slightly different visions of the future.

1 Isolation: Emma Goldman (1869–1940)

Emma Goldman was an anarchist: it should come as no surprise that anarchists as a group are resistant to definition. In her book, *Anarchist Women 1870–1920*, Margaret Marsh (1981), cautious as she is about characterising anarchism as a 'movement', none the less states that broadly speaking there were two strands among those who declared themselves anarchists. There were the 'individualists' who were of course against all forms of externally imposed authority, who were determined to abolish the existing society and who believed that not infringing the liberties of others should be the only restraint placed upon individual freedom. As far as the 'individualists' were concerned, the greatest obstacle in the way of such freedom was the state – it was the state that they wanted to abolish and they therefore found the issue of private property not much of an issue at all. In stark contrast, the 'Communist-anarchists' – composed predominantly of European-born adherents – 'placed private property itself at the center of their analysis of social and economic oppression' (ibid., p. 13), with the result that *their* abolition of society meant the abolition of private ownership – and the state apparatus which had been erected to protect private property.

Among the anarchists there were feminists; the fact that anarchism assumed the absence of the state interference helped to set the framework for their brand of feminism which was, to say the least, markedly different from that of some of their sisters who were looking towards an extension of the role of the state to improve women's position – for example, with protective legislation for women.

Anarchist-feminists basically believed (as I do) that: 'legal equality with men is a gain that the existing institutional structure can accommodate without fundamental changes in society' (ibid., p. 5) and, because it was fundamental changes in society that they wanted, there did not seem to be much point in putting their energy into the battle for legal equality, which was by the end of the nineteenth century the basic platform of the women's suffrage movement. Not that they all necessarily repudiated legal equality – one may as well be equal as unequal in a perfidious system – but as one anarchist-feminist, Voltairine de Cleyre (1866–1911), stated, 'the ballot hasn't made men free and it won't make us free' (ibid., p. 55).

Emma Goldman scoffed at the very idea that suffrage would change women's lot – or even permit women to bring about change. As for the argument about women 'purifying' politics, she said, it was time people stopped talking about 'corruption in politics in a boarding school tone.

Corruption in politics has nothing to do with the morals, or the laxity of morals, of various political personalities. Its cause is altogether a material one. Politics is the reflex of the business and industrial world . . . There is no hope even that woman, with her right to vote will ever purify politics' (Goldman, in Shulman 1979, p. 135). If you are going to have capitalism – and a state – she argued, you are going to have corruption in politics, and the only process of purification was elimination. Understandably, her politics did not endear her to the suffrage movement.

Anarchist-feminists did not look to the state (or to men) for emancipation; instead they 'insisted that female subordination was rooted in an obsolete system of sexual and familial relationships. Attacking marriage, often urging sexual varietism, insisting on both economic and psychological independence, and sometimes denying maternal responsibility, they argued that personal autonomy was an essential component of sexual equality, and that political and legal rights could not of themselves engender such equality' (Marsh, 1981, p. 5). In their analysis they seem to have more in common with the contemporary women's movement than with the values of the Victorian era, which could suggest that they were exceptional, or that our impressions of the Victorian women have had something omitted.

At a time when many women – such as Frances Willard – were emphasising the differences between women and men (and arguing that woman's right to political participation was based on the different and purer value system she would bring to the political process), anarchist-feminists were drawing on the ideas of Mary Wollstonecraft and Sarah Grimké to assert that *both* sexes were *human*, that women and men had the same human needs and should be governed by the same standard.

They would not condone the 'different but complementary and equal' stand; they would not accept the 'one rule for men and another for women' position, be it in relation to the public or private arena. Women had just as many rights in the workplace and men had just as many responsibilities in domestic terms. Without benefit of the modern vernacular, most anarchist-feminists subscribed to the thesis that all human beings have a right to work, to obtain financial independence, and to enter sexual relationships as equals, and that all human beings were responsible for their own shit-work! This was why it was necessary to restructure the nuclear family completely and to reorganise the household division of labour; and this was where the responsibility for children became a considerable stumbling block.

Many of the male anarchists did not share the women's view on some of these matters; these 'radical' men – in what could be termed classic style – found it advantageous to facilitate the greater sexual availability of women but inconvenient to reciprocate and make their own labour available for the business of daily maintenance. Anarchist-feminists such as Helena Born (1860–1901), Mollie Stiemer (1897–1980), Marie Ganz (1891–(?)), and Voltairine de Cleyre (1866–1911)[1] placed little faith in the

---

[1] These women are all discussed at some length in Margaret Marsh's book *Anarchist Women 1870–1920* (1981), which is highly recommended for further reading.

enlightenment of radical men, and Margaret Marsh states that this was a wise decision on their part, for without exception these four women encountered male colleagues who were firmly of the persuasion that men's problems constituted the human and universal issues while women's concerns (if they were acknowledged to be *real*, and often they were not) were peripheral and would all dissolve with the coming of the revolution. (This is such a tired old story, I wonder sometimes how we can ever take it seriously. I think the next time a 'radical' male assures me that women's *minor* problems will be solved, after *his major* problems are solved, I shall just laugh.)

There *is* a humorous element in the case put forward by the anarchist men, for in general they 'claimed to believe that once anarchism has been achieved, sexual equality would follow' but 'very few thought immediate action was wise or desirable' (ibid., p. 54). Woman was urged to 'join her strength to that of man in *his* effort to establish the proper relations between labor and capital' (ibid.) and was informed that her 'true mission lay in assisting working-class men to create the socialist revolution' (ibid., p. 158).

Many of the anarchist-feminists damned their male colleagues as tyrants. Emma Goldman was an exception. In 1920, Crystal Eastman wrote in *The Liberator* that: 'Many feminists are socialists, many are communists, not a few are active leaders in these movements. But the true feminist, no matter how far to the left she may be in the revolutionary movement, sees the woman's battle as distinct in its objects and different in its methods from the workers' battle for industrial freedom. She knows, of course,' Eastman continues, 'that the vast majority of women as well as men are without property, and are of necessity bread and butter slaves under a system of society which allows the very sources of life to be privately owned by a few, and she counts herself a loyal soldier in the working-class army that is marching to overthrow the system. But', she adds emphatically, 'as a feminist she also knows that the whole of woman's slavery is not summed up in the profit system, nor her complete emancipation assured by the downfall of capitalism' (Eastman in Cook, 1978, p. 53).

I have my suspicions that Emma Goldman would have disagreed. Born into a Jewish family in Russia in 1869, Goldman knew extremes of privation and exploitation from an early age. She had a terrible childhood – directly within her own family where her father seems to have embodied the excesses of male despotism and brute force (Goldman herself said he was the nightmare of her childhood) – and within the larger society where she constantly witnessed the beating of wives and children, the whipping of peasants, the persecution of Jews, and a system of administration based almost exclusively on corruption.

Her flight to America was precipitated when, at the age of 15 she declared she wanted to study and travel, resisted her father's efforts to marry her off, and rebelled when he screamed, 'Girls do not have to learn much,' just how to 'prepare minced fish, cut noodles fine, and give the man plenty of children' (quoted in Shulman, 1979, p. 6).

Goldman had developed a passionate admiration for some of the

Russian women rebels of her time, and was inspired with the determination to *act* in the world, as they did, and it was this commitment to action which largely shaped her response to America when she found not freedom and justice, and an absence of poverty, as she had been led to imagine, but deprivation and exploitation on a scale not dissimilar to that which she had left behind in Russia. Working in Rochester, New York, she found it impossible to subsist on her factory wage, even living in an immigrant ghetto; for a very short time she married a fellow Russian immigrant. She also read many of the pamphlets emanating from the European anarchists.

But this did not alter, only emphasised, the harsh and repressive nature of her existence in the 'land of the free and the home of the brave', and she was inspired once more by the 1866 Chicago Conspiracy Trial (in which four anarchists were hanged for throwing a bomb at the police, on the most dubious of evidence) which convinced her that the only possible reaction was a life of protest and revolt. She went to New York with her only assets 'a sewing machine with which to make her way, five dollars (borrowed) and a passion to join the revolutionary anarchists whose scathing tracts she had read so avidly in Rochester' (ibid., p. 8).

She was soon living in a commune with several other Russian-born anarchists, had met her first great love, Alexander Berkman, with whom her life was enmeshed until his suicide, and assumed an independent life. She set off on lecture tours to rouse the workers to oppose the system and was always searching for that one *event* which would fire them to action and unity, in the same way that she herself had been fired to action. Her goal was to make the revolution. In 1892 the opportunity for the dramatic, inspirational event came. There was a steel workers' strike in Homestead; armed men were called in and the result was carnage. In retaliation, and as a means of uniting and inspiring the workers, it was agreed by the group of which Emma Goldman was a member that an act of political violence was called for. The assassination of the chairman of the company was planned: Goldman was to raise the finance (to buy the gun) and then afterwards use the act for the necessary propaganda purposes; Berkman was to fire the gun.

Berkman *did* shoot the chairman, but he quickly recovered; Goldman *did* try to explain the significance of the deed to the world, but the masses remained uncomprehending and there was no uprising. Berkman was dismissed as a lunatic and served fourteen years in gaol (ibid., p. 11). A year later, Goldman herself was gaoled – for inciting a riot among the unemployed, although no such riot occurred. After her imprisonment she found she had become notorious as 'Red Emma'. Says Shulman, 'she was called enemy of God, law, marriage, the state. There was no one like her in America' (ibid., p. 12).

In 1895 and 1899 she visited Europe and met and talked with fellow anarchists, but in 1901, after the assassination of President McKinley, her public lecturing was curtailed. She was arrested in connection with the assassination – primarily because she was an anarchist not because there was any evidence against her – and while later released, so severe was the backlash against anarchism, she found it impossible to appear in public and was even forced to go 'underground'. She emerged again in 1906 when, with Berkman (who was released from gaol), she began to publish a radical journal, *Mother Earth*. For almost a decade she continued writing and lecturing, in her attempt to bring about the revolution and change the world. But in 1919 – after her anti-war efforts – she was deported to Russia. Within a very short space of time she became disillusioned. The Russian revolution had not realised her dream. She left Russia (with Berkman who had also been deported) and lived a life of exile, settling finally in England and eking out a very meagre existence from her writing.

For me, Goldman poses a problem: I do not like her. Not only must this make a significant contribution to my assessment of her (a warning to readers to beware of negative bias), it also raises the issue of *why* I have no great affection for her. Perhaps I am not alone; I suspect Margaret Marsh (1981) shares some of my reservations about Goldman, for she does not make a practice of extolling Goldman's virtues. Like Alix Kates Shulman, she suggests that Goldman misread the American scene, that she did not appreciate the differences between American and European traditions and, consequently, many of her actions – and ideas – remain incomprehensible in an 'English-speaking context'. But I am sure this is not the source of my alienation from Goldman. On the contrary, it is partly because I find her ideas readily comprehensible that I find myself at times strenuously objecting to them.

This does not detract from my admiration of Goldman; I have much respect for her courage, her disagreeableness and defiance. I could not fail to be impressed by the woman who never went off to lecture without taking a good book – in case she ended up in gaol; or the woman who completely exposed the hypocrisy of the American dream. When deported from the 'free' world for her ideas, she declared, 'I consider it an honor to be the first political agitator deported from the United States' (Shulman, 1979, p. 16). Ironically, it is, however, not what she opposed, but what she did *not* oppose which is, I think, the basis of my disaffection.

Goldman is usually portrayed as the woman who was against everything: ' "The more opposition I encountered," she boasted, "the more I was in my element" ' (ibid., p. 15) and Shulman says that Goldman was 'combative by nature' and a woman who 'presented the most provocative topics in the most dangerous places. . . She talked up free love to puritans, atheism to churchmen, revolution to reformers; she denounced the ballot to suffragists, patriotism to soldiers and patriots' (ibid.).

But I can find no record of her 'talking up' the limitations of men to the 'superior' sex. To her, capitalism was the *sole* source of women's oppression, and she looks no further for evidence and has no need of other explanatory ideas. There is no indictment of *male* power in general and no criticism of males in particular. For one who is against everything, she is significantly silent on the abuses of women, by men. Heterosexuality is not even questioned; rather, love for men, and the maternal instinct, are held up as the positive features of women's existence which have been eroded by women's achievement of emancipation! 'Emancipation as understood by the majority of its adherents', she said, 'is of too narrow a scope to permit the boundless love and ecstasy contained in the deep emotion of the true woman, sweetheart, mother in freedom' (ibid. pp. 136–7), and it is perhaps paradoxical to hear a feminist invoking the cult of true woman-hood and presenting it as a desired and inevitable outcome of the anarchist revolution.

I simply cannot accept Goldman's argument that the 'emancipated' woman is to be pitied. These women who claim to be independent on the grounds that they earn their own living 'paid for it by the suppression of the mainsprings of their own nature' asserts Goldman (1930) for 'fear of public opinion robbed them of love and intimate comradeship. It was pathetic to see how lonely they were, how starved for male affection, and how they craved children.' Hence her conclusion that 'the emancipation of the women was frequently more of a tragedy than traditional marriage would have been' (vol. I; p. 371). She contended that women needed to be 'emancipated from emancipation', for, while it had 'brought woman econ-omic equality with man' (an assertion that would have been no less rigor-ously contested at the turn of the century than now), this 'highly praised independence is, after all, but a slow process of dulling and stifling a woman's nature, her love instinct, her mother instinct' (Shulman, 1979, pp. 135–6).

No one has ever suggested that it is easy, or without penalties, to live as an independent woman in a male-dominated society. On the contrary, most women who have tried to lead such independent lives have outlined the many difficulties this entails, because men do not usually like such independence and have inflicted penalties on independent women precisely because they want to coerce them back into the fold of love for men, and expression of the maternal instinct. I would not want to dispute that many women living without men may find some of the problems faced insur-mountable. They are meant to. But I would never suggest, as Goldman does, that the fault lies with the women. It is on this issue that we most definitely part company.

Goldman could only ever have been classified as radical within a male context; as far as sexual politics are concerned, and in a female context, she is a conservative, if not indeed a reactionary. One of the most significant features of Goldman is that she had no *sisters* – male lovers, yes (and Berkman gets quite a few pats on the back for his generous attitude and lack of jealousy), but sisters, no. She does not admit the collective experi-ence of women to her frame of reference, and this allows her to accept without question the descriptions and explanations provided by men to account for their own circumstances under capitalism. She assumes – with very few exceptions – that it is the same for women, and the issue of women's oppression prior to capitalism, or in cultures that are not capi-talist, does not arise.

There is only one case that I know of where Goldman, at least in part, admits the experience of other women – in her lecture on Mary Wollstone-craft, given in 1911 (see Alice Wexler, 1981), but even here there are qualifications. Wexler says that: 'Goldman's portrait of Wollstonecraft is significant as the most revealing short self portrait she ever wrote' (and had she looked more to women and less to men she might have revealed a different self), but while Goldman identifies with Wollstonecraft, there are problems with such identification. It is 'a sense of identity with the great rebels and martyrs of the past', says Wexler, for 'Mary Wollstonecraft was one of those great rebels. In describing her vision of Wollstonecraft, Goldman also described herself' (ibid., p. 113). Not as a woman, but as a rebel and a martyr (traditionally male categories); not as a protester against male power, but as an 'emancipated' woman with a tragic love life.

Central to Goldman's image of Wollstonecraft was her passion for Imlay, which was 'the great turning point and climax of her life, and one from which she never really recovered' (ibid., p. 124), and at the time she wrote the essay, says Wexler, she 'had been involved for three years in a love affair which she regarded as similar in many ways to Wollstonecraft's passionate involvement' (ibid., p. 127). But instead of pursuing this, Goldman explains it all – over-simply – in terms of the tragedy of emancipated women who have been 'ruined' for love. (Wexler also points out that there were many 'emancipated women' at the time who could not be accommodated by Goldman's theories. 'Most of Goldman's activist and radical women contemporaries would probably have rejected her implied assessment of their lives as tragic. For the autobiographies and correspondence of women such as Charlotte Perkins Gilman, Elizabeth Gurley Flynn, Jane Addams, Crystal Eastman, and Lillian Wald convey their authors' sense of purpose and deep satisfaction with their lives,' ibid., p. 128).

Because 'Goldman projected into her portrait of Wollstonecraft both her greatest hopes and her worst fears about the possibilities of love and freedom' (ibid., p. 132), she provides a glimpse of the *potential* which could have been realised had she sought to perceive herself as part of a community of women and been prepared to start with women's experience as a basis for explaining the world. As it is there is not much of evidence to suggest that Goldman challenges the propositions that male experiences are the norm, male problems the universal problems, and male solutions total solutions. Nor was there any likelihood that these propositions would be challenged while she made no attempt to construct and understand women's reality or to assess the discrepancies between the way men perceived women and the way women perceived themselves.

Her ideas about women under capitalism are valuable, but they are only part of the picture, as Crystal Eastman suggested. The 'traffic in women' is related to low pay for women, but this is not the complete explanation; nor is it a complete explanation to suggest that such 'traffic in women' will be miraculously erased with the coming of revolution. Despite her many assertions which anger me, however, there are ideas which it is only fair to say that I find stimulating and affirming. For example, in her analysis of the workplace, Goldman is prepared to concede that women are in a different position from men, and she anticipates the 'new' formulation of the problem of sexual harassment. 'Nowhere is woman treated according to the merit of her work,' she said, 'but rather as a sex. It is therefore almost inevitable that she should pay for her right to exist, to keep a position in whatever line with sex favors' (Shulman, 1979, p. 145).

Had this insight more frequently been the substance of her discussion, I am sure that trying to empathise with Emma Goldman would not have been such a problem for me. As it is, my hopes have at times been raised, only to be dashed. I was reassured to discover that she was one of the first women in America publicly to advocate birth control,[2] but disappointed to find that it was primarily because it was part of her 'free speech' campaign, and a form of resistance to state interference, and *not* primarily as an issue of women's rights to control their own bodies.

2 Birth strikes: Margaret Sanger (1879–1966)

This was not the stand adopted by Margaret Sanger, who explicitly stated that 'no woman can call herself free who does not own and control her body' (Rossi, 1974, pp. 520–1) and Sanger devoted most of her life's work to assisting women to achieve this freedom. While not an anarchist herself, Sanger shared many of the beliefs of the anarchists, particularly as they related to the non-interference of Church and State in matters of women's rights to control reproduction. She was supported by Emma Goldman when in 1914 she defied the law and published the first issue of her magazine *Woman Rebel*. Sanger was also committed to the class struggle (more openly in the early days of her crusade, before she attempted to enlist the help of the medical profession and faced great pressure to become 'respectable') and saw a reduction in the number of children as a direct threat to capitalism, which required – in those days – a constant stream of workers.

Benefits is a novel written by Zoë Fairbairns (1979b) in which, like Lysistrata and the women of ancient Greece, the women of Britain in the last decades of the twentieth century go on strike and refuse to have children. It is not long, of course, before the men – who theoretically hold all the power – are attempting to meet the women's demands (so that the women will go back to *work*), and Fairbairns creates in fiction a reality which Sanger herself perceived in theory. She envisaged the possibility of a birth strike which would not only break capitalism but would expose the artificial nature of male power and bring about its downfall. This is a proposition I still find very interesting and attractive.

According to Sanger, however (and many of the customary aspersions have been cast on the credibility of her own account), her crusade for birth control had its origins not in any form of analysis of the state – or even initially of male power – but in a direct response to the plight of some of

---

[2] Eliza Sharples, who used the name *Isis*, advocated birth control in England in the 1830s (as did Harriet Martineau – on the economic grounds that the population should be reduced). Anna Wheeler also advocated birth control, see Constance Rover, *Love, Morals and the Feminists*, 1970.

the women she nursed, who were destroyed by numerous and unwanted pregnancies, and who resorted to desperate measures of abortion – and frequently died.

In her book *My Fight for Birth Control* (1931) she is quite clear about the fact that while birth control may have served economic ends, and while it was a practice consistent with her analysis of society, it was none the less a response to women's needs – and not to men's needs of a revolution – that induced her to take on the double task of finding out how pregnancies (and births) could be prevented, and then of distributing the knowledge to women. While today we may think that the greater problem is finding safe and satisfactory means of birth control, in Sanger's time the greater problem was providing women with the information of the means.

The law stated – in Sanger's own words – 'that *no one* could give information to prevent conception to *anyone* for any reason' (1931, p. 152). It was illegal to publish such information or to send such 'obscene' material through the post. Because of this 'conspiracy of silence', it is understandable that many women thought there was a 'secret', known only to the privileged few. This was the case with Sadie Sacks, whose experience Margaret Sanger cites in her own account of her commitment to the struggle for birth control. Mrs Sacks already had three young children when she became pregnant again, and because she could not afford another child, physically or financially, she procured an abortion and Margaret Sanger arrived as the nurse who afterwards battled for her life. The woman survived but was very despondent, informing Sanger that another baby would kill her (either through abortion or birth) and that she was desperate to find a way of preventing it. She asked the doctor what she should do and he treated the whole issue facetiously; he scoffed at the idea that she should want to have her cake and eat it too, and suggested that she 'ban' her husband to the rooftop. After the doctor's departure, Mrs Sacks implored Sanger to tell her the secret, and Sanger states with rage and frustration that she *simply did not know* how you prevented pregnancy.

Sanger too left Mrs Sacks's home and over the next few months felt uneasy – even guilty – about the fate of Mrs Sacks. Then she was called once more; this time Mrs Sacks died from the abortion. Sanger returned to her own home, stunned, but gradually convinced throughout the course of the night that 'uncontrolled breeding' was *the* central social problem and determined to do something about it. She writes that at that moment she renounced all palliative work for ever. 'I would never go back again to nurse women's ailing bodies while their miseries were as vast as the stars. I was now finished with superficial cures, with doctors and nurses and social workers who were brought face to face with this overwhelming truth of women's needs and yet turned to pass on the other side. They must be made to see these facts. I resolved that women should have knowledge of contraception. They have every right to know about their own bodies. . . . I would tell the world what was going on in the lives of these poor women. I *would* be heard. No matter what it should cost. *I would be heard*' (ibid., p. 56).

In 1916, Sanger opened a birth control clinic in Brooklyn – the main emphasis being on contraception, not abortion – and while it was designed to provide women with information it was also a deliberate attempt to test the law. News of the clinic quickly spread, women flocked to its doors, and poured out their feelings of terror and pain on this issue which haunted their lives but which was a socially and legally taboo topic. The premises were raided, the women arrested and Sanger says, 'We were not surprised at being arrested, but the shock and horror of it was that a *woman*, with a squad of five plain clothes men, conducted the raid and made the arrest. A woman – the irony of it!' (ibid., p. 158). There can be no doubt that Sanger saw women as a group, with shared interests and a common cause. There was panic among the women in the waiting room – who were being bullied by the police in the attempt to obtain their names so that they could later be subpoenad to testify – and there was chaos outside (women, baby carriages, children – all waiting to get into the clinic). When Sanger and Tania Mindell were taken away, one woman ran after them, screaming wildly for them to come back and help her. The clinic was closed; the court declared it a 'public nuisance'. Sanger was imprisoned but went on to fight again – and again.

The issue of contraception helps to illustrate the way men have been able to control so many facets of society in their own interest. It is not too much to suggest that if men were to give birth, huge amounts of money would be invested in research on *safe* contraception (decreeing that the consequences of the pill or coil are *side*-effects is an evaluation that could only be made from a male frame of reference; for the women who experience them they are *the* effects). If men were to give birth, information about it (and its prevention) would no doubt be readily available, and contraceptives would in all probability be free – as a *public* service, given that men's problems *are* the social problems. But perhaps even more significantly, if men were to give birth, the topic of birth and birth control, would be a *prestigious* one, a means of distinguishing those with problems of central and profound significance from those who were excluded from such an event.

It is not the capacity to give birth which in itself constitutes a liability or an asset in social arrangements. Whether giving birth is a mark of penance or a sign of superior powers depends largely on which sex controls social organisation and produces the meanings for society. In our society where men hold power, the capacity to give birth has been used against women – from being a reason for their exclusion from paid employment to being a sign of their disfavour in the eyes of God. Instead of being a testimony of women's power – as it would most certainly be if women were in charge of social meanings – it has been *stolen* by men for their own purposes, used to enhance their power and to degrade and debilitate women. As Lysistrata and Zoë Fairbairns have demonstrated (not to mention Charlotte Perkins Gilman, Adrienne Rich and Ann Oakley), birthing could readily be a basis for women's *strength*, and the fact that it is frequently conceptualised as a *weakness* reveals more about the power arrangements in society than about birth, or women.

That men have seen their own prowess enhanced through their control over birth is a point starkly and illuminatingly made by Laurence Housman (1912). When, in walking beside one of London's parks one day, he witnessed 'A poor woman, about to become a mother [who], was on her way home when unexpectedly her pains overtook her and she could go no further. A policeman came to her aid, and went to find a conveyance; and while she waited a crowd gathered, men and boys; and as they watched her they laughed and made jokes. She was a symbol to them of what sex meant; some man had given her a lesson and now she was learning it; to their minds it was a highly satisfactory spectacle' (p. 50).

From Elizabeth Cady Stanton to Mary Daly has come the claim that men have conflated the image of god and themselves, and the correlation between this attitude of teaching women a lesson with that of god's supposed injunction to go forth and multiply in pain, as penance, is not coincidental. One of the reasons so many men were so fiercely resistant to the issue of birth control was because they saw it as depriving them of this constructed source of power,[3] of taking away their 'mastery', particularly if contraception were placed in the hands of women.

Of course they did not always give this as their reason for opposing birth control. Their arguments were more likely to be couched in the terms that contraception was part of prostitutes' 'lore' and that women who even knew of its existence were of prostitute status (see Constance Rover, 1970, p. 99). They asserted that contraception was unnatural and unhealthy. Bertrand Russell (1967) states that when as a young man he tried to find out about it he was given the medical advice that it was invariably gravely injurious to health, and his family hinted that it was his father's use of contraception that resulted in his epilepsy (p. 81).

If these were insufficient grounds to oppose it (and to defy women to use it at their peril) there were also the additional ones that it contravened the scriptures and constituted murder. However, these objections were in one sense superficial and helped to conceal the underlying issues which were at stake – those of control. The introduction of birth control – particularly if practised by women – was a threat to the power structure that had been established in relation to birth; it enabled women to have resources *outside the influence of men*. With safe and sure contraception women would no longer be available to men as they had been – not as objects to be taught a lesson, not as 'breeders', not as docile helpmates 'barefoot, pregnant and in the kitchen'.

Birth control would give women some degree of autonomy; men would no longer be able to *inflict* their demands on women. Indeed, quite the opposite could occur where, before a woman agreed to a pregnancy, a man might have to meet certain criteria which she set. This is why so many men found birth control such a threatening issue and why they erected all manner of obstacles, legal ones included, to block its introduction (and why there is still such deeply entrenched resistance to the idea that women

---

[3] Matilda Joslyn Gage (1893) argued that it was when wise women were using their healing skills to reduce women's child-bearing pains that the clergy were incensed and the witch-hunts intensified.

should control their own bodies). I have always believed that it has been in the interest of the preservation of male power for women to be kept too busy and too tired to organise and protest, and constant pregnancy is one way of keeping women too busy, too tired, and, of course dependent. As Margaret Sanger found (along with Marie Stopes in Britain), many women just 'gave up' under the pressure and pain of unwanted repeated pregnancies which were often perceived as their 'just deserts'.

This raises the question of women's attitude towards sex – or more precisely, towards heterosexuality. I am weary of reading about the prudish women of the nineteenth century who failed to adjust to adult sexual relationships and whose refusal to risk unwanted pregnancies (and venereal disease) is viewed as neurosis. Had women been writing the records (as did Margaret Sanger, Marie Stopes, 1918, and Christabel Pankhurst, 1913), these women could have appeared as rational. I can only envisage what it must have been like for women when every act of sexual intercourse brought with it the risk of pregnancy, but I can perfectly well understand any decision (or rationale according to the conventions of the time) to be sexually unavailable to men. It seems to me a fairly healthy and independent response.

When Margaret Sanger took it upon herself to find a means of preventing conception and realised that a 'side'-effect could be a threat to capitalism and male power, she recognised nothing less than many men had seen. This was one of the reasons that their attitude towards birth control was so repressive. Sanger aroused even greater fear among men when she insisted that contraception was a woman's problem and that the knowledge and its application should reside in women's hands. It was one thing to suggest that it might not be necessary for women to be consistently pregnant, even though this in itself was threatening, but it was quite another to insist that it should be women who made the decisions about pregnancy, for what role did this leave for men? Sanger argued that it might be possible in an ideal society for birth control to be a *parental* issue, but in a society which was far from ideal, in which men held power and women bore the consequences, it was a woman's right to protect (defend?) herself. Women needed their own resources, she argued, and not dependence on male benevolence, which could be conditional.

I think her argument still applies. Today the issue should not be that a male-dominated medical profession has come up with contraception for women, but that it has produced *unsafe* contraception for women. Questions should be asked about the criteria for safety; would men have different (and better) standards for themselves? But it is difficult to be critical of the fact that it has been women in general for whom contraception has been designed. I have known too many women who, if contraception had been in the hands of men, would have had unwanted pregnancies inflicted upon them in the name of an 'accident'. When the consequences of sexual intercourse are not the same for both sexes, the realities are different, pose different problems and call for different solutions. Therefore I unhesitatingly agree with Sanger that reproduction belongs to women. Pauline Bart

(1981) has advocated that women should 'seize the means of reproduction' and this is precisely what Margaret Sanger attempted to do.

She was aware of the reasons that men passed laws to keep reproduction under their control and she saw men's position in relation to reproduction as artificial, absurd, and readily undermined. That is why I think she would have approved wholeheartedly of some of the more recent developments among women completely to circumvent man-made laws aimed at depriving women of control through abortion. It is argued that terminating a pregnancy is a skill which bears no more relation to the medical profession than does the skill of cooking: it is possible to get an infection from one and food poisoning from the other, but if knowledge about the processes is freely available and care is taken, such undesirable outcomes are unlikely and the services of the medical profession unnecessary. If women can cook for themselves (and others), they can also terminate pregnancies for themselves (and others) and male edicts and laws are quite superfluous!

Like Sanger I would prefer prevention to cure, but prevention is not always possible and cures are sometimes called for, and a number of women in America have demonstrated that this has nothing to do with either the medical profession or the law. It appeals to my sense of subversion to have men pass as many laws as they please while women distribute knowledge among themselves and safely, and undetectedly control their own bodies and terminate their own pregnancies if they so desire. Passing laws against women cooking would probably be easier to enforce.

Margaret Sanger's battle for contraception and for women's right to control their own bodies was not a 'single-issue' movement but part of her radical programme for social revolution. She questioned the whole edifice of male power and indicated that reproduction was only one area where men had usurped power, and where beliefs about birth were only one set of values which had to be resisted. She urged women to look at other areas of their lives and to be wary of accepting men's justifications for the existing social arrangements. Women must not reproduce men's values which assist men, she argued, but gain independence and formulate their own, in their own interest.

'Women are too much inclined to follow in the footsteps of men,' she warned, 'to try to think as men think, to try to solve the general problems of life as men solve them. If after attaining their freedom, women accept conditions in the spheres of government, industry, art, morals and religion, as they find them, they will be but taking a leaf out of men's book. The woman is not needed to do man's work. She is not needed to think man's thoughts.' She adds cuttingly and revealingly: 'She need not fear that the masculine mind, almost universally dominant, will fail to take care of its own' (Sanger, 1920, quoted in Rossi, 1974, p. 535).

Birth control (or its more euphemistic and less-threatening counterpart 'family planning') may be acceptable in most quarters today. Once won, like the vote, it no longer constitutes a radical demand. But in Margaret Sanger's day it was one of *the* most radical and outrageous demands, and many men and some women thought its introduction would secure drastic changes in the balance of power. It was a source of freedom for woman, argued Sanger, which would give her time, energy, and resources 'not to enhance the masculine spirit' nor 'to preserve a man made world' but to create a world in which women were fully represented and in which their values and concerns would prevail – at least half the time (ibid.).

Sanger's aspirations have not been realised. The creation of a human world, which Sanger called for and which necessitated a social revolution, has not materialised.

3 Cerebration and celebration: Charlotte Perkins Gilman (1860–1935)

Another woman who saw women as fully human (and men and their lop-sided values and creations as only partially human) was Charlotte Perkins Gilman, who refused to declare herself a feminist on the grounds that the term was inaccurate. The world was a man-made one, she argued (the title of one of her books being *The Man Made World or our Androcentric Culture*, 1911), permeated with androcentric or masculine values, and rather than be seen as simply representing the 'other' side – the meaning she attributed to 'feminist' – she claimed humanity for herself. This is both an interesting and subversive view, and very typical of Gilman (with whom I have no 'identity' problems), who was quite good at making propaganda points. She defiantly asserted that it was the women who protested against tyranny, injustice, oppression and exploitation who were the human norm, against which masculist values could be measured and found wanting.

Of all the women writing and lecturing about women's position and the problem of men at the beginning of the twentieth century, I think Charlotte Perkins Gilman (who is referred to by Alice Rossi, 1974, and Carl Degler, 1966, as the leading feminist intellectual in the first two decades of the century) comes closest to sharing the assumptions and aims of the contemporary women's movement. It is very affirming to know she said what she did, but it is frustrating – even enraging – to recognise that her ideas were lost, in such a short time, and had to be painstakingly forged again and she herself re-discovered.

Her feminism was forged from practical experience: her father left her mother when Charlotte was young and he provided little or no financial support over the years. Charlotte had every reason to be suspicious of the ideology of marriage and motherhood, says her biographer, Mary Hill (1980), for images of romantic love had been replaced by the reality of too-frequent pregnancies, and notions of domestic security had given way to the experience of an itinerant and precarious lifestyle, for which Charlotte frequently blamed her father (who did not find steady work compatible with his nature and who seemed to have little compunction about evading his family responsibilities). If a man did not want to fulfil the obligations inherent in the marriage contract, what was there to stop him? As Frances Power Cobbe had pointed out – nothing!

Charlotte, her brother and her mother were for some time in the unenviable position of being forced to seek shelter with relatives, but in 1874 her mother took the very radical step of moving into a Swedenborgian co-operative household: 'Here was a group of religious non-conformists, a group of divorcees at that, cooperating on housework, communing on their mystic faith, and forming what would seem to many a threatening substitute for the traditional family model' (Hill, 1980, p. 37). And here Charlotte's mother, Mary Perkins, thrived, gaining in strength, assurance and self-esteem.

When later Charlotte Perkins Gilman came to advocate co-operative and communal living and the collectivisation of housework, and when she suggested that women could create self-sufficient and satisfying communities – on their own – as she did, for example, in *Herland*, her vision for women was not merely a dream, but substantiated from her own personal experience. Her early encounters helped her to develop as a woman – identified woman, both in the way she lived her life and the way she formulated her theories of women's oppression. She herself 'publicly and proudly proclaimed the "deep personal happiness" she had known in female friendship' (ibid., p. 82) and at 21 formed a romantic friendship with Martha Luther which, while fulfilling, was also threatened by the prospect of Martha's marriage and the agony of accepting that relationships with women were classified as a 'substitute'.

But it was not just love which claimed her attention. She had always responded to crises and distress by turning to books and writing (and it is the fact that she wrote so much – including diaries and letters, that helps make this biography of Hill's so rich and interesting). She consistently made herself schedules and fought to be disciplined. But it is her energy, exuberance and enthusiasm which makes her such an attractive person.

To be physically fit was part of her discipline and a manifestation of her energy. She was interested in being physically strong and in performing athletic feats and for a while *How to Get Strong and Stay So* was her bible. She took up weight-lifting and gymnastics and highly recommended the virtues of regularly running a seven-minute mile. 'Not only did she delight in her own physicality,' says Hill, 'she delighted in the effort to control her body as part of the larger effort to control her life. She locked the door "actually and metaphorically," sat up all night because it was forbidden, slept on the floor once, out on the roof another (again, mother told her not to), and generally indulged in, or "wasted (her) substance in," equivalent "riotous-virtues" ' (ibid., p. 67).

Her early affairs with the opposite sex proved to be unsatisfactory, partly because she recognised that few were the males who wanted strong women and many were the males who required ego-massaging. She experienced the conflict so common among women between being independent and being acceptable. When she settled for acceptability – as she often did in these early years – she later fumed and felt decidedly shabby. She prided herself on her intelligence and her physical ability, she gloried in being a strong-minded woman; but there were still occasions when it was easier to give in and conform to the approved image, and tears, when she experienced rejection.

Then Martha got married and Charlotte met Walter Stetson. An aspiring artist, committed to his work, sombre, well-read, noble, protective, kind, intensely proper, *and* attractive, Hill describes him as having 'a strikingly attractive body – broad shouldered, vigorous, and physically imposing' (ibid., p. 92). He asked Charlotte to marry him; she didn't know what to do. They had an erratic courtship in which Charlotte said she would, she wouldn't, and she might – later! She herself recognised that she 'plummeted into the doldrums under Walker's loving gaze' and regained her buoyancy and spunk when he was not around (ibid., p. 101). But she finally agreed and then experienced a raging internal battle as the wedding day approached (ibid., p. 119).

My own past floods in on me as I read her accounts of the early days of wedded bliss as she plunged herself into a frenzy of domestic activity only to find that the harder she tried the worse she felt – and the harder she tried. Having frenetically washed and wiped plates until they gleamed – and then smashed them – I know how she felt. I know if I had been able to read Charlotte Perkins Gilman's description and explanation of the state of mind of the new housewife when I was experiencing the first 'shocks' of such an existence, I would have felt reassured rather than irrational. But I did not know she existed at that stage of my life.

She gave up trying harder and, for one for whom physical fitness and vitality was so important, the lethargy in which she took refuge was a mark of her despair. She became pregnant, she got even worse, she experienced acute post-natal depression. She also felt extremely *guilty*. Why could she not live up to the image of blissfully happy wife and mother? What was wrong with her? Where had she failed? A familiar tale among women; an indication of female neurosis to men. She tried to break the pattern of her existence. In 1886 she attended her first suffrage convention (and was amazed to find that Lucy Stone, far from being the harridan that she had been portrayed, was sweet and kind). In 1887 she started writing a regular suffrage column for the periodical *People*. But while her column became increasingly radical, she became increasingly debilitated until in 1887 she was sent to the famous Dr S. Weir Mitchell for his infamous rest cure.

She arrived in Philadelphia for the 'cure' for her nervous troubles, and was immediately given the standard treatment: complete rest in bed, over-fed, no stimulation – no books, writing, or conversation – on the premise that 'freed from the taxing pressures of "inappropriate" ambition, the "hysterical woman" would begin to accept life's blessings calmly' (ibid., p. 148). Ha! Hill states that Mitchell's treatment of women, while granted the status of 'medical science', was – of course – a product of his considerable prejudice against women, a punishment even of strong-minded women of whom he completely disapproved. He deliberately set out to 'cure' such women of what he saw as their dominating, destructive and predatory nature by forcing passivity and vacuousness upon them, this would teach them to adjust to their 'femininity' and to become what he considered 'healthy'. His attitude towards Charlotte – as to his other patients (or victims) – was to make her believe that domesticity was a *cure* and not a *cause* of her distress (ibid., p. 149).

She herself later stated – partly in her fiction *The Yellow Wallpaper* – that the effect of this treatment was to bring her perilously close to losing her mind. The 'cure' did not work. Charlotte came to recognise that she was better when not in Walter's company and even better still when not expected to be a housewife. They separated, and in 1894 were divorced. Grace Channing, a close friend of Charlotte's (and who *remained* a close friend), married Walter and with him assumed responsibility for Charlotte's daughter, Kate. 'This double departure from the traditional attitude of the divorced wife was too much for the newspapers,' says Carl Degler (1966) 'which pilloried her as the woman who gave away her husband and her child to another woman' (p. xii). Ann J. Lane (1980) says that Gilman 'was so unnerved by the scandal that she literally gave up her home. She left California and took to the road for five years of lecturing' (p. xii).

In her travels Gilman found – what Betty Friedan was to 'rediscover' in the 1950s and 1960s – 'the problem without a name'. Everywhere she went she met women who were questioning their role in life and who were responding to the pressures of their existence with resentment or rebellion, despair or defiance. The more she saw, the more she was convinced that her task in life – her passion – was 'to understand the whys and wherefores of women's situation, to organize within the women's movement, and to preach the idea that self-respect, satisfying work, and economic independence were women's basic rights' (Hill, 1980, p. 185).

Through working and living with women (and through her relationship with Adeline Knapp) Gilman came to believe that the solution for women lay in perceiving themselves as a united class and in working co-operatively together. She did not look to men to bring about the emancipation of women (or even to assist in the task), but spoke of 'woman supporting woman' as the means by which women would recognise their potential and realise their power. Her personal/political identification with women was explicit: 'I know women best, and care more for them. I have an intense and endless love for women,' she wrote (ibid., p. 188–9).

It is in this context that many of Gilman's ideas were formed and shaped and expressed. In the course of her life she not only had to her credit 'countless nationally and internationally applauded lectures,' states Mary Hill, 'but some twenty volumes of published work besides' (ibid., p. 6).

After her breakdown, her ordeal with Mitchell, her divorce and disentanglement from Walter's loving gaze, her harassment by the press, she recovered her health, renounced feminity, preached rebellion, and developed a feminist framework which in its fundamental respects is equally applicable today. At the turn of the century she married Houghton Gilman, a man who endorsed her values and her commitment to her work, and who provided her with emotional and intellectual support. In 1935, in a way that was characteristic of her life, she brought about her own death, when, incapacitated by pain, she decided that she preferred 'chloroform to cancer'. Her death was 'an act of will, of rationality, of affirmation,' says Ann J.

Lane (1981) and she bequeathed to women a rich legacy of her ideas, her writing, her lectures, her example (p. ix).

The titles of some of her books and articles are clear statements of her values:

His Religion and Hers: A Study of the Faith of Our Fathers and the Work of Our Mothers
The Home: Its Work and Influence
Human Work
The Man Made World: Our Androcentric Culture
and her most famous book, *Women and Economics*

Among her articles are 'Divorce and Birth Control', 'Do Women Dress to Please Men?', 'Her Own Money: Is a Wife Entitled to the Money She Earns?' 'The Labor Movement', 'Making Towns Fit to Live In', and there is her fiction – her short stories (see Ann J. Lane, 1981), *Herland,* and *The Yellow Wallpaper.*

With regard to women and men, Gilman had little time for theories which tried to justify the relationship between the sexes in terms of 'nature' or 'divine ordination'; she firmly believed in the 'plasticity' of human beings and wrote extensively and illuminatingly on the process of socialisation and the role played by conditioning. She was unequivocal in her stance that the relationship between the sexes was primarily an economic one; men held power and used it to make economic arrangements which consolidated and maintained that power. But she also saw that women's work – which was arduous but neither acknowledged nor valued by men – led not just to economic dependence but to psychological disturbance. Perhaps it was a result of her own personal experience that Charlotte Perkins Gilman reconceptualised the nature of 'mental illness' among women: she came to see it as a form of resistance and a logical reaction to a 'kind and benevolent *enemy*' one was not permitted openly to fight. Foreshadowing so much current work (Jessie Bernard, 1972; Phyllis Chesler, 1972; Jean Baker Miller, 1978; Naomi Weisstein, 1970), Gilman suspected that in a 'sick' society, women who reacted, far from being *ill,* were demonstrating a healthy and positive response.

Women and Economics (1899) begins with her fundamental thesis that marriage is *not* a union of two souls or a partnership of equals and that, far from representing the most developed form of relationship in the animal kingdom, it constitutes the most degraded: 'We are the only animal species in which the female depends on the male for food, the only animal species in which the sex relation is also an economic relation. With us an entire sex lives in a relation of economic dependence on the other sex' (in Gilman, 1899, p. 5). So much for progress and civilisation!

Women work harder than men and longer than men, she argued, and yet they are impoverished in comparison to men. The reason for this is perfectly simple as, *for women, their livelihood does not depend on their labour, but on the goodwill of men* (and given women's current share of the world's resources it seems that the goodwill of men towards women is almost non-existent!). Using arguments similar to those of Matilda Joslyn Gage, Gilman contends that men have appropriated women's resources in order to augment their own.

Part of that appropriation of resources is the right men have reserved to themselves of providing the explanations for society. Women's experience is omitted from the social reservoir of knowledge and this leaves men free to produce arguments which, while they may be logical to men, make no sense at all to women who insist on the authenticity of their own lives: 'The human female the world over', writes Gilman, 'works at extra-maternal duties for hours enough to provide her with an independent living, and then is denied independence on the ground that motherhood prevents her working!' (ibid., p. 21). Only men could have issued such an absurd edict, argues Gilman, as only men could have devised the codified system of *economics* which assumes the non-existence of half of humanity.

Gilman challenged the whole conceptual framework of economics in much the same was as Lisa Leghorn and Kathy Parker were to do in 1981; *economics* as a system has its origin in a male frame of reference and is designed to account for male experience. And women's experience, argues Gilman, is fundamentally and drastically different. What work women do – particularly in terms of emotional management and psychological support – does not count as *work*, for the very reason that men don't do it. For women there is no relationship between education and remuneration, between work and wealth (unless it be an inverse one where middle-class and upper-class women who work *less* have access to *more* resources by virtue of the wealth of the men to whom they belong). But when women's economic basis is *sex attraction,* Gilman asserts, access to male resources can be a very precarious business indeed (as she well knew) and ultimately women can find that they are all of *one* class: 'when the woman, left alone with no man to "support" her, tries to meet her own economic necessities, the difficulties which confront her, prove conclusively what the general economic status of the woman is' (ibid., p. 10).

The argument that woman's work is *necessary* for man and that he therefore values it, or that it therefore offers woman any self-esteem or autonomy, simply won't stand up, says Gilman: 'the labor of the woman in the house, certainly, enables men to produce more wealth than they otherwise could; and in this way women are economic factors in society,' but, she adds with customary irreverence, 'so are horses. The labor of horses enables men to produce more wealth than they otherwise could. The horse is an economic factor in society. But the horse is not economically independent, nor is the woman' (ibid., p. 13). It is even easier to argue, she suggests, that the relationship of horses and men is more a relationship of *equals* than the relationship between women and men, for horses are not required to work from a sense of *duty* and are usually well cared for as an investment. The same cannot be said of wives!

The only thing men have allowed women to retain and to sell is themselves, says Gilman – their bodies, their labour, their emotional resources. But they are not even permitted to *trade* openly. They are repudiated and made outcasts if they realistically sell their wares as prostitutes, and if they do not, they are reduced to economic beggary. Any woman who openly classifies marriage as a market and seeks to make a mercenary match is condemned, yet she is only behaving reasonably, particularly in a society where men are admired for *their* ability to *accumulate* wealth. Women are even scorned if they are perceived as putting any energy into their 'occupation' and it is mandatory that they attempt to secure a livelihood without being seen to do so! And women who do not secure a livelihood – spinsters and old maids – are despised because they have no value; the explanation is that there are no buyers for their sex attraction and, as they are permitted no other resources, they are, in their 'failure', nothing but figures of fun and ridicule.

Gilman recognises that, by controlling all the resources, men have been able to ensure that they are materially necessary to women and that women, therefore, are obliged to align themselves with men – regardless of the way women feel about it and regardless of the way men may treat them. This is what Adrienne Rich (1981) referred to as compulsory heterosexuality. It is what Gilman perceived as the means of controlling women, and of defining women purely and simply in relationship to men so that a woman who tries to remain outside the net is *not* seen to be making a *choice* of independence but is mocked and maligned for her *failure* to 'get a man'.

Marriage – which men have claimed to be the only legitimate relationship between the sexes – as socially, psychologically and economically constructed, asserts Gilman, has nothing to offer women. 'The fear exhibited that women generally, once fully independent will not marry, is proof of how well it has been known that only dependence forced them to marriage as it was' (ibid., p. 91).

Gilman was such a prolific writer, and her ideas so many and varied, it is not possible to begin to summarise her contribution to feminist theory and understandings. I know of no current issue that she did not address and many topics that she raised which have not been pursued. Her thesis in relation to women's mental health – rediscovered by Friedan (1963) without the knowledge that the subject had been explored before, and since researched by numerous individuals – has, to my mind, still not been matched in terms of the insights it affords into women's dilemma in a male-dominated society. *The Yellow Wallpaper* (a copy of which she sent to Dr S. Weir Mitchell and which he never acknowledged), and her later explanation for writing it, stand in direct contradiction to Freud's conceptualisations and it is superfluous to add that in relation to women the *authentic* voice of Gilman was eclipsed by the *spectator's* – Freud's. Gilman repudiated many of Freud's theories in a way which we are only now beginning to recognise as reasonable.

At the risk of inviting contemporary wrath, I would like to comment on Gilman's position on women's sexuality (bearing in mind Freud's contribution to our current view of the world). To Gilman, human beings were 'plastic' and could come to be socialised into accepting as natural and reasonable just about every conceivable form of social organisation (as both history and anthropology suggest). The interpretation, the value – and the reasons for them – placed upon human actions varied from one culture to another and it was on this basis that she examined the interpretations and justifications for arrangements in her own society. It is not surprising that she should have included sexuality and subjected it to critical scrutiny; what would have been surprising would have been its omission.

During her lifetime she saw the interpretation placed upon sexuality – particularly for women but also for men – undergo a dramatic change, as the Victorian era gave way to the more permissive 1920s, and the injunction that a 'full sex life' was necessary for fulfilment. She is frequently portrayed as resisting this trend, and this is usually commented upon in a negative light and has even given rise to the accusation that she was a prude and possibly frigid. That there was something wrong with her sexuality (a charge invariably levelled at women no matter what form their sexual behaviour takes) is an assertion that is lent greater weight by some of the uncomprehending (and I suspect Freudian influenced) explanations of her reaction to marriage and motherhood with Walter Stetson. It has been said that Gilman and Lucy Stone (who experienced a similar crisis, and who may have found it just as impossible to display any hostility to the sympathetic, loving, and just, Henry Blackwell) were both 'unable to make the transition to adult life with an easy or mature acceptance of themselves as women, and this difficulty manifested itself in an undercurrent of psychological rejection of adult sexuality and maternity.' Apart from the fact that this is a standard means of discrediting women's ideas and casting doubts on the reliability of *all* their work, it seems as if this assessment of Gilman – bolstered by her refusal to declare sexuality as central to women's happiness – just wasn't true.

Gilman's own accounts of her early married life are quite remarkable, and both Mary Hill (1980) and Ann J. Lane (1981) suggest that the physically fit and exuberant Charlotte shocked the more sedate Walter: Charlotte wrote in her diary that she was sad because she was too affectionately expressive and had to learn to control herself, and in conformity to the Victorian picture of ideal womanhood – wait to be asked! (Hill, 1980, pp. 123–4; Lane, 1981, pp. xi–xii). Since sex has been accorded central significance in our society, one is not permitted to be unenthusiastic about it, and its absence as a focus in Charlotte Perkins Gilman's philosophy (and fiction) has been used against her on occasion. Perhaps, however, the current centrality of sex and its correlation with fulfilment and its obvious links with capitalism and consumerism is but a passing phase and the time will come when this 'social construct' is challenged and dismissed (along with Freud) as superstition, and Gilman's questions about its value and importance – for women – will enjoy popularity.

Overall, the work of Charlotte Perkins Gilman still stands at the forefront of feminist theory. Her 'cosmic world view utilized history, sociology, philosophy, psychology, and ethics in an effort to understand the past and, more important to project a vision of the future. Her sociological and historical works analyze the past from her peculiar humanist-socialist perspective. . . . In her fiction she suggests the kind of world we could have if we worked at it; the kinds of choices we could make, if we insisted on them; the kinds of relationships we could achieve, if we went ahead and demanded them. The fiction illustrates the human drama inherent in the history and sociology, for, as she said, "Until we see what we are, we cannot take steps to become what we should be" ' (Lane, 1981, p. xiv).

Gilman sought a social and socialist revolution; she envisaged a society where women freed themselves by leaving the nuclear family *(The Home: Its Work and Influence,* 1903a); where more thoughtful and loving care and socialisation was provided for children in co-operative communities *(Concerning Children,* 1900); where housework was collectivised and lost its designation as women's work, becoming instead human work, no different from other areas of endeavour related to shelter and sustenance – such as house building or heating maintenance *(Human Work,* 1903b); where all human beings were independent, economically and psychologically *(Women and Economics,* 1899); where their beings were equally valid *(His Religion and Hers,* 1923); where they were equally represented in the formulation and justification of social arrangements *(The Man Made World or Our Androcentric Culture,* 1911): in short, where all human beings were equal. She recognised that the vision was not as appealing to men as it was to women.

4 Equality means the same: Crystal Eastman (1881–1928)

Charlotte Perkins Gilman and Crystal Eastman are among my favourite feminists; in some respects they have much in common. They both had a vision of what the world could be and committed their lives to promoting that vision and transforming it into reality. They both wanted a social revolution and equal distribution of the world's resources; they both saw men, their values and their power, as a problem and a major obstacle to the construction of more equitable social arrangements; they were both 'woman-identified women' who worked not for male approval but female autonomy and strength. Both saw strength in psychological, intellectual and physical terms, with Eastman just as concerned about women's athletic development as was Gilman. Eastman (tall, and athletic herself) lectured consistently on 'women's right to physical equality with men' and firmly believed that 'when women were expected to be agile, they became agile; when they expected to be brave, they developed courage; when they had to endure, their endurance broke all records' (quoted in Blanche Wiesen Cook, 1978, p. 9). Eastman's ideas about socialisation and expectation and the implications of these processes for the construction of sex differences are very close to Gilman's ideas on the 'plasticity' of human beings.

But they shared certain experiences as well. Like Gilman, Eastman was ambivalent about marriage. During the period when she was trying to decide whether to marry Wallace Benedict she was sick; after she was married she was depressed. She did make links between her own marriage, and 'melancholy' (as it was called), but did not pursue them to the lengths that Gilman did. Eastman was quite unabashed about declaring that housework made her physically ill. After two years of marriage and un-characteristic depression, Eastman separated from her husband in 1913.

As Gilman had done, she also married again. While Eastman's rela-tionship with her second husband (Walter Fuller) was not without its difficulties, and constituted a liberated marriage for the time (with one of her articles, 'Marriage Under Two Roofs' reflecting some of her ideas on the subject), it proved to be more satisfactory than her first marriage had been. And like Gilman, one of the biggest struggles Crystal Eastman ex-perienced was that of trying to achieve the economic independence she believed to be absolutely basic for all 'proper grown ups'.

Crystal Eastman used to declare that she was 'born a feminist'. She attributed this in the main to her mother who had fought for women's rights, who had at times been the family breadwinner and who was, along with her father, an ordained minister. Her mother was a model for her, not only in terms of embodying permission for Crystal to be independent, to be active, questioning, and to develop aspirations and self-esteem, but also in more mundane and practical matters, such as organising a form of communal living when on vacation. During the summer, spent like 'most middle class small town American families, in a cottage by the lake,' wrote Eastman, her mother 'organized a system of cooperative housekeeping with three other families on the hillside, and it lasted for years' (Eastman in Cook, 1978, p. 43).[4] As an adult, such co-operative arrangements were to be Eastman's chosen lifestyle (not that they were always achieved).

It was within her own family that Eastman developed some of her fundamental ideas that *equal means the same*. This was her feminist frame-work throughout her life and the source of considerable difference in opinion between her and some other feminists who were, for example, fighting for protective legislation for women in the workforce. In her own family it was not just her mother who supported her stand that *equal means the same*; her father was also encouraging and supportive. 'When I insisted that the boys must make their beds if I had to make mine, he stood by me,' she wrote in 1927, and, 'When I said if there was dishwashing to be done they should take their turn, he stood by me. And when I declared there was no such thing in our family as boys' work and girls' work, and that I must be allowed to do my share of wood chopping and outdoor chores, he took me seriously and let me try' (ibid., p. 45). Given her own athletic prowess, she no doubt excelled.

'Equal means the same', however, applied not just to sexual divisions in labour, it also applied to sexual differences in morals and manners. Crystal Eastman (she never changed her name), having discarded the con-ventional and restrictive bathing garb considered appropriate for girls in the nineteenth century, recounts the occasion on which her father was

---

[4] All references to Eastman are from Blanche Wiesen Cook's (1978) selection of her writings but this particular article is also included in Elaine Showalter's (1978) illuminating volume *These Modern Women: Autobiographical Essays from the Twenties*, pp. 87–91, which serves to illustrate what women were thinking and how 'Freudian theories' shaped the response to them.

confronted one Sunday morning by the other fathers, demanding that he use his influence with her to ensure that in future she was decently clothed. 'I don't know what he said to them,' Eastman writes, 'but he never said a word to me. He was, I know, startled and embarrassed to see his only daughter in a man's bathing suit with bare brown legs for all the world to see. But he himself had been a swimmer; he knew he would not want to swim in a skirt and stockings. Why then should I?' (ibid.)

While the behaviour of the sexes was so rigidly hedged in by conventions which were designed to create major differences in women and men, Eastman showed not the slightest compunction about throwing convention to the winds, and practising the premise that 'equal means the same'. This does not mean that she advocated that women should behave in the same way as men – she was more likely to argue that what was good for the goose was good for the gander and that it was about time that the gander tasted the 'joys of life' he so carefully circumscribed for the goose. But she did insist that the same opportunities be available to both sexes, that they be permitted the same education, the same employment prospects, the same pay (and if protective legislation were to be introduced that it be the same for both sexes); and, of course, she argued that both sexes be subjected to the same moral standard.

It was on summer vacation with her family that Crystal Eastman, at the age of 15, gave her first feminist paper. Within the summer community 'symposiums' were organised and Eastman presented 'Woman' for discussion. In it, she insisted it was women's right and responsibility to have work of their own, for 'the only way to be happy is to have an absorbing interest in life which is not bound up with any particular person.' She also argued that such work should provide economic independence, for no one who has to depend on another person for a living is 'really grown up' (ibid., p. 43). Looking back on that paper at the age of 46 Eastman remained quite satisfied with it, feeling that it embodied all the feminist principles which she believed important and which she had worked to put into practice. The only difference was, she said, that she was not quite so solemn at 46.

Those who have commented on Eastman (and of course, there haven't been very many) emphasise her vivacity, her wit, her exuberance. Blanche Wiesen Cook says that she loved life, was free and bold, firm and aggressive. 'She spoke in a deep and musical voice and could be entirely captivating as she dashed about the country on behalf of suffrage or peace or to organise against an injustice. Her sincerity was absolute and she frequently grew red with anger. She was impulsive and passionate. . . .' (ibid., p. 3).

Jeanette Lowe, her close friend, said of her that 'you wouldn't believe her freedom – she was entirely free, open, full of joy in life' (ibid.) and on her death, in 1928, Freda Kirchwey wrote in *The Nation* that wherever Eastman 'moved she carried with her the breath of courage and a contagious belief in the coming triumph of freedom and decent human relations . . . as feminist, pacifist, socialist – she fought for her faith. Her strength, her beauty, her vitality and her enthusiasm, her rich and compelling personality – these she threw with reckless vigor into every cause that promised

a finer life to the world. She spent herself wholly, and died – too young'
(quoted in Cook, 1978, pp. 371–2).

There is no way that Crystal Eastman fits the picture of the shrill
embittered and humourless feminist (there's probably no way any woman
does) so endeared to patriarchy, which is probably one of the reasons she
disappeared; it was easier to bury her than transform her! She was an
energetic, outspoken, flamboyant figure who made it clear that she 'neither
sought male approval nor courted male protection' (ibid., p. 3). She obviously delighted in the company of women, and not only loudly proclaimed
this but, in a manner which was often seen as 'unfathomable' at the time,
preached and practised the idea that women should dress for themselves
and each other.

'There was nothing simple about her work, her political vision, or the
nature of her personal relationships', says Cook, 'And her vision demanded
radical, profound and absolute changes. Crystal Eastman's ideas were heretical and dangerous. Her life, by its very example, embodied a threat to
customary order' (ibid.). Predictably, she encountered many forms of harassment; she was criticised by many women and condemned by many men.
One of the reasons she encountered such difficulty in her attempt to be
economically self-sufficient (and support her two children) was because she
was blacklisted and could not get work.

Preparing papers for the community symposiums must have stood
Eastman in good stead for she went on to obtain her M.A. in sociology,
and then in 1907 her law degree. She then joined the Russell Sage Foundation and for over a year was involved in 'the first in-depth sociological
investigation of industrial accidents ever undertaken' (ibid., p. 6). In 1909
she was appointed as the first woman commissioner to the Employer's
Liability Commission, where she proceeded to draft New York State's first
worker's compensation law. Her work received international acclaim and
the law was soon used as a model by many other states.

She was a socialist and wanted a complete transformation of the
realtionship between labour and capital. But like many other women she
had little faith in the efficacy of violent revolution (although she later hailed
the Russian revolution as a victory and was critical of Dora Russell's
reservations about the possibility of replacing one tyranny with another,
see Russell, 1977) and was more inclined to see change occurring in terms
of a social revolution, over a period of time. Blanche Wiesen Cook says:
'Very early on Crystal believed that revolution was a process and not an
event' (ibid., p. 8). Her labour law reform was consistent with this view.

She was not, of course, always patient, waiting for people's attitudes
to change and the social revolution to be ushered in. '*We will not wait for
the Social Revolution to bring us the freedom we should have won in the
19th century,*' she declared at the first Feminist Congress in the United
States (1 March 1919: New York). At this Congress she outlined – clearly
and concisely – the position of women on the public-participation-in-pol-
itics index, and stated that four-fifths of women were still without voting
rights, only one woman had held a seat in the United States Congress, that
only twenty-one women were sitting in the forty-eight state legislatures,

that higher executive offices were reserved for men, that women sat on juries in only six states, that with very few exceptions (in lower courts) there were no women judges, that while twelve million women were in the workforce, even where their productive capacity was greater they were paid less, that women were still excluded from most of the trade unions, that marriage laws (and other laws) were still designed to perpetuate the economic dependence of a wife, that voluntary motherhood was still an ideal and that: 'Women are still denied by law the right to that scientific knowledge necessary to control the size of their families, which means that among the poor where the law is effective, marriage can become virtual slavery for women.' Finally, 'Laws, judges, courts, police and social customs still disgrace, punish and "regulate" the woman prostitute and leave uncensured the man who trades with her – though in case of all other forbidden vices the buyer as well as the seller suffers if caught' (ibid., pp. 49–50). This differential treatment of the sexes incensed Eastman.

Her anger, her passion, her impatience were invariably demonstrated and her lack of caution and circumspection was often a source of irritation and discomfort to other feminists who, while they may have agreed with her in private, deplored her confrontational tactics in public. There was a series of 'dissociations' and it is interesting to note that Blanche Wiesen Cook points out that those who tried to protect their 'respectability' lived to find out that it was *illusory*: ultimately it didn't much matter whether they were cautious or confrontationist, they were judged in much the same way (ibid., p. 22).

But the dissociations became divisions when in 1916 feminists were required to support *either* women's suffrage, *or* peace. Eastman had put enormous energy into women's suffrage (she was the campaign manager for the 1911 women's suffrage referendum in Wisconsin) but when it was a matter of choosing for president between 'Hughes, who seemed to promise suffrage with war, or Wilson who promised peace without suffrage' (ibid., p. 16), she was not prepared – as were some of her feminist contemporaries – to put *suffrage first*! She chose peace. (She too lived to find out you cannot trust politicians, seeing Wilson brought war while also denying suffrage.)

Crystal Eastman was passionately against war and worked unceasingly for peace. (Cook says that with the birth of her baby imminent, she worked sixteen to twenty hours a day in the months prior to the declaration of war, in the United States, in April 1917.) As early as November 1914 she invited Emmeline Pethick-Lawrence to come and speak, and organised the Woman's Peace Party of New York, a party based more on the style of the British Suffragettes or Alice Paul's Congressional Union (also based on the Suffragettes) than on the 'respectable' and conventional lines usually associated with a women's peace movement. A national Woman's Peace Party was formed (with the assistance of Jane Addams) and the American Union Against Militarism was also formed with Crystal Eastman as its executive director.

Eastman's methods of working for peace were frequently unorthodox, designed to embarrass the government, and generally confrontational (she is referred to as a militant-pacifist). As the government moved into its 'prepare for war' campaign, Eastman, in 1915, launched in flamboyant style the 'Truth About Preparedness Campaign' in which she demonstrated how much profit was being made by those who were advocating preparation for war. She also tried to show again and again how civil liberties were undermined when a nation began to think in militaristic terms, how individual freedom counted for nothing in the face of the 'national interest'. Her analysis of war and strategies for peace were based primarily on the understanding that the workers of different countries had more to unite them in peace than divide them in war. She believed strongly in the principle of private mediation and lobbying, and public confrontation and publicity, and many of her ideas about the prevention of war and promotion of peace deserve serious consideration today.

The threat of war hung over the United States and Mexico in 1916 and, through the American Union Against Militarism, Eastman put her energy into averting such a catastrophe. Convinced as she was that those who are in a position to make declarations of war rarely suffer directly from the consequences of their actions (and quite frequently *profit*), she sought to bring together workers from 'opposing' sides, who *would suffer* in the event of war and who therefore had a vested interest in avoiding, not promoting, it. Three Mexican and three American anti-militarists met in El Paso in 1916 and every effort was made by them to remove the points of contention. Wide publicity was given to their meeting and their recommendations, and President Wilson responded by appointing a Commission to Mexico to mediate the differences.

There was no war. Writing suggestions for future policy to the American Union Against Militarism, Eastman said: 'we must make the most of our Mexican experience. We must make it known to everybody that *people* acting directly – not through their governments or diplomats or armies – stopped the war and can stop all wars if enough of them will act together and act quickly' (ibid., p. 16).

Of course, knowledge such as this is usually 'lost' in a patriarchal system, selected *out*, so that students may be drilled in the conventional 'Causes of the First World War' (with little or no reference made to who profits) or required to memorise the so-called 'Allied Victories', but where rarely, if at all, attention is given to the ways and means of *averting* war. How real are the reasons for peace in our society? How many peace movements are the substance of educational curricula? And where they are mentioned how often are they presented as items of 'human interest', as social, rather than *political* history? This is one of the reasons Virginia Woolf (1938) equated patriarchal education and war – and one of the reasons Quentin Bell said she was not political and had some strange ideas (see Naomi Black, 1982).

The war divided many women in the United States and it was not just simply in terms of whether they were or were not prepared to put their energy into war work, as the division between Crystal Eastman and Alice Paul reveals.

5 Suffrage first: Alice Paul (1885–1977) and Crystal Eastman

Alice Paul had worked with the suffragettes in Britain; she had studied their tactics, participated in their activities (been gaoled and forcibly fed when she went on hunger strike) and had been radicalised by the experience. (I must admit I enjoyed writing that last phrase.) She returned to the United States in 1910 to find a very demoralised suffrage movement and she determined to put some new life back into it with an injection of Pankhurst philosophy. By 1913, along with Lucy Burns, Crystal Eastman and Mary Ritter Beard (among others), she helped to put women's suffrage back on the map as a political issue in much the same way as the militants had done in Britain. (And, in much the same way that Millicent Fawcett had acknowledged the achievement of the militants without condoning their actions, Carrie Chapman Catt, again the leader of the National American Woman Suffrage Assocation after the resignation of Anna Howard Shaw, gave Alice Paul's militants credit for the achievement, but did not want the movement to be associated with such radical activities, particularly after the prospect of war became more imminent.)

The Congressional Union (as it was first called because it concentrated on the passage of a federal amendment through Congress rather than the exhausting piece-by-piece state activities) brought women's suffrage into the political arena the day before President Wilson's inauguration, with a huge march of 5,000 women. When Wilson arrived in Washington, expecting a welcoming crowd, he was greeted instead by deserted streets and the information that the population was elsewhere – watching the women's parade. For a man who was against women's suffrage this could have been a salutary lesson; Wilson, however, did not learn. But if this protest was a taste of things to come for Wilson, it was also a taste of things to come for the women in the march: 'police protection broke down' and there were many ugly and vicious incidents.

In 1914 links between the Congressional Union and the National American Woman's Suffrage Association were severed, and by 1916 the Congressional Union had become the Woman's Party and was picketing the White House. The women stood silent and motionless, holding their banners which asked when women would get the vote, and they were treated sometimes with sympathy, sometimes as harmless curiosities, until America declared war. Once war was declared it seemed imperative to Eastman that every ounce of energy should be put into the radical *peace* movement, with its three goals of ending the war, ensuring a just peace, and removing the military mind-set which had deprived the country of civil liberties. This was not how it appeared to Alice Paul; to her it was suffrage first. Women were not going to be diverted from their task by the barbaric behaviour of men. (Even now, with the benefit of hindsight, I find it difficult to decide between these two forms of analyses: what is not difficult to see is the way that men, when in power, determine the choices faced by women.)

The banners of the pickets at the White House reflected the knowledge that there was a war going on, and exploited the war for propaganda purposes. 'Kaiser Wilson' and 'Democracy Should Begin at Home' were among some of the slogans. In a country now well fuelled by an extensive propaganda machine, the pickets of the Woman's Party were no longer harmless curiosities: they were often attacked and from 22 June 1917 were arrested. However, as the women were breaking no law, they could only be charged with committing a nuisance. At first they were dismissed, but as arrest and dismissal did not stop them, they were gaoled, at first for days, then weeks, then months. They went on hunger strike to protest at the illegality of their arrests, their treatment, and the conditions under which they were kept; they were forcibly fed.

To Eastman, what was happening to these women was more evidence of the way civil liberties were suspended 'in the national interest'. Eleanor Flexner (1979) states that these women 'were actually among the earliest victims in this country of the abrogation of civil liberties in wartime . . . once the suffrage arrests began, they were invariably confined to the pickets and never included the men who tore the banners from their hands and destroyed them, and often physically maltreated the women. While their slogans obviously were inflammatory, the suffragists were never once arrested for disturbing the peace, inciting to riot, or jeopardizing the security of the country or its Chief Executive' (p. 295). Needless to say, this is not an isolated example of the 'double standard'.

Crystal Eastman and Alice Paul had their differences of opinion – then and later – and Eastman wrote about some of them ('Alice Paul's Convention', 'Personalities and Power: Alice Paul') and confronted the difficult problem – today still unresolved – of how to be critical of the philosophy of other women, without providing men with abundant ammunition. But divisions among women were not confined to those between Eastman and Paul; Eastman had many other critics as well. Some of the women within the peace movement expressed considerable disapproval of her conduct. The Woman's Peace Party had its own respectable contingent which tried to prevent Eastman, in 1919, from attending the Second International Congress of Women on the grounds 'that her "extreme" radicalism and her "casual sex life" would confuse their mission and increase their difficulties' (Cook, 1978, p. 22). The former was in reference to her endorsement of the Russian revolution and the latter in reference to her relationship with the British pacifist Walter Fuller whom she married in 1916.

There must have been many occasions when Eastman felt an outsider, unable to discern the reason for her exclusion. Cook says that during the 1920s she occupied an increasingly isolated political position; 'She was generally the only socialist at feminist meetings, one of the very few feminists at socialist meetings' (ibid., p. 1), and this, with her inability to find paid work (after she resigned as editor of *The Liberator*, one of the few international and socialist periodicals, in 1922) was a constant source of concern to her. 'Her inability to find work, the fact that she was actually barred from the work she sought, was the hardest for her to comprehend' says Cook, 'Today we are more familiar with the facts and effects of political blacklists. But Crystal Eastman, attorney, social investigator, noted orator and author, could not understand why a militant feminist, antimilitarist and socialist could not between 1922 and 1928 find regular employment' (ibid., p. 29).

Her husband too had considerable difficulty. He returned to Britain and from 1922 to 1927 – always burdened with financial worries – she and her two children travelled backwards and forwards between the United States and England (in much the same way as Vera Brittain) living very much the life she had described in 'Marriage Under Two Roofs'.

In Britain she became good friends with Lady Rhondda, editor of *Time and Tide* magazine (so called, because 'Time and Tide waits for no man') and was one of the regular contributors to the journal along with Rebecca West, Vera Brittain, Winifred Holtby. But Lady Rhondda, much admired by Eastman, was an aristocratic heiress 'without a socialist bone in her body', and despite Eastman's friendship with Hazel Hunkins Hallinan – a fellow American in self-imposed exile – she hungered for permanent, steady and rewarding work in her native land. In 1927 she returned to try and find it; Walter was to join her when she had got a job. But a few weeks later Walter Fuller died of a stroke and within ten months, Crystal Eastman had died of nephritis, at the age of 46. Her death was painful, and her last concerns were about all the work she had left undone – and her two children.

Eastman's writing ranges over many topics and through many moods: there are well-planned programmes of practical feminism and light-hearted, but none the less serious, questions about a British woman who changes her name to that of her (eminent) husband, in the absence of a 'Lucy Stone Society' ('Who is, Dora Black?'). There are diatribes and jibes ('All feminists are familiar with the revolutionary leader who "can't see" the woman's movement. "What's the matter with the women? My wife's all right," he says. And his wife, one usually finds, is raising his children in a Bronx flat or a dreary suburb, to which he returns occasionally for food and sleep when all possible excitement and stimulus have been wrung from the fight. If we should graduate into communism tomorrow this man's attitude to his wife would not be changed' (ibid., p. 53).

'Equal means the same' in the domestic arena, as well as the public one, argues Eastman, and places the emphasis not on the emergence of 'true womanhood' after the revolution, but male responsibility in the home as a *part* of the process of revolution. 'It must be womanly as well as manly to earn your own living, to stand on your own feet,' she wrote in 1920, but also, 'it must be manly as well as womanly to know how to cook and sew and clean and take care of yourself in the ordinary exigencies of life,' and, she adds cryptically, 'I need not add that the second part of this revolution will be more passionately resisted than the first.' She goes straight to the heart of the matter when with irony she states 'Men will not give up their privilege of helplessness without a struggle' (ibid., p. 54). In 1970, Pat Mainardi's 'The Politics of Housework' was a revelation to me. I did not know, and I am sure Mainardi did not know, that Eastman had analysed it all before: every fifty years we 're-invent' the wheel.

'Two self-supporting adults decide to make a home together: if both are women it is a pleasant partnership, more fun than work,' says Eastman, arguing that women know and feel responsibility, but, 'if one is a man, it is almost never a partnership – the woman simply adds running the home to her regular outside job' (ibid., p. 55). It seems that the solution is clear, either men change, or it is more satisfactory for women to live with women.

I enjoy Eastman's journalistic coverage of contemporary events, from 'Socialist Women of Eighteen Countries Meet at Marseilles' to an account of Lady Rhondda's public (and successful) debate with G. K. Chesterton on the topic 'That Women of Leisure are "Menace" '. I have been moved by some of her articles against war, and for peace, ('To Make War Unthinkable') and I think that she has a timely contribution to make today. But I must admit experiencing a distinct sense of déjà vu when I came across her articles on the sexist representation of women in the media, on the pros and cons of a woman's page, on sexism in children's books and sexism in the curriculum. In 1923 she reviewed a book which examined the literature on sex differences, entitled *The Dominant Sex*, by Mathilde and Mathias Vaerting. Eastman comes to the same conclusion as the authors 'that the time honored division of labour between the sexes was not due to woman's physique or reproductive faculties, but was a natural division "between a dominant and subordinate sex" ' (ibid., p. 85). Men took for themselves the tasks they considered desirable: the rest were allocated to women. Power was the basis of the sexual division of labour and *this was supported by the research findings on sex differences*. At times, I almost despair.

6 Nowhere to go

For Eastman, Gilman, Sanger and Goldman – and many, many more – were effectively buried along with their ideas. Alix Kates Shulman (1979) says of Goldman that prior to the 1960s 'anarchism and feminism seemed irrelevant anachronisms to most Americans, each an old joke which in one version had Emma Goldman as the punchline' (p. 3). If and when she was remembered at all it was as someone 'laughably naive', whose values and lifestyle had long since ceased to be relevant, and whose silly ideas could not possibly be significant. Any legacy which she had left was tinged with a pathetic tone, and in any context in which she was cited she was customarily mocked; 'figures of fun' are not frequently fertile ground for philosophic enquiry. She is not an 'isolated case'; there is nothing out of the ordinary in her disappearance, and nothing unusual in the manner in which it was achieved.

The actions of Margaret Sanger cannot be challenged, so instead her motives have been questioned in the attempt to deprive her of an honourable place in history. Her commitment to the alleviation and elimination of some of the specific misery and pain suffered by women is undeniable, so attempts to minimise her and her contribution have taken the form of casting her in the role of a publicity seeker, a 'self-proclaimed heroine' and the authenticity of her motives and her accounts of the struggle have been called into question. David Kennedy (1970) has outlined her 'exaggerations' and of course, carefully and authoritatively corrected them, suggesting that it was her psychological need for attention that prompted her melodramatic campaign.

I have heard it all before: Margaret Fuller and Margaret Sanger could have had a fine time comparing the notes of their respective biographers and listing all the psychological deficiencies they had in common; they could also have commented on their biographers' deficiencies and their psychological need as men, for superiority.

Instead of her ideas being seen as a viable alternative to Freud's (and I would argue that Gilman's explanations of women's mental complexities leave Freud looking like an amateur), we find that one of the most pervasive reasons given for Gilman's journey to obscurity was her repudiation of Freud. *Her* sexuality constitutes sufficient grounds for her demise; in the land of the double standard, Freud's does not. We are reminded that we are not to take her work too seriously (I have just realised that I have *never* read such a warning in relation to Freud) for, in the case of *Women and Economics*, for example, 'it is easy to be beguiled into thinking it is a scientific study, rather than the reform tract that it is' (Degler, 1966, p. xxix). It is 'not the result of elaborate or new research' (ibid., p. xxx) but one woman's personal experience, even 'autobiographical' experience, and therefore not something to be generalised from. (Contrast that with the reverence and praise for Freud's 'scientific theories' in which woman is defined in relation to man! I give up.)

Like Wollstonecraft, Gilman is often criticised because she wrote too quickly: her 'style' therefore is not good. *Women and Economics*, written as it was in several months of intense writing, ran into many editions, was translated into many languages, was acclaimed as the most significant book on the subject since *The Subjection of Woman* was 'probably the most devastating indictment of traditional nineteenth century motherhood ever written' (ibid., p. xxvi) *but* ... unfortunately 'her subsequent books had all been adumbrated in that first effort; those that followed largely elaborated a position already clearly staked out, even if not thoroughly explored' (ibid., p. xiii). No doubt if her name had been John Stuart Mill, later books would have been perceived as an attempt to develop and refine her principles: frequently, to men, one feminist book (of for that matter, one feminist) looks the same as any other.

One of the problems is that there is nowhere for these books to go; there is no heading for them in our inventory of knowledge. Despite the hundreds (thousands?) of them that have been written, there is no name for them, no genre under which they can be filed. Libraries today that still resist classification schemes which include women's studies, or feminism, merely serve to illustrate this problem whereby hundreds of books can 'disappear' without trace into their general system and are unlikely to be found again for twenty years. (It is a recurrent dream of mine to enter the British Library and find feminist non-fiction grouped together: it would stand as a visible testament to women's activity. That is why it is not done

– the library today is much the same as it was when Virginia Woolf described it in *A Room of One's Own*, a collection of men's literature, much of which is about women. It is no accident that most of the books that I have requested are not even kept on the premises and have to be ordered two days ahead. Florence Howe has said that feminist courses on campus are usually in the smallest, darkest places, the furthest removed from the 'main' centre of activity; so are feminist books.)

The categories of knowledge themselves have been devised by men in line with their own experience, which is one of the reasons books such as *Women and Economics* have no place to go! They are neither permitted entry into men's categories nor allowed to stand as categories on their own. I doubt if there would be anywhere where *Women and Economics* was classified as 'economics'. Despite the fact that it still stands as a fundamental conceptualisation of the economic position of half the population I have no evidence that it is a popular text on economic courses or a prominently displayed entry in bibliographies on economics. And yet there is no other categorisation for it.

Whole systems have been erected around individual men whose names have been lent to particular theoretical frameworks, but I have spent the last fifteen minutes *inventing* comparable classifications for women. We have Newtonian Theory, Freudian Theory, Marxist Theory; there is no Somervillian Theory, Cheslerian Theory, Gagist Theory or Dalyist Theory. I know of Keynsian Economics but not Gilmanian Economics; there are Althusserian principles but not Eastmanian ones. This is not just an interesting side issue; nor is it a mere oversight that while men label the categories, women have nowhere to go. It is one of the most blatant means of consigning women to oblivion. It is an example of the way men appropriate women's intellectual resources and maintain their ownership of theory. While it persists there is no basis for according women's ideas *general* application or for treating women as intellectual beings capable of producing their own theories in relation to their own experience.

That there is no place for Crystal Eastman's theories of women and revolution is well understood by Blanche Wiesen Cook, who says in her opening paragraph that: 'For fifty years our entire culture militated so vigorously against our discovering Crystal Eastman's ideas and finding them usable that she practically disappeared from history' (1978, p. v) and Cook continues to expose what I now see as a familiar pattern. There was no one to 'speak for' her after her death so that from 'that year to this not one essay, not one book has been entirely devoted to her work or to her life'. There have been the customary 'distortions' with the one historian who does refer to her stating that she 'had no audience for her views; the unpublished nature of her writing attests the fact that the publishers did not consider her concerns worthy of print' (ibid).

Cook states that: 'It is no accident that her work has for so long remained unknown – along with her joy in life and exuberance for people. The neglect and disappearance of Crystal Eastman's work is partly explained by the fact that history tends to bury what it seeks to reject' (ibid., p. 2), and while men are in charge of ideas, and history, they will consistently reject and bury ideas such as those of Eastman, in the same way they have consistently rejected and buried Behn, Astell, Macaulay, Martineau, Fuller, Taylor, Gage, Gilman – and all the rest of those many women.

And what are our chances of uncovering them? Cook describes how she inadvertently came upon Eastman, even how she knew at one level of Eastman's existence but at another did not know of her significance, did not find her attractive: 'I did not fully realize Crystal Eastman's importance until the women's movement altered my own consciousness and I began to think about all the women – activists and writers – who came before, and whom we have been, until recently, programmed to deny.' (ibid., p. vi).

Before accepting the thesis that: 'once we were blind but now we can see', it is well to remember that we are not the first generation to recognise that we have been programmed to the invisibility of women, we are not the first generation to discover that women have had their intellectual and creative energy and efforts taken away. In more recent times Virginia Woolf went back and constructed the tradition of women's ideas and contribution; before her it was Matilda Joslyn Gage and fifty years before her it was Margaret Fuller. We could simply be part of a tradition of 'lost and found' unless and until we have control over our own work and knowledge and are then in a position to ensure the transmission of that tradition from one generation to the next. At the moment I do not think we are any closer to achieving that status than were our foremothers. I have no illusions: this book is not being published because of the contribution it will make to the history of ideas (as many of the male authors are evaluated) but because it is believed that it will sell, and there's a recession. Nothing has changed – Fuller, Gilman, Eastman – they 'sold' as well!

There are many other women – of the calibre of Goldman, Sanger, Gilman, Eastman and Paul – whom I would have liked to include, but space does not permit. I must emphasise again that I am not concerned with providing a comprehensive coverage so much as uncovering the pattern of women's treatment in a patriarchal society. That the virtues of Anna Howard Shaw, the political acumen of Carrie Chapman Catt or the theories and practice of social transformation as put forward by Jane Addams are not topics for discussion reflects no value judgements about their importance, for an analysis of their treatment could be equally illuminating and would help to establish that whether a woman is agreeable or disagreeable, lady-like or social outcast, 'history' will consign her to much the same place. When women's resources are taken by men it is ultimately of little matter whether those resources are palatable or not at the time; if men can use such resources to their own advantage, they will do so – presenting ideas that have originated with women as their own if need be (see Ruth Hubbard, 1979); if men find such resources threatening they will bury them. Either way, the active resistance of women can be denied while men determine what is known and what makes sense, in a system based on male supremacy.

(B)

MILITANT AND MALIGNED

1 Decades of denial

Josephine Kamm (1966) begins her chapter on the Pankhursts with the statement that: 'The militant suffrage movement is, of course, inextricably bound up with the names of Richard Pankhurst's wife and daughters' (p. 141) which seems to be a particularly blatant attempt to define women exclusively in relation to men, given that Richard Pankhurst had long been dead when the Women's Social and Political (WSPU) Union was formed in 1903, and when, even later, the militant suffrage movement began. It is my opinion that one of the reasons the Pankhurst women – and other militants – have been so misrepresented and maliciously maligned, is because of their independence of men (predictably referred to repeatedly as man-hating). Kamm's introduction of the Pankhursts, like that of so many other commentators, can be seen as a response to the militant's autonomy and as a means of quickly 'putting them back in their proper place'.

So extensive and extreme are the distortions of the Pankhursts in much of the literature (including contemporary accounts), that the portrayal of them, alone, in the literary and historical records, could constitute the basis of a convincing argument that for women there is no relationship between their actions and male-controlled representations of them – unless it be an inverse one, in which those who comprise the greatest threat receive the harshest treatment. If this is the case, we can assume that the Pankhursts posed a substantial challenge to male power as far as men were concerned.

The derisory way in which they have been portrayed also raises another issue: while there is a general thesis that people do research on the lives of those individuals whom they find attractive, this most definitely does not apply to the Pankhursts. David Mitchell's (1977) *Queen Christabel: A Biography of Christabel Pankhurst* is one of the most devastatingly damaging (and just plain nasty) accounts I have ever read of one person's life, and is only surpassed in venom and viciousness by Piers Brendon's (1979) account of Mrs Pankhurst. These portrayals are much more likely to have been motivated by a desire (or obsession) to prove how *unattractive* these women are (in the same way that Marie Mitchell Olesen Urbanski, 1980, suggests the editors of Margaret Fuller's *Memoirs* were motivated) than by any desire to illuminate their lives, personalities and ideas of the women.

I am not alone in my conclusion that these accounts reveal more about the fears of the authors than the lives of the women they profess to portray: in the case of David Mitchell's version of Christabel Pankhurst, Martin Pugh (1980) declares, in an unsolicited comment on further sources, that it is 'a particularly hostile biography'. However, before crediting Pugh with impartiality, it should be noted that he states that 'the militants' accounts are largely fantasy' and this because they were either trying to establish their own claims (a practice common among male politicians giving their accounts of their careers, I should have thought), or because they were written 'simply to perpetuate the image of martyrdom'. So, even *within* the confines of the 'double standard', Pugh still sees Mitchell as particularly hostile to Christabel Pankhurst; readers be warned!

Sylvia Pankhurst once wrote about her mother's reluctance to write, and how Emmeline Pankhurst's autobiography *My Own Story* (1914) was produced with the assistance of an American journalist from talks with Mrs Pankhurst and from reference to suffragette literature (Sylvia Pankhurst, 1931, p. 268), another practice not unknown among men. To Martin Pugh, however, this is reason to label *My Own Story* as 'a bogus autobiography', while to Andrew Rosen (1974) it becomes 'primarily the work of Rita Childe Dorr, an American journalist' and is described as: 'Produced hurriedly in 1914 when Mrs Pankhurst was at the height of her fame', and is therefore, 'so replete with errors and glossings over as to be virtually useless to the historian' (p. 167). Apart from being tempted to argue that I have in the main found 'the historian virtually useless to women', I have my reservations about Rosen's assessment as well. On the same page he states that Emmeline Pethick-Lawrence and Frederick Pethick-Lawrence both wrote their respective autobiographies but 'that of F. W. Pethick-Lawrence is somewhat more reliable' (ibid.). It should also be noted that far from being an 'exploitive journalist' – the image encouraged here, Rheta Childe Dorr (1910) is the author of the excellent book *What Eight Million Women Want* and was in a commanding position to 'help' Mrs Pankhurst with her autobiography.

One of the points Rosen does make is that 'professional historians have paid no more than passing attention to women's suffrage movements,' with the results that what is readily known about the period is not 'grounded in extensive archival research' but based more upon 'general knowledge' (ibid., p. xvi). Neither the papers of Sylvia Pankhurst nor those of Teresa Billington-Greig (to name but two of the many sources) have ever been made use of by anyone doing research on the militant suffragettes, declares Rosen, pointing to the deficiencies in the historical and literary accounts of the period and the people, and, while I fully appreciate the significance of his argument, I could only share his sense of outrage if I thought this neglect of sources was an isolated incident, confined to the history of the Women's Social and Political Union (WSPU). Having recognised that from Aphra Behn to Margaret Fuller, from Mary Wollstonecraft to Christabel Pankhurst, the 'gatekeepers' of history have had little or no respect for original sources in relation to women, and a great deal of respect for their own male superiority. I find yet another example rather wearying and am more inclined to ask 'what's new?'.

Only if one believed that there was a 'pure' process for the construction of history could one be indignant about this particular 'departure'. If it is recognised that the historical record is a social product, which means for us that it is created in the context of a male-dominated society where male control over knowledge is demonstrably established, then one would be more 'shocked' to find women's past treated with scrupulous attention, care and respect, than one is to find it conveniently shaped to fit male fears and fantasies.

What the militants do help to illustrate is the particular and fundamental problem of trying to represent the ideas and political actions of women in a society in which women are not treated seriously as intellectual, political, or active beings. Such women are an anomaly in a patriarchal society, where it is men's ideas that are considered intellectual and men's activities that are taken as political. For women who try to assert their *different* but *autonomous* intellectual and political identity there can be no validity within a male scheme of values that accepts male experience as total.

Men may talk politics in the pub, but women boycotting a supermarket are on a 'housewive's jaunt'; the differences in power among men are serious and of a political nature, but the differences in power between women and men as conceptualised by women are silly, and of a neurotic nature. Men may treat parliament as a boys' club and still be 'political', but the women who were denied membership to the club and who therefore treated all the boys the same showed 'no political understanding' and 'no grasp of (male) party politics'. The relationship between the football manager and the players may be political, but when Virginia Woolf linked patriarchy and fascism, her nephew and biographer Quentin Bell (1972) called her apolitical and explained her stance in terms of her irrationality over 'the beastly masculine' (see Naomi Black, 1982 in press and Berenice Carroll, 1978).

Because it is fundamental to the frame of reference in a patriarchal society that men are the political creatures, the political activists and theorists, women's activities in relation to power are *denatured*, classified as something else. Either it is denied that the women are concerned about power (the women have got the issue all wrong) or else it is asserted that the women are not real women (the women themselves are wrong), for it is mandatory that the deficiency be found in the women and not in the means of interpreting the world.

We are back with Elizabeth Cady Stanton: no matter what women do it is not given the same value as men, for value depends on sex and not the activity. We are back with Matilda Joslyn Gage: women's energy is stolen by men to reinforce their own resources and power. In this context the avowedly political and effective women militants have little chance of being reported seriously and of being accepted as genuine political theorists and activists. Virtually all the portrayals of them suggest that they either misread the issues or that they were most unattractive women. From my perspective it is not difficult to portray them differently.

2 The Pankhursts

We could begin with Emmeline Goulden, born in 1858 in the north of England, which was 'an effectual school of politics and economics' and where the 'seamy side of industrialism, and the manifold need of reform, appear there in reality' (Christabel Pankhurst, 1959, p. 15).[1] She had a comfortable and secure existence (her father owned a business), but still learnt early some of the lessons of life that always stayed with her. She was 'near enough to the other and poorer half of the world to know how it lived – to gain an understanding of wrong social conditions and the hardship of the working masses that prepared her for the work of her later life' (ibid., p. 16). She also learnt what it meant to be female.

Emmeline Pankhurst states that she first suspected that there was something different about boys and girls when the education of her brothers was treated as a matter of grave importance and discussed at length, whereas that of the daughters was never mentioned: 'A girl's education at that time seemed to have for its prime object the art of "making home attractive" – presumably to migratory male relatives', she said. 'It used to puzzle me to understand why I was under such a particular obligation to make home attractive to my brothers. We were on excellent terms of friendship, but it was never suggested to them as a duty that they make home attractive to me. Why not? Nobody seemed to know.' Her suspicion that boys were more valued was confirmed when one evening, believing Emmeline to be asleep, her father leaned over her bed and said: 'What a pity she wasn't born a lad.'

Relating this incident later, Emmeline Pankhurst said that she resisted the impulse to jump up and protest and, in thinking on the matter, decided that she didn't regret her sex, even if her father did. What she began to understand, however, was 'that men considered themselves superior to women, and that women apparently acquiesced in that belief.' This did not seem at all a satisfactory arrangement (quoted in Midge Mackenzie, 1975, p. 5).

Her education – which was never discussed – was a reasonable one for a female of her time: she 'went to a carefully selected girls' school' where 'the headmistress was a gentlewoman' (ibid.), and she also had access to some books and a few lectures. And there was a period of schooling in France. But with her schooldays over, the eldest daughter among ten children returned to her family and the appropriate and narrow domestic routine. She found her duties unfulfilling, to say the least: 'Her ardent nature moved her to desire to do some great thing, and little seemed possible in those times for a woman' (C. Pankhurst, 1959, p. 18). She was interested in politics, and particularly in women's suffrage, but there was little stimulus and less outlet for her interest.

---

[1] In line with the general thesis it should be noted that both Christabel Pankhurst and Sylvia Pankhurst are frequently considered unreliable sources on their mother and each other (except when they make an unflattering remark) because of their relationship. That Leonard Woolf and Quentin Bell *were* related to Virginia Woolf, however, is often seen as evidence of their greater veracity. Sex makes a difference.

Until she met Richard Pankhurst. 'They were made for one another,' says Christabel Pankhurst (ibid., p. 21), and in 1879 they were married – despite the fact that Emmeline's father did not approve and did not provide her with a dowry. Richard Pankhurst was an advocate of 'struggling causes', always in advance of his time; he was a brilliant barrister whose integrity was high, with the result that his income was quite low. 'Nowadays extreme Socialists can make fortunes at the Bar,' said Christabel Pankhurst commenting on his financial straits, for 'the extremity of their views merely lends piquancy to their professional exploits and in no way detracts from their prosperity. But in Father's day it was not so. Bang went briefs every time he made a political move. His championship of woman suffrage was the action that counted most against him, especially when he began it in the 1860's' (ibid., p. 24).

Obviously there was much about him that endeared him to Emmeline, who, as with some other women (Millicent Fawcett, for example) found that her 'career began with her marriage,' for she found herself admitted to her husband's political circle, included in debates, and involved in political activities. She shared his idealism, passionately wanted to help rather than hinder his freedom of thought and action, and instead of being a 'sobering' influence, persuading him to abandon his unpopular causes and to acquire respectability and resources (as many urged her to do), she made it quite clear that her 'ambition for him was that he should do great things for the people to deliver them from poverty and bad housing and overwork, and that he should work for the cause of international peace' (ibid., p. 23).

Emmeline Pankhurst did not want to tie her husband down; on the contrary she wanted to help him, and not just by providing emotional support. She wanted to provide financial support so that he could be free of money worries and devote himself entirely to (unpopular and unprofitable) public work. This was why she later opened a shop in London (Emerson's) so that she too could make a financial contribution to the maintenance of the household.

While actively involved in his political life, however, for Emmeline Pankhurst it wasn't all politics. She had four children (Christabel, Sylvia, Francis Henry called Frank, and Adela; they moved from Manchester to London where she thought there was greater scope for Dr Pankhurst's political potential. But while there were happy times, there were also tragedies. Frank died from diphtheria, and, in giving birth to her youngest child (Francis Henry, but called Harry), Mrs Pankhurst almost died. And the shop proved to be more of a financial drain than a source of extra income.

Never embroiled in domesticity to the exclusion of all else (a factor not always quoted in her favour), Emmeline Pankhurst maintained her commitment to the working class and to women. The London house had been obtained with a view to holding meetings, and meetings there were with the children attending likely as not. Richard Pankhurst's maxim for the development of his children was: 'If you do not work for others, you will not have been worth the upbringing', and they were encouraged (some might say 'pushed') into considering the major social and political issues of the day. In the Pankhurst's London home the Women's Franchise League was formed in 1889 – with Elizabeth Cady Stanton being one of the members and speakers – and Christabel and Sylvia, particularly, could not have remained impervious to the discussion and debate around them.

The disadvantages of London, however, were that Emmeline and Richard Pankhurst were often separated, for while Dr Pankhurst's potential may have decreed London to be his habitat, his bank balance decreed that he should spend a considerable part of his time in Manchester, where he obtained his income. So they decided to return to Manchester, and there they both became increasingly more involved with the Labour movement.

Commenting on this period, Christabel Pankhurst said that: 'The Labour leaders who in time became national figures came to the house. Some were of the bourgeoisie and privileged in education; among these were women as well as men. Others were proletarians, largely self educated and among these were very few, if any, women. It seemed very difficult for working women to overcome the handicap of poverty, and the domestic cares which fettered them. . . . Mother regretted the disadvantages suffered by working women, but she hoped that the developing Labour movement would charge itself with getting votes for women' (ibid., p. 32).

Emmeline Pankhurst also began her own political career and was elected to the Board of Poor Law Guardians after attempting (unsuccessfully) to gain a place on the school board. As a Poor Law Guardian, she said, I soon 'found that the law was being very harshly administered. The old board had been made up of the kind of men who are known as rate savers. They were guardians not of the poor but of the rates, and, as I soon discovered, not very astute guardians even of money' (quoted in Mackenzie, 1975, p. 9). It was as a Poor Law Guardian that Emmeline Pankhurst began to think of the vote not as a right, but as necessity. If men could make such a mess at a local level and be responsible for the harsh and wasteful regimes as she saw in the work-house, how much worse must it be at national level?

With her family of growing children becoming ever more independent, Emmeline Pankhurst was able to devote a considerable amount of her time to public affairs, and within the constraints imposed upon women she gained a great deal of political experience. But in 1898, when she was in Geneva, where she had taken the 17-year-old Christabel to stay with friends (as a prelude to her future, but as yet undecided, occupation), a telegram arrived from Sylvia stating that Dr Pankhurst was ill. Mrs Pankhurst left for home immediately, but on her arrival in London she saw the newspaper headlines 'Dr Pankhurst Dead'.

It seemed that her lifestyle had ended, indeed it seemed as if the family unit had collapsed. Among the issues that Emmeline Pankhurst had to face was that of supporting her four children, for there was no money. It was not an easy task for, as Christabel said, 'Mother now had to fulfil a man's responsibilities in a world that wholly underrated the economic value of its political outlaws, women' (1959, p. 37).

Friends came to the fore and suggested possible solutions, among them that an appeal be launched, particularly for the education of the children;

Robert Blatchford went as far as announcing such an appeal in the *Clarion*. But Mrs Pankhurst would have none of it and adamantly insisted 'that she did not wish working people to subscribe for an education for her children which they could not provide for their own. She urged that the fund Blatchford proposed in memory of the Doctor should be used to build a socialist hall' (Sylvia Pankhurst, 1931, p. 153).

The matter of earning a living remained, and the options were as few for a mature woman with no formal training at the end of the nineteenth century as they had been in the previous centuries. It seems that 'taking up the pen' (from Sylvia's account) was not a possibility, and Emmeline Pankhurst would never entertain the idea of opening a school, so there was really only the option of opening a shop. Despite the failure of the earlier 'Emerson's', Mrs Pankhurst resolved to try again hoping that her prospects would be improved by the location of the premises in Manchester (overheads were less) and by the assistance of Christabel who could return to this occupation.

The other children were also 'settled': Harry was in grammar school, Adela looked set on the path of becoming a teacher and, by fortuitous circumstances rather than foresight, Sylvia was at the Municipal School of Art. When a friend had come to advise on the sale of paintings on Dr Pankhurst's death, he had declared Sylvia's drawings more promising than the paintings and had sent them to the School who had awarded her a free studentship. 'What joys that opened up to me,' said Sylvia (ibid., p. 155). Christabel, on the other hand, seemed to find little joy in working in the shop with her mother.

In Sylvia's words, while Christabel expressed no other desires or plans for her future, 'she detested Emerson's. She arrived there as late as she could each morning, took a couple of hours off for lunch and got away as early as possible in the afternoon, stifling her thoughts by a constant succession of novels' (ibid., p. 156). Christabel was bored and listless, but interestingly she seems never to have succumbed to the pressures of this purposeless existence in the manner society intended and as many of her contemporaries did; there is no account of her ever viewing marriage as a possible escape route.

What she did do was attend some lectures at the university, where she met Esther Roper and Eva Gore Booth, and this probably helped to change the direction of her life. She got back into politics in a way that she had not done since her father's death, becoming an active member of the North of England Women's Suffrage Society, and an executive of the Women's Trade Union Council. And it was partly at the suggestion of these two active suffragists that Christabel decided to switch from doing a few 'interesting' lectures, to undertaking the more rigorous and arduous task of completing a law degree. This was a shift from a young lady, playing the dilettante, engaging in some social and political issues to wile away the hours, to a young woman who made a total commitment to a course of action, and pursued it with thorough and uncompromising single-mindedness. There were few precedents for such behaviour in England, but many known penalties.

For a woman to enrol in law at the turn of the century in Britain was an act of courage and defiance. There were two obvious risk areas: the first one was that such a woman would risk losing her femininity; in the phraseology of the times she would become unsexed and brand herself as a strong-minded woman. One would have to be prepared to dispense with the 'approval' given to young ladies if one was seriously to take on 'competing' in this male domain. And of course competition itself entailed a considerable risk. What if one were to fail? What mileage that would give those who opposed women's rights and insisted on women's intellectual inferiority.

Christabel Pankhurst was realistic enough to recognise that she was not even beginning on the same footing as men. Her education had not been systematic and it certainly had not been planned with a view to pursuing such a profession as law. She first had to study for matriculation. But there were other more subtle factors operating as well, for males had been reared with the expectation that they would work in the world and that they could influence the environment, and she had not. Liberal as her training may have been for the time within the family circle, it was still located within the context of woman's sphere. Christabel Pankhurst had her own doubts to conquer. And she also knew that it might not even be a fair 'competition' – for Sylvia was well aware of this at art school, where girls were well placed when students were anonymous but where they were evaluated as not up to standard when their sex was known (see Sylvia Pankhurst, 1931, p. 71). Undaunted by all these risks, Christabel proceeded, and in doing so demonstrated much of that nerve and audacity which would today place her among the ranks of the 'uppity women'.

It was all for a *purpose*: law was not an end in itself but a useful tool in achieving her aims. 'There then was an aim in life for me – the liberation of politically fettered woman-hood. One decision I came to firmly: it was that this vote question must be settled. Mine was the third generation of women to claim the vote and the vote must now be obtained. To go on hopelessly pleading was undignified. Strong and urgent demand was needed. Success must be hastened . . .' (Christabel Pankhurst, 1959, p. 42).

While Christabel was moving towards the recognition that women must be a force to be reckoned with, Emmeline Pankhurst was also finding herself propelled towards the acceptance of more drastic measures in order to obtain the full representation and influence for women in public life. Upon the death of her husband, Emeline Pankhurst had resigned from the Poor Law Guardians and had later been appointed to the salaried office of Registrar of Births and Deaths. Her district was a working-class one and because she appreciated many of the difficulties of working women she took the simple step of introducing evening office hours twice a week, where she found herself over and over again hearing some of the most dreadful stories from women about the conditions of their existence. She was shocked to the core: 'I have had little girls of thirteen come to my office to register the births of their babies, illegitimate of course. In many of the cases I found that the child's own father or some near relative was responsible for her state. There was nothing that could be done in most cases. . . . During my term of office a very young mother of an illegitimate child exposed her baby, and it died. The girl was tried for murder and sentenced to death. This was afterwards commuted it is true but . . . the wretch who was from the point of view of justice, the real murderer of the baby received no punishment at all' (quoted in Mackenzie, 1975, p. 15).

Emmeline Pankhurst believed – as did many women and men of her time – that when women played an equal part in policy- and law-making processes, policies and laws, particularly as they related to the lives of women, would be very different. She also believed – and she was not alone – that when women were in such influential positions, the status of their sex in general would be elevated. Women as a group would be treated more seriously when they had to be taken into account as voters, and as potential and real policy- and law-makers. 'It was rapidly becoming clear to my mind', she said from her experience as Registrar 'that men regarded women as a servant class in the community, and that women were going to remain in that servant class until they lifted themselves out of it. I asked myself many times . . . what was to be done' (ibid.). It was most definitely to women, and not to men, that Mrs Pankhurst looked for a solution (which in itself distinguishes her from many of the nineteenth-century suffragists) and she was becoming increasingly impatient for action.

Mrs Pankhurst, Christabel and Sylvia initially had high hopes of the Labour movement which, unlike other parties, professed itself to be in favour of women's suffrage, but they were to find (as women had been finding in many countries of the world once they claimed the right to vote) that there was a great discrepancy between a commitment in theory and the test of practice. They encountered the argument that there were many more important issues than women's suffrage; these important issues of course related to men.

Keir Hardie was one of the few staunch supporters (if not the only one). Many of the other men – past colleagues of Dr Pankhurst – who came to the Pankhurst house to talk politics were extensively grilled by Christabel on their stand on woman's suffrage, and none of them gave satisfactory answers as far as the Pankhursts were concerned. 'Bruce Glasier,' states Sylvia, 'far from realizing the new spirit that had taken possession of our home, offended badly. It was not essential, he argued, that the whole people should be enfranchised. So long as the division were not upon class lines.' An old and familiar argument. But Glasier went further and argued as John Stuart Mill's father had done about eighty years before that 'those outside the suffrage would be represented by those within; their interests would be the same. There was no distinction of interest on sex, but only on class lines' (S. Pankhurst, 1931, p. 167). As Anna Wheeler had been enraged by James Mill, the Pankhursts were infuriated by Bruce Glasier and his colleagues: 'This opinion, common enough amongst Socialists of the time was bitterly resented,' states Sylvia (ibid.).

Men did not and do not hear what women are saying. So what was to be done? As far as the Pankhursts were concerned they decided *it was a waste of energy to keep telling men!* If after so many years of discussion and debate, of clear and cogent argument, 'radical' men could persist with their line of reason that women had no specific grievances and what minor 'difficulties' did exist would be ironed out after men had fixed up the world for themselves, one would have to be a dunce or a masochist to pursue a policy of trying to change men's minds. That women should stop talking to men about what was to be done, and start talking to each other, was a strategy that gained in popularity among the Pankhursts over the incident of the Pankhurst Hall.

The Hall had been financed by the appeal launched on Dr Pankhurst's death. The Pankhurst women were quite involved in its construction, with Sylvia giving much of her time to it by assuming the responsibility for its decoration. One can imagine their anger, then, when they found they were not allowed to use Pankhurst Hall, for women were not permitted to become members of that particular branch of the Independent Labour Party. This humiliation was rendered even more galling when they discovered that men who chose not to be members of the ILP, were nevertheless permitted to use it. This was too much: it 'proved the last straw which caused Mrs Pankhurst to decide on the formation of a new organization of women', said Sylvia (ibid.). She came to the conclusion that 'she had wasted her time in the ILP' (ibid., p. 68), and she wasn't going to waste it any more. There was nothing else for women to do but to assume responsibility for their own quest for political representation: on 10 October 1903 the Women's Social and Political Union was formed. Sylvia reports that the break with the Labour party was not undertaken lightly by Mrs Pankhurst, and that she was extremely distressed, but under the circumstances she thought women had no choice but to work for themselves.

The WSPU was a Manchester-based organisation and for Sylvia, Manchester was no longer her place of residence. In the scholarship examination (in which the candidates were anonymous) she had secured a first-class certificate in all but one subject and had 'headed the list of competitors for the whole country' (S Pankhurst, 1931, p. 170). She went to London to pursue her art studies, and while in these early days she was a 'contact' in London for those in Manchester, it was Manchester where the policy of the WSPU was being forged.

3 Recruits: Annie Kenney (1879–1953) and Teresa Billington-Greig (1877–1964)

Among some of the first members of the WSPU (apart from the Pankhurst family) were Annie Kenney and Teresa Billington. From financial pressure Annie Kenney had begun work in a textile factory at the age of 10 as a half-timer, and as an adult she experienced a distinct sense of loss – of childhood, education, culture, leisure. Her four younger sisters had attended night school and, while Annie Kenney found this not a viable option, their activities helped to give substance to her idea that there was something more that she was missing. She had become involved with the Labour movement, but had not seriously considered the issue of women's suffrage until, in the name of the newly formed WSPU, Christabel came to speak. And Annie Kenney was one of the first of many, many recruits.

Christabel Pankhurst must have been a charismatic speaker – one does not even have to look far in the often otherwise unfavourable reports on her to find praise for her skills as a public speaker. But charisma was only part of it (and not the major part, as some of her critics have suggested in the attempt to devalue her), for she had a philosophy and a practice which fell on welcoming ears. She offered women hope and she instilled in them a sense of purpose and strength. Christabel, says Sylvia 'talked not of women's woes and helplessness, but of the young working women who were to come forward and take their own part in politics' (ibid., p. 186). It seemed like a dream, but Christabel Pankhurst made it seem that it was a dream that would come true – soon! 'She urged them to rise up and fight for their rights', says Sylvia, and, 'To Annie Kenney the words were a personal appeal' (ibid.). She was invited to 62 Nelson Street, the Pankhurst home and WSPU headquarters, and immediately and unhesitatingly took to the lecture platform. It was she who suggested that platforms be set up at the local fairs in Lancashire.

The number of speakers was growing and Teresa Billington also joined the ranks. She was a school teacher, a socialist and an agnostic, who came to know Mrs Pankhurst as a member of the Education Committee when she looked like losing her job for her refusal to teach religious instruction. Mrs Pankhurst was instrumental in helping to have her transferred to a Jewish school where no such problem arose. Teresa Billington was also the secretary of the Manchester Equal Pay League and had not only thought long and hard about women's rights, but had decided that the time for action had come. She was energetic, exuberant, physically robust and a symbol of strength; she was also uncompromising in her attitude towards equality and positively determined that women would get their way.

While Mrs Pankhurst, Christabel, Annie Kenney and Teresa Billington were rousing women in Manchester and its environs, it is usually suggested that the WSPU, in the form that we recognise today, was born on 12 May 1905 when, for the umpteenth time, women's hopes for the franchise were once more dashed by the male politicians. Mrs Pankhurst had descended on Sylvia in February (and Sylvia's art studies had to take a very secondary place) to start lobbying for votes for women. By 12 May hopes were high and many women (including Nellie Alma Martel from Australia, who had stood for Parliament) gathered at the House amid much excitement and great anticipation. Only half an hour remained when the much-awaited Bill was introduced. There were roars of laughter in the House. The Bill was talked out. Derision and defeat.

There was frustration and desperation as so many women representing so many different organisations stood around the Stranger's Entrance and felt the full extent of their powerlessness. Elizabeth Wollstoneholme Elmy, almost in her seventies, began to make a speech on how the movement had started forty years before and how it was no closer to achieving its objective now than it had been then. The police pushed the women away. They moved to the statue of Richard I, but the police hustled them on again.

Under the protection of Keir Hardie they were permitted to remain in Broad Sanctuary, where they held a meeting expressing their indignation and passed a resolution against the Government.

4 Confrontation and confirmation

Christabel was not present: she was in Manchester concentrating her mind – and not only on her law degree! She had already begun to formulate and test some of the tactics that would help break the wearying mould of repeated defeat.

On 19 February 1904 she had attended a meeting in the Free Trade Hall in Manchester where Winston Churchill had spoken for an hour and a half (on the advantages of free trade), when she proposed an amendment to Churchill's resolution which would have the words expressed in the masculine gender in the Representation of the People Acts construed to include women. The Chairman refused to allow the amendment, but for quite some time Christabel would not give way. She was finally howled down, and for Christabel, this 'was the first militant step – the hardest to me, because it *was* the first. To move from my place on the platform to the speaker's table in the teeth of the astonishment and opposition of will of that immense throng, those civil and county leaders and those Members of Parliament was the most difficult thing I have ever done' (1959, p. 46). But the world did not end: the first and worst feat had been accomplished; the way was open to further 'militant' steps.

What Christabel discovered in the process was an insight not unknown to many of her foremothers (Florence Nightingale among them) even if not previously recognised by herself: that when women cease to be willing, men are either obliged to give way to women's demands or else they are required to demonstrate their greater power and force to keep women in their place. The manners of chivalry can only be maintained while women willingly abide by the restrictive rules men have imposed upon them; once women challenge those rules, chivalry is dead. It would be impossible for men to argue that women have all the rights and respect that they need, that they are treated with deference and consideration, *at the same time as the same men abused and assaulted women*. For Christabel this policy of challenging men had much to recommend it, for either way women could gain; either men would immediately concede the vote for women, or the whole pretence of respect for women would be dropped and would stand exposed as a pretence.

This was the analysis behind the 'altercation' that Christabel provoked at the Manchester Free Trade Hall on 13 October 1905. She planned that she and Annie Kenney should go to gaol (she set out from home on the night of the meeting stating gaily, 'I shall sleep in prison tonight!' S. Pankhurst, 1931, p. 189), not just for the publicity (although it *was* important, for there was no point to the exercise unless people knew about it), but because it would demonstrate – perhaps even once and for all –

that men were prepared to use their power to imprison women for stepping out of their sphere. Asking whether the government would give women the vote at a public political meeting may not seem to be such a significant issue, and without the benefit of hindsight it might have been said that Christabel was being over-optimistic in believing that this would be a sufficiently inflammatory challenge (and this was almost the case), but the whole point was to make 'the enemy show his hand' and in this respect, Christabel was certainly successful.

The question put forward was not the traditional one of asking the Member of Parliament whether he was in favour of votes for women – hundreds of members had been in favour of the vote in principle for decades and nothing had happened. Christabel was not about to risk the enterprise by allowing Sir Edward Grey to say he was in favour of the vote for women, and then allowing the matter to be dropped. The question was 'Will The Liberal Government give women the vote?' and the implications were not lost on Grey. At the meeting a banner with 'Votes for Women' suddenly appeared and Annie Kenney put the question first. 'Other questions were answered: that question was ignored,' states Sylvia. 'When it was persisted in, Annie Kenney was dragged down by the men sitting near her, and one of the stewards put a hat over her face. Christabel repeated the question. The hall was full of conflicting cries,' and the Chief Constable came and told the women to put the question in writing and it would be answered later. The question was passsed around among those on the platform who were somewhat bemused, but no one deigned to answer it. 'When Sir Edward Grey rose to acknowledge a vote of thanks, Annie stood on a chair to ask again, whilst Christabel strove to prevent her removal: but Liberal stewards and policemen in plain clothes soon dragged both from the hall.' But, adds Sylvia 'Determined to secure imprisonment Christabel fought against ejection' (1931, p. 189).

It wasn't all that easy, but it was necessary. Christabel tried technical assault: she hit one policeman and spat at another, and it was when she addressed the crowd that she achieved her goal, although the charge she faced was spitting at a police superintendent and an inspector.

Back inside the Free Trade Hall, Edward Grey found it necessary to provide an 'explanation' and stated that the question was one he would not deal with 'because it is not, and I do not think it is likely to be, a *party* question' (ibid., p. 190, my emphasis). Christabel had struck the nail on the head. Grey knew the significance of making the question a *party* issue and Churchill knew the significance of the gaol sentence – he went to try and pay the fines so the women would be released. And women everywhere, interested in the vote, knew that a new phase had arrived.

Christabel and Annie went to gaol and in many respects Christabel's policy had paid off; the only difficulty was the thorny issue of spitting. It was fundamental to her tactics that the world should see what men would do to women whom they professed to protect and respect. Women who *spat* were not 'ladies' and could be said to have put themselves beyond the pale. This was the stance adopted by some of the newspapers and was a stumbling block for her former intimate companions Esther Roper and Eva

Gore Booth, for whom the matter was primarily one of whether Christabel did or did not spit. If she had spat at a police inspector then there was some reason for the punishment, but if not – then it was an outrage that such a young woman should be sent to prison.

To evaluate Christabel's actions in this way is to miss the point completely (not that this has discouraged historians who have wished to portray her as a harridan and who have therefore attached great significance to the *spitting* and ignored the element of technical assault). As far as Christabel was concerned it was immaterial *which* facet of her behaviour the police lighted upon, the purpose was for a lady to get arrested and imprisoned on the issue of 'Votes for Women' and there was not much else she could do but spit when her arms were pinioned at her side. But spitting was never used again; it was too likely to backfire.

I have not been able to determine how much the Pankhursts knew about Annie Besant (1847–1933), but she had definitely ventured into the territory where the Pankhursts were now to tread. An extraordinary woman (the two volumes of her biography are entitled *The First Five Lives of Annie Besant* (1961) and *The Last Four Lives of Annie Besant* (1963) in her biographer Nethercot's attempt to indicate the range and diversity of her actions), she had deliberately courted arrest and trial in order to have the case for birth control placed on the official and public records. A suffragist, she stated her position clearly when she declared that men's argument that the vote would prevent woman from performing her proper work led ultimately to the position that only the idle should be enfranchised (see Constance Rover, 1970, p. 102). Unhappily married (to a clergyman) and infuriated by the bondage in which married women were kept, she left her husband (but was not allowed custody of her daughter because she was an atheist), and began to champion the right to free speech, and birth control.

Because publications which dealt with the issue were 'obscene', she formed, with Charles Bradlaugh, the Freethought Publishing Company, and republished a book on the issue which had been circulating for forty years (it was Charles Knowlton's *Fruits of Philosophy*, first published in 1832). She and Bradlaugh were brought to trial in 1877: 'Both conducted their own defence. Mrs Besant eloquently pleaded the case for family limitation as a means of relief to working class women. . . . Like Marie Stopes after her, she wished to help working class women living in poverty, and felt it unjust that such women should be deprived of knowledge that could contribute to their happiness' (Rover, 1970, p. 104). And by arrest and publicity she helped to make the topic an issue and to expose male treatment of women in general and of working-class women in particular.

Whether or not Christabel knew of this precedent and chose to emulate it, there can be no doubt that for she and Annie getting gaoled produced the goods – although it must not be forgotten that gaol meant humiliation and deprivation. Anyone who has ever spent a night in gaol knows how harrowing the experience can be and I have no wish to romanticise or minimise what price these two women paid – as did the hundreds of others who later joined them (six hundred ex-prisoners marched in one demonstration alone). Because I think it important to know what prison – and hunger strikes and forcible feeding – meant, but because it is not strictly relevant in this context I have included an appendix (page 533) which contains some of the accounts of the suffragettes themselves. But even though it was a traumatising experience, as far as Christabel and Annie were concerned, the results were worth the pain.

The 'conspiracy of silence' in the news media was broken as 'Votes for Women' became a headline. Women flocked to suffrage meetings as protests were held throughout the country. The two women emerged from prison to be greeted by supporters in the Free Trade Hall where 'Christabel insisted that no reference should be made to their prison experiences, in order that attention might be fully concentrated on Votes for Women' (S. Pankhurst, 1977, p. 191). The only negative outcome was that Christabel 'was now threatened with expulsion from Owens College, and as a condition of remaining to take her degree was obliged to pledge herself to refrain from making any further disturbance' (ibid.). She kept her pledge; she was the only woman enrolled but she took the prize in international law and graduated equal first. Given the demands of her political activities, this was no mean feat.

But it was to London that the WSPU began to look. Annie Kenney and Teresa Billington had been thrown out of a meeting addressed by Campbell-Bannerman at the Albert Hall on 21 December 1905 when Teresa Billington had released from the balcony a nine-foot-long banner demanding 'Will the Liberal Government give Justice to Working Women?', and then in 1906 Annie Kenney arrived on Sylvia's doorstep with £2 and the instruction to 'rouse London'.

This was quite a tall order, but Sylvia decided that on 19 February, the day of the King's Speech, the WSPU would hold a meeting, and Caxton Hall was engaged. Mrs Pankhurst arrived and was aghast at the size of the hall thinking that there was no likelihood of their filling it and that they would look ridiculous. But the meeting – and afterwards a march on Parliament – had been widely advertised, and so they had to go ahead. But steps were taken to make sure that more than a handful of people attended. Ultimately, they proved to be unnecessary.

Annie Kenney went to Canning Town, Poplar, and Limehouse, to drum up support among women and on the day, three hundred women from the East End arrived at Caxton Hall, which was soon filled with women from virtually every walk of life. News came that there had been no mention of women's suffrage in the King's Speech, and the march through the rain to the House of Commons began. Only twenty women at a time were permitted to lobby the indifferent politicians, and for almost two hours women stood outside in the cold and rain, waiting their turn.

5 The treasure: Emmeline Pethick-Lawrence (1867–1964)

But if the experience in itself had been demoralising, the significance attached to the event was helpful. It had been a large meeting, it was newsworthy, and more women came forward. Among them was Emmeline Pethick-Lawrence, who proved to be literally a *treasure*.

Emmeline Pethick came from a very comfortable (but apparently unaffectionate) family, and as a young woman had taken up social and philanthropic work with working-class girls. She was deeply committed to social reform and quite averse to marriage, even when she met Frederick William Lawrence in 1899. She was 32 years old and not interested when he proposed marriage, fearing, quite justifiably, that it would deprive her of her independence, her freedom, and her work. Besides, she was a socialist, and he was not. They separated, and by the time they met again in 1901, he had moved towards the left in politics, and was also able to convince her that marriage would not infringe on her freedom. They were married, with both of them taking the name 'Pethick-Lawrence' as a symbol of her continued individual identity, and his commitment to it.

In 1905 the Pethick-Lawrences visited South Africa where they formed a firm and lasting friendship with Olive Schreiner (and where they read about Christabel Pankhurst's and Annie Kenney's exploits in the newspaper), and when they returned, Keir Hardie introduced the two Emmelines, on the basis that a friendship might be mutually beneficial. Emmeline Pethick-Lawrence agreed to become treasurer for the WSPU and with her entry to the group (and her money-raising skills) the WSPU in many respects ceased to be an informal family concern and became an organisation. Sylvia Pankhurst was honorary secretary, Annie Kenney was formally made an organiser on a weekly salary of £2, and other members of the committee were Irene Fenwick Miller, Mrs Drummond (commonly referred to as the 'General'), Mrs Clarke (Mrs Pankhurst's sister) and Mrs Martel (who evidently preferred the struggle in London to the achievement of Australia).

With the WSPU organised, the task was now to act. Sylvia Pankhurst outlined the initial actions of the women who stood behind the motto: 'Deeds not Words!' 'Our first move was to secure an interview with the Prime Minister. My written request being refused, I replied that we could accept no denial, and that some of our members would call upon him at the official residence in Downing Street on March 2nd. The visit proved abortive; the Prime Minister was ill. . . . Again we wrote for an interview, and again were refused. On March 9th thirty women proceeded to Downing Street. Two detectives opened the Prime Minister's door and ordered them away. Irene Miller knocked again and was arrested. Mrs Drummond pulled at a little brass knob she thought a bell; the door flew open; in she ran, and was thrown out and arrested. Annie Kenney jumping into somebody's motor-car began to make a speech and was taken in charge. The three were detained at Cannon Row police station for an hour. Then a message was brought that the Prime Minister would shortly receive a deputation from the Women's Social and Political Union, either individually or in conjunction with other organizations. The prisoners were released and came home jubilant' (Sylvia Pankhurst, 1931, p. 207–8).

It worked!

The *style* of the WSPU had emerged. It was a women's organisation which not only functioned independently of men but took the unprecedented step of setting itself up in *opposition* to men. Parliament was referred to as the 'Men's Parliament'; women started to hold their (huge) meetings in nearby premises and to refer to them as the 'Women's Parliament'. Whereas previous suffrage organisations had tried to convince men that they had nothing to fear from women's enfranchisement, the WSPU began its policy of convincing men that they had *much* to fear if women were *not* enfranchised.

6 Sex-war

It wasn't that the members of the WSPU ignored the warnings that they were promoting a sex-war, it was that they *wanted* a sex-war, because that seemed the only way of obtaining the vote. They deliberately set out to accentuate the differences between women and men in order to end – once and for all – the ridiculous argument put forward by men that women's best interests were served by men. They promoted confrontation between the sexes in the firm belief that men would reveal the extent to which they were prepared to go to keep women in their place. They called for a *battle* in order to *rob* men of the rationale that women were in a privileged position they could not possibly want to jeopardise. They called for a confrontation to *rob* men of the rationale that women were happy as they were, perfectly content with their lot.

Talk of protection and privilege became impossible when 'respectable' women were being beaten and gaoled. If and when enough of the women who had lived within the confines of true womanhood – denying their protests and grievances – and who had helped to sustain this image ceased to do so, if they stepped forward and demonstrated that there was no distinction between true womanhood and the women who were assaulted and imprisoned, not only would there be the practical difficulty that soon there would be insufficient women left for men to protect, there was also the danger that the whole male classification scheme and appropriation of power could break down.

The women who joined the WSPU had nothing to lose and were therefore able to call men's bluff. The argument that they were putting back women's cause would stand up no longer. As far as the WSPU were concerned it couldn't go back any further. The argument that men wouldn't like them if they behaved in this way was not valid. Men didn't like women anyway; if they did they would concede women the vote. The argument that it was unladylike and uncivilised to behave in this militant fashion could be readily countered with the argument that they took their standards from men who were behaving in an ungentleman-like, uncivilised, and treacherous fashion in relation to women's suffrage, and women's struggle.

The women of the WSPU began to set their own terms to which men were required to respond, instead of simply reacting to the terms set by men. The WSPU became an alternative political power base, and this contrasted starkly with the male definition of women's powerlessness, which many women had learnt to accept. Christabel Pankhurst made it perfectly plain that this was a *glorious* struggle, that it was waged in the name of dignity and freedom, that those who joined in were of heroic dimensions, and that for women entry to the militant suffrage campaign meant entry to a realm of purpose, confidence, self-esteem. Given the alternatives available to women at the beginning of the twentieth century, it is hardly surprising that so many of them found this prospect attractive.

The source of much of this success (and later the basis of much of the criticism) was the WSPU insistence that all men be treated as members of *one* party. Among themselves – in a male electorate with male members – men had decided that some would be more powerful than others, but as far as the WSPU was concerned the means by which this hierarchy among men was arranged was *irrelevant* to women. Those who were the government and had the power, had the power to give women the vote, and were therefore held responsible. The composition of the government might change, individual men may come and go, men's parties might rise or fall, but these 'personal' issues among men were of no account to women who focused their attention on an *agency* – the government – and not upon individual men.

Of course, for numerous reasons many felt this practice of the WSPU was unfair, because it wasn't playing by the rules men had set up. Frequent are the comments that Mrs Pankhurst and Christabel *deserted* the Labour party and betrayed its principles (few are the comments by the way that the Labour party deserted women and betrayed women's principles); yet it was fundamental to their analysis that all male parties should be treated the same. There is something suspect about the rationale 'Oh, but my bloke is different' in the same way as there would have been something suspect about the rationale, 'Oh, but my male political party is different.'

There was *not* a lot of mileage to be gained in opposing the Conservatives on the issue of Votes for Women, for Mrs Pankhurst had been opposing the Conservatives for years. As such opposition was not at all new the Conservatives could have been forgiven for treating such a policy as an idle threat, and dismissing it. The mileage lay in opposing the party one had *not* opposed before, in refusing to adhere to male distinctions and treating all men the same. For this made it obvious that the divisions among men, so clearly prized by themselves, were irrelevant to women. (We are back to Adrienne Rich's thesis that it is fear of irrelevance which is the *primary* male fear.)

The WSPU *had* to oppose the Labour party while it refused to make women's suffrage a priority issue. All the Pankhurst women recognised that the franchise had been extended to men by degrees and that the process had not yet been completed. While they argued that full adult suffrage was the ultimate goal, they knew that even the proposal for adult male suffrage had no hope of success (as Sylvia said, 'The very phrase was as a red rag to a bull', 1931, p. 248) and that it was absolutely ludicrous to demand for women more than men were prepared to grant to themselves. So the WSPU argued, quite consistently, that they would settle for the same as men, that the disqualification on the basis of sex should be removed and that women should be admitted to the electoral role *on the same terms as men*.

The sensible nature of this policy has often been wilfully ignored in the past and in the present. 'Adult suffrage was the main refuge of those [men in the Labour party] who did not care for Votes for Women and disliked militant tactics,' states Sylvia Pankhurst (ibid., p. 242) and the Labour party was prepared to leave the whole question of the franchise in abeyance rather than commit itself to Votes for Women. And in none of the other parties was it even an issue. But because the WSPU was making a claim for limited franchise – on the grounds that it was most likely to be successful – their policy has been maligned as elitist: the demand for the vote on the same terms as men was 'a convenient handle to opponents, who insisted that the suffrage movement was bourgeois in leadership and opposed to any but a limited vote' (ibid., p. 205), an assertion which Sylvia hotly disputes, and quotes much evidence to the contrary to support her case.

Besides Sylvia Pankhurst's account of the extent to which women of *all* classes were involved in the suffragette movement, there is Annie Kenney's version (*Memories of a Militant*, 1924) which documents the diversity of backgrounds of many of the women who participated in militancy, and Teresa Billington-Greig's account (*The Militant Suffrage Movement*, 1911), which makes explicit the links between the suffrage movement and working-class women. There is also Hannah Mitchell's posthumous autobiography (*The Hard Way Up*, 1977) and Elizabeth Robins's 'documentary', *The Convert* (1907) as well as numerous testimonies from working-class women in general sources such as Raeburn (1974) and Rosen (1974), and Liddington and Norris's (1978) account of the emergence of the suffrage movement.

In the face of this considerable evidence of the multi-class nature of the movement (where women of all classes expected improvements in their position once the franchise was won), it seems quite remarkable that there are (still) constant allegations (which undoubtedly help to minimise the movement and bring it into disrepute) that it was nothing other than a bourgeois movement which looked for nothing more than limited enfranchisement. I cannot argue (because I do not have sufficient evidence) that women of all classes were equally represented within the movement and stood to gain equal improvements from enfranchisement. I cannot argue – again because I do not have the evidence – that the enfranchisement of *one* section of women would have implications for *all* women. But by the same standard I know that *no one else has sufficient evidence to argue the reverse*.

My question then is: who is trying to throw doubts on this movement and for what purpose? *Are the same allegations made of men's movements?* What I do know is that male political figures who have argued for an extension of the franchise (which women's suffrage undoubtedly was) but who have advocated the wisdom and necessity of proceeding by degree (as the WSPU was doing) have *not* often had *their* championship of liberty called into question.

That past and present women's movements can so readily be disparaged by assertions which, not unintentionally, are almost impossible to repudiate (or to substantiate – but that, of course, is a very different matter) is not the only similarity shared by rebellious women over time. In the period of the suffragettes there were members of parliament, members of the press, and members of the public who professed to be in sympathy with the women's aims, but because they 'deplored their tactics' found themselves unable – unfortunately – to offer support. Having been informed myself on numerous occasions that my arguments are *sound* but my (aggressive) manner 'spoils my case', I can sympathise with the members of the WSPU who, on encountering the same dismissal, were enraged, frustrated, and totally unconvinced by this line of reasoning. It was seen by militant suffragettes then (as I suggest it should be seen by feminists today) as merely an excuse for *not* dealing with women's ideas and experience. It was, and is, an attempt to assert that unless women conduct themselves in ways acceptable to men and male values, they will not get a hearing (see Shirley Ardener, 1975); but as Teresa Billington-Greig (no date) roundly asserted, as soon as women conducted themselves in ways men deemed appropriate, they were dismissed anyway! Damned if you are militant; damned if you are polite! Teresa Billington-Greig presents a powerful case for militancy (which does not suit men) in preference to politeness, or 'good conduct' (which she maintains does not suit women).

The basic principle of our male-dominated society, she argues, is that: 'Men may fight; women should suffer' (p. 3) and it is this fundamental principle that women are challenging. Men are not opposed to rebellion, but to a rebellion of *women*, she says, identifying the major objection to women's militancy. Men themselves have done far worse things and have been treated much more leniently, and the reason men so violently oppose women's challenge is because it *denies* the male view of the world (where women must be docile, decorous and decorative), whereas male challenges *confirm* the male view of the world (where males are aggressive and masterful). A society which depends on a view of women as passive cannot countenance militancy in women.

The early suffragists, argues Billington-Greig, believed men when they said that success for women would lie in reason and justice, in presenting their case in an appropriate manner, but this has proved to be a hoax which has taken up women's time and energy and has led nowhere. 'It might aptly be called the theory of good conduct,' she says, 'for it limited the Suffrage propaganda to the mildest persuasion, the politest and most dignified advocacy, and condemned all warmth, all vigour, all attack, as unworthy of the women's cause. It succeeded in giving the whole movement a character of shadowy unreality, the influence of which infected both the

Suffragists and the politicians they set out to convert. Studied moderation of speech under all circumstances, an over-patient dignity, and an attitude of pleading for privilege, rather than one of claiming a right, became universal on the side of the advocates of women's liberty' (ibid., p. 4).

And it was a trap, she declares. It was exactly what men wanted. Women's claims made in this way were no bother at all. They allowed the politician to display 'a mixture of good humoured toleration and contempt'; it was no threat to the operation of chivalry. It was no threat to the concept of women as non-active creatures. This, states Teresa Billington-Greig, was an absolutely useless way for women to try to obtain the vote. '*Liberty was never won by pleading*, and cannot be purchased' (ibid., p. 6). The only time that power changes hands, argues Billington-Greig, there is a struggle: those who have previously been considered non-existent, invisible, establish their identity and their power.

She was quite open in her acknowledgement that men would never be convinced by *logic* of women's right to vote, and she has no hesitation in revealing her contempt for male logic (and for those who subscribe to its precepts). When men find it perfectly logical to deny the value of women's industrial, social and political work, she argues, it will not stretch their powers of comprehension to find it perfectly logical to deny women the right to vote. Those who place their faith in logic are doomed to failure – while men control logic.

There is no alternative but militancy, declares Teresa Billington-Greig. Women have to start challenging and opposing men – all men! That they are women and the target is men makes the issue of the vote a power contest, as it has always been but which men have been able to camouflage, while women were beguiled into practising good conduct. It was *bad* conduct for women that was necessary. Men will concede the vote to women when they *have* to, she argues, in the same way they have conceded it to groups among themselves when necessity has dictated. But women's militancy is not men's militancy; it is not a crude case of *might is right*. There are different and more subtle processes at work.

The very fact that women are prepared to revolt against male tyranny will cause men to rethink. They cannot sleep safe in their beds at night, secure in the knowledge that women are under control, when women persist in behaving in an uncontrollable manner. Practically it could prove to be well-nigh impossible for men to control women unless women consent to be controlled, and when so many women will no longer consent, many a doubt must be planted in the mind of many a man, who could well begin to decide that discretion is the better part of valour.

It will be the fact that *women are in revolt,* rather than the revolt itself, which will win the day, argues Billington-Greig, because in the end men will just not have the energy or the resources to maintain their position *once women cease supporting them and start opposing them.* While she does not put her case in these precise words, she is suggesting a strategy that is completely consistent with the thesis of Matilda Joslyn Gage and Charlotte Perkins Gilman (and later Mary Ritter Beard) – that men's power depends on the appropriation of women's resources, and when women will not permit their resources to be appropriated, when they cease to make their support available to men, men's power is undermined.

What Billington-Greig does say is that it has to be *all men*. The divisions among them are irrelevant to women, she argues, and should not be taken into account. 'Every Government candidate must be opposed at every by-election,' she insists, for his 'personal professions are of no account to women' (ibid., p.11). (Just as a side-line what this must have done to men to have their 'serious political differences' perceived as personal problems is interesting to contemplate.)

Drawing her firm dividing line between the interests of women and the interests of men, Billington-Greig declares that: 'Insistent demand in season and out of season – for the non-voter is always out of season – backed up by every constitutional and unconstitutional protest is necessary to carry the day. The refusal to pay taxes, the refusal to acknowledge man-made laws, must be used,' (ibid.). And she was as good as her word. On 21 June 1906 she and Annie Kenney were arrested for causing a disturbance outside Mr Asquith's house (Teresa being charged with slapping P.C. Warman three times, and kicking him) and when she appeared in court she refused to testify, declaring: 'I do not recognize the authority of the Police, of this Court, or any other Court of law made by man' (Metropolitan Police Report, 21 June 1906; quoted in Rosen, 1974 p.68).

Teresa Billington-Greig, along with Charlotte Despard[2] (and Edith How Martyn, and Irene Fenwick Miller) set up the Women's Freedom League after a disagreement about the way the WSPU should be run, and pursued a vigorous policy of what could be called passive resistance. Charlotte Despard regularly refused to pay her taxes, regularly had her furniture seized and sold to meet the debt, with the result that her friends became quite accustomed to frequenting auction rooms to buy back her furniture for her.

It was the Women's Freedom League that organised the boycott of the 1911 Census, where all over the country women left their homes for the night on the basis of 'No Vote – No Census!' 'Marian Lawson, a brilliant and enterprising member of the Women's Freedom League, spent the whole night on roller skates at the Aldwych Skating Rink. "We were very tired the next morning, but we were so pleased to have diddled the government about a few names on the census" ' (Raeburn, 1974, p. 177).

7 The delight of defiance

This brings me to a glaring omission in the appraisals of the theory and practice of the militants. It is undeniable that the success of their movement depended greatly on attracting large numbers of women to their cause, and

[2] Charlotte Despard (1844–1939) 'Suffragette, Socialist and Sinn Feiner' is one of the most fascinating of the suffragettes and has been too little and too unsympathetically studied. There is a recent biography of her by Andro Linklater, 1980: no comment.

it goes without saying that in order to do this, the movement had to be *attractive* to women. It seems, however, that there is little that is attractive about assault, imprisonment, hunger striking and forcible feeding, yet there were always far more volunteers for these ordeals than were ever needed. Besides, the movement was rarely presented as attractive in the popular press, where the suffragettes were condemned – often crudely, as embittered women,[3] but sometimes more insidiously: 'Officialdom everywhere treated this militancy as a pernicious form of hysteria,' says Sylvia Pankhurst (1931, p. 229) indicating the way women's actions were undermined.

When today it is frequently stated that the women's movement gets such a bad press that it is not surprising that women are discouraged from identifying with it, it is worth remembering that the press the suffragettes received (apart from their own controlled papers) was no better, and probably worse, than that received today. They were subjected to the same harassment as all other women who have dared to protest, but in their case the harassment seems not to have worked. The question is *WHY?*

For even as the press called them childish, spoilt, frustrated, embittered, humourless, and wicked, still women came in droves to join the movement. The number of branches mushroomed: for example, on the 28 February 1907 there were forty-seven branches of the WSPU, on the 10 May there were fifty-eight and on the 31 August there were seventy. And it wasn't just the numbers which grew, it was the finances as well. 'Women everywhere were practising "self-denial" to give money to the cause. The more acts of militancy, the more rolled in: the income rose with increasing momentum; reaching £3,000 in 1906–7, £7,000 in 1907–8, £20,000 in 1908–9, £32,000 in 1909–10. Then there came a truce for nine months; the income decreased somewhat, but was still enormous, being £29,000 in 1910–11,' states Sylvia Pankhurst, and 'every other organization in the country wondered at the income of the WSPU' (ibid., p. 222). Yet no one tried to explain it – at least not in terms other than 'a fad', a form of hysteria, an aberration – the customary way women's behaviour is explained when it differs from men's. But even less effort then or now has gone into satisfactorily explaining the growth of this movement.

Elizabeth Cady Stanton (rebuked by Gail Parker in 1975 for savouring the struggle more than the success) could have explained it. The attraction was the sheer joy and exhilaration of *defiance* after so many years of *denial;* it was the luxury of (bold) deeds as distinct from (polite) words; it was freedom from those oppressively inhibiting rules of proper behaviour; it was the alternative to repressing anger, it was solidarity, sisterhood and *fun!* It was the joy at being active, visible, alive! (Freud could not have explained it; he would have had the *entire* female population classified as maladjusted and envious of men before he could have perceived the attraction of militancy to women.)

Women had learnt the skills of managing men's emotional state (at

---

[3] I suggest that some research be done on the research done by men. So many of them take pains to *count* the number of prominent suffragettes who were – wait for it – unmarried! No doubt this is methodologically sound – in male terms.

the expense of their own) and they were therefore in a very commanding position to know what men would find emotionally most irksome. Once the barriers were down and women could see that they didn't have to stay in their psychological place if they didn't want to, they tasted some of the real fruits of liberation. I suspect that much of their emotional energy which previously had been used to prop up patriarchy now went into thwarting it: I know that many of the women found this a most enjoyable experience. David Mitchell (1977) has identified this aspect of the suffragette campaign (although he gives it a different emphasis from the one that I do) and has said that the Liberal Government looked on Christabel as a 'witch', inspiring women to obstruct the government's programme and to steal 'away their manhood by force of ridicule' (pp. 4–5).

The militants 'arrived in all sorts of guises, and appeared in all sorts of places,' says Ray Strachey (1928). 'Now one would appear as a messenger boy. Once they chained themselves to the railing in Downing Street, and so gained time to make some longish speeches before being hauled off to Bow Street; another was found chained to a statue in the lobby of the House of Commons, a thoroughly strategic position. They sprang out of organ lofts, they peered through roof windows, and leapt out of innocent looking furniture vans; they materialised on station platforms, they harangued the terrace of the House from the river, and whenever they were least expected, there they were' (p. 312).

It simply isn't possible to describe even a small proportion of the incidents they promoted (most of the papers referred to them as 'antics' with the usual derision) but their tactic of digging up golf courses, and leaving the message 'No Votes – No Golf' has a certain amount of appeal to me today as the media assaults me with the football news – but then 'No equality – No football' does not have the same ring as 'No Vote', which is one of the reasons it was fixed on as a symbol. (Perhaps 'No Disarmament – No Football,' might be an appropriate strategy.)

Asquith – whom Millicent Fawcett described as an enemy of women whose actions were calculated to drive even the most complacent woman into a frenzy – was a particularly popular target. As he was followed by women everywhere he went, and he couldn't turn around without confronting a sign or hearing the cry 'Votes for Women', every precaution was taken to keep women away from him and to exclude them from his meetings. After his visit to Sheffield in 1909 the *Sheffield Daily Telegraph* contained the following report:

> The methods for conveying Mr Asquith from the station to the hotel were highly successful but not particularly English. The railway officials rigged up a platform adjacent to a sort of back door, and from that Mr Asquith was smuggled to the hotel as if he were a bale of contraband goods. Time was when a British Premier was proud to face the people – but now! It was surely a little undignified for a British Prime Minister to be making unexpected entrances and mysterious exists like a trap-door artist in a Christmas pantomime (quoted in Raeburn, 1974, pp. 114–15).

The suffragettes loved it. Gaol was not such a harsh price to pay for this sense of power.

But all the resources of British security couldn't make it safe for Asquith. Asquith held a house party for some of his colleagues at Clovelly Court in Devon and Elsie Howey, Jessie Kenney (Annie's younger sister – the four of them eventually became organisers for the WSPU) and Vera Wentworth also went to Clovelly for the weekend. Asquith found their presence in church on Sunday considerably disconcerting and left hurriedly by a side door. He awoke the next morning to find the rhododendron bushes painstakingly decorated 'with three inch *Votes for Women* discs, inscribed on the reverse side REMEMBER PATRICIA WOODLOCK (undergoing three months imprisonment . . .) and RECEIVE OUR DEPUTATION ON JUNE 29' (ibid., p. 115).

On 5 September (after a few more betrayals by Asquith) the same three once more disturbed the peace of the Asquith family circle, this time in Kent. Christabel Pankhurst says that: 'a golf course was the scene of their encounter. Mr Asquith, accompanied by Mr Gladstone, was seen emerging from the clubhouse. The three ladies approached them, but Mr Asquith and his colleague tried to escape and instead of a discussion of votes for women, quite a fight ensued, home truths being all the time delivered to the Ministers, who were warned that the leaders of the movement would not be able to control women much longer unless the Government granted the vote. A visit to Lympne Castle (where Asquith was staying) was then planned. Voyaging by boat to the landing place, the three made their way to the Castle Wall just at dinner time. One was hoisted up to the window of the dining room and saw Mr Asquith and the whole party at table. Leaning through the open window, she called out in a loud voice: "Mr Asquith, we shall go on pestering you until you give women the vote." Stones struck the window by way of parting shots' (1959, p. 137).

Militancy wasn't just pestering, however; it was Asquith, who stated that there was no evidence that women wanted the vote. (Rosen, 1974 says that, 'His objection to women's enfranchisement was based on a belief that, as far as women were concerned, existing social arrangements were *natural* arrangements; there was no pressing reason to tamper with them . . . Asquith liked them [women] the way they were far too much to be interested in their potential for "serious" endeavours – the qualities of frivolity and sympathy, on which he depended for respite from politics, might be eroded by women's involving themselves in "masculine" pursuits and concerns', p. 97). Women took up the challenge and organised massive demonstrations (which were also fun and a source of celebration), to prove that women did indeed want the vote. It was to advertise a forthcoming demonstration that Mrs Drummond took to boating. The General 'electrified Members of Parliament peacefully taking their tea on the terrace', says Josephine Kamm (1966), 'by appearing on the river in a decorated launch, and urging them through a megaphone to "come to the Park on Sunday . . . There will be no arrests," she promised. "you shall have plenty of police protection." A Member rushed off to call the river police, but by the time they arrived the General had chugged happily away' (p. 161).

Many may have heard of the Wooden Horse of Troy, but have they heard of the Pantechnicon Raid?

Sing a song of Christabel's clever little plan
Four and twenty suffragettes packed in a van
When the van was open they to the Commons ran
Wasn't that a dainty dish for Campbell-Bannerman?
Asquith was in the treasury, counting out the money
Lloyd George among the Liberal women speaking words of honey
And then there came a bright idea to all those little men
'Let's give the women votes,' they cried 'and all be friends again'

(Raeburn, 1974, p. 63)

These lines appeared in the *Daily Mail* two days after the raid, when the women involved had all disappeared into Holloway. This 'had been written by one of the prisoners who had managed to smuggle in a pencil, despite the mandatory stripping and searching ordeal they were all subjected to' (ibid.).

But perhaps one of the most popular incidents was organised by Jessie Kenney. Often showing a penchant for the uniform of a messenger boy (a disguise which enabled her to enter a number of forbidden places), on this occasion she decided to abandon the messenger boy's uniform and instead, to send a message. 'On February 23 Jessie Kenney went to the West Strand Post Office with Elspeth McClelland and Daisy Soloman. "I want to send a human letter." The form was duly handed out, and she completed it, addressing her two comapnions to "The Right Hon H. H. Asquith, 10 Downing Street, SW." When she had paid the threepenny charge, a telegraph boy was called and the party set out. The two women walked briskly along the Strand on either side of the messenger. Daisy Soloman carried a placard bearing the address, while Elspeth McClelland held a still larger board printed with the message: VOTES FOR WOMEN – DEPUTATION – HOUSE OF COMMONS – WEDNESDAY.

'When they arrived at 10 Downing Street they were stopped by the three policemen on duty. The boy showed his way-bill and he was allowed to go forward to Number Ten, but the Suffragettes were told to wait. The messenger rang the bell, handed his note to the butler who opened the door, and he was asked inside.

'A few moments later the door re-opened and the butler came out. "You must be returned." "But we have been paid for!" they protested. "Well then, the post office must deliver you somewhere else. You can't be delivered here." "But the express letter is an official document and must be signed according to the regulations." "It can't be signed, you must be returned, you are dead letters" said the butler firmly, and went back to the house leaving the women to return to Clement's Inn,' WSPU headquarters (ibid., p. 104).

Members of the government were not safe (sometimes not even in Downing Street) as multitudes of women used their ingenuity and energy to find a way of shouting 'Votes for Women' at close quarters. It may seem amazing, but all it took to get arrested was to stand up at a meeting and shout 'Votes for Women' and the procedure went like clockwork. There were women, of course, who believed that it couldn't happen in their city, in their party, or be authorised by their husbands, (who were 'different'), and Christabel Pankhurst quotes a case in point: 'A leading Liberal woman, when Mother remarked that women would certainly be thrown out of the meeting for questioning Mr Asquith, replied that such a thing could not happen in that city, where women had done so much for the Liberal Party. Mother thereupon decided to put the matter to the proof and, accompanied by this trustful Liberal woman, entered the meeting and seated herself in the front row of a section set apart for the wives and daughters of local Liberal leaders. Mother sat silently until Mr Asquith had finished his discourse. Then she rose and told the chairman she would like to put a question to Mr Asquith. Hesitancy on the platform! So she at once inquired whether Mr Asquith did not think that women had a right to influence the government of the country through the vote. The stewards seized her by the arms and shoulders and pushed and dragged her from the hall.

The Liberal woman resigned from the Women's Liberal Association and joined the WSPU' (1959, p. 74).

In essence the WSPU held a simple test for men. They failed it. They readily demonstrated the contempt in which women were held, and once male contempt was blatantly revealed, women made it clear that they would put energy into their own development rather than make it available to men. The prominent Liberal woman was only one of many who deserted her ostensible party when she found it wasn't hers at all. The suffragettes came from *every* party and set themselves up as women against men.

Men retaliated, of course, and not just the members of the government who excluded women from their meetings. The suffragette tactic of constantly holding meetings – everywhere – was an affront to many men who responded with extensive and often brutal harassment (sometimes it was the police and not just the 'hooligan element'). 'Mice, poor little creatures, live and dead flung at us, tomatoes, flour, stones, often concerted and continuous shouting and stamping. Sometimes at the open air meetings we were in positive danger through the roughness of gangs of disturbers and the consequent surging of the crowds,' states Christabel Pankhurst (ibid., p. 73). On one occasion Mrs Pankhurst was badly bruised and her ankle severely sprained when she was pushed into a barrel and rolled down a hill.

Margaret Haig (Viscountess Rhondda) – whose female family members considered it their duty to be imprisoned for the cause and at times took drastic lengths to ensure it – recounts some of the attacks she experienced and which were standard treatment for WSPU speakers: 'I do dislike rotten eggs more than any other political missile I know,' she states (1933, p. 141).

There were threats ('the last suffragettes here were murdered') and there was violence – clothes torn, hair pulled, handbags stolen, bodies pummelled, punched and pinched; none of it stopped the suffragettes! Having had a particularly frightening experience at one meeting in a town in Wales, – which included being attacked in the 'Ladies Toilet', Lady Rhondda (if I refer to her as Haig, you won't find her in the bibliography – but I balk every time I write the title) resolved to go back and hold another meeting: 'It was against every tradition of the WSPU', she says, 'to leave any place alone after a really bad meeting. One was always expected to go back and have a successful, or at least a quiet one, as a follow up. So I went back' (ibid., p. 143). As did so many others. They went back to hold their own meetings and to interrupt at men's.

Male politicians had a real problem on their hands: everywhere they went they came up against 'Votes for Women'; every meeting they attended, there it was again. It had to stop – of that there was no doubt – for not only were all their plans and procedures being disrupted, but they themselves were being mocked. They were often a laughing stock to the public; it was even said that a group of hysterical women were getting the better of them. Their pride was hurt, their dignity offended, their egos were bruised.

8 Unable to 'divide and rule'

According to the male view of the world, the solution should have been simple: everyone knew there were two sorts of women, the proper and the improper (a variation of the Madonna–whore division that incensed Josephine Butler and which she had to a certain degree confounded), and, as it was obviously the improper women who were behaving in this appalling manner, they should be prevented from attending all political meetings and excluded from all decent company. The improper women should be placed beyond the pale of male protection and punished; that would soon teach them to mend their ways.

But the suffragette tactics had suddenly exposed the limitations of the male view of the world and women. When it was important for men to be able to distinguish between the women who would and the women who would not disrupt their meetings, protest, break windows, destroy golf greens, there came the stunning recognition that men could not tell them apart. When it became apparent that certain 'elegant-looking dowagers now carried hammers and stones for window smashing concealed in their muffs' (Kamm, 1966, p. 163), how could a man be expected to be able to identify the enemy? When the opera was disrupted and the King harangued by a well-dressed young woman, when a shower of 'Votes for Women' leaflets descended on the audience while she was being removed, when a young lady presented at court curtseyed to their Royal Highnesses and said, 'Stop forcible feeding, Your Majesty', there was simply no way of knowing who the enemy was, until she struck. It seemed as if the whole female sex would have to be declared the enemy, and treated accordingly, if men were to be protected.

The height of absurdity was reached (from my point of view of course: no doubt it seemed logical to men) when there were mutterings about

deception, about these terrible women who had the gall to disguise themselves as respectable women and gain entry to places where they were not
supposed to be. These dreadful women would not behave according to
plan, was the general verdict; little attention was paid to the artificial and
distorted nature of the plan itself. If *no* woman could be trusted – no
matter how respectable or innocent she may appear – then there was no
alternative but to treat all women in the same punitive way. This response
was precisely the one that Christabel Pankhurst, as the major theorist and
tactician of the WSPU, had banked on. After a very rowdy meeting at the
Albert Hall – where Lloyd George had promised to make a significant
statement on the status of the Votes for Women issue, and where no such
statement was forthcoming – he announced, 'that in future all women
would be excluded from his meetings' (C. Pankhurst, 1959, p. 117). It
wasn't just at political meetings that the total ban applied either: 'It was
with triumphant glee', states Christabel, 'that we read a notice in the Press
stating that "It is understood that no ladies of British nationality are to be
admitted to the dinner given by Mr Harcourt to the members of the
International Peace Conference. The object of course is to prevent a repetition of the Suffragist interruptions that occurred during Mr Lloyd
George's speech at the Queen's Hall". The Suffragettes had certainly scored'
(ibid., p. 99).

'Womanless meetings' became 'the rule for Cabinet Ministers', states
Christabel, as all over the country elaborate precautions were taken to keep
male politicans out of reach of women (ibid., p. 121) and 'by trying to keep
the Suffragettes out of their meetings, the Liberal leaders were driving
women out of the Liberal Party' (ibid., p. 128). So many women who had
spent so much time supporting men, campaigning for them, raising money
for them, addressing envelopes for them, were now off at WSPU headquarters supporting women's issues; they were campaigning, raising money
and addressing envelopes in their own interest. The men felt a distinct loss
as women's resources were withdrawn and were not only no longer available to them but were actually being used against them.

This, however, was not the full extent of the rebellion: that women no
longer showed the same respect for male authority was at least, if not more,
significant. In a society which tends to explain power in economic terms,
the psychological dimensions of power are often overlooked. Yet this dimension had been known to many women (Aphra Behn, Mary Astell,
'Sophia', Frances Wright, Anna Wheeler, Harriet Martineau, Elizabeth
Cady Stanton, Charlotte Perkins Gilman – to name but a few) and was
certainly obvious to Christabel Pankhurst. Despite centuries of warning,
many women have continued to believe the male tale that women were
pure, privileged, and on a pedestal, in no need of a public role or rights of
their own, for men would protect their interests. But now that the mask of
chivalry had been removed and the contempt in which women were held
was there for all to see, women started to feel then (as they did with the
advent of the modern women's movement) that they had been deceived.
Once bitten, twice shy; if men had deceived them on this issue, why not on
others? Instead of being accepted without question, male explanations of

the world began to be openly challenged by women and this represented a considerable shift in psychological power.

Virginia Woolf (1928) stated that for centuries women had been serving as looking glasses for men (1974, p. 37), reflecting them at twice their normal size. This was in part how male superiority was constructed as women used their resources (particularly emotional and psychological ones) to support men, to enhance the image of men at the expense of their own. Once women ceased to believe in male superiority, they ceased to put their energy into helping to construct it, with the result that it had much less chance of 'coming true'. Men began to find themselves looking distinctly foolish when women failed to reflect them at twice their normal size. They began to *blame* women for making them look stupid – and the battle was intensified.

Assault escalated into the sexual violence against women on 'Black Friday',[4] into forcible feeding, legitimately described by women as rape, and condoned by men as 'medical treatment'. It is salutary to note that there is virtually universal condemnation of Christabel Pankhurst for her strategy of stepping up the militancy. Nowhere have I read the suggestion (apart from in the accounts provided by the suffragettes themselves) that increased militancy was a *response* to increased state repression and violence. Always the militant tactics are described as ultimately played out and useless; never is it suggested that they were eminently successful because they revealed the fallacious nature of men's logic and arguments about women's position.

In many, though by no means all, respects, men have judged women's militancy by their own standards and have therefore missed the point as they are so prone to do. They have seen women's militancy as a contest of *force* in which women could never hope to win, and have therefore argued (despite abundant contrary evidence), that the women grew tired of the tactics when there was no prospect of success. But militant tactics were never intended to produce an outcome of 'might is right'; they were intended to expose men as the enemy and to make it clear what men were capable of doing to those whom they claimed to protect. And in this they were spectacularly successful. Women did not tire of these methods (as the number of volunteers for 'dangerous duty' reveals); on the contrary the harsher the methods employed by men (such as raiding WSPU premises, charging the Pethick-Lawrences and Emmeline and Christabel Pankhurst with conspiracy, preventing the publication of *Votes for Women*, imprisoning hundreds of women – Mary Leigh and Gladys Evans for five years – forcibly feeding women), the *more* women were prepared to be militant.

Actually, one *could* argue that the changes in tactics that Christabel made constituted a *decrease* in militancy – if one were concerned with *human* values. Originally the plan was for women to be caught, to be arrested and imprisoned, but after 'Black Friday', when so many women were viciously and sexually mauled and assaulted by the police, and when

---

[4] See Caroline Morrell, 1981, for an excellent coverage of this incident in particular and of violence against women in the suffragette movement in general.

mothers began to say that their daughters might break windows but were not to go on any more demonstrations, the plan was changed to an attack on *property* (beginning with government property), and the idea was that women would try to *avoid* being caught.

'*It is only simple justice that women demand,*' stated Christabel in her pamphlet *Broken Windows*. 'They have worked for their political enfranchisement as men never worked for it, by a constitutional agitation carried on on a far greater scale than any franchise agitation in the past. For fifty years they have been striving, and have met with nothing but trickery and betrayal at the hands of politicians. Cabinet Ministers have taunted them with their reluctance to use the violent methods that were being used by men before they won the extension of the franchise in 1829, in 1832 and in 1867. They have used women's dislike of violence as a reason for withholding from them the rights of citizenship. . . . *The message of the broken pane is that women are determined that the lives of their sisters shall no longer be broken, and that in future those who have to obey the law shall have a voice in saying what the law shall be.* Repression cannot break the spirit of liberty.'

Christabel Pankhurst's analysis of male power (and how to expose it) was often uncannily accurate, so much so that Frederick Pethick-Lawrence described her as the most brilliant political theorist and tactician – ever! She found it relatively easy to set the stage for men to demonstrate that they valued their finances more than they valued women, and when women recognised this many of them became even more angry – and set out to break more windows, dig up more golf greens, and in their worst acts of all, commit arson. To which the government and the judiciary responded with an even greater show of force against women. Such force was not always displayed against men. Christabel was also quite accurate when she stated that the male government treated male militancy very differently. Many more, and more violent, deeds, in which there was often loss of life, were committed by men in the name of Ireland, and the government bent, rather than try to break the men. Most of the prominent suffragettes acknowledged that it was not the militancy itself which men were so indignant about – it was the fact that it was undertaken by women. This was a threat to the whole social order in a way that militancy from men was not.

Christabel Pankhurst's analysis was related to male power, and not just with the way it was manifested in the parliamentary arena. She could not have made her policy clearer, VOTES FOR WOMEN – CHASTITY FOR MEN, although again, men have often missed the point, and have regarded her stand on male sexuality as irrelevant – and a sign of neurosis, of course. Yet for Christabel, male power, male treachery and betrayal of women were much the same in the public political arena as they were in the private political arena. The male record of protection of women on sexual grounds was no better then it was on party political grounds.

Even many men were prepared to acknowledge that the incidence of venereal disease was high among men, but most recommendations that they made for controlling it still fixed women as the source of the disease.

As with all the knowledge generated by women which is offensive to men, the logic and explanations of Josephine Butler had been in the main 'lost', and the old rules that decent women should neither know nor say anything on the matter had been re-instated. Yet it was not difficult to establish that many were the women who had abided by the injunctions to remain pure and innocent, only to find themselves infected with venereal diesase not long after they were married.

More evidence, argued Christabel in *The Great Scourge, and How to End It,* of what odious things men will do to those whom they claim to protect and cherish. The only solution, as she saw it was to extend the political power of women and to curb the sexual demands of men. As such, it is not so far removed from some contemporary demands, and those of us who are at the moment engaged in campaigns against male violence, against rape, sexual harassment and pornography should take full cognisance of the fact that we will no doubt be classified, as Christabel Pankhurst usually is, as prudish, puritan and repressive, and most definitely as neurotic.

The problem we confront as women is not confronted by men, therefore it does not exist: any analysis we might have of the problem is consequently meaningless or invisible. If we protest, as Christabel did, we will be seen, as she was, as 'making a fuss out of nothing' and simply confirming for men the well-entrenched thesis that women are irrational, by their standards.

9 Emotionalism or objectivity

So great is my rage at David Mitchell (1977) that I find it very difficult to relate the substance of his comments on Christabel Pankhurst and the WSPU, but in the interests of substantiating my charges I must quote some of his vituperative statements. The framework in which he has located Christabel is nothing other than vicious and his vindictiveness surfaces page after page – not that it is Christabel alone who comes in for violent treatment in his 'objective' biography. In the second paragraph of his book Mitchell sets the scene when he states that Christabel's imprisonment in Manchester was a 'coldly calculated manoeuvre (which) released a warm, quasi-orgasmic gush of gratitude and heroine worship' (p. 1) among women. This theme is continued throughout the book. In relation to 'Black Friday' and the sexual abuse of women which was associated with many demonstrations but which was more blatant on this occasion, Mitchell says that 'Christabel's oft-repeated taunt that the suffragette agitation could be ended by giving women what they wanted was unfortunately open to various interpretations' (in his male mind) 'and the provocativeness of the maiden warriors gave some men a splendid excuse to wage their own class – and sex – war. As the campaign lengthened and tempers shortened, near (and sometimes actual) rape became a hazard of the tussles in Parliament Square and at the stormier by-elections. Clothes were ripped, hands thrust into upper and middle-class bosoms and up expensive skirts. Hooligans, and occasionally policemen, fell gleefully upon prostrate forms from sheltered backgrounds. Wasn't this they argued, what these women *really* wanted?'

And, add Mitchell, 'Perhaps in some cases, and in a deeply unconscious way, it was' (p. 160). There is no need to comment on Mitchell's needs – conscious or otherwise; his whole treatment of active women, claiming resources for themselves, leaves no doubt about his own fears. But sadly the 'record' that *he* provides is treated too frequently as objective, and not as an emotional, reaction to threat.

Every facet of Christabel Pankhurst's life that he can turn to discrediting account is used by Mitchell; in the one sentence he manages to devalue both Christabel and her mother when, in the attempt to revile her according to his scale of values, he declares that Christabel mixed with lesbians in Paris, among them Natalie Barney and Romaine Brooks, and he says of the latter that her 'lesbianism seems to have been rooted in incestuous feelings of love-hatred for a neurotic mother – an experience which, one feels, was not unknown to Christabel' (ibid., p. 207).

Completely (and perhaps unconsciously, wilfully) missing the point of Christabel's campaign against the excesses of male sexuality, Mitchell says of this Moral Campaign that it had 'a healthy effect on the sales of the *Suffragette* – it appealed to ferocious spinsters ... and to long suffering wives who relished a vicarious revenge' (ibid., p. 226). No sane woman, of course, would object; all those who protest against male power are legitimate targets for abuse in Mitchell's scheme of values; they all have something 'wrong' with them.

Mitchell's concluding chapter is called 'Bitch Power' and in it he uses almost every trick of the male trade to malign her (for further discussion, see Elizabeth Sarah, 1982b, in press). He comments on Christabel's own account of the suffragette movement and the part she played in it *(Unshackled*, 1959) and states that the manuscript was not 'discovered' until after her death, and when published in 1959, 'it did not get a good press' (ibid., p. 317). He then proceeds to quote all the nasty comments the reviewers made – that 'My Mother right or wrong seems to sum up Dame Christabel's creed' (*The Times*) and 'In the *Daily Telegraph* Felicia Lamb questioned Christabel's claim to have a sense of humour – "what she and her comrades never foresaw was that instead of enfranchised women making pilgrimages to Caxton Hall, the suffragettes would become one of the comic side-shows of history like some of the puritan sects" ' (ibid.).

You see she was naive, she just believed in her mother; she was not to be taken seriously. She was nothing but a silly woman who was so lacking in a sense of humour (here we go again) that she did not even know how funny she and her friends appeared to the outside world; and she was even funnier about sex! In a manner which I have come to see as systematic, David Mitchell uses other women to speak for him. He takes critical comments on Christabel, made by contemporary feminists, and strings them together in an inventory of damnation. But those among us who have made these resources available to him are not paid, but are rather paid *back* for our helpful efforts. For Mitchell then proceeds to claim that the criticisms contemporary feminists have levelled at Christabel apply equally to themselves. We are all the same: there is no difference between Juliet Mitchell's movement of women's libbers, and that of Christabel Pankhurst's suffragettes. There is no 'significant difference between Christabel's *Great Scourge* thesis and the wilder rantings of Kate Millet, Ti-Grace Atkinson, Germaine Greer, or Martha Shelley. Millet denounces the beastliness of Henry Miller, D. H. Lawrence and Norman Mailer with a puritanical solemnity hardly matched by Christabel . . .' (ibid., p. 319). I suggest that if we are going to have to suffer with her it is in our interest to support her!

One woman does get a pat on the back from Mitchell – Arianna Stassinopoulos – whom he quotes, revealingly, as saying that 'some degree of male dominance is necessary in sexual relationships' (ibid.), obviously a point of view David Mitchell understands and identifies with. While sympathising with Stassinopoulos's point of view, he heatedly castigates Christabel for her anti-male stand (she did not even approve of a male auxiliary of the WSPU) and says that she 'came as close as she dared to Martha Shelley's claim that "lesbianism is one road to freedom from oppression by men" ' (ibid., p. 320).

In his objective and well-researched summation, David Mitchell declares that: 'Christabel did not rewrite the Bible or hark back to the good old days when God was a woman,' and he adds, leaving no mistake about the contempt in which he holds women, 'this omission has probably lowered her prestige amongst feminist historians and anthropologists' (ibid.).

Mitchell allows no chance to discredit her to slip by. It is beyond his comprehension that Christabel's position was one of autonomy, and that, in a society where women are oppressed, this is significant. So blind is he in his limited male experience of the world, he cannot even accord women responsibility for their own actions. Do you know how he accounts for the suffragette Movement? These bravoes were just 'ultra suggestible' – like Rose Dugdale and Patty Hearst! That women could reach different conclusions on the basis of different evidence yielded by different experience is a possibility that has not entered Mr Mitchell's head. The world, and women, will be made to fit his beliefs – and it is doubtful whether he believes women are part of humanity.

He concludes his biography on Christabel – *the only one there is* – with a self-revealing quote: 'a Bitch occupies a lot of psychological space. You always know she is around. A Bitch takes shit from no one, you may not like her, but you cannot ignore her' (ibid., p. 323). Mr Mitchell is *not* using the term bitch positively, as the original authors intended; Mitchell gives the source of the quote as the 'Bitch Manifesto', quoted in *Norman Mailer*. Honour among thieves.

It is extremely distressing that so little work has been done by women to reclaim Christabel Pankhurst, who has been subjected to some of the most savage patriarchal misrepresentation (with Elizabeth Sarah's 1982b astonishing and excellent account being the exception), and that David

Mitchell stands as the *sole* authority, and continues to portray her as a despicable character. It was he who wrote the article on her in *The Sunday Times* in 1980, in commemoration of the centenary of her birth, and his vituperative pen keeps alive the image of Christabel Pankhurst as a stupid and nasty woman who does not merit serious attention. It is an image I totally reject. At no stage would I want to declare her a flawless feminist, but I do want to suggest, with some passion and some 'proof', that there is much more to her and her ideas than we have been led to believe and that it is because she is of value to us that she has been so systematically maligned.

The basic difference between my own account and that of David Mitchell's is that I have tried to present some of the things she said and did which are useful and illuminating for us today; I have sifted through her writings with an eye for the positive aspects. Mitchell, on the other hand, has looked for ways to discredit her and has presented issues (and elaborations of them) which make her appear repellant. But while there are differences, Mitchell and I share one thing in common: *our stands are equally political*!

Had I chosen to discuss Christabel Pankhurst's lesbianism I should have done so in a context of independence; I should have seen her *decision* to work with women and to reject men as rational and radical. To Mitchell, however, lesbianism is just another means of bringing Christabel Pankhurst into disrepute, and I quote some of his statements as an example (although I must admit I am sorely tempted to ignore them rather than give them print space).

'Herself a Sanctified Sex object', he says derisorily, 'it was not surprising that sexual priggery, or female chauvinism, should become Christabel's distinctive contribution' – no matter what intellectual contribution one makes as a woman it is by sexuality one is judged, and there is no surer way of being judged wrathfully than to reject men. 'She had been edged into a stance of what might now be called political lesbianism' – note she did not even *choose* this position but presumably woke up one morning and found herself occupying it – 'and she was almost certainly a lesbian in the usual meaning of the word (although presumably repressed).' How is that for a clear definition of terms, and as a product of objective, scholarly endeavour?

Devaluing the whole concept of sisterhood by recourse to girls' boarding school imagery, he states that: 'The hot-house conventual atmosphere at WSPU headquarters had encouraged passionate crushes' and under pressure from the outside 'had spread the "Amazonian" spirit throughout the ever more youthful suffragette ranks' (ibid., p. 68). Christabel Pankhurst and the WSPU were a bad influence on young – impressionable – women; and Christabel is the one accused of 'priggery'?

There is no way we can accept David Mitchell's version of Christabel Pankhurst – and no way we can ignore what he has done. Commemorative articles often err on the side of unqualified eulogy; not so the one he wrote. With this article in 1980 we are witnessing part of the process of making one woman – whose ideas could be extremely valuable to us – disappear from the record. Who would want to know more about Christabel Pankhurst after David Mitchell has had his say?

I can only hope that he doesn't come forward in 1982 with a commemorative article on the centenary of Syliva Pankhurst's birth, for he treats her no less severely. For Sylvia the issues were very different and initially inextricably bound up with her desire to be an artist. Her own account of the 'tug of war' that went on inside her as a result of the conflicting demands of the suffragette movement and art makes harrowing reading (see S. Pankhurst, 1931). Her analysis of oppression has a much stronger conventional economic base, but her commitment to women, and to liberation, was no less than Christabel's, even if the vision that inspired it was somewhat different.

Says Mitchell (1977), 'the suffragette campaign was in many respects a projection of the melodrama of the Pankhurst family', for there was something unbalanced about all the Pankhurst women: 'Sylvia, herself subject from an early age to migraine and fainting fits and spectacularly over-sensitive (while painting scenery for a WSPU exhibition in 1909 she nearly swooned when mice ran across the studio – she was afraid they might get hurt)' (p. 28), was also quite disturbed, Mitchell implies. 'Sylvia denies that she was jealous of the fact that Christabel, the only child to be nursed by Mrs Pankhurst . . . was her mother's favourite' (ibid., p. 29), states Mitchell, cunningly constructing the negative image of Sylvia, the Pankhurst family and the suffragette movement. These are not political figures in a political movement – they are silly women drawing the public into a family feud, in which jealousy, incestuous relationships, and frustrated sexuality are the primary motivating sources. This is the *only way* Mitchell can make sense of active, male-power-resisting women!

Summing up the Pankhurst daughters after the suffrage movement, Mitchell says that: 'compared with the vehement activity of Adela (who having left the Communist Party in the early 1920s was interned as a pro-Japanese "fascist" in 1940) and of Sylvia (who championed the cause of Ethiopia with a sentimental passion . . .) Christabel's left-over life was placid to the point of vapidity' (ibid., p. 314). No matter what we do as women we simply won't be treated seriously. That's not all that Mitchell says: actually, I think he gets worse when talking about Mrs Pankhurst, who, as the mother, was – predictably – responsible for it all!

The children had a terrible upbringing, argues Mitchell, 'from the moment they could lisp a sentence or hand out a pamphlet, the children had been saturated in an atmosphere of what Dr Pankhurst liked to call "Noble endeavour". . . . It was a wonder that they did not break under the strain or kick over the traces' (ibid., p. 14). Mrs Pankhurst was the driving force behind all this (so Mitchell argues) for 'she was the sort of person who could never admit failure. Her marriage had to be splendid, her husband a Galahad, her daughter a genius. Criticism of them meant criticism of her, and that was something she could never support. Mrs Pankhurst and her daughters had their full share of the Doctor's unfaltering sense of self-importance and moral superiority. The difference was they were not content with moral victories. They intended to win and they were very bad losers' (ibid., p. 17).

Here they are nothing but selfish petulant women (with not a brain among them); in her own desire for the limelight, the mother put her daughters on the public stage. She *pushed* everyone ('The eager Emmeline drove him [Dr Pankhurst] almost literally to death', ibid., p. 19); she was undisciplined – unable to complete the course of reading her husband set her; no mention of four children, domestic work and support in his political campaigns of course, or of the discipline required for hunger and thirst striking. She was mercenary[5] and pretentious and insisted on a big house in Russell Square where the rent was high and where flowers were demanded (really, I am quoting from Mitchell), and where there could be significant social gatherings over which she could preside (ibid., pp. 20–1). Mitchell presents her as a shallow, grasping creature who wouldn't think of letting her daughters become school teachers and 'who kept the girls away from school on every possible pretext' partly because she was 'jealous of Christabel's wealthy school friends' (ibid., p. 36).

This is the assessment of the woman who started the WSPU (in order to get Christabel away from Eva Gore Booth and Esther Roper of whom she was also jealous according to Mitchell, jealousy seeming to suffice as an adequate explanation for a number of events), who was superb in the significance and stature she gave to the suffrage cause,[6] who by her example inspired thousands of women to take on the government, who worked increasingly in women's interests. But even David Mitchell's version tends to look quite flattering alongside that of Piers Brendon (1979).

In outlining some of the things Mr Brendon says, let me state from the outset that if it is noticed that all the references come from the first part of the article, the explanation is that I simply could not bear to read any more, and I even apologise to readers for inflicting this malicious diatribe upon them. If I did not feel so strongly that we should have no illusions about the way women are treated in a patriarchal society, I should omit Brendon altogether, but I feel confident that having become familiar with his assesssment of Emmeline Pankhurst – which is one of the most recent, and makes a considerable contribution to her representation in contemporary times – it will no longer be a question of how much more evidence do we need? We will have ample!

Mrs Pankhurst, says Brendon in his opening paragraph, was a 'castrating threat' for whom 'violence was less striking as a form of political agitation than as a mode of personal dominance', for she had the 'ruth-

---

[6] There is considerable evidence that Emmeline Pankhurst was not mercenary: she had to make a decision about whether she should keep her salaried job as Registrar (with its pension) or continue with her suffrage activities, even though the Registrarship was her only source of income and it certainly didn't appear as if suffrage would *pay*. She was always trying to earn money – this being the prime reason she went on lecture tours to the States. She once went on such a tour – reluctantly but necessarily – to earn money to pay for Harry's hospital bills.

[6] Years ago when my mother told me (sorry about this, Mum) that she was too old for feminism, I told her that at her age Emmeline Pankhurst was in prison on hunger strike.

lessness and a disposition to "smash" those who challenged her autocracy' (1979, p. 133). Not a pretty picture.

While suffragettes were in general the 'unenjoyed' (the arrogance of the man!), Mrs Pankhurst 'was the very antithesis of the frustrated spinster and the soured old maid'. She looked 'more like a quiet housewife going shopping', she enjoyed 'the drama of a sale and the excitement of employing sharp wits and sharper elbows to secure a bargain' and she 'revelled in the pretty clothes she bought and in adorning herself with a coquettish grace' (ibid., p. 135). Oblivious to any inconsistencies (and I suppose if you just want to be nasty there aren't any inconsistencies here), Brendon continues: 'Mrs Pankhurst had worshipped her husband with all the ardour of a romantic and all the abasement of a domestic' and had reared her children in a ridiculous manner 'insisting that they finish their lumpy porridge, forbidding her astigmatic son to wear spectacles, chastising recalcitrance, and once instructing the servants to tie her second daughter Sylvia to a bed all day for refusing to take her cod liver oil' (ibid., p. 136). Who would want to know more about this terrible woman? (By the way, Brendon quotes no sources!)

While declaring that Emmeline Pankhurst was 'a domestic ornament any man would have been proud to possess' (this is real, I am not making it up), Brendon indicates his complete contempt for the man who was taken in by her charms (and sorcery) and who, as he was unable to 'tame' her, ceases in many respects to qualify as a 'proper man'. 'Richard Marsden Pankhurst', he says, 'with his carroty beard and a piping treble voice which often caused him to be mistaken for a woman, seemed an improbable key to bliss. He was twice Emmeline's age. He had always lived with his Baptist parents and never left the house for an hour without telling them where he was going. A scholarly barrister, he was small, unprepossessing and so physically incompetent that his wife had to do all the carving. Still, he had beautiful hands . . .' even though, when he spoke he would claw 'the air with his long, curved finger-nails' (ibid., p. 145).

But if Emmeline Pankhurst got the better of Richard Pankhurst, there were other areas where she was less successful, and Brendon shows a distinct enthusiasm for quoting Ethel Smyth[7] in the interest of portraying Emmeline Pankhurst in a depreciating light. Mrs Pankhurst was 'intensely fastidious' says Brendon, but really it was all to no avail, as 'Being so "meticulously dainty" in her personal habits Mrs Pankhurst could never have realized, so Ethel Smyth reckoned, that during and after hunger-and-thirst strikes, her body feeding off its own tissue, emitted a "strange, pervasive, sweetish odour of corruption" ' (ibid., p. 136). Does such presentation require comment?

The imagery of evil and corruption are blended into Brendon's treat-

---

[7] Here is another woman who deserves much more attention – even if only because David Mitchell and Piers Brendon make so many disparaging statements about her: a musician and composer (she composed the *March of the Women* for which Cicely Hamilton wrote the words), an active suffragette who taught Mrs Pankhurst the art of stone throwing, she is described very positively by Lady Rhondda, in her autobiography (1933).

ment of Mrs Pankhurst, who was dominated by the 'terrific violence of her soul' (ibid., p. 134) and who inflicted it on her children. She was a dreadful mother: 'Christabel alone she nursed', we are informed again and a bond was forged 'between the feline daughter and the passionate mother' (ibid., p. 146). Towards the other children – particularly the sons – Mrs Pankhurst was totally irresponsible. The death of her first son from diphtheria is attributed to her mistreatment of her children (ibid., p. 147) and 'She did not scruple to sacrifice even her frail adolescent Harry' to the cause (ibid., p. 160).

Brendon implies that it wasn't all Mrs Pankhurst's fault that she was such a poor mother; her own mother was hardly a good example, for she too failed to live up to her theory of women's rights in practice, for 'despite the availability of contraceptives she allowed herself to become a breeding machine' (ibid., p. 142). Apart from the offensiveness and wilful misrepresentation involved here (that Mrs Goulden 'allowed herself to become a breeding machine' at a time when women had no rights at all upon marriage, and were legally as well as socially obliged to *submit* to their husbands), I was concerned about the accuracy of this statement in terms of the availability of contraception. With the help of Renate Duelli-Klein I set about finding what 'contraceptives' were available to women in 1858, and as far as we can determine the most used was an abortifacient – lead pills! Enough of them usually resulted in miscarriage and consequent illness, for women were actually giving themselves lead poisoning in order to stop having children (see Patricia Knight, 1977). So Piers Brendon scathingly dismisses Emmeline Pankhurst's mother for not giving herself lead poisoning when it was no great hassle to get lead pills from the chemist.

Trying to account for the driving force behind Emmeline Pankhurst, Brendon says that to her the 'ballot box, with its suggestive orifice (was) as a symbol of man's sovereign promiscuity' (ibid., p. 153), a statement which leaves me astonished, and, while it says little about Mrs Pankhurst, it reveals much about the writer. The depreciating list goes on and on: we are informed that Mrs Pankhurst could not sing (ibid., p. 158) and that her first militant steps were a 'ravishing adventure. The glare of publicity quite made Mrs Pankhurst's skin glow' (ibid., p. 159), and in an attempt to 'ruin the reputation' of Mrs Pankhurst and one of her daughters, Brendon says that in the case of Keir Hardie 'his compassion for women in general was a symptom of his passion for the Pankhurst women in particular. Rumour-mongers scented hanky-panky, hinted that Hardie knew Emmeline better than he should have done. . . . And he undoubtedly did have carnal knowledge of Sylvia' (ibid.). There is more in the same vein.

Brendon weaves a condemnation of Christabel in with that of Mrs Pankhurst and artfully contrives to use them against each other. One such incident he employs for this purpose is that of the 1908 trial. Having issued handbills calling for women to 'rush' parliament, Christabel, Mrs Pankhurst and the General wound up in the dock, charged with inciting the public to wrongful and illegal acts. Christabel conducted a brilliant defence, part of which was to subpoena Lloyd George and Gladstone (who were witnesses of the demonstration) and to have them answer questions about the government's policy – and past and present practices – *under oath*. As Lloyd George had also had his granddaughter with him while he watched the 'rush', Christabel contended that either it was not a dangerous demonstration, or he was an irresponsible grandfather! A transcript of the trial is available at the Fawcett Library and makes entertaining reading; it also promotes admiration for Christabel's considerable skill as a lawyer – not that she was permitted to practise at the Bar, of course. While Brendon admits her defence was 'clever', the real secret of her success however 'lay in her fresh white muslin dress with the broad band of purple, white and green stripes around her lissome waist, of the silky curls with just a hint of gold in them clustering demurely about her neck, of her alabaster skin and rose-petal cheeks, more exquisitely flushed than usual' (ibid., p. 166). This is no compliment; it is the theft of her intelligence.

'But', adds Brendon, 'though she was "bright and dainty as a newly opened flower" and though she up-staged both magistrate and ministers, Christabel could not steal the scene from so experienced a tragedienne as her mother' (ibid.). These are the women who have committed political offences, who are on trial (Mrs Pankhurst was given three months, and Christabel ten weeks, and the conditions were absolutely degrading and demoralising – see Appendix I), who are conducting themselves with courage and conviction. Piers Brendon treats the whole show as a theatrical little game.

It is not just the Pankhurst women either who come in for such virulent attack. Even women who in other sources are portrayed as eminently respectable are ridiculed by Brendon, Lady Constance Lytton (Anna Wheeler's granddaughter) being a case in point. Having once been arrested, gone on hunger strike, and been released without being forcibly fed, Constance Lytton decided that she was getting preferential treatment because of her position. So, next time she threw stones and got arrested she gave her name as 'Jane Warton' and *was* forcibly fed when she went on hunger strike. The publicising of this caused the government even greater embarrassment – particularly as few were prepared to assert that Lady Constance (whose brother Lord Lytton chaired the 'Conciliation Committee' of Members of Parliament) was not a lady. Brendon says of her that she was 'a strict vegetarian won over to the cause by perceiving in the maltreatment of a sheep on its way to the slaughterhouse a revelation of "the position of women throughout the world" ' (ibid.). By this means every woman, and every aspect of women's struggle is increasingly belittled.

While I could keep on quoting his self-revealing perversity and prejudice, I think that this constitutes sufficient evidence of the way women are represented in a male-dominated society. The hostility, and the fear, *he* has of Mrs Pankhurst, her mother and her daughters, is apparent on every page (or more accurately, the ones I have read) and yet few are the critics, I suspect, who would comment on *his* theatrical tricks and melodramatic presentation. Will there be voices raised in protest among the literati about *his* emotionalism, his woman-hating, his lack of intellectual ability? I doubt it. While he refers to Mrs Pankhurst as a member of the 'shrieking sisterhood' there isn't even a comparable epithet with which to label him; men do not perceive themselves as unreasonable in relation to women so they have no need to generate words for a state which, to their mind, does not exist.

But whereas Brendon makes me furious, some of the other accounts of the militants just leave me discouraged. Nowhere have I found a positive appraisal of their stand or an illuminating account of their ideas. Antonia Raeburn (1974), for some inexplicable reason, has J. B. Priestley (whom we have met before) introduce her version of the period and the women, and Priestley offers little hope of reclaiming them when he asks whether the suffragettes were 'manhating shrieking viragos' or whether they possessed 'a naive and even childlike quality which might encourage irrationality and deliberate misbehaviour' (pp. 11–12). It's not much of a choice – again, either way, they are damned. At the risk of repetition, I think I have to say that I have never known a male political rebel to be discussed in terms of 'child-like' and 'misbehaviour'.

And throughout *Militant Suffragettes*, which is undoubtedly the best portrayal we have, there are still the constant disparaging asides which help to reduce the women and render them 'unattractive': 'Christabel was an avid reader and when she spent weekends with the Pethick-Lawrences in Surrey, she was always the first to look at the morning papers. As she finished a page, it was thrown to the floor, and someone had carefully to collect up and reassemble the scattered papers before the master of the house appeared' (1974, pp. 52–3). Where does such detail come from (no sources are given), and what is the point of including it, unless the aim is to discredit her?

Even Ray Strachey (1928), usually so scrupulously careful, doesn't let the suffragettes pass without casting aspersions on them. Her sympathies were with Millicent Garrett Fawcett and the constitutionalists, and perhaps this is the explanation for her derogatory remarks about the militants whose propaganda rang with notes of 'defiance, antagonism, suspicion' and whose 'deliberate policy was to seek sensational achievement rather than anything else' (p. 309). They were publicity seekers, they were dishonourable, they had no scruples about brushing aside the ordinary niceties of procedure, says Strachey, for 'they did not care whom they shocked and antagonised . . . and laughed at all talk of persuasion. What they believed in was moral violence', and she adds, their 'policy of sensational public protest was not one which left much time for the tasks of self-government, nor was democracy much to their taste' (pp. 309–10). She also objected to the air of mystery which constantly surrounded the militants who were 'outside the law'.

And this was in 1928: it is a record written by a feminist who witnessed much of the struggle (she was born in 1887) and who was deliberately helping to construct positive images of women and women's history. I do not think we can afford to treat each other in this way when we do not control knowledge. Everything we say against other women is ultimately used against us. For my part I intend to keep silent on those issues I am encouraged to speak on; I have plenty to keep me talking on those issues which are taboo.

(C)

WRITING AS POLITICS

1 After the battles

After the devastation, disillusionment, and despair that many had experienced with the First World War, the 1920s – on both sides of the Atlantic and in Australasia – ushered in a period of hope for the future. This is understandable; it would have been easy enough at the time to have believed that the war represented the absolute worst that could happen, and that things could only improve after it. If, with hindsight, this may seem a naïve point of view, it is worth bearing in mind that it was probably a necessary point of view – in terms of maintaining one's sanity. So traumatising was the war that many saw it as an end to a particular phase of civilisation, a form of destruction from which man *must* learn, and for those like Crystal Eastman and Vera Brittain (1896–1970) it meant a commitment to uncompromising pacifism, and a conviction that absolutely nothing could justify such depravity. For them hope lay in part in peace movements and their promotion.

But there were other reasons for optimism and for many different expressions of it. In Britain it was not just that the war was over and that a new philosophy and practice for living had to be found, it was also that there were qualitative differences for women – legally, socially and personally – when it came to their 'before and after' war status. To many it looked as though woman's time had come.

The legal impediments no longer applied as they had done. Some women were now enfranchised and a major obstacle to full participation in public life had been removed, for the blatant argument that no woman was fit to hold public office (and therefore that all women had to be legally debarred from doing so) was no longer tenable. And socially the time was propitious, for people were questioning the social values which had led to the war and were prepared to entertain the possibility of alternatives. Many women believed women *did* have an alternative and that the time was ripe for its introduction. Vera Brittain (1953) summed up this position with the statement that it had been: 'The masculine principle of power and tyranny' which had produced the war and that this must now give way to 'the feminine principle of love and co-operation' so that society could be 're-deemed and transformed' (p. 10).

For individual women, the world – and their rights within that world – also looked very different during the 1920s. Prior to this period there are often references within women's literature to the sense of individual inferiority and personal inhibition which prevented women from claiming an equal place in society. In the absence of evidence that women are equal, there are the self-doubts and the fears, as women ask what the consequences will be if and when they take the steps into the unknown. After this 'tradition' it comes as something of a surprise to encounter not only the optimism but the confidence in the future of many women of this period. Rather than seeking permission to enter the male domains, quite a few women assumed they had a perfect right to go in – and not only that, but to go in, have a look around, and to decide whether or not they wanted to join!

One of the reasons for this was the vote. Understandably, many women felt they had *won* the right to do what men did, and after the victory they were not so likely to be intimidated by men, or inhibited by their own fears of inadequacy. There had been a battle and women had won, and now they wanted to get on with the work they had to do. Far from being a single-issue movement which disintegrated once the franchise had been achieved (I am assuming no one has any doubts about the source of this particular historical interpretation), there were many members of the women's movement who loudly proclaimed that their work was about to begin, and not that their movement was about to end. They started to set their sights on future goals which would help to realise equality, widely recognised as being symbolic only in nature, at this stage.

Millicent Garrett Fawcett had argued in the early days of the suffrage movement that it was more a question of what the vote would do for women than what women would do with the vote – and that was long before militant suffrage tactics had been dreamed of. Her prediction seems largely to have been vindicated, partly because of the militancy. While I can find no single study of the significance for women of being able to perceive themselves as possessing power and influence (which is hardly surprising as I suspect the findings of such a study would not be ones you would want to promote in a patriarchal society), some women have provided records about their feelings in the 1920s and these help to explain their air of optimism.

2　Funding for feminism: Lady Rhondda (1883–1958)

Reared among what would have to be the most privileged of circumstances for the time (I am referring to psychological as well as material factors), Margaret Haig (Lady Rhondda) describes, none the less, in her autobiography (1933), her acute lack of confidence and absence of purpose as a young woman, that is, until she joined the WSPU. It brought about a remarkable change. She became a militant, went to prison (despite considerable opposition) and experienced a marked growth in self-esteem. 'I had loved, it is true, every minute of that militant fight before the war', she says, for it 'had to be done. There are times when to change the law is the quickest – indeed the only way to change public opinion. The period of the militant movement had been such a time. But', she adds, oblivious to the interpretation provided by historians, 'even so that fight of ours was only ostensibly concerned with changing the law. The vote was really a symbol. And *the militant fight itself did more to change the status of women – because it did more to alter our own opinions of ourselves* – than ever the vote did' (p. 299, my emphasis).

It was the militancy, the sense of being able to *do* something to influence one's destiny, of being able to act and having those actions taken into account, that for Margaret Haig meant the end of self-doubt and the growth of self-esteem. It was the recognition that she didn't have to remain invisible, that she was not obliged to sacrifice her own interests for those of a man, that helped her to establish her entitlement to her own space in her own right; she changed from a shy, self-effacing housewife to a very assured (and divorced) business-woman.

Her father died in March 1918; she took over his extensive business interests and ran them most successfully. But business on its own was not enough – she still felt the need to *do* something to change the world. As a suffragette a whole new range of possibilities had been presented to her – and not just as they related to how to go to gaol. She had also come across the possibilities of women's knowledge: 'One of the first effects that joining the militant movement had on me, as perhaps on the majority of those of my generation who went into it', she says, 'was that it forced me to educate myself' (ibid., p. 125). She had been forced to find out what women had done, what women's arguments had been, and were (particularly so that she could answer hecklers at public meetings), and she found the process invigorating. She describes how exciting and stimulating it was to read all the feminist literature (although she also adds that there was not a great deal of it), and what strength and joy there was to be found in Cicely Hamilton's *Marriage as a Trade* (1909) and Olive Schreiner's *Woman and Labour* (1911). This was a new and more satisfactory way of looking at the old value system; these were the explanations that had been left out. They were women's view.

But Lady Rhondda found something else as well. By the twentieth century the disciplines had evolved; knowledge had become structured into various discrete departments with few links between them, and she perceived then what many still fail to recognise today – that feminism is not just *another* compartment. She scoffed at the idea that women's knowledge was but a sub-section that could be added on to the existing disciplines, and discovered then what we were to rediscover about fifty years later, that feminism was an alternative to these many man-made divisions. It was women's view on *all* the disciplines; it was a different perspective on the world.

From feminist literature 'a dozen paths led out into other subjects, each of which bore on feminism in one way or another,' she writes, 'and each of which needed exploring. One wanted to read up political science and economics. One wanted to have some general idea of psychology and sociology, and even of anthropology. And one wanted to get to the theories and reasons behind the facts' (1933, p. 126). One wanted to describe and explain the world from the perspective of 'the new woman' – not deferentially or apologetically, but firmly and positively. Yet the place for doing this in a public forum was so rare as to be non-existent.

In trying to give some idea of how restricted the access was to new, challenging knowledge, Lady Rhondda quotes an incident in relation to Havelock Ellis's book *The Psychology of Sex*. 'It was the first thing of its kind I had found', she says, and, 'Though I was far from accepting it all, it opened up a whole new world of thought to me. I discussed it at some length with my father, and he, much interested, went off to buy the set of volumes for himself; but in those days, one could not walk into a shop and buy "The Psychology of Sex"; one had to produce some kind of signed certificate from a doctor or a lawyer to the effect that one was a suitable person to read it' (ibid., pp. 126–7). The reason Lady Rhondda had been able to read it, while her father – to his indignation, could not – was because of the practical provisions made by Ruth Cavendish Bentink who had established a library[1] and who 'was at the time supplying all the young women in the suffrage movement with the books they could not procure in the ordinary way' (ibid., p. 127).

This experience left a deep impression on Margaret Haig. In her own life she had known what it was to be 'kept in ignorance', to be bound to convention and to accept without challenge the prevailing (and man-made) ideologies which curtailed her existence; in stark contrast she had come to know what it was to be freed from those restrictive injunctions, to find the world transformed, to taste the delight and excitement of thinking, explaining, inquiring, debating, the unencoded and unclarified needs and interests of women. In the 1970s no doubt we would have referred to this experience of Lady Rhondda's as consciousness-raising; to Lady Rhondda it was a passionate and urgent desire to understand and change customs, to influence and generate ideas (ibid., p. 300). In the 1970s we started newsletters and networks; in the 1920s – with her own resources – she started the weekly periodical *Time and Tide*, which survived for almost forty years. Such a review had not been founded by a woman before, but this was not the only 'novelty'; the political periodical (based on the format of the *New Statesman*) was to be run by women.

Emerging as it did in the period when the last obstacles to women's political participation were being removed, *Time and Tide* was to have a parliamentary flavour. Its symbol (or logo) contained Big Ben, and the 'tide' flowing under Westminster Bridge. It was to be a journal where women could take their place in political discussion and debate, where they could evaluate policies, and put forward their own ideas. It was to be a 'political pressure' periodical. It was to be a feminist forum, but definitely

---

[1] The library is now the Cavendish Bentink Collection and is housed in the Fawcett Library.

not a 'ghetto' (which would be the contemporary label for the marginal status *Time and Tide* was seeking to avoid).

Besides reporting on international movements, particularly those related to the League of Nations, and to peace movements, it supported women members of parliament (of all parties); it addressed the problems of parliamentary legislation 'in women's interest' (the conflict between 'equality' and 'special' treatment for women); it monitored bills that related to women and reported on the voting patterns of male members of the House when it came to bills relating to women. We have no such mainstream journal today which acts as a woman's 'watchdog' on parliament, reveals who is lobbying whom, and why, or records the voting habits of male members on issues that relate specifically to women.

In 1921, the year after *Time and Tide* was established, Lady Rhondda also inaugurated the Six Point Group – so called because of the six points it formulated for parliamentary action in the interest of women's equality. In January 1923, the 'Six Point Group Supplement' appeared in *Time and Tide*; it was written by Elizabeth Robins and stated that the first point which required parliamentary action was child assault. (Other points were legislation for widows, satisfactory legislation for the unmarried mother and her child, equal guardianship, equal pay, and equality of opportunity in the work force. *Time and Tide* and the Six Point Group may have gone;[2] some of the problems remain.)

Crystal Eastman and Elizabeth Robins were regular contributors to *Time and Tide*; so too were Vera Brittain and Winifred Holtby when they came down from Oxford, with Winifred Holtby becoming a director of the paper in 1926; Rebecca West features prominently in the pages, as do E. M. Delafield and Cicely Hamilton (one of the founding contributors). Here is a group of women making practical use of their newfound comparative equality and freedom; they are openly discussing the political and social issues of their time in a manner which women had not done before – from the premise that they were the political equals of men. Within a context of a community of women they exchanged ideas, generated a framework for the interpretation of political events, formulated social policies and priorities and developed a basis for understanding and influencing the public world from which women had for so long been excluded.

They expected to be economically independent; they expected to be heard, and to be taken seriously. They also assumed the centrality of feminism and expected it to be taken seriously as well. They have left behind a fascinating record (if one can find it) of women's response to their new and relatively more responsible role, and of the nature and development of feminist ideas within this context.

Much has gone with the demise of *Time and Tide*; while its passing makes me sad, however, its *invisibility* makes me mad! It is a case of having

---

[2] The Six Point Group has only recently disbanded: Hazel Hunkins-Hallinan, now in her nineties and one of its most committed members, has lodged the papers of the Six Point Group with the Fawcett Library. (Regrettably, Hazel Hunkins-Hallinan died in May 1982.)

to know about it before one can know about it. Housed as it is in the Colindale 'depot' of the British Library and available on request, it could not be more effectively hidden from enquiring minds; and few are the women likely to stumble over it as a fortuitous accident. Such a radical journal for its time – in some ways it would be a radical journal today – it has been removed from public view and effectively buried. Another part of our immediate heritage virtually erased: with its disappearance we have also lost the contributions of many radical and illuminating women writers and thinkers of the time.

3 On 'showing men up': Cicely Hamilton (1872–1952)

It is not at all surprising that Cicely Hamilton should have been involved in *Time and Tide* from the outset – and not just because Lady Rhondda had been so influenced by *Marriage as a Trade*. At the time, Cicely Hamilton was a highly esteemed writer of fiction and non-fiction and not only shared, but had helped to shape, some of the new values Lady Rhondda had come to adopt and which she now wanted to develop. Cicely Hamilton was a champion of women's independence – her own life was a struggle as a single woman for economic independence which she perceived as necessary for emotional independence – and this was the underlying theme of her writing. (She wrote many novels, a highly successful play, *How the Vote was Won* – performed in 1909 – 'A Pageant of Great Women' for the suffrage exhibition in 1910, two children's plays, travel books, as well as a history of the Old Vic and her critiques of male power and aggression, see Jane Lewis, 1981. Her writing is, of course, not generally known and is rarely – if ever – studied in the halls of learning.)

Cicely Hamilton's life was not an easy one; she had gone from teacher to actress to writer in her quest for economic independence, and it was a hard struggle all the way (see Hamilton, 1935). But she did not pretend that it was easy for women to be autonomous – economically and psychologically – in a male-dominated society; indeed it was central to her argument that in order to make marriage compulsory for women, men had been obliged to establish a whole range of economic and psychological punishments for women who did not marry. But she defied men, not only by remaining single, but by exposing them in her writing. There can be no doubt that she was successful when it came to psychological independence from men, for there is not a semblance of deference to them, or dependence on them, in her description and analysis of society. When women were enjoined to be agreeable as a mark of their (male-defined) womanliness, Cicely Hamilton obviously took great pleasure in confounding their edicts, and she stands as one of the most 'disagreeable' among women.

Her contrariness and her defiance found encouragement and support in the context of women's militancy, and Hamilton assumes (in 1909) that there is a conflict of interest between women and men, and that it is because men have the power and the wealth that their interests have prevailed.

However, contrary to what men would *like* women to believe, Hamilton was convinced that women were not powerless. She argued that women could begin to claim their own autonomy, they could start by being psychologically independent and defining their own lives in their own terms. Men will have to *react*, she argued (as they have had to react to militancy), and part of the power nexus will be broken; women will then be in a better position to claim their share of the world's resources.

In *Marriage as a Trade*, Hamilton certainly practised what she preached. There are continual references to women's emotional management of men, to women's reluctance to 'show men up' in the work place or the home (she includes discussion of sexual harassment as well), and while women continue to behave in this way, she argues, denying their own needs, aspiration, and *anger*, men are allowed to go on feeling superior. This has got to stop, insists Hamilton, and *she* stops emotionally managing men and massaging their egos, with the result that from beginning to end *Marriage as a Trade* is an outspoken denunciation of men and their arrangements for society.

Hamilton gives sound reasons for her stand and they are similar to those used by the suffragettes. Firstly, she argues, most of what we know in our society has been made up by men and they have invented much which is purely and simply a cover-up for their own self-interest – partly because if their motives and practices were openly displayed, they would in all likelihood promote protest. But, she warns, if we accept the explanations that men have provided, then we are bound to accept their 'truth' that they are superior and we are subordinate, and we are bound to live our lives accordingly. If, however, we *know* an alternative, if we generate our own knowledge, our own explanations, in which men are not at all superior and we are not at all subordinate, if we start to construct our own 'truth' about our own equality, then this can become the guiding principle of our lives. We will *act* differently to take account of our *actions*. Men will have to learn in part to accommodate our view of the world, to fit in with our ideas and explanations; it will no longer be a matter of us willingly fitting into their plans.

She appreciates that this is easier said than done. It means women have to claim their own resources for themselves, that they have to overcome the deeply entrenched belief that men know best, and that man is the authoritative sex. But look around you, she urges women of her day, look and learn that it is woman who can define and is defining herself, and in complete contradiction to the prescriptions formulated by man. Of the militant suffragette who has challenged authority, Hamilton says that: 'Authority . . . is a broken reed. Has she not heard and read solemn disquisitions by men of science on the essential limitations of woman's nature and the consequent impossibility of activity in this or that direction? – knowing all the while, that what they swear to her she cannot do she does, is doing day by day' (1909, p. 33).

To dispute man's authority, to decide as a woman for oneself, is to claim full humanity, asserts Hamilton, and it goes without saying that men do not want this to happen (or even, that they will do everything in their power to prevent this happening). Once a class of human beings has reached the stage of doubting the authority of their superiors, once they have found the resources to frame the question 'Why is this?', they 'can no longer be satisfied with the answer "Because I wish it". That is an answer which inevitably provokes the rejoinder "But I do not" – which is the essence and foundation of heresy and high treason' (ibid., pp. 48–9).

In 1980, Adrienne Rich called upon women to be 'disloyal to civilization', to be disloyal to the social values which men had established and which made so much violence and oppression seem sensible and sound; when Cicely Hamilton in 1909 called on women to engage in heresy and high treason in a patriarchal society, she was seeking a very similar protest and form of resistance from women.

Women must 'be allowed to see things in their own way and with an eye to their own interests spiritual and material' (ibid., p. 49) she argues, for becoming *active,* taking back our intelligence and using it to describe, explain and construct our version of the world is one of the initial, and one of the biggest steps, in claiming and establishing our authority. Aphra Behn, 'Sophia', Frances Wright and Matilda Joslyn Gage would all have applauded.

It is in the context of taking back our intelligence as women and using it in a manner that is consistent with our values and our vision, that *Marriage as a Trade* is written. In it Hamilton begins with the acknowledgement that one of the most notable features of woman's existence is its absence. In a manner which Ann Oakley was to adopt again almost seventy years later (*The Sociology of Housework,* 1974), Hamilton states that woman's world has not been documented from the perspective of those who inhabit it and that this is a glaring, significant but 'sensible' omission in a male-dominated world: 'The only excuse for this book', she writes as her opening lines, 'is the lack of books on the subject with which it deals – the trade aspect of marriage' (1909, p. 17).

Why should this be, she asks? Undoubtedly 'an enquiry into the circumstances under which the wife and mother plies her trade seems to me quite as necessary and as justifiable as an enquiry into the conditions of other less important industries – such as mining and cotton spinning' (ibid., p. 17). And her impertinence is offensive; it is meant to be. Not only does she call into question the value of what men do (in the mining and textile industries) but at the same time she asserts that marriage is also an industry, a form of trade. This is being most 'disagreeable', for have not men decreed that marriage is 'different', that women marry for love (not necessity), and that all is explained by romance? Decidedly unromantic, Hamilton asserts that women marry to earn a living (and a very poor one), and *love* is mocked in the process.

Hamilton's case (which she is sure men do not want to hear for the very reason that it seriously undermines their own), is that it is just as reasonable to examine the effect of working conditions upon women as it is upon men, and without the camouflage of 'love and romance' (a complete and convenient male invention according to Hamilton). The working conditions of women appear so appalling that one must ask why it is women enter such employment. And here is the crux of the matter; *it is the only field men have permitted them.*

What a useful arrangement, she says, for men; they have forced women to undertake the tasks which they find distasteful and have thereby removed women as competitors from tasks that are more to male tastes. But they have gone even further than this for, not only have they failed to *pay* women for their labour, they have insisted that women undertake these tasks because they want to, because they like it, because it is 'natural' to them. 'One wonders why it should be "natural" in woman to do so many disagreeable things,' says Hamilton. 'Does the average man really believe that she has an instinctive and unquenchable craving for all the unpleasant and unremunerative jobs?' (ibid., p. 68).

Of course not. The average man believes – because he wants to – that woman is his inferior and it is therefore proper – and even her duty – for her to perform those tasks he would find demanding and demeaning. Because he has made sure that other more rewarding and remunerative jobs are not readily available, the average woman has no choice but to go along with these arrangements and to accept man's explanation that they are 'natural'. The only thing that is natural about this division of labour, argues Hamilton, in tones which echo many of her foremothers, is that the group who has power gets its own way. It is nothing other than 'the right of the strongest to avoid payment' (ibid., p. 60); it is men stealing women's labour.

Hamilton's thesis and her style are in many ways comparable to those of Charlotte Perkins Gilman, and *Marriage as a Trade* could have aptly been entitled *Women and Economics*. Like Gilman, she is concerned to show that men's economic explanations apply only to themselves and that it is no mere accident that women and their work are omitted from consideration. Like Gilman, she wants to demonstrate that man sees himself as the representative human being, and sees his experience and explanation as total, and valid, while woman – who exists only in relation to him – is of a different order, having no autonomy, and no claim to the same human needs and rights that he accords himself.

There is a vast discrepancy, says Hamilton, between the way men see women, and the way women can see themselves. For while it is possible for women to accept themselves as complete entities, it 'is hardly necessary to point out that the mental attitude of the average man towards woman is something quite different. ... As far as I can make out', she adds, 'he looks upon her as something having a definite and physical relation to a man; without that definite and necessary relation she is, as the cant phrase goes, incomplete' (ibid., p. 20).

Hamilton makes no attempt to conceal her scorn for this ridiculous form of reasoning which has led men to argue – seriously – that a woman 'is not a woman at all – until man has made her so. Until the moment when he takes her in hand she is merely the raw material of womanhood – the undeveloped and unfinished article' (ibid.). What advantages this line of reasoning has for man, she says with biting wit; we 'must sympathise with the pleasurable sense of importance, creative power, even of artistry, which such a conviction must impart. To take the imperfect and undeveloped creature and, with a kiss upon her lips and a ring upon her finger, to make her a woman, perfect and complete.' It is indeed a 'most admirable, most enviable' skill that man informs us he possesses (ibid., pp. 20–1).

This, however, bad enough as it is, is not the end of it, says Hamilton, for man's limited logic has led him to other ludicrous conclusions. Because he has come to believe that he has the power to transform the raw material into the finished product, he has a habit of seeing woman as incomplete without him, as waiting for him to materialise and make his magic. He has come to the conclusion, she says, that woman 'exists only for the purpose of attaining completeness through him' (ibid., p. 21) and, while it may be highly advantageous for man to believe this, woman believes him at her peril!

Man would like woman to believe that he is psychologically necessary to her, that it is through him she will find fulfilment, says Hamilton, but perhaps woman does not believe it at all. That she does not *contradict* him cannot be taken as evidence of agreement, for, in Hamilton's terms, where marriage is a trade, it may be that in the interest of keeping her job a woman finds it politic to agree with her employer! Looking at marriage from the perspective of women, through the lens of economics, certainly makes a difference to the way it is described and explained, and it is understandable that this should be a description and explanation that men might not want to hear, for it does not reflect simply on their social arrangements – but on themselves! There is the distinct possibility that they may not be the blessing to women that they have portrayed themselves to be.

In more primitive times, argues Hamilton, even men admit that they had to take a woman by force, for when a woman was capable of supplying her own needs she was unlikely to be enthusiastic, or even willing, to enter permanent servitude: her 'wants being few and easily supplied by herself' – her reluctance was comprehensible enough 'for there was no need for her to exchange the possession of her person for the means of existence' (ibid., p. 22). But in contemporary times, argues Hamilton, when man has deprived her of the means of supplying her own wants, she has no choice but to form a relationship with a man to provide him with her person, surrender all her resources, in order to exist. Force is no longer necessary, for no other alternatives for her exist.

Women, states Hamilton, with a note of menace, do not keep themselves alive to find a husband as many a man would like to believe, but find a husband to keep themselves alive (ibid., p. 25). It may be flattering for man to think the former – that he is the prime reason for woman's existence – but the time has come, she argues, for woman boldly to state the latter, that she is required to be his servant and breeding machine because there is no other way she can support herself. This is not emotional management of men; it is no ego-massage-message, but a deliberate assault on male pride and male power, with the avowed intention of breaking the psychological hold man has over woman.

Men, says Hamilton, have made marriage compulsory in order to make themselves necessary to women. They have used every trick of the marketplace to ensure that women must look to them for survival. They have made it almost impossible for a woman to support herself (and Hamilton speaks from bitter experience), and they have heaped ridicule on those women who have attempted to do so. They have insisted that *all* women should be destined and educated from birth, for the one calling, marriage, and when such a large body of persons has no choice in the market, and when 'every other calling and means of livelihood is barred to them you have all the conditions necessary for the forcing down of wages to the lowest possible point to which they will go – subsistence point' (ibid., p. 66).

Women, says Hamilton, should go on strike. They should organise, withdraw their labour, be their own persons, take back their own resources. But this possibility men have also foreseen and have attempted to preempt: 'I need scarcely point out that man, like every other wage payer, has done his level best and utmost to suppress the spirit of combination, and encourage distrust and division, amongst the wage earners in the matrimonial market; and that the trade of marriage, owing to the isolation of the workers, has offered unexampled opportunities for such suppression of unity and encouragement of distrust and division' (ibid., p. 39).

Marriage was a means whereby men divided women, and ruled; a means whereby men stole women's labour; a means whereby men made themselves necessary to women and at the same time ensured their superiority, both real and apparent. The whole system of marriage worked wonderfully well – for men, argued Hamilton, but the foundations on which it rested were precarious. Marriage depended for its continued existence in large measure on the willingness of women to say that it was what they wanted, to agree (can you believe?) that it suited them, and that they were content. Once women started to assert that they did not want it, it would not work so well; those foundations on which it rested were likely to crumble and even to collapse. It was in women's power to defy men's ideas, to challenge their authority.

Hamilton was influenced by the militant movement and the militant movement was influenced by Hamilton, as Lady Rhondda, Winifred Holtby, and many more testified. This was women using their energy, their resources, and their intelligence, to act in women's interest, and there was every reason to believe that it worked.

Cicely Hamilton recognised what a few contemporary commentators on her have not – that it was necessary for woman to be *seen* as independent of man – economically, psychologically and *sexually*. While she never used the term 'heterosexuality', there can be no misunderstanding her meaning when she declares that man has made marriage compulsory for woman in order to ensure that he is necessary, and that a spinster, far from being *unchosen* and a figure of fun and foolishness, can be a woman who has made a *choice*. Because that choice is not a man, then men must confront 'the unpalatable fact that sexual intercourse was not for every woman an absolute necessity' (ibid., p. 36). Man must face the fact that he is not the centre of a woman's universe, not necessary to her existence. To me this foreshadows the radical feminist stance of Adrienne Rich: goddess deliver me from those who insist upon it as a prudish, reactionary stand and an inexplicable defence of celibacy!

In 1909 Cicely Hamilton was arguing from a position of women's strength; she was arguing for women's independence and positive self-esteem, and she saw the relationship between the sexes as an area of conflict. By the 1920s interpretations had shifted and feminists in general were more inclined to argue that the sexes were *inter*-dependent, and that women should be seeking a means of conciliation, rather than confrontation, with men.

It was in keeping with the values of the time for Cicely Hamilton to insist in *Marriage as a Trade* that man denied women's intellectual resources: man says that 'women could not think even if they tried,' she wrote (p. 51), and when women defy his injunction and demonstrate that they can and do think, it is discounted as 'intuition', a secondary, inferior, undisciplined, uncontrolled and 'lucky' method of reaching conclusions, but still another way of robbing women of their intelligence (ibid., p. 52). By the 1920s such a stand would not have been so popular when there was more of a consensus among feminists – particularly some of those who worked at *Time and Tide* – that women were the intellectual equals of men and that there could be a mutual exchange of ideas between the sexes. Given that most of the women suffered a similar fate whether they believed in conciliation or confrontation, there doesn't seem to be much point in trying to decide which interpretation was 'right' and which was 'wrong'; differences among women fade into insignificance in a male-dominated society where, in the end, most women are treated the same way on the basis of their sex.

But I have quoted Cicely Hamilton at some length because I see *Marriage as a Trade* as part of the tradition of 'fighting words' which resurfaced again in the 1970s. Dilys Laing (1906–1960) once wrote of one of her foremothers, the poet Anne Finch, Countess of Winchilsea (1661–1720) with whom she identified,

> Lost lady! Gentle fighter!
> Separate in time, we mutiny together
> (Laing, 1974, p. 329)

It is very much how I feel about Cicely Hamilton (not that she was such a 'gentle fighter' in 1909).

In 1923, an unsigned article appeared in *Time and Tide* on Cicely Hamilton. The writer lists many of the plays Hamilton wrote and produced, comments on her prominence as a suffragist and her success as a journalist, speaks of her irreverent humour and states that Hamilton was 'unhelpful' at the interview – when asked how she would like herself portrayed, she replied 'Whatever you say I don't suppose it will matter to me one way or another a year from now' (Anon, 1923a, p. 83). But the writer is undaunted – Hamilton's biographers, she says, '(it seems probable that she will have them)' (ibid., p. 84), will put the record right. Hamilton has not had her biographers; the record is grossly distorted.

4 A different documentary: Elizabeth Robins (1862–1952)

Nor is the record right when it comes to one of Hamilton's contemporaries who was also a woman of fighting words – Elizabeth Robins. Sharing many of Hamilton's ideas, she has also shared a similar fate. A contributor to *Time and Tide* and a militant suffragette along with Lady Rhondda (Robins was a member of the WSPU committee from its inception and *agreed* with WSPU policy – not that this is ever commented upon; the ones who are quoted in sources are, predictably, generally those who disagreed), she had also been an actress and a writer, like Cicely Hamilton. Born in America, and having run away to go on the stage when she was sent away to college, Elizabeth Robins married for a short period of time (her husband was drowned) and then, in Jane Marcus's words she 'rejected the demands of the heterosexual life and turned to a network of women' (1980a, p. vi).

She spent her life working with and helping to organise women – even in the fields of acting and writing. When she arrived in England in the late 1880s she was quickly involved in the struggle for women's rights and helped to organise women in the Actresses' Franchise League – a group which was of considerable assistance at WSPU demonstrations and exhibitions. She lived her feminist ideas, insisting on the value of the experience of all women (even when there were apparent contradictions), insisting on the diversity and not the divisions. While an active member of the WSPU, she did not condemn the constitutionalists, and held Millicent Garrett Fawcett in high regard, dividing the profits from some of her feminist writing between the constitutionalists and the WSPU.

Having made her reputation as an actress (one of the best England had ever had according to popular opinion of the time), in the 1890s she turned to writing, where she made exceptionally good use of her skills as an actress – her ear for dialogue, her understanding of drama, her construction of character and of scene, are all reflected in her novels and her play *Votes for Women* (1907). She also made exceptionally good use of her militant feminism.

Her novel, *The Convert* (also 1907), is unusual and exciting. It is a realistic documentary of the suffragette campaign, and the 'fictional' element is used largely to link the speeches of the militants – particularly those of Christabel Pankhurst (who is only thinly disguised and who is presented as very likeable, which defies the conventional definition of her). The suffragette speeches were reconstructed largely from transcripts of the actual events; they make marvellously exciting, illuminating (and entertaining) reading. (Marcus states that in 'The Robins Papers, Fales Collection, New York University, are several transcripts of actual suffrage meetings, and demonstrations in Trafalgar Square, with each speech captured word by word, including the comments of the hecklers in the crowd and the responses of the speakers', 1980a, p. viii.)

No doubt, if the writer had been a man, reporting on a significant period in men's history, this 'factional' reconstruction would be acclaimed as a unique historical record and would be treated as an authoritative source (as in the case of Samuel Pepys' *Diary*, for example). As the writer was a woman, depicting an episode of woman's history, the work – where acknowledged, which is so rare as to be almost non-existent – is dismissed as propaganda (and Robins labelled with the derogatory term, 'propagoose'), classified as unreliable, and consigned to oblivion.

The Convert stands in direct contradiction to the official interpretation of events of the time (which is probably one of the reasons it has been erased) and not just in the positive images it presents of the Pankhursts. In this documentary the evidence is that women of *all* classes were involved in the suffrage movement, for women of all classes were united in their belief that the vote would improve their position in society. While the conventional image of the suffragettes is of a movement 'relentlessly middle class in its membership and goals', Robins demonstrates that this simply was not true, states Marcus, for all the speakers in the movement (and this is verifed by reference to other suffragette literature of the time) came from all classes and 'demanded votes on the grounds that women at the bottom, working class women and the despised and rejected prostitutes, will benefit most' (ibid., p. xi).

Written as a record of the confrontation which the militants were eager to promote, Elizabeth Robins makes no attempt to hide the confrontation, or the militancy, and the reasons for this stand (and the positive dividends it has for women) are amplified throughout the course of the novel. Robins was not at all reluctant to name men as the enemy – indeed, she even went so far as to call some of those prominent men who wanted to *appear* as friends the *enemy*; she stated that she did not believe G. B. Shaw's feminism and openly denounced H. G. Wells as an unprincipled opportunist.

Her fighting feminist philosophy is outlined in her collection of essays, *Way Stations* (1913), where Robins makes it clear that women should act together in their own interests, making their resources available to each other, in the effort to combat the combined resources of men. Always trying to draw women together, to make links between women and to establish 'networks', Robins emphasised the international nature of women's struggle. She acted as 'the apostle of British militancy in the American press where she published essay after essay explaining the necessity of militant action,' says Jane Marcus, and some of these essays are included in *Way Stations* which she 'dedicated to her sister-in-law, Margaret Dreier Robins, head of the Woman's Trade Union League of America' (1980a, p. viii). She did her utmost to promote alliances between the WSPU and the American Women's Trade Movement, convinced that for women the solution lay, in part, in the establishment of an international, organised, autonomous women's movement which was a force to be reckoned with.

Acknowledged as England's first great intellectual actress, praised by

Henry James and propositioned by George Bernard Shaw, acknowledged as an inspiration by Virginia Woolf on behalf of her self and other women writers, Elizabeth Robins lived a woman-centred life and dedicated herself to the promotion of women's interests, before and after the vote was won. Patronised as a propagandist, she was criticised for sacrificing her art to a transitory political cause, which is but another way men have legitimated their dismissal of women writers who display a different and autonomous set of values which undermine their own. Boldly advocating that women have power, and can use it if they want to (and feel good about it), it is not surprising that Elizabeth Robins should be excised from the literary and historical records. She might have been a very bad influence, as far as men were concerned.

5 Feminism old and new: Winifred Holtby (1898–1935)

Robins was undeniably influential among the women of her time (as Virginia Woolf has testified, see Marcus, 1979) but how much direct influence she exerted over the women at *Time and Tide* is difficult to say. But while I cannot ascertain whether Robins was a model for Winifred Holtby, there can be no doubt that Cicely Hamilton was. In 1934, when Holtby published her book *Women*, she dedicated it to Ethel Smyth and Cicely Hamilton, 'who did more than write "The March of the Women".' Born in Yorkshire, Winifred Holtby went to Somerville College, Oxford, after serving as a member of the Women's Auxiliary Army Corps in the First World War. At Oxford, she met Vera Brittain, and the strong and celebratory friendship, the feminism, the aspirations to be writers, shared by these two women, is well documented in Brittain's biography of Holtby, *Testament of Friendship* (1940). In her short life Winifred Holtby certainly achieved her ambition to be a writer (even if the height of her transitory fame occurred after her death). She was the author of novels, short stories and essays, a regular contributor to the *Manchester Guardian*, the *News Chronicle* and *Time and Tide* (as well as a reviewer for *Good Housekeeping* and a columnist for *The Schoolmistress*, see Rosalind Delmar, 1980); she also wrote a critical study of Virgina Woolf, 1932 (a refreshing change after the customary 'lit-crit' interpretation) and *Women* (1934).

Winifred Holtby's feminism typifies a shift in the mood of the 1920s, and Vera Brittain sums up Holtby's position as one of a new breed (not unknown to us today) when she says that her 'feminist opinions knew no bitterness, since they had not originated in any sense of grievance. Never having found it a disadvantage to be a woman, she brought to the service of women ideas which were positive and constructive' (1940, p. 134). For most of her (short) life, Holtby seems to have taken it for granted that women and men were to be treated equally (a stand that would not have been possible during the nineteenth century, prior to the suffragettes), and she seems to have been genuinely surprised when she encountered an absence of 'fair play', assuming that it was an anomaly that could, once recognised, be remedied.

To her the major battle had been won (although the peace terms were still a matter of some dispute); to her, Mary Astell, Catherine Macaulay and Mary Wollstonecraft had made the first demands and from that time there had been a slow but steady movement towards the attainment of the goals they had set forward. She was aware of her heritage (*Women* is primarily a construction of the part women had played, from Mary Astell, and assumes, with one exception I will comment on later, a model of change and progress), and very conscious of the debt she owed to women who had gone before. Brittain relates how the two of them 'attended the All Night Watch Service for Mrs Pankhurst and together kept part of the vigil beside her coffin. . . . To us, grown to maturity after the suffrage campaign, she had existed mainly as a legend, but a sense of obligation for our heritage of *comparative freedom and equality* brought us through the midnight streets of Westminster to the shadowed church where her body was lying in state' (ibid., p. 273, my emphasis). But for all this, there is a sense in which Holtby sees herself as an inheritor of comparative equality, not as someone who is passionately incensed by injustice, and whose over-riding concern is to bring about radical change. 'Political emancipation is a condition of freedom: it is not freedom itself', she warns in *Women* (1934, p. 53) but I think there can be little doubt that she sees 'political emancipation' as fundamental; having achieved it, freedom is now possible in a way it was not before.

This is why she describes herself as one of the 'old' feminists, as an 'equality' feminist, in the debates conducted within the pages of *Time and Tide*, where the 'new' feminists were those who were looking towards parliamentary processes for the 'protection' of women and, rather than asserting women's equality with men, were arguing for women's *special* position. Holtby argues that she is an 'equality' feminist because she wants to see both sexes as human, that she wants to concentrate on what women and men have in common, and not on what divides them. In *Time and Tide* (6 August 1906) she wrote: 'Old Feminism, with its motto "Equality First" and its concentration upon those parts of national life where sex differentiation still prevails, may seem conservative, hysterical or blindly loyal as old catchwords. This is not the truth. The Old Feminism emphasises the importance of the human being . . .' (quoted in Delmar, 1980, p. 450).

Holtby gives the impression that she is not an 'Old Feminist' because she *wants* to be, but because she *has* to be, when she writes for the *Yorkshire Post*: 'I am a feminist because I dislike everything that feminism implies. I desire an end of the whole business, the demands for equality the suggestion of sex warfare, the very name of feminist. I want to be about the work in which my real interests lie, the study of inter-race relationships, the writing of novels and so forth. But while the inequality exists, while injustice is done and opportunity denied to the great majority of women, I shall have to be a feminist with the motto Equality First' (quoted in Brittain, 1940, p. 134).

Journalism, of course, imposes its own restraints. The *Yorkshire Post* might not have accepted a radical feminist protest, and while Holtby suggests that it is somewhat tiresome to have to be a feminist in her day and age, and to fix up those problems that still remain, she is adamant that she *is* a feminist and it is because of the discrimination that is practised against the great majority of women. But if in the 1920s Holtby was taking part in a debate about the changing nature of feminism, I think that by the 1930s her own feminism has also changed.

This was when she wrote *Women* (1934), which begins with a damning portrait of an arrogant male flexing his muscles on a bus to Brighton, complaining about women pacifists (' "All those women, cooped up together" he lordly and loudly proclaims to his devoted companion, "scratching each other's eyes out. Women weren't intended for that sort of thing",' p. 1); and he puts forward the proposal that as there were too many of them, poking their noses into too many things, what was needed was a huge tidal wave to carry two million women off, and to level things up.

'I am not going to suggest that the homicidal aspirations of the gentleman on the bus were typical of his generation,' says Holtby, 'but it is a matter of common observation that, in the second quarter of the twentieth century, the very existence of women appears to challenge controversy' (ibid., p. 2).

Emphasising the fundamental nature of the problem – the repudiation of women's very right to exist – and the fact that this should occur in the second quarter of the twentieth century, with all the implications that this has for the so-called hardwon gains of the first quarter of the twentieth century, represents a considerable change in Holtby's feminist analysis. Here, the 'honeymoon' of comparative equality and coexistence with men appears to be over, and the disillusionment and sense of betrayal with the reality of inequality and the recognition of conflicting interests, has begun. Holtby hasn't modified her belief about progress; indeed, I suspect that this is partly why she finds the attitude of men difficult to explain and resorts to seeing it as an aberration, but she does go so far as to say that there is a feeling of 'bitterness' in the air, as women begin to concentrate their minds on *not* what they had achieved, but *how far* there was to go, when men would not even recognise women's right to exist.

Had she lived longer she may have developed this new frame of reference and 'spoken bitterness' (the term used by Chinese women who, as a consciousness-raising process, cultivated the technique of 'speaking bitterness' against men). We might have been able to follow the shifts in Holtby's feminism over time, as we can for example with Brittain's – assuming that her writing was known and available. Such a study would have helped to dispel the myths that feminism is only a passing phase in the lives of many women, and that the women's movement evaporated when the vote was won. As it is, Winifred Holtby stands as an example of one of the women who, handed her comparative freedom and equality, came to understand that she was more than comparatively oppressed. She contradicts the prevailing belief that feminism was wound down in the 1920s, and had faded from sight in the 1930s, by revealing that her own feminism became increasingly more wound up over this period. As the growth and development of her ideas are unlikely to be of assistance in substantiating the patriarchal version of women's 'progress', it is not surprising that her work should be, in the main, unknown and unacclaimed.

6 The whole duty of woman: Vera Brittain (1896–1970)

When Winifred Holtby died, many women offered words of praise in recognition of the contribution she had made to their lives, individually and generally. Lady Rhondda stated that she doubted 'whether *Time and Tide* would be in existence now if it wasn't for Winifred' (1937, p. 207), and Vera Brittain wrote the most memorable testament to her as, 'The best friend whom life has given me' (1940, p. 4). Almost all who knew her deeply regretted that she had been so generous to others with her time and emotional support (and all seem to have suffered guilt feelings), and that, as she was so eminently interruptable and self-sacrificing (she is frequently referred to as a 'saint'), she had not been left the time and the space that she wanted for pursuing her own writing. And it is here that Vera Brittain – who shared so much of her life and her self with Winifred Holtby, reveals some of the areas in which she differed from Holtby, when she writes in the closing pages of *Testament of Friendship* that had Winifred lived longer 'she might have learnt that one's self, and not the demanding, exploiting world is the rightful judge of how one's time should be spent' (ibid., p. 441).

Unlike Holtby, Brittain's feminism was born of 'bitter experience' as *Testament of Youth* (1933) readily reveals. Brittain knew that *time* was a precious resource and that women were consistently robbed of it; she knew that creativity, intelligence, development and action were resources, and that women were frequently denied them in a variety of ways. So integral to her was the understanding that women were expected to be available, and were made to feel immediate and immeasurable guilt if they were not, that while she shared the optimism of her time and believed that there were many new opportunities available to women who would use them well, she also had reservations, because she believed there was much in the way that women had been trained which would effectively prevent them from making use of the new freedoms technically available to them. There is a tension reflected in her feminism as, on the one hand, she looks to a future in which women will realise their potential and the world will be a better place for it, while, on the other hand, she appreciates that there are so many factors working against women in the male-dominated world, where it is the proper duty of woman to *give* herself to others (as Winifred had done) so that there is little time, energy or inclination left to develop her *self*.

Brittain's ideas on this subject emerge early and are a constant concern over the decades. When she published 'The Whole Duty of Woman' in 1928, in *Time and Tide*, she no doubt thought that it represented her position as a feminist, and she may have known that it was representative of a long line of women's ideas; what she could not have known, however, was how relevant it could be in the 1980s. 'The Whole Duty of Woman' is a review which with its curiously contemporary connotations could be republished today without amendment. It is introduced with the statement that it is 'on an article entitled "Sex and Intelligence" which dealt with the Report on the Differentiation of the Curriculum for Boys and Girls in Secondary Schools' (1928b, p. 216). (Fifty years later there are other comparable reports of course – which many of us believed to be 'new' and which had to be refuted in much the same way as Brittain had done.)

The Report reveals the basic mechanisms of a male-dominated society at work. Here was an institution set up by men for themselves – education – and to which women had only relatively recently been conceded entry, after years of struggle, and here were these institutional standards, formulated by men, being used to assess the performance of women, the newcomers; and the newcomers were performing differently. It takes patriarchal assumptions to suggest that this difference means there is something wrong with the girls; it takes patriarchal assumptions to raise the question – so significant in our society – 'of whether any inherent inferiority in the female intellect determined that differentiation'? (ibid.). Much can be understood about the 'code' of a society which is prepared to ask whether the different behaviour of a substantial group of its members is because they were 'born that way', with a handicap that cannot be remedied and for which nothing can be done. Vera Brittain understood.

Her rage and fury, and bitterness, although controlled, make their presence felt in every paragraph, as she argues that every facet of society has been arranged by men to provide their sex with the maximum advantages so that they can then compare themselves to women and find themselves superior. Vera Brittain argues that men demand that women make their resources available to others, that men help themselves liberally to such resources, and then blame women because they have so few left for themselves. Brittain saw time, and will, and intelligence as part of those resources men had taken from women.

Because, as with so many of the ideas women wish to put forward, there are so few established concepts and words available to name them (another by-product of what is not experienced by men does not exist), Brittain makes use of analogy to map out what it is that she means, and begins with the illustration of Charlotte Brontë who at one stage had determined to use her resources for herself, to run her own life, and write, but whose plan for independence crumbled in the face of the demands of her family. Duty, modesty, gentleness, womanliness all decreed that she should abandon her plans for autonomy and stay 'at home to care for a sick father, a drunken brother, a sister whose proud independence of soul approached very nearly to something which at the present day we should probably describe as obstinate stupidity. She sacrificed herself,' says Brittain; why, and for what?

'For, in the end, her years of uneasy martyrdom at Haworth could save neither her father from sorrow, her brother from sin, nor herself and her sisters from premature death. One wonders whether a calm and resolute refusal to remain in the dark house on the edge of the churchyard for the sake of an invalid might not have had the effect of removing both her family and herself to a healthier sphere, and thus saving the lives of them all. But,' adds Brittain, 'in the days of Charlotte Brontë not resolution but submission was the whole duty of woman' (ibid., p. 217). Brittain did not think much had changed since the days of Brontë; I do not think much has changed since the days of Brittain.

To me this represents a fundamental dilemma, as it did to Brittain: it is because it has suited men to have women's emotional, psychological, intellectual resources available to them (and their children) that they have allocated a nurturing role to women. Our nurturance is not 'biological', not an inherent 'deficiency', as Margaret Mead (1950) and many more demonstrated with cross-cultural studies which show women in semi-non-nurturing roles. But despite the fact that we have had no choice in the matter, that nurturance has been assigned to us, we have become skilled at it and have come to appreciate its value. We want to assert that it is in the interest of society for all its members (not just half) to be nurturant, for we believe this to be a more sensible and productive basis for organising the world. But we find ourselves in the position of being *the nurturing sex in an exploitative society*; our nurturance is taken and used by men. We must confront the problem of how to make ourselves nurturantly unavailable for exploitation – and oppression – without repudiating nurturing itself.

Annie Cornbleet (1982) has suggested that it is our very nurturance as mothers, wives, teachers, nurses, social workers, secretaries, etc., that allows the exploitative society to continue functioning, and that by making our emotional energy and our time available to these ends we are *colluding*, helping to maintain patriarchy (and leaving ourselves little time and energy to construct our own alternative). But any suggestions that we should stop playing our nurturing role – that Charlotte Brontë should have left her family and gone off to London, that Vera Brittain should have left her husband and her children (periodically) to pursue her own work, that women should choose to be 'childfree' (Robyn Rowland, forthcoming) – are often accompanied by accusations of 'selfishness' and condemnation as 'hard' (and I speculate on the origins of this label and its significance), with such women sometimes being dismissed as 'behaving just like a man'. We construct an immense burden of guilt for women who elect to make their emotional resources unavailable. Because men are not required to conform to the expectations of nurturing it is a guilt which they do not experience when they do not conform to its demands.

Almost every woman who has protested against male power has raised the issue of women's emotional availability to men – from the obvious examples of putting one's energy into a husband's 'success' at the expense of one's own development, through to the more subtle areas of agreeing with men's view of the world, supporting their conversation topics, 'saving men's face' in public as Cicely Hamilton put it, in the workplace, the home, or the school. Vera Brittain calls this *submission*; Annie Cornbleet calls it *collusion*. I see it as a dilemma, one that was perceived by George Eliot, for if we acknowledge that it is through our nurturing that we are exploited and oppressed, and if we decide that it is a question of nurturance *or* liberation (which is by no means inevitable and says more about the rules for making sense of the world in patriarchy, than about the choices available), we could well decide that we prefer oppression.

To Vera Brittain it was largely the emotional demands made on females which were responsible for their different performance in secondary school (or work). Females do not go to school, or work, she argued and then return home for respite and replenishment (as do their brothers), but return home for more work, recharging male batteries while their own are flattened in the process. To this I would add that, even in the workplace or the school, in mixed-sex contexts, women are still doing two jobs while men are doing only one, for whether they be students, teachers, social workers, or engineers, women are still emotionally managing and recharging men, an activity which is not reciprocated (and which again, therefore, in the minds of most men is non-existent), and which is *over and above* the demands of many jobs. Why do women often state they prefer to work just with women? Because it is easier! It removes a considerable *work load!*

Vera Brittain recognised this in her relationship with Winifred Holtby. The emotional availability of one woman to another is not a *visible* element in our social arrangements, yet it is often reciprocal and as such, mutually enhancing and immensely rewarding. For as long as we have had records, states Brittain, 'The friendships of men have enjoyed glory and acclamation, but the friendships of women . . . have usually been not merely unsung, but mocked, belittled and falsely interpreted' (1940, p. 2).

There are many reasons for women's 'friendships' remaining invisible. One is of course that it is an area from which men are excluded and of which they have no direct experience, and it is therefore an area that has not been accorded validity and elaborated upon. But another is that it is *divisions* among women, not *alliances*, that are facilitated in a male-dominated world, and testimonies like those of Virginia Woolf – that Chloe liked Olivia – and of Vera Brittain to Winifred Holtby, are subversive and dangerous. When women put their energy into other women and find the process satisfying and replenishing where does that leave men? It is not just that they are no longer central to women's existence – which may be a blow to their pride and promote an identity crisis – it is also that women's resources are not available to men for the taking. It should be no surprise that 'women only' groups should constitute a considerable threat to patriarchy.

Vera Brittain appreciated the threat that the unavailability of women's resources could pose in a male-dominated society; she thought about it, wrote about it, and lived it. From the Oxford days she and Winifred Holtby shared a flat in London and, despite the economic difficulties, and the rejection from publishers (on occasion), Brittain's description of that period of her life leaves no doubts that it was a joyous time. But then Brittain married in 1925 (and Holtby had to deal with her loss, as so many women have done, but which is again not a common social topic), and went to America to join her husband at the university in Ithaca. Brittain found herself doing the housework, and writing in isolation, and her writing was rejected. American editors could not be persuaded to publish her articles; back they came 'with devastating regularity, accompanied by complimentary letters filled with amiable excuses which conveyed the dismal certainty that residence in Ithaca meant full stop to a writer's progress' (1957, p. 33).

Work of her own was not available to Brittain in America. After one year of marriage, she wrote: 'In England I had been regarded as a promising young writer, whose work dealt with subjects that mattered, but in the United States I was less than dust. Whereas G. (her husband) was now happily contributing to *The New Republic*, *Harper's Magazine*, *Current History*, and several other academic publications, I had failed to place one article in an American magazine. I could not even persuade some minor periodical to appoint me as its representative at the coming League of Nations Assembly' (ibid., p. 37).

The future looked bleak to Brittain, who compared herself to Florence Nightingale – deprived of mental food and under threat of 'death from starvation'. She faced the fact that the future offered nothing more than being a 'Faculty Wife' and Brittain could see then what was to be to Betty Friedan (and millions of other women) a revelation in the 1950s – that such a life was depressing, frustrating and embittering. She wanted to return to England. But her husband's work was in America. Should she think of him, or herself? Should she pursue her own ideals or sacrifice them and stay? Could she cope with the criticism – and the guilt – that would accompany the declaration that while having a satisfying relationship with her husband, *it wasn't enough*, and that she was prepared to go to another continent and embark on a 'semi-detached marriage' in order that her own life was more complete and rewarding?

Brittain recognised that she was confronted with a difficult choice and that her 'generation of women was so ruthlessly trained in childhood to put persons before convictions that its members have never been able to pursue an impersonal ideal without remorse' (ibid., pp. 38–9). She took the risk; she changed her marriage to a 'semi-detached' one, returned to England (and Winifred), dealt with the accusations that she was a poor wife, a selfish woman, a shirker of duty – and never regretted it. She felt no remorse.

Brittain's feminism spans decades and gives the lie to the belief that there have only been phases, or short episodes, of feminist concern during the twentieth century. She was a feminist in 1923 and no less a feminist in 1953 when she wrote *Lady Into Woman* during a period when many insist that feminism was unknown and perceived to be unnecessary. *Lady Into Woman*, subtitled 'A History of Women from Victoria to Elizabeth', is Brittain's reflection on fifty years of women's history, from the perspective of one who has been involved in shaping that history, for much of the time. It begins with the recognition of the necessity for women to pass on to the next generation what it is they have come to learn and understand from experience, otherwise the 'insights' will be lost; future generations of women will have to start again. Brittain opens the book with a letter to her daughter; it is a reminder that she has been fortunate in her upbringing and a rejoinder that all is not yet well with the position of women.

To Brittain, the movement towards a welfare state, to a society which cared for all its members, had been a triumph of 'feminine' principles over 'masculine' ones, and she reminds her daughter that women fought for the health and baby services which were in part responsible for her physical wellbeing. Brittain also reminds her daughter that she was reared 'free from the implanted sense of inferiority that handicaps so many women by undermining the self-confidence' and that, unlike Elizabeth Cady Stanton or Emmeline Pankhurst, for example, she was 'deeply desired as a *daughter*' (1953, p. xiv). The daughter will not have to spend the time and energy learning to believe in herself and her purpose as the mother had to.

And, in comparison, the daughter had reaped other rewards as a result of the mother's feminism. 'Thirdly', says Brittain, 'you belong to a household in which a woman's work has been constantly in progress', where it has not been valued less than a man's, or approached with any less seriousness or purpose than the work of a man. But in counselling her daughter in this way, Brittain is also emphasising the unusual nature of the ('semi-detached') household, and warning that in general society does not practise what this particular home preaches.

In 1953 Brittain reasserts her feminism to her daughter. She acknowledges that with the best will in the world the problem cannot be solved – even at an *individual* level. 'I could have written much better if I had been interrupted much less,' she says, returning to her theme of the availability of women, to the understanding that a woman's time is not her own. Her wish for her daughter is the elimination of interruption – few women, I think, have ever given such public and subversive advice to their daughters. *Lady Into Woman* reflects on the way women have changed over the century, and the way men have changed *as a response*! Brittain recognises that woman 'still inhabits a male dominated world, but thanks to the past half century of revolution the men belong to a different type from that of her grandfather and even her father' (ibid., p. 9) and while I would not want to get wildly enthusiastic about the progress men have made (and Brittain herself goes on to add that even in the 1950s there are those men who flatter themselves that one of their number is, in itself, sufficient compensation to a woman for a life of her own), I do try and keep in mind what a revolution it was to Brittain, and women of her generation, who lived through Edwardian parentage and looked forward to their daughters taking a place in the public world – not just unopposed, but positively encouraged. I am prepared to call the changes that have occurred in my own life over the last fifteen years a social revolution; the changes Brittain lived through, were, I think greater.

Some of the things she was prepared to settle for would not satisfy us today. She was pleased that women were not so often required to cook and wash up alone; she suggested that 'a voluntary partner is more flattering to self-esteem than a compulsory slave' and that men should understand this, for the price they pay for the privilege of companionship and respect is small – 'It amounts to no more than help with the housework and occasional shopping, in addition to the more constant society of his children and an understanding of their care which benefits both him and them' (ibid., p. 10). John Stuart Mill might have supported this stand, but Harriet Taylor would not – nor would Charlotte Perkins Gilman, Virginia Woolf, or Ann Oakley. So much for trying to show the gradual improvements in women's position.

Many of us today would also have difficulty countenancing Vera Brittain's justification for her relationship with Winifred Holtby. Lillian Faderman (1981) has pointed out that relationships between women are not threatening to the patriarchal social order if they are seen as an 'apprenticeship' to a relationship with a man; as long as a man ultimately reaps the reward almost anything goes. It comes of something as a surprise to find Brittain asserting that 'loyalty and affection between women is a noble relationship which, far from impoverishing, actually enhances the love of a girl for her lover' (one assumes male), 'of a wife for her husband, of a mother for her children' (1940, p. 2).

I can only try to understand this position in the light of my own experience, for I cannot afford to be critical. Had I been writing in the late 1950s or early 1960s I know that someone could probably confront me now with one of my statements of 'I would rather talk to men than women because men are so much more interesting' or 'You can't trust other women', etc. Times change. In the pre-contemporary women's movement days I inhabited a different world from the one I do now; Vera Brittain inhabited a different one again. Given how many feminist precedents she set in her own time, it is more likely that she would be at the vanguard than the rearguard of feminist interpretations today. No doubt she would even revise her defence of Radclyffe Hall (1968).

Vera Brittain was one of the thirty-nine witnesses to defend Radclyffe Hall's book at the obscenity trial. Basically her argument was that it was not offensive; it was a plea for openness and for tolerance – towards the abnormal woman (see 1928a). What is important is *the defence* – of Radclyffe Hall, and of her relationship (and her celebration of that relationship) with Winifred Holtby. Few else would have dared.

Brittain herself indicates that she was always ready to change the ways and means, but never to abandon the principle. In looking back on her earlier feminism (when she, with Holtby, was one of the 'old' equality feminists) she states that the 'chief error of the older feminists was to use men as yardsticks. What matters to the modern woman is not how men have tackled problems in the past, but how she herself is going to tackle them in the future' (1953, p. 2).

This is one of her tenets that still applies – as does much of her analysis and many of her recommendations in relation to women's work. She wanted homemaking and motherhood to be valued as *work* but she also wanted women who wished to do other forms of work to experience equality of opportunity. She wrote *Women's Work in Modern England* (1928c), which was an attempt on the one hand to awaken women to the job possibilities that were available to them, but a documentation on the other hand of the forms of discrimination that were practised against them. The workplace was a crucial focus for Brittain, who always held that there was no independence without economic independence. The unity of Brittain's feminism and pacifism is also illuminating, and her ideas deserve greater attention today when once again (almost fifty years later) we are reforging the connections between feminism and pacifism (see Birgit Brock-Utne, 1982). An 'old equality' feminist Brittain may have been at one time, but she would never have entertained the possibility that the principle of equality applied to war and that it was legitimate to work for women's equality within the armed services. War was totally unjustifiable under any circumstances, and while she was prepared to accept the reasonableness of the proposition that it was women's role to 'patch up' the casualties of the First World War, even this proposition looked less reasonable with the outbreak of the Second World War, and the recognition that all that 'patching up', that all those resources women had made available to mend and repair, were misused. By the Second World War Brittain believed that women could not support war, they must resist.

There is no contradiction in her approach; questioning the nurturing role did not mean (as some would like to insist) adopting an aggressive role. On the contrary, it was perfectly consistent for her to argue that women should use their own resources to create a society in which voluntary support and co-operation were valued, and that these resources should not be taken by men for their own use, whether that use was ostensibly 'peaceful' or obviously aggressive.

One omission from her analysis that I find significant is that she does not raise the issue that even for feminist-pacifists men call the tune, and that during the war all her energy was taken in the effort to resist, in the effort to endure the ostracism and the condemnation, in the effort to repudiate the male arguments that justified war. This was not a woman independently choosing the issues but one whose entire energy went into reacting to the issues that men decreed. Not that I want to suggest that Brittain had a choice; I just find it somewhat surprising that, given her awareness of the way women's energy is appropriated, she does not comment on it in relation to pacifism. In the absence of aggression and war, the concept of pacifism would not even exist.

I have no criticisms to level at Brittain's feminism, only deep admiration for a woman who, for over a period of almost fifty years, reasserted her feminism again and again, and loudly proclaimed the existence of women's 'difference' along with the right and the necessity for that difference to be an equally powerful force in the structuring of 'human' and the organising of society.

Were I not aware of what happens to women and women's ideas in a male-dominated society, I would be baffled by the fact that a woman who wrote well into the 1960s, who was innovative with literary forms (the blend of autobiography, biography, history and documentary that comprise the trilogy of the 'Testaments' has few counterparts), who was a prolific feminist novelist, who explored in fiction the realities of woman's existence (see for example *Honourable Estate*, 1936), who wrote critiques of patriarchy (*Women's Work in Modern England*, 1928c; *Lady Into Woman*, 1953; *The Women at Oxford*, 1960; *Radclyffe Hall: A Case of Obscenity?* 1968) should have been so overlooked in Elaine Moers's *Lit-*

erary Women (1978), which is such a careful and extensive documentation of 'lost' women writers but which makes no mention of Brittain. Nor am I surprised that there should have been – despite the overlap – so few links initially between Brittain and the modern women's movement.

Many of Brittain's most illuminating insights are contained within her journalism and as she stated, the 'tragedy of journalism lies in its impermanence' (1940, p. 269) and, while this applies to men, it has even greater implications for women, for I am not necessarily obliged to know what it is I am looking for when (and if) I wish to read what many of the master journalists have written. Their work is often available in anthologies or readily accessible in the British Library. To me it is a source of considerable regret that there is no contemporary collection of Vera Brittain's (or Winifred Holtby's, or Charlotte Perkis Gilman's) essays.

7 Current culpability: Rebecca West (1892–   )

But I suspect that the problem of discontinuity between one generation of feminists and another goes even deeper than the published availability (or non-availability) of women's ideas. Fundamental to feminist analyses are the principles that gulf-like divisions are created among women and also, that where women are perceived as male property, they are accorded their greatest value in their youth. The development of ideas about ageism has helped us to understand that whereas the worth of a man may increase with age in a society ordered by men (so that life merely begins at forty) that of a woman decreases with age (so that life ends at thirty – see Spender, 1982a), with the result that, while society may sit at the feet of elderly male gurus, women almost never experience such veneration.

An 'old woman' is a term of abuse; while it may have been encoded by men its meaning could well be shared by women (see Spender, 1980). Just as women help to construct sexism, perhaps we make our contribution to ageism by accepting rather than challenging the belief that 'old women' have little of intellectual value to offer. This could be the explanation for Rebecca West's statement in 1975 that: 'No Women's Lib people have ever shown the slightest interest in me' (see Connell, 1975). Yet Jane Marcus (1980b) has stated that Rebecca West 'has become this century's great feminist literary critic, philosopher, novelist, historian and journalist' (p. 5). Her feminist ideas virtually span the twentieth century to date (her first published item on women's suffrage was in *The Scotsman* in 1904, when she was 14 years of age) and her commitment to feminism is no less now than it was at the beginning of the century.

I have thought about this and come to the conclusion that I am culpable, that I have been too ready to dismiss some of my immediate foremothers as misguided, and too ready to be contemptuous of what I *perceived* to be but a battle for the vote, and an attempt to place as many women as possible in positions of influence that have been traditionally held by men. Now I am more inclined to ask questions about the *origins* of those perceptions, and the effects for women when one generation – on the basis of received impressions as distinct from direct evidence – severs connections with a generation that has gone before. The pattern does not seem to vary much, for many of us today, by failing to establish links with Rebecca West (and Dora Russell, and Hazel Hunkins-Hallinan, and Mary Stott, and Constance Rover – and many many more)[3] are playing our own part in ensuring that feminist insights are *not* handed down and that the process of women's disappearance is facilitated. We need *actively* to resist, not to aid and abet the dismissal and erasure of women, particularly when, as has been the case for me, *direct* evidence has revealed that there is not one shred of plausibility in the premise that these, our foremothers, experienced arrested development with the advent of the suffrage movement, and have little or nothing of intellectual value to offer us. To believe this of them is to be taken in by patriarchal misrepresentation; many of us have been misled, and *it is our loss*.

Rebecca West was born Cicily Isabel Fairfield[4] in 1892. Significantly she took the pen-name Rebecca West after playing the strong-willed character of that name in Ibsen's *Rosmersholm* in her late teens. At the age of 19, West was a journalist for the feminist *Freewoman* (one of the twenty-one feminist periodicals in Britain at the time, which together commanded an immense audience that today makes our own 'constituency' look fairly fragile, see Elizabeth Sarah, 1982 a, b, c) and she also served her journalist apprenticeship on the socialist *Clarion*. By 1920 it was claimed by an anonymous writer in *Time and Tide* (reprinted in 1923) that West was 'conspicuous to a degree that . . . is quite extraordinary. She is now twenty seven years of age and the reading public has been aware of her for eight years' (1923b, p. 149). The writer in *Time and Tide* says that West has been a feminist from a very young age, partly because 'She had the good fortune to be thrown in with Mary Gawthorpe[5] when she was still a schoolgirl and that witty and loveable and courageous personality made her understand the nature of the Feminist Movement . . .' (ibid., p. 150). Evidently Mary Gawthorpe was a very good teacher!

Jane Marcus (1980b) – and the writer in *Time and Tide* – are impressed by Rebecca West's candour (as were the two journalists who interviewed her in the 1970s) and there is much admiration expressed for the courageous way in which she brought to the fore issues that were customarily discreetly ignored or dismissed. Her feminist novel, *The Judge* (1922; 1980), is an example. Prefaced with the statement that: 'Every mother is a judge who sentences the children for the sins of the father,' the novel

[3] I am currently engaged in interviewing these elder stateswomen of feminism in an attempt to develop an oral history of twentieth-century feminism: hopefully this information will appear in a forthcoming publication *There's Always Been A Women's Movement*.

[4] Virago, and Jane Marcus, 1980b, give her name as 'Cicily'; the *Evening Standard*, 1 November 1930 as 'Cicely' and the *Guardian*, 26 October 1959 as 'Cecily'. In the interest of accuracy I have settled for the feminist version of the spelling.

[5] The name Mary Gawthorpe arises again and again, always with the most positive connotations but little elucidation attached.

deals with the forces at work in a patriarchal society, and addresses the issues of rape, and unmarried mothers – as well as the issue of suffrage. Rebecca West is right in the middle of things, and many of her time would have preferred them to be left unnoticed and unsaid. Jane Marcus states that: 'Those who have wished Jane Austen at Waterloo or Charlotte Brontë out of Haworth parsonage, find their literary daughter, Rebecca West, on the barricades' (1980b, p. 4).

West's own status as an unmarried mother was well known and she deals with the topic (and with that of women's freedom) with a passion, vehemence, candour and complexity that is impressive to many. Her name was a household word to independent women, says Marcus, and these women understandably displayed keen interest in her ideas. One critic's response to *The Judge* was that: 'She puts the male into the dock and convicts him before a jury of women' (quoted in Marcus, 1980b, p. 6).

But, probably for much the same reason that many women found West's stand admirable, some men found it reprehensible. West was exploring the whole realm of women's experience and disclosing many aspects of it which were dramatically different from the experience of men (the position of the rapist and the unmarried father being qualitively different from the one who is raped – note even the absence of a word – and from that of the unmarried mother), and because what she was describing was outside the experience of the authoritative, representative, male, there were those who thought it of insufficient substance to be worthy of serious treatment. This was sensationalism, not literature. It is revolting, said one critic, that the unwed mother should be the subject of serious fiction; it was not rape, and the persecution of the single mother, that he found offensive, but the presumption that these distasteful forms of titillation should be included within the ambit of literature.

West introduced *women's politics*, and Jane Marcus suggests that one of the reasons she was able partially to resist consignment to the secondary ranks of the literary ladies who produced melodramas was because she already enjoyed a considerable reputation as a journalist within the realms of *men's politics*. In 1922 she tried to make sexual politics a serious issue, and to put them on a par with the other political issues with which she dealt.

Where Rebecca West stood, then and now, with male political creeds is, unlike her feminism, difficult to determine. She was, and is, critical of both Right and Left and is, of course, in the position of an *outsider* (which raises the question of why it is that women who are 'outsiders' have not been seen to be more 'objective' in male political debate than those involved, namely men themselves). The writer in *Time and Tide* emphasised the independence of West's position, which endeared her to neither side, and said: 'It is probable that if there is ever an English Revolution there will come a point when the Reds and Whites will sink their differences for ten minutes while they guillotine Miss West for making remarks that both sides have found intolerably wounding' (1923b, p. 150). (Vera Brittain occupied a comparable position during the Second World War when she was perceived as an enemy by British and German authorities alike.) That in the space of one sentence West should be able to reveal her distance from both ends of the political spectrum (and win favour with neither) is revealed in a statement she made in an interview for *The Times* in 1975, when among some positive comments upon Marxism (as distinct from Marxists) she said: '*Das Kapital* is a dreary book, except for that chapter of wild praise for the achievement of the bourgeoisie' (Connell, 1975).

Writing in 1972 after interviewing Rebecca West (on her eightieth birthday), Rivers Scott stated that while it was still difficult to pin down West's position in terms of male-defined political issues, there could be no mistaking her unwavering allegiance to women's issues. She was and always had been for the emancipation for women, which in her words had little to do with the vote and a lot to do with the repudiation of an obligation for women to be what men alleged they were. With Scott, Rebecca West discussed at length the idea that, in a male-dominated society, women are in the 'wrong', their experience questionable and their authority impugned. Far from seeing women's position as one of steady improvement throughout the twentieth century, West could identify areas where things were getting worse and where, old obstacles overcome, new and sometimes bigger ones were erected in their place. One such creation, in her view, was Freud, and she referred to the 'fundamental folly of Freudianism'.

'Freud was a great enemy of women,' she said. 'All that nonsense about suffering from penis envy, which presupposes that the unconscious does not tell little girls that they have perfectly good sex organs within themselves, but apparently gives them full information about the male sex organs though the little girls may never have seen or heard of them. If you could believe that', she says scornfully, 'you could believe anything.' But she knows it was and is believed and that this must be accounted for; and she has very strong ideas on how it is that a society can come to believe so much stupid nonsense about women while still taking seriously so many ridiculous complaints of men. 'Thanks to Freud', says West, in a tone which is unmistakeable in its contempt, 'the whole of the United States is covered with millions and millions of grown men grizzling about the way they were treated by their mothers, who are usually dead.' And she includes Norman Mailer among their number: 'For Mr Mailer I have nothing but distaste. He isn't much and makes such a noise about it.' We should have been listening, and long before 1972.

For all of her working life Rebecca West has shown her defiance of male authority and demonstrated her audacity. She has shown not the slightest respect or deference to men and has been passionately concerned with (and I would say has in many respects succeeded in) preserving her autonomy and integrity. The implicit and explicit theme of much of her writing over the decades has been the responsibility and the necessity for women to define and develop their own intellectual area, which fosters their own values and reflects their own priorities. She has reversed the patriarchal order and assumed the negative nature of many male qualities (which men pride in themselves), equating male aggression, mastery and control with exploitation and destruction; she has presumed the positive nature of many of women's attributes – seeing women as life-giving and constructive. And she has never hesitated to make her own opinions known nor to express them in a manner which may be unacceptable to men. On many counts she could be classified as 'disagreeable' in a 'man-governed' (her term) world.

Feminists do not usually get a good press – particularly not disagreeable ones, particularly not in *The Sunday Telegraph*, nor in 1972 – yet here is Rebecca West condemning the male establishment, indicting Freud and Mailer, and delivering clear and loud feminist signals which I suspect met little or no answering response. In British feminist circles she remains relatively ignored, despite her immense literary output and her unquestionable feminism.

Where do we get the idea that women become increasingly 'unreliable' with age? Why do we practise (even if we do not explicitly preach) the tenet that there are no words of wisdom, no 'old wives' tales' which can be profitably passed from one generation to the next? Why do we make it so easy for male domination to continue, for men to divide and rule?

Some of Rebecca West's writing is currently in vogue (see Rebecca West *A Celebration*, 1977; 1978) and all the evidence points to her being misrepresented and disposed of in the same way as women who have gone before, and in the same way as we are likely to be treated, unless we can disrupt the process. It is interesting to note that already it is her specifically feminist writing which is seen to be 'not up to standard'; it is her personality that is coming under discussion. While one of her most salient characteristics is seen to be her struggle to establish the autonomy of women's thinking and writing, we are asked to be reassured that this does not detract from her work, and to accept that she still has a contribution to make to the 'mainstream'. The first signs of her dismissal could not be along more predictable lines.

Neither *The Judge* nor *Harriet Hume* (1929) is included in the recent selection of her writings (*A Celebration*) and Samuel Hynes (1978) gives the reason for this: '*The Judge*', he says, is 'a long, melodramatic story of sex, guilt and power, interesting for the autobiographical beginning in Edinburgh, and for the remarks about the nature of the man–woman relations' but with *Harriet Hume* ranks as her 'least successful novels' (p. xii). If she was not seen as a melodramatic (autobiographical) literary lady in the 1920s, there are reasons to suspect that she is beginning to be seen that way now – and yet, there is no feminist work on Rebecca West which will help to refute this assessment or prevent this move towards her erasure.

Among Rebecca West's ideas are the principles that the world is man-governed, and that this includes the realm of intelligence and creativity, of thought and artistry. She could see how it was that women came to adopt masculine values as the basis of their thinking and their work, and she argued that women should resist, that they should mirror themselves and not men, that they should refuse to make their resources available to the world of men. She has had many years of experience in the resistance movement; one suspects that she has had some successes and some failures. But we have only 'clues' about the movement and the battles that have been fought. Elizabeth Cady Stanton, Susan B. Anthony and Matilda Joslyn Gage put us all to shame.

8 Interdependence: Olive Schreiner (1855–1920)

One of her foremothers to whom Rebecca West paid attention – indeed to whom Lady Rhondda, Elizabeth Robins, Cicely Hamilton, Winifred Holtby, Vera Brittain and Rebecca West all paid attention, was Olive Schreiner. In the words of Schreiner's recent biographers, Ruth First and Ann Scott (1980), her book *Woman and Labour* (1911) was 'a central text of the women's movement during the first decades of this century' (p. 15).

Schreiner did not just write *Woman and Labour*, a treatise on women's disinheritance from labour and their consequent economic inequality, she also wrote novels (*The Story of An African Farm*, 1883, being the best known) and revealed herself to be a woman of many parts. Born on a mission station on the Basutoland border, Schreiner became a socialist, a friend of Eleanor Marx, Edward Carpenter and Havelock Ellis, a supporter of the Boers against the British, and of the blacks against both Boers and British. Her diversity, complexity, and contradictions have allowed her to be 'dismembered' (First and Scott, 1980, p. 17), with one aspect of her work frequently being used to discredit the other. Despite the fact that Schreiner saw herself and her work as one and the same thing, with an essential unity, those who do not like her 'politics' (particularly her feminist and anti-racist politics) have used them against her literature, and those who do not like her literature have used it to devalue her politics. Her dismissal too, has been along fairly predictable lines. 'Since her death', state First and Scott, 'she has been seen as a novelist who never mastered the form; as a poet rather than a novelist; as a visionary rather than a cogent political thinker. In her lifetime she was similarly contained' (ibid.). In other words her intellectual, creative, and political contribution has been denied on just about all fronts, and the conflict she faced, the illness she experienced, the unhappiness she knew, have been conveniently utilised to slot her in almost as an eccentric artist (who nevertheless failed to achieve); and the fact that she was so enormously influential among so many women in the earlier part of the twentieth century is seen as of no consequence or else conveniently 'forgotten'.

Woman and Labour ('the "Bible of the women's movement"' Jane Graves, 1978, p. 9), is concerned with women's exclusion from productive work. Schreiner suggests that women and men had shared a comparable position in the past, but that men (for reasons not quite understood) have moved into women's territory, making drudges of working-class women and dolls of middle-class women. What was required was for women to find a place in the new administrative and intellectual occupations (a philosophy that would have appealed to those associated with *Time and Tide*), thereby gaining access to economic resources, and helping to restore the old equilibrium between the sexes. While a socialist, Schreiner accepted that socialism itself would not bring about parity and that there was an economic problem that related specifically to women.

Unlike Charlotte Perkins Gilman who shows what men have left out of economic explanations (and who shrewdly suggests what their motivation for this has been), and who attempts to develop an economic framework in which the work of women and men is accorded equal value, Schreiner's framework is more the conventional male one. I think it fair to say that whereas Gilman tried to transform the conceptualisation of work and money, Schreiner tried to ensure that women had a more equitable place within existing conceptualisations.[6]

One of the reasons for this was Schreiner's reluctance to repudiate male authority. To her, it seemed that the sexes were obliged to live and work together and, because of their interrelationship, men would begin to understand that equality was the best basis for harmony and development. The whole society would suffer, as far as Schreiner was concerned, if men were to think only of themselves, and men she believed were sensible enough to see this.

To me, there are two striking features about Olive Schreiner: the first is that she had such a wretched childhood and appears to have been extremely unhappy as an adult; the second is that she displayed such sympathy and concern for men, who had difficulty in understanding that custom was unfair to women, and difficulty in trying to adjust to more egalitarian arrangements in society. I tend to think that her unhappiness – and her inability to name men as the enemy – were related. I do not mean this in a simplistic sense, that the problems of unhappy women will be solved if they begin to be more critical of men. What I do mean is that Olive Schreiner experienced oppression – as a woman – personally, intensely, and continuously, and yet because she believed in the *inter*dependence of the sexes and the necessity of goodwill and understanding between the sexes, she did not often allow herself to see men as a force, as a competing interest group, and therefore had no real target for change, and no means of resolving her own conflict. When those without power try to cultivate the good will and understanding of those with power, they are often doomed to disappointment and may even intensify their internalisation of oppression – which on Schreiner's own admission, was a source of constant distress to her. Her 'solution' I think, was one which is not uncommon among women: unable to 'blame' men, she blamed herself.

Barbara Scott Winkler (1980) has compared Olive Schreiner and Charlotte Perkins Gilman and has indicated how much the two women had in common; they both had ineffectual fathers, mothers who insisted on obedience and submission and who saw defiance as sin; they both experienced

---

[6] I knew this would happen sooner or later: since writing this account of Schreiner, I have read Liz Stanley's excellent article reappraising Schreiner – and find I have fallen into many of the traps I have been cautioning against. I could have rewritten my discussion of Schreiner, but upon reflection decided to let it stand as an example of being 'conned', primarily by the Freudian framework in which Schreiner has been evaluated. Readers should not, therefore, 'trust' my assessment of Olive Schreiner – and are recommended to read Liz Stanley's account.

Victorian upbringings and were drilled in the proper duties of a woman; both were determined to be 'free', to break away from their subordination and both saw economic independence as a first step, but were aware of the structural obstacles in the way. Both saw marriage as an oppressive insti- tution for women and yet sought to be married, and both were ill in the months preceding their marriages (Schreiner's asthma worsened, and four months before her marriage 'she had an attack of hysterical paralysis that affected her speech', ibid., p. 25.) Both were insistent that women had sexual needs but at times experienced conflict about expressing them.

However, what Winkler does not comment on is where they were different. Charlotte Perkins Gilman was prepared to repudiate male au- thority. After her traumatising personal experience she was prepared to reject the advice of the experts (and this meant rejection of many of the established values of her time), and she made the conscious decision to shape her own life in a way that was consistent with her own personal experience and beliefs; and she found the process – although painful at times – liberating and self-affirming. No such option seems to have been available to Schreiner, who sought friendship, not enmity, with men, who saw women and men sharing many of the same interests rather than having fundamentally conflicting interests. Given this framework, it is easy to see how any 'conflict' she experienced with men could be interpreted as a 'failure' on her part, rather than as a clash between two opposing groups.

First and Scott (1980) say that they 'have tried to understand her illness and unhappiness as an expression of the split between the sense of her own needs and the reality of what was possible for women in the cultures in which she lived' (p. 23) and I think (or used to think, before reading Liz Stanley) that this was an accurate interpretation of Schreiner's life, but I would suggest that if she had not needed to see men in such a positive light, the split between her own desires and the context in which she found herself (and which manifested itself in illness and unhappiness) might not have been so great. Unable to challenge male authority, unable to challenge men's good opinion of themselves (including their self-pro- fessed attributes of reason and justice), Schreiner was only able to blame herself for her shortcomings in dealing with men.

Schreiner attributed some of her difficulties to her harsh upbringing, and certainly it would seem to have been almost impossible to have endured what she did, without marks being left. Accounts of her childhood are distressing in the extreme and it is obvious that she early understood the pain and humiliation of submission – which was routinely exacted by her mother. Brought up in a middle-class home in London, Rebecca Lyndall had become 'proficient in French and Italian, flower painting and music . . . expected to be ornamental, modest, pious and submissive' (Winkler, 1980, p. 3) and then had fallen victim to the Wesleyan Evangelical revival, had married Gottlob Schreiner, a missionary, and departed for Africa to take the gospel to the heathen. Nothing in her London life could have prepared her for what she had to face – another woman disillusioned and made desperate by the reality of wifedom.

The Schreiners 'lived in poverty, moving from one isolated missionary station to another, sometimes having to build their own straw-thatched mud floor shack', and in these harsh and hazardous circumstances Rebecca gave birth to twelve children only six of whom survived to adulthood. There was an immense contrast between the ideal of service (to husband, God and the heathen) and the reality of this grinding poverty and hardship. From the young lady of 'accomplishments' and refined taste she became a woman 'faced with the numbing routine of cooking and cleaning, nursing and burying her babies and clothing and educating those that survived' (ibid., p. 4).

Of course she was conscious of the transformation: she became increasingly disillusioned and bitter about the nonsense of 'teaching the heathen' and she became increasingly irreverent about her husband's sermons. But in terms of explaining her own life, she questioned the efficacy of the arrangement of sending ill-equipped missionaries to South Africa rather than the circumstances in which such 'solutions' were offered for civilisation. Critical of the detail, she did not repudiate the authority, but resigned herself to her God-determined fate. In some respects I see Olive Schreiner replicating this pattern.

Rebecca's disenchantment was intensified when her husband was forced to give up his position and his ministry in 1865, basically because of his incompetence. Instead of declaring the whole thing ridiculous and impossible, however, Rebecca herself was trapped by cultural constraints and her own conditioning, and saw no alternative but to persevere with privation. She was only sustained through rigid adherence to her religious precepts and, in a way described by Mary Daly (1978), tried to ensure that her daughters conformed to the same code, regardless of how destructive that might be.

Resolved that they should be good Christians (as distinct from evangelical missionaries), Rebecca steadfastly believed in submission as a virtue and reared her daughters 'in conformance with the evangelical mode of child rearing to conquer their wills and ensure their obedience to their elders and their fear of God. Her chief method of discipline was the rod' (Winkler, 1978, p. 56) and she did not spare it; it was used even for the most paltry and insignificant infringements of her code – such as using the Afrikaans term 'ach' as an expression of surprise.

Winkler suggests that it was because Olive's mother and sister treated her so harshly that she was unable to identify fully with women (despite many women friends), for she knew 'women, like her mother and her elder sister Ettie, could also persecute other women unjustly, disciplining members of their own sex to conform to a code of female behaviour that in the wider culture operated ultimately to the benefit of men. Thus Schreiner would "hate" as well as "love" her own sex and recognize the colonized self inside her' (ibid., p. 12).

I don't want to minimise the brutality – physical and psychological – used by Rebecca against her daughter, but I do want to suggest, in the terms outlined by Mary Daly (1978), that 'deforming' one's daughters in accordance with the standards of a patriarchal model, and in the interest of gaining patriarchal approval, is a form of behaviour not unexpected in a patriarchal society which is structured so that it is necessary for women to gain male approval. Rebecca Schreiner was hardly a free agent making a choice from a range of viable or positive options, but a woman who believed – as she was meant to – that there were *no* choices. When it came to the relationship of women and men, Olive Schreiner seems to have shared this frame of reference – there were no options, the two sexes *must* be able to live together in harmony. What I find surprising is that Olive Schreiner – who queried the origin of so many other beliefs – should not have queried this one, and did not ask who gained when women believed that they must accept and condone the behaviour of men in the interest of the mutual good. (Liz Stanley's account would suggest that I am completely misled, and that Olive Schreiner *did* query the origin of this belief; it is superfluous to add that Stanley's *positive* interpretation serves women better than my *negative* one.)

For it wasn't that Schreiner did not rebel, she most certainly did, and even as a young child refused to become the submissive daughter, and developed instead an analysis of oppression, based on personal experience. And the personal experience of oppression did not end with childhood but continued into adulthood, with her first job as a governess at the age of 18. It was her rebellious nature again which helped her to break away from this deadening and depressed existence and in 1881 she left for England to train as a nurse (an occupation she had to abandon because of her asthma). For almost a decade she lived a nomadic existence in England, moving from one boarding house to another, constantly plagued by ill-health. But in this time she also published *The Story of an African Farm* (under a male pseudonym) which met with considerable success and which brought her into contact with many of the distinguished intellectuals of her time.

While on the one hand, it is suggested that 'she wanted to find men who would regard her not merely as a woman, but as a co-worker, with whom she could have "love and friendship without any sex element" ' (First and Scott, 1980, p. 18), this being the basis of amicability between the sexes, on the other hand, Schreiner argued that women's sexual needs were comparable to those of men and that the denial of them was equally as debilitating as it was for men. Evidently she did not entertain the possibility of finding sexual expression with women and she did not think it an option to have a sexual relationship with a man outside marriage, which meant that she placed herself in the predicament where, in order to satisfy some of her needs (sexual) she had to sacrifice other needs (for freedom and autonomy), and this was part of the conflict that manifested itself in her illness and unhappiness.

Winkler argues that Schreiner perfectly well understood that marriage meant a loss of freedom and the adoption of a subordinate role but that nevertheless 'the idea of marriage to a sexually aggressive, intellectually sophisticated man continued to fascinate her and she was disappointed when Havelock Ellis proved incapable of fulfilling this role' (1980, p. 24). The sources for this line of reasoning come primarily from the man Schreiner did ultimately marry (and the flattering element present in such an evaluation can hardly go unnoticed) and who presented Olive Schreiner as someone who believed that celibacy was no good for the brain of a continual brainworker (see Cronwright-Schreiner, 1924b, p. 130).

Despite the acknowledged or unacknowledged contradictions, marriage Olive Schreiner decided upon and sick she got when in 1894 she married Samuel Cronwright, a former member of the Cape Parliament, and, according to Jane Graves (1978), 'a strange choice – pedantic, priggish and reserved. A farmer who shared her love of open air life, he was also more significantly, the typical dominating male for which part of her nature longed' (p. 6).

Those Freudian interpretations raise their ugly heads again; with descriptions such as this abounding – who wants to know more about masochistic Olive Schreiner? Certainly, I was put-off by the abundance of negative comment and felt relieved (though foolish) when Stanley showed me the error of men's ways – but ways which I none the less had imitated.

'Explaining' Schreiner in this way is too much like blaming Schreiner for the limitations of the society in which she lived (and in which she is being evaluated), and which through a variety of circumstances led her to believe that she had *no* choice other than to enter marriage with a *strong* male who could accommodate her individuality, her creativity, her desire for freedom *and* her sexual needs. That this did not eventuate says more about the misleading nature of the social rationales than about Schreiner's judgement. *If*, as Winkler suggests, Schreiner did accept 'the idea that the man must be the dominant partner in any marriage' (1980, p. 21), it was after all, a lesson which had been thoroughly taught and one which just helped to make her conflict greater.

Whether she ever acknowledged that she had been just as misled by myths as her mother before her, or whether she just felt inadequate, is difficult to determine. She did not publicly admit that her marriage was unsatisfactory, despite the fact that she lived away from her husband most of the time. Again, we are led to believe that instead of repudiating the institution she rationalised the arrangement: 'Where Cron could work, she could not live: where she could breathe, he could not find work' (Graves, 1978, p. 8). In 1913 she returned to England and her wandering boarding-house existence, and became increasingly ill; in 1920 she went back to South Africa, where she died, the same year, in a boarding house.

There is so much about Olive Schreiner which is saddening. Even her book *Woman and Labour* is a fragment, a recollection based, she says, on a much more substantial manuscript, worked on for years, and which was destroyed during the Boer War. She constantly castigated herself for her own inefficiency, her illness, her writer's blocks, her failure to finish her work or her failure to finish it quickly. She blamed herself for not being healthier, not being happier. We have no need to endorse this assessment.

She could stand as an example of a woman caught between the pressures of subordination and the pressures of trying to conceptualise alternative social and economic arrangements. She could be seen as a woman who, despite all the restrictions placed on her, wrote some superbly illuminating novels about women's oppression, some influential pamphlets and treatises on women's emancipation, and who worked for women's suffrage and against racism (she resigned as Vice President from the Women's Enfranchisement League in Cape Town when she found black women were not to be included in the franchise or permitted to vote within the League). Without benefit of formal education, reared in repressive and isolated circumstances, plagued by ill-health and disturbed by internal conflict, Olive Schreiner could be said to have utilised every resource available to her to promote women's liberation in a hostile climate. This is not usually how she is judged; there is frequently the suggestion that she was her own worst enemy. The verdict is one of a neurotic, eccentric woman – who is therefore 'unreliable' and not to be seen as authoritative.

This view of her was facilitated in part by her husband who through a biography of her (1924a) attempted to construct a particular and palatable image of her – from his perspective. 'In many respects, Cronwright had barely understood his wife,' state First and Scott, 'but his presentation of her personality and behaviour created the Olive Schreiner of most subsequent biographies and commentary. For Cronwright was not only concerned to build a monument of her as a writer, but also, by destroying much of the material to which he had access, to perpetuate a view of Olive acceptable to himself' (1980, p. 20). The same old story of fashioning an image of a woman in a way that enhances a man's image of himself.

The picture Cronwright-Schreiner painted was of a woman who was hampered by her creative sensitivity, a woman who was highly strung, nervous, naïve as a child, who had no sense of the relations between her own ideas and her actions, and who was morally irresponsible. She is completely removed from the realm of the intellectual, from the realm of serious and authoritative philosophy and politics, and becomes instead the irresponsible 'artiste' moved by the muse and beyond the framework of ordinary mortals. No attempt is made to examine the context in which she lived and worked, the conflict that she faced, the analysis she developed of society.

'Some of Olive's close women friends', state First and Scott, refused to co-operate with Cronwright on his biography of Olive Schreiner which they described as 'Cronwright's autobiography of his wife' (ibid.). But despite their protests it of course became 'authoritative', and his portrayal of her as irresponsible and unreliable was elaborated and reinforced by Johannes Meintjes's (1965) biography in which readers are warned against taking Olive Schreiner's diary entries seriously – for after all, they were melodramatic, neurotic, a form of self-dramatisation. A man knows these things; it is his interpretation that counts.

Even among some feminist accounts I detect a sense of disapproval in relation to Olive Schreiner. She wasn't disapproved of by women of her own time for whom she was a source of inspiration. I think it important that we celebrate that contribution that she made (and which is still a contribution) and that we hold society – not Schreiner – accountable for the debilitating conflict she endured. To blame her is to fail to learn from her experience.

9 Remember our heritage: Ray Strachey (1887–1940)

If the women associated with *Time and Tide* were influenced by Olive Schreiner, a slightly later generation of feminists were influenced by Ray Strachey – albeit it in a somewhat different manner. Mary Stott (1982), one of the first 'flapper voters' in 1929, an active feminst and journalist throughout her life, when asked how she had become a feminist said that there was one major cause – *The Cause* (1928) by Ray Strachey.

It must have been the first book of its kind – 'a short history of the women's movement in Great Britain' – and it made visible women's tradition, and responsibility. It was not only a celebration, a reminder of the energy so many women had invested in order that their 'heirs' might participate fully in political life, not only a salutary account of the struggle and the resistance and hostility that women encountered, it was also a call for future effort from women. Strachey did not for a minute believe that the battle was won with the vote, and *The Cause* embodies an insistent demand for women to live up to the example and the expectations of their foremothers, to build on what they had already achieved so that sexaul equality could become a reality. It seems that a new generation of women responded to her message and a link was forged between the old and the new.

Partly because of her own family circumstances, Ray Strachey placed great value on handing on a feminist tradition. She came from a long line of writing-feminists, but this was not the only unusual feature her family possessed. Her grandmother, Hannah Whittall (1832–1911), married Robert Pearsall Smith in their native America and, according to Ray Strachey's daughter, Barbara Strachey (1980), became 'wrong way' immigrants to Britain in the 1880s. Hannah – who was a formative influence in Ray Strachey's life – appears to have been a most formidable woman with her two famous sons-in-law (Bernard Berenson and Bertrand Russell) expressing considerable dislike for her and her domineering ways. Hannah obviously had great zest and enthusiasm for life, became more radical as she grew older, and never ceased to write: the archive inherited by her great-granddaughter Barbara Strachey contains over 20,000 of Hannah's letters, and of course she wrote books and pamphlets as well.

'Hannah was a fierce feminist and a doting mother,' says Barbara Strachey, and, 'She was even a more adoring grandmother, providing a home for Ray and Karin when their mother (Mary) ran away from her first husband, Frank Costelloe, with Berenson. Ray, her favourite, grew up to follow in her feminist footsteps and married a brother of Lytton Strachey, while Karin who was not quite so admiring, became one of the best Freudian psychoanalysts and married the brother of Virginia Woolf' (1980, p. 13).

That within the family circle women were strong and competent, perfectly capable of looking after themselves and entitled to have their opinions taken seriously and acted upon was an understanding that was fundamental to the Whittall women, as they were inclined to call themselves in honour of Hannah. 'One of the most notable characteristics of the family was its matriarchal nature,' says Barbara Strachey. 'Descent ran, without question, from mother to daughter, and being the eldest daughter of the eldest daughter, of the eldest daughter I was always aware of being considered the "heir" to the family traditions' (ibid., p. 15). It was this sense of tradition, of passing on a heritage, that was a major part of Ray Strachey's motivation for writing.

What does emerge from Barbara Strachey's account of the Pearsall Smith family, and, indeed an item that she comments on, is the extent to which some of the most prominent intellectual and suffrage figures of the time formed part of a relatively small circle. Ray Strachey had access to a community in which ideas were shared and explored. Mary, Ray's mother, was a close friend of Walt Whitman's; her uncle, Logan (himself a writer), and her aunt, Alys (married to Bertrand Russell), were friends of Henry James. There was of course constant discussion and debate with Bertrand Russell (who encouraged Ray's interest in politics and coached Karin for her Cambridge exams), and then Ray married Oliver Strachey, after first being introduced to Maynard Keynes as a possible suitor. Mary's cousin was Carey Thomas – president of Bryn Mawr and a family influence – and Karin and Adrian Stephen's daughter, Ann, married R. Llewelyn Davies.

While not members, both Ray and Karin had contact with the 'Bloomsbury Group' (Ray's mother called it the 'Gloomsbury Group'), and Virginia Woolf stayed with the Pearsall Smith family (Virginia did not exactly approve of Ray but was even more critical of her sister-in-law, Karin). With all this intermingling of relations and friends, Ray Strachey did not lack food for thought, and it was in this context she began her career as a writer – writing about women.

Perhaps it is just as well to say little about Ray Strachey's first venture into the world of print – it was a biography of one of her grandmother's friends, and was entitled *Frances Willard: Her Life and Work* (1912). Understandably Ray was familiar with American feminist traditions not just through her grandmother's connections and through Carey Thomas, but because Ray herself spent time in America and went on a lecture tour with another elder stateswoman whom she admired, Anna Howard Shaw, who was (after Carrie Chapman Catt's short term) Susan B. Anthony's successor as president of the National American Woman's Suffrage Association.

Ray Strachey seems to have had few inhibitions about claiming her rights won by previous generations of women, and just as there was no question about her right to write, nor was there any question about her right to education. She read mathematics at Cambridge (although by her own admission, and her results, she wasn't very good at it, not that she seems to have found this unduly disturbing) and later, electrical engineering at Oxford. Her sister, Karin, while very different in many respects, also seems to have shared the belief that women had every right to education, and even to excel. Coached by Bertrand Russell (who admired her intellect, 'as a woman'), she did three years' work in two, at Cambridge, to obtain First Class Honours in the first tripos in 1910, and she was the first woman at Cambridge to be given the 'Star' or Distinction in Philosophy.

While Ray was dedicated to her writing, says Barbara Strachey, it was only half of her life; the other half was suffrage. She fought for women and her writing was part of the battle. Ray Strachey was a devoted follower of Millicent Fawcett's (she published a biography of Fawcett in 1931) and a tireless organiser, speaker, writer, within the suffrage movement. She was also determined that women should use and enjoy the political rights they were acquiring, in the same way as they should use and enjoy educational rights.

Ray Strachey undeniably dispensed with many of the nineteenth-century conventions which had restricted women's activities; she strode through life. She was remarkably unconcerned about her appearance – there are quite a few stories about her wearing her dress inside out, and claiming that no one would notice – she puffed a pipe, and she built her own home, aptly called Mud House in reference to the material from which she built it. Upon her marriage to Oliver Strachey (who couldn't find a job), she attempted to implement a feminist lifestyle – with familiar consequences. As Oliver had no employment, they decided to write a book together on Indian history, and to share domestic responsibilities. Ray wrote that they agreed that Oliver was 'to do all the food and foodbills and everything appertaining to meals, and I am to do the rest . . . Oliver is reading cookery books and anxiously discussing . . . how to use up scraps, and I believe he is going to make a great success of it.' He didn't. He did not get beyond a leg of mutton – every day – and says Barbara Strachey, 'Ray soon had to take the whole thing over herself' (1980, p. 267). Ray Strachey's feminism was not a theory divorced from reality; she lived it.

During the war Ray Strachey continued to work unceasingly for women's interests. She was 'engaged in great battles with the War Office over their attempts to inflict unequal pay and totally unsuitable conditions of employment on the vital women workers in munitions: she was conducting equally urgent negotiations with the big Trade Unions on their behalf, and also lobbying politicians of all parties on the forthcoming National Service scheme. Finally as 1917 drew on, the Suffragists turned all their energies to the new Representation of the People Bill, which in their opinion had to be steered firmly towards some inclusion of the women's vote' (ibid., p. 273). When in 1918 a further – and unexpected – Act permitting women to stand for parliament was passed, Ray Strachey was one of the sixteen women who stood for election and tried to organise a campaign in the three weeks that were available to them. She was unsuccessful (they all were, with the exception of Countess Markiewicz who did not take her seat as part of the Irish Republican protest) and was also unsuccessful in her two later attempts in 1922 and 1923.

She believed strongly that women should get into the political arena and work for change; and she also believed that it was vitally important that women should be seen as politically competent. When in 1919 Nancy Astor was elected to parliament, 'Ray offered her services, without pay, as part-time Parliamentary Secretary and adviser', for, as she wrote to her mother, 'It is very important that the first woman MP should act sensibly, and she, though full of good sense of a kind, is lamentably ignorant of everything she ought to know' (ibid., p. 287).

On other fronts Strachey fought to open new professions and trades to women, and she founded, ran, and raised funds for the Women's Employment Federation. She took over as editor of the old suffrage paper *The Common Cause,* renamed *The Woman's Leader,* and she became deeply involved in work for the League of Nations. She also found time to broadcast almost weekly on current affairs, to introduce and edit her grandmother's Fanaticism Papers, and to write her influential books and articles.

While Ray Strachey was also one of the generation who had witnessed a revolution in woman's position in society, she was well aware of just how much further there was to go. But it is typical of her style that she could keep reminding women of just how much had been achieved, for she believed this to be the most effective spur for further action. In 1931 she edited *Our Freedom and its Results* in which five women (including herself and the MP Eleanor Rathbone) evaluated the changes that had occurred in public life, in the law, in sex morality, in employment and in social life, and in this, the case was again clear: there were grounds for encouragement but also the need for much more work to be done. Women had much to be proud of, given where they had begun, but the revolution was not yet completed.

What has happened to Ray Strachey? She died in 1940 after an operation and seems to just disappear. She is introduced to the modern women's movement through the republication of *The Cause* (1978) which seems to have had a comparable effect now to that which it produced among women when first published – a reminder of the heritage and a call for future action, which does not go unheeded. But of Ray Strachey, one of our immediate foremothers, so little is known.

10 Friend or enemy?

One cannot read about Ray Strachey and her family environment without encountering constant references to Bertrand Russell. His reputation has ensured sustained interest in him in a variety of sources, but it is more his personal qualities than his internationally proclaimed philosophical expertise which was of concern to the Pearsall Smith family. Undoubtedly he encouraged the women of the family to develop their minds and to become politically active – on behalf of their sex – but it was within prescribed limits, despite his avowed pro-feminism and his interest in women's suffrage. For Russell, the intellect of a woman was not like that of a man, and there is no mystery about which he valued most. If the great intellectual Bertrand Russell could not admit women's intellectual equality with men, there was little likelihood that lesser mortals would be the recipients of contrary credible insights!

When Alys Pearsall Smith agreed to marry Bertrand Russell – after much hesitation and with considerable apprehension which later proved to be well founded – she expressed some misgivings about being his intellectual equal, and therefore about being a suitable companion, to which Russell replied – reassuringly – 'You really need not trouble yourself about your exact degree of intellect. . . . No woman's intellect is really good enough to give me pleasure as intellect' (quoted in Strachey, 1980, pp. 252–3). When it is recognised that for many at the time Russell was *the* champion of women's rights (he once stood as a women's suffrage candidate for parliament), then there do not seem to be too many advantages in permitting prominent and powerful men to represent women's interests.

Having reassured Alys that she couldn't hope to be his intellectual companion – with the comforting counsel that no woman could – and that she was not to trouble herself about such minor details, Russell added in his letter that 'love is altogether strange' (ibid., p. 253) and in his case, this was probably something of an understatement. He succeeded in making Alys's life miserable. He did not treat her as someone who had the same human needs as himself and he used his power, personal and structural, to deprive her of her identity and confidence. This was accomplished in part by his rejection of her, and his affairs with other women (including Lady Ottoline Morrell) which served as a constant (and I suspect intentional) reminder of her inadequacy, in his (clever and not to be questioned) eyes.

After insisting that Alys give up her own life for his (and his requirements in relation to his daily existence were not easily met), it could be said that he waited until she was depleted of resources of her own before he insisted with equal firmness that they should each live their own lives. By this time, Alys did not really know what her own life could or should be, after so many years of denying her own needs and catering exclusively for his. Distressed by his injunction that she should be responsible for herself while his career – and his affairs – sustained him, Alys, unable to perceive any viable alternative, went along with this arrangement, painful though it was to her: 'In 1920 she received yet another blow. Bertie wanted to marry Dora Black to ensure that their coming child – who might be a son and therefore in line for his brother's earldom – should be legitimate, though Dora herself would have preferred to remain unmarried. Alys fell once more into sleeplessness and depression but she agreed immediately to the divorce, and also to support Bertie's plea to cut short the waiting period, since the child was soon to be born' (ibid., p. 292).

11 Out from under: Dora Russell (1894–)

And so enters Dora Black. This was the woman whom Crystal Eastman was to ask at a later date about the reason for her change of name ('Who is Dora Black?' 1978, pp. 114–18) and who was to encounter the reassuring response of the *husband*, who informed her: 'I admit I should not like to have become Mr Dora Black' (ibid., p. 114), but who added, 'To tell the truth . . . it never occurred to us that Dora might keep her own name when we were married' (ibid., p. 115). Russell was indeed extremely helpful in speaking for his new wife (as he had for his old), and Eastman reports that, despite her request to speak to Dora Russell, Mr Russell stayed throughout the entire interview and 'graciously helped us on' (ibid.). In his second marriage Russell seems to have given a repeat performance.

In her autobiography, *The Tamarisk Tree* (1977), Dora Russell makes no attempt to analyse Russell's treatment of his first wife, Alys, and in *her* account of the Pearsall Smith family, Barbara Strachey makes no reference to his treatment of his second wife, yet when the two marriages are viewed side by side they reveal some remarkable similarities. Both expose Russell's attitude to women, and both indicate that he showed little compunction in robbing his wives of their youthful resources, and then leaving them with few of their own.

This is, of course, not the usual portrayal of Russell which is coloured by reverence for his ability as a scholar, and by admiration for his pro-feminist stand. But then, the source of this representation is often Russell himself. Alys never provided her public version of the man and Dora Russell says in 1977 that until then, her voice had not been heard (p. 10). In the absence of contrary evidence, Russell's good opinion of himself prevailed. Dora Russell is still not completely free to speak. She stated in 1977 that: 'The copyright law is such that although the right to publish letters written by me is mine, the recipient, in possession of the actual paper, can prevent publication. Russell placed on my letters to him an embargo until five years after my death' (ibid., p. 11). Very convenient; needless to say Russell did not operate under such restrictions.

Upon marriage Dora too found that as well as her livelihood, she had to give up many of her friends (though not her mother) as Alys had done, and take on Bertie's, despite the fact that his were considerably older. Dora was thus effectively removed from a circle of women such as those who were associated with *Time and Tide*. There were contacts, of course, such as the interview with Crystal Eastman, a visit from Sylvia Pankhurst, meetings of the Congress of the World League for Sexual Reform (of which she and Bertie were both members), where Vera Brittain gave a paper, and luncheons such as the one at which Emma Goldman spoke and 'over which Rebecca West, young, slender and beautiful, presided with considerable grace and courage' (ibid., p. 97). But basically Dora Russell was isolated by her marriage and there were other problems as well.

She found herself many times an unacknowledged appendage of her famous husband – the philosopher, socialist, parliamentary candidate, writer. Visitors who came to their house, she said, would 'address them-selves solely to Bertie, leaving me as the dispenser of tea' (ibid., p. 162). If she made any intellectual contribution to the discussion among Bertie's friends, it was assumed that her ideas came from him. 'I had to live in the shadow of his reputation,' she wrote (ibid., p. 164), and it does not seem to have been a very enhancing existence.

Like Alys, who had contributed a chapter entitled 'The Woman Ques-tion' to Russell's *German Social Democracy* in 1926, Dora contributed a chapter to his *The Prospects of Industrial Civilization*, 1923 (which is in Russell's name although she is acknowledged as a collaborator) but, understandably, she wanted work of her own. She says she did not tell Russell about her need for her *own* work; one can guess why.

Dora Russell says she was discouraged from pursuing her ideas about questioning the 'solution' of technology and the premise that only men could have invented 'life-denying machines'. Her position, which might be appreciated today, was so advanced in the 1920s that it was usually considered strange, and she was met with non-comprehension, which in the circumstances would no doubt be sufficient to induce anyone to abandon their stand – particularly a woman in contact with the intellectual giants of the time who failed to understand what she was saying. An avid feminist from an early age, a brilliant scholar with a future ahead of her at Cambridge (she was made a Fellow of Girton after the First World War), an independent and competent woman (who got herself into Russia without a visa, no mean feat, in order to see first hand the results of the revolution), a woman who had been extremely critical of marriage and its conventions, Dora Russell found herself married, isolated, demoralised, deprived of the work she wanted to do and, as wife and mother, required to do a great deal of unpaid work she did not want to do. And the gap between the possibility of work and the reality of her daily life became greater. She was also informed by Russell that women's intellects were not of the same standard as men's.

What I do find somewhat surprising is that she did not react in the way described by Charlotte Perkins Gilman, for Dora Russell must have felt conflict: what does one do when the champion of women puts one down? In society's terms, Russell was above reproach and attack in his attitude to women, yet Dora Russell's domestic reality points to a male tyrant – who appropriated so many of her resources (in a very clever way of course) but who could not be criticised. At this stage of her life it would have been very difficult for Dora Russell to have labelled her husband as an enemy of woman; there is little chance that anyone would have believed her anyway – a common predicament for women.

Even though Dora Russell had been acutely aware of the way women were exploited through marriage, she still found herself caught to some extent in the 'trap' she had so assiduously sought to avoid. Like Tillie Olsen (1980) and Adrienne Rich (1980, p. 197), who have raised the issue of the conflict between *wanting* to meet the needs of children, and at the same time wanting one's own autonomous existence, Dora Russell stated that for 'a woman, marriage presents not only practical problems, but she finds herself emotionally pulled all ways, and tends by tradition and impulse to put the needs of others before her own' (1977, p. 167). Another example of the thesis that it is through nurturance that the weapon for women's oppression is forged?

Dora Russell readily acknowledged that married women and mothers who wanted their own paid work (or were obliged from necessity to find such work, as she herself was, at a later stage) were simply adding yet another job to their already overburdened lives. She could see the emerging shape of the 'superwoman', expected to cope with home and work, and she detected the danger. Awareness of its own, however, was not sufficient to solve the problem; Dora Russell knew she had to have stimulating and active work which was her own. She needed it, and the positive feedback it could provide, not just in terms of her competence, but in order to confirm her existence.

But what sort of work? Cut off from many of the women of her own age who shared her interests, there was little access to the broad women's movement; she was unable to indulge her desire to be an actress, and it appeared futile to attempt anything in the intellectual domain where Bertie so demonstrably dominated. There were few options, but she began by representing women's specific interests (a difficult stand even for Bertie to adopt) in the political circles in which she and her husband moved. She started to explore and appreciate the significance and centrality of birth control in women's lives (in her relationship with Bertrand Russell this was not an insight born of personal experience, given that the issue was for her to become pregnant, not to prevent it), and she began to recognise the implications of men making it legal to withhold this vital knowledge from women who desperately needed it.

Dora Russell was outraged when in 1923 a cheap pamphlet written by Margaret Sanger 'explaining about sex and contraception in terms which, it was thought, uneducated women would understand' (1977, p. 169) was seized and destroyed as obscene. She organised an appeal, but the magistrates refused to hear the evidence, declaring that they would make up their own minds. Dora Russell says, 'It seemed to me that what worried them most was the question and answer in the pamphlet, "Should a woman enjoy sexual intercourse? Yes, she should." What would be the effect of this information coming to the knowledge of their wives and daughters?' (ibid.).

Frequently Dora Russell made the links between women's 'ignorance' and men's power, and rightly argued that women should possess any knowledge which men had constructed – though this did not mean of course that women were obliged to accept it. Many men felt differently.

At that time government policy on the issue of birth control was quite clear: the policy of the Ministry of Health was 'to threaten with dismissal doctors or health visitors who gave such advice, as well as indicating that grants to health centres might be withheld' (ibid., p. 170). It did not escape Dora Russell's attention that it was men who were delivering these edicts which had so many effects on women's lives, and that men in general appeared threatened by any attempts on women's part to control their own fertility. Nor did it escape her attention that these decisions men made were blatantly discriminatory against poor women. Dora Russell was incensed that 'information which a middle class woman could get from her doctor should be withheld from a poorer woman who might need it far more', although she admitted that: 'In actual fact, ignorance about contraception and the importance of family limitation were then fairly widespread among all classes' (ibid., p. 169). But it was working-class women who suffered most.

Recognising the class bias in the distribution of knowledge on contraception, Dora Russell turned to socialist men for support. She did not get it. It is worth noting that she was informed by many of the men in the Labour Party and Trade Union movement that it was *more money* the working class needed, not *less children*. Most of them remained unimpressed with her argument that even if a woman lived in Buckingham Palace she would not want a baby every year.

The divisions between women's politics and men's politics were marked, and there was many a bitter wrangle. It should come as no surprise to find that Dora Russell was warned to keep sex out of politics, and told that her efforts would split the Labour movement. After being taken to task by the woman organiser of the Labour party who instructed her to withdraw the disruptive resolution on birth control, Dora Russell wrote that this 'interview revealed to me that the Labour Woman Organiser existed not so much to support the demands of women, as to keep them in order from the point of view of the male politicians' (ibid., p. 172). An old and familiar tactic.

Dora Russell was completely convinced, however, that the women did not share the men's point of view. Working-class (and middle-class) women *did* want contraceptive advice (understandably) and saw it as an issue of the greatest priority. There was widespread recognition, says Dora Russell, that emancipation for women at the most fundamental level meant emancipation from continual and unwanted pregnancies. At one Labour Women's Conference, Russell says she was 'astounded at the fury against child bearing displayed by the delegates. . . . Here were women fiercely repudiating what had been preached at us as the noblest fulfilment of our womanhood' (ibid., p. 175).

It was one thing to think that continual and unwanted pregnancies were part of the natural order, inevitable, and to be endured, and quite another to discover that there was an alternative, that they could be prevented, but that men were against this. I am not surprised that the women expressed such fury; men's behaviour constituted a blatant example of male power and could be neither rationalised nor ignored. Whenever power is exposed in this way it seems to me that women invariably get angry, for the mask of mutual concern just falls away.

Dora Russell played a considerable role in unmasking the operation of power, in making birth control a *political* issue, and in exposing the value system of men. She helped to coin a particularly effective and unanswerable slogan: 'IT IS FOUR TIMES AS DANGEROUS TO BEAR A CHILD AS TO WORK IN A MINE: AND MINING IS MAN'S MOST DANGEROUS TRADE.'

If men were so concerned about the dangers of mining and prepared to devote so much energy to removing these dangers, why were they not only *silent* when it came to the even more dangerous (and more extensive) occupation of motherhood, but went so far as to put their energy into preventing changes which would reduce the dangers? Was it possible, asked Dora Russell, that dangers for women did not count in the same way as dangers for men?

Dora Russell made an impressive contribution to the campaign for birth control, but the campaign also helped her resolve in part some of her personal difficulties, by providing her with useful and meaningful work which was very much her own. She was able to build on her understandings and consolidate her position with the publication of her book, *Hypatia, or Women and Knowledge,* in 1925, although in her interview with Crystal Eastman she revealed (unintentionally I suspect) some of the problems she was up against.

In her interview with Eastman, Dora Russell said of the book: 'I wanted to publish the book as Dora Russell . . . but the publisher persuaded me to allow him to put "Mrs Bertrand Russell" in parentheses under my name, on the title page. He said it would add two thousand to the sales, and the thing I cared most about was to get the book read, to make my ideas known, and besides we needed the money . . . So I agreed. You see, I used to write a great deal, but I could not get any paper to print what I wrote when I was Dora Black' (and this could have been a point made at Eastman's expense, for Eastman had rejected a letter from Dora Black – defending Russell's book to which she had contributed – when she was editor of *The Liberator*). 'So', says Eastman, 'there you have it; a spirited young woman of great promise marries an older man of many achievements and considerable fame. Shall she struggle on as "Dora Black" until she has won a hearing for herself on her own merits and such distinction as her achievements entitle her to? Or shall she make the most of her husband's name?' (1978, p. 117). What is clear is that for women it is a choice between the lesser of two evils!

Hypatia is today still a good read; Dora Russell's analysis shares much with contemporary feminism, even if her optimism of the time appears slightly misplaced in retrospect. The book is dedicated to her daughter Kate and the Preface helps to set the tone for much to follow: 'Hypatia was a University lecturer denounced by Church dignitaries and torn to pieces by Christians. Such will probably be the fate of this book: therefore it bears her name. What I have written here I believe and shall not retract or change for similar episcopal denunciations.'

There has been a sex-war for the last twenty or twenty-five years, writes Dora Russell, and women started it, because they had no choice. It has been a rebellion against male tyranny despite the fact that men prefer not to see it in this light (and despite the fact that men have the power to impose their interpretations upon women). Writing from her experience with male politicians, Russell states that, 'the politician has yet to be found who will realize that the sex problem is as fundamental in politics as the class war, and more fundamental than foreign trade or imperial expansion' (1925, p. 4). There can be no mistaking her meaning as she challenges men's definitions of the world, of women and politics, and in the first part of the book, no attempt is made to sugar coat the pill. 'Birth control is . . . displeasing to the male' (ibid., p. 10), she states, therefore women shall not have it; and women who seek it are mocked and ridiculed. This is unquestionably the behaviour of tyrants; this is why sex-war is necessary.

Women want and need knowledge, and knowledge which is consistent with their own experience, argues Dora Russell. Male power has been based upon women's *ignorance* (which along with beauty have been the two qualities most admired in women – and for reasons that are not difficult to fathom as far as men are concerned), but women have proved that they have minds (this, a reference to women's battle for education and their consequent success), and the time has now come for them to assert that they also have bodies. There is no room any longer for nineteenth-century-type denials of women's sexual needs.

Russell's demand was a radical one in the 1920s – and no less risky then, than it is now. Feminists, she claimed, have been pushed into denying their biological capacities in order to prove that they have intellectual ones, because patriarchy has used woman's *different* biology to 'prove' that she is intellectually inferior. Denying woman's capacity as 'life giver', as 'nurturer', however, was to Russell dangerous. For this was the stance that men adopted, it was a 'philosophy' that would lead to soulless destruction.

Anticipating what we would call today the 'ecological frame of reference', as early as the 1920s (and without a sympathetic audience), Russell was trying to argue for the human race as but one constituent in a living and organic universe; she was trying to assert the value of life – all life – and the necessity of learning to live a replenishing existence on the planet, rather than trying to 'master' it and ruin it. Arguing as she did that only men could think of themselves as differentiated from nature, as 'above' it, with their reverence for divorcing all elements of 'living' from their 'logic', she undoubtedly did not receive a wildy enthusiastic reception from her husband (who epitomised the distinction between the 'intellectual' and the contaminating 'personal' – although I am assured on good authority, for I have neither the time nor inclination to read his work, that he later abandoned this position).

Today's rereading of Dora Russell is complicated by the fact that 'woman and nature', and the 'biology' of women, have become tricky concepts, and are assiduously avoided within the contemporary women's movement as a reaction against 'biological determinism'; but I cannot help but wonder whether women are intended to turn away from the conceptualisation of human beings as part of the animal kingdom, with a responsibility towards finding a way to live at one with all forms of life – including that of our own species. (This is discussed in more detail in the last section.)

Where I do detect a difference between Dora Russell's philosophy and that forged in the last decade is on the issue of heterosexuality. Russell acknowledged the necessity of the sex-war, but suggested that the unsatisfactory nature of heterosexual relationships could be resolved; she believed that men could change, that they could accommodate woman's full humanity, even to the extent of learning from women and adopting some of women's more productive values. I think that men will *not* change, *unless they have to*. Their investment in the present arrangements – no matter how absurd or destructive those arrangements may be shown to be – is so great (I would argue) that it is unlikely that they will voluntarily abandon them and willingly follow, rather than deny, women.

In relation to *Hypatia*, Dora Russell informed Crystal Eastman that: 'Feminists have emphasized for a long time the importance of each woman's individual entity and the necessity of economic independence. Perhaps it was necessary. But now I think we need some emphasis on the instinctive side of life, sex and motherhood. I am writing another book now called "The Right to be Happy" and trying to say what I mean. Life isn't all earning your living. Unfortunately we fall in love and Feminism must take that into consideration' (Eastman 1978, p. 118).

For anyone looking for a modern rationale for women, I suggest they read the last chapter of 'The Right to be Happy' rather than dismiss this statement of Russell's, for she intended the term 'love' in the widest possible nurturing sense of the word. Perhaps having a go at Bertrand, she suggests that the answer to life lies in life itself – and not in the stars! She is trying to establish that there is more to life than 'economics' (and 'the machines' that serve them), which she sees as a product of male consciousness; to Dora Russell there is absolutely no doubt that women's consciousness has been excluded completely from the current ways of thinking about the world, and she wants to re-establish women's nururance as a basis for social values. We do not have to be cowed into denying our life-enhancing values, she argues, simply because men have been able to use those values against us in the past.

But how many Dora Russell scholars are there? I wouldn't even like to hazard a guess on how many people are engaged in protecting her ex-husband's interests (ensuring that his letters are not published, his papers preserved in the university, the trust funds properly administered). Her books are out of print, her work on children and education (and it was in the establishment of a school that she helped to find her own space and identity) is relatively unknown, her name missing from any inventory of philosophers, educationalists, intellectuals – and sometimes of feminists. We have been most remiss.

12 Tough politics: Virginia Woolf (1882–1941)

Unlike Dora Russell, a veritable industry has been built up around Virginia Woolf, whose book *A Room of One's Own* was published but three years after *Hypatia*.

I do not propose to embark here on a detailed study of Virginia Woolf's feminism – her ideas have been discussed by so many people in so many places, that in some respects it could be argued that she defies the thesis that women who protest disappear. But I do want to draw attention to the *way* she has been portrayed, and by *whom*, for while Woolf may not have been erased (as yet?) she has none the less been given 'the treatment' of a patriarchal culture.

Until relatively recently (and the feminist 'revival'), Virginia Woolf was known primarily as an artist and not as a thinker (and there is a world of difference for women) with her novels enjoying some status, but her feminist writings little or none. *Three Guineas* (1938), her most outspoken denunciation of patriarchy, *had* virtually disappeared. And the portrayal of Virginia Woolf had been reflected almost exclusively through the filters of two men – Leonard Woolf and Quentin Bell. They may have had personal reasons for wanting to represent her in a particular way, but there may also have been limitations in their view of Virginia Woolf and her work. In Woolf's own words, a woman 'will find she is perpetually wishing to alter the established values – to make serious what appears insignificant to man, and trivial what is to him important. And for that of course she will be criticized; for the critic of the opposite sex will be genuinely puzzled and surprised by an attempt to alter the current scale of values, and will see in it not merely a difference of view, but a view that is weak, or trivial, or sentimental because it differs from his own' (1929; 1972, p. 146). Virginia Woolf would have disputed Leonard Woolf's and Quentin Bell's ability and authority to categorise herself and her work, and for very sound reasons. There is considerable and growing evidence that where Woolf did not fit their preconceived notions and definitions they have found her to be 'meaningless', 'eccentric' or misguided.

'Virginia Woolf is seldom seen as a political writer, least of all as a successful or influential political writer, and almost never as a theorist with a comprehensive and penetrating grasp of the social and political fabric of the society we inhabit,' states Berenice Carroll (1978) in her marvellously illuminating reappraisal of Virginia Woolf. For the most part, Woolf's political writing passes unnoticed, adds Carroll, and points directly to the part played by Leonard and Quentin in this process – she didn't fit their definitions of politics and in typical patriarchal style they therefore determined that she was not political. 'Leonard Woolf, . . . wrote that she was "the least political animal that has lived since Aristotle invented the definition." Quentin Bell, her . . . biographer, devoted scarcely a handful of pages to her political awareness in the first 400 pages of his two-volume biography, and remarked of her in the year 1934 (when she was fifty-two years old) that "as yet Virginia was not really worried about politics" ' (ibid., p. 99). No, their discussion of Virginia Woolf was related to her personal 'idiosyncrasies', their discussion of her work to 'the aesthetic qualities of her art, the "lyric mode" of her novels, the techniques of interior monologue, the form and style and symbolism of her writing, her success or failure in creating "character", and the allegedly internal (or even "egoistic") focus of her work' (ibid.).

We have heard all this before: it is the means whereby 'women's novels (are) applauded for a certain elegance of style, an attention to detail or nuance, and then . . . curtly dismissed for their inevitably "feminine" lack of humor, weighty truths, or universal significance', says Annette Kolodny (1981, p. 23), so that women's art becomes 'peculiar pathology' while men remain the serious artists and thinkers. While Virginia Woolf conformed to this pattern all was well. But what happened when she stepped outside it, as she did in *A Room of One's Own* (1928) and *Three Guineas*?

This was not art, was the verdict, but propaganda, and a failure.

This is a verdict to be expected in a male-dominated society, but it could well change if it were women doing the judging, and not the men. Much that the male critics have passed over as insignificant, dismissed as meaningless, bridled over as absurd, could assume entirely different connotations when women who share some of the values of Virginia Woolf make their selection. The representation of her and her work that we have received could undergo some remarkable changes. Leonard might well have believed that Virginia Woolf needed to be protected from the world, but those for whom Charlotte Perkins Gilman's *The Yellow Wallpaper* strikes a chord might suggest that Virginia Woolf needed protection from him. Quentin Bell might well have thought her apolitical, over-sensitive and irrational in her denunciation of masculine values, but those who link aggression, force, conquest, violence and control with masculinity might suggest that Woolf's analysis is the essence of a rational politics.

Virginia Woolf's politics are not (male) party politics, but feminist politics, and I think that there are few areas of feminist thought to which she has not made a contribution. Her fundamental thesis that those who are in power perceive the world differently (and determine the scale of values) from those outside the power structure (and whose values are therefore decreed to be deviant, eccentric, neurotic, irrational, inexplicable) is for me one of the touchstones of feminism, and helps to explain the way she has been treated, removed from the realms of philosopher or political analyst, and cast into the mould of delicate and elaborate artist. (There is even a jarring of images if one tries to visualise Virginia Woolf as a tough political thinker — which indicates how pervasive the portrayal has been — yet in *Three Guineas*, which she carefully planned in order to 'strike very sharp and clear on a hot iron' (Carroll, 1978, p. 103), her avowed intention was — as is the title of Carroll's essay — 'To Crush Him In Our Own Country', which is a tough stand in the face of the drift to war.)

Woolf herself would not have been surprised at the treatment she has received, consigned to a separate and acceptable women's sphere outside the mainstream of intellectual recognition, for after all, were women not literally locked out of men's libraries? She understood this process and it was precisely the one she was attempting to subvert with the documentation of women's heritage — and possibilities — in *A Room of One's Own*. She tried to construct a coherent context in which women's values were meaningful and invested with layers of symbolism, and celebration — no mean feat in a society in which the symbolism of the phallus is so pervasive and where men consistently celebrate their own achievements, but where women's imagery and celebration is invisible. And she tried to do this because she recognised the political nature and the significance of the act of creating a different and autonomous women's culture *outside* the control of men, although still rooted in the culture of men, and in opposition to it.

When Florence Howe asserts that women's studies is not a *ghetto* but the *centre* of the construction of knowledge, based on the experience of half the population (with the implication that it is men's studies which is on a side-track), she is doing nothing less than Virginia Woolf, who made it a virtue to be an *outsider* in an exploitative and oppressive society. Women can best help society, can best serve the interests of achieving freedom, equality and peace, by *not* helping men, argues Woolf, in *Three Guineas*, by *not* imitating them or supporting them in their aggression, violence, and war. She urges women to stay out of patriarchal institutions, to find their own critical and creative means of promoting change (1938, p. 206), and to remain *free from unreal loyalties*, to remain *outside* that 'loyalty to old schools, old colleges, old churches, old ceremonies, old countries' (ibid., p. 142).

This was the book Leonard Woolf decreed as not very good, indeed to which he was hostile: ' "Maynard Keynes was both angry and contemptuous: it was, he declared, a silly argument and not very well written." E. M. Forster thought it "the worst of her books." Quentin Bell perhaps best displayed the depth of incomprehension of the book in reporting his own reactions: "What really seemed wrong . . . was the attempt to involve a discussion of women's rights with the far more agonising and immediate question of what we were to do in order to meet the ever growing menace of Fascism and War. The connection between the two questions seemed tenuous and the positive suggestions wholly inadequate" ' (Carroll, 1978, p. 119). Bell missed Virginia Woolf's thesis that tyranny begins at home; Adrienne Rich (1980) did not. In her appeal to women to be 'Disloyal to Civilization' she quotes and builds upon Woolf's concept of 'freedom from unreal loyalties'. To Rich, as to Woolf, it was the values of a society controlled by men which women must disown, and challenge, in the interest of freedom, equality and peace.

But Woolf did not make a cult of the patriarchal opposite of aggression, nurturance. She saw nurturance, as it was constructed under patriarchy, as an enemy of women, as a means of depleting their resources and depriving them of independence and identity. When Virginia Woolf evokes the image of 'The Angel in the House', the woman who is 'utterly unselfish', who excels 'in the difficult art of family life', who sacrifices herself daily, who is pure (1929, p. 285), she sets up the image only to knock it down. Woolf says of her own battle with The Angel, 'I turned upon her and caught her by the throat. I did my best to kill her. . . . Had I not killed her, she would have killed me' (ibid., p. 286).

For Woolf there is no mystery about the existence and purpose of The Angel, the image to which women are obliged to conform, and no doubt about what has to be done to this image. Women are without financial resources, argues Woolf. It is the underlying theme of *A Room of One's Own* and *Three Guineas* that, because men control wealth, women, of necessity, must find favour with men. Women 'must charm, they must conciliate, they must – to put it bluntly – tell lies if they are to succeed' (ibid.). Success for women depends on approval from men – even the success of earning one's living or finding one's own board and lodging in return for service – and men have made it quite clear that it is The Angel who suits them, and of whom they approve. That is why she must go.

Economic independence, and freedom from the interruption of being emotionally available (the sanctuary of 'A Room of One's Own'), are fundamental tenets of Woolf's feminism. She understood, and deplored, the way women were required to make their resources available to men (and in this context what construction is to be placed on her 'frigidity' and her retreat into madness, which by her own admission she found profitable?), to distort their needs in order to meet those of men, to lie not just to succeed, but to survive.

A Room of One's Own and 'Women and Fiction' (1929) contain not abstract theories but are the direct product of personal experience where, as a writer, Virginia Woolf knew the reality of persistent seduction to flatter men and gain their approval in order to earn her living. She learnt early, says Berenice Carroll, 'of the need to be circumspect about seeming to preach to the master race', after Clive Bell informed her that her prejudice against men made her didactic and priggish. While deciding that man was not a very impartial or good judge of his own sex, Woolf none the less became cautious and took to veiling her meaning. While seeming to approve all the while she attempted to undermine, which was not quite as satisfactory as a more direct approach (1978, p. 102).

Woolf knew the reality: 'Secrecy is essential,' she wrote in *Three Guineas*, 'we must still hide what we are doing and thinking' because there are penalties to be paid for criticising your master (1938, pp. 217–18). One loses one's livelihood. By the time she wrote *Three Guineas* I suspect this was not such an issue. She undertook the direct approach and gives every indication that she enjoyed her new freedom – even to the extent of savouring the hostile reviews of the critics (of whom Queenie Leavis was one of the harshest; food for thought? See Marion Glastonbury, 1978).

While the approval of men might have been necessary for earning a living, it wasn't necessary for identity or a sense of emotional wellbeing, as far as Woolf was concerned. In comparison to Adrienne Rich's (1981) direct attack on compulsory heterosexuality, Virginia Woolf's meanings are veiled – but they are still there. She sees the links between male control of resources and between economic and psychological dependence for women. She clearly sees the price women pay for access to male-controlled wealth but she also sees what price men would pay if women ceased to make them the centre of the universe. Virginia Woolf wants to get rid of The Angel who is required to reflect men at twice their normal size, in the interest of women; but she also appreciates that if women begin 'to tell the truth', it will undermine the interests of men, for when man is reflected as woman sees him, and not how he demands to be seen, she argues, 'the figure in the looking glass shrinks: his fitness for life is diminished' (1928, p. 37). In using her resources for herself, woman takes them away from man.

And there can be no doubt that Woolf wants women to use their resources to promote women's values and culture. Despite the way she has been presented, her sense of sisterhood was a powerful force in her life. Regardless of 'allegations of "snobbishness" and class bias levelled against her, Woolf represents as well as any of our contemporaries the recognition that "every woman is my sister" ', says Carroll. 'Collaborationists must be exposed and resisted but beneath the surface of every woman's life Woolf sees a core of doubt, of suffering, of alienation, even of resistance. That this resistance is often secret and silent she thought inevitable under present conditions. But she saw in every woman the potential "to live differently" ' (1978, pp. 122–3).

This aspect of Woolf's feminism is well captured by Louise Bernikow

(1980), who comments on the significance of Woolf's radical concept in a patriarchal society – that 'Chloe liked Olivia'; it was Woolf, says Bernikow, who raised the possibilities for her of relationships among women, and who has been her guide. Among women, states Bernikow – and Woolf – women communicate differently from the way they do when men are present, but because it is men who decree the shape and substance of the world, who see women through the eyes of men and in relation to men, and who *do not have access* to the exclusive world of women, then this aspect of women's existence becomes invisible. It is not part of male experience, therefore it does not exist in a patriarchal society.

But this pattern of communication, these shared values and ways of expression are very real among women, argues Bernikow (and Woolf and many more, see D. Spender, 1980), for 'Woolf spoke of the "very fine instinct wireless telepathy nothing to it – in women . . ."' (1980, p. 10) and 'of "purity" of the "disinterested" quality between women. She is pointing to the political,' adds Bernikow, to the absence of a power dimension with the absence of men for: 'She imagines that women are natural with each other, that when a man walks into a room, women mask themselves. Her descriptions of how this happens and her analysis of why it does runs all through her work. One's feeling for a man does not exist apart from ways of being in the world, from the necessity that women please men to survive' (ibid., p. 11).

As a woman writer addressing herself to women – but finding she must please men, and therefore resorting to a sub-text at times in order to achieve her purpose – Woolf takes away some of the mask women don in a patriarchal society, and explores the ramifications – for women – of male power. And she puts forward a programme for change, particularly in her non-fiction. 'Woolf's political program was neither the "androgynous vision" for which she has often been praised', says Berenice Carroll, 'nor the "self-indulgent," "neurotic" outburst for which she has been attacked. It was a program which combined limited support for conventional political or reform action with a strong focus on alternative modes of political struggle: truth-telling, "living differently," and commitment to the duties of an outsider' (1978, p. 125).

There is little in her philosophy and practice that is not applicable today. 'Like many radical feminists today, she saw patriarchy as the central pillar, where domestic politics, institutional politics, and state politics converge, where the "personal is political"' (ibid., p. 118). That this was beyond the comprehension of Leonard Woolf and Quentin Bell is not at all surprising – although Berenice Carroll does suggest that Virginia Woolf didn't always reflect the men around her at twice *their* normal size: they might have been 'prepared', or they might have been hostile. 'In her personal life, it was only in rare moments – and those called "insanity" – that Woolf ever felt free enough to tell . . . men of her own intimate circle the truth' (ibid., p. 121).

Despite her 'status' as an artist, Virginia Woolf has not always enjoyed a positive reputation – and it's not just her 'madness', 'frigidity' or 'child-free' state that has been emphasised, in representations of her. She has been seen as elitist, as removed from the world of ordinary women and from the struggles which some of her contemporaries were engaged in. Few are the references to her membership of the Labour party (and the fact that she was secretary of the Rodmell branch for some time),[7] and many are the comments on her refusal to call herself feminist (for precisely the same reason as Florence Nightingale avoided the term – it was not radical enough). Where her Introductory Letter to the essays of the women of the Women's Cooperative Guild (edited by Margaret Llewelyn Davies, 1931; 1977), is mentioned, it is often perceived as an aberration on Woolf's part – as are her contributions to other feminist publications such as *The Woman's Leader* – and not as an expression of her coherent feminist philosophy. Yet Margaret Llewelyn Davies was her friend, women's issues her cause, and undermining men's values one of her primary goals (and Virginia Woolf recognised the power of women's voices in *Life As We Have Known It* to undermine male values and assert the different existence of women, women's culture and values).

But because in the main she was aloof from party politics, and the party political issues which preoccupied men, because she was outside the suffrage movement (the only activity of women which men perceived as political and only then, after it impinged on their own politics and on which they bestowed an accompanying assessment of many of the women and their policies as misguided), and because men construct the representations of women in a patriarchal society, we have been asked to accept a picture of Virginia Woolf as an apolitical, neurotic, isolated aesthete.

13 Writing with a vengeance

Divide and Rule!

It was a slogan not unknown to Woolf, with its implications for divisions among women. She recognised the way women were isolated from one another and herself did much to circumvent the process. She was, however, divided from Katherine Mansfield, and on Mansfield's early death wrote in 'the privacy of her journal . . . that with Mansfield dead there was no one to write for' (Bernikow, 1980, p. 27). Mansfield was exploring similar themes in her fiction, to those of Woolf; she has also suffered a similar fate from being represented primarily through the eyes of John Middleton Murry.

Not that Mansfield was the only woman of the time using fiction to suggest the shape of women's world. Fifty years later Adrienne Rich (1980) could speak of a new generation of women writers working out towards a new space on the boundaries of patriarchy (p. 49) but this description was equally applicable to the early decades of the twentieth century, when Edith Wharton was showing just what Henry James was leaving out, when

[7] I am indebted to Naomi Black 1982 (in press) for this and other insights in relation to Virginia Woolf.

Colette was making a mockery of men (after she took back her writing in her own name instead of allowing her husband to masquerade as the author – see Margaret Crosland, 1973), where Dorothy Richardson was exploring women's experience and insisting on its authenticity in a style later appropriated by James Joyce (Gillian Hanscombe, 1979); and in Australia, Miles Franklin was challenging the patriarchal structure – a daunting task (Verna Coleman, 1980).

The printing presses were bringing forth non-fiction as well. In 1913 Maud Pember Reeves in *Round about a Pound a Week* put paid once (but not for all) to the myth that working-class poverty and malnutrition were self-induced and a product of ignorance, when she documented the resources on which working-class women were required to manage and the conditions under which they lived. *The Working Life of Women in the Seventeenth Century* was published in 1919 and in it Alice Clark presented one of the most detailed accounts of women's life and work during the period – she helped to establish women's visibility and repudiate the myths that suggested women had never worked, and that it was a new and challenging demand to claim the right to do so. Margaret Llewelyn Davies had first published working-class women's horrific experience of enforced pregnancy in 1915 in *Maternity: Letters from Working Women* in a bid to establish the conditions of women's existence, and to put the case for birth control, and in 1931 she followed this up and the Hogarth Press brought out *Life as We Have Known It*. Ivy Pinchbeck's *Women Workers and the Industrial Revolution* was published in 1930 and once more the existence of women in the workforce (and their exploitation) was made visible, along with the implications of industrialisation for women (which existed only as a footnote in the annals of men), which were significantly different from many of the implications for men. And in 1939 there was Margery Spring Rice's *Working Class Wives* which documented the harsh social and economic realities of the lives of many women.[8]

All of these publications form part of a heritage of women studying women; all of them were attempts to make women's life and experience visible and to give women a voice. Today, they have been 'reclaimed' and are a rich resource, yet there is no reason to believe that an error of the past has been rectified and that they now enjoy a rightful place in the tradition of women's history. These records of the past, along with records of the present, could again be easily erased.

In 1938 Dorothy Sayers also came out and registered her protest against men who wanted women to go back into the home and stated: 'It is perfectly idiotic to take away woman's traditional occupations and then complain because she looks for new ones' (1971, p. 25). She too recognised that men were not against women working – women were everywhere working from dawn to dusk at domestic labour and in the poorest-paid, least-skilled and most exploited conditions. What men were against, she

---

[8] All of these publications have since been reissued in current times: most of them had been out of print for decades.

argued, was women obtaining jobs that were pleasant, exciting and profitable (ibid., p. 43), and which they wished to reserve for themselves.

By the time of the Second World War there was a considerable amount of feminist literature – there was documentation, explanation and analysis across English-speaking countries. Contrary to conventional wisdom, the efforts had not abated once the vote was won, and, contrary to conventional wisdom, feminism was not dead and buried once the war was over.

14 The 'other' politics

If, however, many women took up the pen as politics, they did not show comparable enthusiasm when it came to entering what had been men's preserve. It is not my intention here to provide any coverage of women's participation in politics but to introduce some examples in order to raise some questions. When we have been told that women have not used the vote they fought so hard to win, and even that the women's movement disintegrated once the vote was won, we must examine these 'explanations' and their origins, for their purpose does not seem to be to enhance the image of women, and I am therefore suspicious of them.

After years of campaigning for women's representation in 'men's politics' – on the grounds that it would make a difference to national and international affairs – women in Australia, America, Canada and Britain *did* try to take 'women's issues' into the men's arena, once they were permitted to do so. Some of them did not get past the early hurdles; Christabel Pankhurst, Dora Russell and Ray Strachey were among those who did not get elected. But there were others who did become politicians and whose actions leave little doubt that they had ideas about the *special* contribution women could make to legislation.

In Britain, not anticipating the advent of the contemporary women's movement, Josephine Kamm (whose book is subtitled 'The Women's Movement and its Aftermath', 1966) concludes her account with a chapter on 'Women in Parliament'. She begins with Nancy Astor, the first woman MP in 1919, who 'inherited' her husband's seat after his elevation to the House of Lords. She was followed in 1921 by Margaret Wintringham – who also took what Eleanor Flexner (1979) refers to as 'the widow's route'; Margaret Wintringham 'was billed everywhere as the first British-born MP,' states Josephine Kamm, and adds that: 'Lady Astor showed not a trace of jealousy towards her popular rival' (1966, p. 208).

Where Kamm is more helpful is in the Appendix where she provides 'Bills Brought in by Women MPs' (ibid., pp. 225–9), for this indicates that for good or ill, women politicians (at least in Britain) have been associated with a particular – and predictable – kind of legislation, centred on issues associated with the removal of 'disabilities' from women's status, the introduction of protective legislation, education, poor law reforms, and consumer affairs. It seems that few, if any, financial or foreign affairs bills have been introduced by women (with one glaring contemporary exception) and one wonders whether this is through choice, or necessity.

There were three socialists among the early women MPs in Britain and all deserve considerably more attention. There was Margaret Bondfield, who had worked as a shop assistant, and then as a trade unionist (building on the work and traditions of Emma Paterson), both before and after her parliamentary contribution. There was Susan Lawrence who was converted from conservatism, who is regularly ridiculed, and who could clearly be thoroughly disagreeable when she chose. The third was Ellen Wilkinson, who appears literally and metaphorically the most colourful, being known as 'Red Ellen' for the colour of her hair and her political persuasions, but her 'prominence' could also be partly explained by the fact that information about her is more readily available (see, for example, Betty Vernon's recent biography of her). Wilkinson was a passionate believer in the equitable distribution of resources and her ideas about politics deserve more attention than they have received in the past.

In 1929, Eleanor Rathbone entered parliament as the Independent Member for the Combined English Universities (a seat abolished in 1948), and for many reasons she, too, warrants further study. She had for many years been closely involved with the women's movement and at the centre of a controversy with Millicent Fawcett. Committed to women's economic independence, and recognising that women bore and reared children in the existing society, Rathbone formulated the arguments and policy for family endowment, presented in a pamphlet in 1918, *Equal Pay and the Family*. Millicent Fawcett opposed the measure and resigned from the National Union over it.

But it is also the fact that Eleanor Rathbone was an *Independent* Member that makes her interesting. She remained free from (male) party alignments (see Mary Stocks, 1949, and Ray Strachey, 1931), which, says Josephine Kamm, is the reason she never held office. But being an 'outsider' in the political arena poses many interesting questions.

There was no great rush of women into the Congress or the Senate in America, where Jeannette Rankin was the first 'anomaly' (being a member for Montana four years before the federal amendment was finalised), and where she was followed by Alice Robertson, who showed a distinct disinclination to espouse the women's view, opposing a much-worked-for measure put forward by the Women's Joint Congressional Committee in the interest of providing better infant and pre-natal maternity care. Summing up women's political participation in America, Eleanor Flexner has said that: 'Women have shown the same tendency as men to divide along orthodox party lines' and even at the polling booth, their participation 'still does not match their growth in the total population (they now outnumber men), nor does it adequately reflect potential political power' (1979, p. 338).

As far as I can determine from my perusal of treatises on women's participation in politics, I am asked to accept that women are either apathetic, showing little or no interest in the political process – an explanation I find hard to accept given their active participation prior to achieving the vote – or else they are stupid! The implication is that despite the vote women have had the 'good sense' to leave the serious world of politics to men, appreciating their own ineptitude in that field of endeavour.

I don't find either explanation particularly useful. From my perspective, given women's low political profile and my bias towards positive interpretations, the question is either whether women are *boycotting* politics, or whether they are being *prevented* from participating. Needless to say, both these questions assume the active and autonomous nature of women, rather than the traditional view which would have them as apathetic and foolish.

After the promise of women like Flora MacDonald Denison in Canada (a woman who 'supported divorce, birth control and even attacked the sanctity of the nuclear family', who worked as a dressmaker, and had some appreciation of the economic basis of women's oppression, and who became the leader of Canada's national suffrage association from 1911 to 1914, see Gorham, 1979, p. 49), there was no great rush to storm the citadel once women received the vote. And the contrast in Australia is perhaps even greater.

It is with joy – if not glee – that I can suggest that at the beginning of the century, it was Australian women who were looked to as 'models'. In 1902 and 1903 women across the English-speaking world heard that Australian women had gained the vote and fielded candidates at an election. Despite the convenient myth that somehow or other for Australian women the vote just descended from heaven, and that they didn't have to struggle for it, women like Rose Scott[9] had been working for years to secure women's political representation (see Marie Knuckey, 1980). So too had Vida Goldstein, who in 1899 had become the leader of the United Council for Women's Suffrage, and who from 1900 owned and edited the (feminist) paper, *The Australian Woman's Sphere*.

Australian women were internationally hailed (then) as politically sophisticated, and their advice and counsel were sought; in 1901, Vida Goldstein was invited to Washington for the founding of the International Woman's Suffrage Society (and became the conference secretary). She returned to Australia to help found the Women's (Federal) Political Association which eventually became a 'women only' party (see Gaby Weiner, 1982a),[10] and in 1903 she stood as its first parliamentary candidate – on a women's platform!

Her campaign was directed towards women and, despite the fact that she was not elected, her considerable success was remarkable, in the face of the opposition of the male candidates operating the party system and availing themselves of more than financial resources (the press was hardly flattering to Goldstein). In 1909 she began the periodical *The Woman Voter* and in 1910 again stood for election (on a women's platform). In 1911 she visited England and offered a helping hand to the WSPU.

Vida Goldstein stands at the start of the century as a symbol of what

---

[9] I want to thank my mother, Ivy Spender, for all the valuable research she undertook on Rose Scott and which I cannot now fit in but which I am sure will not go to 'waste'.

[10] I am grateful to Gaby Weiner for drawing my attention to Vida Goldstein.

women might do in the male political arena. She embodied many of the
fears held by men that the enfranchisement of women would undermine
male party politics and split the electorate on the basis of sex. Her conceptualisation of politics, her formulation of priorities and policies based on
women's needs, interests and experience, stood in stark contrast to the
framework presented by men and she, and many other women, had every
reason to believe that political and personal life would be transformed once
women were voting, and voting women into politics. Many men certainly
believed this.

What happened? I think I am surprised that more questions have not
been asked in this area. According to Margaret Stacey and Marion Price
(1981) the question should not be why are there so *few* women in politics,
but why, when nothing else changed, have so *many* women been able to
find their way into this male-controlled domain. When men still control
the institutions they set up for themselves, when they still manage the party
machines that reflect their 'personal' views (as Teresa Billington-Greig put
it), how is it that so many women have found a place?

The enfranchisement of women changed none of these practices; nor
did it prove to be a weapon for changing the division of labour. While
women are still expected to bear the brunt of domestic responsibility, and
while it is almost mandatory for every political figure to have the material
and emotional services of a *wife*, how is it that so many *wives* (albeit a
disproportionate number of widows, I suspect), have been able to fulfil this
role? How have so many single women ('wifeless politicians') been able to
run the gauntlet and bring women's issues to the floor of the House?

But if Stacey and Price are suggesting that women have been *prevented*
from participating fully in politics, Dora Russell (1982) offers a different
explanation; she suggests that women have been registering a vote – a
protest vote! The whole model of politics, like the law, says Russell, is a
product of men's consciousness and is based on *conflict*. The party system,
which demands 'adversary' politics that fly in the face of common sense –
or conscience – is simply antipathetic to women's way of operating in the
world. It allows no room for co-operation, it leaves no place for consensus.
Women cannot see the 'sense' of such a system, she argues, and this is
reflected in their choice to stay outside. (It should be noted that this line of
reasoning is also being put forward in relation to women's non-partici-
pation in 'science'.)

I find the explanations of Stacey and Price, and Russell, attractive, but
I still have many unanswered questions and tend to find the whole issue
relatively perplexing. I recognise that women know little about 'power',
that it is an issue we have often shied away from. Most of what we know
has its origins in the 'powerful', as Elizabeth Janeway and Jean Baker
Miller have pointed out; we have little reason to trust their explanations
in which they establish and justify their own power. By them we are defined
in many contexts as powerless, and if we accept that view, no doubt we
will *feel* powerless.

Undeniably women do not possess the resources which men have
declared the substance of power; materially we are impoverished, politically

we are almost without representation. But are these the only sources of power, or the sources of power only under patriarchy? Is there a future as outsiders? I know there are times when I/we do feel powerless; in the face of the world's nuclear insanity, its destructive drive, its unequal, absurd and cruel distribution of resources, I feel very powerless. Yet I cannot accept that if there were an equal number of women in politics, the prospects would look different. So what do women do? We have desperate need of ideas. Ones which originate in our view of the world.

(D)

AND WHEN THERE WERE NONE...

1 Woman as force: Mary Ritter Beard (1876–1958)

In 1946, in Britain, Margaret Goldsmith published a book entitled *Women and the Future* in which she gave the historical background to women's struggle for equality, and discussed the implications of women's new 'freedom' which had been a product of the war years. Goldsmith confessed that she thought this freedom was fragile and that there were historical, social, and patriarchal, reasons for it being at risk; but she also warned that women were not likely to be the docile creatures they might once have been, and predicted a return to the conflict and sex-war of the suffragette days if women were mocked in their desire to participate fully in social reconstruction, and were forced back into the private sphere. She had a fair idea what was on men's minds, but women, she argued, were a force to be reckoned with. Today, I find her book painful to read.

That women had always been a force to be reckoned with was the thesis of Mary Ritter Beard's most famous work, *Woman as Force in History*, published in the same year. Fifty-three years after Matilda Joslyn Gage's *Women, Church and State*, Mary Ritter Beard produced a comparable and positive reconstruction of women's past. Her thesis that women have *always* been a very real, although unrecognised, force in society grew from her own experience, says Ann J. Lane (1977)[1] in her *Source Book* on Beard, who, like Gage, left insufficient personal records to permit a full-scale biography. 'Women have been active, assertive, competent contributors to their societies' was Beard's message, and any other representation of them was not only false, but pernicious, for making women passive and invisible, as historical records had done, was to facilitate women's acceptance of themselves as powerless. When women believe they are passive, and without influence, argued Beard, 'their collective strength is undermined. The very idea of women's oppression takes hold of women's minds and oppresses them. But women could be freed from that ideological bondage by discovering their own powerful creative history and using the knowledge to create new social relations' (Lane, 1977, p. 1).

What has happened to Mary Ritter Beard and her powerful message

---

[1] I am grateful to Ann J. Lane for her insights on Mary Ritter Beard.

about women's power? As with Gage, 'Mary Beard devoted her life to reconstructing women's pasts in an effort to end that invisibility,' says Ann Lane. Yet again, as with Gage, 'it is as if she herself – her life and her work – were a demonstration of that thesis' (ibid., p. 2). Even today in feminist circles Beard is still largely neglected, rarely quoted, and relegated at times to the status of her husband's collaborator.

While Mary Beard was a scholar, she was by no means confined to an ivory tower or secluded in a library; like Gage, she was a political activist and among the most radical of the suffragists. After her marriage in 1900 she departed for Manchester, where she discovered the militant women's movement, met and worked with English radical suffragists, and developed a keen understanding of class politics. When she returned to America it was with Crystal Eastman and Alice Paul that she joined forces in the effort to gain the vote, and it was her understanding, in this context, that women who were essentially without power were proving to be quite powerful, which was to be the basis of many of her ideas about women.

Mary Beard could see that there was strength and power in a community of women and, while it was undeniable that women were outside the traditional power structure, it was equally undeniable that for as long as women acted as a community, they were able to exert influence. How was this phenomenon of *woman-power*, which flew in the face of what was known about women's powerlessness, to be explained?

There were some apparent contradictions which demanded investigation. Beard began with the recognition that there were no concepts of women's power in society, no realities of women's strength, and no description or theories about this aspect of women's experience. There was no 'explanation' of the influence women were wielding in Britain or America, and it was as if even while women were being active, influential, and powerful, their activity, influence and power did not exist. With no conceptualisation of women as strong, as a force, women's power was 'invisible' even at the same time as it was demonstrable.

To Beard it seemed that as a society we believed that power resided in institutions and, as women were not members of influential institutions, we assumed that women were powerless. This assumption, however, appeared to be false and in need of modification. It was not difficult to see that men were the members of influential institutions from which the definitions of power emanated. It was not difficult to determine that it had been men who had encoded the concepts and theories of power in their customary manner, and that they had described themselves, and their offices, as powerful. It was not difficult to reach the conclusion that in the process of describing themselves and asserting the universal nature of their experience, men had, once more, left women out of the conceptualisation of power. But what was even worse, as far as Beard was concerned, was that women had come to accept their omission, to take on the powerlessness men accorded them, and so we are back to the understandings of women such as Frances Wright and Matilda Joslyn Gage that men have much to gain if women believe they are without power and influence in the world.

Insights born of her involvement with women and the struggle for equality were built upon by Mary Ritter Beard during the 1930s, which were, states Ann Lane, productive years for Beard. Lane draws attention to the fact that the creative periods of women's lives are often very different, and occur much later than in men's, when women, understandably, find themselves free from child care and able to commit themselves to work, and as with Stanton and Gage, and Russell and Hunkins-Hallinan, gives the lie to the belief that women become conservative in their old age.

In 1931 Beard published *Understanding Women*, which is a vision of women's power and force, and then, 'she wrote in 1934, an extraordinary fifty page pamphlet entitled "A Changing Political Economy as It Affects Women" which was in effect an extensive women's studies program. In 1933 she also edited a reader, *America Through Women's Eyes*, which she used to show that American women were an integral part of the development of the United States from colonial to contemporary times, a power equal to, if not surpassing, men. Also in 1934, she co-authored with Martha Bruère, *Laughing Their Way: Women's Humor in America*' (Lane, 1977, p. 33).

It was not as if Mary Beard just wrote one book and disappeared; she wrote six books of her own and collaborated with her husband, a celebrated scholar, on seven others, and she was a prolific writer of essays and pamphlets and known to a wide cross-section of the community – even to those rare and elusive souls, feminists with a sense of humour! It is sadly ironic that she knew so well that women disappear, that she put an enormous amount of energy into turning this process round, and that she believed, I suspect, that she had had some small success.

Out of her conviction that one of the reasons for women's disappearance is women's complicity – that is, that we let women disappear without actively resisting the process – came her commitment to the establishment of a Women's Archive dedicated to preserving the records of women's contributions and activity (again there is a similarity with Gage, and of course, with Stanton and Anthony). For five years, from 1934, says Lane, Beard 'tried to establish, finance, organize, structure, house and publicize what became known as the World Center for Women's Archives' (ibid.). Not even the women's colleges had attempted to follow Stanton, Anthony and Gage's example and to 'secure for posterity' the records of women, with the result that women were 'invisible' even while they lived, and likely to disappear without trace upon their death. Beard gathered round her committed women and they brought together an impressive array of documents but in the end the venture failed – for lack of funds.

The Center was dissolved in 1940 and in 1941 she turned her attention to the *Encyclopaedia Britannica*, its systematic exclusion of women, and the effect this had on compounding women's invisibility and powerlessness. She received some encouragement from the editor-in-chief, who seemed not averse to changing some of his patriarchal ways, and with high hopes Mary Beard and three other women worked for eighteen months on a multi-disciplinary critique of the information contained in the *Encyclopaedia*, and a list of recommendations for a rewrite which would include women. (Beard also entertained the idea of publishing a women's encyclopaedia.)

A forty-page report was prepared entitled 'A Study of the Encyclopaedia Britannica in Relation to its Treatment of Women' and was presented to the editor-in-chief. Nothing came of it. Lane says it is difficult to determine what actually happened but not difficult to establish that the report was never acted upon: the 'long neglect of women in the compendium', which the editor-in-chief had declared would be rectified, never was, and the critique prepared by Beard and her colleagues is just as pertinent today as it was then, says Lane (ibid., p. 49). For Beard it was eighteen months' work 'wasted'; it was all to no avail.

While Beard has much in common with Matilda Joslyn Gage, she also shares some similarities with Virginia Woolf. Although never using the term *outsiders*, there is no doubt that Beard believed that power and influence could reside among the outsiders, that being *outside* was a fruitful place to be, and conducive to creative and constructive change. What was required, she argued, was a change in consciousness, a reconceptualisation and redefinition of the world from women's perspective, and with women central, visible and influential within that framework. Like Virginia Woolf, Beard urged women to stay outside, to resist the temptation of joining and imitating men's ways. She too wanted women to be 'free from unreal loyalties', for once women joined the institutions, they were too likely to be co-opted and to have the prevailing values reinforced rather than challenged and changed. There are many overlaps between Virginia Woolf's critique of patriarchal education in *Three Guineas* and Beard's passionate insistence that women should be independent learners outside the institutions of higher education, for 'Bright, ambitious women, caught up in the careerism and conformity that are fostered in the university, lose their innovative potential in their scramble for a place in the Congressional Office, the physics laboratory, or the elitist academic institution', argued Beard. 'They jeopardise the power that comes from independence' (Lane, 1977, p. 64). Her words of wisdom were not available to us when we began our tentative steps to establish women's studies courses. We would have felt very much more confident – and reasonable – if they had been, for, in line with Beard's own thesis, our case, having been stated before, would have seemed more real; we would have had a concept of power, not powerlessness. But less than twenty-five years after the publication of *Woman as Force in History* few of us even knew that Mary Ritter Beard had existed.

One exception was Gerda Lerner who, on finding Mary Beard, saw in her, in her life and her work, a model worthy of emulation: 'Early in my undergraduate studies I had first read Mary Beard's *Woman as Force in History*, states Lerner (who was a mature student undergraduate in the early 1960s) and, 'Somehow, I was able to . . . connect with her central idea, that women have always been active and at the center of history. I was struck as by a sudden illumination, by the simplicity and truth of her insight. Mary Beard had arrived at that conviction the same way I had, by herself having been an engaged participant in women's work in society. In her narrative I recognized a world I knew from experience, a world in which women were active participants in the building of community and of institutions' (1981, p. xxxi).

Mary Beard's work helped to change one woman's consciousness at least, but as Lerner reports, it was not easy to pursue the path which this shift in consciousness required. When Lerner informed the interviewers at Columbia University prior to her admission to the PhD programme that she wanted to complete the work begun by Mary Beard, the 'announcement was, not surprisingly, greeted by astonished silence' (ibid., p. xix).

This experience of Gerda Lerner's deserves closer attention, for it is not necessarily that her interviewing committee were unusually ignorant or excessively nasty, but more likely that they were playing their part in consigning women to oblivion in a male-designed and controlled institution – where male values predominate! So widespread is this practice that it formed part of Beard's thesis, and she was by no means the first, of course, to have observed and explained its operation. It was one of the reasons that she objected to women entering men's education (and one of the reasons that I would argue as well, that educational gains for women have been no gains at all in many respects, see D. Spender 1981b), for ' "Equal education," for which women have clamored', wrote Beard in 'A Changing Political Economy as It Affects Women', has brought no change in the structure and content of knowledge which men have produced and distributed in their own institutions, and women's entry to these institutions 'has meant merely the extension to women of men's education in their own history and judgement of themselves' (Lane, 1977, p. 204).

Lerner's experience was the standard experience of women who question male centrality and *dare* to posit an alternative of the positive and visible nature of women. Within the academy (devoted, needless to say, to the ostensible pursuit of truth and knowledge) Lerner encountered considerable harassment as she persisted in her attempt to develop Beard's thesis and to 'legitimate' women's history. She states how difficult it was at times to persevere and explains how in the face of such opposition she did not abandon her goal. 'Had I been a young woman just out of college,' she writes, 'I probably could not have withstood the social pressure, subtle ridicule, constant discouragement, and, not infrequently, open disapproval' (1981, p. xx).

Lerner, of course, was meant to give up, and to take on a more serious and substantial (and less subversive) topic. The reason she did not accept such advice was precisely the same reason that she was urged to – knowing about Mary Beard made a difference: 'Long before the new feminism surfaced, reading Mary Beard raised my feminist consciousness,' says Lerner (ibid., p. xxii). What would happen, one might ask, if Mary Beard, then, were to become part of the substance of education? Perhaps the consciousness of many might be changed; perhaps the image of woman as powerless, as passive victim, might be dislodged; perhaps invisibility could give way to visibility; perhaps women could believe in themselves as a force, to *act* as a force and to make women's power a reality, with concepts and theories to designate it; perhaps patriarchy couldn't take it.

This was the thesis of Mary Beard and many of her predecessors –

Virginia Woolf and Matilda Joslyn Gage among them. The invisibility (and ostensible powerlessness) of women is not a by-product of patriarchy but a foundation stone of it: to challenge the patriarchal representation of women is to challenge patriarchy at its roots. This is a common and central idea among the women who have questioned male power, and been 'victims' of it as they have fulfilled patriarchal expectation and disappeared. From Aphra Behn to Adrienne Rich it has been suggested that among the most subversive and powerful activities women can engage in are the activities of constructing women's visible and forceful traditions, of making *real* our *positive* existence, of celebrating our lives and of resisting disappearance in the process.

This, however, is not an easy task to accomplish in a patriarchal society and any attempt to put these ideas into practice invites conflict with the 'legitimated values'. What outrageous *bias* in a male-dominated society to emphasise the positive aspects of women's lives and work! What a disreputable and misleading approach *deliberately* to 'gloss over' the negative features. Justice demands 'constructive criticism' (ring the voices of past tutors in my ears, and I try to concentrate instead on an equivalent to Woolf's 'Angel in the House' and to dismiss the 'noise').

If I choose *not* to refer to certain ideas of various women or to make condemnatory comments about their writing style (or personality) it is not just because I think these are arbitrary value judgements which can change from one generation to the next, nor is it because I am so naive as to believe that all women possess sound and sensible judgement, have perfected an exemplary style, and are just and fair. I am not advocating the simple premise that women can do no wrong.

I am advocating the premise that knowledge is political. I am asserting that in a male-dominated society women do not control the uses that are made of knowledge. I am asserting that a fundamental use of knowledge in a patriarchal society is to enhance the image of men and to negate the image of women. I am asserting what women's resources are appropriated and used to find in favour of men and against women, and that much 'valuable' use is made of any negative evidence we may construct about other women. While it is not in our power (at present) to influence the uses made of negative knowledge about women, *it is well within our power to refuse to make it available.*

I am withdrawing my labour: a knowledge strike. As a political act (and with a considerable amount of pure, positive enjoyment which I can highly recommend) I will persist with the subversive practice of finding in favour of women – of constructing an image of women's force, as Beard suggested – to counteract the patriarchal principle of finding, exclusively, in favour of men, and I will continue to do so (and to face the wrath of patriarchal gods of 'objectivity' and 'truth') until a more equitable balance of power between the sexes is realised. If and when the two sexes are judged equally, and by the same standards, I will be prepared to find in favour of each for 50 per cent of the time. However, while a patriarchal society insists on finding in favour of men – regardless of what they do – and insists on this practice as 'objective', I shall persist with my practice of finding only in favour of women and will insist – with equal justification, that *this* is objective.

I will not make such unsubstantiated (and stereotypical) comments as: Mary Beard's work suffers from 'poor presentation', that it is at times but 'ill-tempered rhetoric' which goes 'too far', for I understand that this 'evidence' can be used to exclude her – justifiably of course – from future consideration. I will, instead, assert the positive nature of her contribution. (And I will not – and have not quoted – the sources of such statements, so that it is very difficult for someone to take and use these negative comments.)

'Essentially, Mary Beard invented the concept of Women's Studies and Women's History,' says Lerner (1981, p. xxii), and while I don't quite concur (Matilda Joslyn Gage, for example, gets no mention in Lerner's book), this simply helps to confirm how successful the process of erasure is. 'It was Mary Beard, first and foremost,' continues Lerner, 'whose critique of an androcentric academic establishment led her to envision new models of education for women.' Among her papers there is 'evidence of Beard's efforts for starting a women's studies course at Radcliffe College and of her protracted work collecting sources for the history of women and establishing a Women's History Archive. I found here a two-page listing of questions, yet to be answered, about women in history, and I found a very few sentences which became my guidelines, as I tried to proceed in this endeavour. In a very real sense I consider Mary Beard, whom I never met, my principal mentor as an historian' (ibid., p. xxii–xxiii).

She made an enormous difference to Gerda Lerner's life: there are many more like her who could make a comparable difference to our lives – if we knew about them.

2 On whose authority? Viola Klein (? –1973)

1946 must have been a good year for questioning the origins of knowledge and the uses to which it was put in a male-dominated society, because in that year Viola Klein's *The Feminine Character: History of an Ideology* was published, and, as the subtitle suggests, in it Klein was to argue that what society knew about women was 'ideological' rather than factual in nature.

Klein's critique is very interesting. Because her concern was with the structure of knowledge in general and not just with the 'mistakes' made within an individual discipline, she was never tempted to suggest that the problem could be solved simply by changing some of the 'rules' (the paradigm) within a particular discipline. How could sociologists, psychologists, anthropologists, etc., eliminate the 'ideology' and leave only the 'facts' in their discipline when the distinction between the two was based on social values and beliefs? One generation's 'facts' were often nothing but 'ideology' (or superstition) to the next generation when values shifted slightly. It was even a manifestation of a particular ideology to believe that it was reasonable and useful to divide the world into fact and fiction in the first place, to insist on the division between objective and subjective, to organise knowledge into a range of disciplines with experts in charge, and to believe that the experts had access to 'truth' in a way that 'lay persons' did not (see Stanley and Wise, forthcoming, for further discussion).

The values of society influenced the production of knowledge and quite simply Viola Klein argued that in a male-dominated society male dominance was reflected in the knowledge that was constructed, and that it was absurd to suggest that the disciplines could be objective and 'fair' to women, when society was not. For the disciplines were encoded by men who also encoded the social values. Implicitly asking the same question as Mary Wollstonecraft had done, Klein demanded to know by what authority males decreed the human values and 'judged' women?

In her introduction Klein states that she proposes to demonstrate that the 'scientific method' of constructing knowledge cannot be 'represented as a completely detached and autonomous mental act', for knowledge 'does not exist in splendid isolation, but is an organic part of a coherent cultural system' (1946, p. 2). Knowledge, she argues, and the means by which it is constructed is influenced *by* the culture in which it is produced, while at the same time it influences the culture *in* which it is produced. You can tell a great deal about a society and its values, says Klein, by looking at the knowledge it creates, and she casts an enquiring eye in the direction of Havelock Ellis and Sigmund Freud.

Klein's method is really quite ingenious – although she was to pay for it later – for she asserts that her focus is the sociology of knowledge and that women are cited merely as an example of the process. This is a 'veiled' rather than a 'direct' approach, which permits her to remain in the 'mainstream' while still dealing with women – or, more precisely the knowledge that has been constructed about women, in a male-dominated society.

She has elected to look at the knowledge encoded about *women* – as distinct from knowledge about food, or domestic pets, or transport systems, for example – because it is an area where bias is more readily detectable. 'The scholars' views on women reflect: (a) the status of women in a given society; (b) the prevailing ideologies concerning women in a certain historical period; and (c) the author's personal attitude towards women' (ibid., p. 3–4) and, she argues (innocently) that while these considerations are no less applicable to food or transport systems, they are more readily discernible in the case of women, where sometimes the theory about women 'amounts, in the last resort, to the use of a scientific apparatus for the rational justification of emotional attitudes' (ibid., p. 4).

When in 1976 Joan Roberts stated that in 'the search for relevant facts and concepts, some of us came to realise that neither facts nor concepts about females existed in critical scholarly areas,' and that, 'we find repeatedly that the "scientific" methods are essentially reasserting with new terminological "weightiness", the same biases against women' (p. 5), she did not know that thirty years previously Viola Klein had made the same points. Joan Roberts, with hundreds of thousands of other women, was in the process of beginning again, not building on insights and understanding arrived at in previous times.

Viola Klein looked at the theories that existed about women in a male-dominated society – at the theories put forward by Havelock Ellis, Otto Weininger, Sigmund Freud, L. M. Terman and C. I. Mills, and Helen Thompson, Mathias and Mathilda Vaerting (whose work Crystal Eastman had reviewed and recommended) and Margaret Mead, and she then put forward a theory to account for these theories about women. She suggested that: 'In a society whose standards are predominantly masculine, women form an "out group" distinguished from the dominant strata by physical characteristics, historical tradition, social role and a different process of socialization' (1946, p. 4) and that these differences are evaluated as *deficiencies*, with the result that women's 'inferiority' is justified. A convenient 'closed circle' argument is constructed on the values of male dominance, and which leads to no other conclusion but that males are dominant – and that's the truth!

Every theory, argued Viola Klein, has to be able to account for the person (or persons) who produced it, and in the ostensibly simple task of accounting for those who have made the theories about women, she uncovers the pervasiveness of ideology, or prejudice, while she systematically explores the value system of many theorists. I shall deal only with Freud as an example (and fairly briefly).

The limits of Freud's scientific theory, says Klein, are the limits of the Victorian morality which constitute his world, but *he* did not suggest that his theory – which may have been an adequate explanation for him – was confined to his particular and peculiar view of the world. Instead he insisted (with considerable arrogance) that *his* view of the world was the only view of the world, that what was not represented within it did not exist, and that, far from being a partial explanation of a partial description, it was a total explanation which applied to the whole world. 'The standards of his own culture he took for unalterable laws,' states Klein, 'and he was convinced that the division of labour in force in the middle class of his period was based on innate sexual differences' (ibid., p. 75). One could argue that he was quite gullible.

Freud began with the assumption that males were superior, and then proceeded to interpret evidence or more accurately, to construct it (including physical evidence), through the prism of male superiority, and not surprisingly, therefore, he came up with the conclusion that males were superior. Because males were superior, women could be 'explained' in terms of trying to adjust to this fact of life – that was; many women envied males and their vulnerable appendages! (As Klein says, it is strange 'that one half of humanity should have *biological* reasons to feel at a disadvantage for not having what the other half possesses (but not vice versa)', ibid., p. 83–4).

Evidently this one-sided explanation did not find favour with one woman, Karen Horney, who had been trained in Freudian 'science', but who seemed to want to describe and explain the world somewhat differently from her own perspective. Klein says that she inverted Freud's theory when she stated that it was not women who envied men's vulnerable appendage, but on the contrary, men who envied women's capacity for motherhood, and who had developed a whole range of compensatory values (including that of defining vulnerable appendages as a source of strength and power), so that the battle between Freud and Horney – based on the same scientific theory – looked 'like a bid for supremacy between two highly interested competitors', adds Klein (ibid., p. 80). Hardly an image of dignified, disinterested, scholarly endeavour.

Within Freud's theoretical framework men owned everything that was considered prestigious, says Klein (and under the circumstances Karen Horney deserves considerable praise for her effort): sexuality was masculine, even bi-sexuality was masculine, libido was masculine, power and activity were masculine. Sigmund Freud seemed to indulge in a considerable amount of wishful thinking, which needless to say, went 'unanalysed'.

So what has Freud contributed to the reservoir of knowledge about women, asks Klein? When his theory is translated into ordinary language, she says, it 'means that women are by their organic nature, excluded from participation in cultural and creative activities. *The old argument about the intellectual faculties of woman has been transferred onto a different plane; clad in a new jargon the traditional view of feminine inferiority is here presented afresh*' (ibid., p. 76, my emphasis). His representation of woman is of 'an envious, hysterical person with limited intellectual interests and a hostile attitude towards cultural achievements' (ibid., p. 78). Understandably, perhaps, women have found it difficult to live up to his representation of them!

Within Freud's terms the reason that women are not visible in the culture, why they are not equal shareholders in power and prestige, why they are perceived as passive and acted upon, is not because men are unjust, tyrannical, or misogynist (and make up the meanings), but because it is in woman's nature to be this way. The fault lies in women and not with men, according to Freud's explanation and, unfortunately, as this fault is an innate and universal deficiency, nothing can be done about it. There is no point in women protesting – or arguing that it does not feel innate – for this is simply evidence that they are 'maladjusted'. Women must adjust to these laws so fortuitously discovered by men, they must come to terms with the 'femininity' men have allocated them, they must resign themselves to being passive victims. Here is the twentieth-century version of Eve's fall from grace, and the edict to go forth, multiply, in pain and in sorrow, and without hope of redemption; failure to comply is not 'sin' but 'sickness'. Authority for these prescriptions is not men's religion, but men's science. The existence – and the credibility – of Freud stands as a testimony that for women, *progress* is an absurd concept. In so many respects our position remains much the same, vis á vis men – what 'progresses' is their increasedly sophisticated rationale of our inferiority, particularly our *intellectual inferiority*.

There is little need to point out that Freud continued to be elaborated while Klein was erased. Despite her initial assertion that she was working within the parameters of the sociology of knowledge, that her concern was 'neutral', and an examination of the way cultural values influenced the nature and content of scientific theories (with the relationship of women and men but a side issue), the critics were not deceived; they saw this (and I suspect they were accurate) as an attack on male authority.

In 1971, *The Feminine Character: History of an Ideology* was reprinted, and it was with empathy for Viola Klein (and animosity for her critics – although one of them was a woman) that I read her 'Preface to the Second Edition'. 'This book has been out of print for a number of years. Yet, despite recurrent demands for a new edition, both the author and publishers were doubtful about the wisdom of reprinting it in its original form,' she begins, for, 'The author did her best to put her cards on the table and to make her dual aim clear from the outset. It seems however that the reading public, by and large, were not prepared to take her word for it that the book was concerned with an analysis of existing theories about feminine psychology rather than being itself a psychological study of women. The misunderstanding of the author's intentions went so far that some critics – Rose Macaulay among them – accused her of using "secondary sources" instead of doing "original research", when in fact the investigation of those sources was the very object of the exercise. . . . Books have their own destiny, and this one had a considerable influence on the author's subsequent fate' (1971, p. xv).[2]

I can only guess at what might have happened but it is an 'educated guess' based on the observation of what has happened to Viola Klein's foremothers and on the theory that in a male-dominated society women have little or no control over the production and distribution of knowledge, with the result that their ideas may be used against them, their intellectual ability denied, and their very existence and presence negated.

What I do know is that in 1956 – the decade when nothing happened – Alva Myrdal and Viola Klein's book, *Women's Two Roles*, was published and that it was instrumental in raising the consciousness of a number of women. In 1958, Viola Klein's *Working Wives* was published, and in 1965, *Britain's Married Women Workers*. Hannah Gavron (1966) cites Viola Klein as the broadcaster of a BBC Talk 'The Emancipation of Women: Its Motives and Achievements' (1949) in a series 'Ideas and Beliefs of the Victorians'. Klein has made a considerable contribution to our traditions. I rarely hear her quoted; I know of no one making a study of her life and work.

3 Men have their cake – and eat it too: Mirra Komarovsky

Another woman who made a significant contribution (and who also published an important paper in 1946) was Mirra Komarovsky, again fre-

---

[2] When I attempted to contact Viola Klein about the reception to her book I was informed that she had died in 1973; her publishers have no record about the criticism of the initial publication or her apprehension about republication.

quently overlooked today. Komarovsky was familiar with the male structuring of reality; she was a witness to male benevolence – education and employment had been opened up to women; she was asked to be a witness to the fact that, despite these new opportunities, women were still abandoning their careers in favour of domestic service; she was asked to accept – from the male perspective – that while men had done everything for women, women would do nothing for themselves. They were 'naturally' withdrawing to the private sphere (one assumes in much the same way as they were 'naturally' withdrawing from politics), regardless of educational and employment opportunities men had made available to them.

It neither looked nor felt that way to Komarovsky. It looked as though men were establishing a good image of themselves and at the same time were retaining all the home comforts. It neither looked nor felt at all natural for a woman to be expected to avail herself of the increased educational possibilities which demanded a display of intellectual competence, and *at the same time*, win a husband who was unlikely to be impressed by intellectual ability and inconvenienced, if not actually challenged, by a wife with a career. It felt like an enormous contradiction, stated Komarovsky, and her 1946 paper was entitled 'Cultural Contradictions and Sex Roles'.

While ostensibly preparing for a public role and developing their intellectual capacity, women were *also* supposed to be engaged in the 'natural' task of obtaining a husband and demonstrating their aptitude for domesticity and their facility for not being too bright. What may have appeared to be an eminently sensible arrangement to a man was an absurdity to a woman, stated Komarovsky, touching on what I believe to be one of the most crucial and sensitive patriarchal issues. Women were expected to live a contradiction, while men blithely decreed women's actions could be explained by 'choice'. That women were choosing marriage and motherhood in preference to equal representation in the workforce with men was a rationale that only men could devise, and was peculiarly and dramatically ahistorical given that during the Second World War women had demonstrated their capacity and willingness for paid work.

But then, as Jean Baker Miller has pointed out, it is the dominant group which defines the acceptable role for subordinates. This usually involves performing services that the dominant group does not want to perform for itself, and the definition of roles is accompanied by the myth that the subordinates are unable or unwilling (the familiar phenomena of apathy or foolishness) to fulfil wider or more socially prestigious roles. A likely story, but one which is believed. The myth 'is challenged only when a drastic event disrupts the usual arrangements,' says Miller. 'For instance, in the emergency situation of World War II, "incompetent" women suddenly "manned" the factories with great skill' (1978, p. 6–7).

But by 1946 it was 'back to normal'. Women were again being consigned the tasks the dominant group did not want to perform for itself, and again beginning to believe the myth of their own ineptitude; they were expelled from those tasks the dominant group wanted to preserve for itself and the whole process was justified on the basis of 'women's choice' – a product of their nature. Mirra Komarovsky was not going back to the private sphere without a protest. She made it perfectly clear that women were not simply allowing their natures to unfold but were trying to meet conflicting demands. Had she had recourse to Cicely Hamilton's or Mary Astell's critique of marriage (or Adrienne Rich's, of compulsory heterosexuality), she might have been more vociferous and more vehement in her stand. Her argument, as it was formulated, was at least as old as Mary Wollstonecraft.

In 1953 – again the decade when nothing happened – Komarovsky went on to develop these arguments in *Women in the Modern World: Their Education and Their Dilemmas*; in 1964, *Blue Collar Marriage* was published. For more than twenty years Komarovsky asserted the authenticity of women's different view of the world (a low-status area of sociology, as Ann Oakley, 1974, suggests) but has received little acknowledgement from women for her effort.

4 Selective breeding: Ruth Herschberger (1917–   )

More in line with Viola Klein's arguments, however, were those put forward by Ruth Herschberger in 1948 in *Adam's Rib*. Anticipating the development of (and the arguments against) what we have come to call sociobiology, Herschberger insisted that it was not just in the social sciences that social values were reflected, but even in the more sacred areas of biology and medicine, the 'objective truths' which were constructed were often nothing but the 'legitimated' prejudice against women, which was a feature of a male-dominated society.

Hindered by an absence of vocabulary or concepts to express a reality of female-force or independence, Herschberger was able to get round the problem to some extent by providing an illustration of an experiment with two chimpanzees – Josie and Jack. Her book begins with a dramatised account (it is humorous as well) of Josie and Jack, in captivity, being observed, in order to determine which was the dominant sex. Josie, of course, carries the burden of being the representative of all womanhood, and the experiment on her and Jack was so designed that the possibility that they would emerge as equal was circumvented from the outset.

The dominant sex was to be the one that obtained the most food which was delivered sparingly via the means of a food chute. For a while Jack took most of the food, but during the period of tumescence (when Josie was in heat) Josie took most of the food; after tumescence Jack again appropriated most of the food. 'Science had made an interesting discovery', states Herschberger. 'All that remained was the routine work of communicating the results to the public' (1948, p. 6). But routine communication in a male-dominated society is a matter of showing the male in a flattering light – and this of course, was precisely what happened. From the chimpanzees' thirty-two days at the food chute an eminent male scientist was able to claim 'not only that males were "naturally dominant" over females but that the biological basis of prostitution stood revealed in certain aspects of Josie's behaviour' (ibid., p. 7).

No explanation was offered for the fact that the naturally dominant Jack, 'lost' 44 per cent of the time – even though he was very much bigger than Josie (no mention was made of the fact that he was *the biggest* male chimpanzee in the colony). No questions were asked about the extent to which chimpanzees behaved like human beings, or human beings like animals (despite the fact the human beings are rarely fed by chute – in insufficient quantities – and that human females do not experience tumescence).

To the eminent scientist there was no doubt that Josie (and woman-hood) were naturally subordinate (and no matter what happened in the experiment this would be the result). Of course, to present this finding meant stating that when Josie was being 'aggressive' (as she was during tumescence) that her behaviour was *receptive* to the male, that when she was being 'sexually demanding' she was actually being *sexually submissive*, and that when she was 'dominant', 44 per cent of the time (despite her much smaller proportions), she was still, *naturally subordinate*. Her sexual cycle was an 'aberration'; in Josie's dramatised words: 'Some woman scien-tist ought to start passing it round that males must be unnatural because they don't have cyclical changes during the month' (ibid., p. 9).

The male scientist's conclusions should not be surprising; the know-ledge that men appropriate women's resources and that they deny and negate women's activity, while women are in the process of being active beings, has been present among women in various forms for a very long time. Herschberger is simply demonstrating here how these understandings apply to and are used by the biological sciences, where the values of a male-dominated human community are imposed on chimpanzees, so that a male-dominated science can prove that human beings are just like chim-panzees – who behave like humans. Round and round we go.

If it were not that these little games were taken so seriously, and used so often, to legitimate male supremacy, the elements of the absurd they contain could be quite amusing; it is actually quite humorous (at times) to see that this is a demonstration of the 'rigorous logic' that men hold in such high esteem! Ruth Herschberger treats much of 'biological science' as a game. This is not the case, however, in her section on rape, where once again we are able to see men negating women's force – even when women are active. By this process, *No* is *not* taken to mean *No*. Because men are not raped by women they can deny the reality of women being raped by men. In a male-dominated society a woman must *actively resist* before rape can be deemed to have occurred, yet in a male-dominated society there are no concepts, meanings, words, *for active resistance in women*; such resist-ance is invisible, non-existent even when women are engaged in it. As Herschberger pointed out when Josie was sexually active, she was termed sexually receptive; when women sexually *resist* they can be called sexually *inviting*. This is how our force, power, strength, integrity, autonomy, are denied; it is not because we are not forceful, strong, autonomous, but because when we are we are called by another name. There is no word for a woman resisting rape; only the term rape *victim*.

The way men construct the world to enhance their image of themselves (appropriating women's resources and denying women's *being* in the process) is explored at some (satirical) length by Herschberger. One section of her book is entitled 'Patriarchal Society Writes Biology' and in it she outlines the definitions and theories with which we are familiar, and in which men have interpreted phenomena to provide themselves with a favoured place. But then she has a section entitled 'Matriarchal Society Writes Biology' in which she provides alternative definitions and theories, in which women are provided with a favoured place, and the contrast is dramatic.

Having given a customary account of the development of the embryo, from a male point of view, in which the male embryo is the positive norm, Herschberger proceeds to describe the embryo and its development from a woman's point of view: 'The male, we find, does not develop in any important way from the asexual or early embryonic state,' she writes. 'His sexual organs remain in an infantile condition, displaying an early arrest of development' (ibid., p. 79). This amounts to 'outrageous distortion' because it reserves 'activity' for the female and reduces the male to a 'passive' and 'invisible' state, and Herschberger continues with other 'outrageous distortions' along the same lines. 'The male sperm', she says, 'is produced in superfluously great numbers since the survival of any one sperm or its contact with an egg is so hazardous and indeed, improbable. The egg, being more resilient, and endowed with solidity, toughness, and endurance, can be produced singly and yet effect reproduction' (ibid., p. 82).

The world looks very different when female imagery is invested with centrality, visibility, and strength. 'After the sperm are drawn into the vicinity of the egg,' she states, appropriating for female the motion of the sperm, in exactly the same way that males have appropriated female activity for themselves in the past, 'the egg by some little known mechanism selects one cell from the many present. Sometimes none of the sperm suits the egg, in which case there is no fertilization' (ibid., p. 84). It is not the (usual) active, daring, venturesome little sperm that goes off to transform a passive egg, that we see here, but a central, strong, independent and selective egg that surveys the offerings it has commanded, and sometimes chooses not to have anything to do with any of them. Herschberger's point is that one description is no more valid, at this stage, than the other.

She makes a very good case for females taking the initiative in sexual intercourse, partly because (and this is a long time before Masters and Johnson, 1970) the clitoris is capable of multiple orgasm, and she says, 'If the woman obtains an orgasm before he obtains his it is absolutely essential that she see that he too receives an orgasm. This is especially true if fertilization is desired . . . but also for humanitarian reasons in order to release the congestion of the penis' (ibid., p. 83). Herschberger's *reversal* makes the point admirably (and makes it almost impossible for one to ever again take seriously the pronouncements of the 'biological sciences'), but I particularly like her reversal of frigidity and impotence.

'*Frigidity*: Frigidity in males in which sexual desire or the ability to reach a climax is lacking. This is very frequent and the theory may be advanced that the cause of this, more frequently than usually realized, is an actual organic inadequacy in the human male, perhaps resulting from the rigors of evolution. The frigidity of a husband should not interfere any more than necessary with the normal gratification of the woman's sexual impulse.

Impotence: Impotence is the occasional inability of a woman to obtain erection or to enjoy intercourse, either because of revulsion to the man, indifference, or because of a psychological barrier' (ibid., p. 87).

While the point Herschberger is making is simple (so simple it is of the 'why didn't I see it before' variety), the creative and intellectual component of her analysis should not be underestimated. It is exceedingly difficult to visualise 'alternatives' to the social reality, particularly ones as radical as these, and inordinately frustrating to attempt to conceptualise, explain and substantiate them, in a society which does not admit their existence. Her basic premise of reversal in 'Matriarchal Society Writes Biology' is to make the female central and active, to construct a reality in which, 'Nature seems to be inviting ... the sperm [to] sacrifice its independence for the larger destiny of the egg' (ibid., p. 84). It is one in which the male is *deficient*, in which male means a lack of certain essential elements (the male *lacks* the ability to reach a climax) while the female *chooses* not to participate (out of revulsion or indifference). It is a savage way to treat half of humanity; but we know how to do it by studying the way males have treated the 'other' half of humanity.

While Ruth Herschberger's critique is still among the most radical challenges to the conventional male wisdom of sociobiology, it was not sufficient in its time to call the whole area into disrepute or to pre-empt it from continuing to expand. Viola Klein argued for the necessity of examining the conditions under which theories are produced, for accounting for the theorist, but we must also examine the conditions under which theories are received, and account for the critics. For women who in a male-dominated society have no control over the production or distribution of knowledge it is not enough just to critique the theories produced by men; it is equally as important to know what happens to the theories produced by women. We have become quite proficient at the former but have given little attention to the latter; we know a great deal about what was wrong with Freud, and why it is ridiculous to attach much significance to food trials with chimpanzees, but we know very little about what happened to the ideas of Mary Ritter Beard, Viola Klein and Ruth Herschberger. Understanding the mechanics of the 'disappearance', 'erasure', 'negation', 'invisibility', of women could well provide us with a valuable tool for promoting the 'disappearance', 'erasure', 'negation', 'invisibility', of patriarchy.

5 The philosophy of 'wrongness': Simone de Beauvoir (1908–   )

So effectively are women, their work and their ideas erased from social consciousness, that it is not so long ago since I would have been prepared to argue that the only feminist contribution to be made between Virginia Woolf's *Three Guineas* in 1938 and Betty Friedan's *The Feminine Mystique* in 1963, was Simone de Beauvoir's *The Second Sex* in 1949. I know now that they are but the tips of the iceberg, and I suspect that what I know now is but a first glimpse of what lies underneath.

While Simone de Beauvoir has not always enjoyed her present popularity, she has never been in danger of disappearing into oblivion. For forty years she has been writing – philosophy, autobiography, novels, essays – and receiving attention, in varying degrees and not always in desirable forms. But it is interesting to note that, unlike Virginia Woolf who was also a prolific writer of diverse forms over a period of time, Simone de Beauvoir is more frequently represented as a philosopher – while Virginia Woolf is portrayed as a novelist. There is added interest in the fact that while de Beauvoir's novels are often used by critics to cast light on her philosophy, Woolf's philosophy (as reflected in *A Room of One's Own*, *Three Guineas*, and her essays) is often used to shed light on her novels.

This may, of course, be an observation on my part which is inconsequential and insignificant, but as I am aware that women are defined in relation to men and through the eyes of men (an understanding put forward by both Woolf and de Beauvoir with insistence and clarity), I wonder what role the men in these two women's lives have played in the construction of their images. If Leonard had been a Jean-Paul, would Virginia Woolf be thought of primarily as a philosopher and *Three Guineas* be considered one of her best books rather than her worst? If Jean-Paul had been a Leonard, and had helped to establish the Hogarth Press, would Simone de Beauvoir be thought of in the main as a novelist and artist, and *The Second Sex* viewed as an aberration and not at all commended?

Simone de Beauvoir has been a source of considerable influence among women in the English-speaking[3] world, with almost every feminist writer since 1949 acknowledging a debt to her, and I am not going to attempt here to deal comprehensively with her ideas or the evaluations of them. My purpose in including de Beauvoir is to establish the chronological tradition of feminist ideas, and to examine her contemporary relevance – which is why I am grateful to Mary Lowenthal Felstiner who in her essay 'Seeing *The Second Sex* Through The Second Wave' (1980) helps to assess de Beauvoir's significance today.

I am also grateful to Felstiner for the early acknowledgement in her

---

[3] The only other women writers I know of who have been translated into English, and who have been possibly as influential in the past, are the Swedish feminist novelist, Frederika Bremer (1801–1865) (see Birgitta Holm, 1980), Georges Sand, and Colette. Currently there are translations which may prove to be extremely influential in the future – Alexandra Kollontai, for example, and perhaps even Flora Tristan.

essay that *The Second Sex* is a difficult book to read. Having on numerous occasions started it with the determination to finish it, I do not feel quite so guilty about my lack of success. Felstiner sees some of the difficulties in terms of translation, but she also suggests that they reflect the difficult conditions under which de Beauvoir wrote – in isolation, without the benefit of a community of women writers, and very much on the defensive (which could also have had something to do with Sartre). In *The Second Sex* de Beauvoir consistently makes the point that it is difficult to assert the validity of female reality, and as *The Second Sex* is quite explicitly an assertion of the validity of female reality in the face of male opposition and denial, one should expect this process to make its presence felt in the text. Felstiner sees the complexity and the length of *The Second Sex* as directly related to de Beauvoir's attempt to cover every possible objection and refutation; under these circumstances it could have been longer, and even more complex.

But despite its difficulty there can be no doubt that *The Second Sex* did – and still does – make a considerable contribution to feminist theory, particularly with its conceptualisation of male as the norm and women as 'other', a conceptualisation which has been incorporated into feminist explanations at a very fundamental level. While other women have put forward this idea in different times and in different ways, de Beauvoir elaborated it, and clarified it to the extent that it has become part of the taken-for-granted feminist reality.

It would be easy today, with the benefit of hindsight, to go back to *The Second Sex* and to point to the 'omissions' and 'false assumptions' in a sanctimonious manner (for, after all, that is a tradition into which many of us have been initiated), and because Mary Lowenthal Felstiner is able to link de Beauvoir's work to contemporary feminism and does *not* resort to this practice of discrediting her, or her ideas, I have great admiration for her method. She sensitively contextualises de Beauvoir's ideas and emphasises our common patriarchal reality, rather than accentuating our differences and calling on that spurious notion of 'progress' to suggest that change is for the better.

Summing up de Beauvoir's contribution, Felstiner says: 'now that our movement has fully absorbed Simone de Beauvoir's argument – that the prevailing inequality between the sexes is a social form, not a natural one – we have the basis for stepping off once more, asking just what is natural about the very recognition of two genders, and about the natural pairing between them. So her unexplained assumptions become our questions. Later on the assumptions *we* don't even know we're making can become questions too' (1980, p. 270), for this is what a tradition can be, when we build on what has gone before – instead of discarding it. Through studying *The Second Sex*, says Felstiner, 'we find out that feminist theory, not just hers but ours, has to count on being timely and time bound' (ibid., p. 271).

When our tradition is one of constant interruption and silence, when we can see that women are made to disappear, it is as well to be wary and to try to ensure that we are not accomplices in the process. In her treatment of de Beauvoir, Felstiner deals with de Beauvoir's relevance today without providing ready 'ammunition' which can later be used against women: 'I believe there are historical reasons why *The Second Sex* uncovers the pervasion of sexism more than the potential of feminism,' says Felstiner (ibid., p. 269), which effectively removes de Beauvoir from the realm of culpability (the position women habitually occupy under patriarchy) and points to the positive force of her analysis.

Throughout *The Second Sex*, de Beauvoir asserts again and again that what women know comes through men, and in that knowledge males are portrayed positively and females are portrayed negatively. While men control knowledge and reality, women are 'other' than genuinely human, she argues, and are characterised by their inherent wrongness. 'In the midst of an abstract discussion', says de Beauvoir, 'it is vexing to hear a man say: "You think thus and so because you are a woman": but I know that my only defence is to reply: "I think thus and so because it is true," thereby removing my subjective self from the argument. It would be out of the question to reply: "And you think the contrary because you are a man," for it is understood that the fact of being a man is no peculiarity. A man is in the right being a man; it is the woman who is in the wrong' (1972, p. 15).

So fully have de Beauvoir's concepts been absorbed that we frequently lose sight of their radical nature in the context in which they were produced. That women were made, not born, that man and not nature is the maker, and that man sees himself as the norm, the positive and central reference point in reality, and thereby makes woman 'other' and 'wrong' are such accepted principles these days (within select circles) that they rarely promote excitement. But one can sense de Beauvoir's feeling of excitement in the formulation of these principles. Simone de Beauvoir has detected the prevalence of 'male bias'; in a way she shows that she has 'cracked the code' of a patriarchal society, and she indicates that she has found a new sense of liberation in being able to *see through* the existing systems of knowledge of her time. She gives the impression that because she has seen how it works she feels free of it, outside it. I suspect that many feminists today would be more cynical and more likely to share Mary Daly's (1978) position – that even while we struggle to escape the 'mind-set' of patriarchy, it still exerts a firm hold over our consciousness.

When today de Beauvoir's assumptions of 1949 are also *her* questions, it would be interesting to know if she still had the same confidence. What does she make of her omission of the treatment of witches in her documentation of women's history, for example? Of course, one can always ask her. To be asking a woman, however, what changes thirty years and more have wrought in her ideas is almost a unique opportunity for women. Our past is usually wiped out more swiftly. So quickly is our force negated and our presence denied that even living women 'disappear' from our understandings and consciousness. Has anyone seriously addressed the question of the relative absence of older women in the women's movement when there have been so many life-long feminists? I do not think they disappear because they abandon their feminism – a stand I might have taken in the not so dim past – but because in a sense, we abandon them. When we have so few means of conceptualising and elaborating their force, their existence, their being, they just simply fade away.

This has not happened to Simone de Beauvoir. Perhaps she marks the beginning of a new era for feminists – when our fate is not necessarily to disappear.

6 Putting it in perspective: Margaret Mead (1901–1978)

To a certain extent, Margaret Mead has also broken the mould. Mead has not been at the centre of feminist discussion like de Beauvoir, for I know of no feminist conferences devoted to Mead's work, such as the one held at New York University in September 1979 to commemorate and celebrate the thirtieth anniversary of the publication of *The Second Sex*. But Mead, none the less, has been visible and influential, with much of her work also integrated into contemporary feminist ideas and explanations. And her work has been very *useful*; in a century where great weight has usually been attached to empirical evidence, Margaret Mead has often helped to provide it, and her cross-cultural comparisons have frequently served as more convincing 'evidence' in sceptical circles than de Beauvoir's philosophical arguments.

The degree to which Margaret Mead was motivated by feminist principles is difficult to discern, and in the long run, it probably doesn't matter anyway. We do know from her autobiographical account that she was reared with a sense of injustice in relation to women's subordination (*Blackberry Winter*, 1972; 1975) and we do know that in her work she helped to expose some of the accepted arguments for that subordination.

Mead was fortunate in that both her mother and her grandmother (who lived with them and who was a major influence in Mead's life) believed in women's rights, even if they expressed that belief in different ways. 'Grandma had no sense at all of ever having been handicapped by being a woman,' says Mead (1975, p. 49), for 'she began school teaching quite young at a time when it was still somewhat unusual for a girl to teach school. When my grandfather, who was also a teacher, came home from the Civil War, he married my grandmother and they went to college together. They also graduated together. She gave a graduation address in the morning and my grandfather, who gave one on the afternoon, was introduced as the husband of Mrs Mead who spoke this morning' (ibid., p. 47). This was not so long after Lucy Stone; things must have changed considerably.

Mead says (significantly) that: 'it was my grandmother who gave me my ease in being a woman. She was unquestionably feminine . . . and wholly without masculine protest or feminist aggrievement' (ibid., p. 55). This was in stark contrast to Mead's mother, who 'was filled with passionate resentment about the condition of women' (ibid.), much of it, it seems, arising out of her own domestic situation. In 1919, Mead's father was unwilling to send her to college: 'The reason he gave was that, since I was going to get married, I would not need a college education – he having married a wife who was working for a doctorate when I was born! And besides, he commented, I would have the same old-maid teachers at Wellesley who had been there when my mother was a student' (ibid., p. 34).

Her doctorate abandoned, five children, a husband who engaged in infidelities and who had financial problems, a void in her life on the departure of her children – it was not surprising that Mead's mother was filled with passionate resentment about the position of women. And while I suspect that Mead did not wish to emulate her mother on this issue, there were other areas where her mother did serve as an example: 'The two women I knew best were mothers and had professional training,' says Mead, so some of the customary conflict experienced by women was absent, for 'I had no reason to doubt that brains were suitable for a woman,' she says. 'I learned that the mind was not sex-typed' (ibid., p. 55) – an unusual lesson to learn, even today, in a male-dominated society.

Margaret Mead overcame the objections of her father and went to college; she became an anthropologist of international repute. In 1935 *Sex and Temperament* was published and in 1950[4] *Male and Female*. In these books, by *including* women, and by demonstrating that what is considered the natural behaviour of the sexes in one culture is considered decidedly unnatural in another, Mead was able to establish that the laws of behaviour for the sexes, and the division of labour between them, were not the unalterable laws which Freud, for example, had asserted, but were culturally specific customs. Whereas it would be futile to protest against unalterable laws (unjust though they may be), it was reasonable and advisable to protest against unjust customs.

Margaret Mead helped to change the basis of the debate about women's subordination. In terms which men could understand, which they respected, indeed which they had set up, and which were difficult to refute by their own standards, Margaret Mead produced the empirical evidence which sharply contradicted patriarchal justifications for women's subordination. Today, when we take cross-cultural comparisons for granted – and when they can still provide many fresh insights – it is easy to lose sight of the radical nature of Mead's contribution – which unlike Klein's, or Beard's, was much more widely disseminated (oh, for a different word!).

'Some peoples think of women as too weak to work out of doors,' writes Mead, going to what is often the crux of the justification for women's inferiority in English-speaking societies, but 'others regard women as the appropriate bearers of heavy burdens' (1950, 1971, p. 30). Now, she argues, if we are going to have universal laws of human behaviour, it cannot be that women are *both* too *weak* and too *strong*; if we are going to have universal laws, they will have to take account of the fact that in some societies women's heads are thought of as too weak for load-carrying, while in other societies it is men's heads that are considered too weak for load-bearing. If there is any law, it has to be that much of the differential

---

[4] A number of sources give 1949 as the original publication date, but my (well-worn) Penguin edition gives 1950.

behaviour of the sexes, and even some of the physical characteristics, are dependent on social custom. This 'law' of Mead's, which delivered quite a blow to a well-entrenched belief system, is often still fiercely resisted today.

Mead resisted the temptation of assuming that because women in some societies were considered stronger, or more capable of physical work, or more competent in trade, that they were therefore the superior sex. Instead she concluded from cross-cultural comparisons that it was not the *activity* but the *sex* which determined 'superiority', for, 'Men may cook or weave or dress dolls or hunt humming birds, but if such activities are appropriate occupations of men, then the whole society, men and women alike, notes them as important; when the same occupations are performed by women, they are regarded as less important' (ibid., p. 151).

Mead recognised – as Elizabeth Cady Stanton had done – that even where women engage in the same activities as men, and even where their performance may be comparable (or better), they are not considered of the same nature. This understanding – which for me has central significance – is often disregarded even today. What does it mean for women to be half the population in public life, to comprise 50 per cent of the politicians, economists, scientists, lawyers, etc., if a woman does not count as much as a man? What does it mean for women to equal or even surpass men in levels of competence or achievement, if women are not valued in the same way as men, if their attributed *wrongness* persists?

But there is yet another way of looking at this question. According to Mead's thesis, if men were to be the home-makers and child-rearers in our society, then the whole society, women and men alike, would consider home-making and child-rearing as the most important and prestigious activities. If such circumstances prevailed today the women's liberation movement could find itself arguing for women's right to stay at home. Margaret Mead raised many interesting questions which not only remain unanswered, but often seem to have been forgotten. Certainly I can find few traces of them being taken up or explored during the 1950s.

7 Facing the 1950s

That I have found little material published during the 1950s could mean that I have not looked hard enough, or it could mean (as I have often been informed) that nothing happened during the 1950s. Yet the publication of some books – already mentioned – tends to belie this. Vera Brittain was still protesting and writing (*Lady into Woman*, 1953); Mirra Komarovsky was still making her points (*Women in the Modern World*, 1953) and Viola Klein may have been discouraged, but she hadn't given up (Myrdal and Klein, *Women's Two Roles*, 1956; Klein, *Working Wives*, 1958). But no *new* women seem to appear, and this is puzzling.

Lynne Spender (forthcoming) has suggested that there is little correlation between what women write and what a male-controlled publishing institution publishes, and it could be that, except for their already published authors, who, presumably had met with some measure of commercial success, publishers during the 1950s were not prepared to publish 'risky' feminist material. Alison Thorne[5] seems to hold this view for she had a manuscript which in its exploration of the invasion of the domestic sphere by male 'experts' foreshadowed the work of Barbara Ehrenreich and Deirdre English (1978). But Alison Thorne could not find a publisher.

Obviously, the fact that on the surface I can find so little material during this decade does not begin to suggest to me that this was a period when women had no ideas about their own subordination, but it does suggest that the taboos against any expression of these ideas on the part of women or men may have been greater then than in other recent decades. However, I must qualify this by adding that when I asked Hazel Hunkins-Hallinan whether she thought the 1950s had been a harsh period for women, she said, 'My dear, when you have been fighting for women's liberation for over seventy years, one decade looks much the same as any other.' Mary Stott, however, another life-long feminist, declares that the 1950s *were* different — although the significance of that difference is only clear in retrospect: can we only see that we have been 'conned' when we look back?[6]

Nevertheless, while there was much more than *The Second Sex* between *Three Guineas* and *The Feminine Mystique* — with the development of some of the most persuasive and powerful ideas which have shaped the direction of the modern women's movement — it still seems fair to assume that the 1950s were atypical in the silence that was imposed on women.

8 Setting the scene: the 1960s

But Betty Friedan did not burst onto the scene in 1963 without precedents. Already there were signs that the whole value system of society was being questioned and that the silence of women, if not indeed broken, was concealing considerable doubt. This was surely what Doris Lessing was doing in fiction with *The Golden Notebook* (1962) and, at the other pole, it was what Rachel Carson was doing in *Silent Spring* (1962). Carson questioned the implications of the prevailing philosophy in which the universe was divided into discrete compartments, for the purpose of control and exploitation, and she established that in ignoring the interrelatedness of the universe man was not just guilty of making an occasional error, but was poisoning the whole human environment. (Her thesis was not dissimilar to the one proposed decades before by Dora Russell.) Today when we as women take an ecological model of the world for granted and have developed — at least partially — our consciousness of the interconnected nature of the world, when we have begun to query the god of science, we

[5] Private communication.
[6] The comments of Hazel Hunkins-Hallinan and Mary Stott are from taped interviews with me, February and March, 1982.

should remember that Rachel Carson was one of the first heretics, and reaped the wrath of a very vengeful god.

So wilfully was Rachel Carson distorted and misrepresented that Shirley Briggs (1981) has provided 'A Corrective Memoir' in which she discloses that the pattern of harassment inflicted on Carson has changed little since Aphra Behn dared to 'show men up'. 'After the publication of *Silent Spring*', says Briggs, 'the part of the chemical industry that felt itself threatened by the book went to great lengths to try to establish a public image of Miss Carson as an emotional, reclusive, unstable person' for, by calling her female personality into question, the possibility of having to confront her ideas was considerably reduced. That Rachel Carson possessed none of the ostensibly negative characteristics attributed to her 'did not deter them, any more than the contents of the book and its supporting scientific data prevented them from denying the truth of what she said and the things they only claimed she had said' (1981, p. 1).

It was 'anti-female fear that lay at the base of a great proportion of this controversy,' states Briggs, quoting from Joseph White. 'The American technocrat could not stand the pain of having his achievements deflated by the pen of this slight woman' (ibid.). Even now, says Briggs, 'some industry spokesmen continue to parrot the old charges, and these are found in twisted form in supposedly friendly commentaries' (ibid.). The charges were of the 'embittered-spinster-with-an-axe-to-grind' variety and reveal the depths to which men can go to belittle and devalue. Briggs suggests that Rachel Carson was to a certain extent 'protected' from this abuse: it was partly because she was an 'outsider' that she was able to distance herself from the establishment and to formulate her critique, and it was because she was financially independent and it therefore involved no risk to her means of earning a living that she was able to publish it. But such abuse still takes its toll no matter what the protection.

That this abuse of women who spoke out was considered reasonable and normal in society was a point at which Betty Friedan began in 1963. She started with 'the problem that has no name' and demonstrated that it was partly women's fear of such abuse which kept it nameless. Attributing much of the blame for the acceptance of such abuse of women to Freud's failure of reasoning power, Friedan stated that in the preceding fifteen years women had been 'taught to pity neurotic, unfeminine, unhappy women who wanted to be poets or physicists or presidents. They learned that truly feminine women do not want careers, higher education, political rights – the independence and the opportunities that the old fashioned feminists fought for' (1963, p. 13). Instead they had learned to 'want' true happiness and fulfilment which they were told lay in marriage and motherhood. Yet even while they followed the advice of the male experts to the full, even while they put all their energy into slavishly trying to live up to the images of the ideal woman, they found that they were not happy, that their lives were strangely empty, that they even often wondered who they were.

Protesting or complaining was made difficult; not only did prevailing wisdom insist that they had everything they could possibly want, that they were the most fortunate women that the world had ever seen, it also insisted that any woman who didn't know and appreciate this had only herself to blame. An ungrateful woman, an unhappy woman, was a 'sick' woman; there was stigma and shame attached to her *personal* failure to be happy and fulfilled.

Friedan stated that it had 'been popular in recent years to laugh at feminism as one of history's dirty jokes:[7] to pity, sniggering, those old fashioned feminists who fought for women's rights to higher education, careers, the vote. They were neurotic victims of penis envy who wanted to be men' (ibid., p. 71). Any woman who displayed similar tendencies was liable to be the recipient of similar treatment, and this was enough to promote silence. Florence Nightingale would have understood why women were likely to persist in asserting that they were happy, and grateful, while underneath they were 'dying from starvation'; and Charlotte Perkins Gilman could have given women the benefit of her experience.

Although protest was effectively blocked, women began communicating in their own way – a concept which in itself has become more real as women have described and explained it – and, says Friedan, one 'April morning in 1959, I heard a mother of four having coffee with four other mothers in a suburban development fifteen miles from New York, say in a tone of quiet desperation, "the problem". And the others knew, without words, that she was not talking about a problem with her husband, or her children, or her home' – the only valid area of problems for women whose only role was wife and mother – and 'suddenly they realized they all shared the same problem, the problem that has no name. They began hesitantly to talk about it. Later . . . two of the women cried, in sheer relief, just to know they were not alone' (ibid., p. 17). Once a problem has been named, once it has been conceptualised, it can be explored and explained. Once women started exploring, explaining – and exclaiming – there was virtually an explosion!

To Betty Friedan it became perfectly clear that the social image of what women were supposed to be and feel did not fit with women's experience of their own lives (and one of the reasons that this revelation had not been made before was because women's lives were not studied). She was courageous to come out and take her stand when much of her evidence rested on the knowledge that women who do protest are ridiculed and abused. She threw in her lot with the 'sick', 'unhappy', and 'misguided' women of the past who had wanted more – or less – than their allocated separate sphere afforded them, and she was prepared to take the consequences of identification with them. She broke the silence and many women heard the message.

But while defiantly returning to an image of the activist pioneers, commending them for their courage, re-evaluating their aims and their lives and asserting that what they had wanted was not unreasonable, it is worth noting that so effectively had women of the past been buried, Betty Friedan

---

[7] This observation is substantiated by reference to the treatment of Rachel Carson, and also by the treatment Diana Trilling handed out to Harriet Taylor in 1952, and by the reception Christabel Pankhurst's *Unshackled* enjoyed in 1959.

seems not to have known of contributions like those of Charlotte Perkins Gilman (or Viola Klein or Ruth Herschberger). Had she known of them, had she known by way of Gilman that women were experiencing a 'repeat performance', in the space of approximately fifty years, she might have been even angrier, and she would certainly have been more confident; the problem had been around for a few centuries and had even been named before – but the name, and the namers, had been lost. Freud had been popularised, Gilman had been erased.

During the 1950s it seems to have been fashionable (and objective) to study women – very occasionally – through the eyes of men, and in terms of the problems they created for men, hence the pronouncements against 'working' wives (where there might be an accompanying decline in the standard of domestic service) and the warnings against maternal depriva- tion when children (the mother's responsibility) showed less inclination to conform to the images that had been constructed for them, and refused more openly to be grateful and well-adjusted. Betty Friedan made a radical move when she began to study women's lives from the perspective of the women who lived them, and for whom the 'problems' were dramatically different from those put forward by men. But – as is so often the case – Betty Friedan was not alone. In England, Hannah Gavron (*The Captive Wife: Conflicts of Housebound Mothers*, 1966) was also examining the realities of women's world in a heterosexual society and her findings were 'defying the evidence' (Elaine Reuben's terminology, 1978) constructed in a patriarchal world.

In line with the work of Mirra Komarovsky, Alva Myrdal and Viola Klein, Gavron examined some of the many contradictions and sources of conflict in women's lives and she implied that society as then constructed did not permit the means of resolution. Despite the prevalence of male pronouncements on the characteristics of true womanhood, we know very little (says Gavron referring to the work of Margaret Mead) about women's lives and women's psychological make-up. We do not even acknowledge that women are placed in conflict situations and that this might have ramifications for their psychological state. When women cannot meet the conflicting demands (which go unacknowledged and are not therefore 'real'), what are they supposed to do?

A fundamental conflict is that women find themselves engaged in long and arduous work, and yet they are told – and they often believe – that they do not work. As Myrdal and Klein (1956) point out, says Gavron, '2,340 million hours are spent annually by housewives in Sweden on this "non work" while industry only uses 1,290 million hours' (1966, pp. 131– 2). How can women make sense of their lives? 'In a society where leisure is coming increasingly to be prized, the housewife is left out' (ibid., p. 132); yet the accepted social reality is one where her life *is* leisure, for she does not 'work'.

Hannah Gavron points out that a woman has not been prepared for the hard work or the contradictions. She has often hurried into marriage, lured by the romantic myth and convinced of the prospect of true happiness, and nothing has prepared her 'for the relentless boredom of scrubbing floors and ironing shirts' nor for the 'feeling that being at home is not as important as being at work' (ibid.). She has been told that she will do herself harm if she does not have children, and that she will do herself good if she does, and yet she finds that, contrary to the image of the 'smiling mother with enchanting babies', 'the advent of children brings with it isolation, confusion and insecurity'; it is 'a time which involves a great loss of confidence to many a young woman' (ibid., p. 133). But there seems no way out. In a heterosexual society where women are defined by marriage and motherhood, there are no viable alternatives for a woman; and yet marriage and motherhood makes her a *captive*, who must persistently profess that she is free.

Betty Friedan and Hannah Gavron mapped a primary realm of women's experience and laid the foundations for future exploration. Jessie Bernard followed up their lead with her assessment of women's version of marriage as contrasted with men's (1972), and her recognition that socio-logy – the discipline in which such questions *should* have been explored – was a male-controlled discipline which exclusively studied male experi-ence (1974). Ann Oakley – who made much use of Margaret Mead's cross-cultural comparions (1972) – went on to make one of the first sys-tematic studies of women's *non-work* in the tradition established by Myrdal and Klein, and Gavron (see Oakley, 1974).

But there was yet another tradition emerging which would help to set the scene for Kate Millett and Germaine Greer, who adopted a different approach from Friedan and Gavron; it was Mary Ellmann's *Thinking about Women* (1968). Mary Ellmann was concerned with women's voice – as it was expressed through literature, and the way men responded to it. It was not the ostensible standards of literary criticism, she argued, which were used to judge women's writing; it was *phallic criticism*. Coming from a different direction from Mary Beard, Viola Klein and Ruth Herschberger, Ellmann none the less found herself arriving at a similar place. She acknowl-edged that it was men who produced and legitimated society's reservoir of knowledge, and in it, men were central, positive, various, active, admirable, while women were sex-objects, seen only in relation to men; women were 'other', where they were deemed to exist at all.

By the end of the 1960s, parameters had been forged once again, problems had been named in history, education, psychology, anthropology, sociology, philosophy, literature, the biological sciences and ecology. That future discussion about women was going to break out of disciplinary strait-jackets was predictable. That it was the *invisibility* of women in society that was reflected in the disciplines, and not the individual limita-tions of a particular discipline which was responsible for the exclusion of women from the encoding of knowledge, was soon to be an established and unchallenged assumption of feminist reality.

But it was not a new 'discovery'. In 1968 a book entitled *In Her Own Right* appeared. It was subtitled 'A discussion conducted by *The Six Point Group*', the group established in 1921 by Lady Rhondda. The first essay is entitled 'A Revolution Unfinished' and is by Hazel Hunkins-Hallinan, who was 78 at the time and had been watching the revolution for quite a few years, since the days of the Woman's Party and the picketing of the White House (in which she had been involved, and for which she had been gaoled, and in the name of protest for which she had gone on hunger strike). 'The great crusading spirit for equality which was so strong at the turn of the century has petered out and the most dramatic revolution of all times has never been brought to fruition,' she states. 'Generation after generation of little girls have become adults completely conditioned to an overwhelmingly masculine society, restricting the development of women until they have no vision of anything different before them.' In 'an environment steeped in subtle masculine propaganda' women have come to hear and to accept that they are not to be taken seriously, she says (1968, pp. 9– 10).

One can sense the sadness, the frustration – and the hope: 'In this book it is our hope to open the eyes of teenage girls starting out in life, about to enter jobs that lead nowhere so that they will demand a better chance; to persuade newly-married wives not to abdicate their rights as people to an unequal partnership in marriage; to reach those older women who have shied away from "women's movements" and who learn late in life what odds are stacked against them. We want to make these thousands realise what their actual status is and then we hope that the emancipation of women, as a movement will come alive' (ibid., p. 10).

'Did you talk like this, in the 1920s?' I asked her: 'Oh no, we were much more radical then,' she replied. And to my deep, deep regret, there is every chance that in 1968 I might have spurned these cautious, but passionately optimistic words.

(E)

REINVENTING REBELLION

1 The old, old story

Recently, an eminent male critic – who for my purposes will remain name-less – wrote a review of *The Handbook of Non-Sexist Writing* for a respectable English newspaper. It began, in bold print, with a statement about the authors: 'From the photograph supplied by Ms Casey Miller and Kate Swift I should judge that neither was sexually attractive,' and contin-ued with, 'I refuse to accept that speculation along these lines is irrelevant to a study of the book.' And why? Because it is the considered opinion of this reputable reviewer that women he decrees as sexually unattractive are intellectually unreliable and incapable of writing a reasonable book.

Before it is assumed that in order to be a good writer (or at least, to get good reviews) it is necessary to be sexually attractive to the male critic, it is worth noting that 'acceptable' women are no more likely to be rated positively than 'unacceptable' ones. Had the photographs of the authors been 'pin-ups' whom the reviewer *did* find sexually attractive they could just as easily have been discredited on the same grounds of unreliability. 'Beautiful' women are presumed to be without 'brains', and women with 'brains' to have no 'beauty', so no matter *how* women appear to men, either way their writing is damned, for it is their sex and not their writing which disqualifies them. As this critic reveals, an intellectually competent woman writer is a contradiction in terms.

In the eye of this beholder, Miller and Swift are without beauty; they are 'plain' women, he says, and therefore not to be trusted, for they write out of a sense of grievance and frustration. He readily acknowledges that men have treated plain women badly – but this is no excuse. 'Plain women have had a pretty rough time through the ages,' he says. 'Some were shut up in nunneries, others burned as witches and even the kindest treatment of leaving them alone to find whatever employment they could was accom-panied by various symbols of disapproval, if not revulsion.' Our critic remains unconcerned about this treatment of women. If women who found him sexually unattractive were in a position to inflict social derision – or violence – on him, or to deny him a livelihood, his consciousness would probably undergo a dramatic change, but because the possibility does not arise, this standard treatment of women poses no problem. His review is part of that standard treatment which imposes punishments on women who do not try to make themselves available (or 'attractive') to men.

Drawing on accumulated meanings of patriarchal wisdom – but without acknowledging the complete lack of originality of his view – our critic continues with the observation 'that the human race now divides into three sexes – men, women and feminists',[1] and adds that this 'should not be seen as a cheap sneer so much as the statement of an important and agonizingly uncomfortable truth' which is that feminists do not 'fit into the established social relationships between the sexes'.

In a sense I agree with him. Feminists *do not* fit into the established social relationships between the sexes, but whereas our critic believes it is because they *cannot*, I know from personal experience (and it is experience not available to the male reviewer) that because it is men who have established the social relationships between the sexes and because they have done so with an eye to their own advantage, feminists *will not* fit in. We do not *fail*, we *choose* not to conform to the dominant group's definition of our subordination. But it is none the less a measure of our subordination that our autonomy and our action can be denied. It is a measure of male dominance that this critic can be considered credible, that his fears and fantasies can be taken as facts.

Accustomed as I am to the limitations of male logic, this man of letters still has the power to astonish me. While asserting that the authors are ugly, discontented, unfortunate, and write out of a sense of grievance and are therefore to be pitied, the reviewer states that: 'simple good manners – no need to use such sexually loaded images as "chivalry" – require that women should not be insulted or belittled in speech or writing by virtue of their sex alone.' What does he think he has been doing in the preceding paragraphs? This is an example of the male intellect in operation: this critic has been behaving in the very way described by Casey Miller and Kate Swift while he continues to insist that such behaviour is 'unchivalrous' (and might even be the substance of a good book!)

The authors are ridiculous, states the critic, for making changes in the English language will not improve their lot at all. Everyone knows what they need. The only thing they have succeeded in doing is to imitate with their pedantry. He concludes by wishing them no luck with their work; his response to women who do not flatter him is the traditional one.

2 Payment in kind

There are many reasons for my inclusion of this review and in this particular form. Firstly, the reviewer is anonymous and will remain so because throughout this book and, as a 'positive learning experience', I have intentionally treated (some) men in the manner in which men customarily treat women. There are quite a few 'husbands' and a few males who are men-

---

[1] Roger Fulford, David Mitchell and Piers Brendon also make use of this same 'joke'.

tioned in the text but whose work is not cited in the references. I have deliberately made some men invisible and I have deliberately denied this critic the 'ownership' of his contribution. If he knows he has been 'robbed', it is even possible that 'invisibility' might become for him a serious issue.

But even as I appropriate his words in this way I am aware that he might respond. It is not an entirely remote possibility that he might review this book. I take refuge in the thought that he would not get this far (unless he is the type to read only the last pages) or else he will render me invisible and this book will go unreviewed as many others before it. But if he ever does want to comment, I look to Caroline Norton for guidance – let him claim the copyright if he will! It is only by these means that we can protect ourselves while men control knowledge and its distribution. Currently, women have no intellectual power-base, no equivalent means of ensuring that our meanings get a fair hearing, are positively presented or widely distributed.

A recurring 'dream' of mine is to have a woman-controlled book programme on television, in prime time, and to invite male publishers to 'explain' their disproportionate rejection of manuscripts written by women and their disproportionate publication of manuscripts written by men (see Lynne Spender, forthcoming). I would like to ask reviewers to be the guests, and to have them justify their treatment of women writers, or men of letters in educational institutions to account for their failure to include women writers in their courses. Naturally it would be women who were defining the terms, who would select who would speak, on what and for how long. Naturally, women would 'edit' the programme and present women's case in the most positive light. And naturally we would be accused of the most flagrant bias, misrepresentation, distortion and deception. We would be called embittered, aggrieved and humourless, no doubt. But we might be able to influence the construction of knowledge, to modify what is known, for half an hour per week – through one medium.

Such a small sphere of influence remains still a 'dream' (I did make a proposal to a television channel but it was rejected). The reality is one where males determine problems, priorities and policies, in which it is assumed that women are available to men and those who are not are legitimately abused for their inadequacy. It is a reality where men can take from women what they need, and use it, and it seems that they frequently need to take women's resources to use against women. What is not needed is easily discredited or discarded, and can soon disappear.

3 Progress or repetition?

Another reason for my inclusion of this review is to demonstrate that literary sexual harassment is no less today than it was in the time of Josephine Butler, Elizabeth Cady Stanton, or the Grimké sisters. Of course, the critic quoted sees little wrong with depriving 'unattractive' women of their livelihood and feels no compunction about wishing Miller and Swift no luck with their work. By dismissing the authors on his sexual grounds he is not obliged to refer to – let alone repudiate – their ideas and he ridicules and reviles them in the same way as his forefathers treated our foremother Mary Wollstonecraft.

That perhaps there has been no progress for women when it comes to the recognition that women exist creatively and intellectually in their own right is a concept difficult to formulate in a patriarchal culture, partly because the belief in progress is so deeply entrenched. It is a belief bolstered by the premises of growth and expansion which underlie capitalism, by the justification of evolutionary theory, and the construction of history as a steady march of human improvement. It is almost beyond our comprehension to question the notion of progress.

The absurdity of this concept is not challenged by the insanity of nuclear weapons, the wilful and increasing destruction and pollution of this planet or by the grossly inequitable distribution of resources. Society needs the concept of progress to legitimate as the high point of civilisation many of its current barbaric practices. Yet this concept of progress, and all that goes with it, has its origins in men's consciousness. It is formed from the perspective of dominance and demands the denial of life-sustaining values, including the denial of women and our thinking/explaining existence.

This is what Matilda Joslyn Gage argued; without benefit of Gage's ideas, it was what Dora Russell started to argue from the 1920s and what she is still arguing today. There are many other women with similar views – Carolyn Merchant, Jean Baker Miller, Robin Morgan, Ann Oakley, Mary O'Brien, Dorothy Smith, Adrienne Rich – who arrived at their conclusions without knowledge of Gage or Russell. This is more like the repetition of the same pattern, than 'progress', the pattern of interruption and silence, which denies women's consciousness so that men's creations can be justified. It is the pattern which constitutes women's culture, says Michelle Cliff (1979), where women's intellectual and creative resources are taken away by repeated interruptions partly through the role men have imposed on them.

Anna Coote and Beatrix Campbell (1982) agree. In their review of the 'modern' women's liberation movement in Britain, they state that progress is the prerogative of men; even the male lifestyle is based on the premise of uninterrupted progress. From school to apprenticeship to work there is the concept of continued advancement with greater prospects, pay and pensions. This is not the case for most women, for men have arranged the world so that women are the ones who must take 'time out'. Ann Lane (1977) has also pointed out that the pattern of women's lives is very different from that of men, with women frequently enjoying their capacity for chosen creative work at a much later age when they have been freed from the demands made upon them.

This daily reality of interruption, argue Coote and Campbell is also the historic reality for women where again and again women are cut off from their past and must start afresh. It is lamentable, they say, 'that generations of girls . . . have grown up in ignorance of their grandmothers'

politics. Only when they reinvent rebellion for themselves do they begin to
disinter the buried remains of that knowledge. Each time they find that
although the setting is new, the battle they are fighting is essentially the
same' (pp. 9–10).

While I have been searching for a means to convey these ideas, I have
seen a play, *Time Pieces*, devised, written and acted by The Women's
Theatre Group, in which the meanings cut with clarity across the consciousness of women. The play begins with 16-year-old Sharon trying to
explain to her mother that she wants to make a man the centre of her life,
'to give up everything and make him happy'. Her mother is anguished by
this 'choice' of her daughter, but cannot communicate her concern and fear
for many (patriarchal) reasons. But Sharon's (feminist) aunt comes to the
rescue, with a photograph album of mother, aunts, grandmother, great-
aunts, and even great-grandmother, and each woman in the album acts out
her own story; those who 'give up everything for a man' tell the *same*
story. It is a story of disenchantment, disillusionment, dependence and
denial, and it is a story which because it defies patriarchal reality defies
transmission to the daughter – who goes on to repeat the same mistake.

Learning for oneself but being prevented from passing the lesson on
is the substance of women's culture, says Michelle Cliff. It is a tradition we
must explore and explain and in the process we will understand that it is
a tradition which has been imposed on us and which has been structured
on the denial of women's consciousness, the repudiation of our resources,
our values, our insights. It is a tradition we must change.

I do not think it is a superficial or indulgent activity to argue for
women's intellectual resources in the current crisis context; I think it an
absolute necessity. We must assert the validity of our own consciousness
and that of our foremothers. We are not the first women to have known
what we know, we are not without precedents – despite the frequency with
which we and our foremothers are presented as new. We are not inventing
our rebellion, but reinventing it.

4 Active non co-operation

The fundamental question is how do we find the ways to influence the
construction and distribution of knowledge, how do we find the means to
break this male hold over what we know so that our meanings are positively
represented and passed around? I have no solutions, only some ideas, ideas
rediscovered and reinvented.

First of all I think we must replace our reverence for male reason and
logic with a very healthy scepticism – at least. It is clear that in the name
of fair reporting (or reviewing), in the name of scholarly research, objectivity, authority and truth, men have systematically robbed women of their
resources and have engaged in practices of distortion and deception with
regard to women and our ideas. It is not the 'unethical' ones who have
been exposed, not merely those 'exceptions' who have 'fallen short of the

required standards'. *This treatment of women is the standard.* That men may not recognise it is their limitation.

Virginia Woolf and Adrienne Rich are among those who urge us to be 'disloyal to civilisation', to free ourselves from the unreal loyalties to male institutions of politics, economics, science and technology. They ask us to re-examine what we know and to reject what is life-destructive; they implore us to cease reflecting men at twice their normal size and instead to call their methods madness and their logic lies.

Their message is not a new one: Mary Astell, Elizabeth Cady Stanton, Charlotte Perkins Gilman and Phyllis Chesler have all argued that for women it is healthy to rebel and sickness to succumb. We have a history rich in these meanings, and we are advocating not something new, but something old when we ask that women look not to men, but to each other for validation and approval. It is to women we must look for authority; it is women freed from unreal loyalties to whom we must turn and check our meanings. And we must be concerned with consensus about our common and diverse experience. Our own tradition teaches us about interruption and silence and we cannot impose on members of our sex the denial of a voice.

But even while we do this we must keep in mind that we are generating our ideas in a male-dominated society. Again, hundreds of women have recognised this, but understanding the process has not protected them from it. In very few respects are we different; we are deluded if we think we have created the first, or even a superior or sophisticated form of rebellion. There have been shifts – certainly – but the critiques of marriage from Mary Astell on merge with Adrienne Rich's critique of compulsory heterosexuality now that the marriage ceremony itself is not so necessary.

Matilda Joslyn Gage's critique of the male dogma of religion has given way to Dora Russell's and Carolyn Merchant's critique of male science and technology, but the principle is much the same. 'Sophia's' critique of male logic resurfaces again and again from Mary Wollstonecraft to Viola Klein and encompasses many reasonable and rigorously rebellious women along the way. Frances Power Cobbe's understandings about law, and male violence, fit very well with Susan Brownmiller and Andrea Dworkin. Catherine MacKinnon's argument that sexual harassment is the normal pattern of relationship between the sexes when women are defined in terms of sexuality fits with Susan Griffin's case that pornography is the patriarchal way of life with its origins in male consciousness and its denial of women's and both have links with Simone de Beauvoir's philosophy of women 'being in the wrong' and Elizabeth Cady Stanton's insight that it is the sex that is the 'sin'. And the analysis of the Grimké sisters and the protests of Sojourner Truth and Ida Wells-Barnett have their counterpart in Barbara Smith's (1979) analysis. About the only 'unprecedented' idea – and I am even very cautious in asserting it – is Shulamith Firestone's 'science-fiction' which is rapidly moving to a reality, where reproduction will be a technological event and women will be 'freed' from its interruption.

Men allocate to women the qualities they despise in themselves, said Mary Astell three hundred years ago, laying the foundations for the analysis of male misogyny. While there have been periods when women have shown a preference for not acknowledging the hatred of men towards women, there have also been times when this understanding has been well to the fore. Germaine Greer and Kate Millett burst upon the contemporary scene with detailed documentation of the contempt in which women are and have been held and Mary Daly provided overwhelming evidence in the systematic violence against women in patriarchal cultures, a violence which has its origins in revulsion, hatred and fear.

This is a very uncomfortable understanding to accommodate, partly because the only frame of reference in which we can explain it in patriarchal society is in terms of sex-*war*, with men as the *enemy*, and women seeking a *victory*. Another reason that this is seen as unacceptable is that while it is reasonable for men to be contemptuous of women in a patriarchal society, it is outrageous for women to be contemptuous of men. Writing prior to the support and approval of the contemporary women's movement, Constance Rover stated in 1970 that women who resist male power are accused of hating not the power, but the men. 'To the charge that some feminists were man-haters', she argues, 'one can make the counter-charge that there is ample evidence of woman hatred. . . . Perhaps the answer to the question of why it has been looked upon as so much worse for women to dislike men than the converse is the belief that the sole justification for the existence of women is that they should be wives (or at least sexual partners) and mothers' (p. 150). We are back to where we began; there must be some way out of the trap.

While I cannot in good conscience advocate a *war* against men with the purpose of *conquest*, I can none the less see that there is a conflict of interest between women and men while the world is arranged in its present form, and that it is self-destructive for women to deny this conflict and the power base that underlies it. I do not seek a victory over men, I do not wish to deny in full their values and their creations but I do want to deny, again and again that their values and creations are the only ones that society can utilise. I want co-existence.

I want the intellectual and creative resources of women to be equally represented and valued in the cultural meanings of society. I want an end to the double standard that would have men's problems as the social problems and women's as 'personal deviancy'. I want an end to the division of male authority and reason, and female unreliability and emotion. I want an end to men's activities being revered as objective, as art, as science, while women's are dismissed as subjective, as accomplishment or foolishness. I want an end to these value judgements for the framework in which they are made is a manifestation of male consciousness in which women's thinking/explaining/acting being is denied.

I want women actively to resist, to refrain from co-operating with men, to cease making our resources available to men who are likely to then use against us what they have taken. I want men to be 'irrelevant' to our enterprise of constructing our own knowledge; I do not want them 'revered'. I am advocating non-violent non co-operation.

It is ironic that it is Mahatma Gandhi who is held up as the originator of this method of resistance. Elizabeth Sarah informs me that in 1906 he visited Britain and on his own ready admission stated that it was from the suffragettes that he learned the power of non co-operation. As they refused to pay fines and were imprisoned, as they refused to acknowledge the authority of the law or its makers, as they 'invented' the method of hunger striking they revealed that a group defined as powerless, excluded from political participation (for they were kept out of meetings), were able to exert a great deal of power. They were able to *act* and the oppressor had to *react*. The oppressor could change his ways or he could show that his rule is maintained by force, but either way his ideology that the oppressed are content with their lot is seriously challenged.

As males cannot be authorities on women's experiences, what they make of this thesis does not much matter; but as they possess enormous power what does matter is what they can take and use. I have tried to practise what I preach and to provide them with as little as possible. I cannot condone violence against the enemy, but I can withdraw my labour from the exploiter and will not be swayed by the argument that he has more rights, that his interest is greater, his authority more legitimate.

I do not believe that women are now of age so that it is perfectly in order for us to start criticising (attacking, condemning, demolishing, deriding) each other in public forums, for I know, as women have found again and again, that our words will be taken down and used as evidence against us. We play into men's hands when we represent our sex negatively; we oblige them by doing some of their work for them. I *know* we are perfectly capable of generating our own valid meanings and I know that we do not all agree. I even know that I will never agree with some women; but my 'criticisms' are in private until the view of a woman carries the same weight as a man's, and is not just the raw data for his patriarchal products. While the world is arranged as it is I *choose* to assert my intellectual and creative existence as a woman and to promote a positive representation of women's lives, values, and ideas. Let men do what they will with this.

APPENDIX:

LIFE IN PRISON

From Sylvia Pankhurst (1931:1977)
The Suffragette Movement,
Virago, London

For many hours after our friends had gone we waited in the dim stone corridor connecting the filthy cells, crouching together on the stone steps by the gate at the end. Mrs. Lawrence read aloud to us from Browning, 'The Statue and the Bust.' In the afternoon the prison van, 'Black Maria,' came to take us to Holloway. We were locked in the stuffy darkness of its little compartments, each just large enough to contain a seated person, bumping against the wooden sides as the springless vehicle jolted over the stones. Some women in the van, taken up from another police court, were shrieking strange words I had never before heard, their voices in the inky blackness lending a horrible misery to the experience. The lamps had long been lit when we reached the prison. We passed between high, forbidding walls, through heavy doors, opened and shut by tall wardresses with great jangling keys hanging at their waists. They locked us into pitch-dark cubicles, with no other seat than a lidless w.c., where we waited until late in the night, whilst batches of prisoners were brought in and locked up, the new-comers thrust in with the earlier occupants of the cubicles, sometimes four or five of them together, shouting those strange words in high-pitched voices. Hearing them with mingled pity and disgust, I stood shivering in the darkness, trembling with fatigue, but afraid of coming into contact with uncleanliness by sitting down. Again and again that night we were called by the wardresses to state our name, age, occupation, religion, sentence, and whether we could read and write and sew. At last we were ranged in line to see the doctor. 'All of you unfasten your chests!' the wardress shouted repeatedly. We filed in and out of the small room, where the doctor was sitting. 'Are you all right?' 'Are you all right?' he asked mechanically, not waiting a reply, touching us lightly with his stethoscope, but not pausing to apply his ear to it. Cases of infectious and contagious disease could easily escape him; no doubt they did. Back to the cubicles; more long hours in the cold and darkness. Finally we were marched off to a large room where, four or five at a time, we were called out to undress in view of the rest, given a short, coarse cotton chemise to cover our nakedness, and ordered to carry our clothing to an officer, who, bundling hat, shoes and all roughly together, thrust our belongings on to a shelf, to remain there till our discharge. We were marched about barefoot from place to place, here to give up our money, there to be searched, raising our arms in the air whilst an officer rubbed her hands over us and examined our hair to ensure we had nothing concealed about us. All the prisoners were quiet now: all seemed cowed; there was an atmosphere of fear. My companions had been taken some other way. They were in the Second Division; I amongst strangers in the Third. Next we went marching to the bath and dressingroom; a miserable place with piles of clothing heaped on the floor in the dim light. The baths were indescribably dirty, their paint discoloured and worn off in patches, showing the black iron beneath, the woodwork encasing them sodden and slimy. They were separated from the room outside by a halfdoor, revealing one's shoulders above and feet beneath. I shuddered at stepping into the water clouded with the scum of previous occupants. A wardress shouted: 'Make haste and get dressed!' as she hung a towel and some clothing over the door – strange-looking garments, all plentifully marked with the 'broad arrow,' black on light colours, white on dark; stockings of harsh, thick wool, black with red rings round the legs; long cotton drawers, red striped to match the chemise; huge, thick petticoats – as bunchy and full at the top as those of a Dutch peasant, but without their neatness, cobbled into a broad waistband of capacious girth, which one overlapped around one's person as best one could, and tied with tapes fastened in front; a curious sort of corset reaching from neck to knees.

'You have not put on your stays!' the wardress screamed at me, with indignant scorn. 'I don't wear them.' 'Unless you were not wearing stays when you came in, you must put them on at once!' 'Did she bring any stays in with her?' A long discussion ensued.

The prisoners were scrambling for dresses of dark, chocolate-coloured serge in the heaps on the floor. 'Make haste! Make haste!' cried the officers. I pulled from the pile a skirt many feet too wide, of the same pattern as the petticoats, and a bodice with several large rents, badly cobbled together. The broad arrows daubed with white paint on the dresses were fully four inches long. The bodices were fastened with only one button at the neck, and gaped absurdly.

'Look sharp! Put on your shoes!'

We grabbed them from a rack where they had been tumbled; no chance of finding a pair! They were made of stiff, hard leather with heavy soles, like those of a navvy, and leather laces which broke as one sought to tie them. An officer handed us each a little white cap, like a Dutch bonnet, with strings under the chin, and two pieces of cotton stuff, blue and white plaid, like the dusters one buys from the draper. One of them with tapes stitched to it was to be worn as an apron, the other was the weekly handkerchief. Did I say weekly? Weekly in theory; even in the reformed period of 1921, after the appointment of a woman prison inspector, I have known prisoners to be left six weeks without a change of clothing. A wardress explained to me that this handkerchief must hang from the waist-band by one corner, no pockets being supplied. Those wide, thick stockings, none too long, were flapping about my ankles. 'Could I have something to keep them up with?' 'No garters here!' – an indignant shout, as though one had asked for a luxury of rare price.

We were marched through a strange sort of skeleton building, painted a drab stone colour with black ironwork, passing through great pavilions, lined with tier upon tier of cells, the doors studded with black nails and bearing in the centre a round spy-hole covered with a flap from outside. The stone corridors by which the cells were reached jutted out from the walls of the pavilion like shelves, bordered by railings of iron trellis-work, and connected by iron staircases. One could see from the floor of the pavilion to its roof, in spite of a strong wire netting stretched across at each tier of cells to catch any prisoner who might attempt to commit suicide by throwing herself over the railings.

We stopped at a little office and gave once more our names, ages, sentences, religion, profession, and so on, and received a pair of sheets, a Bible, a hymn-book, a religious tract called 'The Narrow Way,' and a small book, 'A Healthy Home and How to Keep It,' which enjoined one to take a daily bath and to sleep with open windows; excellent maxims, but impossible of performance in Holloway Prison. Waiting by the office I saw again my fellow Suffragettes with a few others of the Second Class. Dressed in dark green to distinguish them from the rest of us in the Third Class chocolate brown, they were regarded as a trifle more respectable than the common herd. A motley crowd we were; all the little women seemed to be wearing the long dresses, the tall women, the short. Those strange, clumsy garments made us look squat and awkward. Weariness and decrepitude preponderating amongst us, we formed a striking contrast to the tall, straight, well-drilled officers. Some of the Suffragettes had little brown loaves in their hands, left from their supper, they told me. Evidently there was not enough to go round in the Third Division, for I had seen none of it. Mrs. Baldock broke off half her loaf and begged me to take it.

The Suffragettes marched away; clack, clack, their footsteps sounded echoing through the long corridors.

At last I was in my cell. It measured perhaps seven feet by five, with a stone floor and a little barred window, not made to open, high up near the ceiling. A flickering gas jet, lighted from the corridor outside, was set in an opening in the wall, covered outside by a piece of tin and separated from me by a thick semi-opaque pane of glass. Under the gas jet was a little wooden shelf called the table. Across one corner another little shelf held the worn, discoloured old wooden spoon, which remained in the cell for prisoner after prisoner, as did the large wooden salt cellar and its contents, so long as they lasted, the tin pint measure from which one drank the time-honoured prison 'skilly,'[1] a tin plate, a piece of hard yellow soap, a small scrubbing-brush, to be used for brushing one's hair, and a three-inch comb, also come cards containing the prison rules and a morning and

[1] A thin gruel of oatmeal and water.

evening prayer. Beneath these the mattress and blankets were rolled up on a lower corner shelf. Ranged on the floor under the window, in positions never to be varied, and all made of block tin, were a dustpan, a water-can with a capacity of about three pints, a small wash-basin and a slop-pail, also a little round scrubbing brush to be used for sweeping. Reared against the wall, with a pillow on top, was the famous plank bed, its cross-boards raising it about two inches from the floor when put down for the night. A thin towel, like a small dish-cloth, and a wooden stool completed the furniture. Hanging on a nail was a disk of yellow cloth, as big as the top of a cup, bearing the number of the cell, which happened to be twelve. It was the prisoner's badge, and by this number I should henceforth be known.

The door opened. 'What! You have not made your bed! The light will go out soon!' 'Please may I have a nightdress?' 'No!' The door banged.

Sleep? Certainly not. The mattress and pillow – round like a bolster – both filled with a kind of shrub, seemed as hard and comfortless as stone. (Prisoners usually put the pillow under the mattress as the least of various evils.) The blankets and sheets were too narrow to cover one, the cell airless and cold. The night was not still. Heavy steps passed and repassed, voices sounded, occasionally a cry. All night I was cold, and every night of the imprisonment.

Long before daylight arose a tremendous clatter; great ringing of bells, great tramping of feet. The light was turned on. One learnt quickly the daily routine. One washed in the little basin and dressed hurriedly, emerged to empty one's slops at the word of command and the clangour of opening doors, rolled up the bedding, cleaned and polished the tins, with brickdust scoured off on the floor, and with the bit of yellow soap also used for washing the person, one scrubbed the floor of the cell, the bed and the table. The sheets were changed for each prisoner; but the blankets remained in the cell.[2] So, too, the little scraps of torn rag used for cleaning the tins, the same rags being employed for all the utensils – even the drinking measure and the slop-pail. If the tins[3] were not bright enough, or the water used for scrubbing not sufficiently discoloured, the wardress would require the work to be done a second time, as she did of me on more than one occasion. I obeyed with meekness, for we had agreed to submit ourselves to the prison discipline.

Again the door opened. 'Where's your pint, 12?' A thin gruel of oatmeal and water was poured into the measure, 6 oz. of brown bread tossed on to the plate. The door slammed. The food eaten, one must set to work – a sheet to hem, a mail-bag, or a man's shirt to make. At 8.30 the

[2] When I was in the prison hospital under the D.O.R.A. in 1921 a woman with a baby occupied the next cell. The woman had scabies. On her release the prisoner employed in cleaning that row of cells complained to me that although the baby had stained the blankets, they had not been changed. When another prisoner was put into that cell she shouted to me that the blankets were stained and smelt as though a baby had dirtied them.

[3] An earthenware mug and plate were substituted in later years, a metal spoon replaced the wooden one.

officers shouted: 'Chapel!' The doors flew open, the prisoners emerged, and were marshalled in single file amid a running fire of rebuke: 'Who is that speaking? I heard someone speaking!' 'Tie up your cap strings, 27! You look like a cinder picker; you must learn to dress decently here!' 'Hold up your head, 30; don't shuffle your feet!' 'Don't look about you, 12!' The chapel was filled with prisoners; row upon row of careworn faces. The majority seemed quite old. The wardresses kept watch in high-raised seats. The chaplain spoke with harsh severity and many a hard word for the sinner. Old women bowed their heads and wept. At his mention of children the mothers sobbed. Tears flowed at the playing of the organ, and voices broke with weeping in the hymns. To me all this was misery. I wept with those poor souls; and when the cell door closed on me again, the shrunken forms of frail old grannies, with their scant white hair, their shaking hands and piteous, withered faces, and the tense, white looks and burning eyes of younger women haunted me. Unnerved by lack of sleep and food – for I had not eaten the morning porridge, I cried till my head ached; and shrank from the sound of footsteps, which foretold that frequent flinging open of the door, fearing the officials would believe me sorry I had come.

'Inspection!' the wardress shouted as she unlocked the door. A pallid woman in black uniform peered in and passed in silence. 'Doctor!' 'Governor and matron!' 'Visiting Magistrate!' they each passed by in silence. To procure a word from any of these powers, an advance application must be made to the officer who opened the doors at 6 a.m. The chaplain alone was apt to converse for a moment or two without having an express application from the prisoner.

At twelve o'clock came the clatter of tins; dinner, a pint of oatmeal porridge, unseasoned, like the breakfast gruel, but cold and stiff instead of thin and hot; two days a week 8 oz. of small, sodden potatoes of poor quality, and the two remaining days 6 oz. of what was called suet pudding, a small, stiff, waxy slice, heavy and unsweetened. 6 oz. of bread were added to each meal. The dietary contained no sugar at all, no fat save in the twice-weekly pudding. After dinner followed sewing till 3 p.m., when we were called out to fetch water for the next day. Then sewing again, and at five supper of gruel and bread, as at breakfast. The cell door was now shut for the night: prisoners might cease work. The light in my cell was too poor for me to read the small print of the Bible without strain, and as a Third Division prisoner I was not yet eligible for a book from the prison library. Twice in the twenty-four hours the prisoners had a brief opportunity, harried by the perpetual shout of 'Make haste! Make haste!' to run to the w.c. in the corridor. It was protected only by a half-door without fastening, like that of a cowshed. The haste, the lack of privacy, the character of the food, the want of exercise, the solitary confinement, the airless condition of the cell told their tale on most prisoners, producing digestive and other disorders. In numbers of cases imprisonment as a Suffragette proved the onset of an illness eventually necessitating a surgical operation.

At 8 p.m. came a noisy knocking at every door, and the cry: 'Are you all right? Are you all right?' The flap over the spy-hole was raised. An eye peered in. Then the light was turned out, and another cold, sleepless night began. Twice a week I went out to exercise for half an hour, in a yard surrounded by giant walls and huge gaunt buildings, chequered by the tiny, barred windows of the cells. We marched in slow file, with a space of three or four yards between each prisoner. I remember a showery day, the sun shining gaily on puddles and raindrops, the white clouds driving briskly across a sky of strong, clear blue, and the wind whisking our bonnets and skirts in playful gusts. The pigeons, dear harbingers of freedom, dwelling in great numbers about that dreary prison, flew low and strutted near us. How gladly my eyes sought the varied hues of their glossy plumage. Then I turned to the prisoners, plodding around with dull gaze bent downward, treading, without heed through the water on sunk stones, though there was dry ground within reach.

How grim seemed the narrow, dull-lit cell when the door slammed again and the key turned in the lock at my back! I was without news of my fellow prisoners, till one morning the chaplain paused at my door and told me that though as a prisoner in the Third Division I was not entitled to have a library book, my sister Adela had requested that an exception might be made for me, and he had granted her request.

In the country outside was a great clamour. 'Richard Cobden's daughter in prison!' From her well-ordered home on the Upper Mall, Hammersmith, beautified by the works of the William Morris circle,[4] this gracious lady, devoted to good works amongst women and children, the gentle hostess of artists, humanitarians, Socialists, and a couple of generations of Liberal politicans, had settled down to life in Holloway with genial equanimity. In the dock she had asked to be allowed to take the whole responsibility of the demonstration: 'If anyone is guilty it is I. I was arrested as one of the ringleaders, and as the eldest I was most responsible.' She quoted the President of the Local Government Board, John Burns, on his trial for incitement in the 'eighties: 'I am a law breaker because I want to be a law maker'; but at this the Magistrate was scandalized, and refused to permit her another word.

Keir Hardie, Lord Robert Cecil[5] and others in Parliament were demanding for us the status of political prisoners. The Government declared itself unable to interfere with the Magistrate's decision. On October 28th Mrs. Pethick Lawrence became seriously ill. In response to the insistence of her husband and a message from Mrs. Pankhurst, she gave the undertaking for six months which would procure her release. Next day Mrs. Montefiore, horrified to discover her head infested by lice, owing to the lack of precautions against the spread of vermin in the prison, precipitately gave the same undertaking and came out. A few days later my solitude was broken by a wardress who led me to a room where I met my fellow Suffragettes; and, wonder of wonders, Elizabeth Robins, the novelist. How had this brilliant creature obtained permission to visit us in defiance of

---

[4] Her husband, the late T. J. Cobden Sanderson, of the famous Doves' book-bindery, a co-worker of William Morris, is recognized as having revived the art of gold tooling.
[5] Afterwards Lord Cecil of Chelwood.

rule? In our curious garb we clustered about her, her arms encircling as many of us as possible, telling us in delightful images of the agitation outside. On the eight day of our imprisonment the matron announced to us a Home Office order to transfer us to the First Division. I was told to take up my bed linen and the sheets I had been given to hem, and thus encumbered, was bustled along the corridor by a shepherding wardress, when I met the other Suffragettes similarly engaged. We were turned into a row of dingy cells in the Remand Hospital, where we indignantly discovered that untried prisoners were treated much like the convicted, though they might presently be proved innocent of all offence. We were now offered the privileges of wearing our own clothes and getting food sent in to us from outside at our own expense. We refused to accept these concessions. No First Division dress existed, but some new ones of grey serge, of precisely the same pattern as the others, were made, to define our new position. We were served with the food supplied to prisoners of the Second Class.[6] We accepted the privileges, meagre in extent, though precious in kind, of receiving and writing a fortnightly letter,[7] and having books and a daily newspaper sent in by our friends. This, of course, was by no means the First Division treatment accorded to W. T. Stead, Dr. Jameson, and others, who had been permitted correspondence and visits without restriction. On consulting the rule card, I saw that First Class misdemeanants may exercise their profession, provided prison dicipline be not thereby disturbed. I therefore claimed the right to send for drawing-paper, pen, ink and pencils. These being granted, I busied myself in reproducing prison scenes.

From Antonia Raeburn (1974)
Militant Suffragettes,
New English Library, London

On the evening of June 29, before the appointed hour of battle, small groups of volunteers assembled secretly in some thirty different offices in the Westminster area. Each team of seven or eight women was under the supervision of an organiser, who gave instructions and kept up morale. Some Suffragettes were to attempt to get into the House and as it was rumoured that they would receive rough treatment, several wore hockey dress, with an added home-made, papier mâché corset as armour under-

[6] Dietary of the Second Class: breakfast: 1 pint tea, 6 oz. bread. Dinner: Monday, 8 oz. haricot beans, 1 oz. fat bacon, 8 oz. potatoes, 6 oz. bread. Tuesday, 1 pint soup, 8 oz. potatoes, 6 oz. bread. Wednesday, 8 oz. suet pudding, 8 oz. potatoes, 6 oz. bread. Thursday, 8 oz. potatoes, 3 oz. cooked meat stewed together, 6 oz. bread. Sunday, 3 oz. pressed meat, 8 oz. potatoes, 6 oz. bread. Supper: 1 pint cocoa, evidently made in the boilers used for the meat, as it always had bits of meat floating in it. This dietary was supplied to Third Class prisoners also after the first month.
[7] The Second Division prisoners wrote and received a letter monthly, the Third Division monthly after the first two months.

neath the thick sports jersey. Other groups were to make an attack on Whitehall and each woman was issued with a striped denim dorothy bag containing stones wrapped in brown paper and tied with string. The dorothy bags were attached round the waist under the skirt and at the signal for the 'smash up', the stones could be reached through a placket pocket.

On June 29 Mrs Blathwayt wrote in her diary:

> This is the terrible night when Mrs Pankhurst is going to lead the deputation from the Caxton Hall, which Asquith says he will not receive. It is a very anxious time for all. Asquith was asked in Parliament if he would be responsible for tonight, but he would not answer.

Just after half past seven Vera Holme, in riding habit and a tricolor sash, came cantering from the Caxton Hall with a message for the Prime Minister. Hundreds of yelling youths ran after her and her horse pushed its passage through the crowd in front, which scattered on either side. At St Stephen's Church she was stopped by a cordon of police; she handed her document to a mounted inspector who dropped it and told her to go away. As she made the return journey to the Caxton Hall, admiring crowds cheered and clapped.

Pressmen saw the deputation appear: 'By the side of Inspector Isaacs came the frail undaunted figure of Mrs Pankhurst, nervously followed by the white-haired Mrs Saul Soloman wearing a black mantle and a bonnet.' The seventy-six-year-old headmistress, Miss Neligan, walked behind, followed by the other five members of the distinguished deputation – the Hon. Mrs Haverfield, Mrs Mansel, Mrs Corbett, Miss Maud Joachim and Miss Catherine Margesson. As they marched swiftly towards the House of Commons, a way was cleared for them through the dense cheering crowds. They finally arrived at the steps of the Strangers' Entrance, to be met by Inspector Scantlebury and Inspector Jarvis. A letter from Asquith was handed to Mrs Pankhurst. It was a note expressing regret that he could not receive the deputation. Mrs Pankhurst read it out loud to the women, dropped it and demanded entrance. Inspector Jarvis began to push her away. Mrs Pankhurst foresaw the usual struggle. 'I had to take into account that I was accompanied by two fragile old ladies who could not possibly endure what I knew must follow. I quickly decided that I should have to force an immediate arrest.' Mrs Pankhurst slapped Jarvis's face. 'I understand why you did that,' he said, but he did not arrest her. She struck him again and then she was taken in charge.

Soon the main attack began. The stone throwers left base and each made her way to the specified area in Whitehall where she was to break a window. Ada Wright was one of the volunteers:

> To women of culture and refinement and of sheltered unbringing and deliberate throwing of a stone, even as a protest, in order to break a window, requires an enormous amount of moral courage. After much tension and hesitation, I threw my stone through the

window of the Office of Works. To my relief, I was at once arrested and marched off by two policemen, the tremendous crowd making way for us and cheering to the echo, all the way to Cannon Row Police Station.

Of the nightmare walk, I remember Laurence Housman suddenly detaching himself from the crowd, cheering louder than anyone else. Slapping me heartily on the back, he shouted out, 'Well done!' and waved his top hat in the air.

Laurence Housman had just been thrown out of St Stephen's Hall for making a speech: 'Fellow citizens, outside this House the people's right of petition is being violated. Women are being treated in a way that no decent government would allow.'

Other Suffragette teams swarmed out of the offices just as the sun was setting and made their way towards the House. The crowd watched, terrified, as the women stood their ground fearlessly under the rearing police horses. The Suffragettes were pledged not to give in until arrested and by the end of the evening one hundred and eight prisoners had been taken.

The next morning they all appeared for trial at Bow Street. Many had come dressed for court in smart, fashionable gowns of purple, white and green, with large picture hats, and the policemen had some difficulty in recognising and identifying their battered prisoners of the previous evening. The women were charged with obstruction, assaulting the police, and doing malicious damage. As test cases, the first taken were those of Mrs Pankhurst and the Hon. Mrs Haverfield. They pleaded that by the Bill of Rights and also by the terms of the Tumultuous Petitions Act, they were legally entitled to petition Asquith as a representative of the King. The magistrate was uncertain on this point and all the cases were adjourned until further advice could be taken.

The cases of the fourteen stone throwers were heard separately at Bow Street on July 12. Gladys Roberts of Leeds, a former solicitor's clerk, was sentenced to one month in the second division. On the day of her trial she started to keep a diary in shorthand:

We left Bow Street at about 4.30. Mrs May [a pillar of the Clement's Inn staff] and Mrs Leigh stayed to the last, teaching us songs. There were eighteen of us in black Maria. The atmosphere and the jolting were indescribable. A regalia, floating from the end of an umbrella, was held through a hole in the roof all the way.

On arriving at Holloway, we were taken into the corridor outside the reception cells. Our names were called and we answered. Miss Wright then asked to see the governor. The wardress, who had tow-coloured hair and was very disagreeable, fetched the matron who wanted us to answer to our names again. We refused and asked once more to see the governor. At last he was sent for. After hearing from Miss Wright that we intended to rebel against all the second-division rules, the governor said he would let us keep our clothing and bags until he communicated with the Home Secretary, if we went quietly to our cells, and on the understanding that we were not allowed to go to chapel or exercise.

I am in bed which is not so bad, and it's about 2.30. Delightful to be able to rest at last.

Tuesday, July 13.
Breakfast just arrived which consists of another lump of that horrible brown bread and tea. I read *Votes*, and tried to eat some of the bread, but failed. To my joy, I found scratched on that bit of tin curved at one end, called a knife:

> Glorious Christabel.
> Courage! brave heart, victory is sure,
> Help comes to those who work and endure.

A wardress has just been in and removed my knife. This does not matter as I have my own old hedger . . .

I hear Miss Garnett in the distance. On her way back from the lavatory she knocked at each door and yelled, 'Votes for women' . . . I find that by putting my chair against the pipes under the window and standing on the back of it, I can see more outside . . . I saw a lot of prisoners in brown dresses filing into what I take to be the laundry. Also prisoners carrying rubbish to the ash pit, and others wheeling barrows of dirty clothes . . .

I have been having conversations with Miss Spong in the next cell. I can't make Kathleen Brown hear. Miss Spong says it's 10.15. How slowly time passes! I have stuffed my peephole with paper. When the doctor came, the wardresses pulled it out, but I have put it back again. I wonder how long we shall be kept in close confinement. My tie is such a comfort and inspiration. It is delightful to have the dear old colours to look at when the walls seem so close in.

The governor has just been, accompanied by the matron. He says he duly reported our wishes to Herbert Gladstone last night, but he has not yet received any reply. The position is just the same. I asked for a form of petition. The governor smelt rather of spirits; he looks rather worried . . .

The Suffragettes had prearranged the course they would follow if political prisoner treatment was not forthcoming.

. . . Finished dinner. I mounted my chair with shoe in hand. We all knocked through to each other. I smashed three panes . . .
Wardresses came running. One white with rage, with several others to back her up, burst into my cell. 'Uncover your inspection hole.' 'Uncover my what?' 'Your inspection hole,' pointing to the peephole. 'No,' I said. 'No, I won't.' 'Then we shall – that is what we are here to do;' and with that she pulled out the piece of paper and flung it down into my drinking water. 'Every time you cover it up, it will be

uncovered!' Bang goes the door. Another half minute and they come: 'What is your name?' Then one sees it on the card outside the door and they retire.

All is quiet now. Oh for a good square meal fit to eat!

A wardress brought a petition form and pen and ink and blotting paper . . . I've finished my petition and pulled in my belt to the tightest hole. Theresa Garnett peeped in my peephole as she passed. Just going to read – What's the matter now? It was a wardress to count the number of panes I had broken. Read until tea came – or is it supper? Another knife with 'Votes for women' scratched on it. I scratched on the other side:

> Asquith's reign has passed away,
> Winston Churchill's had his day,
> Suffragettes have come to stay,
> Therefore give them votes.

Just as I finished it, the wardress came for the knife. Tea consisted of the usual loaf. I could only manage a few crumbs – it's so vile – my fat will soon be reduced!

A few minutes ago, someone in a cell lower down called three cheers for Mrs Pankhurst, then Christabel, then Annie Kenney. I can't make Kathleen Brown hear me . . .

Wednesday, July 14.
I hear Theresa Garnett in the distance. We are all greatly excited. Theresa has been able to make a woman in one of the adjoining gardens hear, and has told her to send word to Clement's Inn and the Press.

I waved my tie out of a broken pane to a woman at a window. Her husband came, and they brought the baby and held it up for us to see.

Christabel has been and two photographers. We all stuck something out of our windows. The drum and fife band is coming tonight and other visitors.

A magistrate has been to see Miss Spong – one of those who were about to try us for mutiny. He told her that he knew that we were right, but that he would have to punish us. We were all taken down separately. My bag and hat were taken from me by six wardresses. I told the magistrates I was not sorry for breaking windows, and that I did not intend to comply with any second-division rules, so was sentenced to seven days' close confinement and was brought down to this cell, with nothing in it except a block of wood fixed to the wall for a chair and a plank bed and pillow . . . unbreakable opaque windows, and double iron doors – God help me to stick it! I can hear the others singing, thank goodness!

They have brought us a pint of cocoa and a lump of the usual bread. Hunger strike commences. The drum and fife band is coming at eight o'clock. I wonder if we shall hear it. We seem to be buried alive.

Thursday, July 15.
I heard a bell this morning so I dressed. Wardresses came. 'Any applications?' I asked for the governor and the doctor. I lie on the bed – I feel so weak – breakfast has just been put in. I said I didn't want any. God help me! I wonder if those outside are thinking about us. I am a coward. A day of reckoning will come for this Government. No sunshine can get into this cell and at night there is a gas jet burning over the door. Always a dull light. However, my room at Stamford and Metcalfe where I sat for four years was not much lighter than this.

I have seen the doctor. He argued with me about the unreasonableness of our conduct . . . The chaplain came. He was rather nice. He asked if there was anything I wanted. I said I wanted a good many things, and I supposed we would not be allowed a library book . . . He said he was very sorry to see us here, and I couldn't keep back a few tears when he had gone. I feel so weak. A wardress brought in a Bible, Prayer Book and Hymn Book. I read the marriage service over. I thought it would get my blood up, so I read Paul's opinion on the duties of a wife.

I suppose Mother and Father are enjoying the sea air at Bridlington. Thank God they don't know where I am. The bang of the double doors is terrible. It seems strange to think of all whom we love going about their business in the normal way while we – Oh, I do feel blubbery. I expect it's because I'm losing my strength. I'm not usually given to weeping, but I feel I should like to have a jolly good cry.

I hear knocking on the walls, and all the prisoners are shouting that they have not eaten their food. Neither have I. Dinner consisted of an egg and potatoes and a pint of milk and (oh, awful temptation!) a boiled onion. I am getting disinclined to write even.

The governor's been. I asked if yesterday's proceedings were to be considered as Herbert Gladstone's reply. He said that the visiting magistrates were a separate body, and acted on their own initiative. Herbert Gladstone had not replied. I expect the visiting magistrates get their orders from Gladstone as I saw my sentence was written down before I was tried.

Friday, July 16.
The wardress said to me this morning, 'Get your clothes on. We shall want to take your bed out.' I wonder if they will. Miss Carwin didn't have hers all day yesterday. Part of the process seems to be to degrade us by not allowing us to wash properly. This morning I have had only my drinking can of water to wash in. May Gladstone's downfall be speedy!

. . . I saw through the peephole, which was accidentally left open,

Mrs Holtwhite Simmons go out of the cell opposite looking ghastly. I wonder if I look likewise. Fifty-four hours without food! God help me to hold out! I feel so choky when I think of the world outside.

Saturday, July 17.
I can't get up this morning. The cleaner came and swept out my cell. She smiled at me and it made me so weepy. The doctor has been and tried to persuade me to give up the hunger strike by saying that I was not so robust as the others. What would my mother and father say, and so on. I had to make a fool of myself after he had gone.

It is now seventy-two hours since I tasted food. The governor and matron have just been to say that Herbert Gladstone had written that he has fully considered the petitions, but sees no reason why he should take action in the matter which proves he could, if he would.

Tremendous excitement – Mary Allen has just come down to the cell next to mine. She broke more windows when she heard Herbert Gladstone's reply. It has quite bucked me up.

There has been a butterfly in my cell all day. It beat itself against the window all night and made such a noise until I got up and put it in a paper bag.

Sunday, July 18.
Had a fairly good night, but dreaming of food all the time. I feel more cheerful today. I've had quite long talks with Mary Allen through the wall. We've beaten Miss Wallace Dunlop's record! Dinner time today will be ninety-six hours without food . . .

Monday, July 19.
I had rather a bad night. The bed, I was sure, must be stuffed with stones, and my poor bones ached terribly. At a little after twelve o'clock, just after dinner had been thrust in, the hospital matron and two prisoners with a carrying chair came for me and carried me to the hospital. They put me to bed and gave me a hot-water bottle and brought me jelly, milk, and bread and butter, which of course I refused. The doctor came and talked and talked, but I wouldn't budge. Then he came and asked me where I wanted what was left of me to be sent at the end of the month. I said I did not think that there would be any to send anywhere. I gave him Clement's Inn and Miss Jones's address.

At 6.20. the governor came with the matron and said: 'Are you feeling miserable?' I said: 'Not at all, I'm very comfortable.' He said: 'Are you still obstinate?' 'Yes.' 'Well, I have some news for you – you are to be released.'

He told me to be very quiet and move about slowly, and he would send a wardress to dress me and also some brandy in a beaten egg. He said he would send to Miss Jones and see if she could take me. As soon as he had gone, I got up and waited, and at about 7.20, after the matron had brought my bag, a wardress came for me and I was taken in a cab to the Joneses.

At about eight o'clock, the drum and fife band came, and they fetched Mrs Leigh in to see me, and then Mrs Lawrence and Christabel came just as I was put to bed. I was never so happy in my life.

CHRONOLOGICAL TABLE

1640–1680	Aphra Behn
1660–1720	Mary Pix
1661–1720	Anne Finch
1668–1731	Mary Astell
1672–1724	Mary de la Rivière Manley
1689–1762	Lady Mary Wortley Montagu
1693–1756	Eliza Haywood
1700–1788	Mrs Delaney
1715–1791	Mrs Vesey
1717–1806	Mrs Elizabeth Carter
1720–1800	Mrs Elizabeth Montagu
1727–1801	Hester Chapone
1728–1814	Mercy Otis Warren
1731–1791	Catherine Macaulay
1739–1829	Eleanor Butler
1741–1821	Mrs Thrale (Piozzi)
1742–1809	Anna Seward
1744–1818	Abigail Adams
1745–1833	Hannah More
1745–1793	Olympe de Gouges
1746–1830	Madame de Genlis
1750–1848	Caroline Herschel
1751–1820	Judith Sargent Murray
1752–1840	Fanny Burney
1754–1793	Madame Roland
1755–1831	Sarah Ponsonby
1759–1797	Mary Wollstonecraft
1760–1843	Mary Hays
1766–1817	Madame de Staël
1780–1872	Mary Somerville
1780–1845	Elizabeth Fry
1785– ?	Anna Wheeler

1792–1860	Lady Byron
1792–1873	Sarah Grimké
1793–1880	Lucretia Mott
1794–1860	Anna Jameson
1795–1852	Frances Wright
1801–1865	Frederika Bremer
1802–1876	Harriet Martineau
1803–1844	Flora Tristan
1804–1876	Georges Sand
1805–1879	Angelina Grimké
1806–1893	Elizabeth Oakes Smith
1807–1877	Mary Carpenter
1807–1858	Harriet Taylor
1808–1884	Frances Dana Gage
1808–1877	Caroline Norton
1810–1850	Margaret Fuller
1810–1892	Ernestine L. Rose
1813–1876	Paulina Wright Davis
1814–1897	Emily Shirreff
1814–1906	Angela Burdett-Coutts
1815–1902	Elizabeth Cady Stanton
1818–1893	Lucy Stone
1818–1889	Maria Mitchell
1819–1880	George Eliot
1820–1906	Susan B. Anthony
1820–1891	Ann Jemima Clough
1820–1912	Louisa Twining
1820–1910	Florence Nightingale
1821–1910	Elizabeth Blackwell
1822–1904	Frances Power Cobbe
1825–1921	Antoinette Brown Blackwell
1825–1864	Adelaide Ann Proctor
1825–1905	Jessie Boucherett

1826–1898	Matilda Joslyn Gage
1827–1890	Lydia Becker
1827–1891	Barbara Bodichon
1827–1894	Frances Mary Buss
1828–1906	Josephine Butler
1828–1895	Jessie Rayner Parkes
1829–1903	Maria Susan Rye
1830–1921	Emily Davies
1831–1903	Isa Craig
1831–1906	Dorothea Beale
1832–1888	Louisa May Alcott
1832–1911	Hannah Pearsall Smith
1834–1918	Elizabeth Wolstenholme Elmy
1835–1895	Emily Faithfull
1836–1917	Elizabeth Garrett Anderson
1838–1912	Octavia Hill
1839–1898	Frances Willard
1840–1912	Sophia Jex-Blake
1842–1924	Josephine Ruffin
1842–1903	Helen Blackburn
1844–1939	Charlotte Despard
1847–1919	Anna Howard Shaw
1847–1933	Annie Besant
1847–1929	Millicent Garrett Fawcett
1847–1925	Rose Scott
1848–1886	Emma Paterson
1855–1920	Olive Schreiner
1857–1950	Alice Stone Blackwell
1858–1944	Ethel Smyth
1858–1928	Emmeline Pankhurst
1859–1947	Carrie Chapman Catt
1860–1935	Charlotte Perkins Gilman
1860–1935	Jane Addams
1862–1952	Elizabeth Robins
1862–1931	Ida B. Wells-Barnett
1867–1954	Emmeline Pethick-Lawrence
1869–1923	Constance Lytton
1869–1940	Emma Goldman
1869–1949	Viola Goldstein
1870–1938	Esther Roper
1871–1947	Susan Lawrence
1872–1952	Cicely Hamilton
1872–1952	Alexandra Kollontai
1872–1946	Eleanor Rathbone
1873–1953	Margaret Bondfield
1873–1954	Colette
1875–1926	Eva Gore Booth
1875–1958	Dorothy Sayers
1876–1958	Mary Ritter Beard
1876–1949	Flora Drummond
1876–1927	Constance Markievicz
1877–1964	Teresa Billington-Greig
1879–1966	Margaret Sanger
1879–1964	Lady Astor
1879–1953	Annie Kenney
1880–1958	Christabel Pankhurst
1881–1928	Crystal Eastman
1882–1941	Virginia Woolf
1882–1960	Sylvia Pankhurst
1883–1958	Lady Rhondda
1885–1977	Alice Paul
1887–1940	Ray Strachey
1890–1982	Hazel Hunkins-Hallinan
1891–1947	Ellen Wilkinson
1892–	Rebecca West
1894–	Dora Russell
1896–1970	Vera Brittain
1898–1935	Winifred Holtby
1901–1978	Margaret Mead
1906–1960	Dilys Laing
1907–1964	Rachel Carson
1908–	Simone de Beauvoir
1919–	Doris Lessing
1921–	Betty Friedan
1934–	Kate Millett
1936–1965	Hannah Gavron
1939–	Germaine Greer

BIBLIOGRAPHY

ABB, Ellen Doughty, 1937, *What Fools We Women Be*, Cassell, London.

ADAM, Ruth, 1975, *A Woman's Place, 1910–1975*, Chatto & Windus, London.

ADAMS, Abigail, 1771–1776, ' "Remember the Ladies": Abigail Adams vs John Adams. Selected Letters from the Adams Family Correspondence', in Alice S. Rossi (ed.), 1974, *The Feminist Papers: From Adams to de Beauvoir*, Bantam Books, New York, pp. 8–15.

ADBURGHAM, Alison, 1972, *Women in Print: Writing Women and Women's Magazines from the Restoration to the Accession of Victoria*, George Allen & Unwin, London.

ALCOTT, Louisa May, 1873, *Work: A Study of Experience*, Roberts Bros, Boston. Reprinted 1977 by Schocken Books, New York.

ALTBACH, Edith Hoshino, 1971, *From Feminism to Liberation*, Schenkman, Cambridge, Mass.

ANONYMOUS, 1632, *The Lawes Resolution of the Rights of Women*.

ANONYMOUS, 1640, *The Women's Sharp Revenge*.

ANONYMOUS, 1672, *On Account of Marriage*.

ANONYMOUS, 1675, *A Broadside Against Marriage*.

ANONYMOUS, 1688, *Sylvia's Revenge, or a Satyr Against Man*.

ANONYMOUS, 1688, *Sylvia's Complaint of her Sex's Unhappiness . . . the Second Part of Sylvia's Revenge*.

ANONYMOUS, 1690, *Against Marriage*.

ANONYMOUS, 1696, *The Whole Duty of a Woman*.

ANONYMOUS, 1696, *History of the Life and Memoirs of Mrs Aphra Behn: by One of the Fair Sex*.

ANONYMOUS, 1696, *An Essay in Defence of the Female Sex*.

ANONYMOUS, 1923a, 'Personalities and Powers: Cicely Hamilton', *Time and Tide*, 26 Jan. pp. 83–4.

ANONYMOUS, 1923b, 'Personalities and Powers: Rebecca West', *Time and Tide*, 9 Feb. pp. 149–50.

ANTHONY, Katherine, 1954, *Susan B. Anthony: Her Personal History and her Era*, Doubleday, New York.

ANTHONY, Susan B. and Ida Husted HARPER (eds), 1902, *History of Woman Suffrage*, Hollenbeck Press, Indianapolis.

ARDENER, Shirley (ed.), 1975, *Perceiving Women*, Malaby, London.

ARDITTI, Rita, Pat BRENNAN and Steve CAVRAK (eds.), 1980, *Science and Liberation*, Black Rose, Montreal.

ASTELL, Mary, 1694, 'A Serious Proposal to the Ladies', reprinted in Katharine

M. Rogers (ed.), 1979, *Before Their Time: Six Women Writers of the Eighteenth Century*, Frederick Ungar, New York, pp. 28–38.

ASTELL, Mary, 1700, 'Some Reflections Upon Marriage, Occasioned by the Duchess of Mazarine's Case', reprinted in Katharine M. Rogers (ed.), 1979, *Before Their Time: Six Women Writers of the Eighteenth Century*, Frederick Ungar, New York, pp. 38–47.

BANKS, Olive, 1981, *Faces of Feminism*, Martin Robertson, Oxford.

BARRETT BROWNING, Elizabeth, 1978, *Aurora Leigh and Other Poems*, The Women's Press, London (originally published in 1857).

BART, Pauline, 1981, 'Seizing the Means of Reproduction: An Illegal Feminist Abortion Collective – How and Why it Worked', in Helen Roberts (ed.), *Women, Health and Reproduction*, Routledge & Kegan Paul, London and Boston, pp. 109–28.

BARTLETT, Elizabeth Ann, 1981, 'Liberty, Equality, Sorority: Origins and Interpretations of American Feminist Thought: Frances Wright, Margaret Fuller and Sarah Grimké', unpublished Ph.D. Thesis, University of Minnesota.

BAUER, Carol and Lawrence RITT (eds), 1979, *Free and Ennobled: Source Readings in the Development of Victorian Feminism*, Pergamon Press, Oxford.

BEARD, Mary Ritter, 1931, *On Understanding Women*, Grosset & Dunlap, New York.

BEARD, Mary Ritter (ed.), 1933, *America Through Women's Eyes*, Macmillan, New York.

BEARD, Mary Ritter, 1934, 'A Changing Political Economy as It Affects Women', National Headquarters, American Association of University Women, reprinted (in part), Ann J. Lane (ed.), 1977, *Mary Ritter Beard: A Source Book*, Schocken Books, New York, pp. 203–9.

BEARD, Mary Ritter, 1946, *Woman as Force in History*, Macmillan, New York.

BEARD, Mary Ritter, 1977, *A Source Book*, Ann J. Lane (ed.), Schocken Books, New York.

BEARD, Mary Ritter and Martha Bensley BRUÈRE, 1934, *Laughing Their Way: Women's Humor in America*, Macmillan, New York.

de BEAUVOIR, Simone, 1972, *The Second Sex*, Penguin, Harmondsworth (originally published in France, 1949).

BECKER, Lydia, 1864, *Botany for Novices*, Remington, Rugby.

BELL, E. Moberly, 1962, *Josephine Butler: Flame of Fire*, Constable, London.

BELL, Quentin, 1972, *Virginia Woolf: A Biography*, Hogarth Press, London.

BERG, Barbara J., 1978, *The Remembered Gate: Origins of American Feminism: The Woman and the City, 1800–1860*, Oxford University Press, London, New York.

BERNARD, Jessie, 1972, *The Future of Marriage*, World Publishing, New York.

BERNARD, Jessie, 1974, 'My Four Revolutions: An Autobiographical History of the A.S.A.', in Joan Huber (ed.), *Changing Women in a Changing Society*, University of Chicago Press, pp. 11–29.

BERNBAUM, Ernest, 1913, 'Mrs Behn's Biography: A Fiction', *PMLA*, vol. 28, pp. 432–53.

BERNIKOW, Louise, 1980, *Among Women*, Harmony Books, New York.

BESANT, Annie, 1893, *An Autobiography*, T. Fisher Unwin, London.

BIGGS, Caroline Ashurst, 1886, 'Great Britain', in Elizabeth Cady Stanton, Susan B. Anthony, Matilda Joslyn Gage (eds), *History of Woman Suffrage* vol. III, Fowler & Wells, New York, pp. 837–94.

BILLINGTON-GREIG, Teresa (n.d.), *Suffragist Tactics: Past and Present*, Women's Freedom League, London.

BILLINGTON-GREIG, Teresa, 1911, *The Militant Suffrage Movement*, Frank Palmer, London.

BIRNEY, Catherine, H., 1885, *The Grimké Sisters: Sarah and Angelina Grimké: The First American Women Advocates of Abolition and Woman's Rights*, reprinted 1969, Greenwood Press, Westport, Conn.

BLACK, Naomi, 1982, in press, ' "The Life of Natural Happiness": Virginia Woolf's Feminism', in Dale Spender (ed.), *Feminist Theorists: Three Centuries of Feminist Intellectual Traditions*, The Women's Press, London.

BLACKBURN, Helen, 1902, *Women's Suffrage: A Record of the Women's Suffrage Movement in the British Isles with Biographical Sketches of Miss Becker*, Williams & Norgate, London and Oxford, reprinted 1971, Kraus Reprint Co., New York.

BLACKWELL, Alice Stone, 1930, *Lucy Stone: Pioneer of Woman's Rights*, Little Brown, Boston, reprinted 1971, Kraus Reprint Co., New York.

BLACKWELL, Antoinette Brown, 1875, *The Sexes Throughout Nature*, G. P. Putnam's Sons, New York.

BLACKWELL, Elizabeth, 1895, *Pioneer Work in Opening the Medical Profession to Women. Autobiographical Sketches*, Longmans Green, London and New York, reprinted 1977, Introduction by Mary Roth Walsh, Schocken Books, New York.

BLATCH, Harriet Stanton and Alma LUTZ, 1940, *Challenging Years: The Memoirs of Harriet Stanton Blatch*, G. Putnam's Sons, New York.

BLUH, Bonnie Charles, 1974, *Woman to Woman: European Feminists*, Starogubski Press, New York.

BODICHON, Barbara, 1857, *Women and Work*, Pamphlet reprint, Fawcett Library, London.

BODICHON, Barbara, 1866, *Reasons for the Enfranchisement of Women*, Social Science Association, Pamphlet reprint, Fawcett Library.

BODICHON, Barbara, 1867, 'Authorities and Precedents for Giving the Suffrage to Qualified Women', *Englishwoman's Review*, no. 11, January, pp. 63–73.

BOOS, Florence, S., 1976, 'Catherine Macaulay's *Letters on Education* (1790): An Early Feminist Polemic', *University of Michigan Papers in Women's Studies*, vol. 2, no. 2, pp. 64–78.

BOSANQUET, Theodora, 1927, *Harriet Martineau: An Essay in Comprehension*, Etchells & MacDonald, London.

BOULDING, Elise, 1976, *The Underside of History: A View of Women through Time*, Westview Press, Boulder, Colorado.

BRENDON, Piers, 1979, 'Mrs Pankhurst', *Eminent Edwardians*, Penguin, Harmondsworth, pp. 131–94.

BRIGGS, Shirley, 1981, 'Rachel Carson: A Corrective Memoir', *Heresies*, 13 (Feminism and Ecology) vol. 4, no. 1, p. 2.

BRINK, J. R., 1980, 'Bathsua Makin: Educator and Linguist (English, 1608(?)–1675)', in J. R. Brink (ed.), *Female Scholars: A Tradition of Learned Women before 1800*, Eden Press, Montreal, pp. 86–100.

BRITTAIN, Vera, 1928a, 'Radclyffe Hall', *Time and Tide*, vol. 10, p. 48.

BRITTAIN, Vera, 1928b, 'The Whole Duty of Woman', *Time and Tide*, 23 Feb. pp. 216–17.

BRITTAIN, Vera, 1928c, *Women's Work in Modern England*, Noel Douglas, London.

BRITTAIN, Vera, 1933, *Testament of Youth*, Gollancz, London, reprinted 1978, Virago, London.

BRITTAIN, Vera, 1936, *Honourable Estate*, Macmillan, New York.

BRITTAIN, Vera, 1940, *Testament of Friendship*, Macmillan, London, reprinted 1980, Virago, London.

BRITTAIN, Vera, 1953, *Lady into Woman: A History of Women from Victoria to Elizabeth II*, Andrew Dakers, London.

BRITTAIN, Vera, 1957, *Testament of Experience*, Victor Gollancz, London, reprinted 1979, Virago, London, and 1981, Fontana, London.

BRITTAIN, Vera, 1960, *The Women at Oxford: A Fragment of History*, George Harrap, London.

BRITTAIN, Vera, 1963, *Pethick-Lawrence: A Portrait*, George Allen & Unwin, London.

BRITTAIN, Vera, 1968, *Radclyffe Hall: A Case of Obscenity?* Femina Books, London.

BROCK-UTNE, Birgit, 1981, 'Girls and the Hidden Curriculum of the Compulsory School', mimeo paper.

BROCK-UTNE, Birgit, 1982, *The Role of Women in Peace Research*, Peace Research Institute, Oslo, Paper S-4/82.

BROVERMAN, Inge K., et al., 1970, 'Sex Role Stereotypes and a Clinical Judgement of Mental Health', *Journal of Consulting and Clinical Psychology*, vol. 34.

BROWNMILLER, Susan, 1977, *Against our Will: Men, Women and Rape*, Penguin, Harmondsworth.

BRYANT, Margaret, 1979, *The Unexpected Revolution: A Study in the History of the Education of Women and Girls in the Nineteenth Century*, University of London Institute of Education.

BUHLE, Mari Jo and Paul (eds), 1978, *The Concise History of Woman Suffrage*, University of Illinois Press.

BURSTYN, Joan N., 1980, *Victorian Education and the Ideal of Womanhood*, Croom Helm, London.

BURTON, Hester, 1949, *Barbara Bodichon*, John Murray, London.

BUTLER, Josephine, 1869, *Women's Work and Women's Culture*, Macmillan, London.

BUTLER, Josephine, 1893, *An Autobiographical Memoir*, George W. and Lucy A. Johnson (eds), Simpkin, Marshall, Hamilton, Kent, London, reprinted 1913.

BUTLER, Josephine, 1898, *Personal Reminiscences of a Great Crusade*, Marshall, London.

BYRNE, Eileen, 1978, *Women and Education*, Tavistock, London.

CAPUTI, Jane, 1974, 'Matilda Joslyn Gage: Philosopher of Feminism', unpublished paper quoted in Mary Daly, 1978, *Gyn/Ecology*, Beacon Press, Boston, Mass., pp. 216–17.

CARDEN, Maren Lockwood, 1974, *The New Feminist Movement*, Russell Sage Foundation, New York.

CARHART, Margaret S., 1923, *The Life and Work of Joanna Baillie*, Yale University Press.

CARROLL, Berenice, A., 1978, ' "To Crush Him in Our Own Country": The Political Thought of Virginia Woolf', *Feminist Studies*, vol. 4, no. 1. Feb., pp. 99–132.

CARROLL, Berenice, A., 1981, 'The Politics of "Originality": Women Scholars and Intellectuals', Paper presented at session 'Women Intellectuals and Scholars: Issues and Methodologies', *Berkshire Conference on Women's History*, Vassar College, 17 June.

CARSON, Rachel, 1962, *Silent Spring*, Houghton Mifflin, Boston, reprinted 1979, Penguin, Harmondsworth.

CASKIE, Helen C., 1981, 'Frances Power Cobbe: Victorian Feminist', unpublished dissertation: available Fawcett Library.

CHAPMAN, Maria Weston (ed.), 1877, *Harriet Martineau's Autobiography*, James R. Osgood, Boston.

CHESLER, Phyllis, 1972, *Women and Madness*, Allen Lane, London.

CHESLER, Phyllis and Emily Jane GOODMAN, 1976, *Women, Money and Power*, William Morrow, New York.

CHEVIGNY, Bell Gale, 1976, *The Woman and the Myth: Margaret Fuller's Life and Writings*, The Feminist Press, Old Westbury, New York.

CHICAGO, Judy, 1979, *The Dinner Party: A Symbol of our Heritage*, Anchor Press, Doubleday, New York.

CHODOROW, Nancy, 1978, *The Reproduction of Mothering: Psychoanalysis and the Sociology of Gender*, University of California Press.

CHUDLEIGH, Lady Mary, 1701, *The Ladies Defense*.

CLARK, Alice, 1919, *The Working Life of Women in the Seventeenth Century*, Routledge, London, reprinted 1982, Routledge & Kegan Paul, London.

CLARRICOATES, Katherine, 1978, ' "Dinosaurs in the Classroom": A Re-examination of Some Aspects of the Hidden Curriculum in Primary Schools', *Women's Studies International Quarterly*, vol. I, no. 4, pp. 353–64.

CLIFF, Michelle, 1979, 'The Resonance of Interruption', *Chrysalis*, no. 8, pp. 29–37.

COBBE, Frances Power, 1868, 'Criminals, Idiots, Women and Minors: Is the Classification Sound?' *Fraser's Magazine*, 8 Dec., Fawcett Library Pamphlet.

COBBE, Frances Power, 1869, 'The Final Cause of Women', in Josephine Butler (ed.), *Women's Work and Women's Culture*, Macmillan, London, pp. 1–26.

COBBE, Frances Power, 1888, *The Duties of Women*, Williams & Norgate, London.

COLEMAN, Verna, 1980, 'Foreword', to Miles Franklin *My Career Goes Bung*, Angus & Robertson, Sydney, pp. 1–4.

CONNELL, Brian, 1975, 'Dame Rebecca West: A Critic in Perpetual Motion', *The Times*, 1 Sept.

CONRAD, Susan, 1976, *Perish the Thought: Intellectual Women in Romantic America, 1830–1860*, Oxford University Press.

COOK, Blanche Wiesen (ed.), 1978, *Crystal Eastman on Women and Revolution*, Oxford University Press.

COOTE, Anna and Beatrix CAMPBELL, 1982, *Sweet Freedom: The Struggle for Women's Liberation*, Picador, London.

CORNBLEET, Annie, 1982, private communication.

COURTNEY, Janet E., 1933, *The Adventurous Thirties: A Chapter in the Women's Movement*, Oxford University Press.

CRONWRIGHT-SCHREINER, Samuel Cron, 1924a, *The Life of Olive Schreiner*, Unwin, London.

CRONWRIGHT-SCHREINER, Samuel Cron, 1924b, *The Letters of Olive Schreiner 1876–1920*, Unwin, London; Little Brown & Co., Boston.

CROSLAND, Margaret, 1973, *Colette: The Difficulty of Loving*, Dell Publishing, New York.

CRUIKSHANK, Margaret, 1980, 'Barbara Bodichon: Victorian feminist', unpublished paper.

DALY, Mary, 1973, *Beyond God the Father: Toward a Philosophy of Women's Liberation*, Beacon Press, Boston.

DALY, Mary, 1978, *Gyn/Ecology: The Metaethics of Radical Feminism*, Beacon Press, Boston.

DALY, Mary, 1980, 'Foreword', to Matilda Joslyn Gage, 1980 (1893), *Woman, Church and State: The Original Exposé of Male Collaboration against the Female Sex*, Persephone Press, Watertown, Mass., pp. vii–x.

DAVIES, Margaret Llewelyn (ed.), 1915, *Maternity: Letters from Working Women*, G. Bell & Sons, London, reprinted 1978, Virago, London.

DAVIES, Margaret Llewelyn (ed.), 1931, *Life as We Have Known It: By Co-operative Working Women*, The Hogarth Press, London, reprinted 1977, Virago, London.

DAVIS, Allen F., 1975, *American Heroine: The Life and Legend of Jane Addams*, Oxford University Press.

DAVIS, Paulina, W., 1871, *A History of the National Woman's Rights Movement for Twenty Years with the Proceedings of the Decade Meeting held at Apollo Hall, Oct. 20, 1870, from 1850–1870*, Journeymen Printers, New York, reprinted 1971, Kraus Reprint Co., New York.

DEGLER, Carl N., 1966, 'Introduction' to Charlotte Perkins Gilman, *Women and Economics*, Harper & Row, New York, pp. vi–xxxv.

DELAMONT, Sara and Lorna DUFFIN (eds), 1978, *The Nineteenth Century Woman: Her Cultural and Physical World*, Croom Helm, London; Barnes & Noble, New York.

DELMAR, Rosalind, 1980, 'Afterword', Vera Brittain, *Testament of Friendship*, Virago, London.

DIJKSTRA, Sandra, 1980, 'Simone de Beauvoir and Betty Friedan: The Politics of Omission', *Feminist Studies*, vol. 6, no. 2, pp. 290–303.

DONNELLY, Lucy Martin, 1949, 'The Celebrated Mrs Macaulay', *William and Mary Quarterly*, vol. 6, pp. 173–207.

DORR, Rheta Childe, 1910, *What Eight Million Women Want*, Small Maynard, Boston, reprinted 1971, Kraus Reprint Co., New York.

DOUGLAS, Emily Taft, 1970, *Margaret Sanger: Pioneer of the Future*, Holt, Rinehart & Winston, New York.

DUFFY, Maureen, 1977, *The Passionate Shepherdess*, Jonathan Cape, London.

DWORKIN, Andrea, 1974, *Woman Hating*, E. P. Dutton, New York.

DWORKIN, Andrea, 1981, *Pornography: Men Possessing Women*, The Women's Press; London.

DYHOUSE, Carol, 1977, 'Good Wives and Little Mothers: Social Anxieties and the School Girls' Curriculum 1890–1920', *Oxford Review of Education*, vol. III, no. 1, pp. 21–35.

DYHOUSE, Carol, 1981, *Girls growing up in Late Victorian and Edwardian England*, Routledge & Kegan Paul, London.

EASTMAN, Crystal, 1978, *On Women and Revolution*, in Blanche Wiesen Cook (ed.), Oxford University Press.

ECHOLS, Alice, 1978, 'The Demise of Female Intimacy in the Twentieth Century', *Michigan Occasional Papers*, no. 6.

EHRENREICH, Barbara & Deirdre ENGLISH, 1973, *Complaints and Disorders: The Sexual Politics of Sickness*, Writers & Readers, London.

EHRENREICH, Barbara and Deirdre ENGLISH, 1978, *For Her Own Good: 150 years of the Experts Advice to Women*, Anchor Press, Doubleday, New York; 1979, Pluto Press, London.

EICHLER, Margrit, 1980, *The Double Standard: A Feminist Critique of Feminist Social Science*, Croom Helm, London.

ELBERT, Sarah, 1977, 'Introduction' to Louisa May Alcott, *Work: A Story of Experience*, Schocken Books, New York, pp. ix–xliv.

ELBERT, Sarah, 1978, 'Work: A Study of Experience', in Sarah Elbert and Marion

Glastonbury, *Inspiration and Drudgery: Notes on Literature and Domestic Labour in the Nineteenth Century*, Women's Research & Resources Centre, London, pp. 11–26.

ELIOT, George, 1855, 'Margaret Fuller and Mary Wollstonecraft', *Leader*, vol. IV, 13 Oct. pp. 988–9, reprinted 1963, in Thomas Pinney (ed.), *Essays of George Eliot*, Routledge & Kegan Paul, London, pp. 199–206.

ELLIS, Gran. A. (ed.), 1874, *Life Works of Mrs Barbauld*, USA.

ELLMANN, Mary, 1968, *Thinking About Women*, Harcourt, Brace, Jovanovich, New York, reprinted 1979, Virago, London.

ELLSWORTH, Edward W., 1979, *Liberators of the Female Mind: The Shirreff Sisters, Educational Reform and the Women's Movement*, Greenwood Press, Westport, Conn.

FADERMAN, Lillian, 1981, *Surpassing the Love of Men: Romantic Friendship and Love Between Women from the Renaissance to the Present*, William Morrow, New York.

FAIRBAIRNS, Zoë, 1979a, 'The Cohabitation Rule – Why it makes Sense', *Women's Studies International Quarterly*, vol. II, no. 3, pp. 319–28.

FAIRBAIRNS, Zoë, 1979b, *Benefits*, Virago, London.

FAWCETT, Millicent, 1911, *Women's Suffrage*, T. C. & E. C. Jack, London.

FAWCETT, Millicent, 1920, *The Women's Victory and After*, Sidgwick & Jackson, London.

FAWCETT, Millicent, 1922, 'Progress of the Women's Movement in the United Kingdom' in Ida Husted Harper (ed.) *History of Woman Suffrage*, vol. VI, pp. 725–51.

FAWCETT, Millicent, 1924, *What I Remember*, T. Fisher Unwin, London.

FAWCETT, Millicent Garrett (n.d.), *Some Eminent Women of Our Time* (biographical Sketches of Foremost Women of the Nineteenth Century: magazine articles plus one volume: reprinted as pamphlets of National Union of Women's Suffrage Societies).

FAWCETT, Millicent, and E. M. TURNER, 1927, *Josephine Butler: Her Work and Principles and their Meaning for the Twentieth Century*, Association for Moral and Social Hygiene, London.

FELSTINER, Mary Lowenthal, 1980, 'Seeing *The Second Sex* through the Second Wave', *Feminist Studies*, vol. 6, no. 2, pp. 247–77.

FENNEMA, Elizabeth, 1980, 'Success in Maths', Paper presented to *Sex Differentiation and Schooling*, Churchill College, Cambridge, 2 Jan.

FIELD, Vena Bernadette, 1931, *Constantia: A Study of the Life and Works of Judith Sargent Murray, 1751–1820*, University of Maine Studies, Second Series, no. 17, University of Maine Press, Orono, Maine.

FIGES, Eva, 1970, *Patriarchal Attitudes: My Case for Women to Revolt*, Faber & Faber, London.

FINCH, Anne, 1974, quoted in Joan Goulianos (ed.), *By a Woman Writt*, New English Library, London.

FIRESTONE, Shulamith, 1971, *The Dialectics of Sex: The Case for Feminist Revolution*, Jonathan Cape, reprinted 1979, The Women's Press, London.

FIRST, Ruth, and Ann SCOTT, 1980, *Olive Schreiner: A Biography*, Andre Deutsch, London.

FISHMAN, Pamela, 1977, 'Interactional Shitwork', *Heresies*, no. 2, May, pp. 99–101.

FLEXNER, Eleanor, 1979, *Century of Struggle: The Woman's Rights Movement in the United States* (revised edition, first published 1959) Belknap Press and Harvard University Press, Cambridge, Mass.

FOSS, Sonja, 1976, 'The Feminists: A Rhetorical Analysis of the Radical Feminist Movement', *University of Michigan Papers in Women's Studies*, vol. II, no. 2, pp. 79–95.

FRANKAU, Pamela, 1970, 'Introduction', *Mary Wollstonecraft; the Rights of Woman: John Stuart Mill; the Subjection of Women* (first published 1929), Dent, London, pp. vii–xi.

FRANKLIN, Miles, 1901, *My Brilliant Career*, reprinted 1980, Angus & Robertson, Sydney.

FRANKLIN, Miles, 1946, *My Career Goes Bung*, reprinted 1980, Angus & Robertson, Sydney.

FREEMAN, Jo, 1975, *The Politics of Women's Liberation*, David McKay, New York.

FRIEDAN, Betty, 1963, *The Feminine Mystique*, W. W. Norton, New York; 1965, Penguin, Harmondsworth.

FULFORD, Roger, 1958, *Votes for Women: The Story of a Struggle*, Faber & Faber, London.

FULLER, Arthur Buckminster, 1855, *Woman in the Nineteenth Century and Kindred Papers by Margaret Fuller Ossoli*, John P. Jewett, Boston.

FULLER, Margaret S., 1845, *Woman in the Nineteenth Century*, Greeley & McElrath, New York, reprinted 1980, Facsimile Reprint, University of Southern Carolina Press, Columbia.

GAGE, Matilda Joslyn, 1870, 'Woman as Inventor', *Woman Suffrage Tracts*, no. 1, F. A. Darling, printer, Fayetteville, New York.

GAGE, Matilda Joslyn, 1880, 'Who Planned the Tennessee Campaign of 1862?' *National Citizen Tract*, no. 1.

GAGE, Matilda Joslyn, 1873, *Woman, Church and State: The Original Exposé of Male Collaboration against the Female Sex*, Charles Kerr, Chicago, reprinted 1980, Persephone Press, Watertown, Mass.

GARDINER, Dorothy, 1929, *English Girlhood at School: A Study of Women's Education through Twelve Centuries*, Oxford University Press.

GARDNER, Katy, 1981, 'Well Woman Clinics: A Positive Approach to Women's Health', in Helen Roberts (ed.), *Women, Health and Reproduction*, Routledge & Kegan Paul, London, pp. 129–43.

GAVRON, Hannah, 1966, *The Captive Wife: Conflicts of Housebound Mothers*, Routledge & Kegan Paul, London; 1968, Penguin, Harmondsworth.

GELPI, Barbara Charlesworth, 1981, 'Introduction', in Erna Olafson Hellerstein et al. (eds), *Victorian Women: A Documentary Account of Women's Lives in Nineteenth Century England, France and the United States*, Harvester Press, Brighton, pp. 8–21.

GEORGE, Margaret, 1970, *One Woman's 'Situation': A Study of Mary Wollstonecraft*, University of Illinois Press.

GILMAN, Charlotte Perkins, 1892a, 'The Yellow Wall-paper', *New England Magazine*, vol. V, Jan., pp. 647–59 (as Charlotte Perkins STETSON), reprinted in Ann J. Lane, (ed.), 1981, *The Charlotte Perkins Gilman Reader*, The Women's Press, London, pp. 3–20.

GILMAN, Charlotte Perkins, 1892b, 'The Labor Movement', Prize essay read before Trades & Labor Unions of Alameda County, 5 Sept., Oakland, Calif. (as Charlotte Perkins STETSON).

GILMAN, Charlotte Perkins, 1899, *Women and Economics: The Economic Factor between Men and Women as a Factor in Social Revolution*, Small Maynard, Boston, reprinted 1966, Harper & Row, New York.

GILMAN, Charlotte Perkins, 1900, *Concerning Children*, Small Maynard, Boston.

GILMAN, Charlotte Perkins, 1903a, *The Home: Its Work and Influence*, McClure, Phillips, New York, reprinted 1972, (introduction by William L. O'Neill), University of Illinois Press.

GILMAN, Charlotte Perkins, 1903b, *Human Work*, McClure, Phillips, New York.

GILMAN, Charlotte Perkins, 1911, *The Man Made World or our Androcentric Culture*, Charlton, New York.

GILMAN, Charlotte Perkins, 1912, 'Her Own Money: Is a Wife Entitled to the Money she Earns?' *Mother's Magazine*, vol. VII, Feb., pp. 5–7.

GILMAN, Charlotte Perkins, 1915, *Herland* serialised *Forerunner* reprinted 1980, The Women's Press, London.

GILMAN, Charlotte Perkins, 1921, 'Making Towns Fit to Live In', *Century Magazine*, vol CII, July, pp. 361–6.

GILMAN, Charlotte Perkins, 1922, 'Do Women Dress to Please Men?' *Century Magazine*, vol. CIII, March, pp. 651–9 (with Alexander Black).

GILMAN, Charlotte Perkins, 1923, *His Religion and Hers: A Study of the Faith of our Fathers and the Work of our Mothers*, Century Company, New York.

GILMAN, Charlotte Perkins, 1928, 'Divorce and Birth-control', *Outlook*, vol. CXLVIII, 25 Jan., pp. 130–31, 153.

GILMAN, Charlotte Perkins, 1935, *The Living of Charlotte Perkins Gilman*, D. Appleton – Century, New York.

GILSON, Sarah, 1909, 'Antoinette Brown Blackwell: Biographical Sketch', unpublished manuscript: Schlesinger Library, Radcliffe College.

GLASTONBURY, Marion, 1978, 'Holding the Pens', in Sarah Elbert and Marion Glastonbury, *Inspiration and Drudgery: Notes on Literature and Domestic Labour in the Nineteenth Century*, Women's Research and Resources Centre, London, pp. 27–46.

GLASTONBURY, Marion, 1979, 'The Best Kept Secret – How Working Class Women Live and What They Know', *Women's Studies International Quarterly*, vol. II, no. 2, pp. 171–83.

GOLDBERG, Phillip, 1974, 'Are Women Prejudiced against Women?' in Judith Stacey et al. (eds), *And Jill Came Tumbling After: Sexism in American Education*, Dell Publishing, New York, pp. 37–42.

GOLDMAN, Emma, 1930, *Living My Life* (2 vols.) Alfred Knopf, New York, reprinted 1970, Dover Publications, New York.

GOLDMAN, Emma, 1970, *The Traffic in Women and Other Essays on Feminism*, Times Change Press, New York.

GOLDMAN, Emma, 1979, *Red Emma Speaks: Selected Writings and Speeches by Emma Goldman*, Alix Kates Shulman (ed.), Wildwood House, London.

GOLDMAN, Harold, 1974, *Emma Paterson: She Led Women into a Man's World*, Lawrence & Wishart, London.

GOLDSMITH, Margaret, 1946, *Women and the Future*, Lindsay Drummond, London.

GORDON, Anna A., 1898, *The Beautiful Life of Frances E. Willard*, Woman's Temperance Publishing, Chicago.

GOREAU, Angeline, 1980, *Reconstructing Aphra: A Social Biography of Aphra Behn*, The Dial Press, New York.

GORHAM, Deborah, 1979, 'Flora MacDonald Denison: Canadian Feminist', in Linda Kealey (ed.), *A Not Unreasonable Claim: Women and Reform in Canada 1880s–1920s*, The Women's Press, Toronto, pp. 47–70.

GOULD DAVIS, Elizabeth, 1973, *The First Sex*, J. M. Dent, London.

GOULIANOS, Joan (ed.), 1974, *By A Woman Writt: Literature from Six Centuries by and about Women*, New English Library, London.

GRAVES, Jane, 1978, 'Introduction', Olive Schreiner, *Woman and Labour*, Virago, London.

GREER, Germaine, 1970, *The Female Eunuch*, McGibbon & Kee, London.

GREER, Germaine, 1974, 'Flying Pigs and Double Standards', *Times Literary Supplement*, 26 July.

GREER, Germaine, 1979, *The Obstacle Race*, Secker & Warburg, London.

GRIFFIN, Susan, 1981, *Pornography and Silence*, The Women's Press, London.

GRIMKÉ, Angelina Emily, 1836a, 'An Appeal to the Christian Women of the South', *The Anti-Slavery Examiner*, vol. I, no. 2, pp. 16–26.

GRIMKÉ, Angelina Emily, 1836b, *Letters to Catherine Beecher*, Isaac Knapp, Boston.

GRIMKÉ, Sarah, 1838, *Letters on the Equality of the Sexes and the Condition of Women*, Isaac Knapp, Boston.

GURKO, Miriam, 1976, *The Ladies of Seneca Falls: The Birth of the Woman's Rights Movement*, Schocken Books, New York.

GUTWORTH, Madelyn, 1978, *Madame de Staël, Novelist: The Emergence of the Artist as Woman*, University of Illinois Press.

HABER, Barbara (ed.), 1981, *The Women's Annual: 1980: The Year in Review*, G. K. Hall, Boston.

HALE, Sarah Josepha, 1855, *Woman's Record: Or, Sketches of All Distinguished Women from the Creation to* A.D. *1854*, reprinted 1970, Source Book Press, New York.

HALL, Ruth (ed.), 1981, *Dear Dr Stopes: Sex in the 1920s*, Penguin, Harmondsworth.

HALLOWELL, A. D. (ed.), 1884, *James and Lucretia Mott: Life and Letters*, USA.

HALSBAND, Robert (ed.), 1947, *The Nonsense of Common Sense, 1737–38, by Lady Mary Wortley Montagu*, Northwestern University Press, Evanston.

HAMILTON, Cicely, 1909, *Marriage as a Trade*, reprinted 1981, The Women's Press, London.

HAMILTON, Cicely, 1935, *Life Errant*, J. M. Dent, London.

HANSCOMBE, Gillian E., 1979, 'Introduction', to Dorothy Richardson, *Pilgrimage I*, Virago, London, pp. 1–7.

HARE, Lloyd C. M., 1937, *The Greatest American Woman: Lucretia Mott*, American Historical Society, New York, reprinted 1970, Greenwood Press, Westport, Conn.

HARPER, Ida Husted, 1899, *The Life and Work of Susan B. Anthony*, Hollenbeck Press, Indianapolis and Kansas City.

HARPER, Ida Husted (ed.), 1922, *The History of Woman Suffrage*, vol. V/VI, National American Woman Suffrage Association. (For earlier vols. see Stanton et al.)

HARRIS, Barbara J., 1978, *Beyond Her Sphere: Women and the Professions in American History*, Greenwood Press, Westport, Conn.

HARTSOCK, Nancy, 1981, 'Mary Wollstonecraft's Two Vindications', Paper presented *Berkshire Conference on Women's History*, Vassar, 18 June.

HAYEK, F. A., 1969, *John Stuart Mill and Harriet Taylor: Their Friendship and Subsequent Marriage*, Routledge & Kegan Paul, London.

HAYS, Elinor Rice, 1961, *Morning Star: A Biography of Lucy Stone*, Harcourt, Brace & World, New York.

HAYS, Elinor Rice, 1967, *Those Extraordinary Blackwells*, Harcourt, Brace & World, New York.

HAYS, Mary, 1798, *An Appeal to the Men of Great Britain in Behalf of Women*, reprinted, 1974, Garland Publishing, New York.

HAYS, Mary, 1803, *Female Biography, or Memoirs of Illustrious and Celebrated Women of All Ages and Countries, Alphabetically Arranged* (6 vols.), Richard Phillips, London.

HAYWOOD, Eliza, 1929, *The Female Spectator: Being Selections from Mrs Eliza Haywood's periodical (1744–46)*, Mary Priestley (ed.), Bodley Head, London.

HELLERSTEIN, Erna Olafson, Leslie Parker HUME and Karen M. OFFEN (eds), 1981, *Victorian Women: A Documentary Account of Women's Lives in Nineteenth-century England, France and the United States*, Harvester Press, Brighton.

HEMLOW, Joyce, 1958, *The History of Fanny Burney*, Clarendon Press, Oxford.

HEROLD, J. Christopher, 1958, *Mistress to an Age: A Life of Madame de Staël*, Bobbs-Merrill, New York.

HERSCHBERGER, Ruth, 1948, *Adam's Rib*, Pellegrini & Cudahy, New York, reprinted 1970, Harper & Row, New York.

HEWITT, Margaret, 1958, *Wives and Mothers in Victorian Industry*, Rockliff, London.

HILL, Mary A., 1980, *Charlotte Perkins Gilman: the making of a Radical Feminist 1860–1896*, Temple University Press, Philadelphia.

HITE, Shere, 1977, *The Hite Report: A Nationwide Study on Female Sexuality*, Talmy Franklin, London.

HOLE, Judith & Ellen LEVINE (eds), 1971, *Rebirth of Feminism*, Quadrangle Books, New York.

HOLLIS, Patricia (ed.), 1979, *Women in Public: The Women's Movement 1850–1900*, George Allen & Unwin, London.

HOLM, Birgitta, 1980, *Romanens mödrar I: Fredrika Bremer och den borgerliga romanens födelse* (Mothers of the Novel I: Fredrika Bremer and the birth of the bourgeois novel), Norstedts, Sweden.

HOLTBY, Winifred, 1939, *Women*, Bodley Head, London. (First published 1934).

HOLTBY, Winifred, 1978, *Virginia Woolf: A Critical Memoir*, Cassandra Editions, Academy Press, Chicago, originally published 1932.

HORNER, Matina S., 1974, 'Toward an Understanding of Achievement – related Conflicts in Women', in Judith Stacey et al. (eds), *And Jill Came Tumbling After*, Dell Publishing, New York, pp. 43–62.

HOUSMAN, Laurence, 1912, *The Sex-War and Woman's Suffrage*, Women's Freedom League, London.

HOWE, Florence, 1974, 'The Education of Women', in Judith Stacey et al. (eds), *And Jill Came Tumbling After*, Dell Publishing, New York, pp. 64–74.

HUBBARD, Ruth, 1979, 'Reflections on the Story of the Double Helix', *Women's Studies International Quarterly*, vol. II, no. 3, pp. 261–74.

HUBBARD, Ruth, 1981, 'The Emperor Doesn't Wear Any Clothes: The Impact of Feminism on Biology', in Dale Spender (ed.), *Men's Studies Modified*, Pergamon Press, Oxford, pp. 213–36.

HUNKINS-HALLINAN, Hazel, 1968, 'A Revolution Unfinished', in Hazel Hunkins-Hallinan (ed.), *In Her Own Right: A Discussion Conducted by the Six Point Group*, George G. Harrap, London, pp. 9–17.

HUNKINS-HALLINAN, Hazel, 1982, taped interview.

HYNES, Samuel, 1978, 'Introduction: In Communion with Reality', in Rebecca West, *A Celebration*, Penguin, Harmondsworth, pp. ix–xviii.

IRWIN, Joyce L., 1980, 'Anna Maria van Schurman: The Star of Utrecht (1607–1678)' in J. R. Brink (ed.), *Female Scholars*, Eden Press, Montreal, pp. 68–85.

JAMESON, Anna, 1856, *The Communion of Labour*, Longman, Brown, Green, London.

JAMESON, Elizabeth, 1974, 'To be All Human: Sex Role and Transcendence in Margaret Fuller's Life and Thought', *University of Michigan Papers in Women's Studies*, vol. I, no. 1, pp. 91–126.

JANEWAY, Elizabeth, 1980, *Powers of the Weak*, Knopf, New York.

JOHNSTON, Johanna, 1979, *The Life, Manners and Travels of Fanny Trollope*, Constable, London.

JONES, Ann, 1980, *Women Who Kill*, Holt, Rinehart & Winston, New York.

JONES, Dorothy and Jennifer JONES (forthcoming), *Single Women*.

JONES, Enid Huws, 1973, *Mrs Humphrey Ward*, Heinemann, London.

JONG, Erica, 1980, *Fanny: Being the True History of the Adventures of Fanny Hackabout-Jones*, Granada Publishing, London.

JUSTITIA (Mrs Henry David Pochin), 1855, *The Right of Women to Exercise the Elective Franchise*, Chapman & Hall, London.

KAMM, Josephine, 1966, *Rapiers and Battleaxes: The Women's Movement and its Aftermath*, George Allen & Unwin, London.

KANNER, Barbara (ed.), 1980, *The Women of England: From Anglo-Saxon Times to the Present: Interpretive Bibliographical Essays*, Mansell, London.

KAPLAN, Cora, 1978, 'Introduction', *'Aurora Leigh' and other poems: Elizabeth Barrett Browning*, The Women's Press, London, pp. 5–36.

KAPP, Yvonne, 1979a, *Eleanor Marx Family Life 1855–1883*, vol. I, Virago, London.

KAPP, Yvonne, 1979b, *Eleanor Marx: The Crowded Years, 1884–1898*, vol. II, Virago, London.

KATZ, Esther and Anita KAPONE (eds), 1980, *Women's Experience in America: An Historical Anthology*, Transaction Books, Brunswick and London.

KEALEY, Linda (ed.), 1979, *A Not Unreasonable Claim: Women and Reform in Canada 1880s–1920s*, The Women's Press, Toronto.

KELLOG, Grace, 1965, *The Two Lives of Edith Wharton: The Woman and her Work*, Appleton-Century, New York.

KEMPF, Beatrix, 1972, *Suffragette for Peace: The Life of Bertha von Suttner*, Oswald Wolff, London.

KENNEY, Annie, 1924, *Memories of a Militant*, Edward Arnold, London.

KENNEDY, David M., 1970, *Birth Control in America: The Career of Margaret Sanger*, Yale University Press, New Haven, Conn.

KERBER, Linda K., 1980, *Women of the Republic: Intellect and Ideology in Revolutionary America*, University of North Carolina Press.

KILPATRICK, Sarah, 1980, *Fanny Burney*, David & Charles, Newton Abbot.

KINGSTON, Beverley, 1977, *My Wife, My Daughter, and Poor Maryann: Woman and Work in Australia*, Nelson, Melbourne.

KINNAIRD, Joan, K., 1979, 'Mary Astell and the Conservative Contribution to English Feminism', *The Journal of British Studies*, vol. XIX, no. 2, pp. 53–75.

KINNAIRD, Joan K., 1982, 'Mary Astell', in Dale Spender (ed.), *Feminist Theorists*, The Women's Press, London.

KIRCHWEY, Freda, 1928, 'Crystal Eastman', *The Nation*, 8 August, reprinted Blanche Wiesen Cook (ed.), 1978, *Crystal Eastman on Women and Revolution*, Oxford University Press, pp. 371–5.

KLEIN, Viola, 1946, *The Feminine Character: History of an Ideology*, Routledge & Kegan Paul, London, reprinted 1971, 1975, University of Illinois Press.

KLEIN, Viola, 1958, *Working Wives*, Institute of Personnel Management, Occasional Papers, no. 15.

KLEIN, Viola, 1965, *Britain's Married Women Workers*, Routledge & Kegan Paul, London.

KNIGHT, Anne, circa 1847, 'Women's Suffrage', Facsimile Reprint, Helen Blackburn, 1902, *Women's Suffrage*, Williams & Norgate, London and Oxford, p. 19.

KNIGHT, Patricia, 1977, 'Women and Abortion in Victorian and Edwardian England', *History Workshop Journal*, vol. IV, pp. 57–69.

KNUCKEY, Marie, 1980, 'Rose Scott: Influence was her Weapon', *Sydney Morning Herald*, 13 May, p. 12.

KOEDT, Anne, Ellen LEVINE, and Anita RAPONE (eds), *Radical Feminism*, Quadrangle, New York.

KOLODNY, Annette, 1981, 'Dancing through the Minefield: Some Observations on Theory, Practice and Politics of a Feminist Literary Criticism', in Dale Spender (ed.), *Men's Studies Modified*, Pergamon Press, Oxford, pp. 23–42.

KOMAROVSKY, Mirra, 1946, 'Cultural Contradictions and Sex Roles', *American Journal of Sociology*, Nov.

KOMAROVSKY, Mirra, 1953, *Women in the Modern World: Their Education and Their Dilemmas*, Little Brown, Boston.

KOMAROVSKY, Mirra, 1964, *Blue Collar Marriage*, Random House, New York.

KRADITOR, Aileen S., 1965, *The Ideas of the Woman Suffrage Movement*, Columbia University Press, New York.

KRAMNICK, Miriam (ed.), 1978, *Wollstonecraft: Vindication of the Rights of Woman*, Penguin, Harmondsworth.

KURTZ, Benjamin P., and Carrie C. AUTREY (eds), 1937, *Four New Letters of Mary Wollstonecraft and Helen M. Williams*, University of California Press, Berkeley.

LA FOLLETTE, Suzanne, 1926, *Concerning Women*, Albert & Charles Bonni, New York.

LAING, Dilys, 1974, 'Sonnet to a Sister in Error', in Joan Goulianos (ed.), *By a Woman Writt*, New English Library, London, p. 239.

LANE, Ann J., 1977, *Mary Ritter Beard: A Source Book*, Schocken Books, New York.

LANE, Ann J., 1981, 'The Fictional World of Charlotte Perkins Gilman', in Ann J. Lane (ed.), *The Charlotte Perkins Gilman Reader*, The Women's Press, London, pp. ix–xlii.

LANGDELL, Cheri Davis (in press), *Writing Against the Current*, Routledge & Kegan Paul, London.

LAVIGUEUR, Jill, 1980, 'Co-education and the Tradition of Separate Needs', in Dale Spender and Elizabeth Sarah (eds), *Learning to Lose: Sexism and Education*, The Women's Press, London, pp. 180–90.

LEACH, William, 1981, *True Love and Perfect Union: The Feminist Reform of Sex and Society*, Routledge & Kegan Paul, London.

LECKY, W. E. H., 1883–1887, *The History of England in the Eighteenth Century* (8 Vols), Longmans Green, London.

LEGHORN, Lisa and Katherine PARKER, 1981, *Woman's Worth: Sexual Economics and the World of Women*, Routledge and Kegan Paul, Boston and London.

LERNER, Gerda, 1971, *The Grimké Sisters from South Carolina: Pioneers for Woman's Rights and Abolition*, Schocken Books, New York.

LERNER, Gerda (ed.), 1973, *Black Women in White America: A Documentary History*, Vintage Books, New York.

LERNER, Gerda, 1977, *The Female Experience: An American Documentary*, Bobbs–Merrill, New York.

LERNER, Gerda, 1981, *The Majority Finds its Past: Placing Women in History*, Oxford University Press.

LESSING, Doris, 1962, *The Golden Notebook*, Michael Joseph, London.

LEWIS, Jane, 1981, 'Introduction', to Cicely Hamilton, *Marriage as a Trade*, The Women's Press, London.

LEWIS, R. W. B., 1977, *Edith Wharton: A Biography*, Harper & Row, New York.

LIDDINGTON, Jill and Jill NORRIS, 1978, *One Hand Tied Behind Us: The Rise of the Women's Suffrage Movement*, Virago, London.

LINKLATER, Andro, 1980, *An Unhusbanded Life: Charlotte Despard, Suffragette, Socialist and Sinn Feiner*, Hutchinson, London.

LIPSET, Seymour Martin (ed.), 1962, *Harriet Martineau: Society in America*, Doubleday, New York.

LLOYD, Trevor, 1971, *Suffragettes International: The Worldwide Campaign for Women's Rights*, Library of the 20th Century, Macdonald, London.

LOEWENBERG, Bert James and Ruth BOGIN (eds), 1976, *Black Women in Nineteenth Century American Life: Their Words, their Thoughts, their Feelings*, Pennsylvania State University Press, University Park and London.

LUNDBERG, Ferdinand and Marynia F. FARNHAM, 1959, *Modern Woman: The Lost Sex*, Harper Bros., New York.

LURIA, Gina (ed.), 1974, *The Feminist Controversy in England 1788–1810* (44 titles, 89 vols), Garland Publishing, New York.

LUTZ, Alma, 1940, *Created Equal: A Biography of Elizabeth Cady Stanton*, John Day, New York.

LUTZ, Alma, 1953, *Susan B. Anthony*, Beacon Press, Boston.

MACAULAY, Catherine (1790), *Letters on Education*, reprinted 1974, ed. G. Luria, Garland Publishing, New York.

MACCARTHY, B. G., 1944, *Women Writers: Their Contribution to the English Novel, 1621–1744*, Cork University Press.

MCGUINN, Nicholas, 1978, 'George Eliot and Mary Wollstonecraft', in Sara Delamont and Lorna Duffin (eds), *The Nineteenth Century Woman*, Croom Helm, London, pp. 188–205.

MACKENZIE, Midge, 1975, *Shoulder to Shoulder: A Documentary*, Penguin, Harmondsworth.

MACKINNON, Catharine, 1979, *Sexual Harassment of Working Women*, Yale University Press, New Haven and London.

MACPHERSON, Geraldine, 1878, *Memoirs of Mrs Jameson*, Longmans, Green, London.

MCWILLIAMS–TULLBERG, Rita, 1975, *Women at Cambridge: A Men's University – Though of a Mixed Type*, Victor Gollancz, London.

MAHL, Mary R. and Helene KOON, 1977, *The Female Spectator: English Women Writers before 1800*, The Feminist Press, Old Westbury, New York.

MAINARDI, Pat, 1970, 'The Politics of Housework', Robin Morgan (ed.), *Sisterhood is Powerful*, Vintage Books, New York, pp. 501–9.

MAISON, Margaret, 1965, 'On Adelaide Ann Proctor: Queen Victoria's Favourite Poet', *The Listener*, 29 April, pp. 636–7.

MANLEY, Seon and Susan BELCHER, 1972, *O, Those Extraordinary Women! Or the Joys of Literary Lib*, Chilton, Philadelphia and Ontario.

MANSFIELD, Katherine, 1945, *Collected Stories of Katherine Mansfield*, reprinted 1976, Constable, London.

MANTON, Jo, 1965, *Elizabeth Garrett Anderson*, Methuen, London.

MARCUS, Jane, 1979, '*Night and Day* as a Comic Opera', in Ralph Freedman (ed.), *Virginia Woolf: Revaluation and Continuity*, University of California Press, Berkeley.

MARCUS, Jane, 1980a, 'The Divine Right to be Didactic', in Elizabeth Robins, *The Convert*, The Women's Press, London, pp. v–xvi.

MARCUS, Jane, 1980b, 'Introduction', to Rebecca West, *The Judge*, Virago, London, pp. 3–8.

MARSH, Margaret S., 1981, *Anarchist Women: 1870–1920*, Temple University Press, Philadelphia.

MARTIN, Theodore, 1908, *Queen Victoria as I Knew Her*, William Blackwood, Edinburgh and London.

MARTIN, Wendy, 1972, *The American Sisterhood: Writings of the Feminist Movement from Colonial Times to the Present*, Harper & Row, New York.

MARTINEAU, Harriet, 1837, 'Political Non-existence of Women', *Society in America*, Saunders & Otley, New York, vol. I, pp. 199–207.

MARTINEAU, Harriet, 1859, 'Female Industry', *Edinburgh Review*, vol. 109, p. 336.

MARTINEAU, Harriet, 1877, *Autobiography: With Memorials by Maria Weston Chapman* (3 vols), Smith, Elder, London.

MASEFIELD, Muriel, 1927, *The Story of Fanny Burney*, Cambridge University Press.

MASON, Bertha, 1912, *The Story of the Women's Suffrage Movement*, Sheratt & Hughes, London.

MASTERS, William and Virginia JOHNSON, 1970, *Human Sexual Inadequacy*, Little, Brown, Boston.

MATHEWS, Jacquie, 1981, private communication.

MATHEWS, Jacquie 1982, 'Barbara Bodichon', in Dale Spender (ed.), *Feminist Theorists: Three Centuries of Intellectual Traditions*, The Women's Press, London.

MAVOR, Elizabeth, 1971, *The Ladies of Llangollen*, Michael Joseph, London, reprinted 1976, Penguin, Harmondsworth.

MEAD, Margaret, 1935, *Sex and Temperament*, Routledge, London.

MEAD, Margaret, 1950, *Male and Female*, Gollancz, London, reprinted 1971, Penguin, Harmondsworth.

MEAD, Margaret, 1972, *Blackberry Winter: My Earlier Years*, William Morrow, New York, reprinted 1975, Pocket Books, New York.

MELLOWN, Muriel (forthcoming), 'Vera Brittain: Feminist in a New Age', in Dale Spender (ed.), *Feminist Theorists*, The Women's Press, London.

MERCHANT, Carolyn, 1980, *The Death of Nature: Women, Ecology and the Scientific Revolution*, Harper & Row, New York.

MILL, John Stuart, 1869, *The Subjection of Women*, reprinted 1974, (Introduction by Millicent Garrett Fawcett), Oxford University Press.

MILLER, Casey and Kate SWIFT, 1981, *The Handbook of Non Sexist Writing for Writers, Editors and Speakers*, The Women's Press, London.

MILLER, Mrs F. Fenwick, 1884, *Harriet Martineau*, W. H. Allen, London.

MILLER, Jean Baker, 1978, *Toward a New Psychology of Women*, Penguin, Harmondsworth.

MILLER, Perry, 1957, 'I find no Intellect Comparable to my Own', *American Heritage*, vol. 8, Feb.

MILLETT, Kate, 1970, *Sexual Politics*, Doubleday, New York; 1972, Abacus, London.

MINEKA, Francis E., 1944, *The Dissidence of Dissent*, University of North Carolina Press, Chapel Hill.

MITCHELL, David, 1966, *Women on the Warpath*, Cape, London.

MITCHELL, David, 1967, *The Fighting Pankhursts*, Cape, London.

MITCHELL, David, 1970, *The Pankhursts*, Herron Books, London.

MITCHELL, David, 1977, *Queen Christabel: A Biography of Christabel Pankhurst*, McDonald & Janes, London.

MITCHELL, David, 1980, 'Maiden Warrior', *Sunday Times Magazine*, 21 Sept., pp. 62–8.

MITCHELL, Hannah, 1977, *The Hard Way Up: The Autobiography of Hannah Mitchell, Suffragette and Rebel*, Geoffrey Mitchell (ed.), Preface by Sheila Rowbotham, Virago, London.

MITCHELL, Juliet, 1971, *Woman's Estate*, Penguin, Harmondsworth.

MITCHELL, Juliet, 1974, *Psychoanalysis and Feminism*, Penguin, Harmondsworth.

MITCHELL, Juliet and Ann OAKLEY (eds.), 1976, *The Rights and Wrongs of Women*, Penguin, Harmondsworth.

MITCHELL, Winifred (n.d.), *Fifty Years of Feminist Achievement*, United Associations of Women, Sydney.

MOERS, Elaine, 1978, *Literary Women: The Great Writers*, The Women's Press, London.

MONTAGU, Lady Mary Wortley, 'Letters', reprinted in Katharine M. Rogers (ed.), 1979, *Before Their Time*, Frederick Ungar, New York, pp. 48–75.

MORE, Hannah (1799), *Strictures on the Modern System of Female Education*.

MORGAN, Elaine, 1972, *The Descent of Woman*, Souvenir Press, London; Stein & Day, New York.

MORGAN, Fidelis, 1981, *The Female Wits: Women Playwrights on the London Stage 1660–1720*, Virago, London.

MORGAN, Lady, 1840, *Woman and her Master* (2 vols), Henry Colburn, London.

MORGAN Robin (ed.), 1970, *Sisterhood is Powerful: An Anthology of Writings from the Women's Liberation Movement*, Vintage Books, New York.

MORGAN, Robin, 1978, *Going Too Far: The Personal Chronicle of a Feminist*, Vintage Books, New York.

MORRELL, Caroline, 1981, *'Black Friday' and Violence against Women in the Suffragette Movement*, Women's Research and Resource Centre, London.

MURRAY, Janet Horowitz, 1982, *Strong-Minded Women: and Other Lost Voices from the Nineteenth Century*, Pantheon, New York.

MURRAY, Judith Sargent, 1790, 'On the Equality of the Sexes', *Massachusetts Magazine*, March, pp. 132–5, and April, pp. 223–6, reprinted in Alice S. Rossi (ed.), 1974, *The Feminist Papers: from Adams to de Beauvoir*, Bantam, New York, pp. 18–22.

MYRDAL, Alva and Viola KLEIN, 1956, *Women's Two Roles*, Routledge & Kegan Paul, London.

NATIONAL WOMEN'S SOCIAL AND POLITICAL UNION (n.d.), *The Trial of the Suffragette Leaders*, The Woman's Press, London.

NETHERCOT, G. H., 1961, *The First Five Lives of Annie Besant*, Rupert Hart Davis, London.

NETHERCOT, G. H., 1963, *The Last Four Lives of Annie Besant*, Rupert Hart Davis, London.

NEWTON, Judith Lowder, 1978, '*Pride and Prejudice*: Power, Fantasy and Subversion in Jane Austen', *Feminist Studies*, vol. 4, no. 1, pp. 27–42.

NIES, Judith, 1979, *Seven Women: Portraits from the American Radical Tradition*, Penguin, New York.

NIGHTINGALE, E. Constance, 1962, 'Frances Power Cobbe 1861–1961', *Women in Council*, Winter, p. 24.

NIGHTINGALE, Florence, 1928, 'Cassandra', in Ray Strachey, *The Cause: A Short History of the Women's Movement in Great Britain*, reprinted 1978, Virago, London, pp. 395–418.

NIXON, Edna, 1971, *Mary Wollstonecraft: Her Life and Times*, Dent, London.

NORTON, Caroline, 1837a, 'The Natural Claim of a Mother to the Custody of her Child as affected by the Common Law rights of the Father, Illustrated by Cases of Peculiar Hardship', printed for private circulation by Caroline Norton.

NORTON, Caroline, 1837b, 'Separation of the Mother and Child by the Law of Custody of Infants Considered', printed for private circulation by J. Ridgway.

NOVARRA, Virginia, 1980, *Women's Work, Men's Work: The Ambivalence of Equality*, Marion Boyars, London and Boston.

OAKES SMITH, Elizabeth, 1851, *Woman and Her Needs*, Fowler & Wells, New York.

OAKLEY, Ann, 1972, *Sex, Gender and Society*, Temple Smith, London.

OAKLEY, Ann, 1974, *The Sociology of Housework*, Martin Robertson, Oxford.

OAKLEY Ann, 1980, *Women Confined*, Martin Robertson, Oxford.

OAKLEY, Ann, 1981, *Subject Women*, Martin Robertson, Oxford.

OBENDORF, Clarence P., 1943, *The Psychiatric Novels of Oliver Wendell Holmes*, Columbia University Press, New York.

O'BRIEN, Mary, 1981a, private communication.

O'BRIEN, Mary, 1981b, *The Politics of Reproduction*, Routledge & Kegan Paul, Boston and London.

O'DONNELL, Sherry, 1981, private communication.

OKIN, Susan Moller, 1979, *Women in Western Political Thought*, Princeton University Press.

OLIPHANT, Margaret, 1889, *Literary History of England 1790–1925* (3 vols), Macmillan, London.

OLSEN, Tillie, 1980, *Silences*, Virago, London.

O'NEILL, William L., 1969, *The Woman Movement: Feminism in the United States and England*, Allen & Unwin, London; Barnes & Noble, New York.

O'NEILL, William L., 1972, 'Introduction', to Charlotte Perkins Gilman, *The Home: Its Work and Influence*, University of Illinois Press, pp. vii–xxiii.

ORBACH, Susie, 1978, *Fat is a Feminist Issue*, Paddington Press, New York and London.

ORTON, Diana, 1980, *Made of Gold: A Biography of Angela Burdett-Coutts*, Hamish Hamilton, London.

OSBORNE, Martha Lee (ed.), 1979, *Woman in Western Thought*, Random House, New York.

OSEN, Lynn M., 1974, *Women in Mathematics*, MIT Press, Cambridge, Mass.

PANKHURST, Christabel (n.d.a), 'Some Questions Answered', *Women's Social and Political Union*, leaflet 24, The Woman's Press, London.

PANKHURST, Christabel (n.d.b), 'Militant Methods', *Votes for Women*, leaflet 63, The Woman's Press, London.

PANKHURST, Christabel (n.d.c), 'A Challenge', *Women's Social and Political Union*, leaflet 91, The Women's (sic) Press, London.

PANKHURST, Christabel (n.d.d), 'Burnt letters', *Women's Social and Political Union*, leaflet 100, The Woman's Press, London.

PANKHURST, Christabel, 1912, 'Broken Windows', *Women's Social and Political Union*, leaflet 88, The Women's (sic) Press, London.

PANKHURST, Christabel, 1913, *The Great Scourge and How to End It*, E. Pankhurst, London.

PANKHURST, Christabel, 1959, *Unshackled: The Story of How We Won the Vote*, Hutchinson, London.

PANKHURST, Emmeline, 1914, *My Own Story*, Eveleigh Nash, London, reprinted 1979, Virago, London.

PANKHURST, Richard K. P., 1954, *William Thompson (1755–1833): Britain's Pioneer Socialist, Feminist and Co-operator*, Watts, London.

PANKHURST, Richard K. P., 1979, *Sylvia Pankhurst: Artist and Crusader*, Paddington Press, New York and London.

PANKHURST, Sylvia, 1911, *The Suffragette: The History of the Women's Militant Suffrage Movement, 1905–1910*, Gay & Hancock, London.

PANKHURST, Sylvia, 1931, *The Suffragette Movement*, Longmans, London, reprinted 1977, Virago, London.

PARKER, Gail (ed.), 1975, *Elizabeth Cady Stanton: Eighty Years and More: Reminiscences 1815–1897*, Schocken Books, New York.

PARKER, Rosika and Griselda POLLOCK, 1981, *Old Mistresses*, Routledge & Kegan Paul, London.

PATTERSON, Clara Burdett, 1953, *Angela Burdett-Coutts and the Victorians*, John Murray, London.

PATTERSON, Elizabeth C., 1969, 'Mary Somerville', *British Journal for the History of Science*, vol. 4, pp. 311–39.

PATTERSON, Elizabeth C., 1974, 'The Case of Mary Somerville: An Aspect of Nineteenth Century Science', *Proceedings of the American Philosophical Society*. vol. 118, pp. 269–75.

PEMBER REEVES, Maud, 1913, *Round About a Pound a Week*, G. Bell & Sons, London, reprinted 1979, Virago, London.

PENNELL, Elizabeth Robins, 1885, 'Mary Wollstonecraft Godwin', in John H. Ingram (ed.), *Eminent Women*, W. H. Allen, London.

PERKINS, A. J. and Theresa WOLFSON, 1939, *Frances Wright; Free Enquirer: A Study of a Temperament*, Harper & Bros., New York.

PERRY, Ruth, 1981, 'Mary Astell's Response to the Enlightenment', paper presented *Berkshire Conference on Women's History*, Vassar, 16 June.

PETHICK-LAWRENCE, Emmeline, 1938, *My Part in a Changing World*, Victor Gollancz, London.

PETRIE, Glen, 1971, *A Singular Iniquity: The Campaigns of Josephine Butler*, Macmillan, London.

PHILLIPS, Mary (n.d.), *The Militant Suffrage Campaign in Perspective*, Fawcett Library Pamphlet.

PICHANICK, Valerie Kossew, 1980, *Harriet Martineau: The Woman and Her Work, 1802–1876*, University of Michigan Press, Ann Arbor.

PINCHBECK, Ivy, 1930, *Women Workers of the Industrial Revolution*, Routledge & Kegan Paul, London.

PINNEY, Thomas (ed.), 1963, *Essays of George Eliot*, Routledge & Kegan Paul, London.

PLATT, Ruth (forthcoming), *Women's Collectives*.

POCHIN, Mrs Henry David, 1855, *The Right of Women to Exercise the Elective Franchise*, Chapman & Hall, London.

POPE-HENNESSY, Una, 1929, *Three English Women in America*, Ernest Benn, London.

PORTER, Cathy, 1980, *Alexandra Kollontai: A Biography*, Virago, London.

PRIESTLEY, J. B., 1929, 'Introduction', Mary Priestley (ed.), *The Female Spectator*, Bodley Head, London, pp. vii–xv.

PRIESTLEY, Mary (ed.), 1929, *The Female Spectator: Being Selections from Mrs Eliza Heywood's Periodical 1744–1746*, Bodley Head, London.

PUGH, Martin, 1980, *Women's Suffrage in Britain 1867–1928*, Hart Talbot, Saffron Walden.

PURVIS, A., 1953/54, 'Mrs Aphra Behn', *Amateur Historian*, vol. I. no. 9.

RADCLIFFE, Mary Ann, 1810, *The Female Advocate, or an Attempt to Recover the Rights of Women from Male Usurpation (In: The Memoirs . . . in Familiar Letters to her Female Friend)*, reprinted 1974, Garland Publishing, New York.

RAEBURN, Antonia, 1974, *Militant Suffragettes*, New English Library, London.

RAEBURN, Antonia, 1976, *The Suffrage View*, David & Charles, Newton Abbot.

RAMELSON, Marian, 1967, *The Petticoat Rebellion*, Lawrence & Wishart, London.

RAY, Gordon N., 1974, *H. G. Wells and Rebecca West*, Macmillan, London.

REID, Hugo, Mrs, 1843, *A Plea for Women*, William Tait, Edinburgh.

REITER, Rayna R. (ed.), 1975, *Toward an Anthropology of Women*, Monthly Review Press, New York.

REUBEN, Elaine, 1978, 'In Defiance of the Evidence: Notes on Feminist Scholarship', *Women's Studies International Quarterly*, Vol. I, no. 3, pp. 215–18.

RHONDDA, Viscountess (Margaret Haig), 1933, *This Was My World*, Macmillan, London.

RHONDDA, Viscountess, 1937, *Notes on the Way*, Macmillan, London.

RICE, Margery Spring, 1939, *Working Class Wives: Their Health and Conditions*, Penguin, Harmondsworth, reprinted 1981, Virago, London.

RICH, Adrienne, 1977, *Of Woman Born: Motherhood as Experience and Institution*, Virago, London.

RICH, Adrienne, 1980, *On Lies, Secrets and Silence*, Virago, London.

RICH, Adrienne, 1981, *Compulsory Heterosexuality and Lesbian Existence*, Only Women Press, London.

RICHARDSON, Dorothy, 1979, *Pilgrimage I*, Virago, London.

RITCHIE, Jane (forthcoming), 'Child-rearing Practices and Attitudes of Working and Full-time Mothers', *Women's Studies International Forum*.

ROBERTS, Joan, 1976, 'The Ramifications of the Study of Women', in Joan Roberts (ed.), *Beyond Intellectual Sexism: A New Woman, a New Reality*, David McKay, New York, pp. 3–13.

ROBINS, Elizabeth, 1907, *The Convert*, Methuen, London, reprinted 1980, The Women's Press, London.

ROBINS, Elizabeth, 1913, *Way Stations*, The Women's Press, London.

ROBINS, Elizabeth, 1923, 'Six-Point Group Supplement: Introductory Number: The Six Points and Their Common Centre', *Time and Tide*, 19 Jan., p. 60.

ROGERS, Agnes, 1949, *Women are Here to Stay*, Harper & Bros, New York.

ROGERS, Katharine M. (ed.), 1979, *Before Their Time: Six Women Writers of the Eighteenth-Century*, Frederick Ungar, New York.

ROSE, June, 1980, *Elizabeth Fry: A Biography*, Macmillan, London.

ROSE, Phyllis, 1978, *Woman of Letters: A Life of Virginia Woolf*, Routledge & Kegan Paul, London.

ROSEN, Andrew, 1974, *Rise Up Women! The Militant Campaign of the Women's Social and Political Union 1903–1914*, Routledge & Kegan Paul, London.

ROSSI, Alice S. (ed.), 1970, *Essays on Sex Equality by John Stuart Mill and Harriet Taylor Mill*, University of Chicago Press.

ROSSI, Alice S. (ed.), 1974, *The Feminist Papers: From Adams to de Beauvoir*, Bantam Books, New York.

ROTHSCHILD, Joan (ed.) (1981), 'Women, Technology and Innovation', Special issue, *Women's Studies International Quarterly*, vol. IV, no. 3.

ROVER, Constance, 1967a, *The Punch Book of Women's Rights*, Hutchinson, London.

ROVER, Constance, 1967b, *Women's Suffrage and Party Politics 1866–1914*, Routledge & Kegan Paul, London.

ROVER, Constance, 1970, *Love, Morals and the Feminists*, Routledge & Kegan Paul, London.

ROWBOTHAM, Sheila, 1973a, *Hidden from History*, Pluto Press, London.

ROWBOTHAM, Sheila, 1973b, *Woman's Consciousness: Man's World*, Penguin, Harmondsworth.

ROWLAND, Robyn, (forthcoming), *Childfree*.

RUPRECHT, Nancy, 1975, 'The Critics, Simone de Beauvoir, and *All Said and Done*', *University of Michigan Papers in Women's Studies*, vol. I, no. 4, pp. 129–47.

RUSK, Ralph L., 1949, *The Life of Ralph Waldo Emerson*, Charles Scribner's Sons, New York.

RUSSELL, Bertrand, 1967, *Autobiography Vol I 1872–1914*, Allen & Unwin, London.

RUSSELL, Dora, 1925, *Hypatia or Woman and Knowledge*, Kegan Paul, Trench Trubner, London.

RUSSELL, Dora, 1977, *The Tamarisk Tree: My Quest for Liberty and Love* (vol. I), Virago, London.

RUSSELL, Dora, 1981, *The Tamarisk Tree: My School and the Years of War* (vol. II), Virago, London.

RUSSELL, Dora, 1982, taped interview.

RUTH, Sheila, 1980, *Issues in Feminism: A First Course in Women's Studies*, Houghton Mifflin, Boston.

SABROSKY, Judith A., 1979, *From Rationality to Liberation: The Evolution of Feminist Ideology*, Greenwood Press, Westport, Conn.

SACKVILLE-WEST, Victoria, 1927, *Aphra Behn: The Incomparable Astrea*, Gerald Howe, London.

SAND, Georges, 1977, *The Intimate Journal of Georges Sand* (edited and translated Marie Jenney Howe) Cassandra, Academy Press, Chicago.

SANGER, Margaret, 1917, *Family Limitation*, (pamphlet) New York.

SANGER, Margaret, 1920, *Woman and the New Race*, Brentano, New York.

SANGER, Margaret, 1931, *My Fight for Birth Control*, Farrar-Rinehart, New York.

SAPIRO, Virginia, 1974, 'Feminist Studies and the Discipline: A Study of Mary Wollstonecraft', *University of Michigan Papers in Women's Studies*, vol. I, no. 1, pp. 178–200.

SARAH, Elizabeth, 1980, private communication.

SARAH, Elizabeth (ed.), 1982a, 'First Wave Feminism', special issue, vol 5. no. 3, *Women's Studies International Forum*.

SARAH, Elizabeth (ed.), 1982b, (forthcoming), *The Problem of Men*, The Women's Press, London.

SARAH, Elizabeth, 1982c, 'Reclaiming Christabel Pankhurst', in Dale Spender (ed.), *Feminist Theorists*, The Women's Press, London.

SAYERS, Dorothy L., 1938, 'Are Women Human?' Address given to Women's Society, printed 1971, William B. Eerdman, Grand Rapids, Michigan.

SAYWELL, R., 1936, 'The Development of Feminist Ideas in England', unpublished M.A. Thesis, University of London.

SCHNEIR, Miriam (ed.), 1972, *Feminism: The Essential Historical Writings*, Vintage Books, New York.

SCHREINER, Olive, 1883, *The Story of an African Farm*, Chapman & Hall, London.

SCHREINER, Olive, 1911, *Woman and Labour*, T. Fisher Unwin, London, reprinted 1978, Virago, London.

SCHREINER, Olive, 1926, *From Man to Man: or perhaps only . . .*, Unwin, London, reprinted 1977, Cassandra, Academy Press, Chicago.

SCHURMAN, Anna van, 1641/1659, *The Learned Maid: Or Whether a Maid may be a Scholar*.

SCOTT, Hilda, 1974, *Does Socialism Liberate Women? Experiences from Eastern Europe*, Beacon Press, Boston.

SCOTT, Rivers, 1972, 'Rebecca West: Women's Lib and Why I'm for It', *The Sunday Telegraph*, 24 Dec, p. 6.

SEWARD, Anna, 1811, *Letters of Anna Seward: Written Between the Years 1784–1807*, Archibald Constable, Edinburgh.

SHAW, Anna Howard (with the collaboration of Elizabeth Jordan), 1915, *The Story of a Pioneer*, Harper & Bros., New York & London.

SHIDELER, Mary McDermott, 1971, Introduction, to Dorothy L. Sayers, *Are Women Human?*, William B. Eerdman, Grand Rapids, Michigan, pp. 7–16.

SHOWALTER, Elaine (ed.), 1971, *Women's Liberation and Literature*, Harcourt Brace Jovanovich, New York.

SHOWALTER, Elaine, 1977, *A Literature of Their Own: British Women Novelists from Brontë to Lessing*, Princeton University Press; 1978, Virago, London.

SHOWALTER, Elaine (ed.), 1978, *These Modern Women: Autobiographical Essays from the Twenties*, The Feminist Press, Old Westbury, New York.

SHULMAN, Alix Kates (ed.), 1979, *Red Emma Speaks: Selected Writings and Speeches by Emma Goldman*, Wildwood House, London.

SIMPSON, Hilary, 1979, 'A Literary Trespasser: D. H. Lawrence's Use of Women's Writing', *Women's Studies International Quarterly*, vol. 2, no. 2, pp. 155–70.

SINCLAIR, Andrew, 1966, *The Better Half: The Emancipation of American Women*, Jonathan Cape, London.

SMITH, Barbara, 1979, 'Toward a Black Feminist Criticism', *Women's Studies International Quarterly*, vol. II, no. 2, pp. 183–94.

SMITH, Dorothy, 1978, 'A Peculiar Eclipsing: Women's Exclusion from Man's Culture', *Women's Studies International Quarterly*, vol. I, no. 4, pp. 281–96.

SMITH, Florence, 1916, *Mary Astell*, Columbia University Press, New York.

SMYTH, Dame Ethel, 1934, *Female Pipings in Eden*, Peter Davies, London.

SOMERSET, Lady Henry, 1898, 'Introductory', in Ann A. Gordon, *The Beautiful Life of Frances E. Willard*, Women's Temperance, Chicago, pp. 13–16.

SOMERVILLE, Martha, 1873, *Personal Recollections from Early Life to Old Age*, John Murray, London.

'SOPHIA, a Person of Quality', 1739, *Woman not Inferior to Man*, facsimile reprint, 1975, Bentham Press, London.

SPENDER, Dale, 1980, *Man Made Language*, Routledge & Kegan Paul, London.

SPENDER, Dale (ed.), 1981a, *Men's Studies Modified: The Impact of Feminism on the Academic Disciplines*, Pergamon Press, Oxford.

SPENDER, Dale, 1981b, 'Boys *Own* Education', in David Warren Piper (ed.), *Is Higher Education Fair?*, Society for Research into High Education, London, pp. 104–27.

SPENDER, Dale, 1982a, *Invisible Women: The Schooling Scandal*, Writers and Readers, London.

SPENDER, Dale (ed.), 1982b, *Feminist Theorists: Three Centuries of Women's Intellectual Traditions*, The Women's Press, London.

SPENDER, Dale (forthcoming), *There's Always Been a Women's Movement*, Routledge & Kegan Paul, London.

SPENDER, Lynne (forthcoming), *Unpublished Heritage: The Politics of Selection*, Routledge & Kegan Paul, London.

STACEY, Margaret and Marion PRICE, 1981, *Women, Power and Politics*, Tavistock, London.

STANLEY, Autumn, 1981, 'Daughters of Isis, Daughters of Demeter, When Women Sowed and Reaped', *Women's Studies International Quarterly*, vol. IV, no. 3, pp. 289–304.

STANLEY, Liz, 1982, 'Olive Schreiner', in Dale Spender (ed.), *Feminist Theorists*, The Women's Press, London.

STANLEY, Liz, and Sue WISE (forthcoming), *Breaking Out: Feminist Consciousness and Feminist Research*, Routledge & Kegan Paul, London.

STANTON, Elizabeth Cady, Susan B. ANTHONY, and Matilda Joslyn GAGE (eds), 1881, *History of Woman Suffrage*, vol. I, Fowler & Wells, New York; 1882, vol. II; 1886, vol. III. All reprinted 1969, Arno and The New York Times. (For vol. IV see Anthony and Harper 1902; for vols V and VI see Harper 1922).

STANTON, Elizabeth Cady, 1898a, *Eighty Years and More: Reminiscences 1815–1897*, T. Fisher Unwin, London, reprinted 1975, Schocken Books, New York.

STANTON, Elizabeth Cady (and the Revising Committee) 1898b, *The Woman's Bible*, European Publishing, New York, reprinted 1978 (6th printing), Coalition Task Force on Women and Religion, Seattle.

STANTON, Theodore, 1886, 'Continental Europe', in E. C. Stanton et al. (eds), *History of Woman Suffrage*, vol. III, pp. 895–921.

STANTON, Theodore and Harriot Stanton BLATCH (eds), 1922, *Elizabeth Cady Stanton as Revealed in her Letters, Diary and Reminiscences* (2 vols.), Harper Bros., New York.

STANWORTH, Michelle, 1981, *Gender and Schooling: A Study of Sexual Divisions in the Classroom*, Women's Research and Resources Centre, London.

STATON, Patricia, 1982, private communication.

STEARNS, Bertha, 1932, 'Reform Periodicals and Female Reformers', *American Historical Review*, July, vol. 37, pp. 678–99.

STENTON, Doris Mary, 1977, *The English Woman in History*, Schocken Books, New York; first published by George Allen & Unwin, London, 1957.

STEPHEN, Barbara, 1927, *Emily Davies and Girton College*, Constable, London.

STEPHEN, Leslie and Sidney LEE (eds), 1973 edn, *The Dictionary of National Biography*, Oxford University Press.

STERLING, Dorothy, 1979, *Black Foremothers: Three Lives*, Feminist Press, Old Westbury, New York.

STERN, Madeleine B., 1980, 'Introduction', to Margaret Fuller, *Woman in the Nineteenth Century*, University of Southern Carolina Press, pp. vii–xxxix.

STILLINGER, Jack (ed.), 1961, *The Early Draft of John Stuart Mill's Autobiography*, University of Illinois Press.

STINEMAN, Esther F., 1977, 'Simone de Beauvoir: An Autobiographical Blueprint for Female Liberty', *University of Michigan Papers in Women's Studies*, vol. II, no. 3, pp. 99–122.

STOCKS, Mary, 1949, *Eleanor Rathbone*, Gollancz, London.

STOCKS, Mary, 1970, *My Commonplace Book: An Autobiography*, Peter Davies, London.

STOPES, Charlotte Carmichael, 1894, *British Freewomen: Their Historic Privilege*, Social Science Series, Swann Sonnenschein, London.

STOPES, Marie, 1918, *Wise Parenthood*, A. C. Fairfield, London.

STOTT, Mary, 1975, *Forgetting's No Excuse*, Virago, London.

STOTT, Mary, 1982, private communication.

STRACHEY, Barbara, 1980, *Remarkable Relations: The Story of the Pearsall Smith Family*, Victor Gollancz, London.

STRACHEY, Ray, 1912, *Frances Willard: Her Life and Work*, T. Fisher Unwin, London.

STRACHEY, Ray, 1928, *The Cause: A Short History of the Women's Movement in Great Britain*, G. Bell & Sons, London, reprinted 1979, Virago, London.

STRACHEY, Ray, 1931, *Millicent Garrett Fawcett*, John Murray, London.

STRACHEY, Ray (ed.), 1936, *Our Freedom and Its Results by Five Women*, Hogarth Press, London.

SUNSTEIN, Emily, 1975, A *Different Face: The Life of Mary Wollstonecraft*, Harper & Row, London/New York.

SWANWICK Helen Maria, 1913, *The Future of the Women's Movement*, G. Bell, London.

SWANWICK, Helen Maria, 1935, *Autobiography*, Camelot Press, London.

SWINEY, Frances, 1908, *The Awakening of Women, or Woman's Part in Evolution*, 13th edn, William Reeves, London.

TABOR, Margaret E., 1933, *Pioneer Women*, Sheldon Press, London.

TANNER, Leslie B. (ed.), 1971, *Voices from Women's Liberation*, Signet, New York.

TAYLOR, Kathryn, 1971, *Generations of Denial: 75 Short Biographies of Women in History*, Times Change Press, New York.

THOMAS, Clara, 1967, *Love and Work Enough: The Life of Anna Jameson*, University of Toronto Press.

THOMAS, W. Moy (ed.), 1893, *Letters and Works of Lady Mary Wortley Montagu*.

THOMPSON, William, 1825, *Appeal from One Half the Human Race, Women against the Pretensions of the Other Half, Men, to Retain Them in Political, and thence in Civil and Domestic Slavery, in Reply to a Paragraph of Mr Mill's Celebrated Article on Government*, Longman, Hurst, Rees, Orme, Brown & Green, London.

THORNE, Alison, private communication.

THORP, Margaret, 1949, *Female Persuasion: Six Strong Minded Women*, New Haven, Conn.

TILLOTSON, J. (n.d.), *Lives of Illustrious Women of England or Biographical Treasury: Containing Memoirs of Royal, Noble and Celebrated British Females of the Past and Present Day*, Thomas Holmes, London.

TODD, Margaret, 1918, *The Life of Sophia Jex-Blake*, Macmillan, London.

TOMALIN, Claire, 1977, *The Life and Death of Mary Wollstonecraft*, Penguin, Harmondsworth.

TRILLING, Diana, 1952, 'Mill's Intellectual Beacon', *Partisan Review*, vol. 19, pp. 116–20.

TRISTAN, Flora, 1980, *London Journal, 1840* (first published France, 1840), George Prior, London.

UGLOW, Jennifer (1982), 'Josephine Butler', in Dale Spender (ed.), *Feminist Theorists*, The Women's Press, London.

URBANSKI, Marie Mitchell Olesen, 1980, *Margaret Fuller's 'Woman in the Nine-*

teenth Century': A Literary Study of Form and Content, of Sources and Influence, Greenwood Press, Westport, Conn.

VERNON, Betty D., 1982, *Ellen Wilkinson 1891–1947*, Croom Helm, London.

VICINUS, Martha (ed.), 1973, *Suffer and Be Still: Women in the Victorian Age*, Indiana University Press, Bloomington.

VICINUS, Martha (ed.), 1980, *A Widening Sphere: Changing Roles of Victorian Women*, Methuen, New York & London.

VUILAMMY, C. E., 1935, *Aspasia: Life and Letters of Mary Granville (Mrs Delany)*, Geoff Blees, London.

WADE, Mason, 1940, *Margaret Fuller: Whetstone of Genius*, Viking, New York.

WAGNER, Sally Roesch, 1980, 'Introduction' to Matilda Joslyn Gage (1893), *Woman, Church and State*, Persephone Press, Watertown, Mass., pp. xv–xxxix.

WALKER, Alice (ed.), 1979, *I Love Myself When I am Laughing . . . and then again when I am looking Mean and Impressive: A Zora Hurston Neale Reader*, Feminist Press, Old Westbury, New York.

WALKOWITZ, Judith R., 1980, *Prostitution and Victorian Society: Women, Class and the State*, Cambridge University Press.

WALTERS, Anna, 1980, 'When Women's Reputations are in Male Hands: Elizabeth Gaskell and the Critics', *Women's Studies International Quarterly*, vol. III, no. 4, pp. 405–14.

WALTERS, Margaret, 1976, 'The Rights and Wrongs of Women: Mary Wollstonecraft, Harriet Martineau and Simone de Beauvoir', in Juliet Mitchell and Ann Oakley (eds), *The Rights and Wrongs of Women*, Penguin, Harmondsworth, pp. 304–78.

WARBASSE, Elizabeth B., 1971, 'Gage, Matilda Joslyn', in Edward T. James, Janet Wilson James and Paul S. Boyer (eds), *Notable American Women 1607–1950: A Biographical Dictionary* (3 vols), Harvard University Press, Cambridge, Mass, vol. II, pp. 4–6.

WARDLE, Ralph, M., 1951, *Mary Wollstonecraft: A Critical Biography*, University of Kansas Press, Lawrence.

WARREN, Mercy Otis, 1805, *History of the Rise, Progress and Termination of the American Revolution* (3 vols), Manning & Loring, Boston.

WASHINGTON, Mary Helen, 1979, 'Introduction' to Alice Walker (ed.), *I Love Myself When I am Laughing . . .*, Feminist Press, Old Westbury, New York.

WEINER, Gaby, 1982a, 'Vida Goldstein', in Dale Spender (ed.), *Feminist Theorists*, The Women's Press, London.

WEINER, Gaby, 1982b, 'Harriet Martineau', in Dale Spender (ed.), *Feminist Theorists*, The Women's Press, London.

WEISSTEIN, Naomi, 1970, '"Kinde, Kuche, Kirche" as Scientific Law: Psychology Constructs the Female', in Robin Morgan (ed.), *Sisterhood is Powerful*, Vintage Books, New York, pp. 228–44.

WEST, Rebecca, 1922, *The Judge*, Hutchinson, London, reprinted 1980, Virago, London.

WEST, Rebecca, 1929, *Harriet Hume*, Hutchinson, London, reprinted, 1980, Virago, London.

WEST, Rebecca, 1933, 'Mrs Pankhurst', *The Post Victorians* (introduction by W. R. Inge), Ivor Nicholson & Watson, London, pp. 479–500.

WEST, Rebecca, 1977, *A Celebration*, Viking, New York; 1978, Penguin, Harmondsworth.

WEXLER, Alice (ed.), 1981, 'Emma Goldman on Mary Wollstonecraft', *Feminist Studies*, vol. 7, no. 1, pp. 113–33.

WHARTON, Edith, 1962, *A Backward Glance: Autobiography*, Constable, London.
WHEATLEY, Vera, 1957, *The Life and Work of Harriet Martineau*, Secker & Warburg, London.
WHEELER, Edith Rolt, 1910, *Famous Bluestockings*, Methuen, London.
WHEELER, Lesley, 1981a, private communication.
WHEELER, Leslie (ed.), 1981b, *Loving Warriors: Selected Letters of Lucy Stone and Henry B. Blackwell, 1853–1893*, Dial Press, New York.
WHEELER, Leslie, 1982, 'Lucy Stone', in Dale Spender (ed.), *Feminist Theorists*, The Women's Press, London.
WILLIAMS, Jane, 1861, *The Literary Women of England*, Saunders & Otley, London.
WILLIAMS, Trevor I. (ed.), 1978, *A History of Technology* (Vol. III) *The Twentieth Century: c. 1900 to c. 1950, Part II*, Clarendon Press, Oxford.
WILLIAMSON, Joseph, 1977, *Josephine Butler – The Forgotten Saint*, The Faith Press, Leighton Buzzard.
WINKLER, Barbara Scott, 1980, 'Victorian Daughters: The Lives and Feminism of Charlotte Perkins Gilman and Olive Schreiner', *Michigan Occasional Paper*, no. 13.
WINWAR, Frances, 1950, *The Immortal Lovers: Elizabeth Barrett and Robert Browning*, Hamish Hamilton, London.
WOLLSTONECRAFT, Mary, 1891, *A Vindication of the Rights of Woman* with an introduction to the second edition by Millicent Garret Fawcett, London.
WOOLF, Virginia, 1928, *A Room of One's Own*, Hogarth Press, London, reprinted 1974, Penguin, Harmondsworth.
WOOLF, Virginia, 1929, 'Women and Fiction', *The Forum*, March, reprinted 1972, in Leonard Woolf (ed.), *Collected Essays: Virginia Woolf*, vol. II, Chatto. Windus, London, pp. 141–8.
WOOLF, Virginia, 1938, *Three Guineas*, The Hogarth Press, London, reprinted 1977.
WOOLF, Virginia, 1932, ' "III Mary Wollstonecraft": Four Figures', *Common Reader*, II, reprinted 1969, in Leonard Woolf (ed.), *Collected Essays: Virginia Woolf*, vol. III, Chatto & Windus, London, pp. 193–9.
WOOLF, Virginia (n.d.), 'Professions for Women', paper read to Women's Service League, reprinted 1972, in Leonard Woolf (ed.), *Collected Essays: Virginia Woolf*, vol. II, Chatto & Windus, London, pp. 284–9.
WRIGHT, Frances, 1829, *Course of Popular Lectures*, Free Enquirer, New York.
WYMAN, Mary Alic (ed.), 1924, *Selections from the Autobiography of Elizabeth Oakes Smith*, Lewiston Journal, Memphis.

GENERAL INDEX

Author's note

The major theme of this book is that males have ordered and controlled knowledge in their own interest and that women's ways of classifying and analysing the world have been repeatedly erased. It therefore seemed inappropriate to continue with conventional (male) practices when it came to indexing the subject matter of this book: such an index would have helped to render many of the 'topics' that have been discussed, invisible. So an attempt has been made to conceptualise the categories as they relate to women – even though this has necessitated the coinage of new terms, such as 'completion complex, that is, the incomplete nature of a woman without a man'.

While I have every confidence that women will quickly become familiar with this framework (and optimistically, will find it useful), I am aware that it may be meaningless and mystifying to males.

I would like to thank Anne Whitbread for the tedious and time-consuming work she has undertaken in helping me to do this index, and I promise her I will never do another one again.

169, 210, 441, 531;
autonomous women's
organisations (and role
of men), 205, 206, 209,
210, 211, 437; men's
reactions, 210, 441;
sexual autonomy, *see*
sexuality
availability, 22, 47, 104,
105, 139, 147, 169,
170, 291, 316, 452,
453, 455, 457, 487; *see
also* appropriation

biology: restrictions, 143;
used against women, 59,
482
birth control, 122, 131,
258, 359, 367, 407,
479, 481; campaigns,
369, 479, 480;
contraception, safe, and
side-effects, 369; *see also*
reproduction
Black Friday, 423–4
burial of women's
contributions, 9, 26, 30,
70, 75, 77, 79, 82, 90,
96, 100, 101, 177, 229,
235, 236, 241, 243,
248, 251, 293, 310, 440

censorship and
propaganda, 8, 10
challenges to patriarchy, 7,
8, 22, 28, 31, 46, 49,
51, 59, 63, 77, 81, 87,
88, 106, 137, 189, 217,
239, 243, 351, 370,
371, 388, 394, 410,
414, 423, 458
champions of women's
rights, 98, 104, 164,
187, 475, 476, 478; *see
also* husbands, loving;
'radical' men
children: care of, 263;
custody of, 318, 319
chivalry, non-existent
nature of, 41, 44, 131,
151, 184, 185, 186,
215, 253, 334, 405,
414, 420, 422, 525
choice, 126, 159, 289, 507
classification scheme,
absence of for women,
8, 9, 23, 24, 40, 64, 76,

98, 391–2; attempts at
establishment of, 151
collusion, 20, 50, 118, 498
common experience of
women, 14–15, 17, 27,
37, 41, 101, 102, 103,
112, 125, 151, 173,
174, 259, 266, 270,
337, 339, 345, 368,
369, 378, 448, 520;
legitimation of, 28, 39,
40, 46, 48, 49, 50, 56,
57, 64, 86, 117, 184,
196, 202, 441;
repetition of life
patterns, 528
competition, 50, 123;
among women, 50, 124;
between women and
men, 65, 284, 401
completion complex (i.e.
the incompleteness of a
woman without a man),
111, 125, 126; a man is
not enough, 456; failure
to get a man, 379;
unfinished, raw material,
443, 444
compulsory
heterosexuality, 74, 445;
see also economics,
sexual
conciliation versus
confrontation, 65, 66,
80, 208, 209, 210, 213,
214, 215, 243, 247,
251, 263, 284, 317,
319, 385, 393, 405,
410, 413, 416, 446,
448; theory of good
conduct, 413–14
confidence: crisis of, 134;
deprived of, 6, 7, 20, 25,
39, 45, 127, 206, 208,
213, 214, 216, 231,
285, 436; development
of, 11, 39; success/
avoidance syndrome, 81,
170
conflict of interest between
women and men, 40, 98,
331, 337, 410, 440,
446, 530
consciousness-raising, 36,
37, 117, 123, 132, 247,
437, 438, 500, free
enquiry, 123, 132;
speaking bitterness, 451

Contagious Diseases Acts,
340, 341, 342, 343,
344, 346, 348, 352, 353
contempt for women, 25,
44, 99, 106, 135, 149,
151, 186, 237, 240,
285, 344, 370, 420,
427, 451, 471, 539; *see
also* woman hating
content with woman's lot,
49, 58, 151, 153, 186,
290, 291, 445, 507
co-operation among
women, 36, 191, 435
cross-cultural comparisons,
516

disagreeable women, 27,
28, 29, 40, 44, 51, 56,
57, 77, 94, 97, 105,
117, 118, 119, 122,
125, 138, 140, 142,
158, 161, 186, 190,
192, 210, 216, 225,
251, 255, 287, 316,
319, 364, 440, 442,
463, 464; desirability of,
117, 208
discrepancy, between
ideology and reality, 3,
6, 22, 27, 86, 106, 120,
130, 155, 520
disloyal to civilisation,
422, 486; freedom from
unreal loyalties, 486;
heresy and high treason,
442; outsiders, 462,
485–6, 499, 519
divisions among women,
50, 79, 162, 163, 334,
426, 427, 434, 445,
460, 468, 528
domestic duties:
disillusionment with, 87,
204–8; as proof of
womanliness, 127, 149,
168, 219, 276, 296,
443, 457, 467, 478; as
theft of women's labour,
445, 455, 507
double-bind, 10, 51, 64,
66, 118, 140, 152, 278,
317, 413, 507, 524; *see
also* scapegoat
double standard, 20, 22,
43, 56, 64, 67, 71, 72,
76, 78, 79, 88, 90, 99,
106, 109, 128, 136,

INDEX OF NAMES